DātaMyte

DātaMyte HANDBOOK
Third Edition

A practical guide to computerized data collection for Statistical Process Control

by DataMyte Corporation

DataMyte Corporation
14960 Industrial Road
Minnetonka, Minnesota 55345
612-935-7704
Telex 756648 FAX 612-935-0018

DataMyte Corporation

Corporate Headquarters

DataMyte Corporation
14960 Industrial Road
Minnetonka, Minnesota 55345
612-935-7704
Telex 756648 FAX 612-935-0018

U.S. Sales Offices

DataMyte Corporation
Regional Sales Office
24125 Drake Road
Farmington, Michigan 48024
313-471-0310

For the location of your nearest DataMyte Sales Representative, call (612) 935-7704.

First edition, June 1984, 20,000 copies
Second edition, September 1985, 30,000 copies
Third edition, June 1987, 50,000 copies
Printed in the United States of America
Standard Book Number: ISBN 0-930345-02-9
Library of Congress Catalog Card Number: 84-71481

International Sales Offices

CANADA

CLOSED LOOP SALES
255 Industrial Parkway South
P.O. Box 429
Unit 5
Aurora, Ontario
Canada L4G 3L5
Contact: Dave Harrison
Phone: (416) 727-1977, 78,79

ENGLAND

SIGMA, LTD.
Spring Road
Letchworth, Herts
England SG6 4AJ
Contact: Tony Aspin
Phone: (462)683841
Telex: 851-825535

FRANCE

EMC
71, Rue De Bagnolet
75020 Paris
France
Contact: Michel Trembleau
Phone: 4348.64.04
Telex: 842-210023

WEST GERMANY

UNIVERSAL ELEKTRONIK
Handelsgesellschaft, GmbH
Chemnitzer, Str. 18
3003 Ronnenberg 3
West Germany
Contact: H.F. Rupprath
Phone: (0511) 46 60 13
Telex: 841-922946

ITALY

MICRO GENERAL
Via Della Rocca N35
10123 Torino
Italy
Contact: D. Chiaberge
Phone: 11-835083
Telex: 843-213569

TABLE OF CONTENTS

FOREWARD TO THE THIRD EDITION

The DataMyte Story - Update

In the three year period since the first DataMyte Handbook was published, the company has quadrupled in size. With over 10,000 systems installed in more than 2000 factories worldwide, DataMyte clearly has emerged as the leader in factory data collection for quality and productivity. Much of the growth has been fueled by a constant stream of new products, new applications, and an ever increasing number of gage interfaces. The company built a strong direct sales force, added selected distributors, created a knowledgable technical support and customer service group and just recently launched a training division, all designed to ensure total customer success and satisfaction.

What started out as a predominantly automotive industry dominated business spread to all types of discrete and hybrid manufacturing operations as attended by the diversity of the one hundred applications in this Handbook. Initially, DataMyte made only handheld data collectors that could collect only variable (measurement) data and only from a limited number of gages. The current offerings described in the product section of this Handbook include both handheld and fixed station data collectors for attribute and variable data interfacing to hundreds of different analog and digital gages. Not only has DataMyte's software capability grown tremendously, but through cooperation with many third party software vendors providing bridges to their software, DataMyte has become the de facto standard. DataMyte products can be connected by the various FAN®, Factory Area Networks, thus elevating our products to a total systems solution.

In December 1986, DataMyte became part of the Allen-Bradley Company, Inc. (a Rockwell International Company). Allen-Bradley has long been a leader in providing automation products to the factory floor. The increased resources of our new parent organization (DataMyte will function as a wholly owned subsidiary) should accelerate both our growth and our ability to serve our customers better worldwide.

The authors of this Handbook made every effort to continue to provide the best reference book in this rapidly growing field. Here are the revisions to the Handbook Third Edition:

- 624 pages compared to 560 pages in the Second Edition.
- 128 pages of a two-color products section compared to 96.
- Theory section expanded to include more on regression analysis (chi square test, kurtosis).
- Applications section has 100 applications compared to 65 in the Second Edition.
- A major change was made to arrange the applications section into eight industry-specific chapters:

  Chapter 7—Aerospace and defense
  Chapter 8—Automotive suppliers
  Chapter 9—Electronics and computers
  Chapter 10—Food, cosmetics and health care
  Chapter 11—Furniture and appliance
  Chapter 12—Glass, plastics, paper and chemical
  Chapter 13—Metalworking and machinery
  Chapter 14—Transportation

- Almost twice as many gage interfaces as the Second Edition.
- Chapter 21 on Allen-Bradley quality management products, represents the largest offering of such products in the world.
- Chapter 22 on factory automation for quality includes product offerings from Apollo, AT&T, DEC and HP.

DataMyte Corporation

May 1987

FOREWORD TO THE SECOND EDITION

Since June of 1984, when the First Edition of this Handbook was published, we have distributed over 20,000 copies. The overwhelming majority of the comments which we received have been favorable and complimentary. We have also received some constructive criticism and requests for expanding the treatment on certain subjects. In preparing this expanded Second Edition, we have taken into account all the requests which we could accommodate. The changes and additions enlarge this book by about a third, to 560 pages.

DataMyte itself has also experienced significant growth. Many new products were developed and put to ever increasing new applications. In addition to our original handheld data acquisition systems, the fixed station DataMyte 750 family of products was developed and the new FAN® (Factory Area Network) systems were introduced. The latest development, the DataMyte 2000 system, brings totally new capabilities to the concept of roving inspection. All these products plus new software developments and sensor/gage interfaces are described in the product section of this Handbook and are featured in the greatly expanded applications section. Listed below are the major changes and the four totally new additions.

Chapter 4, on measurement: an addition on gage capability studies.

Chapter 5, on acceptance sampling: an addition on Dr. Deming's statements about acceptance sampling.

Chapter 6, (new) on Just-In-Time (JIT) manufacturing and Total Quality Control (TQC).

Chapter 7, (new) on plant-wide quality control, including 16 new FAN applications. (Of the 40 applications in the First Edition, seven were eliminated and 32 new ones added, bringing the total in this book to 65 applications.)

Chapter 13, (new) on computerized data collection and the FAN (Factory Area Network) systems.

Chapter 17, (new) on SPC software available from other sources. In keeping with our open software architecture, many interfaces were developed between DataMyte data collectors and third party software vendors.

Chapter 18, (new) on SPC training. In addition to DataMyte's training programs on our own equipment, two cooperative programs are described. They are SMIP, from Control Data Corporation, a computer delivered SPC training course, and a video delivered training course from Technicomp Corporation.

It is the continuing interest of the authors and editors of this Handbook to make it a most useful, relevant and informative source of knowledge regarding all aspects of industrial data collection for the improvement of quality and productivity. To this end we again wish to solicit the constructive comments of our readers. These comments, together with the results of our continually expanding search for valuable, pertinent technical information, will be incorporated into future editions of this book.

DATAMYTE CORPORATION

January 1986

FOREWORD TO FIRST EDITION

The DataMyte Story

DataMyte Corporation is a rapidly growing private company in Minnetonka (a suburb of Minneapolis), Minnesota. Started in 1967, the Company has specialized in the design and development of handheld data acquisition systems for the past ten years.

Because DataMyte products are rugged, they are uniquely suited for the factory data collection environment. Because they are a complete user friendly system, comprised of automatic input sensors, a handheld computer and specialized software, they can provide both the data collection and data processing functions required for Statistical Quality Control (SQC).

Interestingly, SQC, which was developed several decades ago as a theory in the United States, found its first wide acceptance among the manufacturing companies of Japan. Superior quality and the resulting competitive advantage explain why.

Well managed companies in this country have adopted quality as a corporate strategy also, and made the necessary top management commitment "to do it right the first time." Hewlett-Packard estimated that as much as 25% of their total manufacturing cost was spent on rework. Others found equally dramatic savings opportunities. The experience of many companies shows that Statistical Quality Control reduces the cost of Quality. DataMyte Corporation has become successful because our systems simplify the implementation of an SQC program and, in turn, pay for themselves in a short time.

Our first volume users were the major automotive companies. Stung by Japanese competition and changing customer preferences for higher quality automobiles, they increasingly turned to SQC and began using DataMytes. We are pleased to have played a part in their overall quality improvement effort.

SQC, SPC — What's the Difference?

Statistical Quality Control (SQC) and Statistical Process Control (SPC) sometimes are used interchangeably, yet to some they mean different things. Without entering the semantic debate, it can be said that SQC is the broader "umbrella" term.

Ultimately, manufacturers hope to have perfect parts, perfect processes and perfect designs, and "just in time delivery." To aim for this perfection, companies are beginning to treat manufacturing as a yield driven *process* , i.e., they set specific defect rates at each step. Key elements of such a program are: performance measures, a test philosophy and Statistical Quality Control.

Why This Book

Data collection in Quality Control is labor intensive. As the use of SQC spreads in American industry, managers as well as practitioners, become more interested in data collection for testing rather than for screening out rejects. To change a process for the desired effect, data must be collected rapidly, accurately, automatically, and should be processed "real time", "on line" rather than later. Here is where DataMyte fills a need.

This handbook is a convenient reference, and a practical guide to the underlying theory, real life applications, and the DataMyte product offerings for the implementation of an SQC program. The presentation is aimed at both the managers and the quality professionals with emphasis on practical problem solutions. Where there are differing theories or methods, this book takes no sides but presents the different views and provides full reference literature where applicable, thus, hopefully, facilitating proper communications. Another aim of this book is to make the implementation and use of an SQC program easier by attempting to share the accumulated technical knowledge of our company, which has specialized in this field for the past decade.

How To Use The Book

This book was prepared as a compendium of articles on many related subjects. The editors made no attempt to homogenize the styles of the different authors. An effort was made however, to make the chapters self-contained and to organize the subject matter in a meaningful way. The definitions in Part I should help readers decide how much background they need to cover.

Some of the information presented is standard reference material, and some probably will not be found elsewhere. Some chapters are quite theoretical, while others focus on the more practical "how to" aspects. Generally the book is organized in three major parts: Theory, Applications, and Products.

This is a handbook, meant to be consulted as a reference as problems arise, rather than being read cover to cover as a student's textbook.

About the Authors

Twenty-three people contributed to the preparation of this book. They comprise the technical staff of DataMyte Corporation, with backgrounds in hardware and software engineering, application and sales support, R & D and training and — most of all — practical problem solving. The authors collectively have over 300 man-years of experience in SQC and data collection -data processing.

In addition to their regular daily work, the authors gave their time generously to make this book possible.

Chapter 15 and 16 require special mention. DataMyte is pleased to have had the cooperation and assistance of two other companies, Hewlett-Packard (Chapter 15) and Allied Corporation (Chapter 16), in presenting a systems approach to quality control. These companies are thanked for providing most of the material contained in these two chapters.

DataMyte Corporation

June 1984

Part I Theory

DEFINITIONS

Acceptable Quality Level (AQL) (for lot acceptance sampling) — Maximum defect rate at which the lot will be accepted.

Acceptance Sampling — Evaluating a sample to determine whether a lot is of acceptable quality; for incoming or outgoing product inspection. **See Chapt. 5.**

Accuracy (of measurement) (vs. precision) — Difference between the average result of a measurement with a particular instrument, and the true value of the quantity being measured. **See p. 4-8.**

AOQL (Average Outgoing Quality Limit) — For an acceptance lot sampling procedure, AOQL is the maximum average percent of defectives for outgoing lots, after correcting defects in the rejected lots. The value of AOQL depends only on the sampling scheme and on the corrective action for defective lots, so that the AOQL gives a guaranteed upper limit on the average outgoing percent of defectives. **See p. 5-11.**

Assignable Causes (of variation) — Those causes of variation in a process which are not random, i.e. which have some source which can be determined and perhaps eliminated. **See p. 1-6.**

Attribute Data (Quality) — Data coming basically from yes/no, pass/fail determinations of whether the units conform to standards. May or may not include weighting by seriousness of defect, etc. **See p. 1-13.**

Average — See Mean.

$$P(B_n:A_m) = \frac{P(A_m:B_n)P(B_n)}{\sum_j P(A_m:B_j)P(B_j)}$$

Bayes Theorem Formula, see p. 5-16.

Bayes Theorem — A theorem of statistics relating conditional probabilities: Suppose that $P(A_i:B_j)$ is the probability that $A = A_i$ given that $B = B_j$, and suppose $P(B_n)$ is the probability that $B = B_n$. Then if we know that $A = A_m$, then $P(B_n)$ is given by the formula. The theorem is used for determining the probability $P(B_n:A_m)$ when we have knowledge of the conditional probability $P(A:B)$.

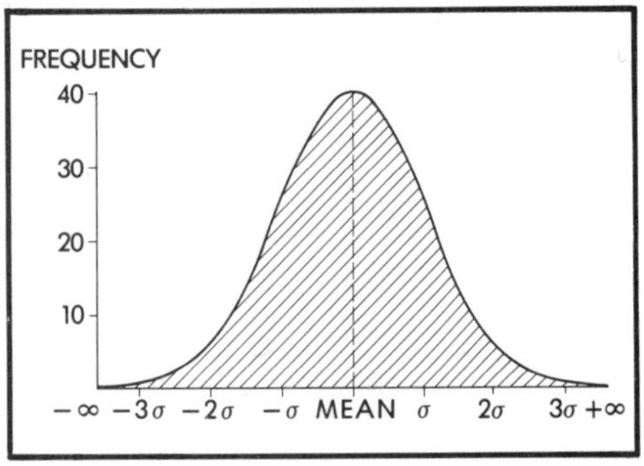

Bell-Shaped Curve, see p. 1-10.

Bell-Shaped Curve — A curve or distribution showing a central peak and tapering off smoothly and symmetrically to "tails" on either side. A normal curve is an example.

Bias (in measurement) — Difference between the average result of repeated measurements with a particular instrument, and the true value of the quantity being measured.

Bimodal Distribution — A frequency distribution which has two peaks.

See p. 3-8.

Binomial Distribution (probability distribution) — given that a trial can have only 2 possible outcomes (yes/no, pass/fail, heads/tails), of which one outcome has probability p and the other probability q ($p+q=1$), the probability that the outcome represented by p occurs r times in n trials is given by the binomial distribution.

$$P(r,n) = \frac{n!(p^r)(q^{n-r})}{r!\,(n-r)\,!}$$

Binomial Distribution Formula, see p. 5-6.

See p. 2-34

c-Chart — For attribute data: A control chart of the number of defects found in a subgroup of fixed size. The c-chart is used where each unit typically has a number of defects.

See p. 4-16.

Calibration (of instrument) — Adjusting an instrument to reduce the difference between the average reading of the instrument and the "true" value of some standard being measured, i.e. to reduce measurement bias.

See p. 3-17.

Camp-Meidell Conditions — For frequency distribution and histograms: A distribution is said to meet Camp-Meidell conditions if its mean and mode are equal and the frequency declines continuously on either side of the mode.

See p. 3-2.

Capability (of process) — The uniformity of product which a process is capable of producing.

Cause and Effect Diagram — See Ishikawa Diagram. **See p. 1-16**

Cell (of frequency distribution and/or histogram) — For a sample based on a continuous variable (or on a discrete variable with an inherent step size smaller than we find convenient), a cell is an interval of the variable for which all the elements falling in that interval will be summed together. Usually the full range of the variable is divided into cells of equal size, and only the total number of elements falling into each cell is used in working with the frequency distribution and/or histogram. This greatly reduces the amount of information which must be dealt with, as opposed to treating each element individually. **See p. 3-4.**

Centerline — For control charts: the horizontal line marking the center of the chart, usually indicating the nominal expected value of the quantity being charted. **See p. 2-10.**

Central Limit Theorem — If samples of a population with size n are drawn, and the values of $\bar{x}$ are calculated, and the distribution of $\bar{x}$ is found, the distribution's shape is found to approach a normal distribution for sufficiently large n. This theorem allows one to use the assumption of a normal distribution when dealing with $\bar{x}$. "Sufficiently large" depends on the population's distribution and on what range of $\bar{x}$ is being considered; for practical purposes, the easiest approach may be to take a number of samples of a desired size and see if their means are normally distributed; if not, the sample size should be increased. **See p. 1-11.**

Central Tendency — A measure of the point about which a group of values is clustered; some measures of central tendency are mean, mode, and median. **See p. 1-7.**

Check Sheet — A sheet for the recording of data on a process or its product. The check sheet is designed to remind the user to record each piece of information required for a particular study, and to reduce the likelihood of errors in recording data. The data from the check sheet can be typed into a computer for analysis when the data collection is complete. **See p. 1-23.**

$$\text{Chi-Square} = \sum \frac{(F(x) - P(x))(N_{tot})^2}{P(x)(N_{tot})}$$

Chi-Square Formula.

Chi-Square — A measure of how well a set of data fits a proposed form. For example, compare a measured frequency distribution F(x) with a probability function P(x) to see if they are significantly different. Let F(x) be the number of elements falling into cell x of the frequency distribution, and N_{tot} be the total number of elements.

The value of chi-square is often divided by the number of degrees of freedom, DF, to get chi-square per degree of freedom. This makes the result relatively independent of the number of cells used. DF is basically the number of cells minus the number of parameters of P(x) which are adjusted to obtain the fit. For example, a normal distribution has 2 parameters: its mean and its width. A chi-square per DF on the order of 1 indicates a reasonable fit; large values indicate a poor fit.

See p. 2-17. *Cluster* — A group with similar properties. For control charts and scatter plots: a group of points falling in the same area of the chart.

See p. 1-5. *Common Causes* — Those sources of variability in a process which are truly random, i.e., inherent in the process itself.

Confidence Interval — Range within which a parameter of a population (e.g. mean, standard deviation, etc) may be expected to fall, on the basis of measurement, with some specified confidence level.

Confidence Level — The estimated probability that a statistcal hypothesis is valid. Example: "The mean of the population lies in the range (X,Y)" is a statistical hypothesis. (X,Y) is called the confidence interval. Confidence level is usually estimated by assuming a normal distribution for the parameter being determined.

Confidence Limits — The upper and lower boundaries of a confidence interval.

Conformance (of product) — Adherence to some standard of the product's properties. The term is used often in attributes studies of product quality, i.e., a given unit of the product is either in conformance to the standard or it is not.

Constant-Cause System — A system or process in which the variations are random and are constant in time.

See p. 1-5.

Consumer's Risk — For acceptance sampling: the probability that a bad lot will be accepted by a given sampling plan.

See p. 5-3.

Continuous Data — Data for a continuous variable (variable data).

See p. 1-13.

Continuous Variable — A variable which can assume any of a range of values; an example would be the measured size of a part.

See p. 1-13.

Control (of process) (statistical) — A process is said to be in a state of statistical control if the process exhibits only random variations (as opposed to systematic variations and/or variations with known sources).

See p. 1-12.

Control (of process) (manufacturing) — Process is in a state of control if its variations fall within specified control limits (this has no relation to statistical control.)

Control Chart — A plot of some parameter of process performance, usually determined by regular sampling of the product, as a function (usually) of time or unit number or other chronological variable. The control limits are also plotted for comparison. The parameter plotted may be the mean value of a particular measurement for a product sample of specified size ($\bar{x}$ chart), the range of values in the sample (R chart), the percent of defective units in the sample (p-chart), etc.

See Chapt. 2.

Control Limits — The limits within which the product of a process is expected (or required) to remain. If the process leaves the limits, it is said to be out of control. Note: control limits are not the same as tolerance limits.

See p. 2-11, 2-25.

Covariance — A measure of whether two variables are related (correlated). It is given by the formula. 'n' is the number of elements in the sample.

$$\sigma_{xy} = \sum_{i=1}^{n} \frac{(x_i-\bar{x})^2(y_i-\bar{y})^2}{n-1}$$

Covariance Formula.

CP — For process capability studies. CP is a capability index defined by the formula. CP may range in value from 0 to infinity, with a larger value indicating a more capable

$$CP = \frac{\text{TOLERANCE}}{6\sigma}$$

CP Formula, see p. 3-12.

process. A value near 1.33 is normally considered acceptable.

$$CPK = \text{The lesser of: } \frac{(USL - MEAN)}{3\sigma} \text{ or } \frac{(MEAN - LSL)}{3\sigma}$$

CPK Formula, see p. 3-14.

CPK — For process capability studies. An index combining CP and K to indicate whether the process will produce units within the tolerance limits. CPK has a value equal to CP if the process is centered on the mean specification; if CPK is negative, the process mean is outside the specification limits; if CPK is between 0 and 1 then some of the 6 sigma spread falls outside the tolerance limits. If CPK is larger than 1, the 6 sigma spread is completely within the tolerance limits.

$$CR = \frac{6\sigma}{TOLERANCE}$$

CR Formula, see p. 3-13.

CR — For process capability studies. The inverse of CP. CR can range from 0 to infinity in value, with a smaller value indicating a more capable process.

See p. 18-7.

Cumulative Sum Chart (Cusum) — A cumulative sum report plots the cumulative difference of each subgroup's difference from the nominal value.

See p. 2-17, 2-30.

Cycle — A recurring pattern.

See 16-38.

DataTruck™ — The DataTruck™ harvests data from several 750s located throughout a plant's unwired FAN® (Factory Area Network) system. The DataTruck™ transfers the data to an IBM PC or printer and it can also transmit setup information from the PC to the 750s.

See p. 4-11.

Deformation — The bending or distorting of an object due to forces applied to it. Deformation can contribute to errors in measurement if the measuring instrument applies enough force.

$$\sigma = \sqrt{\frac{\Sigma (x-\bar{x})^2}{DF}}$$

Standard Deviation Formula

Degrees of Freedom — The number of unconstrained parameters in a statistical determination. For example, in determining $\bar{x}$ (the mean value of a sample of n measurements), the number of degrees of freedom, DF, is n. In determining the standard deviation (STD) of the same population, DF = n − 1 because one parameter entering the determination is eliminated. The STD is obtained from a sum of terms based on the individual measurements — which are unconstrained — but the nth measurement must now be considered "constrained" by the requirement that the values add up to make $\bar{x}$. An equivalent statement is that one degree of freedom is "factored out" because the STD is mathematically indifferent to the value of $\bar{x}$.

Discrete Variable — A variable which assumes only integer values; for example, the number of people in a room is a discrete variable.

Dispersion (of a statistical sample) — The tendency of the values of the elements in a sample to differ from each other. Dispersion is commonly expressed in terms of the range of the sample (difference between the lowest and highest values) or by the standard deviation.

Dispersion Analysis Diagram — An Ishikawa diagram for analysis of the various contributions to variability of a process or product. The main factors contributing to the process are first listed, then the specific causes of variability from each factor are enumerated. A systematic study of each cause can then be performed.

See p. 1-18.

English System — The system of measurement units based on the foot, the pound, and the second.

Evolutionary Operations (EVOP) — A procedure to optimize the performance of a process by making small, known variations in the parameters entering the process and observing the effects of the variation on the product. This seems identical to Response Surface Methodology, except that it is done in a production situation rather than during process development, and the variations must therefore be kept small enough to meet product tolerances.

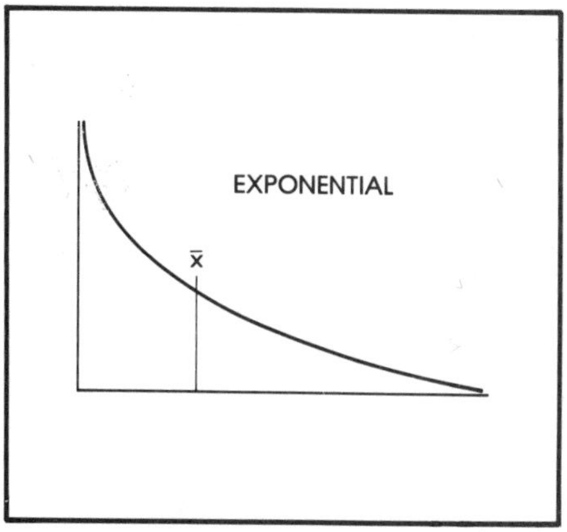

Exponential distribution, see p. 3-8.

Exponential Distribution — A probability distribution mathematically described by an exponential function. Used to describe the probability that a product survives a length of time t in service, under the assumption that the probability of a product failing in any small time interval is independent of time.

$$F = \frac{\sigma_1^2}{\sigma_2^2}$$

F Distribution Formula

F Distribution — The distribution of F, the ratios of variances for pairs of samples taken from the same population. Used to determine whether or not the populations from which two samples were taken have the same standard deviation. The F distribution is usually expressed as a table of the upper limit below which F can be expected to lie with some confidence level, for samples of a specified number of degrees of freedom.

F Test — Test of whether two samples are drawn from populations with the same standard deviation, with some specified confidence level. The test is performed by determining whether F, as defined above, falls below the upper limit given by the F distribution table.

See Chapt. 15.

Factory Area Network (FAN®) — A flexible unwired system for quality control, consisting of DataMyte data collectors and DataTrucks™.

Failure Rate — The average number of failures per unit time. Used for assessing reliablility of a product in service.

See p. 2-20.

False $\bar{x}$ Causes — For $\bar{x}$ control charts: changes in the $\bar{x}$ control chart which are not due to changes in the process mean, but to changes in the corresponding R-chart.

See Chapt. 15.

FANLINK™ — A network controller that provides a hardwired communications link for the FAN® (Factory Area Network) system.

Fault Tree Analysis — A technique for evaluating the possible causes which might lead to the failure of a product. For each possible failure, the possible causes of the failure are determined; then the situations leading to those causes are determined; and so forth, until all paths leading to possible failures have been traced. The result is a flow chart for the failure process. Plans to deal with each path can then be made.

Feedback — Using the results of a process to control it. The feedback principle has wide application: an example would be using control charts to keep production personnel informed on the results of a process. This allows them to make suitable adjustments to the process. Some form of feedback on the results of a process is essential in order to keep the process under control.

Figure of Merit — Generic term for any of several measures of product reliability, including MTTF, MTBF, MTBM, MTFF, mean life, etc.

Fixed Station Data Acquisition Equipment — Data collecting equipment used at a fixed location, for example permanently attached to a particular manufacturing facility or residing in a test lab.

See p. 1-31, Chapt. 16.

Flow Chart (for programs, decision making, process development) -A pictorial representation of a process indicating the main steps, branches, and eventual outcomes of the process.

Frequency Distribution — For a sample drawn from a statistical population, the number of times each outcome was observed.

Goodness of Fit — Any measure of how well a set of data matches a proposed form. Chi-Square is the most common measure for frequency distributions. Simple visual inspection of a histogram is a less quantitative, but equally valid, way to determine goodness-of-fit.

Handheld Data Collector — A portable electronic device for recording data on a process or its product. The data collector serves in place of a check sheet for recording data.

See p. 1-27, Chapt. 16.

Header — For DataMyte® handheld data collectors: an entry at the beginning of a matrix of data used to record the contents of the matrix, i.e., information such as the date, operator, type of data, etc.

See p. 1-28.

Histogram — A graphic representation of a frequency distribution. The range of the variable is divided into a number of intervals of equal size (called cells) and an accumulation is made of the number of observations falling into each cell. The histogram is essentially a bar graph of the results of this accumulation.

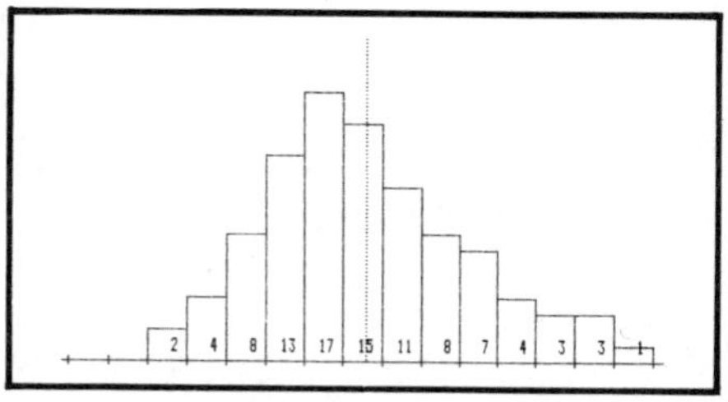

Histogram, see p. 1-7, 3-4.

Hypergeometric Distribution — A probability distribution for the probability of drawing exactly n objects of a given type from a sample of N objects of which r are of the desired type.

$$\frac{\binom{d}{r}\binom{N-d}{n-r}}{\binom{N}{n}}$$

Hypergeometric Distribution Formula, **see p. 5-6.**

Inspection Accuracy — The percentage of defective units which are correctly identified by an inspector. The percentage is determined by having a second inspector review both the accepted and rejected units.

See p. 2-16.

Instability (of a process) — A process is said to show instability if it exhibits variations larger than its control limits, or shows a systematic pattern of variation.

See p. 1-16.

Ishikawa Diagram (Cause-and-Effect diagram) — A pictorial diagram showing all the cause-and-effect relations among the factors which affect a process.

See Chapt. 6.

Just-In-Time (JIT) Manufacturing — Time manufacturing coordinates inventory and production to get away from the batch mode of production in order to improve quality.

$$K = \frac{(\text{MEAN} - \text{MIDPOINT})}{(\text{TOLERANCE}/2)}$$

K Index Formula, **see p. 3-13.**

K — For process capability studies: a measure of difference between the process mean and the specification mean.

See p. 3-8.

Kurtosis — A measure of how well a distribution is fit by a normal curve: If the distribution has larger tails than a normal distribution of the same standard deviation, it is said to have positive kurtosis (platykurtic); if it has smaller tails, then it has negative kurtosis (leptokurtic).

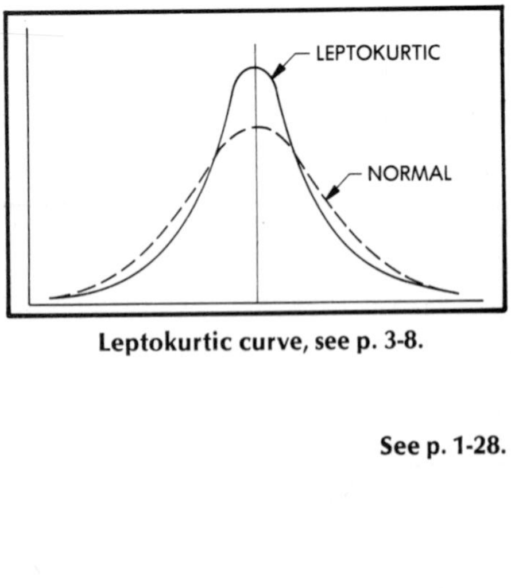

Leptokurtic curve, **see p. 3-8.**

LCL — Lower Control Limit. For control charts: the limit above which the process remains when it is in control.

Leptokurtic — For frequency distributions: a distribution which shows a higher peak and lower "tails" than a normal distribution with the same standard deviation.

See p. 1-28.

Limit Checking — For handheld data collectors: alerting the operator concerning any entries outside the expected range.

See p. 4-7

Linearity — The extent to which a measuring instrument's response varies with the measured quantity.

Lot Formation — The process of collecting units into lots for the purpose of acceptance sampling. The lots are chosen to ensure, as much as possible, that the units have identical properties, i.e., that they were produced by the same process operating under the same conditions.

See p. 5-8.

LSL — Lower Specification Limit. The lowest value of a product dimension or measurement which is acceptable.

Matrix — An array of data arranged in rows and columns. For DataMyte handheld data collectors, the rows of the matrix correspond to different samples, i.e., different manufactured units, while the columns correspond to the different measurements to be made on each unit.

MTBF — Mean Time Before Failure, or Mean Time Between Failures. This is a measure of product reliability.

Mean (of a statistical sample) — The average value of some variable. The mean is given by the formula, where 'x' is the value of the variable for the ith element, and n is the number of elements in the sample.

$$\bar{x} = \frac{x_1 + x_2 + \ldots + x_n}{n}$$

Mean Formula, **see p. 1-7.**

Measurement Accuracy — The extent to which the average result of a repeated measurement tends toward the true value of the measured quantity. The difference between the true value and the average measured value is called the instrument bias, and may be due to such things as improper zero-adjustment, nonlinear instrument response, or even improper use of the instrument.

See p. 4-7.

Measurement Error — The difference between the actual and measured value of a measured quantity.

See p. 4-10.

Measurement Precision — The extent to which a repeated measurement gives the same result. Variations may arise from the inherent capabilities of the instrument, from variations of the operator's use of the instrument, from changes in operating conditions, etc.

See p. 4-8.

Median (of a statistical sample) — For a sample of the values of a variable, the median is the point X such that half the sample elements are below X, and half above X.

See p. 2-3. *Median Chart* — For variable data: a control chart of the median of subgroups.

Metrology — The science of measurement.

See p. 5-11. *MIL-STD-105D* — A set of specifications for acceptance sampling plans based on acceptable quality level (AQL). For a given AQL, lot size, and level of inspection, the specification lists the number of defective units which is acceptable, and the number which requires rejection of the lot. The specifications allow for tightening or loosening of inspection requirements based on previous experience.

See p. 5-12. *MIL-STD-414* — A set of specifications for acceptance sampling plans based on acceptable quality level (AQL) for variables data, using the assumption that the variable is normally distributed.

See p. 2-17. *Mixture* — A combination of two distinct populations. On control charts, a mixture is indicated by an absence of points near the centerline.

Mode (of a statistical sample) — The value of the sample variable which occurs most frequently.

Monte Carlo Simulation — A computer modeling technique to predict the behavior of a system from the known random behaviors and interactions of the system's component parts. A mathematical model of the system is constructed in the computer program, and the response of the model to various operating parameters, conditions, etc. can then be investigated. The technique is useful for handling systems whose complexity prevents analytical calculation.

See p. 2-4. *Moving Average/Moving Range Chart* — A chart having points which are averages or ranges of previous day's data carried forward with the current day. Used to dampen the affects of a single reading when only one reading is made per day, or when a process is strongly linked to a previous day's output.

See p. 1-2. *Nominal Dimension* — For a product whose size is of concern: the desired mean value for the particular dimension.

Nonlinearity (of a measuring instrument) — The deviation of the instrument's response from linearity.

See p. 4-7

Normal Distribution — A probability distribution given mathematically by the formula. The normal distribution is a good approximation for a large class of situations. One example is the distribution resulting from the random additions of a large number of small variations. The Central Limits Theorem expresses this for the distribution of means of samples; the distribution of means results from the random additions of a large number of individual measurements, each of which contributes a small variation of its own.

$$p(x) = \frac{e^{-\frac{(x-\bar{x})^2}{2\sigma^2}}}{\sigma\sqrt{2\pi}}$$

Normal Distribution Formula, see p. 1-10.

np-Chart — For attributes data: a control chart of the number of defective units in a subgroup.

See p. 2-33

Operating Characteristics Curve — For acceptance sampling: a curve showing the percent defective in a lot vs. the probability that the lot will be rejected, for a specified lot size and sampling plan.

See p. 5-4.

Out of Control — A process which exhibits variations larger than the control limits is said to be out of control.

See p. 2-16, 2-29.

p-Chart (percent defective) — A control chart for the percentage of defective units. Used for attribute quality control.

See p. 2-31

Pareto Analysis — An analysis of the frequency of occurrence of various possible concerns. This is a useful way to decide quality control priorities when more than one concern is present. The underlying "Pareto Principle" states that a very small number of concerns is usually responsible for most quality problems.

See p. 1-19.

Pareto Diagram — A "bar graph" showing the frequency of occurrence of various concerns, ordered with the most frequent ones first.

See p. 1-19.

Percent Defective — For acceptance sampling: the percentage of units in a lot which are defective, i.e., of unacceptable quality.

See p. 3-3. *Performance Study* — Analysis of a process to determine the distribution of a run. The process may or may not be in statistical control.

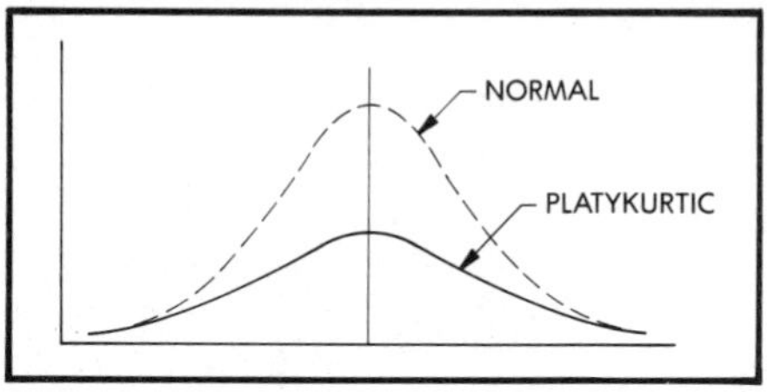

Platykurtic curve, see p. 3-8.

Platykurtic — For frequency distributions: a distribution which has larger "tails" than a normal distribution with the same standard deviation.

Point Estimate (Statistics) — A single-value estimate of a population parameter.

$$P(R)=\frac{(Np)^R(e)^{-Np}}{R!}$$

Poisson Distribution Formula, see p. 5-6.

Poisson Distribution — A probability distribution for the number of occurences of an event; N = number of trials; p = probability that the event occurs for a single trial; R = the number of trials for which the event occurred. The Poisson distribution is a good approximation of the binomial distribution for a case where p is small.

Population (statistical) (universe) — The set of all possible outcomes of a statistical determination. The population is usually considered as an (effectively) infinite set from which a subset called a sample is selected to determine the characteristics of the population, i.e., if a process were to run for an infinite length of time, it would produce an infinite number of units. The outcome of measuring the length of each unit would represent a statistical universe, or population. Any subset of the units produced (say, a hundred of them collected in sequence) would represent a sample of the population.

See Chapt. 15. *Post Processing* — Processing of data done after it is collected, usually by computer.

See p. 4-8. *Precision (of measurement)* — The extent to which repeated measurement of a standard with a given instrument yields the same result.

See p. 4-4. *Primary Reference Standard* — For measurements: a standard maintained by the National Bureau of Standards for a particular measuring unit. The primary reference standard duplicates as nearly as possible the international standard and is used to calibrate other (transfer) standards, which in turn are used to calibrate measuring instruments for industrial use.

Probability (Mathematical) — The likelihood that a particular occurrence (event) has a particular outcome. In mathematical terms, the probability that outcome X occurs is expressed by the formula. Note that, because of this definition, summing up the probabilities for all values of X always gives a total of 1: this is another way of saying that each trial must have exactly one outcome.

$$P(x) = \lim_{N \to \infty} \frac{\left(\text{Number of trials giving outcome X}\right)}{\left(\text{N = total number of trails}\right)}$$

Probability Formula, see p. 1-5.

Probability Distribution — A relation giving the probability of observing each possible outcome of a random event. The relation may be given by a mathematical expression, or it may be given empirically by drawing a frequency distribution for a large enough sample.

Process Analysis Diagram — An Ishikawa diagram for a process. Each step of the process and the factors contributing to it are shown, indicating all cause-and-effect relationships. This allows systematic tracing of any problems that may arise, to identify the source of the problem.

See p. 1-18.

Process Capability — The level of uniformity of product which a process is capable of yielding. Process capability may be expressed by the percent of defective products, the range or standard deviation of some product dimension, etc. Process capability is usually determined by performing measurements on some (or all) of the product units produced by the process.

See Chapt. 3.

Process Control — Maintaining the performance of a process at its capability level. Process control involves a range of activities such as sampling the process product, charting its performance, determining causes of any problems, and taking corrective actions.

See p. 1-3.

Producer's Risk — For acceptance sampling: the probability that a good lot of product will be rejected by a particular sampling plan.

See p. 5-3.

Prompt — For DataMyte handheld data collectors: a message displayed by the DataMyte to indicate to the operator what data should be recorded next. Prompts are input by the user during setup for a particular task.

See p. 1-28

Quality Assurance — The function of assuring acceptable quality levels within an organization. This function is the particular responsibility of one or more upper-management individuals who oversee the entire quality function of the organization.

Quality Characteristic — A particular aspect of a product which relates to its ability to perform its intended function.

See p. 1-2.

Quality Control — The process of maintaining an acceptable level of product quality.

Quality Function — The function of maintaining product quality levels; i.e.,the execution of quality control.

Quality Specifications — Particular specifications of the limits within which each quality characteristic of a product is to be maintained.

See p. 2-5.

R-Chart — A control chart of the range of variation amongst the individual elements of a sample — i.e., the difference between the largest and smallest elements — as a function of time, or lot number, or similar chronological variable.

Random — Varying with no discernable pattern.

See p. 1-8.

Range — The difference between the highest and lowest of a group of values.

See p. 2-14.

Rational Subgrouping — For control charting: a subgroup of units selected to minimize the differences due to assignable causes. Usually samples taken consecutively from a process operating under the same conditions will meet this requirement.

See tests for normality in Chapter 3.

Regression Analysis — A technique for determining the mathematical relation between a measured quantity and the variables it depends on. For example, the method might be used to determine the mathematical form of the probability distribution from which a sample was drawn, by determining which form best "fits" the frequency distribution of the sample. The frequency distribution is the "measured quantity" and the probability distribution is a "mathematical relation."

Rejectable Quality Level (RQL) — The minimum quality level at which a lot will be accepted. The term is usually used in lot inspection by sampling.

Reliability — The probability that a product will function properly for some specified period of time, under specified conditions.

Repeatability (of a measurement) — The extent to which repeated measurements of a particular object with a particular instrument produces the same value. **See p. 4-8.**

Reproducibility — The variation between individual people taking the same measurement and using the same gaging. **See p. 4-20.**

Response Surface Methodology (RSM) — A method of determining the optimum operating conditions and parameters of a process, by varying the process parameters and observing the results on the product. This is the same methodology used in Evolutionary Operations (EVOP), but is used in process development rather than actual production, so that strict adherence to product tolerances need not be maintained. An important aspect of RSM is to consider the relations among the parameters, and the possibility of simultaneously varying two or more parameters to optimize the process.

Resolution (of a measuring instrument) — The smallest unit of measure which an instrument is capable of indicating. **See p. 4-6.**

Route — For inspection, inventory, or other in-plant data collection: the sequence or path that the operator follows in the data collection process. **See p. 1-23.**

Run — A set of consecutive units, i.e., sequential in time. **See p. 2-16, 2-29.**

Sample (Statistics) — A representative group selected from a population. The sample is used to determine the properties of the population. **See p. 1-29.**

Sample Size — The number of elements, or units, in a sample.

Sampling — The process of selecting a sample of a population and determining the properties of the sample. The sample is chosen in such a way that its properties are representative of the population.

Sampling Variation — The variation of a sample's properties from the properties of the population from which it was drawn.

Scatter Plot — For a set of measurements of two variables on each unit of a group: A plot on which each unit is represented as a dot at the x,y position corresponding to the measured values for the unit. The scatter plot is a useful tool for investigating the relations between the two variables.

See p. 4-6. *Sensitivity (of a measuring instrument)* — The smallest change in the measured quantity which the instrument is capable of detecting.

See p. 4-2. *SI System* — The metric system of units of measure. The basic units of the system are the meter, the kilogram, and the second; the system is sometimes called the MKS system for this reason.

See p. 1-9. *Sigma* — The standard deviation of a statistical population.

See p. 3-9. *Sigma Limits* — For histograms: lines marked on the histogram showing the points n standard deviations above and below the mean.

Simulation (modelling) — Using a mathematical model of a system or process to predict the performance of the real system. The model consists of a set of equations or logic rules which operate on numerical values representing the operating parameters of the system. The result of the equations is a prediction of the system's output.

Skew — A nonsymmetric distribution is said to be skewed.

See p. 1-2. *Specification (of a product)* — A listing of the required properties of a product. The specifications may include the desired mean and/or tolerances for certain dimensions or other measurements; the color or texture of surface finish; or any other properties which define the product.

Stability (of a process) — A process is said to be stable if it shows no recognizable pattern of change. See also Control, and Constant Cause System.

See p. 1-11.

Standard (measurement) — A reference item providing a known value of a quantity to be measured. Standards may be primary — i.e., the standard essentially defines the unit of measure — or secondary (transfer) standards, which have been compared to the primary standard (directly or by way of an intermediate transfer standard). Standards are used to calibrate instruments which are then employed to make routine measurements.

$$\sigma = \sqrt{\frac{\sum_{i=1}^{n}(x_i - \bar{x})^2}{n-1}}$$

Standard Deviation Formula, see p. 1-9.

Standard Deviation — A measure of the variation among the members of a statistical sample. If a sample of n values has a mean of $\bar{x}$, its standard deviation is given by the formula.

Statistical Control (of a process) — A process is said to be in a state of statistical control when it exhibits only random variations.

See p. 1-12.

Statistical Inference — The process of drawing conclusions on the basis of statistics.

Statistical Quality Control — The process of maintaining an acceptable level of product quality by means of statistical methods.

See p. 1-3.

Stratification (of a sample) — If a sample is formed by combining units from several lots having different properties, the sample distribution will show a concentration or clumping about the mean value for each lot: this is called stratification. In control charting, if there are changes between subgroups due to stratification, the R-chart points will all tend to be near the centerline.

See p. 2-17, 2-30.

Subgroup — For control charts: a sample of units from a given process, all taken at or near the same time.

Systematic Variation (of a process) — Variations which exhibit a predictable pattern. The pattern may be cyclic (i.e., a recurring pattern) or may progress linearly (trend).

t-Distribution — For a sample with size N drawn from a normally distributed population with mean mu: The distribution is shown where s is the sample variance and $\bar{x}$ is the sample mean. The t-distribution is expressed as a table for a given number of degrees of freedom (= N − 1).

t-Test — A test of the statistical hypothesis that the mean of a population lies within a specified range: a sample is drawn from the population, and the t-distribution is applied to the sample mean, to determine the probability that the population mean lies in the specified range.

See p. 1-2. *Tolerance* — The permissible range of variation in a particular dimension of a product. Tolerances are often set by engineering requirements to ensure that components will function together properly.

See Chapt. 6. *Total Quality Control (TQC)* — A management system of integrated controls, including engineering, purchasing, financial administration, marketing and manufacturing, to ensure customer quality satisfaction and economical costs of quality.

Transcription — Rewriting; copying.

See p. 2-17, 2-30. *Trend* — A gradual, systematic change with time or other variable.

See p. 2-19. *True $\bar{x}$ Causes* — For $\bar{x}$ control charts: changes in the $\bar{x}$ control chart which are due to actual changes in the mean produced by the process. True $\bar{x}$ changes are usually accompanied by a stable pattern in the R-chart.

See p. 2-5. *Type I Error* — In control chart analysis: concluding that a process is unstable when in fact it is stable.

See p. 2-5. *Type II Error* — In control chart analysis: concluding that a process is stable when in fact it is unstable.

See p. 2-36 *u-Chart* — Attribute data: a control chart of the percentage of defects in one subgroup to total defects for an inspection.

UCL — Upper Control Limit. For control charts, the upper limit below which a process remains if it is in control.

Uniform Distribution — This distribution means that all outcomes are equally likely.

USL — Upper Specification Limit: the highest value of a product dimension or measurement which is acceptable.

Variability — The property of exhibiting variation, i.e., changes or differences, in particular in the product of a process. **See p. 1-4.**

Variables — Quantities which are subject to change or variability.

Variable Data — Concerning the values of a variable; as opposed to Attribute Data. **See p. 1-13.**

Variance — The square of the standard deviation.

$\bar{x}$ and R Chart — For variable data: control charts for the average and range of subgroups of data. **See p. 2-5**

$\bar{x}$ and Sigma Chart — For variable data: control charts for the average and standard deviation (sigma) of subgroups of data. **See p. 2-3**

1. INTRODUCTION TO STATISTICAL PROCESS CONTROL

1.1 HOW IT ALL BEGAN

You must have control over an industrial process in order to produce interchangeable parts. Eli Whitney and other forerunners of the industrial revolution discovered this a bit too late. In 1798 Whitney won a contract from the U.S. government to produce 10,000 muskets. He was convinced he could work out a system of making gun parts to a standardized pattern. Nowadays that wouldn't be anything special, but back then it was practically unheard of. The conventional method of manufacturing a gun was to have a skilled craftsman fashion the whole piece, forming and fitting each part. If a part broke, a new one would have to be custom made. For a nation in need of armaments it is easy to see the attraction of the concept of interchangeable parts. Unfortunately, out of Whitney's first manufacturing run of 700 parts only 14 guns could be assembled. The idea temporarily failed for the lack of another.

Quality control was the name for the new idea. Quality control was necessary because mass produced products lacked quality and early manufacturing processes lacked control. The concept of quality control was to ensure that a specification was written and all parts conformed to it. First, a part was evaluated in terms of its function and its meeting the needs and expectations of the customer. Engineering then created a specification (Figure 1.1.1). The specification called out the materials, the dimensions, and the finish. The dimensions were usually expressed as the target dimension, or nominal, and the high and low limit, or tolerance. The job of quality control then was to inspect parts to make sure they conformed to specification and evaluate bad parts to find out why they didn't. As long as a high percentage of good parts were made in a suitably efficient way the process by which they were made was not that important.

The experience of World War I, however, raised doubts about the adequacy of this kind of quality control. The war was America's first experience with supplying vital materials over long distances. The quality of both finished products and replacement parts had to be guaranteed under conditions that prohibited the on-sight evaluation of fail-

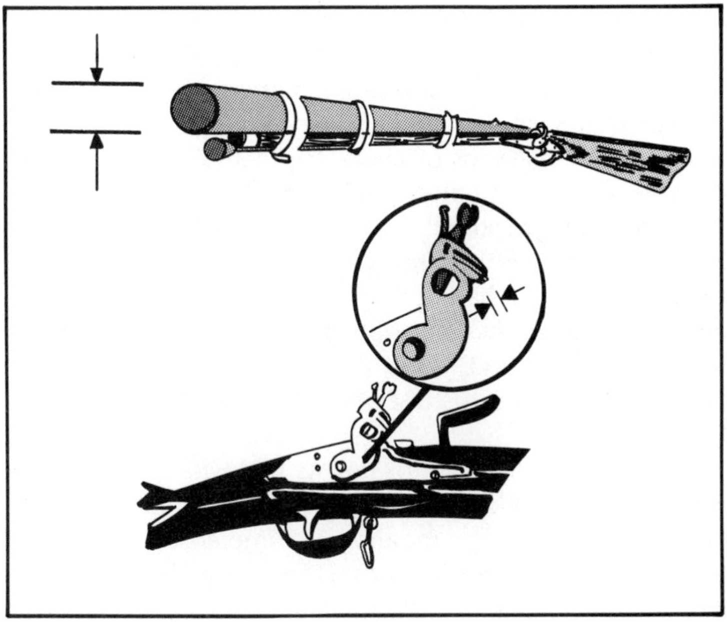

Fig.1.1.1 A specification is a pattern from which to build parts.

ures, and in volumes that made 100% inspection a losing proposition. Quality control was inadequate because it was reactive. It relied too much on the evaluation of parts and parts failures. The logistics of war demanded a more active quality function. The focus had to shift to the home front so to speak — to the manufacturing process. Of course this new emphasis had to have a new name.

Statistical quality control was the new name. It is also called *statistical process control* to emphasize the importance of the process. But the old concept of quality control lacked something else besides a simple shift of emphasis. That something is statistics.

We owe the application of statistics to Dr. Walter A. Shewhart, a physicist at Bell Labs. Shewhart specialized in Brownian movement, the random behavior of small particles in a fluid caused by the collision of molecules. Statistical methods for analyzing large amounts of data were useful to this type of study. It was natural for Shewhart to use his knowledge of statistics when asked to help in the war effort.

Shewhart was assigned the task of designing a standard radio headset for army troops. He began by measuring the head sizes of 10,000 troops (Figure 1.1.2). He arranged the sizes from small to large and marked the frequency of occurrence of individual sizes. What intrigued him was that

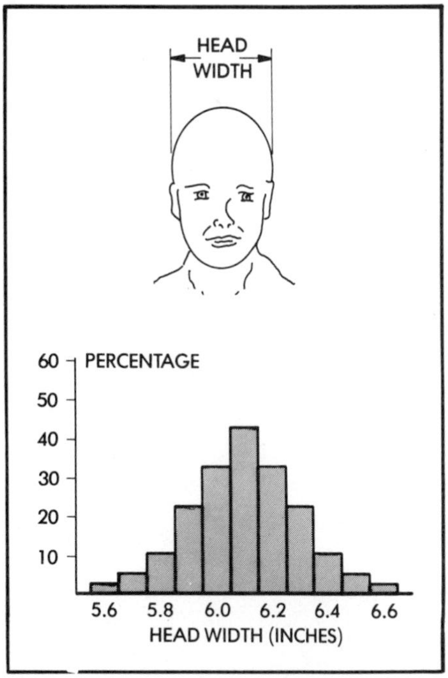

Fig.1.1.2 Distribution of head sizes among army troops.

the pattern of the distribution resembled what is known as the *bell-shaped curve*, or normal distribution, shown in Figure 1.1.2. It was a pattern he encountered when studying Brownian movement, and he wondered whether such patterns and the methods of analyzing them had broader applications. He eventually developed some descriptive statistics to aid in manufacturing and wrote a book published in 1931, *Economic Control of Quality of Manufactured Product*. The book had very little impact at the time it was published, but gradually people became aware of the value of statistical methods. One very important technique he developed is called the Shewhart Control Chart, or $\bar{x}$ & R Chart.

Statistical quality control saw its first widespread application during World War II. The war department required industries making war materials to implement statistical controls, and hired statisticians to help teach them. One of the statisticians was Dr. W. E. Deming, who later helped foster the statistical quality movement in postwar Japan. The Japanese faced much the same problems in guaranteeing quality over long distances that America faced during the war. Lacking in many natural resources, their ability to produce and export manufactured articles was necessary for survival. Fortunately for them, they listened to sound advice and they learned to implement it. The success of their implementation of a basically American methodology has been felt far beyond their shores.

1.2 BASIC STATISTICAL CONCEPTS

What Shewhart discovered in the twenties is that variability is as normal to a manufacturing process as it is to natural phenomena like the movement of molecules in a jar of fluid. No two things can ever be made exactly alike, just like no two things are alike in nature. The key to success in manufacturing is to understand the causes of variability and to have a method which recognizes them. Shewhart found two basic causes of variability, *common causes* and *assignable causes*.

Common Causes of Variability

If we flip a coin and count the number of heads versus tails, at first we may get a few more of one than the other but over the long run they will be fairly even (Figure 1.2.1). We say that the *probability* of heads in a coin toss is 50% or 0.5. The probability is a statistic. For a few coin flips this probability may not be a reliable indicator of the outcome, but it tends to be more reliable as larger groups of coin tosses are counted. Coin tosses vary purely by chance, and chance is what is known as a common cause of variability.

Another example of common causes at work is with dice throws. If we repeatedly throw a pair of dice and record the totals, we'll get an unequal distribution of results. The possible outcomes are the numbers 2 through 12, but as any craps game player will tell us the frequency of their occurrence varies. Dice pair combinations total some numbers more frequently than others, as shown in Figure 1.2.2. The number 7 will occur in six combinations whereas the number 12 has only one. Over the long run the probability of the number 7 occurring is .167 or about 17%, which is greater than the number 2, which is about 3%. A pair of dice produces an example of an unequal frequency distribution, but it is entirely due to common causes. Whenever the outcomes of a process can be expressed in probabilities, and we are certain about the distribution of outcomes over the long run, we have what is known as a *constant-*

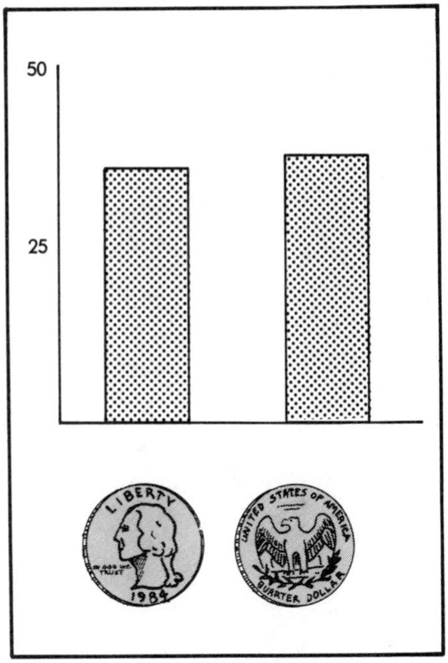

Fig.1.2.1 Probability of coin tosses.

Fig.1.2.2 Probability of dice throws.

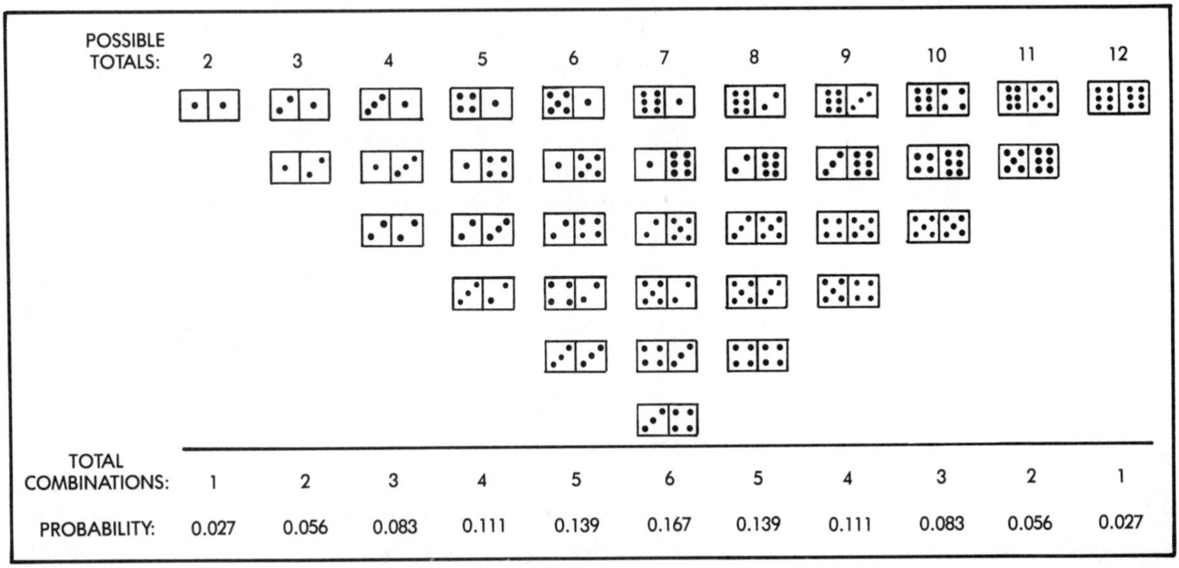

cause system.

As you may have guessed, manufacturing processes sometimes behave like constant/cause systems. The causes of variation are commonplace, like dice throws. If left to produce parts continually without change, the variation would remain. It cannot be altered without changing the process itself. Statististics provide us with ways of recognizing variation due to common causes. The main one is the control chart. By using a control chart we can separate common causes from the second type, which are called assignable causes.

Assignable Causes of Variability

A change of materials, excessive tooling wear, a new operator, these types of things would produce variation in a process that is different from variation due to common causes. They disturb a process so that what it produces seems unnatural. A loaded pair of dice is another example. Since we know what a regular pair of dice produces over a large number of rolls, we can be reasonably sure a pair of dice is loaded if, after a large number of rolls, we have more twelves than sevens.

When we look for problems in a process we are usually just looking for these assignable causes of variability. Assignable causes produce erratic behavior for which a reason can be identified. One might ask why we are going through all the trouble. Why separate assignable causes from common causes when we have to compare parts to a specification anyway? One reason is that we can minimize variability when we know its causes. Variability may result in many parts being out of specification or only a few. If there are many parts out of specification, we have three choices: 1) continually inspecting all parts and using the good ones, 2) improving the process until most or all parts are good, or 3) scrapping the process and building a better one. Since 100% inspection is expensive and inefficient in most cases, we are better off trying to improve the process and reducing our inspection load. Which brings us back to the process. There is no sense in trying to improve a process that won't do the job for us. Also, we don't want to scrap a process that potentially could work like a charm. Therefore, we need a way to determine whether the process can consistently produce good parts. The only reliable method is through the use of control charts to find and eliminate the assignable causes of variation.

The Mean or Central Tendency

Many processes are set up to aim at a target dimension. The parts that come off the process vary of course, but we always hope they are close to the nominal and not too many of them fall outside of the high and low specifications. Parts made in this way exhibit what is called a *central tendency.* That is, they tend to group around a certain dimension (Figure 1.2.3).

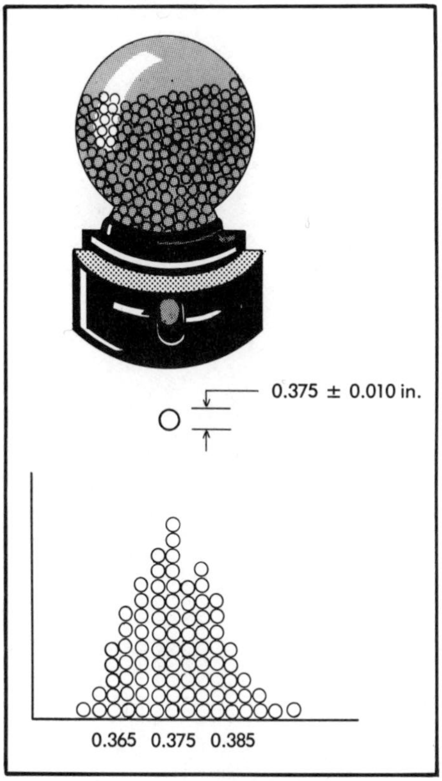

Fig.1.2.3 The central tendency of a process.

The most useful measure of central tendency is the *mean* or average. To find the mean of measurement data, add the data together and divide by the number of measurements taken. The formula would be:

$$\bar{x} = \frac{x_1 + x_2 + \ldots + x_n}{n} \qquad (1.2.1)$$

'x' is the measurement and 'n' is the number of measurements. In statistics the average is symbolized by $\bar{x}$, or x-bar. If we use the Greek letter for summation Σ, the formula can be written as:

$$\bar{x} = \frac{1}{n} \sum_{i=1}^{n} x_i \qquad (1.2.2)$$

Figure 1.2.4 is a *histogram* showing one dimension and its variation among 50 parts. The histogram shows the frequency of parts at each dimension by the height of the bars. Notice that the $\bar{x}$ is not at the most frequent value. The most frequent value is just to the left of it. Now look at Figure 1.2.5. The mean value in this histogram seems to be among the least frequent values that occurred. Obviously, without some kind of statistic that tells us about the spread or *dispersion* of our data, the mean does not tell us enough.

Averages are used in many sports, from bowling to baseball. When we know someone's bowling average or baseball hitting average we have some indication of how good

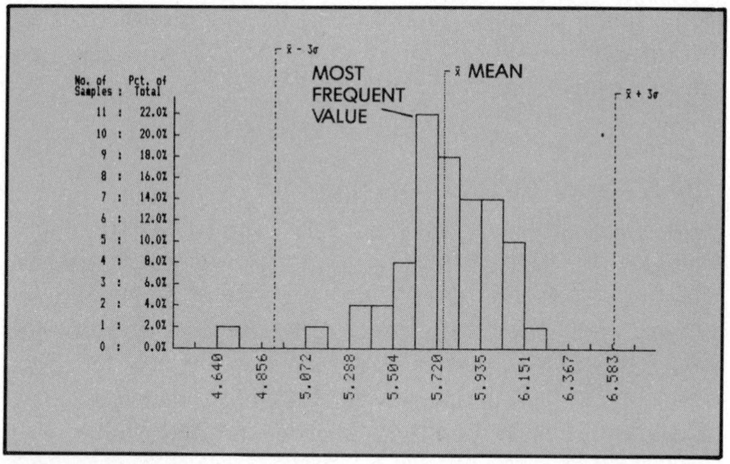

Fig.1.2.4 The mean may not be the most frequent value in a distribution.

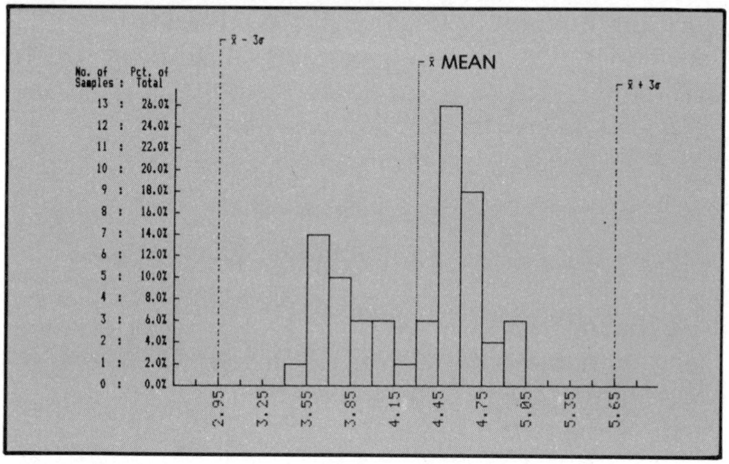

Fig.1.2.5 The mean may even be the least frequent value.

that person is, but not really enough information about consistency. Lurking behind a low average could be a lot of great games and a few very bad ones. A good average could merely be the work of an average player with a few lucky games.

Range and Standard Deviation (Sigma)

Two measures of dispersion are used in statistics, the *range* and the *standard deviation*. The range tells us what the overall spread of the data is. To get the range, subtract the lowest from the highest measurement. The symbol for range is R. The formula is:

$$R = x_{max} - x_{min} \qquad (1.2.3)$$

It means simply to subtract the smallest measurement from the largest. Now that we have a measure of spread and a measure of central tendency, why do we need a third statistic? What does standard deviation tell us that range and average do not? To help answer this we need to look at Figure 1.2.6. Two different histograms are pictured. Rather than using bars, continuous lines are used to show the shape of the distributions. We can imagine that if enough data was collected and if the data was represented by bars of very narrow width, a bar histogram would look nearly like the curves shown here. The two histograms have different shapes, yet the ranges and averages are the same. Obviously, a statistic is needed to tell us something about the shape of the distribution, rather than just the midpoint and the extremes. This is what we use the standard deviation for.

The standard deviation is called *sigma* in statistics and is symbolized by the Greek letter σ. Sigma can be calculated using this formula:

$$\sigma = \sqrt{\frac{\sum_{i=1}^{n} (x_i - \bar{x})^2}{n - 1}} \qquad (1.2.4)$$

$\bar{x}$ is the mean of the data, x is an individual measurement and n is the total number of measurements. The above formula is called the n-1 formula because of its denominator. The more classic standard deviation formula uses n instead of n-1. The n-1 formula will be used here because it provides a closer approximation of the standard deviation of samples coming from a process that is producing continually. Continuous processes are the most common type used in manufacturing.

Sigma has a special relationship to the distribution shown in Figure 1.2.7. The distribution shown is called a *normal distribution* and its special properties are described in the next paragraph. When sigma is calculated from data that takes the form of a normal distribution, and we plot distances of one, two, and three sigma away from the mean, we find these relationships:

Fig.1.2.6 Two histograms having the same mean and range.

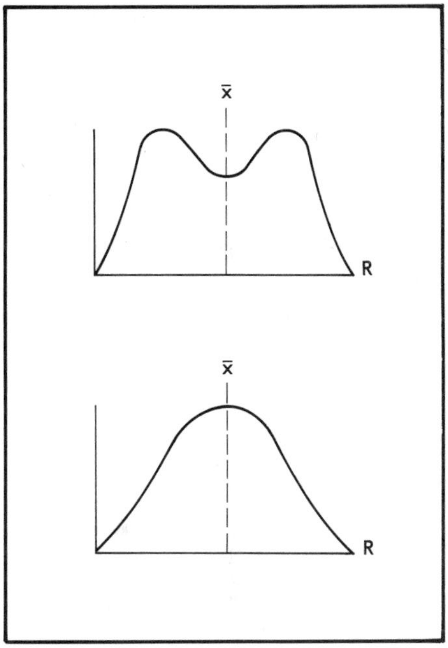

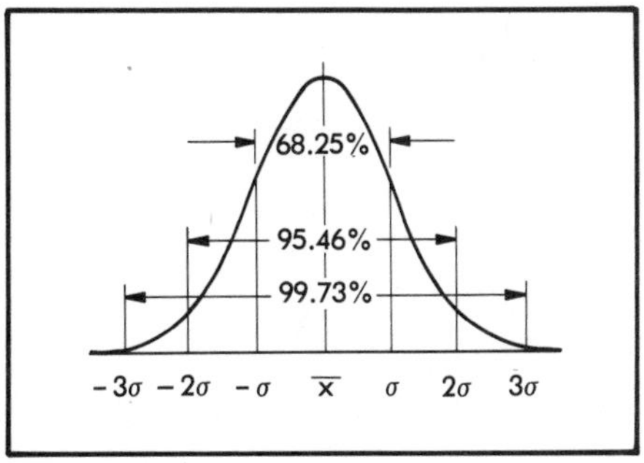

Fig.1.2.7 The relationship of sigma to a normal distribution.

- 68.25% of all measurements lie between $\bar{x} - \sigma$ and $\bar{x} + \sigma$.
- 95.46% of all measurements lie between $\bar{x} - 2\sigma$ and $\bar{x} + 2\sigma$.
- 99.73% of all measurements lie between $\bar{x} - 3\sigma$ and $\bar{x} + 3\sigma$.

The Normal Distribution

There is one type of distribution that can be described entirely by its mean and standard deviation. It is the normal distribution or bell-shaped curve. It has these characteristics (Figure 1.2.8):

Fig.1.2.8 The normal distribution, or bell-shaped curve.

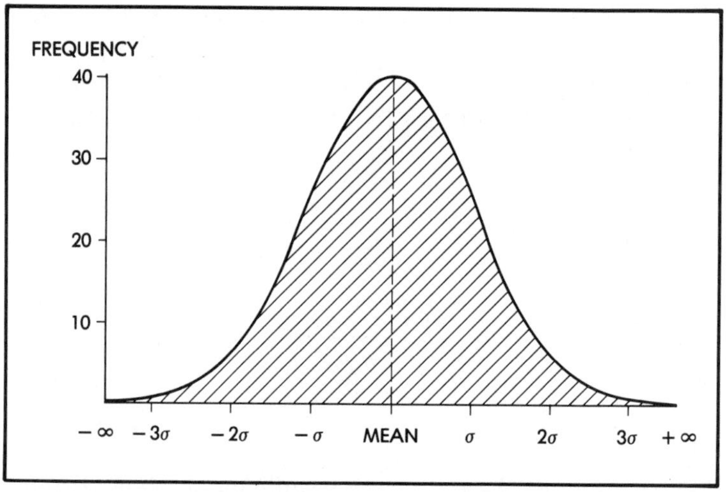

- The point of highest frequency is right at the mean.
- It is symmetrical about the mean.
- On either side it slopes downward to infinity. In other words, its range is seemingly infinite.
- 99.73% of the area under the curve is bounded by the mean plus and minus three sigma ($\bar{x} \pm 3\sigma$)

The equation for a bell-shaped curve is:

$$p(x) = \frac{e^{-\frac{(x-\bar{x})^2}{2\sigma^2}}}{\sigma\sqrt{2\pi}} \qquad (1.2.5)$$

The normal distribution is a valuable tool because we can compare the histogram of a process to it and draw some conclusions about the capability of the process. Before making this type of comparison, however, a process must be monitored for evidence of stability over time. This is done by taking small groups of samples at selected intervals, measuring them, and plotting their averages and ranges on a control chart. The control chart provides us with an indication of whether we have stable variation, in other words a constant-cause system, or a lack of stability due to some assignable causes. Chapter 2 describes the making and using of $\bar{x}$ & R charts in more detail. The reason they work has to do with the *central limit theorem* and the normal distribution curve.

Central Limit Theorem

Shewhart found that the normal distribution curve appears when the averages of subgroups from a constant-cause system are plotted in the form of a histogram. The constant-cause system does not itself have to be a normal distribution. It can be triangular, rectangular or even inverted-pyramid shape like dice combinations, as long as the sample size is reasonably large. The averages of different sized subgroups selected from these distributions, or *universes,* as they are called in statistics, will show a central tendency. The variation of averages will tend to follow the normal curve. This is called the central limit theorem.

Shewhart demonstrated this by using numbered chips and a large bowl. His normal bowl had 998 chips, rectangular bowl had 122, and triangular bowl had 820. The rectangular universe had chips bounded by a certain range and in equal numbers like in Figure 1.2.9. The triangular universe had unequal numbers of various chips as shown in Figure 1.2.10. Shewhart took each chip out of the bowl one at a time, recorded the number and put it back. He then mixed the bowl before choosing another. He averaged every four. The points he plotted fell within or along the edges of the bell-shaped curve. What this meant to him is that a process can be monitored over time by measuring and averaging a standard subgroup of parts. The subgroup could be 2, 4, or even 20. The frequency could be once per hour, or once per day depending upon the output. If the process was a constant-cause system, these averages would fall within a normal curve. One could conclude that the process was *stable.*

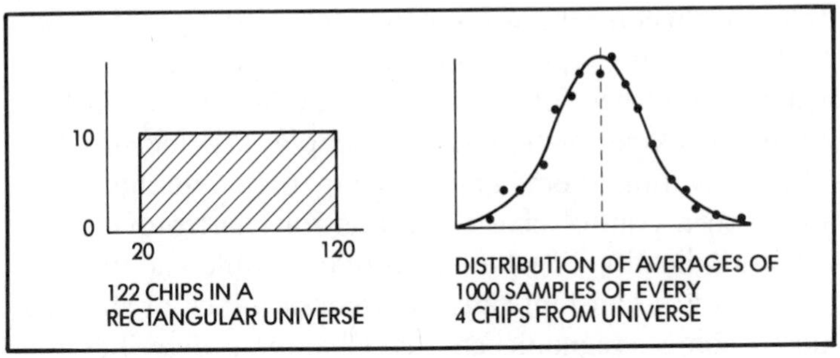

Fig.1.2.9 Averages of large enough subgroups from a rectangular universe tend to follow a normal distribution.

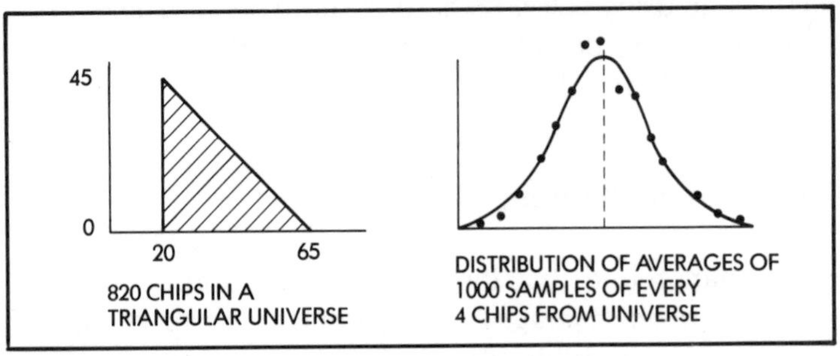

Fig.1.2.10 Averages of large enough subgroups from a triangular universe tend to follow a normal distribution.

By stable, we mean that the variability was entirely due to common causes. Statisticians also use the phrase *in control* to refer to a process that has stable variability over time.

Frequent checking of the averages of subgroups also provides a way to discover when assignable causes are present in a process. When assignable causes appear they will affect the averages to the point where these averages will probably not fit within a normal curve. Once it is known what the stable variation of the process is, the assignable causes will appear in averages of subgroups taken periodically.

The central limit theorem is the reason why control charts work. The charting of averages has this particular advantage over the charting of individual data points. The charting of ranges is also used because subgroup ranges will also show stability if a constant-cause system exists.

1.3 BASIC DATA COLLECTION METHODS

The first part of this chapter introduced the concepts of statistical process control. But before we can apply statistics we must first collect data. The rest of this chapter explains how to identify characteristics and begin the task of collecting data.

Types of Data

Data can be classified in a very general way by how it is collected. Data that is measured is called *variable* data. Data that is counted or classified is called *attribute* data. Variable data has these characteristics:

- It is measurable, by units of length, diameter, weight, temperature or Newton meters for example.
- It is continuous (Figure 1.3.1). How we verify it depends entirely on the accuracy and resolution of our gaging. Something could weigh 2 kilograms on our scale but could weigh 1.98 Kg on a more precise scale and a slightly different weight on other scales.
- Variable data of the same unit of measure can be compared numerically. We can find the mean, range and standard deviation.

Attribute data has one or more of these characteristics:

- It is countable. Either it exists or it does not, such as with defects on a painted surface (Figure 1.3.2).
- It is classified or graded using a scale, such as small, medium and large eggs. Sometimes an arbitrary scale is used as a substitute for measuring when the exact measurement is not important.
- Pass/fail data, such as the picture tube works or does not.

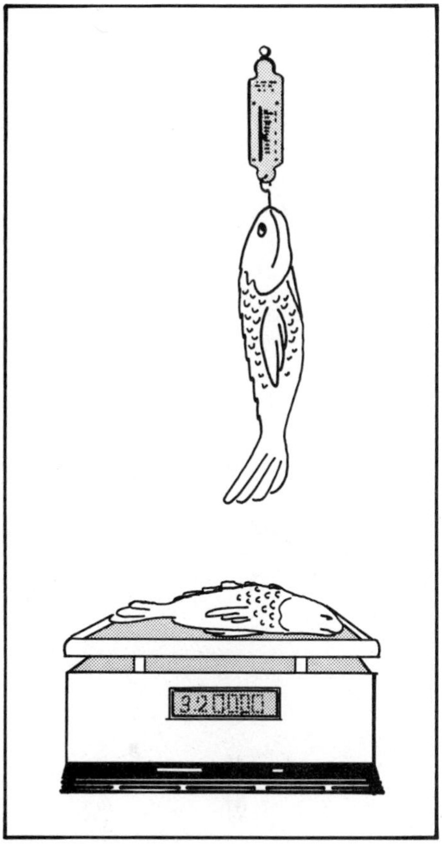

Fig. 1.3.1 Variable data.

Fig. 1.3.2 Attribute data.

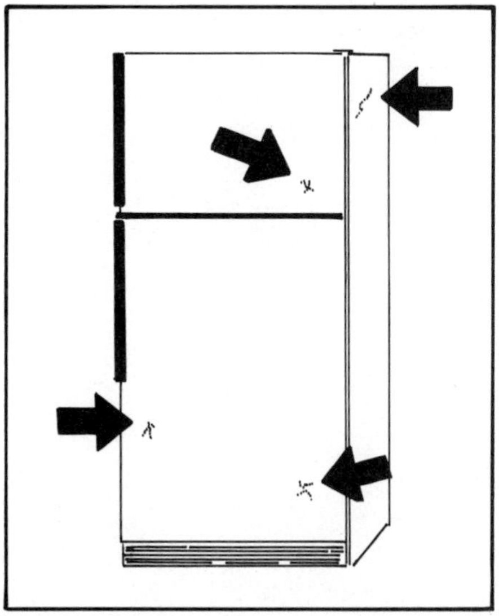

Other types of data such as serial numbers, build sequence numbers and piece counts are used for production control. These types are sometimes used to support the quality control function and very often need to be collected and analyzed for the same purposes. Data collection techniques have their application in many aspects of manufacturing, whether for production control or quality control.

Attribute data is often collected during final inspection. An assembled machine may be composed of parts that can be individually measured, but once assembled it either works or it doesn't. The success of a manufacturing process can be expressed as the percentage of good parts produced. This type of data provides an overall measure of quality improvement when inspection is used, but it does

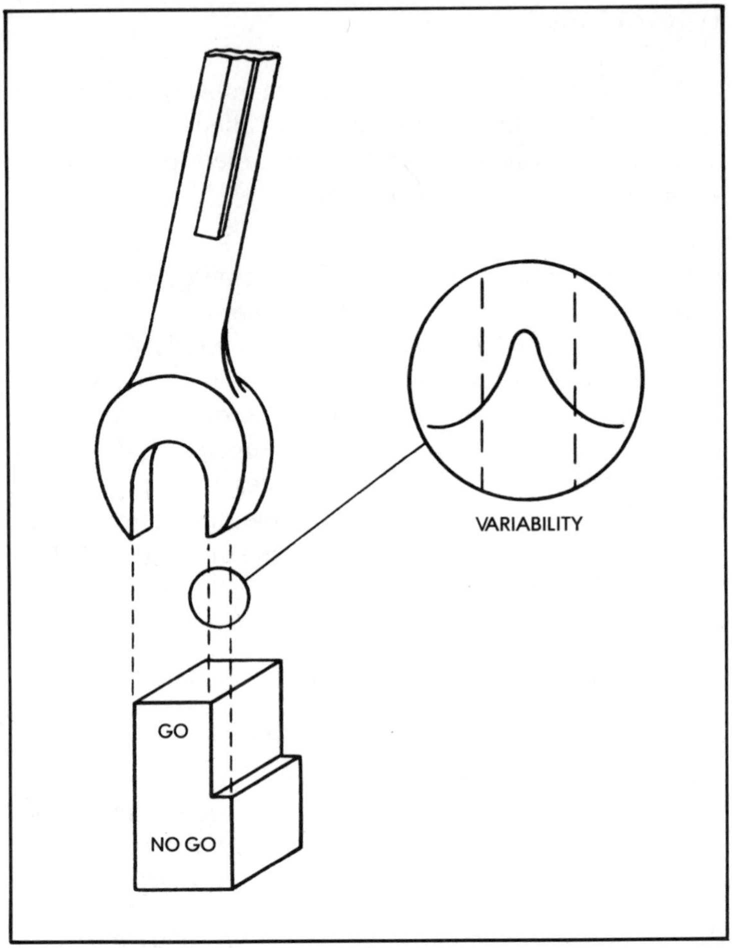

Fig.1.3.3 GO/NO-G0 gages do not detect the variability in a process—the main indicator of process improvement.

not provide a clue as to how to make the improvement. In general, attribute data is not a good substitute for variable data. Improving a process often depends on the ability to distinguish between minute differences in dimension, weight, or some other quality characteristic. The gaging must be able to detect these differences in order to establish the variability of a process. GO/NO-GO gages based on the low and high limits of a part specification do not provide a means for process improvement (Figure 1.3.3).

Selecting Characteristics

To improve quality we must first identify the characteristics of quality in a part. These characteristics may have to do with fit or finish, or perhaps something very intangible such as product desirability. Selecting characteristics involves a clarification of purpose, and aims at identifying these characteristics as either variable or attribute data. Some of the questions that may need asking are:

- *Purpose* — is our purpose a general one, or are we addressing a specific quality problem? Can it be defined?

- *Problem clarification* — Where is the problem noticeable? Where does it appear first? Is it a compound problem? Can it be addressed within our factory? Is there currently a method for detecting the characteristics of this problem?

- *Selecting characteristics* — Can we specify the characteristics? Are they measurable? At what point in the process can they be measured or verified? Can we take action on data collected on these characteristics? Are results verifiable?

The importance of selecting characteristics becomes evident when we are faced with the task of collecting data. To be worthwhile, data collection must serve our objectives. The clarification of these objectives and the selection of characteristics that provide evidence and also serve as a basis for action will allow data collection to provide results. If the problem is not clear or the wrong characteristics are being measured, time will be wasted and we will still have a problem.

Selecting the Means of Analysis

How data is analyzed depends on both the type of data, whether variable or attribute, and the purpose for collecting it. There are also several ways of analyzing data for any one purpose. One or all methods may need to be used. Table 1.3.1 classifies several means of analysis described in this book.

Purpose	Type of Data	Means of Analysis	See Chapter
Process Control	Variable	$\bar{x}$ & R Chart	2
		$\bar{x}$ & Sigma Chart	2
	Attribute	p, np, c-Charts	2
		Pareto Diagrams	1
Process Capability	Variable	Histograms	3
		Capability Studies	3
	Attribute	c-Charts	2
Acceptance Sampling	Variable	Histograms	3, 5
	Attribute	AQL, LTPD, AOQL	5

Table 1.3.1 Means of analysis.

1.4 CAUSE AND EFFECT DIAGRAMS (Ishikawa Diagrams)

Dr. Kauru Ishikawa, a noted Japanese authority on quality and productivity, developed these diagrams for problem solving. A more complete explanation of these diagrams can be found in his book, *Guide to Quality Control,* 1976. A cause and effect diagram is a simple technique for dissecting a problem or process. Making a diagram is possibly the best first step in analyzing a problem prior to data collection. It organizes thinking and provides a plan of attack at the same time. There are three types of cause and effect diagrams:

- *Cause enumeration diagram* — A graphic listing of all the possible causes of a problem.

- *Dispersion analysis diagram* — Used to analyze the causes of variability in a process.

- *Process analysis diagram* — A flow diagram used to study quality problems.

All three diagrams look nearly alike. The dispersion analysis and process analysis diagrams are derivatives of the basic cause enumeration diagram and are used to highlight process control problems.

To create a cause enumeration diagram, first put the problem on the extreme right side of the page as in Figure 1.4.1. Then draw a long-stemmed arrow to it. Along the stem of the arrow draw smaller arrows and label them with the possible causes. It is important to list all possible causes by putting down everything that comes to mind. A good diagram will look extremely complicated and busy, but if everything is included on the chart then the true causes of the problem should be there.

For a compound problem several diagrams may be necessary. Later we might be able to combine the diagrams and organize the causes, using some criterion such as their relative importance, or the sequence of events. When investigating the causes, we use the diagram to note progress. We may be able to eliminate most causes, or even add a few that were not described.

Fig.1.4.1 How to start a cause enumeration diagram.

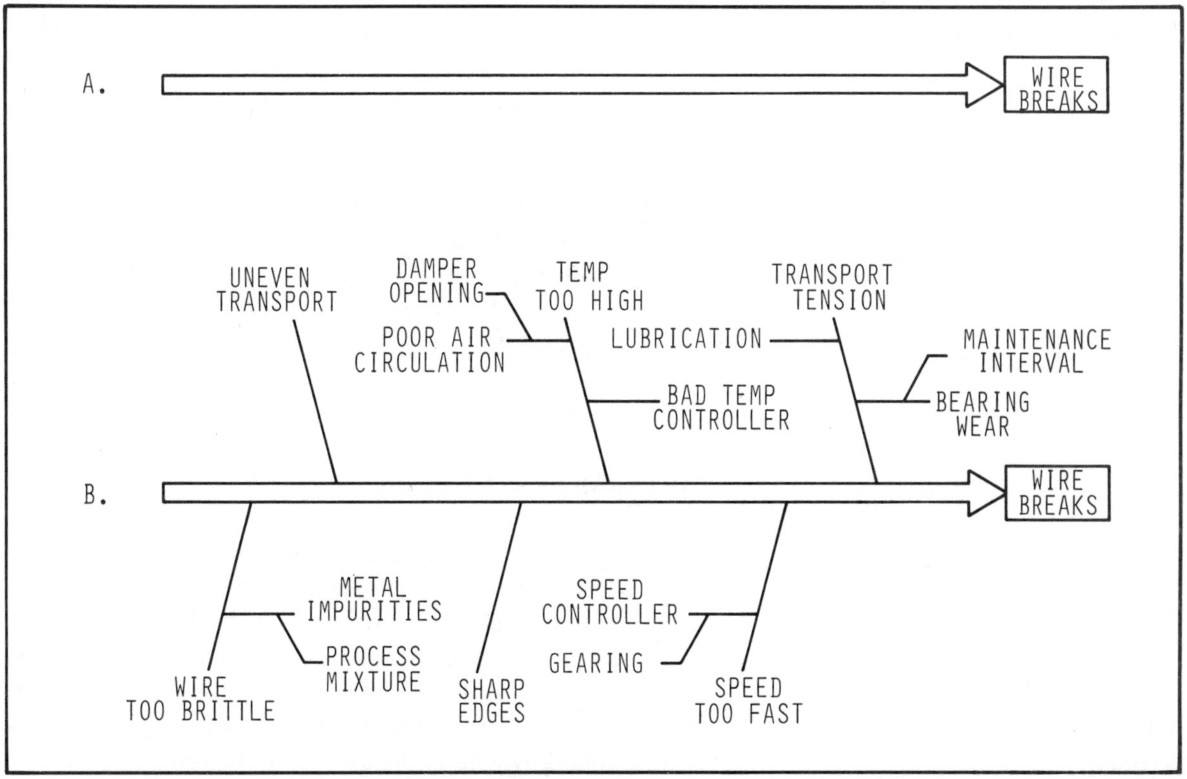

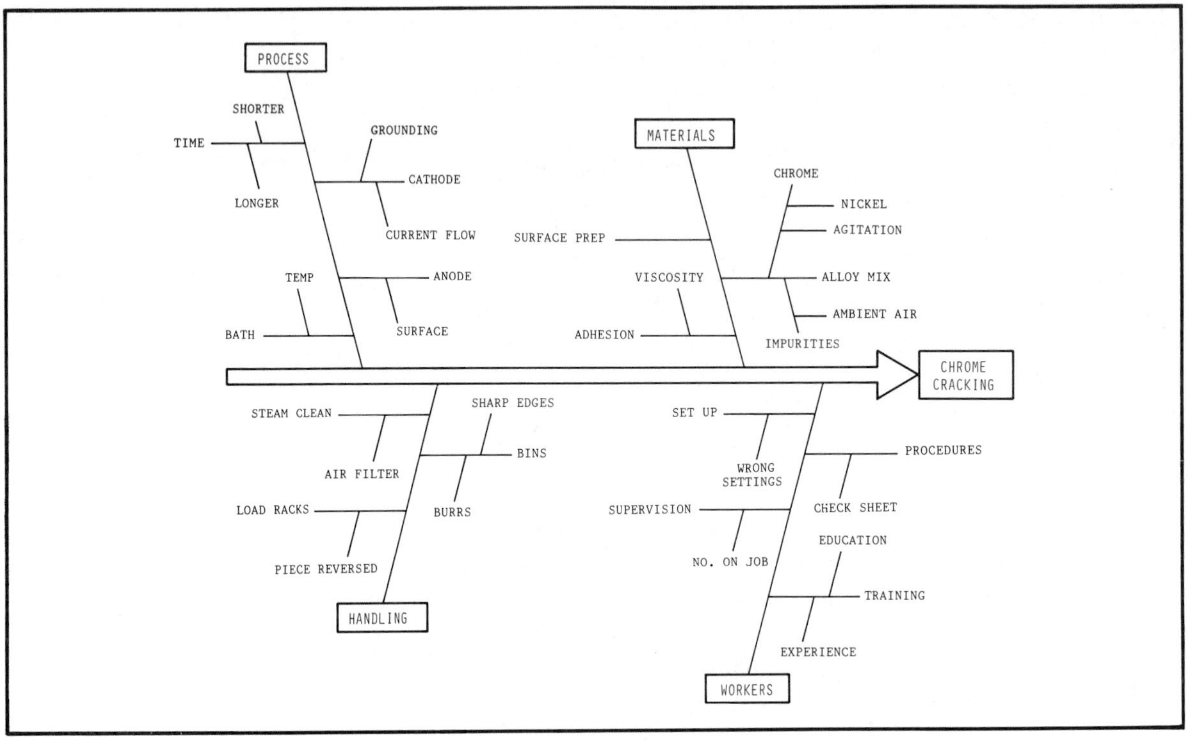

Fig.1.4.2 Dispersion analysis diagram.

Dispersion Analysis Diagram

To make a dispersion analysis diagram, start with the problem on the right and an arrow to it as shown in Figure 1.4.1a. List the main groups that influence the problem by their general category, such as worker, materials, tools, inspection, and machinery (Figure 1.4.2). The next step is to list all details that would contribute to variability by drawing arrows to the branches and labeling them. This organizes the causes into categories that can be focused on one at a time.

Process Analysis Diagram

A process analysis diagram is like a process flow diagram. Each step of a process should be labeled and connected by a line going from left to right (Figure 1.4.3). At each step in the process draw branches and label everything that could influence the quality of the product at that point in the process. This provides a listing of quality problems arranged by when they appear in the process.

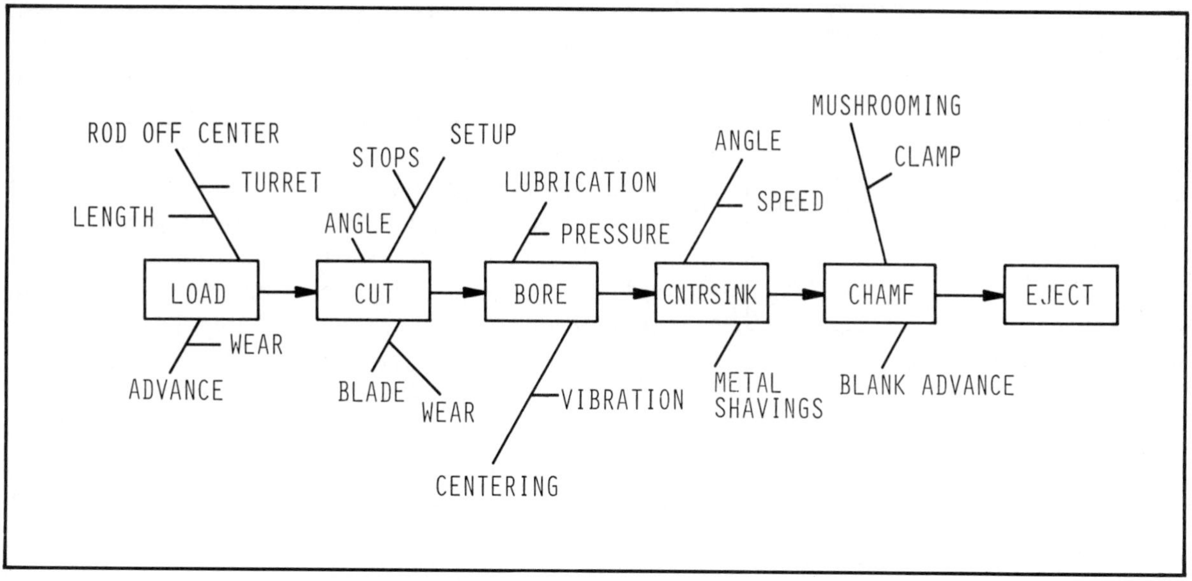

Fig.1.4.3 Process analysis diagram.

Benefits of Ishikawa Diagrams

These diagrams graphically illustrate all influencing factors of a problem. They force one to put everything on paper so that it all becomes known and can be studied. Of course, the main weakness of a diagram is that it depends for its accuracy on the person or group who makes it. The benefits can be summarized as follows:

- All factors can become known, not just the suspected obvious ones.
- They provide a simple plan of attack. Each cause can be investigated and crossed out if not important.
- When the analysis has been completed one can be reasonably sure that everything has been accounted for.

1.5 Pareto Diagrams

Pareto diagrams, named after the Italian economist Vilfredo Pareto (1848-1923), provide a method by which causes of a problem can be arranged by their relative importance. The diagram has as its basis the idea of the "vital few" and the "trivial many". Very often over half of a qual-

Defect	Number
Scratch	13
Crack	42
Off center	6
Plating flaw	78
Burr	25
Other	29
	193

Table 1.5.1 Inspection data.

ity problem is the result of one cause. It is a much better tactic to locate the most important cause and eliminate it than to attempt to eliminate all causes at once. Eliminating the one important cause will result in a dramatic quality improvement with possibly the least amount of effort.

Pareto diagrams can be used with either variable or attribute data, but are probably used most often with attribute data. Usually the data is expressed in percentages. For example, inspection data can be broken down by the number rejected due to various causes. Table 1.5.1 lists some sample inspection data. The first step in making the Pareto diagram is to draw a left vertical axis and label it with a scale going up to the total number rejected. See Figure 1.5.1. Draw a horizontal axis and mark off equal lengths to be labeled with each of the causes. Put the most frequent cause to the left and the rest in descending order. If there is an "other" category, put it on the right side even though it may not be the smallest. The "other" category can be used to group lesser causes and reduce the width of the diagram. Now draw vertical bars of equal width for each cause, each at a height which matches its frequency to the total scale.

If possible, put an additional scale on the left side which

Fig.1.5.1 Steps for constructing a Pareto diagram.

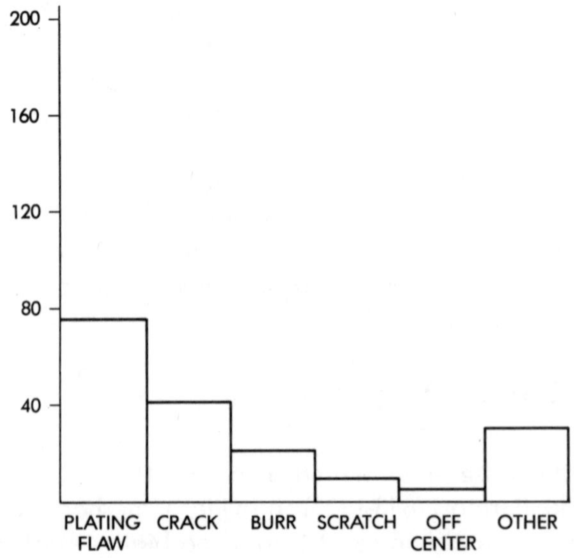

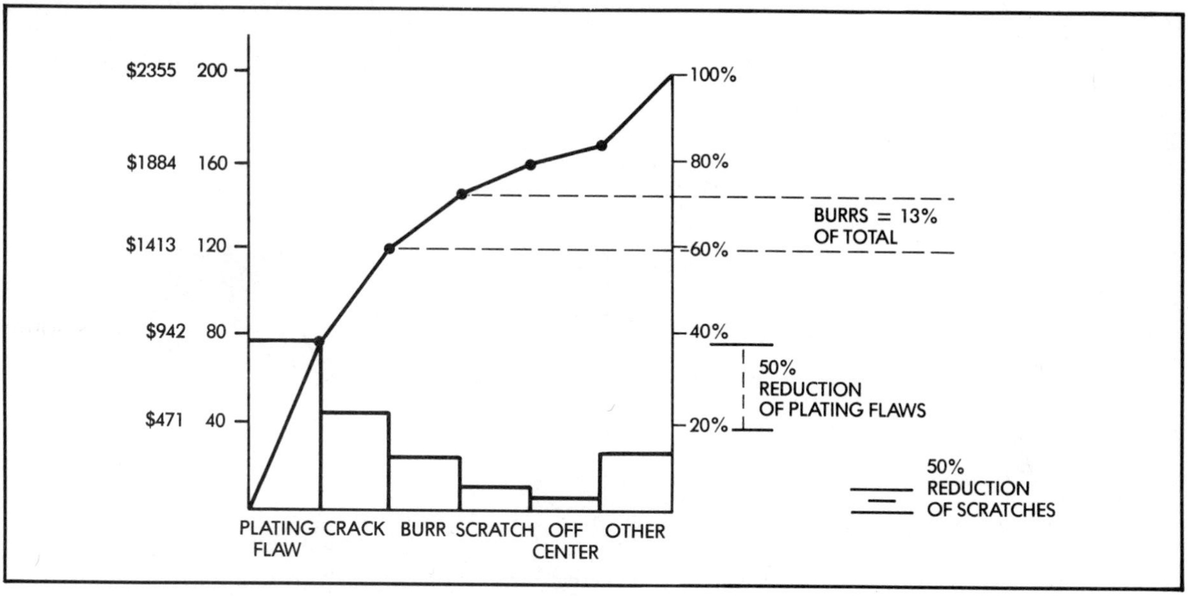

Fig.1.5.2 Completed Pareto diagram.

represents the cost of defectives. On the right side draw a second vertical axis and label it with the percent defective. Finally, draw a segmented line which represents the cumulative percentage, starting at the bottom left corner and ending at the upper right. The completed diagram will be similar to Figure 1.5.2. The segmented line simply totals each defect, but it provides a way to quickly estimate percentages. Simply draw two horizontal lines to the percent scale and subtract to get the percent due to any one cause.

Pareto Diagrams have these usages:

- They highlight the few most important causes. If we were to try to reduce scratches by one-half in Figure 1.5.2, it would not have nearly the effect on reducing total defects as reducing plating flaws by one-half. The effort at reducing either of these might be the same even though the "payoff" is much different. Pareto diagrams help focus on effective solutions to problems in this way.

- They highlight the results of improvements. Diagrams drawn side by side will illustrate the overall results of quality improvements in a before/ after context. Figure 1.5.3 shows the results of improving the main cause of circuits failing a power-on test.

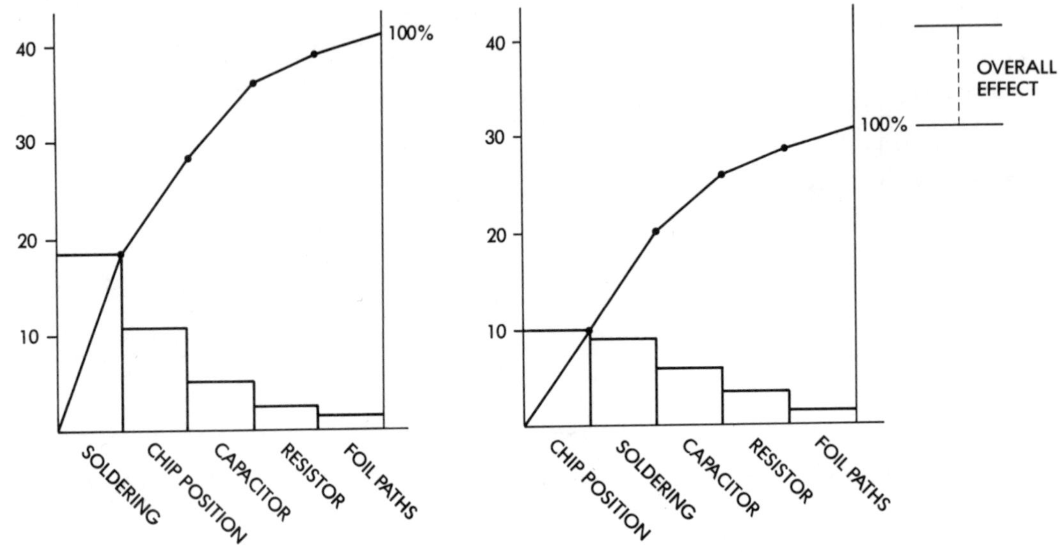

Fig.1.5.3 Side by side diagrams can display the results of improvement.

- Note that it is important to use numbers of defects or costs of defects on the left-hand scale of the diagrams, not the percentages. If percentages were used, the causes in the second diagram would look larger in comparison to the first. Repetitive audits of the causes of this problem should show the main cause shifting to second or third position if attempts at improving the main cause are successful. If repetitive audits show the causes shifting their order without an overall reduction in the magnitude of the problem, then attempts to solve the problem are insufficient. A daily control system that effectively focuses on all aspects of the process should cause a reduction of all causes without much shifting of order.

When used with cause and effect diagrams, Pareto diagrams become an instrument for plotting the course of activity, noting progress, and gaining perspective on a problem at any point during the work. After a cause and effect diagram is made, data must be collected to determine the relative importance of causes. The Pareto diagram can be the first useful document produced after initial data collection.

1.6 RECORDING DATA

Three common ways to record data for process control are:

- Check sheets
- Handheld data collectors
- Fixed station data acquisition equipment

In a factory-wide process control program all three ways would probably be used because each offers certain advantages the others do not have and they are all somewhat complementary.

Check Sheets

Check sheets are the easiest to make and most flexible way to record data. A well designed check sheet enhances all aspects of a study. First, its design allows an auditor to efficiently gather data. Essential information such as the study identification, date, shift, and auditor's name is put on the sheet. If a route is required to collect the data, a description of it is included. Each data collection station is labeled by the type measurement, number of significant digits, the gaging to be used, frequency of measurement, and possibly the high and low specifications. There must be room on the sheet to record all data and include notes about conditions when necessary. A parts drawing with points of measurement clearly marked can also enhance the check sheet as an effective data recording tool.

Secondly, a check sheet should provide some method of on-the-spot analysis. The auditor should be able to verify that the data is reasonable while it is being collected to help minimize measurement error. This is not to say that the auditor should make snap judgments about whether the data indicates a problem. But in the case of critical measurements, where parts out of specification cannot be tolerated, the auditor should be able to recognize out of specification data and mark the parts or proceed according to his responsibilities.

The third aspect of a study the check sheet should enhance is the analysis. The sheet should be designed to minimize transcription errors. Such errors occur more often when copying or reading data along a horizontal line than down a vertical column, so columns should be used to record groups of like data. Some sheets, especially those used to mark frequency of occurrence, invite analysis right on the sheet by taking on the appearance of a histogram. If hand calculations will be performed after the data is collected, provide the space and parameters for it on the back of the check sheet. This way the sheet becomes a complete record of the study. If the data needs to be transferred to a computer, then the sheet should accommodate easy transcription. In some situations where the deviation from nominal is being analyzed or where only the last two digits are significant, the check sheet could be used to record only the deviation number or last two significant digits. The computer can supply the rest.

Check sheets have many usages, from setting up a complicated piece of machinery to testing all functions of a product and making sure all the correct pieces are in a shipping container. For process control there are two basic types, one for variables and another for attribute data.

Check Sheets for Variables

Variable data can be recorded in two ways. One way is in columns arranged by the route and type of measurement. See Figure 1.6.1. This provides for either manual calculations or transcribing for processing by computer. Another way is to use one check sheet for each type of measurement and label the columns by gradations of the measurement scale as shown in Figure 1.6.2. This allows you to simply mark the sheet where each measurement falls. The result will be a histogram. One drawback of a histogram type of check sheet is that the data gets categorized and its resolution is limited by the number of columns on the sheet.

PRODUCT Valve

MFG STAGE Pre-polishing

LOT NO. 2372

SPECIFICATIONS See drawing

AUDITOR Rick Perry

DATE 4/6/84

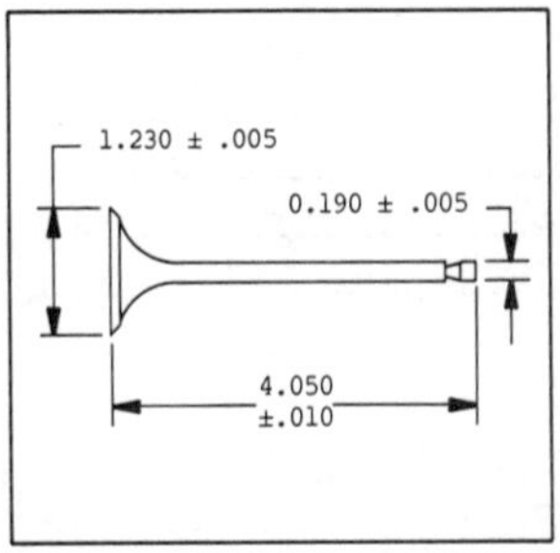

	VALVE DIA	STEM LENGTH	STEM DIA	VALVE DIA	STEM LENGTH	STEM DIA
	1.233	4.003	0.191	1.231	4.001	0.192
	1.215	4.063	0.190	1.235	4.050	0.191
	1.231	4.051	0.193	1.228	4.032	0.189
	1.232	4.048	0.189	1.234	4.053	0.190
	1.230	4.055	0.187	1.229	4.044	0.192
AVE:	1.228	4.044	0.190	1.231	4.036	0.191
RANGE:	0.018	0.06	0.006	0.007	0.052	0.003

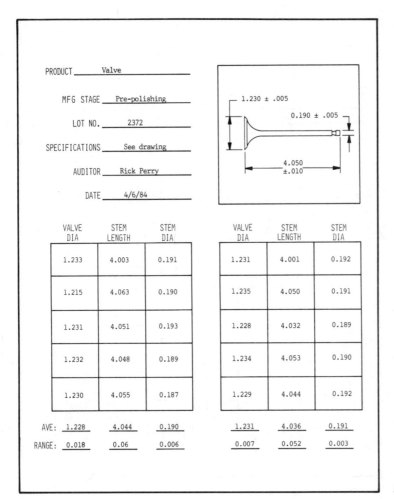

Fig.1.6.1 Check sheet for variables.

Check Sheets for Attributes

There are three basic types of check sheets for attribute data (*Ishikawa*, 1976). The first is *defect-by-item*. See Figure 1.6.3. The types of defects are listed on the left side and checks are made next to them for each type of defect found. The results are then tabulated on the right. This type of sheet translates very easily into a Pareto diagram.

The second type is *defect-by-location*. This sheet is basically a parts drawing with a list of codes for different types of defects. See Figure 1.6.4. The inspector then marks the location on the drawing with the code for the defect. This type of sheet allows quick analysis of problems on large parts or assemblies where the location of a defect provides

PART DIMENSION CHECK SHEET FILE NO. 122

PART NO.	OEX250	SPECIFICATION	1.62 ± .05
DESCRIPTION	Bearing race	NO. INSPECTED	151
AUDITOR	Amy Noyes	NO. BELOW SPEC	5
DATE	4/10/84	NO. ABOVE SPEC	11
ROUTE	101	NOTES	Some of yesterday's batch mixed in with today's.

DIMENSIONS	.54	.55	.56	.57	.58	.59	.60	.61	.62	.63	.64	.65	.66	.67	.68	.69	.70	.71
TOTALS	0	3	2	6	9	7	10	21	12	17	18	10	14	11	4	7	0	0

Fig.1.6.2 Check sheet for variables in the form of a histogram.

Fig.1.6.3 Defect-by-item check sheet.

DEFECT TALLY SHEET

PART NO.	RD400ES	DATE	3/28/84
DESCRIPTION	1/4 H. Pump Assy	STATION	Crating
		INSPECTOR	JP
REMARKS		BIN NO.	3042
		STARTING SEQ NO.	4076508
		ENDING SEQ NO.	4076590

DEFECT	NUMBER	TOTAL BY DEFECT
Piece Missing	HHT HHT HHT //	17
Loose Fastener	HHT HHT HHT HHT HHT HHT ///	33
Foiled Power On	HHT HHT HHT HHT HHT //	27
Scratch	HHT HHT HHT HHT HHT HHT HHT //	37
Other	HHT HHT HHT ///	18
	GRAND TOTAL	132
PARTS REJECTED	HHT HHT HHT HHT HHT HHT HHT HHT HHT HHT HHT HHT HHT HHT HHT HHT //	82

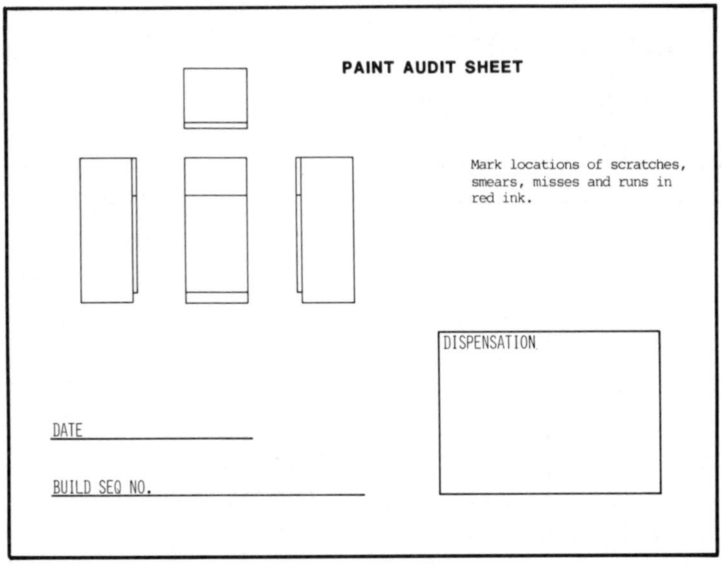

PAINT AUDIT SHEET
Mark locations of scratches, smears, misses and runs in red ink.
DISPENSATION
DATE
BUILD SEQ NO.

Fig.1.6.4 Defect-by-location check sheet.

the key to the cause of a problem. It may be helpful to superimpose a grid on the parts drawing to make the location clearer.

The third type of check sheet is the *defect-by-cause* sheet. See Figure 1.6.5. Defects are recorded against a grid that highlights other variables such as time of day, machine number, and worker. The frequency of defects attributable to these variables can then be checked during data collection. By design, this sheet is very similar to some control charts. In fact, this sheet could be used for ongoing process control as well as for temporary problem solving.

Handheld Data Collectors

See Chapter 16 for descriptions of DataMyte data collectors.

Handheld data collectors have many similarities to check sheets. Because they offer advantages in recording data in computer readable form, and in capturing data directly from electronic gages, they economize with frequent usage. It will help to compare a handheld data collector such as the DataMyte® Statistician™ with the qualities of a check sheet to determine its suitability for various data recording tasks.

First are the requirements of study organization, such as study ID, date, name of operator and notes about the study. Routing information is needed to guide the operator to data collection points and indicate the type of measure-

DATE: 2/21/83 **DEFECT ANALYSIS SHEET** INSPECTOR: G.S.

CODES

A = TAILINGS B = MISFORMED C = OVERSIZE D = UNDERSIZE E = BROKEN

MACHINE	OPER-ATOR	MONDAY		TUESDAY		WEDNESDAY		THURSDAY		FRIDAY		SATURDAY	
		SHFT 1	2	1	2	1	2	1	2	1	2	1	2
FORGE 1	Alex	AA B	CCE AA	CA AA	BA CC	AAAA BB	CCC A	BBA C	CCA BB	CCCC BB	CCCA	AACC CCBB	AAA ACB
	Harv	AA BD	AAB CEE	BBB CCAA	AA	BBD D	AAA	CCCB BCA	BBB AA	DDD BE	DDE	AAB B	BBB A
FORGE 2	Bert	AB	AAA	BBD	E	AAA	CCCA	BBAA AA	AAA BBB	AAAA B	BBAB C	CBAD	CBAD DE
	Ted	AA E	EED	EE DD	BBA	ACAA	AABB	BBAA EE	EEE	DDDE EEE	AAA EEA	AAA BBB	AA

Fig.1.6.5 Defect-by-cause check sheet.

ment. A block of memory is reserved for this type of information, which is called a *header.* Another block for memory is needed to store interactive prompts for route, gage, and type measurement. An example of header and prompt information is shown in Figure 1.6.6. An operator begins a study by entering the appropriate study information, following the route, and recording the data. To facilitate data recording, electronic gaging can be used. If keyboard entry is used, the previous day's data could be left in memory so that only when the data has changed are extra keystrokes necessary.

Another feature handheld data collectors share with check sheets is on-the-spot analysis. A data collector such as the DataMyte displays the mean, range, minimum sample, maximum sample, standard deviation of sample group and other statistical calculations. It also does limit checking, alerting the operator with an audible beep when the data just taken is out of specification.

The third aspect of check sheets, that of enhancing data analysis, is also provided by handheld data collectors. Formatted reports with summary information can be obtained by connecting the data collector to a printer. The data can also be transmitted to a computer for further analysis.

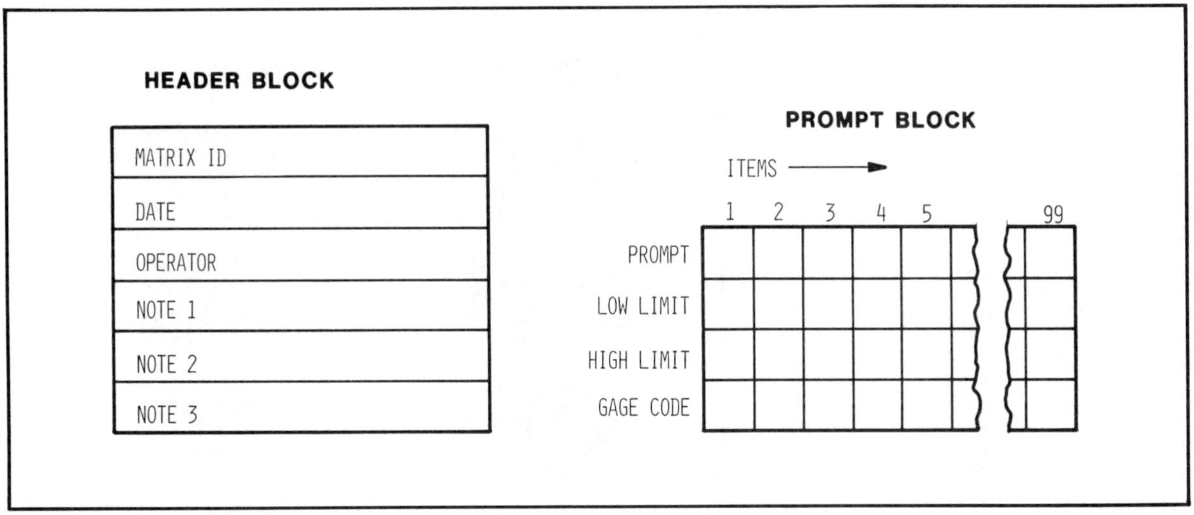

Fig.1.6.6 Data collector memory has header and prompt sections.

Collecting Variable Data

Handheld data collectors are well suited to collecting variable data. A *matrix* is used as shown in Figure 1.6.7. The matrix consists of data cells arranged in columns and rows. One column is used for each type of measurement, or *item*, as it is called. The repeated measurements of each item are called *samples*. The width of a data cell is expressed in terms of the number of significant digits.

Data can be recorded in a matrix by moving horizontally or vertically. Horizontal movement allows one to take samples of each dimension of a part before proceeding to the next part. Vertical movement allows one to take several samples of one item and then proceed to the next. Data in a matrix can be analyzed by rows or by columns and also in aggregate. An intelligent data collector or a computer program can scale each item and produce a series of histograms or other types of graphs.

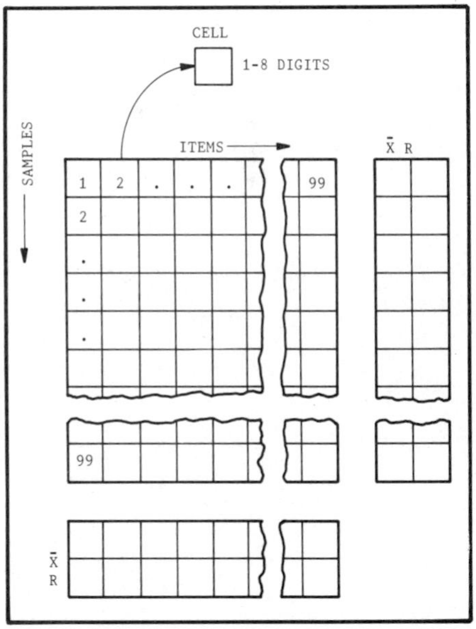

Fig.1.6.7 Data is arranged in a matrix-like memory.

Collecting Attribute Data

Attribute data is recorded in a handheld data collector by coding it. Coding schemes create enough flexibility to record defect-by-item, defect-by-location, or defect-by-cause. A defect-by-item scheme is shown in Figure 1.6.8. One list of codes is used to identify the defects. Each separate code entry counts as a defect type. Fast entry can be

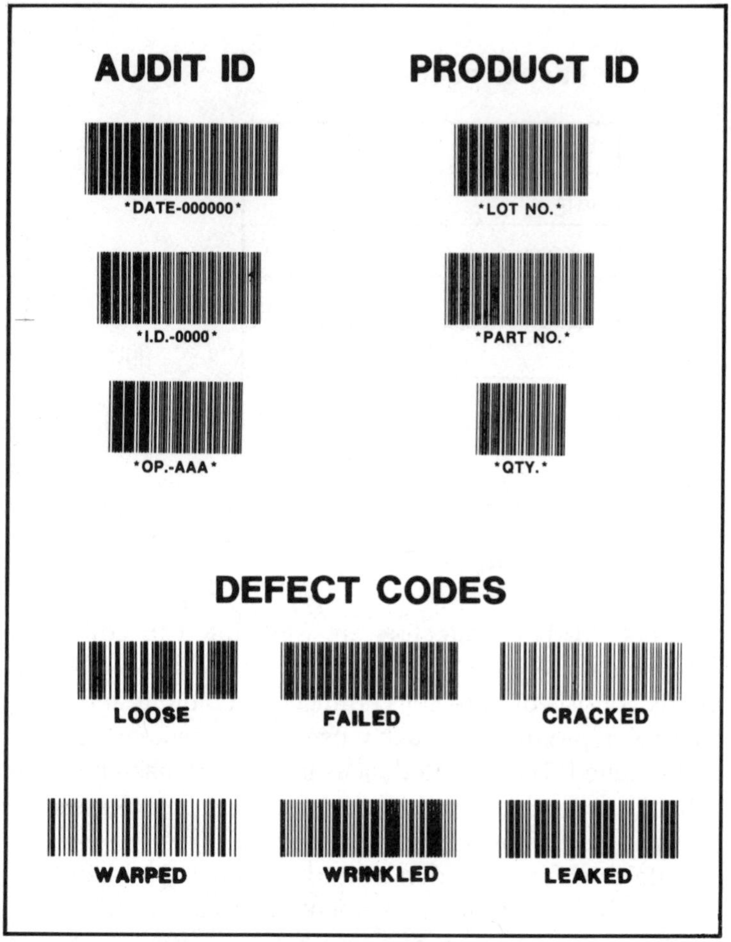

Fig.1.6.8 Bar codes used for fast entry of attribute data.

achieved by using a bar code label or magnetic stripe to identify the defect, and then simply wanding the label when the defect is spotted. The sequence of codes is then sorted by the computer, and a control chart, histogram, or pareto diagram can be formatted and printed.

Defect-by-location and defect-by-cause check sheets can be simulated in essentially the same way. Separate code lists identify the defects, locations, machine, worker, and time of day. Real time can be input automatically by turning on a 24-hour clock built into the data collector. Bar codes or magnetic stripes allow fast data entry and reduced dependence on the operator's command of the codes and ability to key them correctly. The data is then transmitted to a computer for sorting by defect and other variables. The reports can be set up to highlight unusual occurrences.

Fixed Station Data Acquisition Equipment

Fixed station equipment has several levels of sophistication. At the lowest level, it is dedicated to recording data from a single source. The data analysis is rudimentary and not compatible with data collected from other sources. In some cases it requires an operator to oversee data collection and either record it or transmit it to a computer for analysis.

Some types of fixed station equipment have outputs that are compatible with handheld data collectors so that a periodic linkup with the data collector could be a regular route item for the auditor. An example of this is a weigh scale and an electronic linear gage mounted on a fixture.

When volumes are high enough to require frequent data collection, the process operator could use a system dedicated to collecting data for SPC. Dedicated systems are usually more efficient than check sheets, and allow more frequent recording than what would be obtained with a roving auditor using a handheld data collector. A system such as shown in Figure 1.6.9 allows the operator to record data and also do real-time analysis. In essense, it is both a data collection system and a quality control computer. Summary information, control charts and other graphs are displayed on a monitor, giving the operator a means of identifying a problem as soon as it occurs. Such equipment has a variety of applications, including statistical process control of dimensional characteritics (Figure 1.6.9) and packaging weights (Figure 1.6.10).

The more sophisticated types of fixed station equipment are beyond the scope of this book. In many cases they are a part of test stations or bays. Operation is automatic or semi-automatic and a computer is either resident at the station or directly linked. Their singleness of purpose makes them ideal for high volume tasks critical to process control. In some cases system controllers provide some degree of closed loop data analysis and adjustment. If not, the data available from fixed station sources can be analyzed with the methods of statistical quality control described in this book and others.

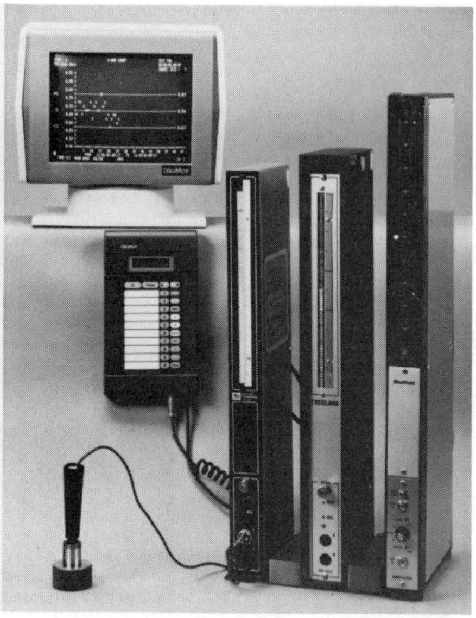

Fig.1.6.9 Fixed station system for dimensional measurements.

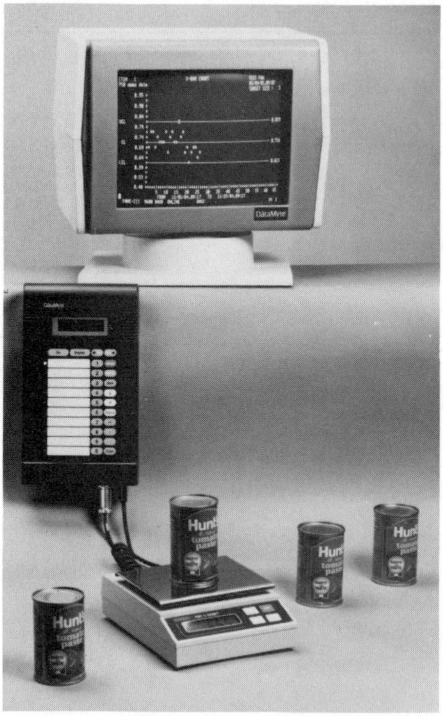

Fig.1.6.10 Fixed station system for weight measurements.

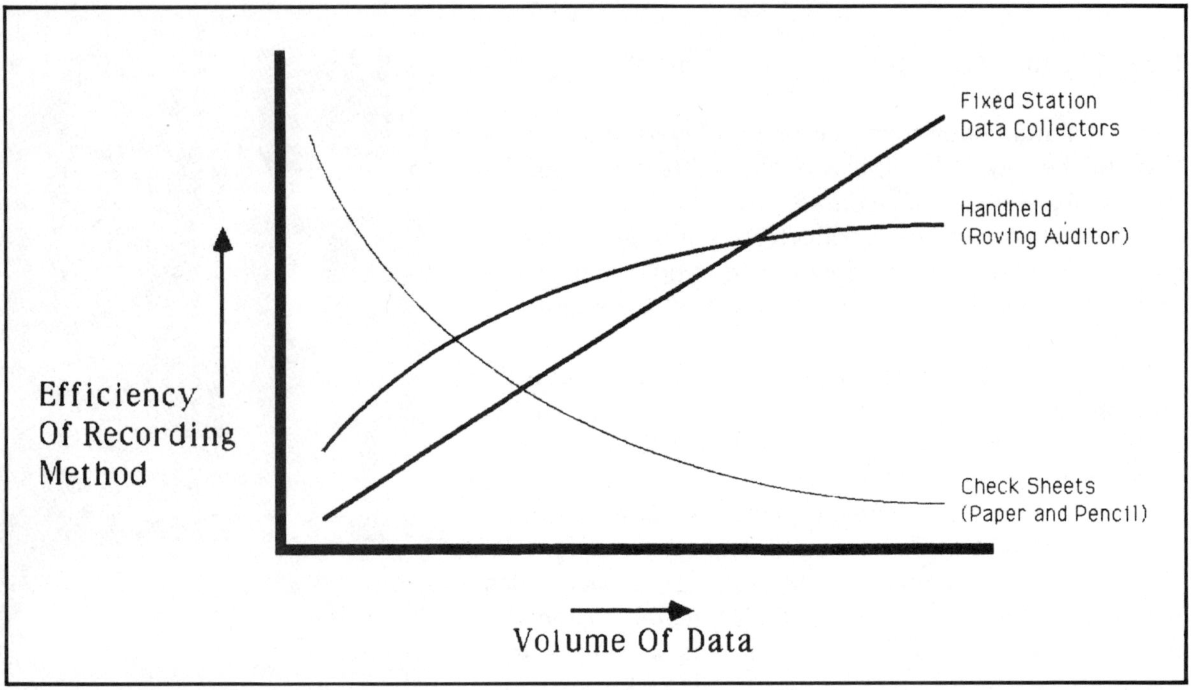

Fig.1.6.11 As the volume of data grows, the efficiency of each of the methods shown in the graph changes. At higher volumes some combination of all three methods are needed.

Comparing Data Recording Methods

Check sheets, handheld and fixed station data collection systems each have distinct advantages for recording data. Most likely a combination of all three would be used in a factory to suit the types of processes and volume of data to be collected.

Although they are simple to construct and easy to use, check sheets become very inefficient when used to gather large amounts of data (Figure 1.6.11). A 1978 study commissioned by the U.S. government found that the handwritten method of data collection can gather information at a rate of 3.3 times per minute, with an error rate of 11.6 percent. When we add together the time to set up a sheet, record the data, and the time to extract data from a sheet for analysis, we find that the check sheet is very labor intensive. Although paper data sheets and control charts provide good permanent records, they are not the most efficient vehicle for data. The data must be keyed into a calculator to figure averages and other statistics, or keypunched into a computer.

Handwritten methods also contribute significant human error to data. Reading errors occur when a person makes a visual observation and wrongly interprets what he sees. Transcription errors occur when a person makes a correct observation but writes it down mistakenly. Keypunching errors occur when a person must enter data from a check sheet into a computer or calculator. Significant error can lead to the false interpretation of data, with nulifies much of the benefit in collecting it in the first place.

It would be better to capture data in computer-readable format right at the source, especially in environments requiring collection of moderate to large amounts of data. This is where handheld and fixed station data collectors are more efficient (Figure 1.6.11). Handheld data collectors can be used by a roving auditor. The auditor is responsible for recording data at several points around a plant. See Figure 1.6.12. By using electronic gages, data is recorded with greater speed and less error.

A factory having many high volume processes is probably better off having each process operator record their own data, rather than a roving auditor. A fixed station data collection system provides each operator a way to continually measure the variability of a process. Whenever necessary, adjustments can be made before quality problems occur. The operators thus gain a more effective influence.

Fig.1.6.12 Roving auditor checking a low volume process.

NOTE: See Chapters 7-14 for examples of companies using both fixed and handheld data collection systems. See Chapter 15 for more information on computerized data collection.

For Further Reference

Burke, James. *Connections.* Boston: Little, Brown and Company, 1978.

Grant, Eugene L., and Leavenworth, Richard S. *Statistical Quality Control,* 5th ed. New York: McGraw-Hill Book Company, 1980.

Green, Constance M. *Eli Whitney and the Birth of American Technology.* Boston: Little, Brown and Company, 1956.

Ishikawa, Kaoru. *Guide to Quality Control.* Hong Kong: Nordica International Limited, 1976.

Quality Control Circles, Inc. *Quality Control Circles.* 2d ed. Saratoga: Quality Control Circles, Inc., 1982.

Shewhart, Walter A. *Economic Control of Quality of Manufactured Product.* Princeton: Van Nostrand Reinhold Company, Inc., 1931.

2. CONTROL CHARTS

2.1 INTRODUCTION

A control chart is a vital part of any process control system. It is a graphic comparison of a measured characteristic against computed control limits. It plots variation over time. The primary use of control charts is to detect assignable causes of variation in a process. By helping to eliminate assignable causes, control charts contribute to increased quality, reduced scrap and rework, and increased productivity. Ideally, only common causes of variation should be present in a process. The control chart distinguishes between the two causes of variation through the use of control limits calculated from the laws of probability. These limits are vital guidelines for determining when action should be taken in a process.

Principal Kinds of Control Charts

There are essentially two kinds of control charts; control charts for variable data (quantitative data or measurements), and control charts for attribute data (qualitative data or counts). See Table 2.1.1. Variables control charts are more sensitive to changes in measured values and therefore are better for process control. Control charts for attribute data are useful for other reasons; attribute data charts are the easiest to obtain data for, cost the least to use, and often do not require a specialized means of data collection.

See the Appendix, Table A-1, for the control limit formulas and constants.

$\bar{x}$ & R Charts — The $\bar{x}$ & R chart is the most common form of a control chart for variable data, and one of the most powerful for tracking and identifying causes of variation. The $\bar{x}$ part of the chart is a continuous plot of subgroup averages. The R chart is a continuous plot of subgroup ranges. A subgroup can be from 2 to 20 samples.

See Chapter 16 for descriptions of data collectors which can print sigma charts.

$\bar{x}$ & s Charts — Known as sigma charts, these charts, like the $\bar{x}$ & R charts, are always used as a pair. The sigma chart is a somewhat more accurate indicator of process variability than an R chart, especially with a larger size subgroup. Disadvantages of the sigma chart are that it is more difficult to calculate sigma.

Type Chart	Parameters Plotted	Primary Usages
$\bar{x}$ & R chart	Averages and ranges of subgroups of variable data.	Process control
$\bar{x}$ & sigma chart	Averages and standard deviations of subgroups of variable data.	Process control
Median chart	Median of subgroups of variable data.	Process control
Chart for individuals	Individual measurements.	Process control
CuSum chart	Cumulative sum of each $\bar{x}$ minus the nominal	Process control
Moving range, average chart	Range or average recalculated for preceeding 3 days	Process control
p-chart	Ratio of defective items to total number inspected.	Inspection sampling Final inspection
np-chart	Actual number of defective items compared to total inspected.	Inspection sampling Final inspection
c-chart	Number of defects on an item for a constant sample of items	Inspection sampling Final inspection
u-chart	Percent nonconformities on item for varying sample.	Inspection sampling Final inspection

Table 2.1.1 Principal kinds of control charts.

Median Charts — This chart combines both the $\bar{x}$ & R information into one graph. The median is the middle value when data is arranged according to size. Median charts yield similar conclusions to the $\bar{x}$ & R charts, and are easy to use. Typically, median charts are used with subgroup sample sizes of 10 or less.

Control Charts for Individuals — Control charts for individual samples are used in cases where it is necessary for process control to be based on individual readings rather than

See the Appendix, Table A-1, for the control limit formulas and constants.

subgroups, such as when measurements are expensive or destructive or the result of a single daily lab test. Control limits for a chart of individuals should be based on the moving range.

See p. 16-9 for an example of a CuSum chart.

Cumulative Sum (CuSum) Chart — A CuSum chart looks at subgroup averages in a different way than an $\bar{x}$ chart. On a CuSum chart, each point represents the cumulative sum of each $\bar{x}$ value minus the nominal value. Basically, it exaggerates the shift from nominal. If successive $\bar{x}$s fall on both sides of the nominal, the chart remains fairly flat. But if two or more succesive $\bar{x}$s fall on the same side of the nominal, the curve begins to rise and fall quite rapidly. The chart, therefore is much more sensitive to a sustained shift away from the nominal.

Moving average, moving Range charts — These charts are used primarily in industries where the output of a process is strongly linked to a previous day's output, such as where the same chemical bath is used each day. For a moving average, each day's reading is averaged with the previous 3 day's readings. Similarly, a moving range chart would plot the range over a 3-day period each day. These charts tend to dampen what would be a single out of control reading on an $\bar{x}$ & R chart, and distribute effects over a longer period in time.

Examples of attribute charts appear later in this chapter.

p-Chart — The p-chart (percentage chart) is an attribute chart for the percentage of defective items in a subgroup, when the subgroup is not necessarily of a constant size from inspection to inspection. *Fraction defective* is the ratio of defective items to the total number of items inspected, which is another way of expressing the percentage. The main purpose of the p-chart is to identify when it is necessary to improve product quality.

np-Chart — The concept of the np-chart is the same as the p-chart except that the np-chart represents the actual number of defective items compared to the total inspected, rather than the fraction. It would be better to use the np-chart if the actual number of defectives is more meaningful or simpler to report than the proportion, or when the subgroup size remains constant from inspection to inspection.

c-Chart — The c-chart is a special type of attribute control chart which uses the number of defects instead of the number of defectives. In cases where a unit can contain many defects the c-chart is a practical alternative. The c-chart should only be used when the sample size remains constant from inspection to inspection. The c-chart is particularly useful where a unit is likely to contain many defects.

u-Chart — The u-chart is similar to the c-chart. The main difference is that the u-chart represents the defects as a percentage of the total defects for an inspection. The u-chart is also effective when collecting data in subgroup sizes that are not constant from one inspection to another.

2.2 $\bar{x}$ & R Charts

This section describes how to make and analyze an $\bar{x}$ & R chart, also known as the Shewhart Control Chart. The $\bar{x}$ & R chart is the most versatile of control charts for variables. There may be specific situations where sigma charts, median charts and charts for individuals have some advantage over the $\bar{x}$ & R chart, but in most applications, the $\bar{x}$ & R chart will do as well or better. Since all are similar in methods of usage and analysis, only the $\bar{x}$ & R chart will be treated in depth.

Rationale for an $\bar{x}$ & R Chart

A control chart is used to establish the *operating level* and *dispersion* of a process. Since the parts coming off a process may be infinite in number, we need a way to establish and monitor this operating level and dispersion without having to measure every part. The $\bar{x}$ & R chart is extremely efficient at this. It also provides a way to avoid the two types of errors that occur when attempting to control a process:

- *Type I error* — saying a process is unstable when actually it is stable.
- *Type II error* — saying a process is stable when actually it is unstable.

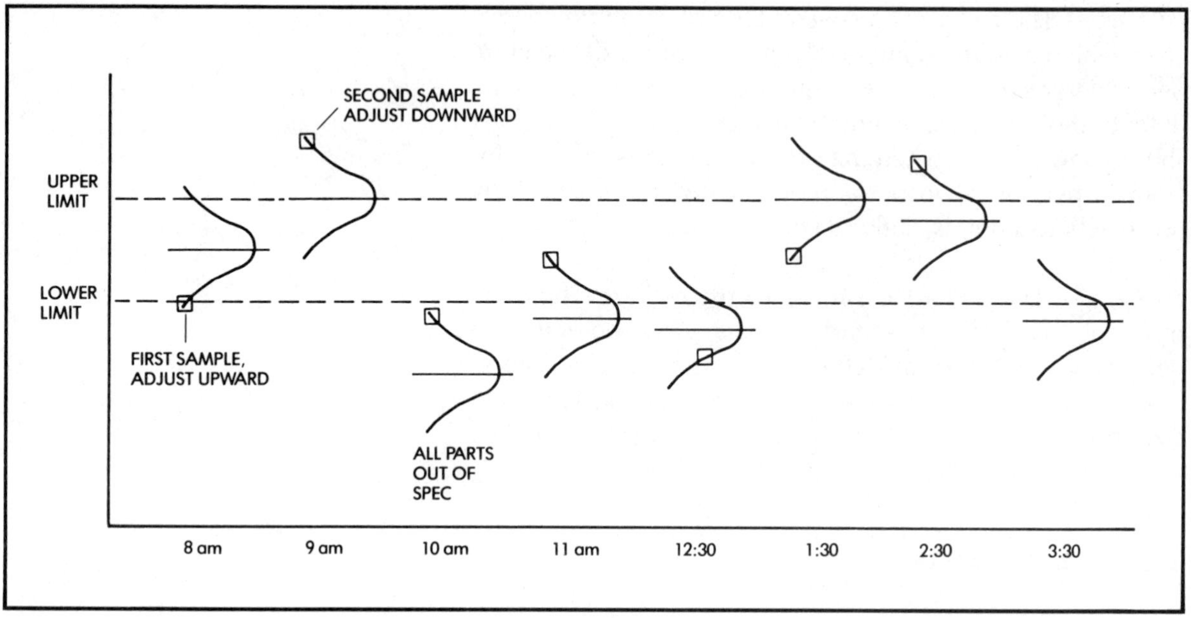

Fig. 2.2.1 Illustration of a Type I error — making adjustments to a process when they are not needed. The curves represent the operating level and dispersion of the process at various hours during the day.

Both of these errors occur when we don't have a method of identifying assignable causes; when we aren't thinking statistically about the data. An example of a Type I error is an operator who adjusts the stops on a turret lathe after taking a single hourly measurement. The data might look like Figure 2.2.1. He starts out at 8:00 a.m. making a batch of 30 parts. The sideways *histogram* represents the distribution of those 30 parts measurements as compared to the nominal and upper and lower limits of the specification. The first batch shows evidence of stable variation (a *normal distribution*). The mean is very close to the nominal and nearly every piece falls within the limits. Is there a need to adjust the stops? Certainly not. But at 9:00 a.m. he picks up one part and measures it. It happens to be right at the lower limit, so he moves the stops outward. This shifts the operating level of his process. After his next batch, he takes a second sample and finds he is way above the upper limit, so he moves the stops inward enough to compensate for the shifts. Between 10:00 a.m. and 11:00 a.m., every part he makes is out of spec. In fact, for the whole day, about half of what he produces is out of spec and unusable. Even though the process is stable and capable of making mostly good parts, mostly bad parts are being produced because the operator is taking only one sample and basing his decisions on it. He is making a Type I error. An $\bar{x}$ & R chart could

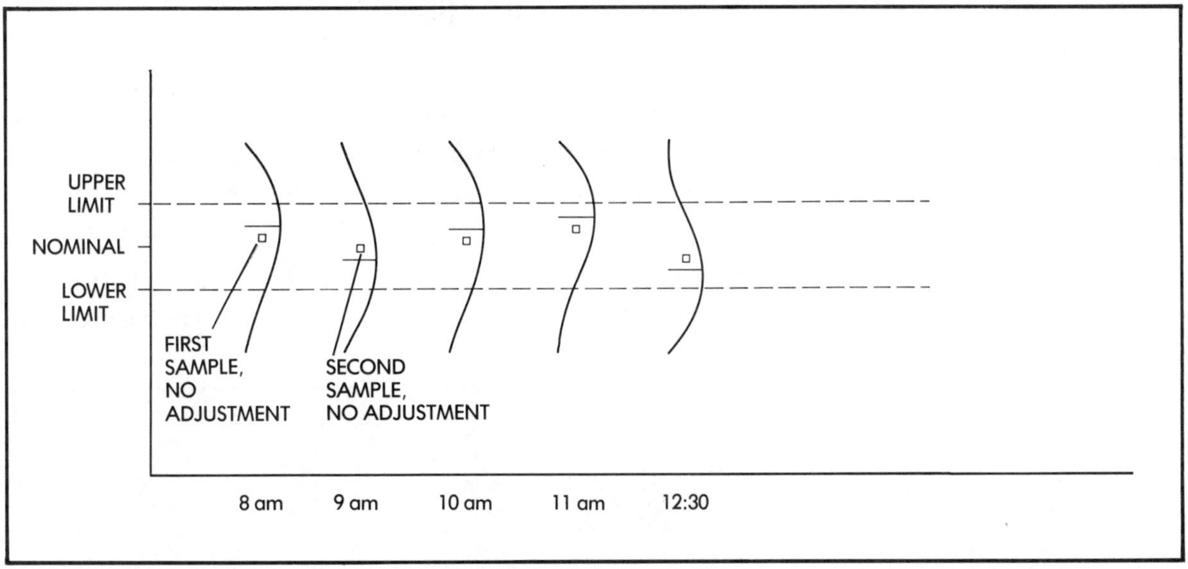

Fig. 2.2.2 Illustration of a Type II error — not making adjustments when they are needed. The curves show that much of the parts being made are out of specification.

have told him when to adjust the operating level, by how much, and just as importantly, when to leave it alone.

A Type II error is just as easy to illustrate, as shown in Figure 2.2.2. In this case the operating level, or *mean*, is always within specification but the distribution of data shows evidence of a lack of stability. You can imagine an operator taking a measurement that happens to fall within spec, and therefore not making any adjustments. An $\bar{x}$ and R chart could possibly have alerted the operator to an out-of-control process after the first hour, and steps could have been taken toward correcting it.

The difference between the chart shown in Figure 2.2.1 and an $\bar{x}$ & R chart is that an $\bar{x}$ & R chart is easier to make. Instead of calculating and graphing small histograms of data subgroups, we graph the averages and ranges on separate charts.

$\bar{x}$ & R charts can be made manually or by computer. Some of the graphs shown in the following pages were produced by a Hewlett Packard series 216 (HP9816) desktop computer and some by an IBM PC computer. Since the main calculations are finding the average and range of a set of 5 or so numbers, the charts could also be done manually. The advantages of a computer lie in minimizing errors, improving the readability of the graph, and freeing the auditor up for the more "human" tasks of analysis, judgment and action.

See Chapter 18 for a description of statistical software for desktop computers.

Creating an $\bar{x}$ & R Chart

To explain the elements of an $\bar{x}$ & R chart, it helps to create one from scratch as if we were to do it manually. This is an illustration of how a computer would generate the chart, but it can also be done manually.

Vertical scale — The vertical scale of the $\bar{x}$ chart should have the average of the data at the midpoint (Figure 2.2.3).

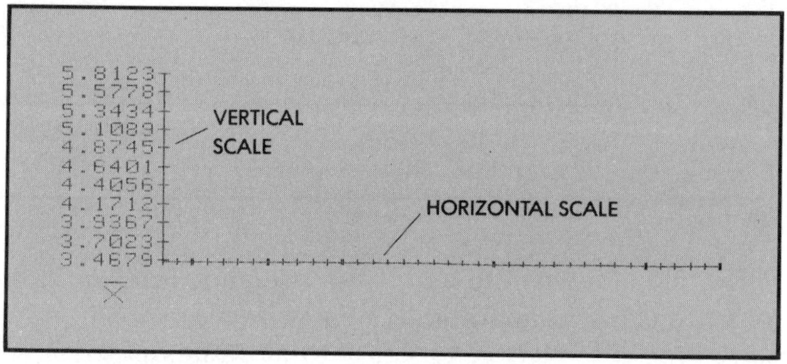

Fig. 2.2.3 Scales used on an $\bar{x}$ chart.

This could also be thought of as the expected operating level of the process. Extending above and below the midpoint should be evenly spaced scale divisions. The scale increments should be sufficiently wide to graph significant changes in average. The scale should extend out enough from the midpoint to take in any expected variation. As a rule of thumb, the scale should extend at least 20% beyond any element that would be put on the graph, such as control limits. The R chart should be scaled similarly, with the expected range at the midpoint and the scale extending at least 40% beyond any element.

Horizontal scale — The horizontal scale should be the same on both charts. The scale divisons correspond to the frequency of sampling and should be labeled by the hour or date when the data was collected, starting at the left. Data should be collected frequently when starting out, perhaps every hour on a high volume process. Once the chart is established and the process has evidence of stability, data can be collected less frequently — every other hour or by shift.

Data Collection — 'x' is the symbol for a single measurement. To start a control chart, at least 100 measurements must be taken. We can begin plotting averages and ranges right away, but we need at least 100 measurements to add the essential elements of the chart. Several considerations must be made to ensure that the 100 measurements are representative of the process:

- Measurement devices must be accurate enough to record the differences between samples. The devices must have high repeatability. See Chapter 4 for a discussion of measurement systems.
- Measurements must be made in small groupings at selected intervals. Determining the groupings and intervals is called *rational subgrouping* and is explained in more detail later. Normally, subgroup size, symbolized by 'n', can be from 2 to 20 consecutive samples, with n = 5 being the most common.

Plotting the Averages — '$\bar{x}$', pronouced X-bar, is the symbol of the average of a subgroup. The data should be arranged in columns of 5 samples each, whether on a sheet or in a handheld data collector (Figure 2.2.4). Each subgroup would then be averaged. The averages would be plotted on

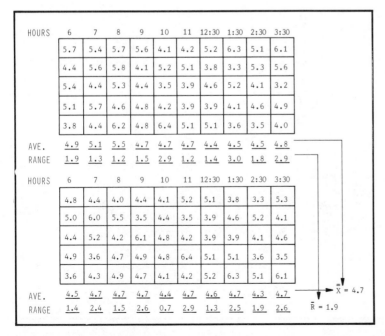

HOURS	6	7	8	9	10	11	12:30	1:30	2:30	3:30
	5.7	5.4	5.7	5.6	4.1	4.2	5.2	6.3	5.1	6.1
	4.4	5.6	5.8	4.1	5.2	5.1	3.8	3.3	5.3	5.6
	5.4	4.4	5.3	4.4	3.5	3.9	4.6	5.2	4.1	3.2
	5.1	5.7	4.6	4.8	4.2	3.9	3.9	4.1	4.6	4.9
	3.8	4.4	6.2	4.8	6.4	5.1	5.1	3.6	3.5	4.0
AVE.	4.9	5.1	5.5	4.7	4.7	4.7	4.4	4.5	4.5	4.8
RANGE	1.9	1.3	1.2	1.5	2.9	1.2	1.4	3.0	1.8	2.9

HOURS	6	7	8	9	10	11	12:30	1:30	2:30	3:30
	4.8	4.4	4.0	4.4	4.1	5.2	5.1	3.8	3.3	5.3
	5.0	6.0	5.5	3.5	4.4	3.5	3.9	4.6	5.2	4.1
	4.4	5.2	4.2	6.1	4.8	4.2	3.9	3.9	4.1	4.6
	4.9	3.6	4.7	4.9	4.8	6.4	5.1	5.1	3.6	3.5
	3.6	4.3	4.9	4.7	4.1	4.2	5.2	6.3	5.1	6.1
AVE.	4.5	4.7	4.7	4.7	4.4	4.7	4.6	4.7	4.3	4.7
RANGE	1.4	2.4	1.5	2.6	0.7	2.9	1.3	2.5	1.9	2.6

$\bar{\bar{X}} = 4.7$

$\bar{R} = 1.9$

Fig. 2.2.4 Sample data used to plot an $\bar{x}$ & R chart.

the chart by the intervals they were collected (Figure 2.2.5). 20 points on the chart will represent 100 measurements in 5-sample subgroups.

Plotting the Ranges — 'R' is the symbol for subgroup ranges. The range of each subgroup in Figure 2.2.4 is plotted against the intervals they were collected.

Centerlines — '$\bar{\bar{X}}$', pronounced X-double bar, is the average

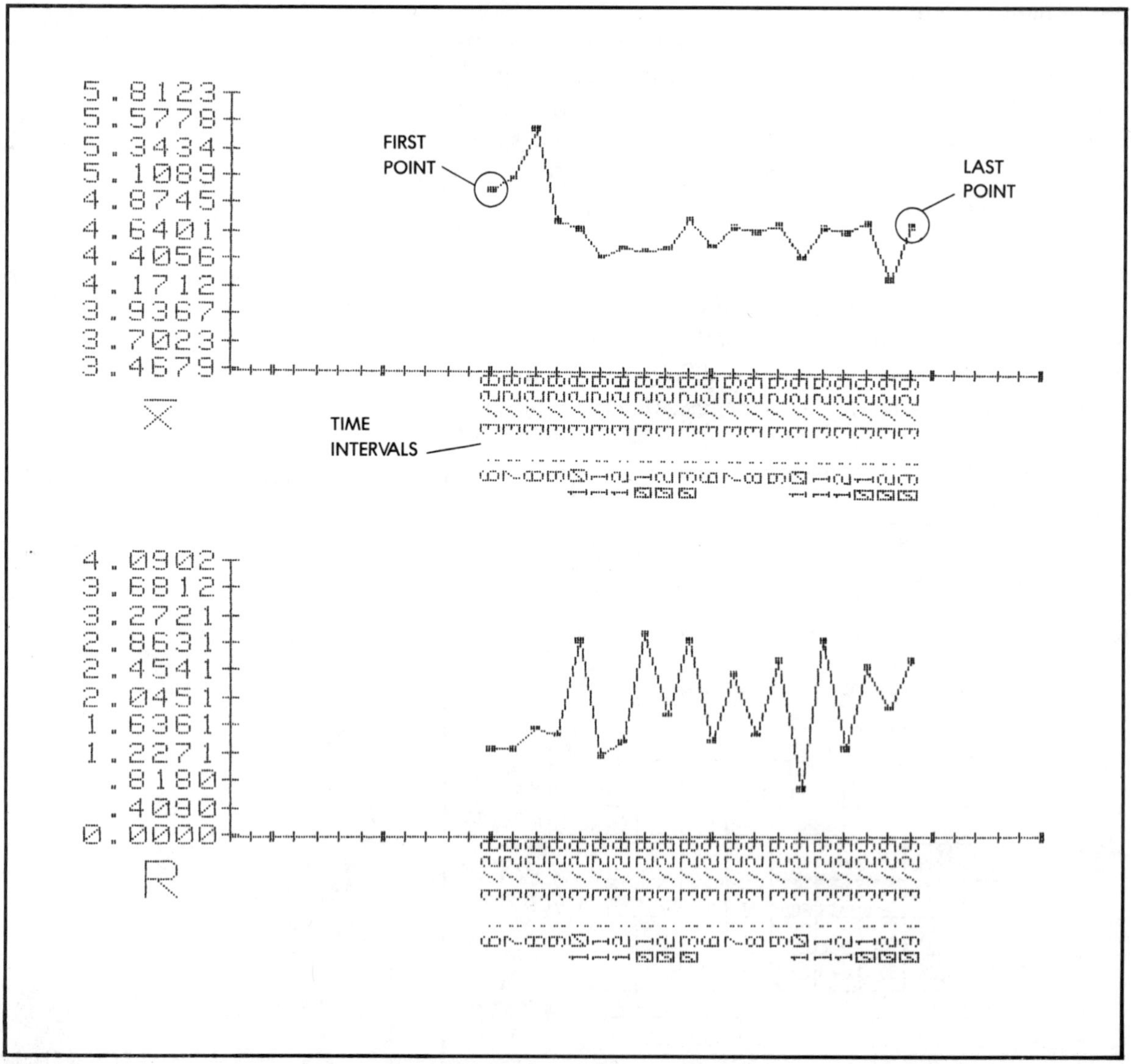

Fig. 2.2.5 Plotting 20 points on the chart.

of the subgroup averages (Figure 2.2.4). R-bar is the average of the centerlines. They get plotted as horizontal dotted lines (Figure 2.2.6). They are your first estimate of the operating level of the process.

Control Limits — The control limits on the chart are the estimated ±3 *sigma limits* for the process. Since sigma must be estimated from samples taken from a continuous process, tables of constants have been developed to make these calculations simple and to reduce error (see Appendix

Fig. 2.2.6 Centerlines represent the average of the subgroups and are plotted as dotted lines.

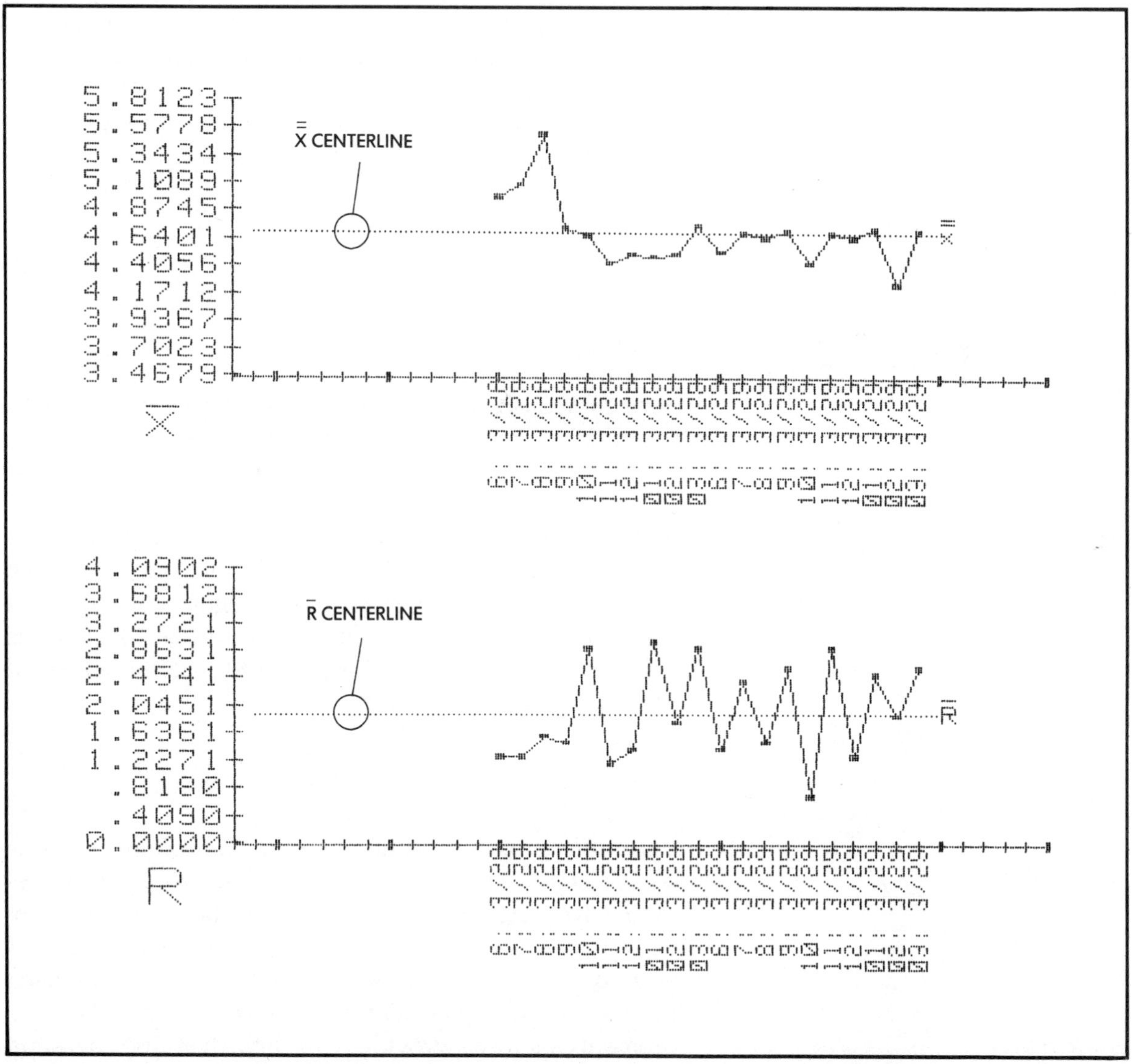

Table A-1 —Constants for Calculating Control Limits). The formulas are:

$$\bar{x} \text{ Upper Control Limit } (UCL_{\bar{x}}) = \bar{\bar{x}} + A_2 \bar{R}$$

$$\bar{x} \text{ Lower Control Limit } (LCL_{\bar{x}}) = \bar{\bar{x}} - A_2 \bar{R} \qquad (2.2.1)$$

$$\text{Range Upper Control Limit } (UCL_R) = D_4 \bar{R}$$

$$\text{Range Lower Control Limit } (LCL_R) = D_3 \bar{R}$$

In the formulas above, A_2, D_4, and D_3 are the constants used for calculating control limits, taken from Table A-1. They vary according to subgroup size (n). For $n = 5$, $A_2 = 0.577$, $D_3 = 0.0$, and $D_4 = 2.114$. The chart in Figure 2.2.6 has an X-double bar of 4.7 and an R-bar of 1.9, so the control limits for the chart would be:

$$UCL_{\bar{x}} = 4.7 + (0.577)(1.9) = 5.8$$

$$LCL_{\bar{x}} = 4.7 - (0.577)(1.9) = 3.6 \qquad (2.2.2)$$

$$UCL_R = (2.114)(1.9) = 4.0$$

Horizontal dash-lines are used to mark the control limits on the graphs (Figure 2.2.7). *By chance alone*, the subgroup averages and ranges should fall within these control limits 99.73% of the time. The variability that occurs between the control limits can be attributed to common causes for the most part. There are certain patterns that occur between the limits that one should learn to recognize, but the most important characteristic to look for is one or more points falling outside the limits. They indicate the influences of assignable causes of variation.

Some Questions About $\bar{x}$ & R Charts

How many points are needed before control limits can be calculated? — The general rule is at least 20 points, representing 100 measurements. For control limits to be meaningful they must be based on a representative sample of the population. There must be a high level of confidence that the sample is representative and that is what 100 measurements or more provide. Any less than 100 measure-

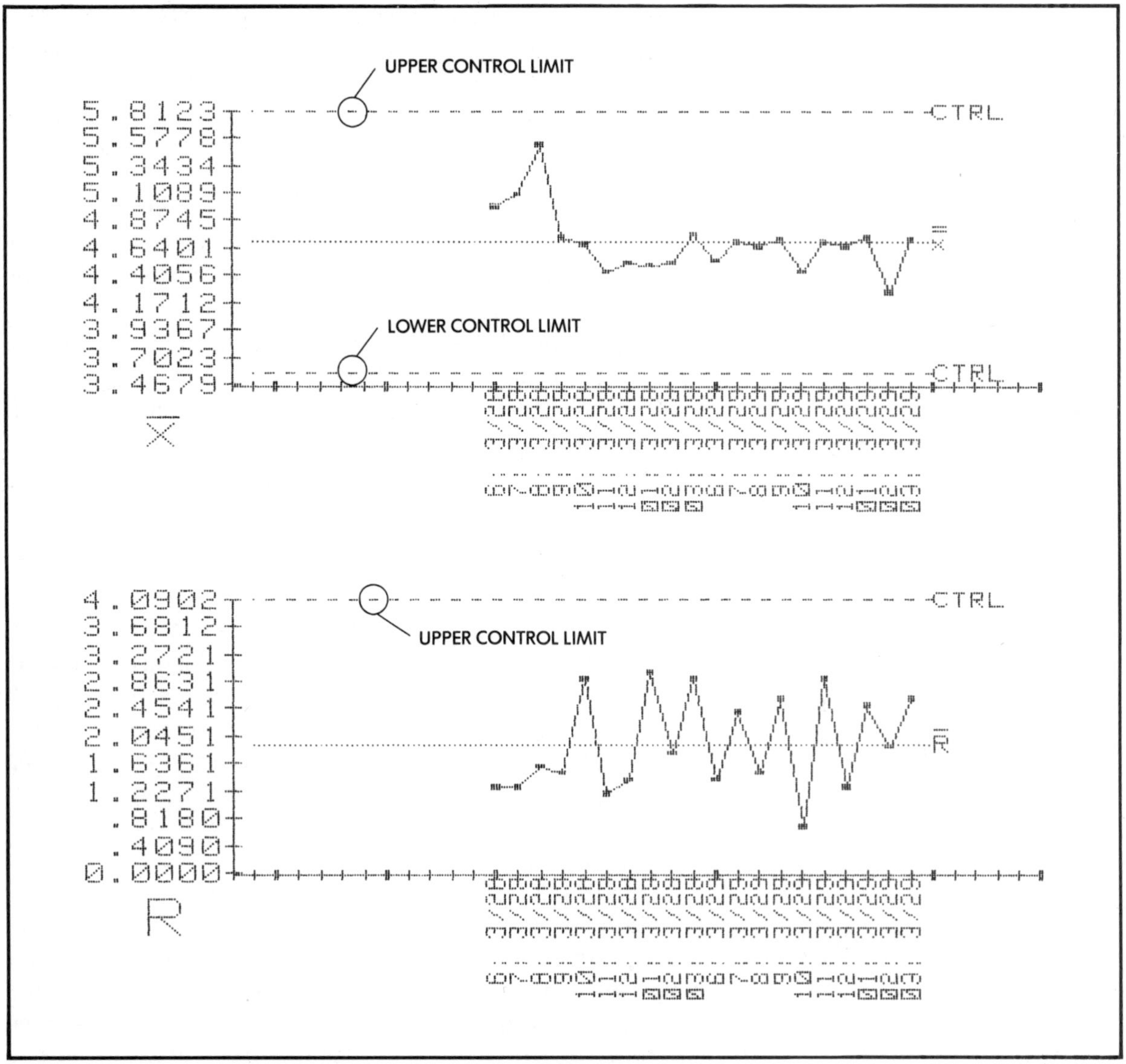

ments very quickly decreases the confidence level. Since we are basing our work effort at improving quality on the ability to detect assignable causes, we should always aim to make the control limits as statistically significant as possible.

Fig. 2.2.7 Control limits are calculated based on the centerlines and subgroup size. See Formulas 2.2.1 and 2.2.2. They get plotted as dashed lines on the chart.

Should engineering limits be put on an $\bar{x}$ chart? — Engineering limits are a demand on a process that is abitrary to the process itself. The points on an $\bar{x}$ chart are averages, so a point at or near an engineering limit can mean many things, including the possibility that one or several data measurements are out of limits. In a pure statistical sense, engineering limits or process objectives do not belong on an $\bar{x}$ & R chart. However, many industries have to live with these specifications as the criteria for a good process, and as such, including them on the chart may serve this goal.

Should the points be connected on the chart? — This is purely a matter of taste. A line connecting the points emphasizes the sequencing of points from left to right. The interpretation of a chart does not depend on this emphasis, so sometimes the sequencing can lead one to the wrong conclusions, like seeing short term "trends" that aren't really there. Lines between points are an ornamentation. If they make the chart more appealing to look at and use, then they may be beneficial.

Rational Subgrouping

To make an $\bar{x}$ & R chart truly useful and easy to interpret, it has to be set up that way. This is analogous to a good family portrait. What on the surface is a simple photograph of a group of people usually has to be done by a professional photographer. Quite a bit of expertise and planning must go into portrait photography, and the same is true with rational subgrouping and $\bar{x}$ & R charts.

The main source of information used for this section on rational subgrouping is the *Statistical Quality Control Handbook*, by Western Electric Co., Inc., 1956. A rational subgroup is one where there is the least possibility of assignable causes creating differences between measurements within the subgroup itself. If a subgroup has 5 measurements, then the opportunities for variation among those measurements must be made deliberately small. This usually means the subgroup should be taken from a batch of pieces made when the process operated under the same settings, one operator, and with no tooling or material changes. Five consecutive pieces might be the easiest to collect.

The logic behind rational subgrouping is that if we can make variability between pieces within a subgroup entirely due to common causes, then the differences in subgroup averages and ranges will be due to assignable causes. The effects of assignable causes will not be buried within a subgroup and dampened by averaging. They will appear on the chart in the form of points that exceed the control limits or have an identifiable pattern. When planning the data collection we must have an understanding of what will constitute a subgroup. If we believe that the time of day a piece is produced contributes to variation between pieces, then one subgroup should be of 5 consecutive pieces from the process. Several subgroups should be collected at selected times throughout the day. If we have a multiple spindle machine and believe that some of the spindles are fine and others not so fine, then the subgroup should be 5 pieces from one spindle and 5 from the next, not 1 piece off each spindle averaged together.

An $\bar{x}$ & R chart is used to plot one system of causes. If several different machines contribute to a single lot of parts, an $\bar{x}$ & R chart of samples taken from the lot will not reveal nearly as much as separate charts on each machine. Using rational subgrouping and working upstream with $\bar{x}$ & R charts, we will find that the charts do indeed help identify assignable causes of variation.

$\bar{x}$ & R Chart Patterns

Characteristics of a process showing stability — The most common feature of a process showing stability, or a constant-cause system in other words, is the absence of any recognizable pattern (*Western Electric*, 1956). Figure 2.2.8 shows such a process. The points on the chart are randomly distributed between the control limits. Since there is a

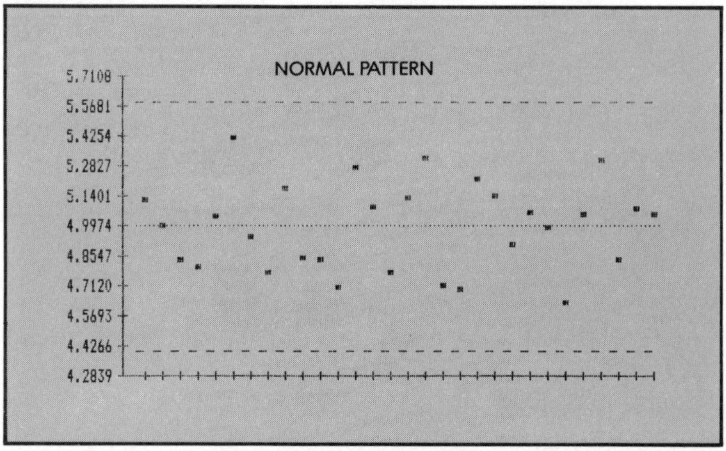

Fig. 2.2.8 Characteristics of a normal pattern are a random distribution with most points near the centerline, some points near the control limits, but no points beyond the control limits.

slight chance of a point falling outside the control limits under normal circumstances, it can happen. A rare point out of limits on a process that has shown stability over the long run can probably be ignored. The characteristics can be summarized as follows:

- Most points are near the centerline.
- Some points are spread out and approach the limits.
- No points beyond the control limits.

Characteristics of a lack of stability — The characteristics of a lack of stability are:

- One or more points outside the control limits (Figure 2.2.9).
- A *run* of 7 or more successive points above or below the centerline (Figure 2.2.10).

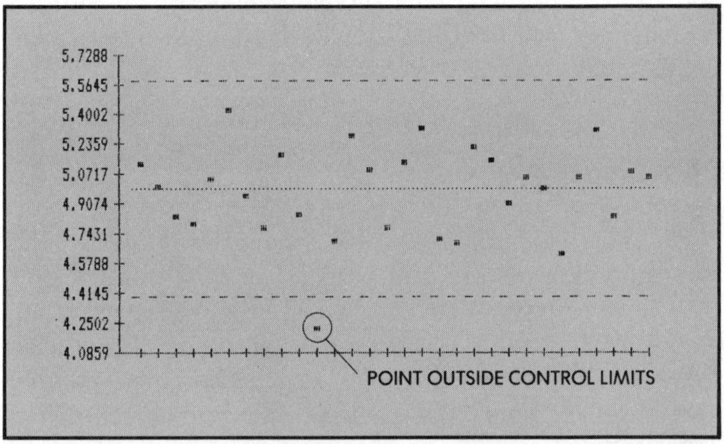

Fig. 2.2.9 A single point outside the control limits is an indication of a lack of stability. Its time of occurrence and possible causes should be investigated.

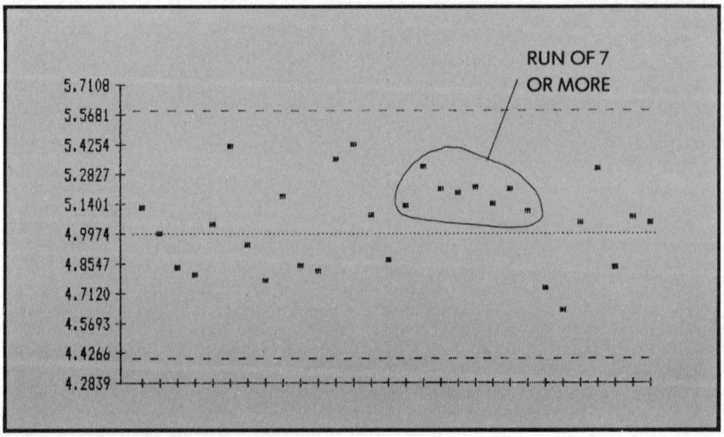

Fig. 2.2.10 This chart has a run of 8 points above the centerline, which calls for an investigation.

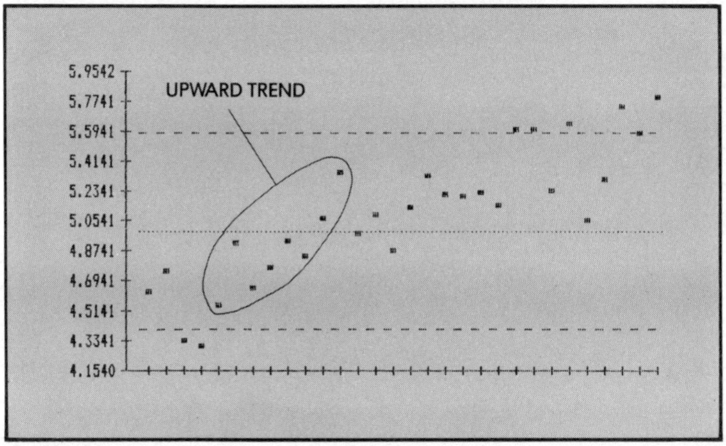

Fig. 2.2.11 *An upward trend sometimes precedes, and forewarns of, the process going out of control. In this case the trend both precedes and follows points out of control, and is the result of overadjustment by the machine operator.*

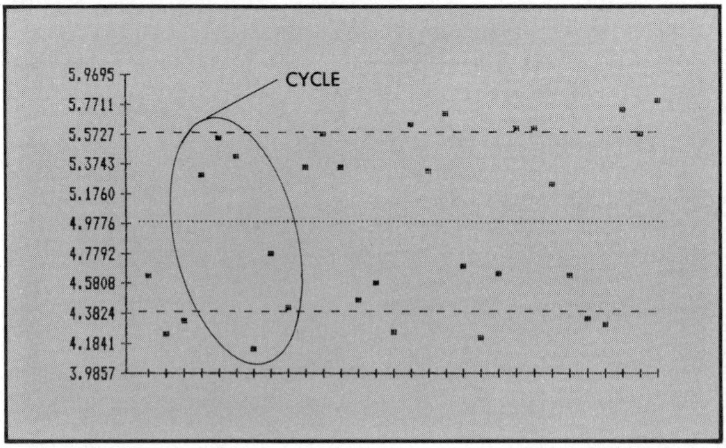

Fig. 2.2.12 *A cycle is a pattern that repeats. In this case it preceded points that are out of control and provided an early indication of instability.*

- A *trend* downward or upward of 7 or more successive points (Figure 2.2.11).
- A *cycle* or pattern that repeats itself (Figure 2.2.12).

In addition, there are several patterns that may appear which are unnatural and should be investigated (*Western Electric*, 1956):

- A *mixture*, identified by an absence of points near the centerline (Figure 2.2.13).
- *Stratification*, identified by 15 or more points consistently hugging the centerline (Figure 2.2.14).
- *Clusters*, or the grouping of points in one area of the chart (Figure 2.2.15).

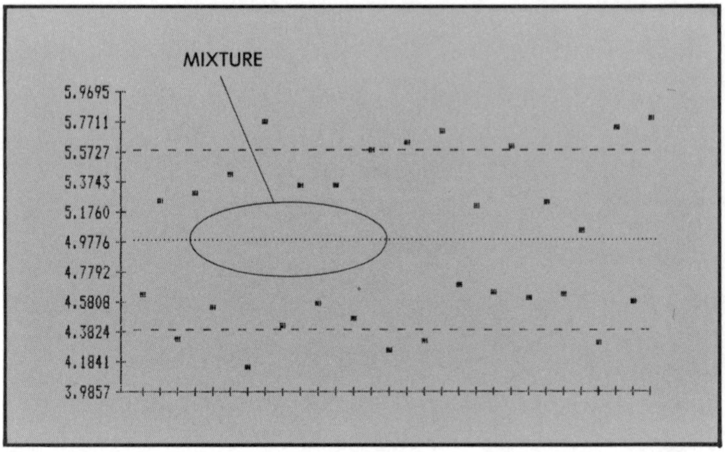

Fig. 2.2.13 Mixtures usually indicate two processes operating at different levels.

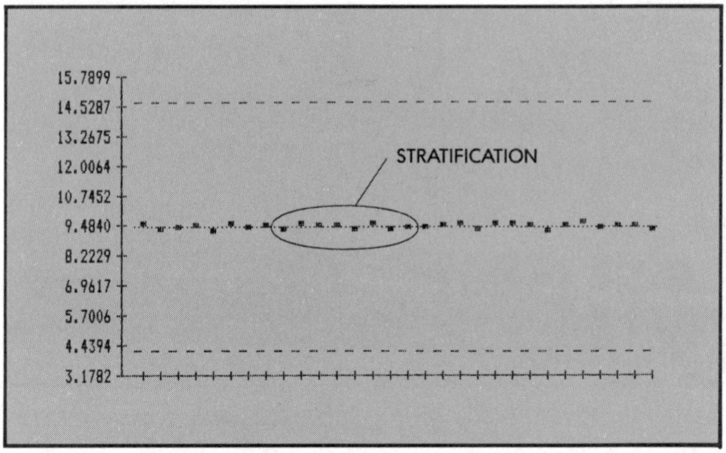

Fig. 2.2.14 Stratification may be an indication of systematic sampling, where the samples consistently offset each other or, as in this case, improperly calculated control limits and chart scales.

Fig. 2.2.15 Clusters are an indication of short duration, assignable causes such as measurement problems, or accidentally sampling from a bad group of parts.

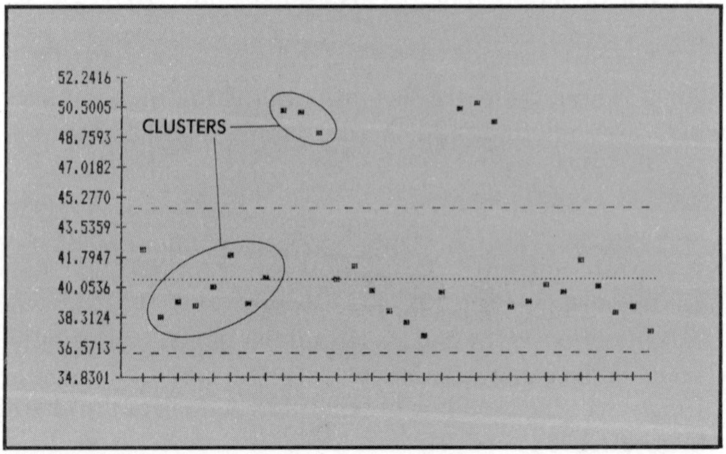

How To Identify Assignable Causes

The first technique to use when looking at an $\bar{x}$ & R chart is to read the R chart first (*Western Electric*, 1956). The R chart is more sensitive to changes in uniformity and consistency. If bad parts start appearing in a process, they will affect the R chart. The variation will increase, so some points will be higher than normal. Generally, the lower the points in the R chart, the more uniform the process. Two machines turning out the same parts can be compared for uniformity by looking at their R charts. Parts mixed together from different processes will also show up in the R chart. Intermittent variation, caused by a switch or relay that sticks occasionally, will cause the R chart to go out of control.

Anything that introduces a new system of causes into the process will show up in the R chart. Any change to the process, such as an inexperienced operator, poorer materials, tool wear, or a lack of maintenance will tend to shift points upward. The biggest clues to an assignable cause on an R chart are the time the characteristic occurs and the fact that some parts are affected more than others.

Since the R chart is more sensitive to change, efforts at improving the process will show up first in the R chart. A steady shift downward in points on the R chart is the best evidence of having successfully eliminated assignable causes of variation.

Once the R chart is stable, we can focus on the $\bar{x}$ chart. When the R chart is unstable, the $\bar{x}$ chart can be very misleading. When both charts are stable, the process is said to be *in control*, and the $\bar{x}$ chart indicates the process operating level at various points in time. Changes in the operating level can be classed by two types: true $\bar{x}$ causes and false $\bar{x}$ causes (*Western Electric*, 1956).

- True $\bar{x}$ causes are causes which change all pieces from a process at pretty much the same rate. This can include a change in materials (thicker or thinner stock), a temperature change, machine calibration or setup, or gradual tooling wear. These things cause a change in level over time that usually can be traced to the moment they occur.

- False $\bar{x}$ causes are causes which show up because the $\bar{x}$ chart reflects changes in the R chart, and those causes are better interpreted in the R chart. They include all the causes mentioned above that create dispersion within a subgroup.

Interpreting the $\bar{x}$ & R Charts Together

The $\bar{x}$ & R charts must be interpreted together as well as separately (*Western Electric*, 1956). As stated, a stable process will have points randomly distributed between the control limits on the charts. With a stable process, the $\bar{x}$ & R points should tend not to follow each other. A lack of stability will sometimes cause them to move together. For example, a process whose population is skewed in a positive direction (Figure 2.2.16) with a long tail to the high side,

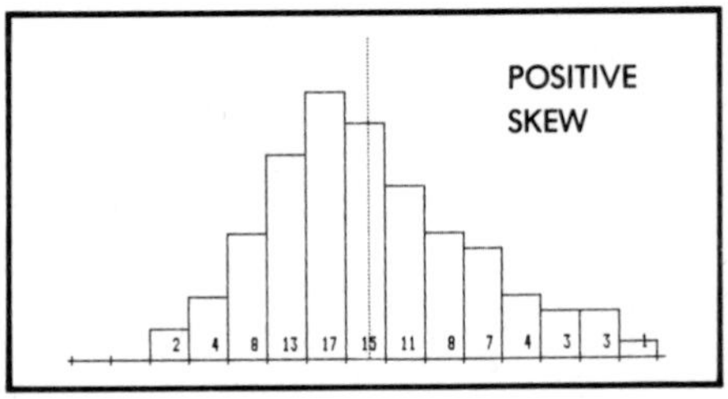

Fig. 2.2.16 The positively skewed distribution shown above can cause positive correlation on the charts, where points tend to follow each other up or down.

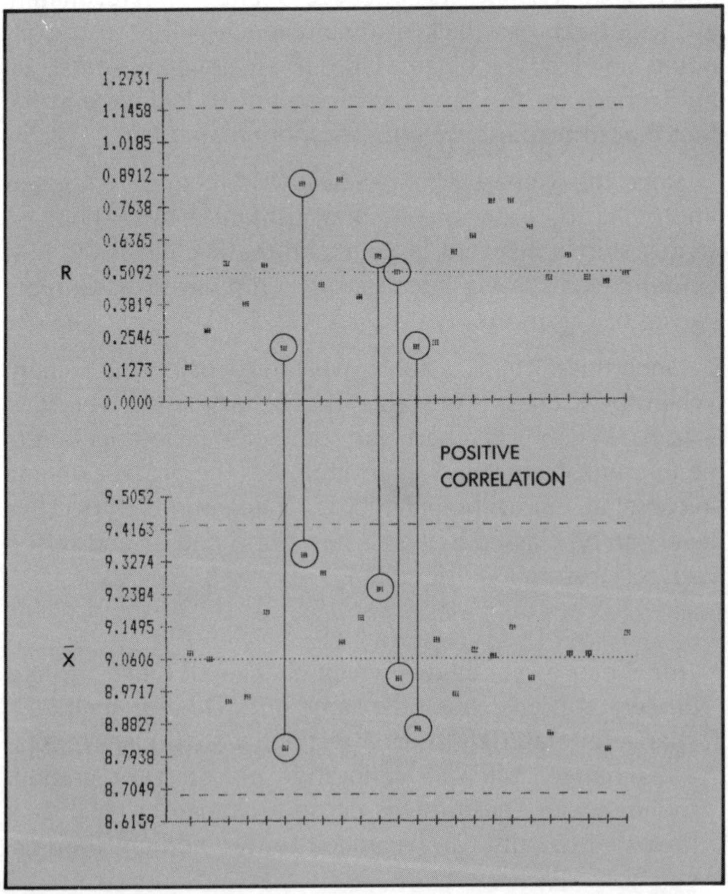

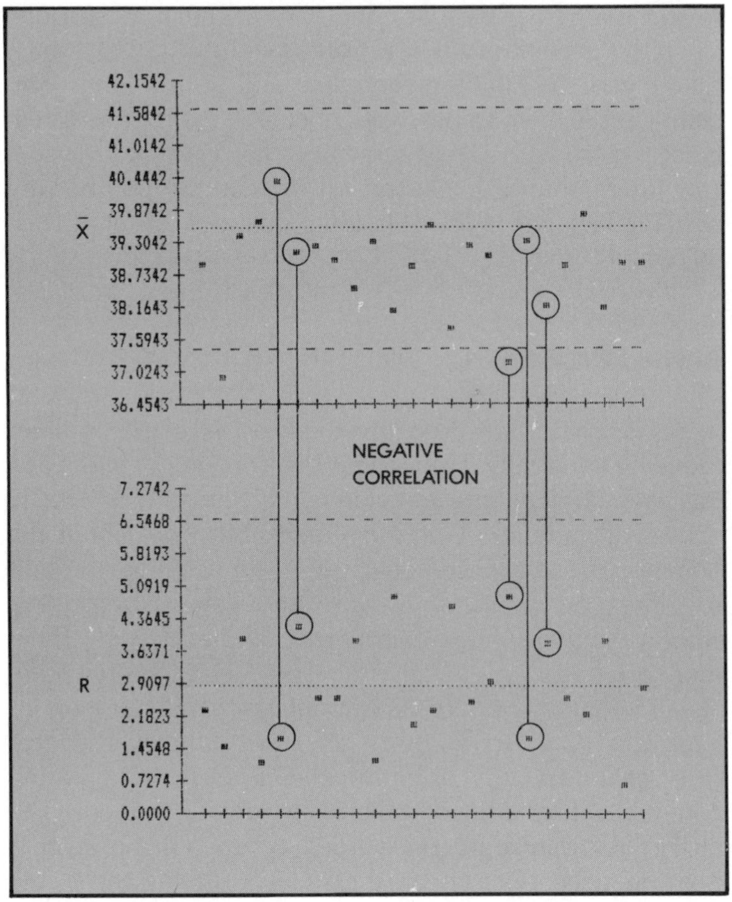

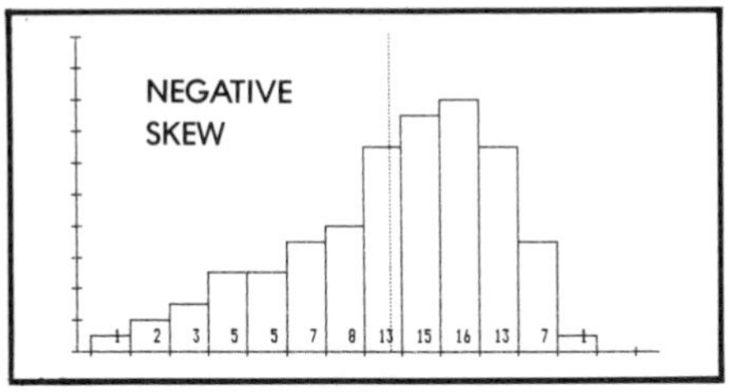

Fig. 2.2.17 A negatively skewed distribution can cause negative correlation on the charts, where the points tend to move in opposite directions.

will cause a positive correlation between the $\bar{x}$ & R charts. In other words, high $\bar{x}$ points will tend to follow high R points. A process with a negatively skewed population will cause a negative correlation between the charts as shown in Figure 2.2.17. The $\bar{x}$ points will tend to follow the R points, but in the opposite direction.

Changes In Level

A sustained change in level in either chart usually calls for a recalculation of the centerline and control limits. This renews the ability of the control limits to be used to detect assignable causes. It also recognizes a change to the process which, for better or worse, is more or less permanent. A chart can be thought of as a moving window. It should reflect the actual present conditions as much as possible, since the present is when action based on the chart must take place. Keeping the centerline and control limits constant causes them to eventually become as arbitrary as engineering limits. We must remember, however, that the control limits should be based on at least 20 points. Any sustained change in level should probably exist for at least 20 points.

Beyond $\bar{x}$ & R Charts

$\bar{x}$ & R charts are probably the most effective tool for reducing variability. Throughout this section, the emphasis has been on detecting and working to eliminate assignable causes of variation. One might ask, "But what about the common causes?" Common causes are much more difficult to address on an everyday level. Often they are part of the whole manufacturing environment, and addressing them more often than not means addressing decisions on materials and equipment purchasing, material handling, shop organization, product and process design, employee education, and company orientation. Obviously, eliminating common causes is beyond the scope of this handbook. The task of assessing a process is a quality function, however. It is known generally as *process capability studies*, and is covered in Chapter 3. *Acceptance sampling* is another aspect of quality control that deals with common causes, and it is covered in Chapter 5.

2.3 CONTROL CHARTS FOR ATTRIBUTES

Attribute data on a control chart is simply the count of products or characteristics of a product that do not conform to some established criteria. The chart becomes a line graph showing the variation in the quality of the process over a period of time. Control limits are drawn on the control chart to aid in analyzing the variation of the process. When the variation is shown by the control chart to be due to common causes, the process is said to be *in a state of statistical control*. If the data on the chart shows abnormal points or patterns then the process has changed due to some assignable or "findable" causes.

Once a process can be said to be in control, the control chart can be used to monitor whether or not the process remains in control. This is because a control chart represents a dynamic or moving picture of what is happening to a process. This is different from a histogram, which can show only a static picture of the variability of the process. Only when a process is in control can it be analyzed for *capability*, or whether or not the process is capable of producing output that meets specifications or tolerances. When assignable or special causes are found, then corrective action can be taken before serious out-of-control conditions occur. A control chart can also show when to leave the process alone. Unnecessary tinkering with the process when the variation is natural and actually indicating statistical control will only inject more variation into the process.

Types of Attribute Control Charts and Data

Attribute data is a count of nonconforming units (defective parts), or the number of nonconformities on a unit (number of defects per part). Attribute data does not require actual measurements such as length, width or torque. It is only necessary to count the number of defects or defective units. Many characteristics of quality can only be measured in this way, such as the presence or absence of a required screw or number of bad solder connections on a printed circuit board. Other attribute data may be the result of data that is measurable but recorded as pass or fail, such as that from a GO/NO-GO gage. Control charts for attribute data have a number of advantages:

- Attribute data is easier to collect and, as a result, less costly to acquire. Inspection skills are not complicated and gages, if used, are simple GO/NO-GO gages. In some cases the data is already available from past inspection records. Large amounts of attribute data can many times be collected at one inspection station.
- Attribute data can be collected from any type of a process. Output from any process can be qualified as conforming or nonconforming.
- Several types of defects can be grouped on one chart. For

complex assemblies it would be very impractical to require a separate control chart for each measured characteristic. Attribute charts in this case can indicate problem areas and suggest where more detailed variable control charts may be needed.

- Attribute data is easy to understand by all personnel. Control charts for attributes are easier to construct and understand.
- Attribute control charts provide an overall picture of the quality of a process and provide useful quality history.

There are also some disadvantages:

- An attribute chart does not always provide detailed data for the analysis of individual characteristics. For attribute charts a part is defective if it has one defective characteristic or many defective characteristics.
- Attribute data does not indicate different degrees of defectiveness. A nonconforming item may be very defective or slightly defective.
- Because of the above disadvantages of attribute data, control charts for attribute data are less sensitive in indicating changes in the process. The charts for attributes also only indicate when a change in the process occurred and offer little information as to why the change occurred.

Control chart types are defined by the type of data being charted. There are four types of control charts for attributes. See Table 2.3.1. Control charts that are for the count of nonconforming units are called *p-charts* and *np-charts*. A unit is nonconforming if it has one or more defects. If the

Table 2.3.1 Summary of types of attribute control charts.

TYPE	WHAT IS COUNTED	SAMPLE SIZE
p-chart	defective items	varies
np-chart	defective items	constant
c-chart	defects on an item	constant
u-chart	defects on an item	varies

data is collected in subgroups of constant size then the chart used is an np-chart. If the data is in subgroups of varying size then the p-chart is used. Control charts that count individual nonconformities or defects on a product are *c-charts* and *u-charts*. c-Charts involve subgroups of constant size and u-charts have subgroups not of constant size.

Elements of a Control Chart for Attributes

A control chart is a two-dimensional line graph (Figure 2.3.1). The plotted points represent the given measure of

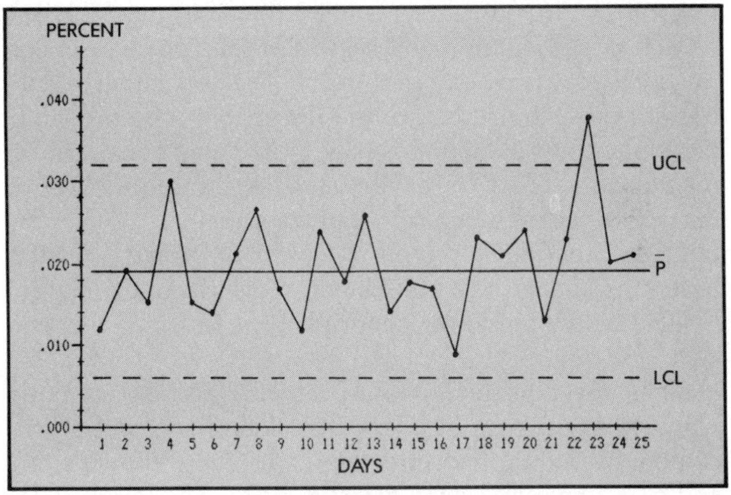

Fig. 2.3.1 Attribute control chart, with centerline and control limits.

quality of the process from the data collected at predetermined periods of time. The horizontal axis is divided into time periods (also called subgroups): hour to hour, day to day, lot to lot, etc. The vertical scale represents the quantity or percentage of defects per unit or defective units. Three control lines are also drawn horizontally on the control chart: a central line, upper control limit line and lower control limit line. The central line is the average of the number of defects or defective units in the process for the total period of the process being charted.

The control limits are the key to control charts. The control limits are the criteria for analyzing a process for statistical control. Control charts use sigma as a measure of variation. The upper control limit is drawn at the central line plus three sigma. The lower control limit is drawn at the central line minus three sigma. The choice of three sigma is somewhat arbitrary but has become fairly standard in the U.S.

The calculation of the three-sigma limits on control charts for attributes is different from that of control charts for variables. For variables it is based on the *normal distribution*. However, for p-charts and np-charts it is based on the *binomial distribution*. For c-charts and u-charts it is based on *Poisson distribution*. When based on the binomial distribution, it is assumed that the possibility of a unit being defective is the same from unit to unit and independent from unit to unit. Each unit has the same chance of being good or bad just as in flipping a coin. When based on the Poisson distribution it is assumed that the possibility for defects occurring on a unit is great but the chances of getting a defect at any one spot is small. Although these distributions differ from the normal distribution, the probabilities of a point falling outside the three sigma control limits on a control chart for attributes is on the same order of magnitude as on a control chart for variables. When only random variation is present on a control chart for attributes, the chance of a point being above the upper control limit or below the lower control limit is less than one percent.

Since the control limits are at plus and minus three sigma from the central line, either side of the central line can be divided up into three zones at plus and minus one and two sigma (*Western Electric*, 1956). These zones, labeled C, B, and A going away from the central line, although not plotted on the chart, also are used in reading a control chart. See Figure 2.3.2.

Application and Construction of Control Charts for Attributes

The following steps describe how to use a control chart for attributes:

- *Select the area or process to be charted.* Give high priority to areas where problems are already occurring Choose characteristics that will provide the type of data needed for finding the problem.

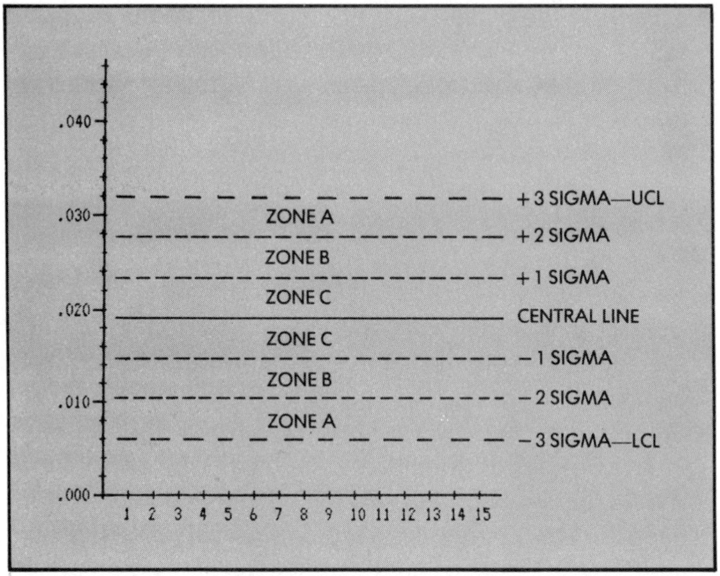

Fig. 2.3.2 Zones used when interpreting a control chart.

- *Decide which attribute chart to use.* This will depend on the type of data that may already be available or the type of data that is desired.
- *Select the frequency of sampling.* In other words, define the subgroups. The subgroup periods may be equal periods of production (hourly, daily, weekly). The periods may also correspond to equal quantities of production (lots, batches). The periods should be chosen to make it easy to find and correct problems. Shorter periods will give faster feedback of problems. It is important that the subgroups be chosen to ensure that there will be minimum variation within a subgroup. This will allow variation to show up on the chart from subgroup to subgroup.
- *Select size of subgroup.* The subgroup size should be large enough to ensure that the subgroup has a strong probability of having some nonconformities. Small subgroup sizes tend to result in control limits being wide and being less accurate in depicting an out of control process. The most effective subgroup size for p and np-charts is greater than 50. For the most effective c and u-charts, the subgroup size should be at least one, but better at five to ten.
- *Gather the data.* Samples within a subgroup should be collected randomly so each item being inspected has an equal chance of having nonconformities.

- *Construct the chart.* Be careful not to make the chart too tall vertically. Plot the data. Calculate and draw the control lines. Many times, the value for the lower control limit will be negative for an attribute control chart. In this case there is no lower control limit. At least 20 to 25 periods should be plotted before control limits are calculated.
- *Analyze the chart for evidence of the process being out of control.* Plotted points indicating a lack of control should be marked with an "x" and investigated. These special causes should be corrected and prevented from recurring.
- *Eliminate causes and recalculate chart.* Once the causes of out of control points are corrected, the control limits should be recalculated, excluding those out of control periods. The chart then should be revaluated with the new limits to look for more out of control conditions.
- *Extend control limits.* When the process is deemed to be in control, the control limits can be extended forward in time on the chart. Future data can then be plotted on the chart to continue evaluating the process for evidence of the process going out of statistical control. As a process continues to improve, the old control limits may be too wide to gain any further improvement in quality. In this case it may be desirable to recalculate the control limits using only the most recent data. Quality is improving when the control limits can be made narrower.

Reading a Control Chart for Attributes

The goal in reading a control chart for attributes is defining which points represent evidence that the process is out of control. Points on a chart that indicate only random or chance variation are the result of common causes and do not indicate the need for corrective action. Points that represent nonrandom variation are due to assignable causes and are the signals for immediate action (*Western Electric*, 1956). Variations above the central line on an attribute chart are called *high spots* and variations below the central line are called *low spots*. The purpose of finding nonrandom variation is to eliminate the special causes that enter a process causing a change in the quality of the output.

A chart with points that are varying in a random fashion is said to have a *natural pattern.* A natural pattern has most of the points near the central line, a few points spread out and approaching the control limits and no points exceeding the control limits. *Unnatural patterns* are those that are missing one or more of the characteristics of a natural pattern. An unnatural pattern on the chart indicates that something is wrong with the process.

The most important thing to look for in a control chart, as has been said before, is points that fall outside of the control limits. Statistically it is extremely unlikely that any point on a control chart will fall outside of the control limits if there are no special causes present in the process. The danger here is finding a point outside of the limits which will signal the need for corrective action when in fact no change has taken place in the process. This is called a Type I error. When no corrective action is taken on a point that is within the control limits, but there really was a change in the process, it is called a Type II error. In order to reduce the chances of these errors, other tests for unnatural variation can be made.

When reading a control chart for attributes it is important to keep in mind that evidence of nonrandomness near the lower control limit (low spots) may seem to indicate that the process is producing too few defects. This may point to areas of a good process and investigation may lead to ways of improving overall quality. Finding reasons why some subgroups have fewer defects than others can cause action for more permanent improvement in quality. Low spots, however, can also indicate that there has been an error in inspection or the need for tighter standards.

Instability — Again, the first and most important test for instability is the presence of one or more points outside of the 3 sigma control lines. See Section 2.4 for an example. Other tests are: 2 out of 3 successive points in zone A or beyond, 4 out of 5 successive points in zone B or beyond and 8 points in a row on one side of the central line. See Section 2.5 for an example. The above tests, also called *runs*, apply separately to either side of the central line (not in combination). Causes of instability above the central line may be operator mistakes, poor maintenance or bad materials. Instability below the central line may indicate better quality of the process output due to operator improvement, better equipment or better materials. Below the central line may also indicate relaxation of criteria for bad output or improper inspection.

Stratification — The characteristic of this unnatural pattern is the absence of points near the control limits. Some causes of this include: non-random sampling, samples coming from different sources, and samples being screened before inspection.

Systematic variation — In this case the pattern has become predictable. An example of this is a low point always being followed by a high one and vice versa. The cause is usually in collecting the data systematically from different sources.

Trends — A trend is a long series of points that are generally moving up or down without a change in direction. See Section 2.6 for an example. Upward trends indicate more defectives, possibly caused by poorer materials or workmanship or the wearing of a tool. Downward trends may be caused by better materials or workmanship or relaxation of standards.

Sudden shifts in level — This is shown by a number of abnormal points suddenly appearing on one side of the central line or the other. This indicates a major change in the process has taken place. See Section 2.7 for an example. Higher shifts in level may be due to a new batch of poorer material, a change to a new operator or poorer machine, or a tightening of inspection criteria. Lower level shifts may indicate a change to better operators, machines, methods or a loosening of standards. Gradual changes in level may also occur with similar causes but over a longer period of time.

Cycles — Cycles are short trends occurring in repeating patterns. They may be caused by regular differences in suppliers or nonrandom data collection.

2.4 p-CHARTS

When the interest is in determining the quantity of defective units and the data is collected in samples that are not of constant size, then the p-chart is appropriate. The p-chart measures the output of a process as the percentage of nonconforming or defective items in a subgroup being inspected. Each item is recorded as being either conforming or nonconforming even if the item has more than one defect. The following symbols are used on a p-chart:

n — The number of units in a subgroup (the subgroup, sample, or subset size).
k — The number of subgroups in the study period.
np — The number of defective or nonconforming units found in a subgroup.
p — The fraction defective in a subgroup (proportion nonconforming). These are the points that are plotted on the chart. The formula is:

$$p = \frac{np}{n} \qquad (2.4.1)$$

p-bar — The average fraction defective (average proportion nonconforming) for the study period. This is drawn as the central line on the chart. It is found by dividing the total number of defective units found in all subgroups of the study period by the total number of units inspected in the study period. The formula is:

$$\bar{p} = \frac{np_1 + np_2 + \ldots + np_k}{n_1 + n_2 + \ldots + n_k} \qquad (2.4.2)$$

How to Make and Use a p-Chart

Refer to the example in Figure 2.4.1.

- Gather and record the data.
- Calculate p-bar.
- Calculate upper and lower control limits. Since the value

Fig. 2.4.1 The percentage of defective light bulbs from a daily inspection is shown in the table below. Note that an average for n is used. The calculations for the chart at right are:

$$\bar{n} = \frac{25068}{25} = 1003$$

$$\bar{p} = \frac{489}{25068} = .019$$

$$UCL = .019 + \frac{3\sqrt{.019(1-.019)}}{\sqrt{1003}} = .032$$

$$LCL = .019 - .013 = .006$$

Note the instability at day 23, indicated by a point out-of-control.

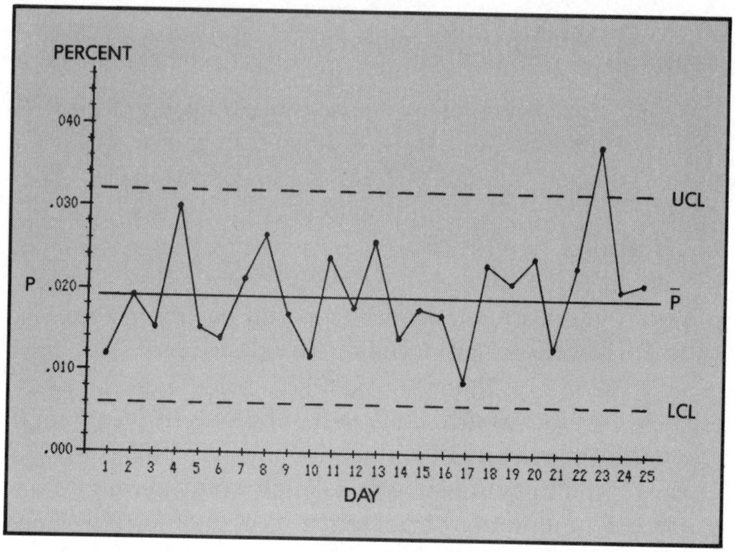

day	n	np	p
1	990	12	.012
2	1134	21	.019
3	960	14	.015
4	1000	30	.030
5	1020	15	.015
6	1024	14	.014
7	1040	22	.021
8	1010	26	.026
9	980	17	.017
10	976	12	.012
11	1010	24	.024
12	1010	18	.018
13	900	23	.026
14	900	13	.014
15	1000	18	.018
16	1000	17	.017
17	1020	9	.009
18	1120	26	.023
19	1024	21	.021
20	1060	25	.024
21	920	12	.013
22	970	22	.023
23	980	37	.038
24	1020	20	.020
25	1000	21	.021
	25068	489	

of n varies from subgroup to subgroup, the control limits must be calculated for each subgroup. This makes the p-chart difficult to read and construct. This nuisance can be avoided by keeping the subgroup size the same or within plus or minus 25% of the average sample size and using an average of n. An alternative is showing two sets of control limits using the maximum and minimum subgroup sizes. The formulas for control limits are:

$$UCL\ \bar{p} = \bar{p} + \frac{3\sqrt{\bar{p}(1-\bar{p})}}{\sqrt{n}} \qquad (2.4.3)$$

$$LCL\ \bar{p} = \bar{p} - \frac{3\sqrt{\bar{p}(1-\bar{p})}}{\sqrt{n}} \qquad (2.4.4)$$

- Decide on a scale and put it on the control chart.
- Plot each p, and add p-bar, and the control limit lines.
- Analyze the data points for evidence of noncontrol.
- Find and correct special causes.
- Recalculate control limits.

2.5 np-CHARTS

When the interest is in determining the quantity of defective units and the data is collected in subgroups that are of constant size, then the np-chart is appropriate. The p-chart could also be used in this case, but the number of nonconforming items rather than the fraction is generally easier to understand. The np-chart measures the output of a process as the actual number of nonconforming or defective items in a subgroup being inspected. Each item is recorded as being either conforming or nonconforming even if the item has more than one defect. Except for plotting the number defective instead of the fraction and the calculation of control limits, the np-chart is the same as the p-chart. The following symbols are used on an np-chart:

n — The number of units in a subgroup (the subgroup, sample, or subset size).
k — The number of subgroups in the study period.
np — The number of defective or nonconforming units found in a subgroup. These are the points plotted on the chart.
np-bar — The average number of defective or nonconforming units for the study period. This is drawn as the central line on the chart. It is found by dividing the total number of defective units found in all subgroups of the study period by the total number of subgroups in the study period. The formula is:

$$n\bar{p} = \frac{np_1 + np_2 + \ldots + np_k}{k} \qquad (2.5.1)$$

How to Make and Use an np-Chart

Refer to the example in Figure 2.5.1

- Gather and record the data.
- Calculate np-bar.
- Calculate the upper and lower control limits. The formulas are:

Fig. 2.5.1 The number of coffee cups manufactured with broken handles is shown in the table below. Inspection is lot-by-lot with each lot consisting of 60 cups. The calculations for the chart at right are:

$$n\bar{p} = \frac{98}{25} = 3.9$$

$$\bar{p} = \frac{3.9}{60} = .065$$

$$UCL = 3.9 + 3\sqrt{3.9(1 - .065)} = 9.6$$

$$LCL = 3.9 - 5.7 = -1.8 \text{ (Assume Zero)}$$

Note the run of 8 above the centerline at lots 18 through 25.

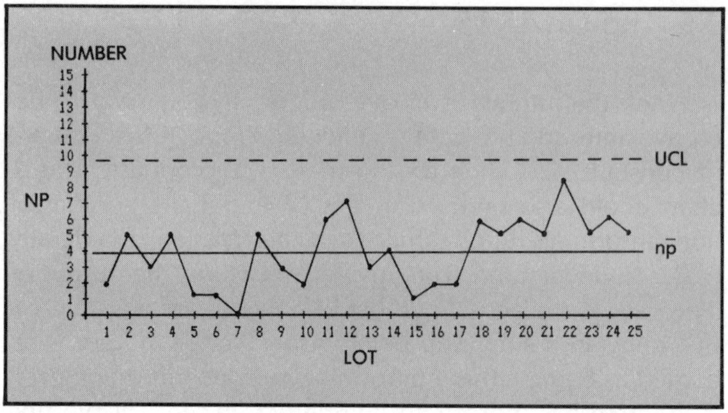

lot	n	np
1	60	2
2	60	5
3	60	3
4	60	5
5	60	1
6	60	1
7	60	0
8	60	5
9	60	3
10	60	2
11	60	6
12	60	7
13	60	3
14	60	4
15	60	1
16	60	2
17	60	2
18	60	6
19	60	5
20	60	6
21	60	5
22	60	8
23	60	5
24	60	6
25	60	5
		98

$$UCL_{n\bar{p}} = n\bar{p} + 3\sqrt{n\bar{p}(1 - \bar{p})} \qquad (2.5.2)$$

$$LCL_{n\bar{p}} = n\bar{p} - 3\sqrt{n\bar{p}(1 - \bar{p})} \qquad (2.5.3)$$

where $\bar{p} = \frac{n\bar{p}}{n}$

- Decide on a scale for the control chart.
- Plot each np, and add np-bar and the control limit lines.
- Analyze the data points for evidence of noncontrol.
- Find and correct special causes.
- Recalculate control limits.

2.6 c-CHARTS

In cases where a single unit of process output is likely to have many defects it may be appropriate to use a c-chart. The c-chart is applied where the defects are scattered continuously throughout the unit output, such as flaws in a roll of paper or bubbles in glass. The interest here is not only that the unit is defective but how many defects it has. Subgroups will be in square yards of cloth, number of glass containers, an area of sheet metal, etc. The areas or number of items for a subgroup must be the same from subgroup to subgroup. c-Charts usually have one item per subgroup but may have two or more. c-Charts also apply where the defects on a single unit, such as individual automobiles, may come from many sources and where no one such source would produce most of the nonconformities. c-Charts are useful in the final inspection of complicated assemblies. Also, they can be used in non-industrial areas such as bookkeeping errors and accidents. The symbols used on a c-chart are:

n — The number of units in a subgroup (the subgroup, sample, or subset size).
k — The number of subgroups in the study period.
c — The number of defects or nonconformities in a subgroup. These are the points that are plotted on the chart.
c-bar — The average number of defects or nonconformities for the study period. This is drawn as the central line on the chart. It is found by dividing the total number of defects found in all subgroups of the study period by the total number of subgroups in the study period. The formula is:

$$\bar{c} = \frac{c_1 + c_2 + \ldots + c_k}{k} \qquad (2.6.1)$$

How to Make and Use a c-Chart

Refer to the example in Figure 2.6.1.

- Gather and record the data. Remember that the size of the inspection sample must be the same (number of units, area of glass, length of wire, etc.).
- Calculate c-bar.
- Calculate upper and lower control limits. The formulas are:

$$UCL_{\bar{c}} = \bar{c} + 3\sqrt{\bar{c}} \qquad (2.6.2)$$

$$LCL_{\bar{c}} = \bar{c} - 3\sqrt{\bar{c}} \qquad (2.6.3)$$

- Decide on a scale for the control chart.
- Plot each c, and add c-bar and the control limit lines

Fig. 2.6.1 The number of assembly errors found in complex circuit board assemblies are shown in the table below. Ten boards were inspected per hour. The calculations for the chart at right are:

$$\bar{c} = \frac{130}{25} = 5.2$$

$$UCL = 5.2 + 3\sqrt{5.2} = 12.0$$

$$LCL = 5.2 - 6.8 = -1.6 \text{ (Assume Zero)}$$

Note the upward trend from hours 16 to 25.

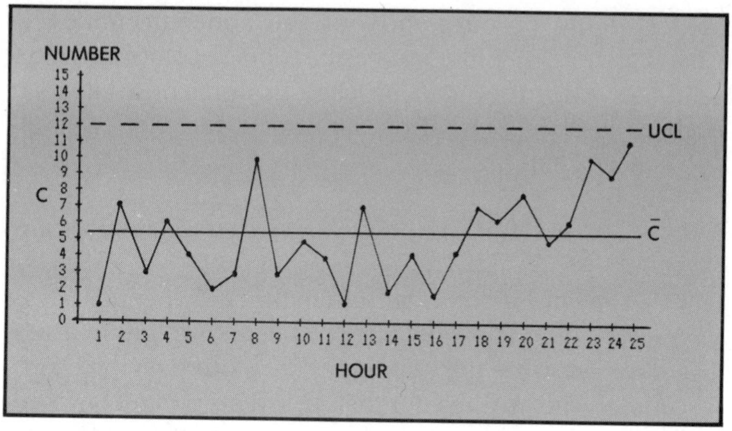

- Analyze the data points for evidence of noncontrol.
- Find and correct special causes.
- Recalculate control limits.

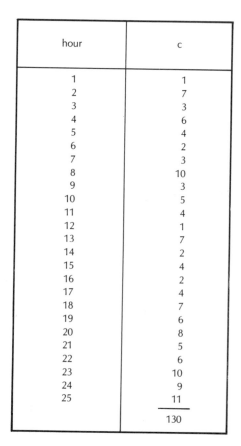

hour	c
1	1
2	7
3	3
4	6
5	4
6	2
7	3
8	10
9	3
10	5
11	4
12	1
13	7
14	2
15	4
16	2
17	4
18	7
19	6
20	8
21	5
22	6
23	10
24	9
25	11
	130

2.7 u-CHARTS

The u-chart is appropriate in the same situations as the c-chart. The differences are in the calculation of control limits and that the plotted points represent number of nonconformities per unit instead of just the number of nonconformities. u-Charts must be used instead of c-charts if the unit size of a subgroup varies from subgroup to subgroup. The following symbols are used on a u-chart:

n — The number of units in a subgroup (the subgroup, sample, or subset size).
k — The number of subgroups in the study period.
c — The number of defects or nonconformities found in a subgroup.
u — The number of defects or nonconformities per unit in a subgroup. These are the points that are plotted on the chart. The formula is:

$$u = \frac{c}{n} \qquad (2.7.1)$$

u-bar — The average number of defects or nonconformities per unit for the study period. This is drawn as the central line on the chart. It is found by dividing the total

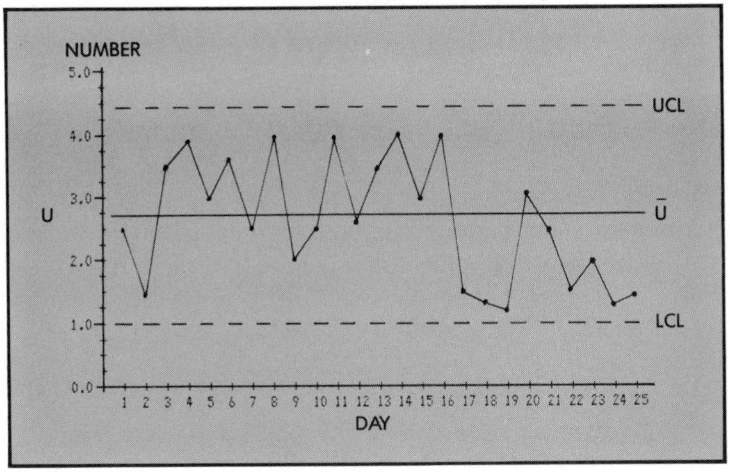

Fig. 2.7.1 The number of dents counted on car hoods per day is shown in the table below. The number of hoods inspected varies from day to day. Note that an average for n is used. The calculations for the chart at left are:

$$\bar{n} = \frac{217}{25} = 8.7$$

$$\bar{u} = \frac{576}{217} = 2.7$$

$$UCL = 2.7 + \frac{3\sqrt{2.7}}{\sqrt{8.7}} = 4.4$$

$$LCL = 2.7 - 1.7 = 1.0$$

Note the sudden shift in level in days 17 through 25.

day	n	c	u
1	10	25	2.5
2	9	13	1.4
3	8	28	3.5
4	9	35	3.9
5	9	27	3.0
6	7	25	3.6
7	8	20	2.5
8	8	32	4.0
9	8	16	2.0
10	8	20	2.5
11	10	40	4.0
12	7	18	2.6
13	11	39	3.5
14	9	36	4.0
15	8	24	3.0
16	10	40	4.0
17	8	12	1.5
18	9	12	1.3
19	9	11	1.2
20	10	30	3.0
21	8	20	2.5
22	8	12	1.5
23	9	18	2.0
24	8	10	1.3
25	9	13	1.4
	217	576	

number of defects found in all subgroups of the study period by the total number of units inspected in the study period. The formula is:

$$\bar{u} = \frac{c_1 + c_2 + \ldots + c_k}{n_1 + n_2 + \ldots + n_k} \qquad (2.7.2)$$

How to Make and Use a u-Chart

Refer to the example in Figure 2.7.1.

- Gather and record the data.
- Calculate u-bar.
- Calculate upper and lower control limits. As is the case with p-charts, the value of n varies from subgroup to subgroup and the control limits must be calculated for each subgroup. Maintaining the sample sizes the same or within plus or minus 25% of the average sample size, and using an average value for n, simplifies the calculation of control limits. The formulas are:

$$UCL_{\bar{u}} = \bar{u} + \frac{3\sqrt{\bar{u}}}{\sqrt{n}} \qquad (2.7.3)$$

$$LCL_{\bar{u}} = \bar{u} - \frac{3\sqrt{\bar{u}}}{\sqrt{n}} \quad (2.7.4)$$

- Decide on a scale for the control chart.
- Plot each u, and add u-bar and the control limit lines.
- Analyze the data points for evidence of noncontrol.
- Find and correct special causes.

For Further Reference

Ford Motor Company. *Process Capability and Continuing Process Control.* Statistical Methods Office, 1983.

Grant, Eugene L., and Leavenworth, Richard S. *Statistical Quality Control*, 5th ed. New York: McGraw-Hill Book Company, 1980.

Ishikawa, Kaoru. *Guide to Quality Control.* Hong Kong: Nordica International Limited, 1976.

Juran, Joseph M., and Gryna, Frank M., *Quality Planning and Analysis.* New York: McGraw-Hill Book Company, 1970.

Quality Control Circles, Inc. *Quality Control Circles.* 2d ed. Saratoga: Quality Control Circles, Inc., 1982.

Western Electric Co., Inc. *Statistical Control Handbook.* 2d ed. Easton: Mack Printing Company, 1956.

3. Capability Studies

3.1 WHAT IS A CAPABILITY STUDY?

The traditional approach to manufacturing is a two step process: production personnel make the product while quality control personnel inspect and eliminate those products which do not meet specifications. This is wasteful and expensive since it allows time and materials to be invested in products that are not always usable. It is also unreliable since even 100 percent inspection would fail to catch all defective products.

In every manufacturing process there is variability. This variability may be large or small, but it is always present. It can be divided into two types:

- Variability due to common causes.
- Variability due to assignable causes.

The first type of variability can be expected to occur naturally within a process. It is attributed to common causes which behave like a constant system of chances. These chances form a unique and describable distribution. This variability can never be completely eliminated from a process. Variability due to assignable causes on the other hand, refers to the variation that can be linked to specific or special causes. If these causes or factors are modified or controlled properly, the process variability associated with them can be eliminated. Assignable causes cannot be described by a single distribution.

A *capability study* (or process capability study) is a technique for analyzing the variability found in a production process. In its most accurate sense, a capability study measures the performance potential of a process when no assignable causes are present. This occurs, by definition, when a process is *in statistical control.* Since the inherent variability of the process can be described by a unique distribution, usually a normal distribution, capability can be evaluated by utilizing the properties of this distribution. *Capability* is expressed as the proportion of process output that remains within product specifications. If capability limits fall outside specification limits, then the process is deemed incapable.

A performance study is the term for a study in cases where it is not practical to determine if the process is in statistical control. Performance studies can be useful for examining incoming lots of materials or short or one-time-only production runs. In the case of an incoming lot, a performance study cannot tell us that the process that produced the parts is in statistical control, but it may tell us by the shape of the distribution what percent of the parts are out of specification or whether the distribution was truncated by the vendor sorting out the obvious bad parts.

3.2 USAGE OF A CAPABILITY STUDY

When we perform a capability study, we are comparing a group of samples against certain manufacturing specifications. As noted above, we should try to verify that the process in question is in control. The capability study can then show whether or not the process can meet specifications. In addition, the study can also provide estimates of the fraction of defective parts that can be expected.

A capability study, therefore, determines the inherent reproducibility of parts created in a process. The practical usages of such a study are numerous, and include the following:

- Evaluating new equipment purchases.
- Predicting whether design tolerances can be met.
- Assigning equipment to production.
- Planning process control checks.
- Analyzing the interrelationship of sequential processes.
- Making adjustments during manufacture.
- Setting specifications.
- Costing out contracts.

Besides their use in manufacturing processes, capability studies can also be used to solve problems in a wide range of situations in manufacturing, administration, engineering, and inspection.

3.3 HOW TO SET UP A CAPABILITY STUDY

Before we set up a study, we must select the critical dimension or variable to be examined. This dimension is the one which must meet product specifications. In the simplest case, the study dimension is the result of a single, direct process. In more complicated studies, the critical dimension may be the result of several processes. It may become necessary in these cases to perform capability studies on each process. Studies on early processes prove to be more valuable than studies on later processes since early processes lay the foundation which may affect later operations.

Once the critical dimension is selected, data measurements can be collected. This can be accomplished manually or by using automatic gaging and fixturing linked to a data collection device. When collecting measurements on a critical dimension, it is important that the measuring instrument be as precise as possible, preferrably one order of magnitude finer than the specification. Otherwise the measuring process will contribute excess variation to the dimension. Using handheld data collectors with automatic gages will help reduce errors introduced by the process of measurement, data recording, and transcription for post processing by computer.

The ideal situation for data collection is to collect as much data as possible over an extended time period. This will yield a capability study which is very reliable since it is based upon a large sample size.

Making a Histogram

Histograms are a graph of one item categorized by the distribution of measurements for that item. See Figure 3.3.1. The horizontal scale is used for the measurement range. The range is divided into cells. Usually about 20 cells provides enough resolution. The vertical scale is used to plot the height of the bars which represent the frequency of measurements at each cell.

The basic construction of a histogram is as follows:

- Collect the data.
- Determine the measurement range.

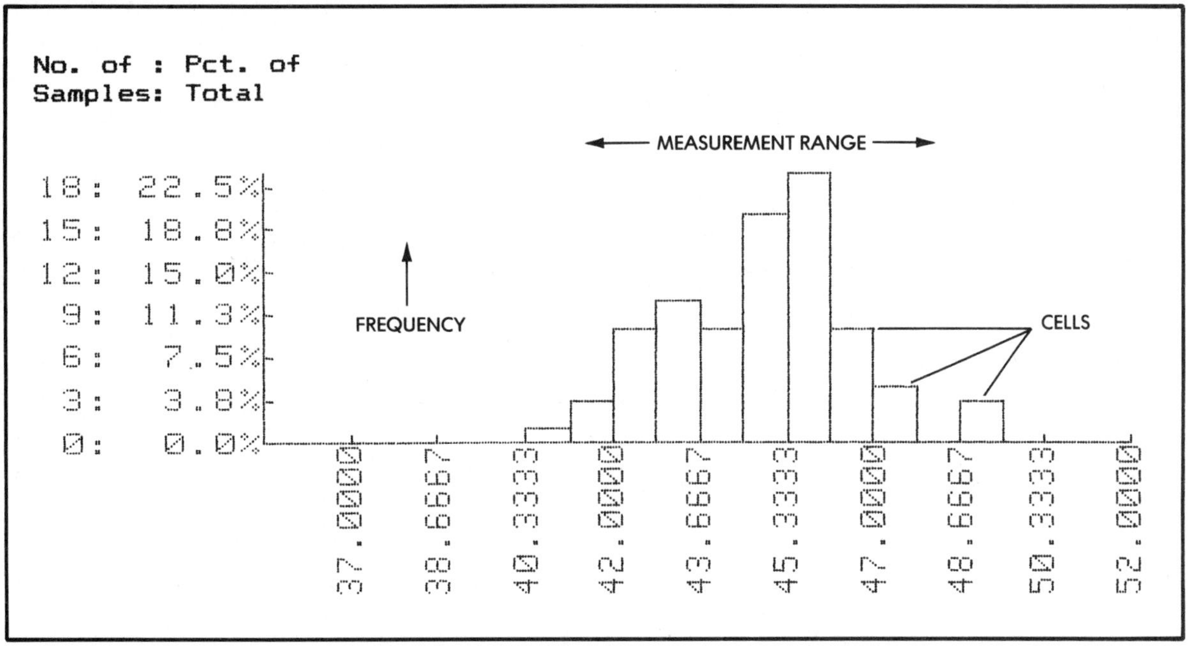

Fig. 3.3.1 A histogram is a graph of measurements of one item or characteristic. The frequency of individual measurements is plotted against the measurement range.

- Divide the range into about 20 equal intervals, or cells.
- Tabulate the number of samples in each cell.
- Use a horizontal scale to label the cells and a vertical scale to number the samples.

A histogram can be constructed manually but it is time consuming. It happens to be a perfect application for a "number cruncher" such as DataMyte data collection system or a desktop computer. A DataMyte data collector not only assists in data collection but will produce a histogram simply by connecting it to a printer or a CRT monitor. After a histogram is made, the DataMyte or computer can superimpose the mean ($\bar{x}$), ± 3 sigma limits, engineering limits, and even a normal curve (Figure 3.3.2).

See Chapters 15 and 16 for descriptions of data collectors for capability studies.

3.4 ANALYZING THE RESULTS OF A CAPABILITY STUDY

Once data collection is complete, analysis and interpretation of the data can proceed. The simplest form of data analysis is the comparison of product tolerance or specification limits with the inherent reproducibility. This can be accomplished graphically by plotting a histogram of the data.

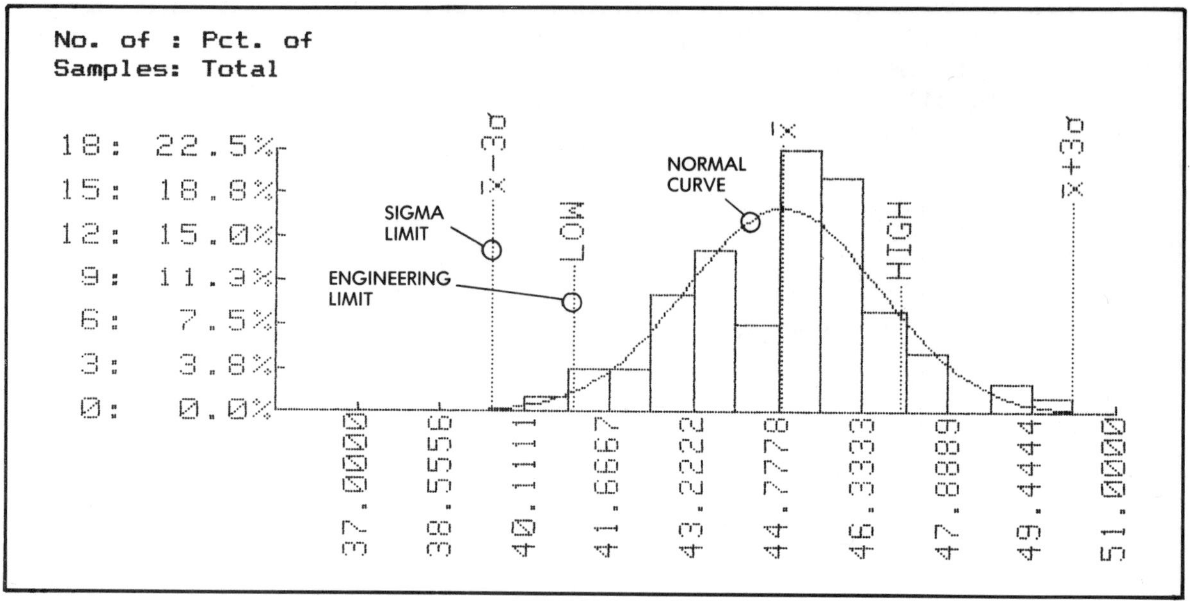

Fig. 3.3.2 The basic histogram can be analyzed by superimposing high and low engineering limits, sigma limits and normal curve.

Using a Histogram

Data from a process that evidences statistical control will form a normal distribution and hence, a normal curve can be fit to the data (Figure 3.4.1). Tolerance limits can be added to the graph and an immediate decision as to whether the process is capable or not can be made visually. This is illustrated in Figure 3.4.2 which shows histograms of two processes; one that is capable and one that is not.

In some cases the measurements do not follow a normal distribution and a different curve must be fit to the data.

Fig. 3.4.1 A histogram that nearly matches the superimposed normal curve.

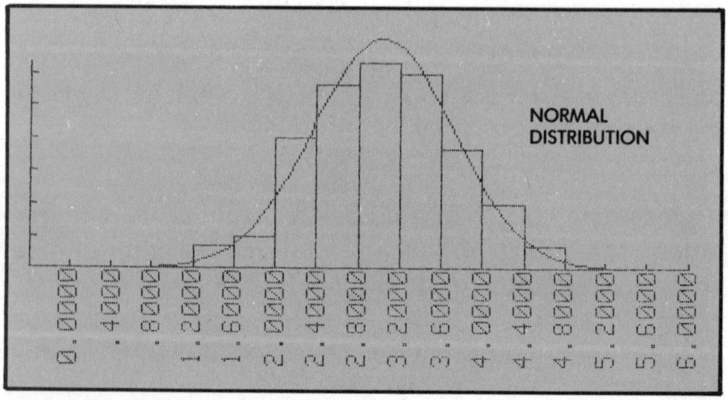

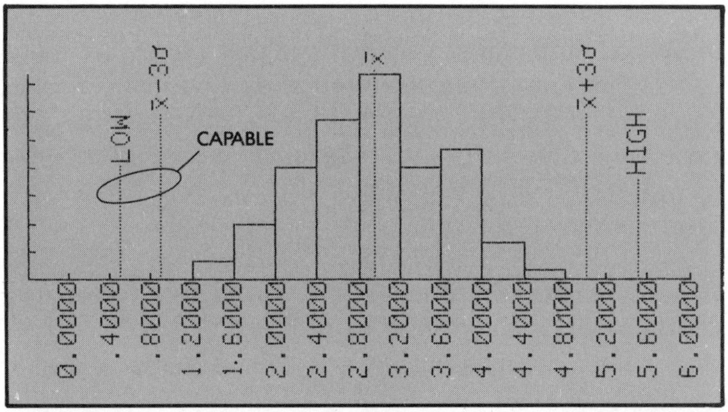

Fig. 3.4.2a A nearly normal histogram with sigma limits inside of engineering limits is evidence of a capable process.

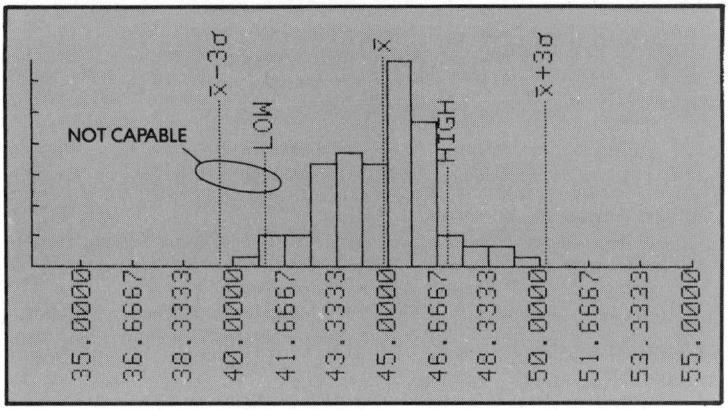

Fig. 3.4.2b A process which is not capable.

Non-Normal Distributions

Non-normal distributions are any distribution other than the normal distribution shown in Figure 3.4.1 and described in Chapter 1. Non-normal distributions may or may not be characteristic of the process itself depending on the size of the sample, the probability of the sample being an accurate reflection of the process, and other factors. A process can be in control and still have a non-normal distribution. Chapter 1, in its explanation of the central limits theorem, provides two examples. Another example would be a part machined using stops which prohibit making it too small. The distribution would have a sharp cutoff at the low end of the specification and more of a tail toward the high end, yet the machining process could be stable under these circumstances.

In the strict sense of a capability study, the shape of a distribution is not as important as where it lies in compari-

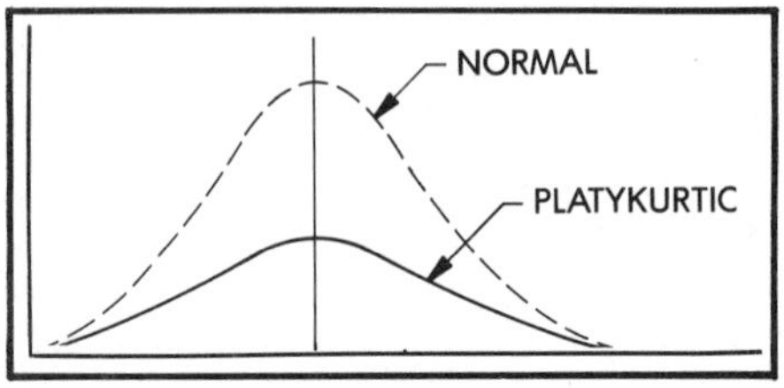

Fig. 3.4.3 Platykurtic curve.

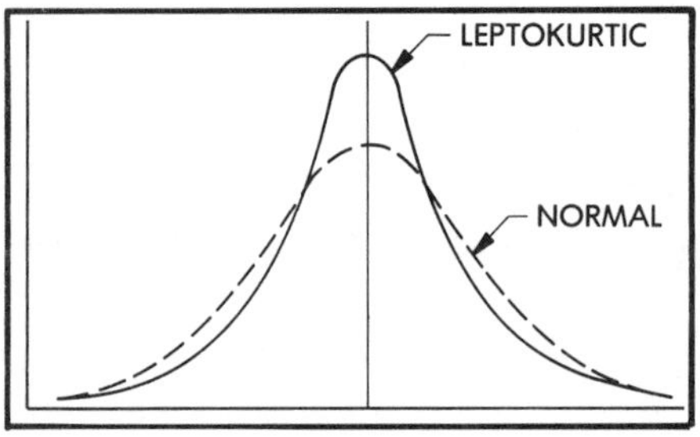

Fig. 3.4.4 Leptokurtic curve.

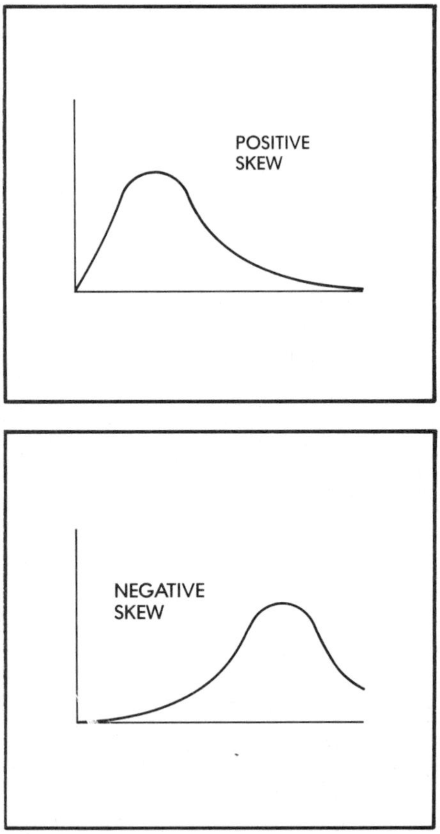

Fig. 3.4.5a & b Skewed distributions.

son to the engineering specifications. But since we will be looking at histograms to analyze capability, it might benefit us to label the various non-normal distributions. In some cases it may help to understand their characteristics and underlying causes. For further reading on this subject refer to the *Statistical Quality Control Handbook*, by Western Electric Company.

Other symmetrical distributions — Kurtosis is a measure of the flatness of a curve and it can be used to describe curves that are symmetrical but are not normal. Kurtosis is symbolized by Υ.

- If $\Upsilon = 0$, the curve is normal.
- If $\Upsilon > 0$, the curve is *platykurtic.*
- If $\Upsilon < 0$, the curve is *leptokurtic.*

A platykurtic curve has a low peak and a large dispersion (Figure 3.4.3). A leptokurtic curve has a very high peak (Figure 3.4.4).

Skewed — Distributions can be skewed in either a positive or negative direction if one tail extends considerably beyond the other (Figure 3.4.5).

Exponential — Exponential curves are encountered often with electronics parts testing. The characteristic is having more observations that occur below the mean than above it (Figure 3.4.6).

Multi-peaked or bimodal — These distributions have more than one peak (Figure 3.4.7). A bimodal distribution is characteristic of two mixed distributions each with separate means. It is possible that two machines produced the lot, or two operators, vendors or materials were involved. When separated, each distribution may be normal, but with a different mean.

Using a Capability Bar Graph

In many instances, analysis of the capability histogram may not yield a clear cut picture. The tail ends of the normal curve may slightly exceed the tolerance limits, raising a very practical question: How much overlap will be allowed before the process is deemed incapable? This can be solved by calculating the *6 sigma limits* of the process and comparing these to the tolerance limits as shown in Figure 3.4.8. The formula for sigma (standard deviation) is:

$$\sigma = \sqrt{\frac{\sum_{i=1}^{n} (x_i - \bar{x})^2}{n-1}} \qquad (3.4.1)$$

The sign σ symbolizes sigma, n is the sample size, x is a sample, and $\bar{x}$ is the mean of the samples. Multiplying sigma by 6 provides the 6 sigma spread of the process, which corresponds to the mean plus and minus 3 sigma ($\bar{x} \pm 3\sigma$). Of course, other sigma limits (such as ± 2 sigma, ± 4 sigma, etc.) could be used but most manufacturers choose the 6 sigma limits since greater than 99% of the measurements fall in this range.

The process standard deviation can be based on the average of the subgroup ranges:

$$\sigma = \frac{\bar{R}}{d_2} \qquad (3.4.2)$$

Sometimes σ is shown as $\hat{\sigma}$ or σ' to denote that it is an estimate. The constant d_2 is based on subgroup size and is listed in Table A-1; $\bar{R}$ is the average of the subgroup ranges for periods with the ranges in control.

The graphing technique shown in Figure 3.4.8 allows for a comparison of the capability of many items at once. The capability of several items, along with their tolerance limits, can be presented on a single page for quick visualization. Figure 3.4.9 illustrates such an example, which was generated by a Hewlett Packard Series 216 (HP9816) desktop computer.

The advantage of a capability report such as Figure 3.4.9 is that items can be compared and sorted. The desktop computer implementation of this report, for the IBM PC, HP9816 and others, allows sorting by certain characteristics. Each item can be placed in order from left to right starting with the worst with respect to the sorting characteristic. The sort and comparison can be made of like processes, all critical items of one process, or the effect of sequential processes on one item. This provides a way to prioritize quality control efforts, judge competitive processes or vendors, allocate inspection load, or analyze the steps in manufacturing.

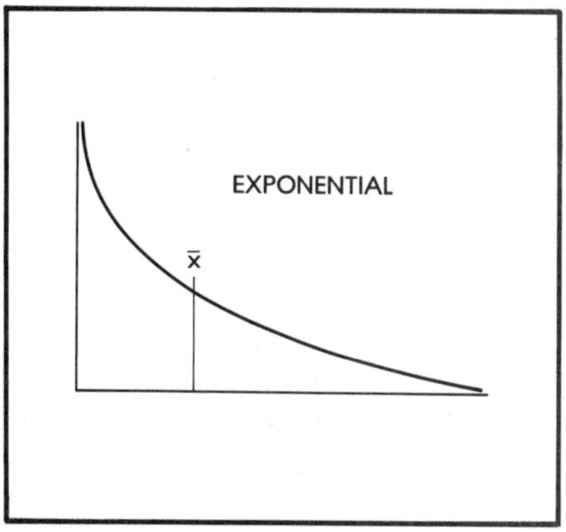

Fig. 3.4.6 Exponential distribution.

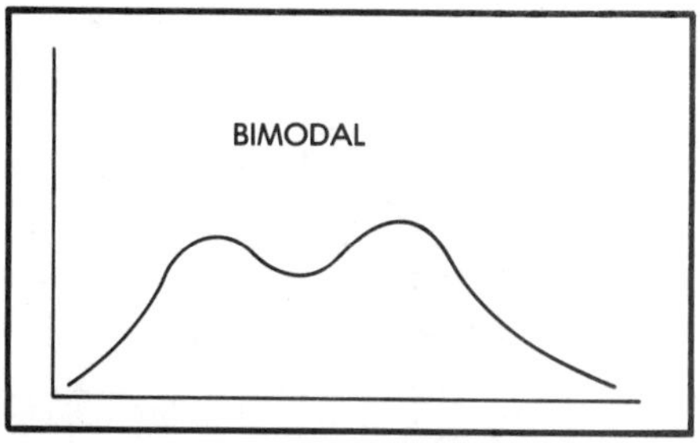

Fig. 3.4.7 Bimodal distribution.

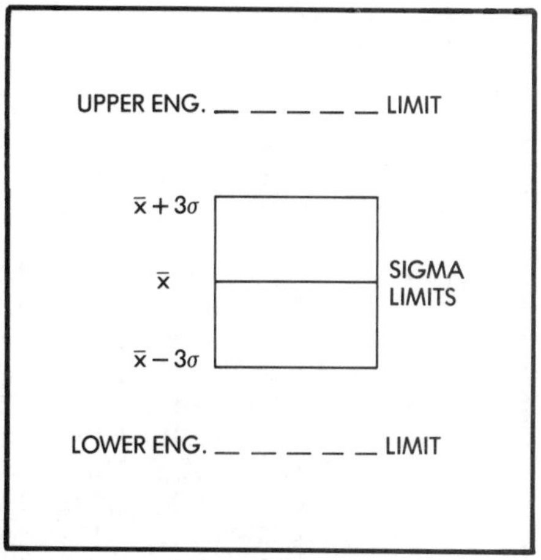

Fig. 3.4.8 Simple representation of capability.

The sorting characteristics most often used on this type of report are:

- *Sort by sigma* — Puts items first with the largest 6 sigma spread. See Figure 3.4.9.
- *Sort by CP* — Puts items first with 6 sigma limits that exceed engineering limits. The characteristic CP is the index of capability and is described in Section 3.5.
- *Sort by CPK* — Puts items first that are most out of center with respect to the limits and that exceed the engineering limits. The characteristic CPK is the index of capability

Fig. 3.4.9 A capability report showing 12 characteristics of a process, in graph and summary form. The items can be sorted from worst to best to provide criteria for improvement.

SORT BY SIGMA

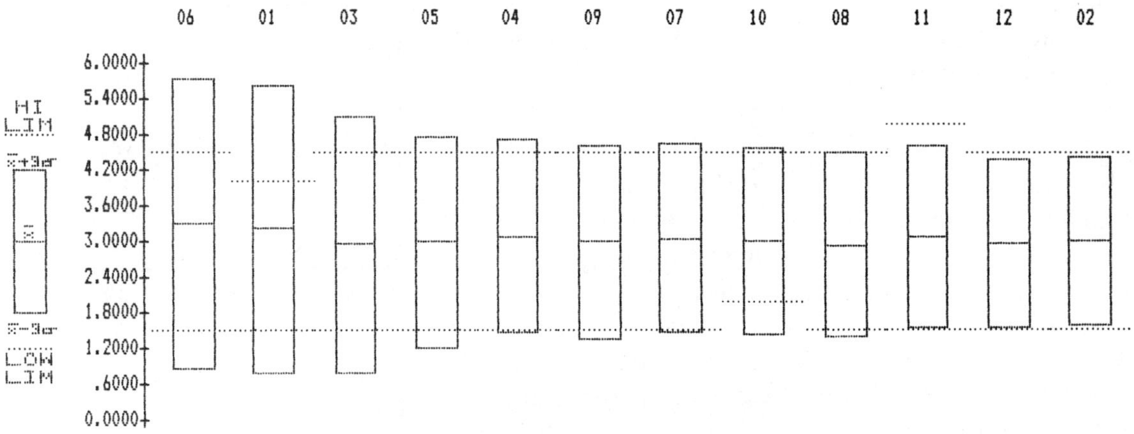

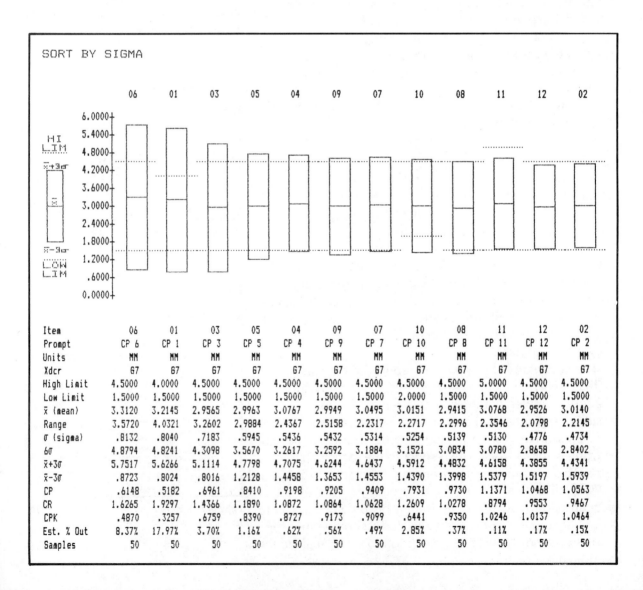

Item	06	01	03	05	04	09	07	10	08	11	12	02
Prompt	CP 6	CP 1	CP 3	CP 5	CP 4	CP 9	CP 7	CP 10	CP 8	CP 11	CP 12	CP 2
Units	MM	MM	MM	MM	MM	MM	MM	MM	MM	MM	MM	MM
Xdcr	G7	G7	G7	G7	G7	G7	G7	G7	G7	G7	G7	G7
High Limit	4.5000	4.0000	4.5000	4.5000	4.5000	4.5000	4.5000	4.5000	4.5000	5.0000	4.5000	4.5000
Low Limit	1.5000	1.5000	1.5000	1.5000	1.5000	1.5000	1.5000	2.0000	1.5000	1.5000	1.5000	1.5000
$\bar{x}$ (mean)	3.3120	3.2145	2.9565	2.9963	3.0767	2.9949	3.0495	3.0151	2.9415	3.0768	2.9526	3.0140
Range	3.5720	4.0321	3.2602	2.9884	2.4367	2.5158	2.2317	2.2717	2.2996	2.3546	2.0798	2.2145
σ (sigma)	.8132	.8040	.7183	.5945	.5436	.5432	.5314	.5254	.5139	.5130	.4776	.4734
6σ	4.8794	4.8241	4.3098	3.5670	3.2617	3.2592	3.1884	3.1521	3.0834	3.0780	2.8658	2.8402
$\bar{x}+3\sigma$	5.7517	5.6266	5.1114	4.7798	4.7075	4.6244	4.6437	4.5912	4.4832	4.6158	4.3855	4.4341
$\bar{x}-3\sigma$	.8723	.8024	.8016	1.2128	1.4458	1.3653	1.4553	1.4390	1.3998	1.5379	1.5197	1.5939
CP	.6148	.5182	.6961	.8410	.9198	.9205	.9409	.7931	.9730	1.1371	1.0468	1.0563
CR	1.6265	1.9297	1.4366	1.1890	1.0872	1.0864	1.0628	1.2609	1.0278	.8794	.9553	.9467
CPK	.4870	.3257	.6759	.8390	.8727	.9173	.9099	.6441	.9350	1.0246	1.0137	1.0464
Est. % Out	8.37%	17.97%	3.70%	1.16%	.62%	.56%	.49%	2.85%	.37%	.11%	.17%	.15%
Samples	50	50	50	50	50	50	50	50	50	50	50	50

and centeredness and is described in Section 3.5.

- *Sort by estimated percent out of spec* — Puts items first with the greatest estimated percentage of samples out of engineering limits (Figure 3.4.10). See Section 3.6 for an explanation of estimating scrap and rework.

3.5 CAPABILITY INDEXES

Capability indexes are useful tools in the statistical analysis of measurement data. The indexes require specifica-

Fig. 3.4.10 Capability report, with items sorted according to estimated percent out of specification.

SORT BY EST. % OUT OF SPEC

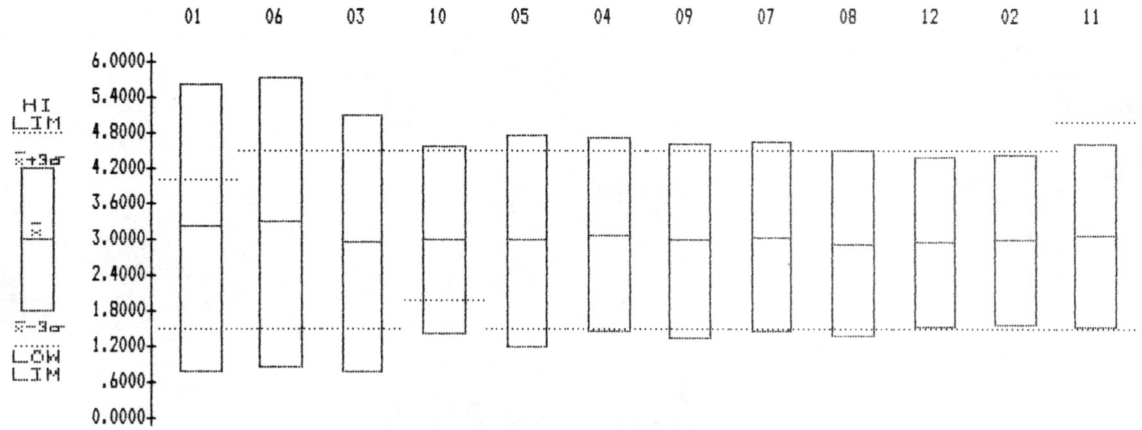

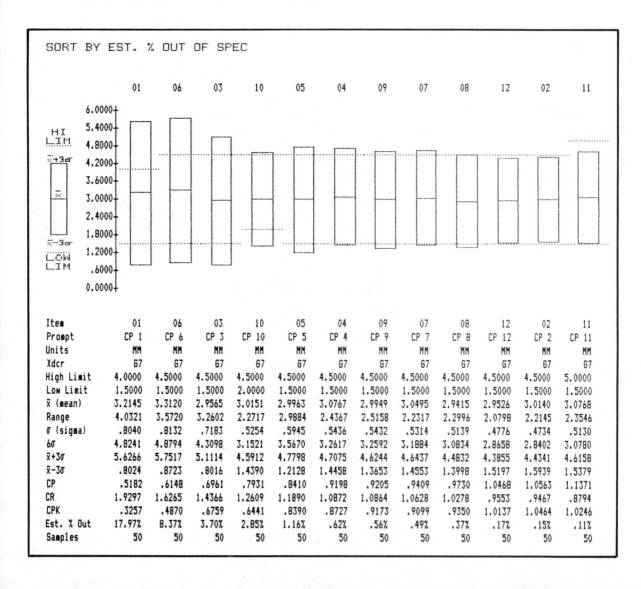

Item	01	06	03	10	05	04	09	07	08	12	02	11
Prompt	CP 1	CP 6	CP 3	CP 10	CP 5	CP 4	CP 9	CP 7	CP 8	CP 12	CP 2	CP 11
Units	MM	MM	MM	MM	MM	MM	MM	MM	MM	MM	MM	MM
Xdcr	G7	G7	G7	G7	G7	G7	G7	G7	G7	G7	G7	G7
High Limit	4.0000	4.5000	4.5000	4.5000	4.5000	4.5000	4.5000	4.5000	4.5000	4.5000	4.5000	5.0000
Low Limit	1.5000	1.5000	1.5000	2.0000	1.5000	1.5000	1.5000	1.5000	1.5000	1.5000	1.5000	1.5000
$\bar{x}$ (mean)	3.2145	3.3120	2.9565	3.0151	2.9963	3.0767	2.9949	3.0495	2.9415	2.9526	3.0140	3.0768
Range	4.0321	3.5720	3.2602	2.2717	2.9884	2.4367	2.5158	2.2317	2.2996	2.0798	2.2145	2.3546
σ (sigma)	.8040	.8132	.7183	.5254	.5945	.5436	.5432	.5314	.5139	.4776	.4734	.5130
6σ	4.8241	4.8794	4.3098	3.1521	3.5670	3.2617	3.2592	3.1884	3.0834	2.8658	2.8402	3.0780
$\bar{x}+3\sigma$	5.6266	5.7517	5.1114	4.5912	4.7798	4.7075	4.6244	4.6437	4.4832	4.3855	4.4341	4.6158
$\bar{x}-3\sigma$	.8024	.8723	.8016	1.4390	1.2128	1.4458	1.3653	1.4553	1.3998	1.5197	1.5939	1.5379
CP	.5182	.6148	.6961	.7931	.8410	.9198	.9205	.9409	.9730	1.0468	1.0563	1.1371
CR	1.9297	1.6265	1.4366	1.2609	1.1890	1.0872	1.0864	1.0628	1.0278	.9553	.9467	.8794
CPK	.3257	.4870	.6759	.6441	.8390	.8727	.9173	.9099	.9350	1.0137	1.0464	1.0246
Est. % Out	17.97%	8.37%	3.70%	2.85%	1.16%	.62%	.56%	.49%	.37%	.17%	.15%	.11%
Samples	50	50	50	50	50	50	50	50	50	50	50	50

tion or tolerance limits for their calculations. Capability indexes take the information present in the histogram and reduce it to a single number which expresses one aspect of capability. The fact that capability indexes are a single number is both an advantage and a disadvantage. As an advantage, a single number is easier to compare. As a disadvantage, this single number is somewhat limited in scope.

Before describing each capability index in detail, there are a couple of formulas that must be defined. USL stands for Upper Specification Limit and LSL for Lower Specification Limit. Midpoint is the center of the specification limits (MIDPOINT = (USL + LSL) ÷ 2). Tolerance is the distance between the specification limits (TOLERANCE = USL − LSL). The examples for each of the capability indexes will use the data from Table 3.5.1 and Figure 3.5.1.

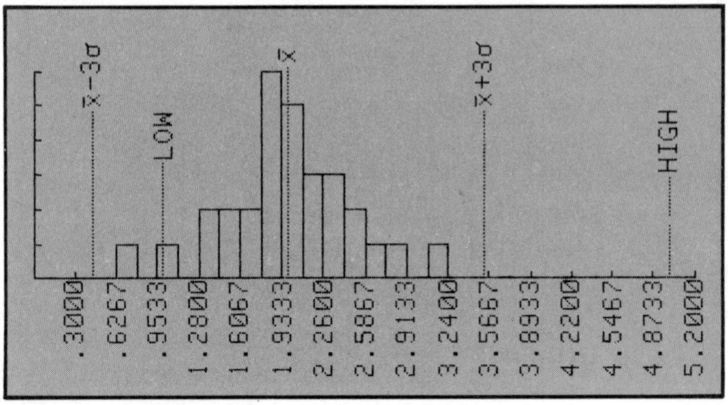

Fig. 3.5.1 This distribution and its summary characteristics shown in the table below can be analyzed with capability indexes.

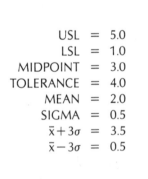

USL	=	5.0
LSL	=	1.0
MIDPOINT	=	3.0
TOLERANCE	=	4.0
MEAN	=	2.0
SIGMA	=	0.5
$\bar{x}+3\sigma$	=	3.5
$\bar{x}-3\sigma$	=	0.5

Table 3.5.1 Data for Fig. 3.5.1.

CP — Inherent Capability of Process

CP is the ratio of tolerance to 6 sigma. The formula is:

$$CP = \frac{\text{TOLERANCE}}{6\sigma} \quad (3.5.1)$$

The CP for the sample item above is:

$$CP = \frac{4.0}{3.0} = 1.33 \quad (3.5.2)$$

Values for CP range from near zero to very large positive numbers. As long as the mean of the measurements is equal to the midpoint of the tolerances, the statements listed in Table 3.5.2 relating CP to capability can be made.

Table 3.5.2 Decision table for the CP index.

CP VALUE	DECISION
Greater than 1.33	Process is capable
Between 1.0 & 1.33	Process is capable, but should be monitored as CP approaches 1.0
Less than 1.00	Process not capable

If the mean of the measurements is not at the midpoint, then the CP values become less precise. In this case the process can be made more capable by shifting the mean (see definition of K below).

CR — Capability Ratio

CR is the inverse of CP. The formula is:

$$CR = \frac{6\sigma}{\text{TOLERANCE}} \qquad (3.5.3)$$

For our sample item,

$$CR = \frac{3.0}{4.0} = 0.75 \qquad (3.5.4)$$

Values of CR less than 0.75 generally indicate capability.

K — Process Mean Versus Spec Mean

K is the comparison of mean and midpoint and tells how centered the data is within the specification limits. The formula is:

$$K = \frac{(\text{MEAN} - \text{MIDPOINT})}{(\text{TOLERANCE}/2)} \qquad (3.5.5)$$

If K is positive, the mean is above the midpoint. If K is negative, the mean is below the midpoint. The best value possible for K is zero, since at this value the mean equals the midpoint. A value of 1.0 or −1.0 for K means that the mean of the data is equal to a specification limit and that about 50% of the parts are bad (require rework or are scrap). If the value for K is above 1.0 or below −1.0, more than 50% of parts produced are bad (because the mean is outside the specification limits). The value of K does not relate directly to capability since K may equal zero, but the process may not be capable (i.e., $CP < 0$).

CPK — Capability in Relation to Spec Mean

CPK tells the capability of a process based upon the worst case view of the data. The formula is:

$$\text{CPK} = \text{The lesser of: } \frac{(\text{USL} - \text{MEAN})}{3\sigma} \text{ or } \frac{(\text{MEAN} - \text{LSL})}{3\sigma} \qquad (3.5.6)$$

For our example,

$$\begin{aligned} \text{CPK} &= \frac{(5.0-2.0)}{1.5} \text{ or } \frac{(2.0-1.0)}{1.5} \\ &= 2.0 \text{ or } 0.67 \\ &= 0.67 \end{aligned} \qquad (3.5.7)$$

A negative value for CPK indicates that the mean is outside the specification limits. A CPK of zero indicates that the mean is equal to one of the specification limits. A CPK between 0 and 1.0 means that part of the 6 sigma limits fall outside the specification limits. A CPK of 1.0 means that one end of the 6 sigma limits falls on a specification limit. A CPK larger than 1.0 means that the 6 sigma limits fall completely within the specification limits.

Capability indexes are useful tools in the analysis of capability data. The most useful index is CPK since it formulates capability in a manner that compensates for shifts in the mean of the distribution away from the midpoint.

3.6 ESTIMATING SCRAP AND REWORK

One of the most valuable applications of statistical quality control is that of reducing scrap and rework. The reduction of scrap and rework alone can pay for the installation of a SQC system in a very short period of time. This section covers calculating the amount and cost of scrap and rework, and possible methods of reducing scrap and rework.

Estimating scrap and rework can be done by analyzing the data that was collected in the capability study. It is done most reliably, if the distribution of the measurements is reasonably normal, by calculating the area under the normal curve that falls outside the specification limits. A normal curve table (Appendix Table A-2) is needed for this calculation. The following procedure is used (USL and LSL stand for upper and lower specification limits):

1) Calculate (LSL − Mean) ÷ sigma.
2) Look up calculated value from areas of normal curve table (Table A-2).
3) Calculate (USL − Mean) ÷ sigma.
4) Look up calculated value from areas of normal curve table (Table A-2).
5) Add 1.0 to the value obtained from step 2 and subtract the value obtained in step 4.

As an example, let's use the data from Table 3.6.1. Calculations are:

USL	=	5.0
LSL	=	1.0
MEAN	=	2.0
SIGMA	=	0.5

Table 3.6.1 Sample data.

1) (LSL − Mean) ÷ sigma = (1.0 − 2.0) ÷ 0.5 = −2.0.
2) Table value = 0.0228.
3) (USL − Mean) ÷ sigma = (5.0 − 2.0) ÷ 0.5 = 6.0.
4) Table value = 1.0.
5) 0.0228 + (1.0 − 1.0) = 0.0228.

Total scrap/rework is thus about 2.28%. In addition to calculating the amount of scrap and rework, one can also arrive at a cost. To estimate the cost of scrap and rework we first must estimate the cost of scrap per part and rework per part. If rework costs more than scrap (this condition should be rare) it is more cost efficient to scrap those parts

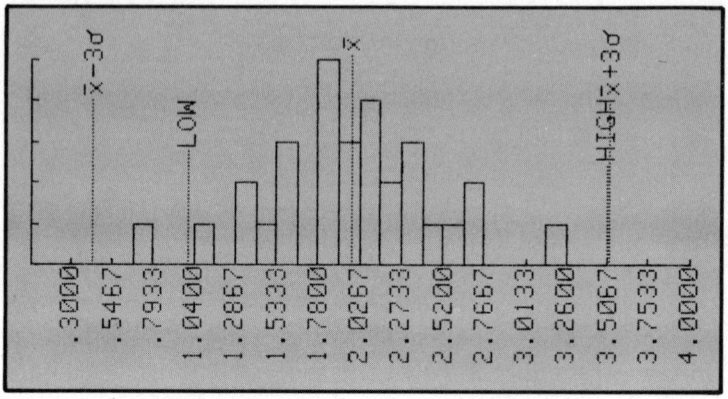

Fig. 3.6.1 Sample distribution for estimating scrap and rework. The table below summarizes the characteristics.

Scrap cost	=	\$5.00
Rework cost	=	\$2.00
USL	=	3.5
LSL	=	1.0
MEAN	=	2.0
SIGMA	=	0.5

Table 3.6.2 Data for Fig. 3.6.1.

that require rework. The cost of scrap and rework is equal to:

Rework cost =	Scrap cost =	
(Rework cost/part)	(Scrap cost/part)	(3.6.1)
(% rework)	(% scrap)	
(number of parts)	(number of parts)	

As an example, let's examine the conditions shown in Figure 3.6.1 and Table 3.6.2. Samples below LSL are scrapped, while samples above USL are reworked. First we must calculate the amount of material above USL and below LSL. This is similar to our example above:

1) (LSL − Mean) ÷ sigma = − 2.0.
2) Table value is 0.0228.
3) (USL − Mean) ÷ sigma = 3.0.
4) Table value is 0.9987 so area above USL is 1 − 0.9987 = 0.0013.

Next we calculate the cost:

Cost of scrap = \$5.00/part × 0.0228 = \$0.114/part
Cost of rework = \$2.00/part × 0.0013 = \$0.0026/part
Total cost = \$0.114 + \$0.0026 = \$0.1166/part

Estimation Using Non-Normal Data

Estimating scrap and rework on non-normal data is less reliable than similar calculations on normal data. This section will separate data into three categories: data that is

Calculated Value	Normal	Camp-Meidell	Other
2.00 – 2.49	2.28	5.6	12.5
2.50 – 2.99	0.62	3.6	8.0
3.00 – 3.49	0.14	2.5	5.6
3.50 – 3.99	0.025	1.8	4.1
4.00 – 4.49	0.003	1.4	3.2
4.50 – 4.99	0.00035	1.1	2.5
5.00 or above	0.00003	0.9	2.0

Table 3.6.3 This table is derived from an area under the normal curve table. Use the 'other' column if data is not normal and does not conform to the Camp-Meidell conditions.

roughly normal, data that conforms to the *Camp-Meidell conditions*, and other data. The Camp-Meidell conditions are: mode is equal to mean (mode is in the tallest bar of a histogram) and frequency declines continuously on both sides of the mode (Table 3.6.3). Use the following procedure for this:

1) Calculate (MEAN − LSL) ÷ sigma.
2) Look up calculated value in Table 3.6.3.
3) Calculate (USL − MEAN) ÷ sigma.
4) Look up calculated value in Table 3.6.3.
5) Sum of the two values looked up is the estimated amount of scrap or rework.

As an example, let's examine the condition shown in Figure 3.6.2 and Table 3.6.4. The data does not meet the Camp-

Fig. 3.6.2 Sample distribution having the characteristics shown in the table below.

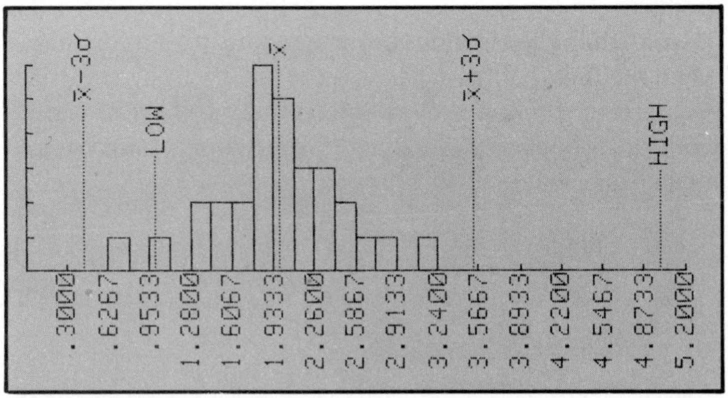

USL	=	5.0
LSL	=	1.0
MEAN	=	2.0
SIGMA	=	0.5

Table 3.6.4 Data for Fig. 3.6.2.

Meidell conditions; therefore, the 'other' column is used on the chart.

1) Index for area under normal curve table (Table A-2) is: $(2.0 - 1.0) \div 0.5 = 2$.
2) Area below LSL is 12.5% (from Table 3.6.3)
3) Index for area under normal curve table is: $(2.0 - 5.0) \div 0.5 = 6$.
4) Area above USL is 2.0% (from Table 3.6.3)
5) Total scrap and rework is: 12.5% + 2.0% = 14.5%.

The best method for reducing scrap and rework is to improve the manufacturing process to make better parts. This option is not always available due to limitations in materials or equipment. A second option that may reduce the cost of scrap and rework involves shifting the mean of a process. We conclude with an example of how shifting a process mean can minimize cost of scrap and rework. Rework costs $0.20 per part and scrap costs $2.00 per part.

Figure 3.6.3a shows a process where scrap accounts for 25% of production and rework accounts for 10% of production. Cost of scrap and rework is $0.52 per part.

After shifting the process to the midpoint of the tolerance, scrap accounts for 15% of production and rework accounts for 15% of production (Figure 3.6.3b). Cost of scrap and rework is $0.33 per part.

When the process is shifted to the extreme of having no scrap, rework accounts for 84% of production (Figure 3.6.3c). The cost of scrap and rework is $0.17 per part. Although the cost of scrap and rework has been reduced significantly, the cost of quality (which includes the labor of checking parts) may actually be more than in the other examples.

Note that the distribution is assumed to remain stable when the mean of the process is shifted. By using statistical methods to monitor the expected amount of scrap and rework, it is possible to reduce costs through fairly simple means (e.g., machine adjustments).

Fig. 3.6.3 (Opposite) An example of maximizing profits by shifting the mean of the distribution.

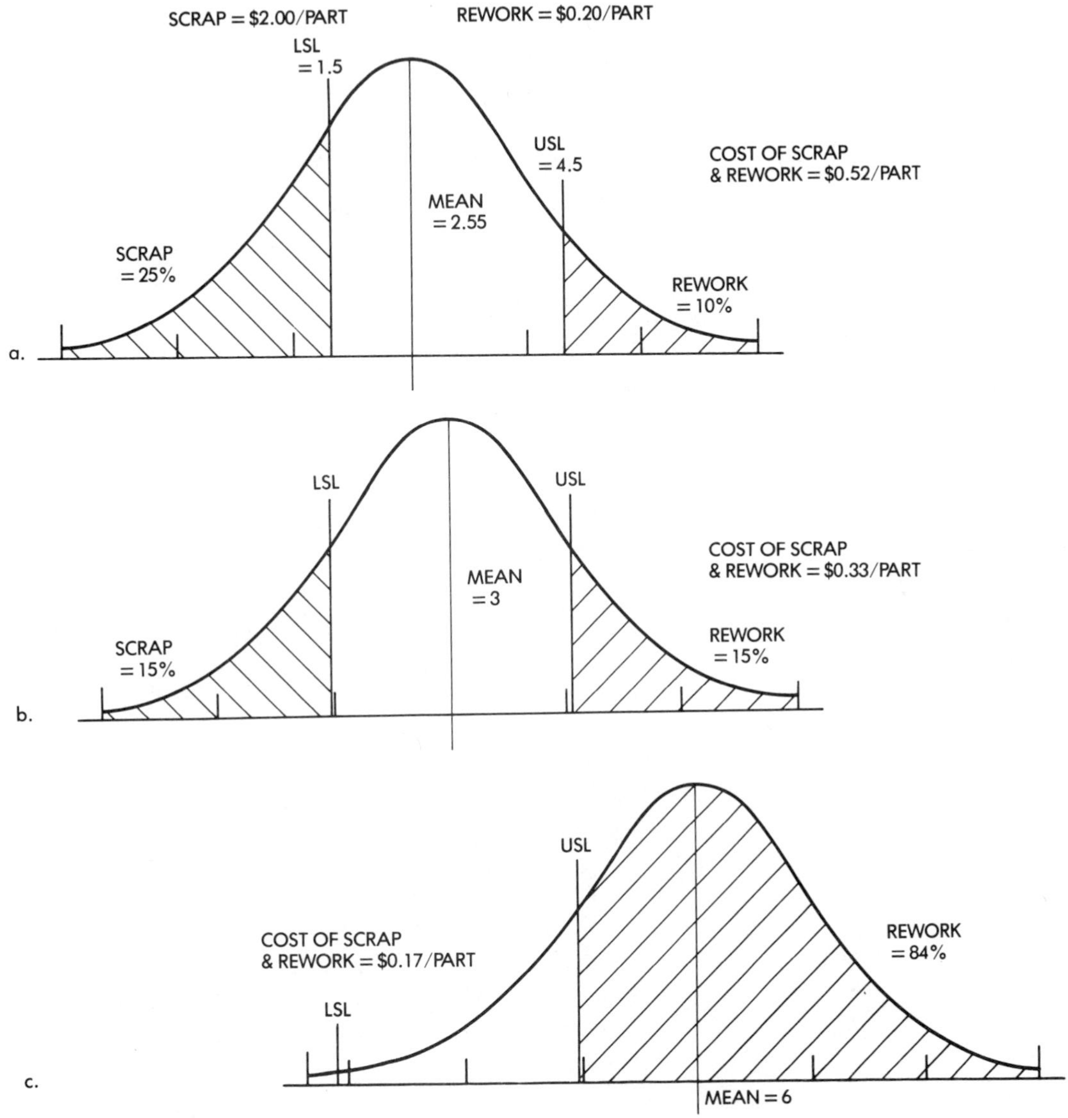
SCRAP = $2.00/PART
REWORK = $0.20/PART
LSL = 1.5
USL = 4.5
MEAN = 2.55
COST OF SCRAP & REWORK = $0.52/PART
SCRAP = 25%
REWORK = 10%
a.
LSL
USL
MEAN = 3
COST OF SCRAP & REWORK = $0.33/PART
SCRAP = 15%
REWORK = 15%
b.
USL
COST OF SCRAP & REWORK = $0.17/PART
REWORK = 84%
LSL
c.
MEAN = 6

3.7 HOW THE DATAMYTE FAN II SOFTWARE PROGRAM CALCULATES CHI-SQUARE, SKEWNESS AND KURTOSIS

Here are the procedures that the DataMyte FAN II Software program follows when it calculates values for chi-square, skewness and kurtosis. All three of these values are put on the printed histogram report.

The Chi-Square Calculation

The program calculates a chi-square value to see how "normal" the data is. The program compares the calculated chi-square value to the "critical chi-square value." The critical chi-square value is stored in a standard table. If the calculated chi-square is less than the critical chi-square, then the program has determined that the data is normal with 95% confidence.

Once the user has determined what data is included in the histogram report, the calculation begins. First, the program finds the range of the first 30 samples of data included in the histogram. This is found by subtracting the lowest value sample from the highest value sample.

$$\text{RANGE} = \text{HIGH} - \text{LOW} \tag{3.7.1}$$

Next, the program calculates the resolution of the data. The resolution is equal to 0.1 raised to the "number of decimal places" power. The number of decimal places is the number of decimal places in each data sample, which has been specified by the user.

$$\text{RESOLUTION} = (0.1) \tag{3.7.2}$$

Now, the program uses the range and resolution for an initial calculation of the number of "classes" of data. A class is like a group of data. Each class has an upper and a lower boundary. The data samples are later sorted into the classes.

$$\text{NUMBER OF CLASSES} = \frac{\text{RANGE}}{1.01 \text{ X RESOLUTION OF DATA}} \tag{3.7.3}$$

If the initial number of classes is greater than 20, the program sets the number of classes to 20. The program divides the range into as many equal segments as there are classes. The program sorts the data samples into the initial classes.

A sample is put into the cell that has a lower boundary and higher boundary than its value.

The program then calculates an "expected probability" for each class. This is the probability that in a normal distribution, a sample will fall in this class.
In order for a class to be "valid," its total expected probability has to be greater than 5.0. The total expected probability is determined by adding together the expected probabilities for each sample in the class.

If necessary, the program combines classes. If a class has an expected value less than 5.0, the program combines it with the next class. This forms a new class. If the new class still has an expected value less than 5.0, the program combines the new with the next class again. The program does this until the class's expected value is 5.0 or greater.

The program then looks at the next class. It continues looking and combining until all the classes have an expected value greater than 5.0. If the last class has an expected value less than 5.0, it is combined with the previous class.

The program has now calculated the final number of classes. The data samples have been reassigned to the classes during the combining.

After computing the final number of classes, the FAN II program calculates the number of degrees of freedom.

$$\text{DEG. OF FREEDOM} = \text{NO. OF FINAL CLASSES} - 3 \qquad (3.7.4)$$

The program calculates chi-square (χ^2).

$$\chi^2 = \sum_{i=1}^{\#\text{ of classes}} \frac{(\text{OBSERVED} - \text{EXPECTED})}{\text{EXPECTED}} \qquad (3.7.5)$$

This chi-square value is called the "calculated chi-square value."

- The program compares the calculated chi-square value to the "critical chi-square value." The critical chi-square value is stored in a standard table. The critical chi-square value is found using a 95% confidence level and the n umber of degrees of freedom already calculated.

- If the calculated chi-square is less than the critical chi-square, then the program has determined that the data is normal with 95% confidence.

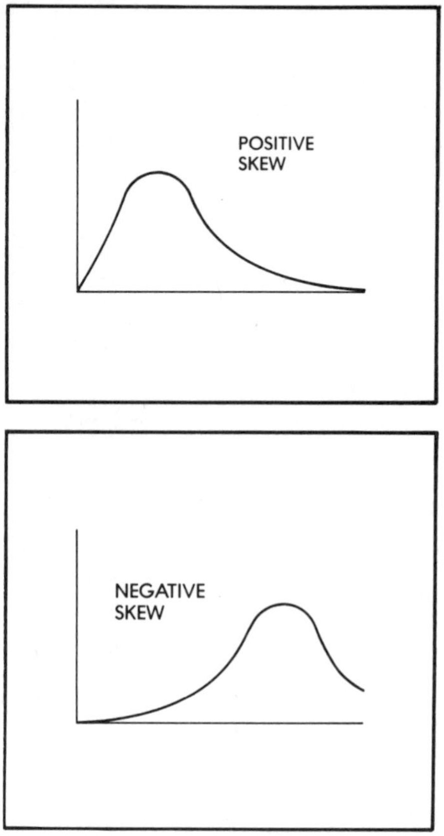

Fig. 3.7.1a & b Skewed distributions.

Skewness

Skewness gives you an idea how far to the right or left your data extends. A positive skew means that the right-hand tail extends considerably to the right. A negative skew means the left-hand tail extends considerably to the left. See Figure 3.7.1.

The Skewness Calculation

First the program finds the mean of all the data included in the histogram:

$$\text{mean of data} = \frac{\Sigma \text{ samples}}{\text{number of samples}} \quad (3.7.8)$$

When calculating skewness, the FAN II program calculates three intermediate numbers, m_2, m_3 and m_4. The program calculates m_2, m_3 and m_4 by "looping through" these formulas:

$$m_2 = \text{old } m_2 + (\text{data point} - \text{mean})^2 \quad (3.7.9)$$
$$m_3 = \text{old } m_3 + (\text{data point} - \text{mean})^3$$
$$m_4 = \text{old } m_4 + (\text{data point} - \text{mean})^4$$

The program plugs each data point, one at a time, into the above formulas. The first time through, old m_2, old m_3 and old m_4 all equal zero.

After the first time through, old m_2, old m_3 and old m_4 become m_2, m_3 and m_4 from the previous iteration.

After going through all the data points, the program has three values: m_2, m_3 and m_4. These numbers are used in the formulas for skewness and kurtosis.

The FAN II program calculates skewness with this formula:

$$\text{skewness} = \frac{m_3}{\sqrt{(m_2)^3}} \quad (3.7.10)$$

The Kurtosis Calculation

The formula for kurtosis is:

$$\text{kurtosis} = \frac{m_4}{(m_2)^2} \quad (3.7.11)$$

The numbers m_2 and m_4 come from the m_2, m_3 and m_4 calculations described above.

Kurtosis

Kurtosis is a measure of the flatness of a curve. Kurtosis helps describe curves that are symmetrical, but not normal. If the kurtosis value calculated by the FAN II program is:

- Equal to 3.0, the curve is normal.
- Greater than 3.0, the curve is platykurtic (Figure 3.7.2).
- Less than 3.0, the curve is leptokurtic (Figure 3.7.3).

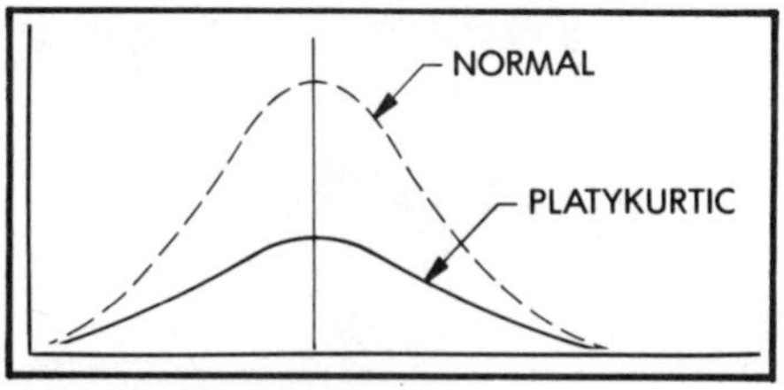

Fig. 3.7.2 Platykurtic curve.

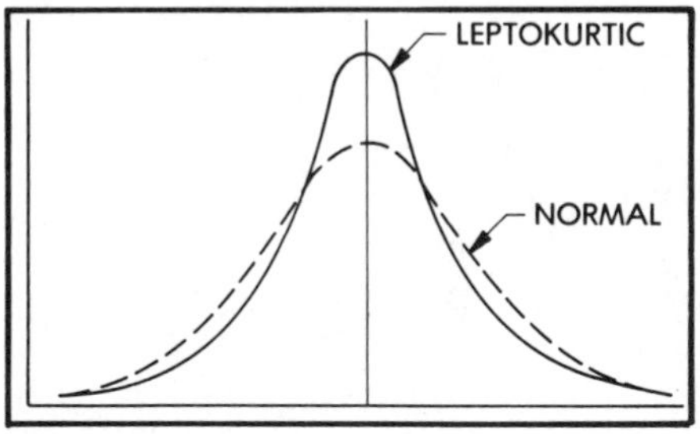

Fig. 3.7.3 Leptokurtic curve.

For Further Reference:

Ford Motor Company. *Quality System Standard.* Product Quality Office, 1983.

Ford Motor Company.*Process Capability and Continuing Process Control.* Statistical Methods Office, 1983.

Ford Motor Company. *Supplier Five Day Seminar on Statistical Thinking.* Ford Motor Body & Assembly Operations Div., 1982.

Grant, Eugene L., and Leavenworth, Richard S. *Statistical Quality Control.* 5th ed. New York: McGraw-Hill Book Company, 1980.

Juran, Joseph M., and Gryna, Frank M. *Quality Planning and Analysis.* New York: McGraw-Hill Book Company, 1970.

Ott, Ellis R. *Process Quality Control.* New York: McGraw-Hill Book Company, 1975.

Western Electric Co., Inc. *Statistical Quality Control Handbook.* 2d ed. Easton: Mack Printing Company, 1956.

4. MEASUREMENT

4.1 INTRODUCTION TO MEASUREMENT

In modern industry, uniformity for interchangeability of parts is vital for cost effective manufacturing. If a machine part fails or wears out, a replacement must be available and must fit. It will if the parts are made according to specific and accurate measurements. Data must be analyzed on parts and processes to determine conformance to product specifications, and data must be fed back to the manufacturing process to prevent production problems. The quantification of data on parts and processes involves the defining of standard units, calibrating instruments to these standard units, and using these instruments to quantify parts and processes. This quantifying is called *measurement.*

What is Measurement?

The term measurement has several meanings. It can be defined as the process of quantification, comparing an unknown magnitude to a known magnitude. Measurement can also mean the resulting number. In the case of quantification (comparing an unknown magnitude to a known magnitude), it is the act of obtaining specific data about a characteristic of a part or a process; i.e., "The measurement was done in the assembly plant." A resulting number is the specific data on a part or a process; i.e., "The measurements on part A all fell within the specified tolerances." The science of measurement is called *metrology*.

4.2 UNITS OF MEASURE

To allow the quantifying of data on parts or processes, defined standard units must be used. These standard units are called *units of measure*. They are definitions of standardized units which are used to quantify characteristics about which we are interested. Metrologists have developed systems of international units of measure for the purpose of international commerce. The primary systems which are in use today are the English, the metric system, and the Systeme International d'Unites (SI). The more preferred system is now the SI system. Table 4.2.1 gives examples of units of measure for the three systems.

Characteristic	English	Metric	SI
Length Force Time Mass	Foot Pound Second Slug	Meter Kilogram Second Kg — Sec^2/Meter	Meter Newton Second Kilogram

Table 4.2.1 Examples of units of measure in the three measuring systems.

The English system was retained by the American colonies when separating from England in 1776. This system consists of units of measures which were developed before the industrial revolution, i.e., a foot is 12 inches, a yard is 3 feet, etc. Only part of the English system is based on decimal multiples.

In 1799 a committee of French scientists, under the direction of the French government, established a system of measures and weights. A basic unit, called the meter, was defined and is the basis for the metric system. This system of measures was primarily concerned with length, area, volume, and mass, based entirely on a decimal system. See Table A-3 in the Appendix for a list of the units of measure used in this system.

By the 1970s all industrialized contries had adopted the metric system with the exception of the United States. Most U.S. companies who have international involvement tend to use the metric system. The metric system is preferred to the English system on a purely technical basis and has been widely accepted by the scientific community. Most of the world is now adopting the SI system, including the United States and the United Kingdom.

The Systeme International d'Unities (SI) system has evolved more recently from the metric system and is an international system. It consists of seven basic units of measure: length, mass, time, temperature, light intensity, electric current and amount of substance. All are fully compatible with the metric system. Two supplemental units are used for solid angles and planes. There is a long list of units of measure derived from the seven basic units of measure, and standardized terminology for subdivisions and multiples of units of measure. Latin prefixes are used

Prefix	Symbol	Multiple or Subdivision
tera	T	1 000 000 000 000 = 10^{12}
giga	G	1 000 000 000 = 10^{9}
mega	M	1 000 000 = 10^{6}
kilo	k	1 000 = 10^{3}
hecto*	h	100 = 10^{2}
deka*	da	10 = 10^{1}
deci*	d	0.1 = 10^{-1}
centi*	c	0.01 = 10^{-2}
milli	m	0.001 = 10^{-3}
micro	μ	0.000 001 = 10^{-6}
nano	n	0.000 000 001 = 10^{-9}
pico	p	0.000 000 000 001 = 10^{-12}
femto	f	0.000 000 000 000 001 = 10^{-15}
atto	a	0.000 000 000 000 000 001 = 10^{-18}

*Use is discouraged

Table 4.2.2 Terminology for subdivisions and multiples of units in the SI system.

to indicate subdivisions, and Greek prefixes to indicate multiples of any standard unit. Table 4.2.2 lists the SI system multiples and subdivisions. Tables A-4 and A-5 in the Appendix are listings of the SI system units of measure and conversion charts for the different systems.

4.3 MEASUREMENT STANDARDS AND TRACEABILITY

Primary Reference Standards

For any standards system to be usable the system must be based on units that are unchangeable. The SI system defines most of its units based on natural phenomena that are unchangeable. An example of this is the definition of a meter. The definitions of a meter and other main units of the SI system can be found in Table 4.3.1. One meter can be reproduced with an accuracy of about ten to the minus eight, which is 0.01mm by definition. These definitions of units are called *standards*.

All countries maintain *primary reference standards* through a "Bureau of Standards" whose purpose is to construct and maintain these standards. The standards consist

UNIT	DEFINITION
Meter (m)	1650763.73 wavelengths (in a vacuum) of the uninterrupted transition $2p_{10}$ to $5d_5$ in Kr^{86}.
Kilogram (kg)	Mass of the international kilogram at Sevres, France.
Seconds (s)	1/315,569,259,747 of the tropical year at 12^h ET, 0 January 1900, supplementally defined 1964 in terms to the cesium F,4; M,0 to F,3: M,0, transition, the frequency assigned being 9,192,931,770 hertz.
Kelvin (K)	**Defined in the thermodynamic scale by assigning 273.15K to the triple point of water (freezing point, at one standard atmosphere). 1K = 1/273.16 of the thermodynamic temperature of the triple point of water.**
Ampere (A)	The constant current which, if maintained in two straight parallel conductors of infinite length, of negligible circular sections, and placed 1 meter apart in a vacuum, will produce between these conductors a force equal to 2×10^{-7} M.K.S. unit of force per meter of length.
Candela (cd)	1/60 of the intensity of one square centimeter of a perfect radiator at the temperature of freezing platinum.
Mole (mol)	**The amount of substance of a system which contains as many elementary entities as there are atoms on 0.012 Kilograms of carbon-12. The elementary entities must be specified.**

Table 4.3.1 Definitions of fundamental units of the SI system.

of copies of the international kilogram and measuring systems which can verify the units and subunits of the defined standards. These standards are then used as a basis for the calibration of equipment. It is not, however, practical for the bureaus of standards and standards laboratories to calibrate all equipment, so secondary and tertiary standards were developed to transfer the primary standards for the calibration of instruments used in general laboratories and manufacturing areas.

Standards Hierarchy

Equipment used by the technicians and inspectors is calibrated against a set of *working standards*. The working standards are referred back to the primary standards through the use of one or more *transfer standards*. This reference from one standard to a higher, more accurate standard is known as *calibration*. Some specialists suggest that a precision of ten to one be used to transfer from one standard to the next. This may not be necessary because the combination of many levels can be represented by the square root of the sum of the squares instead of by the sums of the precisions of the levels. A precision ratio of five to one has been accepted among transfer standards to allow for a longer hierarchy of transfer standards.

When a piece of equipment is calibrated and can be related back to a primary standard through transfer standards, this is known as *traceability*. A system of documented certification of accuracy allows for calibration to be traceable to the National Bureau of Standards, which maintains the primary reference standards. Figure 4.3.1 shows the hierarchy of standards used for traceability.

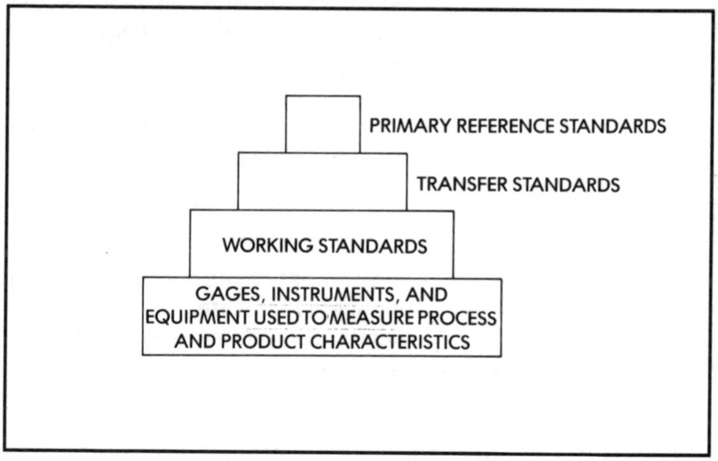

Fig. 4.3.1 Hierarchy of standards used for traceability.

4.4 MEASURING INSTRUMENTS

There are several terms often used when referring to characteristics of measuring instruments. These terms describe how sensitive instruments are to measured quantities, how bias affects the measurements, and how repeatable an instrument is when measuring.

Resolution

Resolution (or sensitivity) is the measure to which an instrument can sense the variation of a quantity to be measured. It is the maximum incremental change in the instrument's output with a change in any specified portion of its measuring range. Figure 4.4.1 shows that there is a discrete change in output for a large enough change in the input measuring range.

Accuracy

Accuracy is the condition or quality of conforming exactly to a standard. The accuracy of an instrument is the extent to which the average of many measurements made by the instrument agrees with the true value or standard being measured. The difference between the average and the true value is the error or inaccuracy. A lack of accuracy is sometimes referred to as a *bias*. This condition, when a result of the measuring instrument, is known as *out of calibration*.

A measuring instrument's accuracy must be considered over the whole range of the measuring instrument. This is often expressed as *linearity*. Linearity is the maximum deviation of the actual measurements from a defined theoretical straight line characteristic. It is expressed as a percentage of the theoretical output and measured output over the total theoretical output characteristic. The ratio can be expressed as follows:

$$\text{Linearity} = 1 - \frac{\Theta - E}{\Theta_T} \qquad (4.4.1)$$

where: Θ is the theoretical output
E is the measured output
Θ_T is the total theoretical output

Often the linearity of an instrument is expressed in terms of *nonlinearity* (1 − linearity ratio). Nonlinearity can be expressed as a percentage of deviation from the theoretical output and measured output over the total theoretical output.

$$\%\ \text{Nonlinearity} = \left(\frac{\Theta - E}{\Theta_T}\right)(100) \qquad (4.4.2)$$

Figure 4.4.2 illustrates graphically the concept of linearity.

Precision

Precision (also known as *repeatability*) is the variation in readings obtained when repeating exactly the same mea-

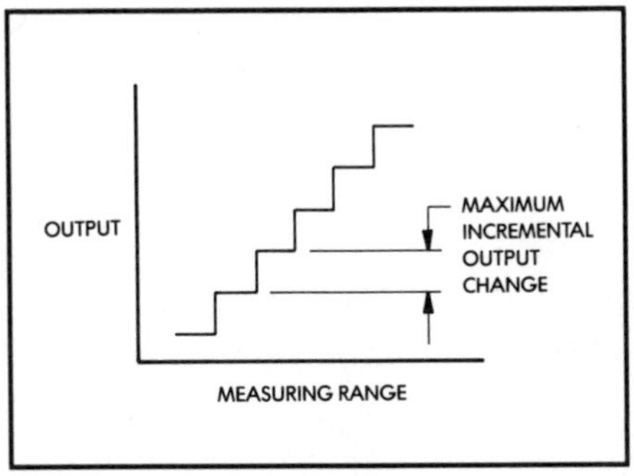

Fig. 4.4.1 Instrument resolution is a measure of the sensitivity, or discrete change in output, for a change in measuring range.

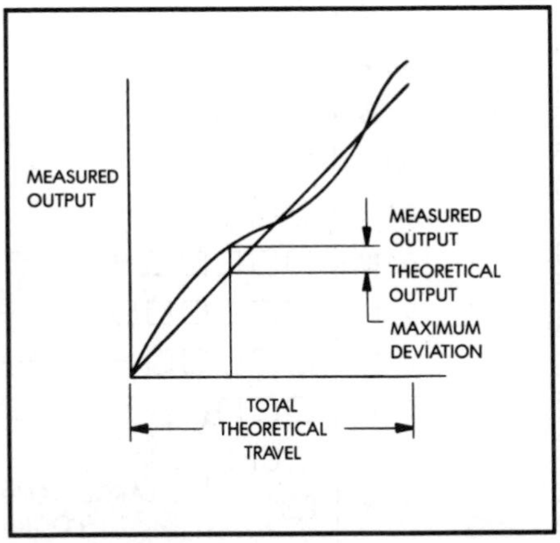

Fig. 4.4.2 Instrument accuracy expressed as a measure of linearity, or deviation from a theoretical straightline characteristic.

surement. The precision of an instrument is the ability to repeat a series of measurements on the same piece and obtain the same results for each measured value. The variation in measured values can be expressed in terms of a standard deviation of the measuring error. The smaller the standard deviation the more precise the instrument.

Accuracy Versus Precision

Confusion often exists between the terms accuracy and precision. The confusion exists because the terms are often interchanged in their usage. Accuracy and precision are two different concepts. The accuracy of an instrument can be improved by recalibrating to reduce its error, but recalibration generally does not improve the instrument's precision. The difference between the two terms will be further clarified in the following examples.

Figure 4.4.3 represents a set of 28 measurements made with the same instrument on the same part which shows good accuracy with little precision. The accuracy is represented by the small difference (error) between the true value of 0.110 and the average of the measurements of

Fig. 4.4.3 Example of accuracy without precision.

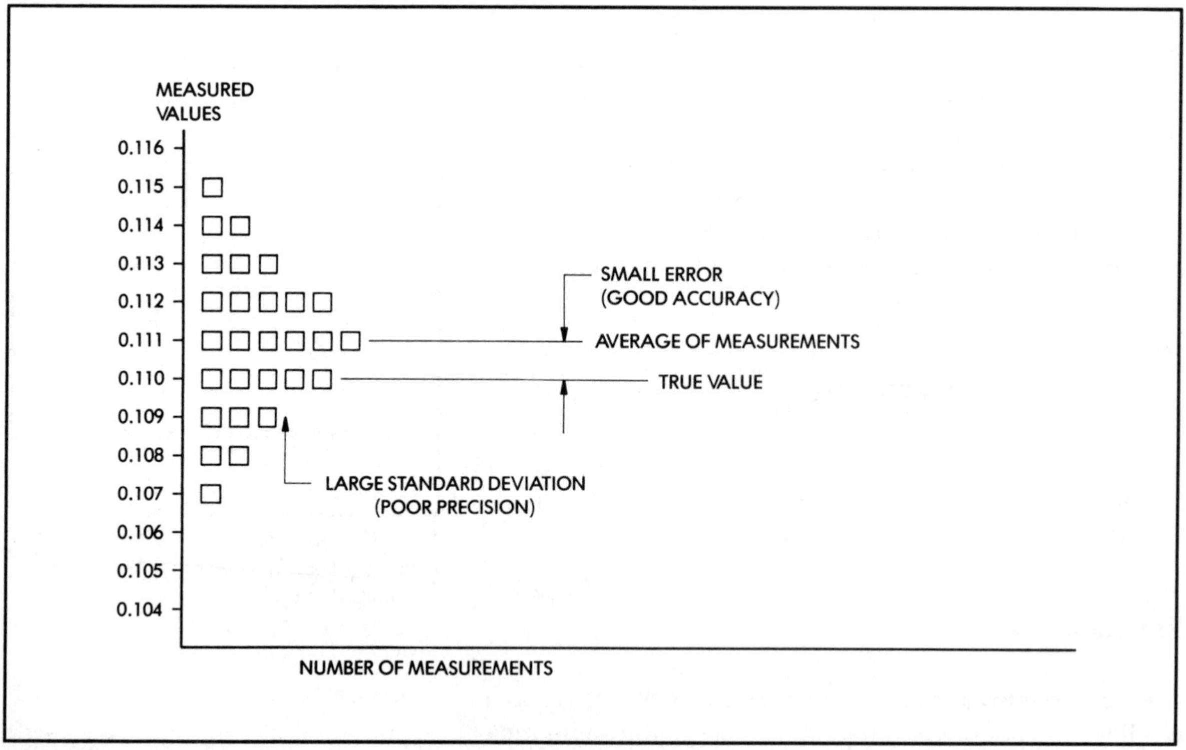

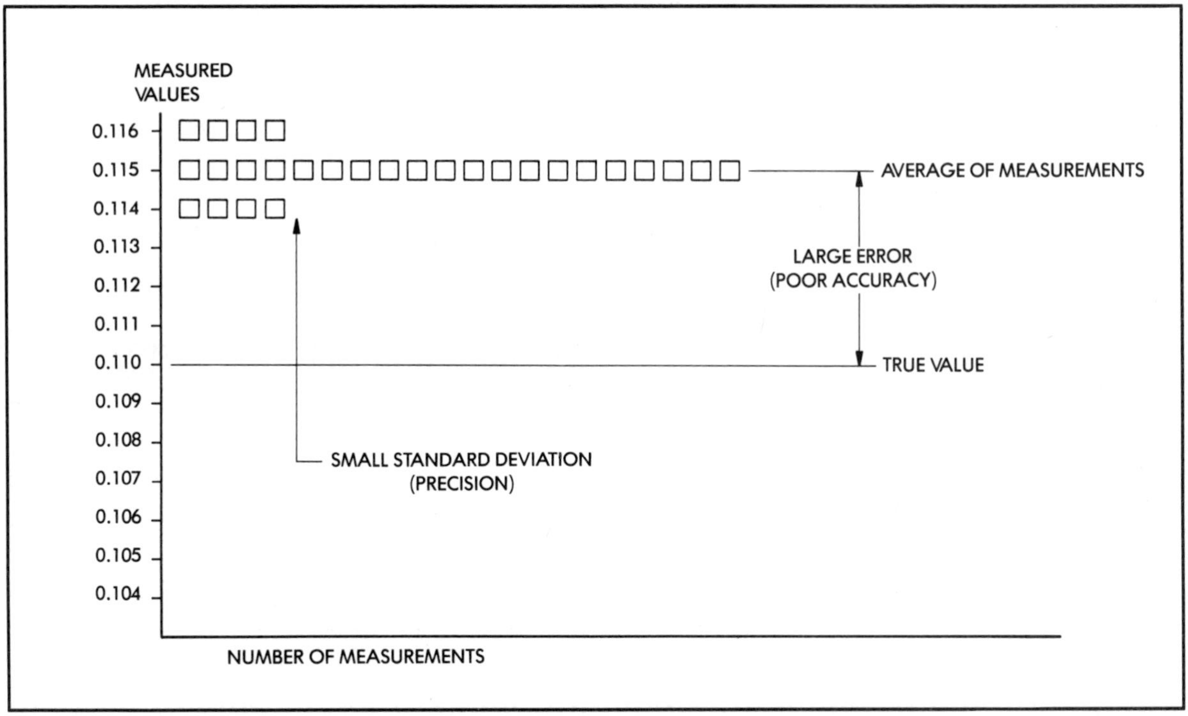

Fig. 4.4.4 Example of precision without accuracy.

0.111, which is 0.001. The precision in this case is poor because of the wide distribution of measurements (ranging from 0.107 to 0.115), as shown by the bar graph (each box represents a measurement). This variation can be expressed in terms of a large *standard deviation of the measurements* error.

Figure 4.4.4 shows 28 measurements taken with a different instrument on the same part as in Figure 4.4.3. It shows that there is precision or good repeatability but that the accuracy is poor. The precision can be seen in the diagram by noting that the distribution of the measurements (ranging from 0.114 to 0.116) is closely grouped around the average (0.115) of the measurements. The standard deviation of the measurements is small in this case. The large error between the true value (0.110) and the average (0.115) of the measurements is 0.005 and represents poor accuracy.

Figure 4.4.5 shows 28 measurements taken with a different instrument on the same part as the two previous examples. It shows that the precision or repeatability is good as well as the accuracy. Note in Figure 4.4.5 that the true value (0.110) and the average value of the measurements

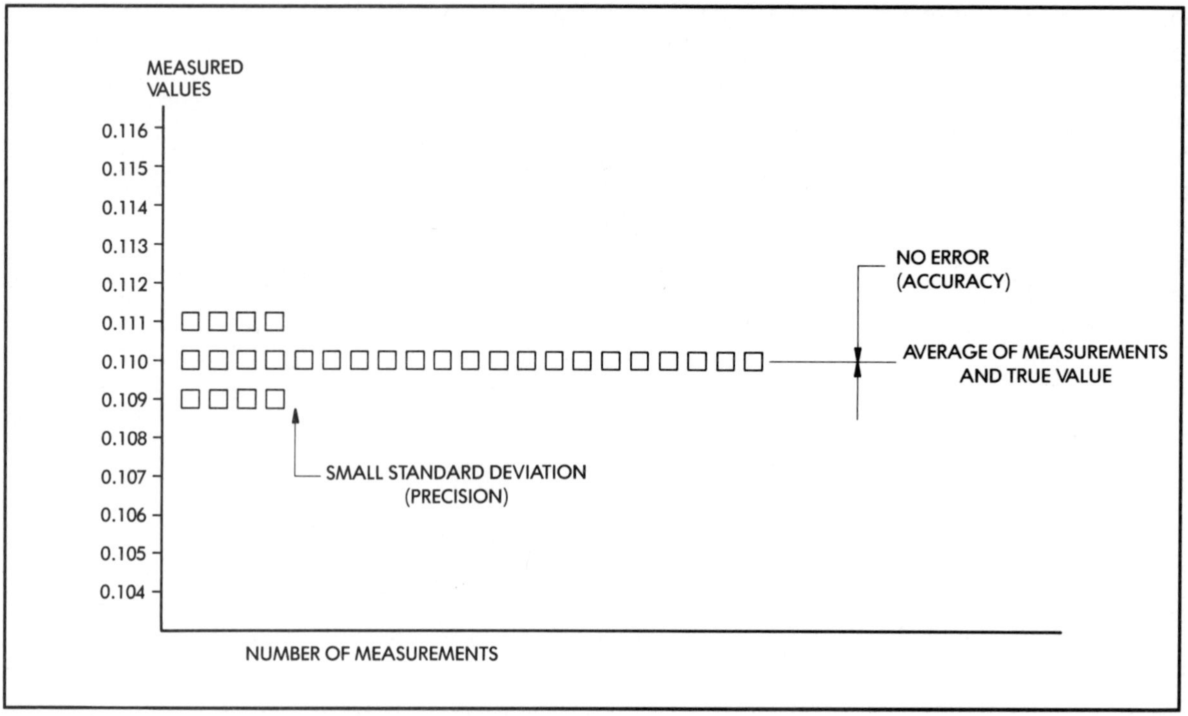

Fig. 4.4.5 Example of accuracy with precision.

(0.110) are the same, indicating that the accuracy is very good. It can also be noted that the variation of the measurements is quite small (ranging from 0.109 to 0.111) which indicates precision or good repeatability.

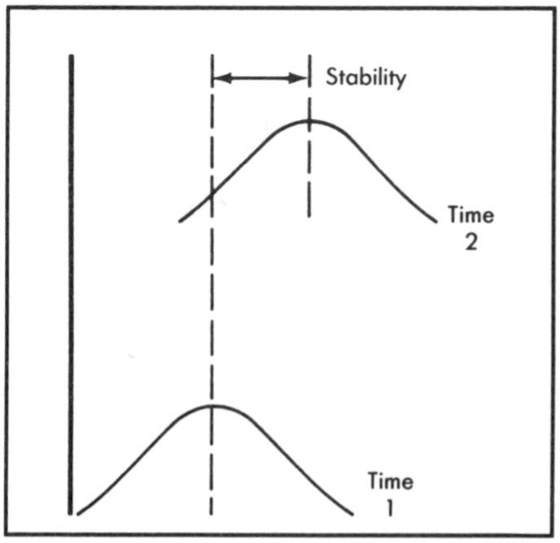

Fig. 4.4.6 Example of lack of stability over time.

Stability

Stability refers to the difference in the average of at least two sets of measurements obtained with the same measuring device on the same parts taken at different times. See Figure 4.4.6.

4.5 SOURCES OF ERRORS IN MEASUREMENT

Error in measurement can result even with the best of equipment and measuring techniques. A measurement error is the difference between the measured value of a magnitude and the true value. This difference from the true value can be a problem of accuracy or precision.

Several sources of error exist in most instruments; for example, nonlinearity, hysteresis (e.g., gear back-lash), and sensitivity to environmental factors such as temperature, magnetic or electrical fields. Instrument error is often magnified by the fixturing required in the measuring process. Poor electrical connection, improper fastening of mechanical linkages, and loose clamps are examples of fixturing problems. Temperature induced error, in addition to its effects on measuring instruments, affects the specimen being measured. As temperature changes, the length (L) of a specimen changes as follows:

$$\Delta L = (L)(\propto)(\Delta T)$$

where: L = Original length of the specimen (4.5.1)
$\propto$ = Thermal expansion coefficient
ΔT = Temperature variation

Table 4.5.1 gives the thermal expansion coefficients for several industrial materials.

Deformation

Deformation is the second largest source of error following temperature. Deformation can be caused by the following:

- Force exerted on a specimen by the measuring instrument.
- Placement of the specimen supports.
- Placement of the instrument supports.

A compression force (within the elastic limit) will cause deformation. The deformation (DL) can be calculated as follows by Hook's law:

$$\Delta L = \frac{(F)(L)}{(E)(A)}$$

where: F = measuring force, Kgf (4.5.2)
L = length of test piece in mm
E = Young's modulus, Kgf/mm^2
A = cross sectional area in mm^2

An example using Hook's law is as follows: a gage block ($A = 9\text{mm} \times 35\text{mm} = 315\text{mm}^2$ and $L = 1000\text{mm}$) is measured with a measuring force of $F = 1\text{kg}$. Young's

Material	Thermal Expansion Coefficient (Per°Celsius)
Aluminum	23.8×10^{-6}
Brass	18.5×10^{-6}
Bronze	17.5×10^{-6}
Carbon Steel	$11.7 - (0.9 \times C\%) \times 10^{-6}$
Cast Iron	9.2 to 11.8×10^{-6}
Ceramics	3.0×10^{-6}
Chromium Steel	11 to 13×10^{-6}
Copper	18.5×10^{-6}
Crown Glass	8.9×10^{-6}
Duralumin	22.6×10^{-6}
Flint Glass	7.9×10^{-6}
Gold	14.2×10^{-6}
Gunmetal	18.0×10^{-6}
Invar (36% nickel)	1.5×10^{-6}
Iron	12.2×10^{-6}
Nickel	13.0×10^{-6}
Nickel-Chromium Steel	13 to 15×10^{-6}
Nickel Steel (58% nickel)	12.0×10^{-6}
Nylon	10 to 15×10^{-6}
Phenol	3 to 4.5×10^{-6}
Plutonium	9.0×10^{-6}
Polyethylene	0.5 to 5.5×10^{-6}
Quartz	0.5×10^{-6}
Silver	19.5×10^{-6}
Steel	11.5×10^{-6}
Tin	23.0×10^{-6}
Vinyl Chloride	0.7 to 2.5×10^{-6}
Zinc	26.7×10^{-6}

Table 4.5.1 Thermal expansion coefficients.

Modulus for steel is $E = 2 \times 10^4$ Kg/mm². The deformation would be as follows:

$$\Delta L = \frac{(1\ \text{Kgf})\ (1000\ \text{mm})}{(2)\ (10^4 \text{Kgf/mm}^2)\ (315\ \text{mm}^2)} \qquad (4.5.3)$$

$$= 0.0001587\ \text{mm}$$
$$= 0.16\ \mu\text{m}$$

Operator Error

There are several sources of operator error which will cause variation in the data that is recorded. An operator of a measuring system can get different results even when measuring the same product and with the same measuring system. This is due to the fact that even with the same operator there will be slight differences in measuring techniques from one measurement to the next. When two operators are measuring the same product with the same measuring instrument, differences will occur in the recorded measurements. These differences can be even greater than with the same operator due to even greater differences in measuring techniques. Depending on the measuring technique, variation in data can be more dispersed or show up as a systematic error.

Variations in recorded measurements can also be evident if different test procedures are used to measure the same product. Different test procedures can introduce variation in measurement technique if they are not carefully designed. Errors in data often occur when the operator takes a reading from the instrument and then enters it on a form or similar media. These errors can consist of transposition of numbers, recording incorrect numbers, or writing them illegibly so transcription errors occur later when the data is analyzed.

4.6 REDUCING MEASUREMENT ERROR

Tolerances and Measurement Error

It is recommended that the ratio of the product tolerance to the precision of the measuring instrument be a 10:1 ratio for an ideal condition. In a worst case condition a 5:1 ratio can be used. These are rules of thumb and should be based on the level of confidence required for each situation. When the tolerance is mixed with the measurement error, a good component may be diagnosed as being bad when, in fact, it was acceptable, or a bad component may be accepted. See Figure 4.6.1 for an example of a 10:1 precision versus part tolerance distribution.

Analysis of Measurement Error (Capability)

Section 4.5 described many sources of measurement error. The error causes variations in the observed values (measurements). Conclusions can be drawn about mea-

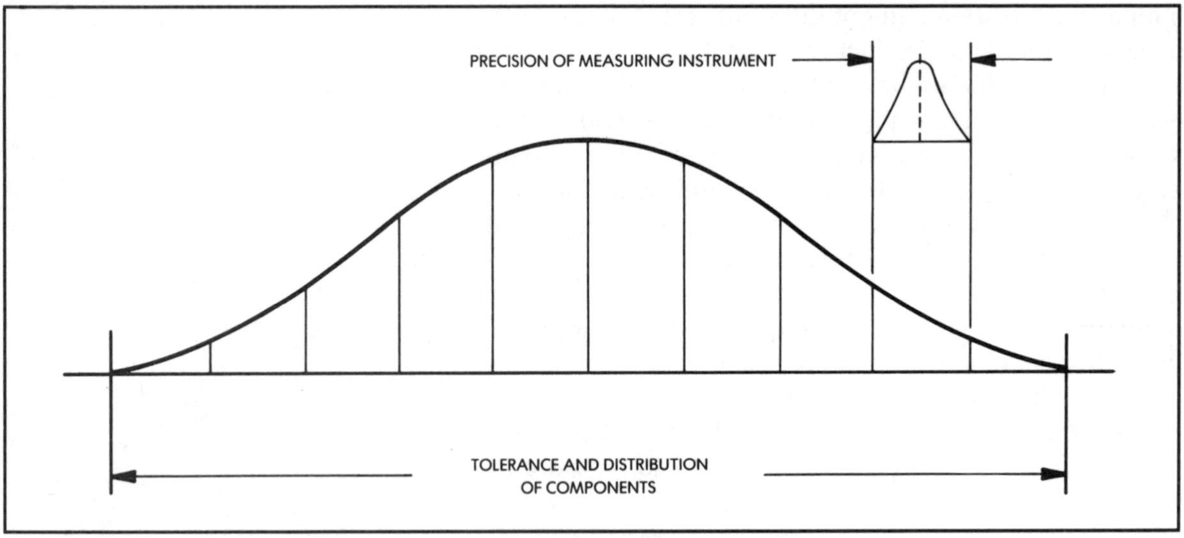

Fig. 4.6.1 The part tolerance compared to the precision of the measuring instrument should be at 10:1 ratio ideally.

surement error based on the formula below. The relationship of various causes is assumed to be independent.

$$\sigma_{obs} = \sqrt{\sigma^2_{cause(a)} + \sigma^2_{cause(b)} + \ldots + \sigma^2_{cause(n)}} \tag{4.6.1}$$

where σ_{obs} = observed variation
$\sigma_{cause(a)}$ = variation due to one cause

The causes are not always easy to identify and may be interrelated. Often it is feasible to identify causes by experiment. Generally, measurement variation occurs because of variation in the system of measurement and the variation of the product being measured. This can be expressed as follows:

$$\sigma_{obs} = \sqrt{\sigma^2_{meas} + \sigma^2_{prod}} \tag{4.6.2}$$

where σ_{meas} = variation due to measurement
σ_{prod} = variation due to product

If the variation in the system of measurement is less than 10% of the observed variation, then the effect upon the variation in product will be less than 1%. The rule of thumb of 10% variation is based on the statement below.

$$\sigma_{prod} = \sqrt{\sigma^2_{obs} - \sigma^2_{meas}} \tag{4.6.3}$$

The following examples will illustrate this concept. The observed variation of a group of product with one instrument was found to be 12 standard deviations. A number of measurements with that instrument were taken on the same product and the variation was found to be 3 standard deviations. The product variation was calculated to be:

$$\begin{aligned} \sigma_{prod} &= \sqrt{12^2 - 3^2} \\ &= \sqrt{135} \\ &= 11.6 \end{aligned} \tag{4.6.4}$$

It can be seen that the measurement variation has a small impact on the product variation by comparing the observed and the calculated product variation. There is about a 3% difference in the observed and product variation.

In another example, the observed variation was 12.6 and the variation of measurement was 9. The product variation was calculated at 8.8.

$$\begin{aligned} \sigma_{prod} &= \sqrt{12.6^2 - 9^2} \\ &= \sqrt{77.8} \\ &= 8.8 \end{aligned} \tag{4.6.5}$$

Where product variation and measurement variation are almost the same, further evaluation is needed determine if the measurement variation can be reduced to a more acceptable level.

Minimizing Instrument Error

Accuracy and precision can be controlled if appropriate steps are taken. If a systematic error is evident, then a correction can be applied to the data. If the accuracy is low then a correction factor can be added to each measurement to adjust the data to the proper reading. An adjustment could also be made to the instrument to bring it back into calibration.

Calibration programs are a means of checking equipment that is used for quality inspection. Calibration control would include provisions for periodic audits on instruments to check their accuracy, precision, and general condition. New equipment should be included in a calibration program to ensure it is properly functioning before use in an inspection process. Inventory control of instruments is often used and records kept to keep track of the use and calibration of instruments. Calibration schedules are kept on instruments as a means to monitor instrument conditions. Elapsed calendar time is the most widely used method. Checks are made at calendar intervals to check the instrument's performance. Another method would be to schedule calibration by the actual usage. This is done by counting the number of measurements an instrument has made. Metering the hours of use would also be a technique to monitor calibration intervals.

Adherence to calibration schedules is probably the most important aspect of calibration control. Without this, the calibration schedule's value would be greatly reduced. Many different systems can be used to accomplish this adherence.

Tool Control Charts

To minimize the effects of calibration intervals on the observed variation of a process, it is recommended that control charts be kept on all auditing tools. The charts can be placed on the gaging fixture or taken on the audit route. An extra reading, the tool control reading, should be included with each subgroup. For example, if 5 samples are taken on each item in an audit route, then the sixth should be the tool control reading, and it should be plotted on a chart.

Tool control charts are the only reliable method of corroborating data from the current process with historical data. The tool control chart can be used to compensate for any bias due to measurement error when trying to equate the data. The charts will also provide a time-independent indication of a need for calibration or repair.

Reducing Operator Errors

Adequate training is required for the operators of instruments to be able to properly utilize them. Many errors can be introduced into measurement by variation in operator technique. With the use of training, these types of errors can be reduced. Proper test procedures and fixturing will also help reduce errors in measurement. Procedures will give a documented systematic approach to the ways a test or inspection is to be performed. These procedures should include enough detail to prevent differences in tests or inspections from one operator to the next. Test procedures themselves should be checked to ensure that they are fully useful and properly designed. It does no good for operators to follow a procedure that does not provide the desired results.

Automation of measurement can be an effective means to reduce operator errors in the recording of data. An instrument that automatically records its measurements will eliminate transposition errors and other types of recording errors. Not only do automated instruments reduce errors, but in many cases the time required to record measurements is markedly reduced.

See Chapter 15 for a dicussion on automation of measurement.

4.7 GAGE CAPABILITY STUDIES

All gages and test equipment have inherent variability. Whether or not this measurement error (capability) precludes using a given gage for a statistical analysis in a specific application can be readily determined using an established methodology.

Consider a sample study: five parts, three inspectors, one gage, a single control dimension and two sets of readings. (The following is reproduced with permission from *Industrial Quality Control*. See reference at end of chapter.)

Five parts are selected and a single dimension specified

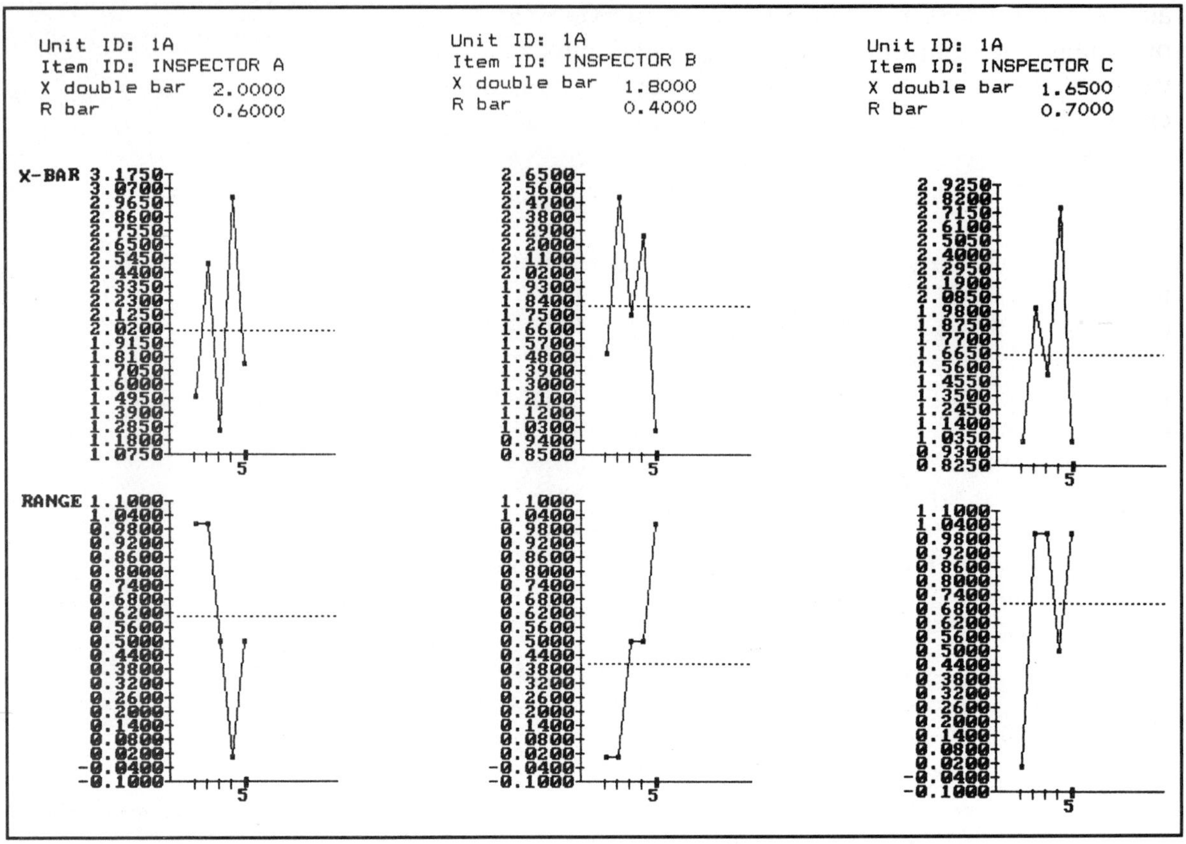

Fig. 4.7.1 The Results of readings made by three inspectors plotted on $\bar{x}$ & R charts, on 5 parts of two readings on each part.

for measurement. The parts are then numbered sequentially, one through five. Three inspectors are selected, each uses the same gaging instrument, and measures the parts in a random order, to assure that any drift or change will be spread randomly throughout the study. When the first set of readings are obtained, the inspectors again measure a second set in a random order. To eliminate the possibility that one inspector could bias another one's reading, the individual conducting the study should be certain that no information is exchanged. In Figure 4.7.1, the results are plotted on an average and range chart. The readings and results will be carried forward and used as a sample capability study.

Gage Repeatability

Repeatability is the variation obtained when one person, using the same measuring instrument, measures the same dimension two or more times. See Figure 4.7.2. In this example only two measurements were made on each piece, or a sample size of two. The standard deviation for these values can be estimated using the average range. In control chart applications this is done using:

$$\hat{\sigma}_x = 1/d_2 \cdot \bar{R} \qquad (4.7.1)$$

The factor, d_2 is essentially independent when the number of samples, k, is larger than 10 or 15. For smaller k values, Table 4.7.1 gives corrected $1/d_2$ factors.

Calculating the estimated standard deviation within parts for each inspector in Figure 4.7.1 (repeatability) gives the following results:

Inspector A

$R = 0.6$

$1/d_2 = 0.840$

$\hat{\sigma}_{\text{(within parts)}} = (0.840)(0.6) = 0.504$

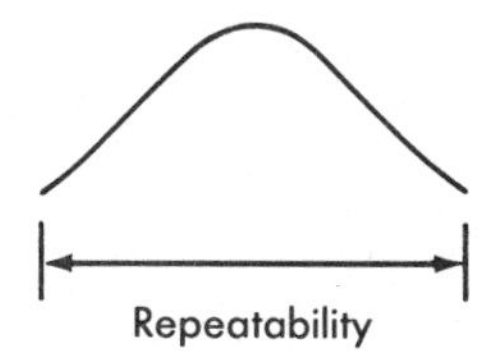

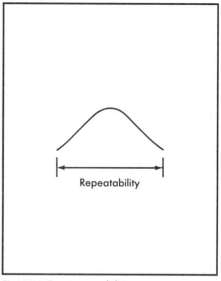

Fig. 4.7.2 Gage repeatability.

Table 4.7.1 Factors for calculating standard deviation.

Factors $1/d_2$* for Converting the Average Range, $\bar{R}$, into a Standard Deviation $\hat{\sigma}_X$.

	k = 1	2	3	4	5	6	7	8
n = 2	0.709	0.781	0.813	0.826	0.840	0.855	0.862	0.885
3	0.524	0.552	0.565	0.571	0.575	0.581	0.581	0.592
4	0.446	0.465	0.472	0.474	0.476	0.481	0.481	0.485
5	0.403	0.417	0.420	0.422	0.424	0.426	0.427	0.429
6	0.375	0.385	0.388	0.389	0.391	0.392	0.392	0.395
7	0.353	0.361	0.364	0.365	0.366	0.368	0.368	0.370
8	0.338	0.344	0.346	0.347	0.348	0.348	0.350	0.351
9	0.325	0.331	0.332	0.333	0.334	0.334	0.336	0.337
10	0.314	0.319	0.322	0.323	0.323	0.324	0.324	0.325

k = Number of Samples (Number of parts measured)
n = Sample Size (Number of times each part was measured)

*Based on d_2 factors, Table D3, p. 910, *Quality Control and Industrial Statistics*, A.J. Duncan.

(d_2 is taken from Table 4.7.1—Sample size is 2 and 5 parts were measured.)

Inspector B

$$R = 0.4$$
$$1/d_2 = 0.840$$
$$\hat{\sigma}_{(\text{within parts})} = (0.840)(0.4) = 0.336$$

Inspector C

$$R = 0.7$$
$$1/d_2 = 0.840$$
$$\hat{\sigma}_{(\text{within parts})} = (0.840)(0.7) = 0.588$$

Assessing these results individually, inspector B has the least variation and the best repeatability. Assuming, however, that all three inspectors normally perform this gaging operation, a standard deviation can be calculated using the average range for all three:

$$R = (0.6 + 0.4 + 0.7) \div 3 = 0.567$$

$$\hat{\sigma}_{(\text{within parts})} = 1/d_2 \times R = (0.855)(0.567) = 0.5018 = 0.502$$

Note that for d_2, k has changed from 5 to 15. From Table 4.7.1, $1/d_2 = 0.885$.

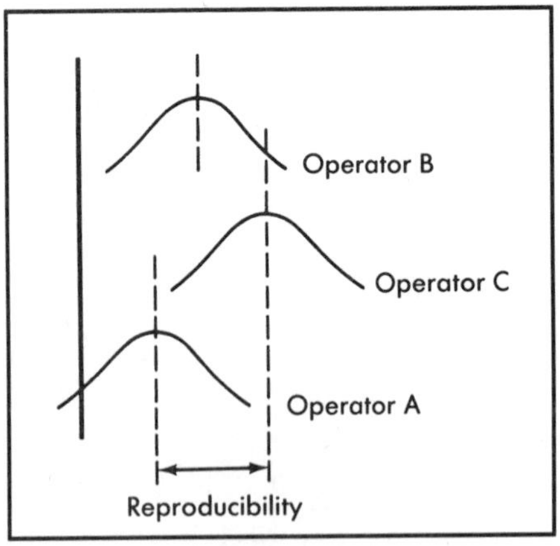

Fig. 4.7.3 Gage reproducibility among three operators.

Gage Reproducibility

Reproducibility is the variation in measurement averages (between-inspector variation), where:

$$\bar{R}_3 = \bar{X}_L - \bar{X}_S \qquad (4.7.2)$$

See Figure 4.7.3. The $1/d_2$ factor is based on one sample, with a sample size equal to three. From Table 4.7.1 this value is 0.524. Then,

$$\hat{\sigma}_{(\text{Between Inspectors})} = 1/d_2 \cdot R_3 = (0.524)(2.0 - 1.65) = 0.183 \qquad (4.7.3)$$

Statistically, variances can be combined to give a single value according to the formula:

$$\sigma_A^2 = \sigma_B^2 + \sigma_C^2 \qquad (4.7.4)$$

This resultant value would be used to measure the repeatability and reproducibility, or

$$\hat{\sigma}_{\text{(Repeatability \& Reproducibility)}} = \sqrt{(0.502)^2 + (0.183)^2} = 0.534 \qquad (4.7.5)$$

It is immediately apparent that reduced variability could be attained by inspector training, which could minimize the differences in averages, or by obtaining a more precise gaging device.

Assume the total tolerance for the parts used in this study is 3.0. A 99 percent spread factor is chosen to provide a high confidence level for the gage repeatability and reproducibility. The tolerance consumed by the measuring system is calculated using this formula:

$$\frac{(5.15)\,(\hat{\sigma}_{R\&R})\,(100)}{\text{Tolerance}_{\text{(Parts)}}} \qquad (4.7.6)$$

$$= \frac{(5.15)\,(0.534)\,(100)}{3.0} = 91.73\%$$

The constant 5.15, is derived from the "Table of Areas Under the Normal Curve" (Table A-2). The constant represents a 99 percent confidence level that any gage R&R readings with these parts, equipment and operators would fall within the same range of variability.

This percentage (91.73) cannot be directly associated with the percent good parts rejected or the percent bad parts accepted. The situation is undesirable, however, since the accepted standard for gage capability is approximately ten percent or less of the total tolerance.

The same information is shown in Figure 4.7.4, using a standardized form which simplifies the calculations required. (This is a form developed by a major automotive manufacturer.) All of the calculations given above are transferred and shown on Figure 4.7.4. What follows is the sequence of operations needed to complete this standardized form.

The procedure for estimating gage R & R summarized in the following steps

1. Select five or more parts and prepare them for gaging (wash, de-burr, and number).
2. Choose two or more appraisers (those who ordinarily use the equipment are preferable). Have each appraiser note any characteristics about the instrument which makes reading difficult. The slightest defect should be corrected before conducting the study.
3. Each appraiser, using the same instrument, measures the parts in a random order and records the values obtained.

a. Appraisers should not see each others readings.

b. Record readings to one more decimal place than the instrument's least count, i.e., if the least count is 0.001, "read to 0.0001". This requires estimating but in many cases is essential.

4. After the first set of measurements have been recorded, each appraiser repeats the measurements — without referring to his first results. (More than one repeat reading can be taken if deemed advisable.)
5. Record the readings in the appropriate columns on a form similar to Figure 4.7.2.
6. Calculate the range (difference between individual appraiser's readings) for each appraiser. Fill in all totals and calculate the averages indicated. Compute R_1.
7. Calculate the upper control limit (circle 1 in Figure 4.7.2) for the ranges and compare individual ranges to this value. Discard points out-of-control and recalculate R_1 (Follow procedure suggested previously.)
8. Determine the standard deviation to measure reproducibility. Calculate R_3, the difference between the largest and smallest appraiser means ($R_3 = \bar{x}L - \bar{x}S$); select appropriate $1/d_2$ factor from Table 4.7.1. (For three appraisers, $n = 3$, $k = 1$.) Calculate the variance and enter at circle 2 in Figure 4.7.4.
9. Determine the standard deviation to measure repeatability. Select appropriate $1/d_2$ factor from Table 4.7.1. (For three appraisers, each measuring five parts twice, $n = 2$, $k = 15$, use $k = \infty$.) Calculate the standard deviation using R_1, the variance, and enter at circle 3 in Figure 4.7.2.
10. Combine the variances calculated at circle 2 and 3, take the square root and enter at circle 4 to determine the standard deviation for reproducibilty and repeatability.
11. To find the percent tolerance consumed by repeatability and reproduceability, multiply the value at circle 4 by 5.15, divide by the drawing tolerance and multiply by 100 to convert to a percent.

Measurement Error Effect on Acceptance Decisions

Previous mention was made concerning the effect that measurement error had on accepting defective material or rejecting good material. This aspect was explored by Alan R. Eagle (See References at end of chapter). The general concept is shown graphically Figure 4.7.5. In this illustration, the gage or testing device is zeroed on the upper and lower specifications, and the measurement errors distributed about these points.

It is obvious that, due to these errors, a probability exists that a good part could be rejected or a bad part accepted. Several assumptions were made in calculating the probabilities involved (a normal practice in statistical analysis).

REPEATABILITY AND REPRODUCIBILITY

GAGE TYPE ______________________ DATE ______________

B/P SPEC. ______________ CHARACTERISTIC ______________ MACH. NO. ______________

PART NUMBER ______________ PART NAME ______________ GAGE NO. ______________

COL. NO.	1	2	3	4	5	6	7	8	9
INSPECTOR	A–			B–			C–		
SAMPLE #	1st TRIAL	2nd TRIAL	DIFF.	1st TRIAL	2nd TRIAL	DIFF.	1st TRIAL	2nd TRIAL	DIFF.
1	2.0	1.0	1.0	1.5	1.5	0	1.0	1.0	0
2	2.0	3.0	1.0	2.5	2.5	0	1.5	2.5	1.0
3	1.5	1.0	.5	2.0	1.5	.5	2.0	1.0	1.0
4	3.0	3.0	0	2.0	2.5	.5	2.5	3.0	.5
5	2.0	1.5	.5	1.5	.5	1.0	1.5	.5	1.0
6									
7									
8									
9									
10									
TOTALS	10.5	9.5	3.0	9.5	8.5	2.0	8.5	8.0	3.5
AVERAGES	2.1	1.9	.6	1.9	1.7	.4	1.7	1.6	.7

	A	B	C
	2.1	1.9	1.7
SUM	4.0	3.6	3.3
$\bar{X}$	$\bar{X}_A$ = 2.0	$\bar{X}_B$ = 1.8	$\bar{X}_C$ = 1.65

($\bar{R}_A$ = .6, $\bar{R}_B$ = .4, $\bar{R}_C$ = .7)

RANGE VARIATION

$\bar{R}_A$ (Col. 3)	0.6
$\bar{R}_B$ (Col. 6)	0.4
$\bar{R}_C$ (Col. 9)	0.7
SUM	1.7
$\bar{R}_1$	0.567

$UCL_R = (3.268)(\bar{R}_1)$

$= (3.268)(0.567)$

$= 1.85$ ①

REPRODUCIBILITY – APPRAISER VARIATION

Difference in Means

$\bar{R}_3 = \bar{X}_L - \bar{X}_S = (2.0) - (1.65) = 0.35$

Standard Deviation (SDM) $= (1/d_2)(\bar{R}_3)$

$= (0.524)(0.35) = 0.183$

Variance $= (SDM)^2 = 0.183^2 = 0.0335$ ②

REPEATABILITY – (EQUIPMENT VARIATION)

Difference in Readings

Standard Deviation (SDR) $= (1/d_2)(\bar{R})$

$= (0.885)(0.567) = 0.502$

Variance $= (SDR)^2 = 0.502^2 = 0.252$ ③

REPRODUCIBILITY AND REPEATABILITY (COMBINED)

Standard Deviation (R & R) $= \sqrt{(SDM)^2 + (SDR)^2} = \sqrt{0.0335 + 0.252}$

SDRR $= 0.5343$ ④

PERCENT TOLERANCE CONSUMED BY REPRODUCIBILITY AND REPEATABILITY

P.T.C. = [(5.15)(SDRR) ÷ DRAWING TOLERANCE](100)

= [(5.15)(0.5343) ÷ 3](100) = 91.73 %

Fig. 4.7.4 Standard Gage Capability Form.

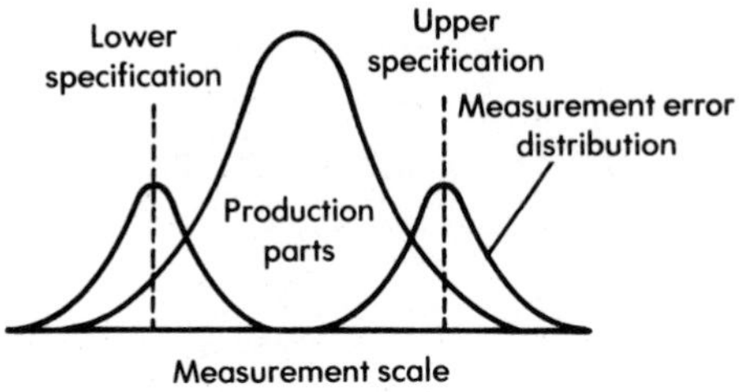

Fig. 4.7.5 Measurement error schematic.

These are:

- The distribution of production parts is normal.
- The parts are centered on the blueprint nominal.
- The specifications intersect the parts distribution at plus and minus two standard deviations.
- The measurement error distribution is normal and distributed about the zero setting.

Using curves developed by Eagle, it is shown that a gage which consumes 91 percent of the specified tolerance would only accept 1.45 percent defective parts on the low end and would reject about 7 percent of parts on the high side. Since these would logically be re-inspected before find rejection, relatively few errors would be made.

In *Quality Planning and Analysis* (See References), a rule of thumb is given:

> *If the ratio of three standard deviations of measurement error to product tolerance is less than about 25 percent, then the effect of measurement error on decisions can usually be ignored."*

For situations where the specifications include more than plus and minus two standard deviations of the parts, the graphs over-estimate the actual probabilities. For the converse situation, i.e., less than two standard deviations included in the specifications, the graphs under estimate, but this latter condition would indicate that the major problem exists in the machine or process, not the gaging.

If the process is not centered or not normal, errors will also exist, and the problem would have to be solved by other methods. Simulation is one technique which could be employed if the conditions warranted such an approach. Also, if the gage is used to obtain data for control chart purposes, the fact that the process mean fluctuates could produce results that would have to be individually analyzed.

This method was presented primarily to reveal that the percent tolerance consumed by repeatability and reproducibility should not be judged solely by its magnitude, but must be further evaluated to determine its effect on potential decision errors.

GAGE REPEATABILITY AND REPRODUCIBILITY DATA SHEET (Long Method)

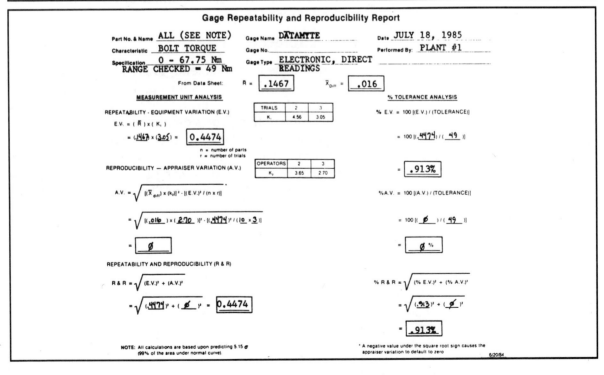

	1	2	3	4	5	6	7	8	9	10	11	12
Operator	A– Marc				B– Jerry				C– Dave			
Sample #	1st Trial	2nd Trial	3rd Trial	Range	1st Trial	2nd Trial	3rd Trial	Range	1st Trial	2nd Trial	3rd Trial	Range
13.6 1	13.6	13.6	13.6	0	13.6	13.6	13.6	0	13.6	13.6	13.6	0
19.0 2	19.0	19.3	19.0	0.3	19.0	19.0	19.0	0	19.0	19.0	19.0	0
24.5 3	24.4	24.7	24.7	0.3	24.4	24.4	24.7	0.3	24.4	24.4	24.7	0.3
29.9 4	30.1	30.1	30.1	0	30.1	29.8	29.8	0.3	29.8	29.8	30.1	0.3
35.0 5	35.3	35.3	35.3	0	35.3	35.3	35.3	0	35.3	35.3	35.3	0
40.8 6	41.0	40.4	40.7	0.6	41.0	40.7	40.7	0.3	40.7	41.0	41.0	0.3
46.2 7	46.4	45.8	46.1	0.6	46.1	46.4	46.1	0.3	46.1	46.1	46.4	0.3
51.7 8	51.8	51.5	51.5	0.3	51.8	51.8	51.8	0	51.5	51.8	51.5	0.3
57.1 9	57.0	57.0	57.0	0	57.2	57.0	57.2	0.2	57.0	57.2	57.2	0.2
62.6 10	62.6	62.6	62.6	0	62.6	62.6	62.6	0	62.4	62.6	62.6	0.2
Totals	381.2	380.3	380.6	2.1	381.1	380.6	380.8	1.4	379.8	380.8	381.4	1.9
		381.2		.21 ($\bar{R}_A$)		381.1		.14 ($\bar{R}_B$)		379.8		.19 ($\bar{R}_C$)
		380.6				380.8				381.4		
Sum		1142.1				1142.5				1142.0		
$\bar{X}$		$\bar{X}_A$ 38.070				$\bar{X}_B$ 38.083				$\bar{X}_C$ 38.067		

$\bar{R}_A$	.21
$\bar{R}_B$	.14
$\bar{R}_C$	.19
Sum	.44
$\bar{\bar{R}}$	.1467

# Trials	D_4
2	3.27
3 ✓	2.58

$(\bar{\bar{R}}) \times (D_4) = UCL_R$*

$(.1467) \times (2.58) = .378$

Max. $\bar{X}$	38.083
Min. $\bar{X}$	38.067
$\bar{X}$ Diff.	.016

* Limit of individual R's. Circle those that are beyond this limit. Identify the cause and correct. Repeat these readings using the same appraiser and unit as originally used or discard values and reaverage and recompute $\bar{\bar{R}}$ and the limiting value UCL_R from the remaining observations.

Gage Repeatability and Reproducibility Report

Part No. & Name: ALL (SEE NOTE) Gage Name: DATAMYTE Date: JULY 18, 1985

Characteristic: BOLT TORQUE Gage No.: Performed By: PLANT #1

Specification: 0 - 67.75 Nm
RANGE CHECKED = 49 Nm Gage Type: ELECTRONIC, DIRECT READINGS

From Data Sheet: $\bar{\bar{R}}$ = **.1467** $\bar{X}_{Diff}$ = **.016**

MEASUREMENT UNIT ANALYSIS

REPEATABILITY - EQUIPMENT VARIATION (E.V.)

TRIALS	2	3
K_1	4.56	3.05

E.V. $= (\bar{\bar{R}}) \times (K_1)$

$= (.1467) \times (3.05) =$ **0.4474**

n = number of parts
r = number of trials

REPRODUCIBILITY — APPRAISER VARIATION (A.V.)

OPERATORS	2	3
K_2	3.65	2.70

A.V. $= \sqrt{[(\bar{X}_{diff}) \times (K_2)]^2 - [(E.V.)^2 / (n \times r)]}$*

$= \sqrt{[(.016) \times (2.70)]^2 - [(.4474)^2 / (10 \times 3)]}$

= **Ø**

REPEATABILITY AND REPRODUCIBILITY (R & R)

R & R $= \sqrt{(E.V.)^2 + (A.V.)^2}$

$= \sqrt{(.4474)^2 + (Ø)^2} =$ **0.4474**

% TOLERANCE ANALYSIS

% E.V. = 100 [(E.V.) / (TOLERANCE)]

= 100 [(.4474) / (49)]

= **.913%**

% A.V. = 100 [(A.V.) / (TOLERANCE)]

= 100 [(Ø) / (49)]

= **Ø %**

% R & R $= \sqrt{(\%\ E.V.)^2 + (\%\ A.V.)^2}$

$= \sqrt{(.913)^2 + (Ø)^2}$

= **.913%**

NOTE: All calculations are based upon predicting 5.15 σ (99% of the area under normal curve).

* A negative value under the square root sign causes the appraiser variation to default to zero

6/20/84

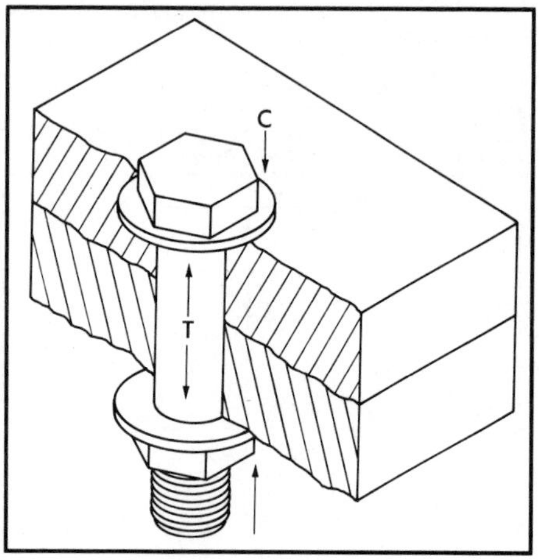

Fig. 4.8.1 Tension and clamping force.

4-8 TORQUE AUDITING

Measuring fastener torque on an ongoing basis for quality control purposes is called *torque auditing*. To help understand the need for torque auditing, it will help to review some of the basic principles of torque measurement. Some case studies of torque auditing appear in the applications section.

How Fasteners Fasten

A special property of fasteners is their *elasticity*. When a fastener is tightened it actually stretches or elongates like a rubber band. A fastener stretched in one direction, such as when tightening a nut down on the threads of a bolt, will provide tension in the opposite direction. As shown in Figure 4.8.1, this tension (T) is what is used to provide the *clamping force* (C) of a joint.

One way to measure tension is to measure the length (or elongation) of the fastener after it is tightened and compare it to its length at rest. This is not very practical in an industrial environment. A more practical but less accurate method is torque measurement.

What is Torque?

Torque is the force that tends to produce rotation or torsion. Figure 4.8.2 illustrates the application of torque and its basic unit of measure, the *pound-foot* (also called a foot-pound). One pound-foot is defined as one pound of force applied perpendicular to, and at a distance of one foot away from, the axis of rotation. The wrench acts like a lever to produce the torsion or twisting effect. The unit of measure for torque in the metric and SI systems is the Newton-

Fig. 4.8.2 Torque applied to a fastener.

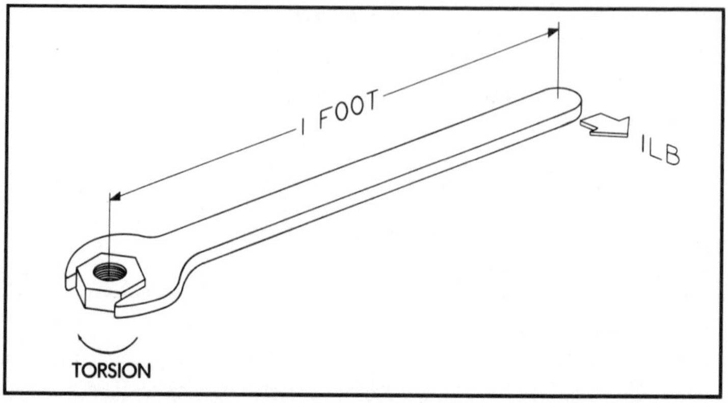

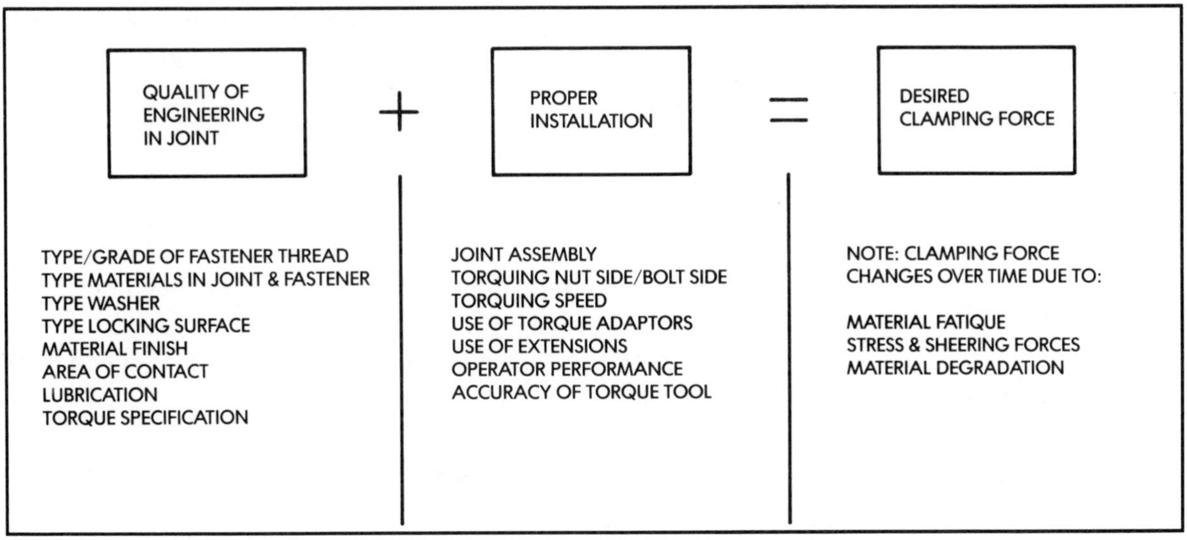

QUALITY OF ENGINEERING IN JOINT
+
PROPER INSTALLATION
=
DESIRED CLAMPING FORCE
TYPE/GRADE OF FASTENER THREAD
TYPE MATERIALS IN JOINT & FASTENER
TYPE WASHER
TYPE LOCKING SURFACE
MATERIAL FINISH
AREA OF CONTACT
LUBRICATION
TORQUE SPECIFICATION
JOINT ASSEMBLY
TORQUING NUT SIDE/BOLT SIDE
TORQUING SPEED
USE OF TORQUE ADAPTORS
USE OF EXTENSIONS
OPERATOR PERFORMANCE
ACCURACY OF TORQUE TOOL
NOTE: CLAMPING FORCE CHANGES OVER TIME DUE TO:
MATERIAL FATIQUE
STRESS & SHEERING FORCES
MATERIAL DEGRADATION

Fig. 4.8.3 Factors that determine clamping force.

meter. A Newton is a measure of force and is equivalent to one Kilogram-meter per second squared (kg-m/sec^2).

Table A-6 in the Appendix provides conversion factors among various units of measure. In an ideal situation, the amount of torque applied to a fastener is a function of the amount of force and the distance at which it is applied. For example, looking at Figure 4.8.2, a torque of 2 pound-foot (lb-ft) will result from either 2 pounds of force on a one foot long wrench or 1 pound of force on a two foot long wrench.

Torque and Clamping Force

Since torque is used to put tension in a fastener, the measurement of fastener torque should tell us something about the clamping force of a joint. But torque measurement is by no means a direct indication of clamping force. Other variables are involved.

For one thing, only a small part of the torque applied to a fastener contributes to clamping force. The rest, as much as 90%, is used to overcome friction. Some torque is also absorbed by the fastener shank when it twists slightly.

The major factors that determine clamping force are shown in Figure 4.8.3. The quality of the engineering of a joint includes the physical characteristics and the torque specification. Proper installation includes both assembly and the application of fastening torque. If everything is done correctly, the desired clamping force results. Any variation will affect clamping force. Differences will be due to changes over time, such as metal fatigue, and the ability of the auditor and torque tool to get an accurate reading.

Torque Auditing Methods

The two most common ways to auditor torque are:

- *Static,* using handheld torque tools to check breakaway torque.
- *Dynamic,* using in-line torque transducers to check peak torque.

See Chapter 17 for torque tools

There is a good deal of difference between these two methods, and advantages and disadvantages to both. The basic characteristics are listed here briefly, and a detailed description follows.

Static torque auditing has these characteristics:

- Checked after installation.
- Reading accuracy is operator dependent.
- Differences between how a fastener is installed and how a torque is checked must be taken into account.
- The time between when a fastener is installed and when torque is checked must be taken into account.
- Fairly uncomplicated gaging is used — A torque wrench or torque driver with dial readout, or an electronic (strain gage) torque tool connected to a handheld data collector.
- A variety of joints and fastener types can be audited with different range torque tools and adapters.

Dynamic torque auditing using in-line torque transducers has these characteristics:

- Checked during installation.
- Readings are operator dependent.
- Used only with powered torque tools, such as nut runners and air ratchets.
- Must be installed in-line with the production tool.
- Strain-gage type output requires an electronic readout or handheld data collector.

Torque Breakaway (Static Torque)

Torque breakaway is the point at which torque applied to a fastener restarts the fastener in a positive direction. The restarting movement is characterized by a momentary drop-off in torque followed by an increase in torque with further rotation in the positive direction. See Figure 4.8.4

There are two ways to check torque breakaway. The first is by having an operator apply torque and feel for the breakaway point, releasing the wrench at the moment it occurs. The dial reading of the wrench indicates the breakaway. The second way is with the use of an intelligent data collector such as the DataMyte, which can sense the drop in load on a strain-gage type torque wrench, and record breakaway automatically. The second way does not depend on the sensitivity of the operator, so it provides a more consistent reading of the breakaway point.

As show in Figure 4.8.5, the breakaway point is a good relative indicator of installation torque, and the clamping force attained, when certain conditions are accounted for. By relative indicator, we mean that there is a positive correlation. Typically, for different types of fasteners and methods of installation, a breakaway reading is either consistently higher by a slight amount or consistently lower than installation torque. Since the purpose is not so much to equate installation specifications with audit data, but rather to monitor a process for control and capability, correlative data is adequate. Given a stable process and a suf-

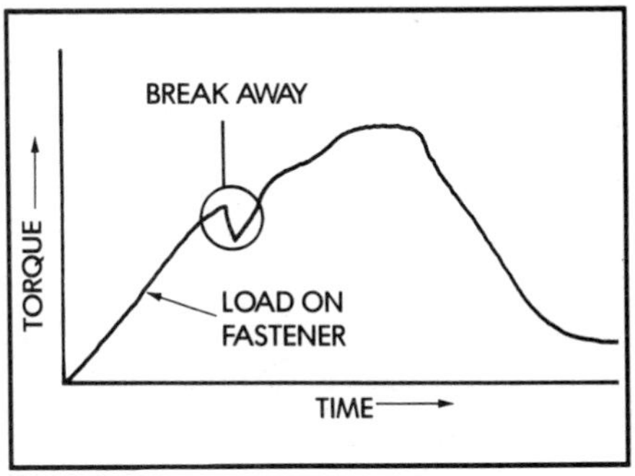

Fig. 4.8.4 A graph of a torque signal.

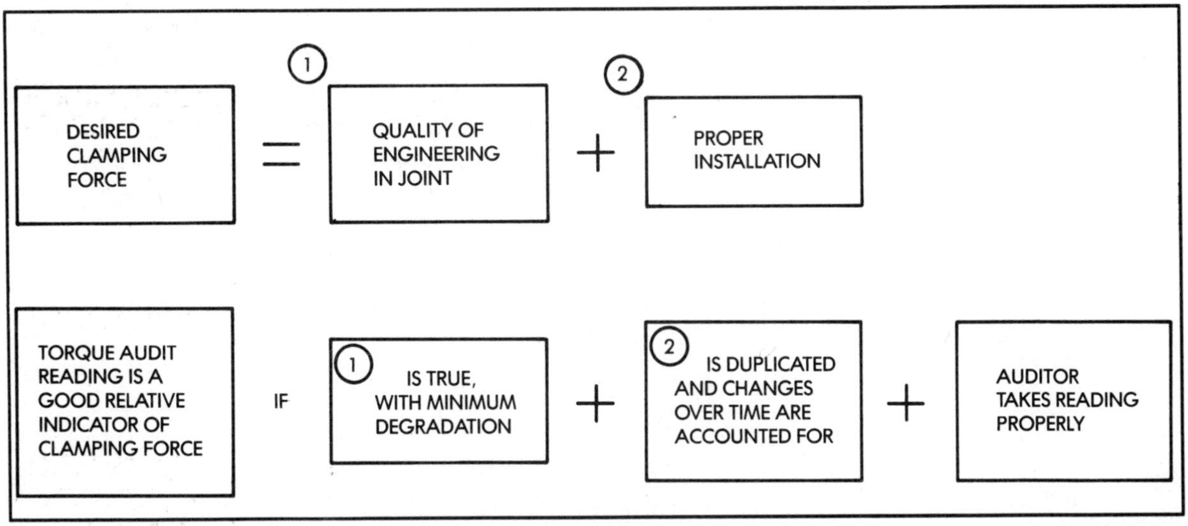

Fig. 4.8.5 Relationship between an audit reading and clamping force.

ficient amount of data, the correlative factor can be accounted for.

Sources of Variation Between Installation and Breakaway Torque

Some of the areas that can make a breakaway reading different from the installation torque specification are:

Actual installation versus the specification — The torque achieved at installation may not be the same as the specification. The design of the joint and fastener, its assembly, the performance of the operator, and the accuracy of the torque tool affect the installation. Use of adaptors, torquing the nut side or bolt side, and tightening speed, all greatly affect actual torque.

Torque fall-off (joint relaxation) — In as little as one hour after installation, the bearing surfaces of a joint will fatigue due to the compression from clamp load. See Fig. 4.8.6. This tends to reduce the torque required to achieve breakaway.

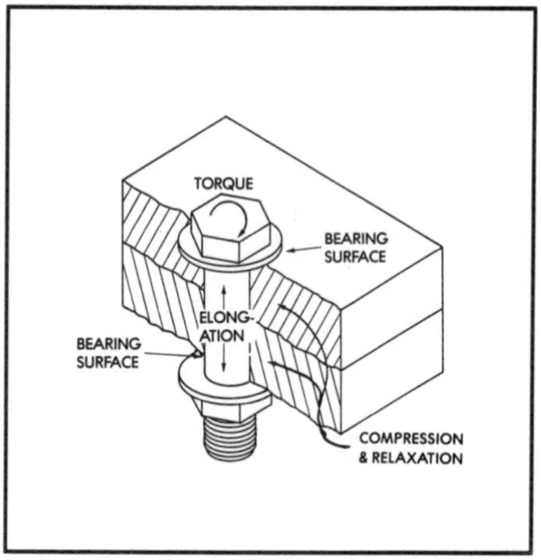

Fig. 4.8.6 Torque fall-off.

Hard joints and soft joints — Hard joints, such as metal-to-metal with a locking fastener will have a more pronounced (and detectable) breakaway than joints using a soft gasket or holding softer materials. Breakaway may be imperceptible in some types of joints, such as pipe threaded junctions, due to the composition of joint materials and the nature of the threads.

Tightening Speed (frictional coefficients) — Speed affects a torque reading because the coefficient of friction varies with it. Since the greatest amount of torque is used to overcome the friction in the joint at rest and restart further tightening motion, friction contributes a great deal to variability among readings. Generally, the tightening speed at installation should be matched during an audit. This is a justification for the use of in-line torque transducers to audit torque on power tools.

Other factors — Other factors that contribute to differences between installation and breakaway torque are:

- Temperature.
- Absorption of torque by the joint.
- Stress and shearing forces.
- Training of the auditor in reading breakaway torque.
- Accuracy of the audit method.

Dynamic Torque

To control torque on an ongoing basis, we can monitor it dynamically; that is, as the torque is applied to the fastener. Individual readings tell us only the torque currently being applied, which may or may not be within suggested tolerance. To apply statistical analysis, we must be able to average a number of readings. The average torque output of a tool supplies criterion for adjusting the tool, and the range or dispersion of measurements becomes criterion for judging the capability of the tool.

A dynamic torque monitoring system, therefore consists of:

- The torque tool, such as a pneumatic nut runner, ratchet, or multi-spindle nut runner.
- An in-line transducer.
- A handheld data collector and analyzer such as the DataMyte Statistician.

See Chapter 16 for a description of data collectors.

The term *transducer* means a device that converts energy from on form to another. In this case, the in-line transducer converts mechanical force into electrical energy. The transducer is termed "in-line" because it is installed in the line of force being applied, as an extension between the driving tool and the socket being driven (See Figure 4.8.7).

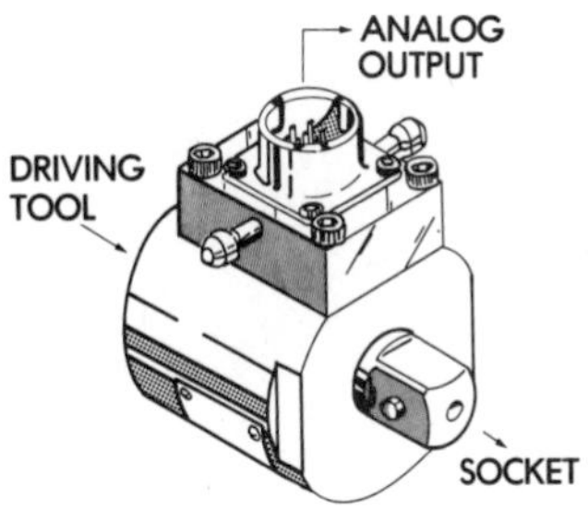

Fig. 4.8.7 In-line torque transducer.

As torque is applied to the fastener, the center shaft of the transducer undergoes a very slight twisting motion. The amount of flex is related to the torque applied. Strain gages are mounted to the shaft in a resistive bridge configuration. When the shaft undergoes a twisting movement, the strain gages twist with it. This motion stretches the resistive gages, causing their resistance to increase.

When the DataMyte is connected to this transducer, it measures the torque by sensing the change in resistance across the strain gages. This signal is converted into a digital count representative of the torque applied. The DataMyte is programmed to record the peak value of torque applied to the fastener. It does this by continually sampling the input signal. When a torque signal appears, the DataMyte continually updates its memory with the highest signal it sees until the torque drops to zero again. It then records the peak value and alerts the operator if the torque recorded falls outside of specified limits.

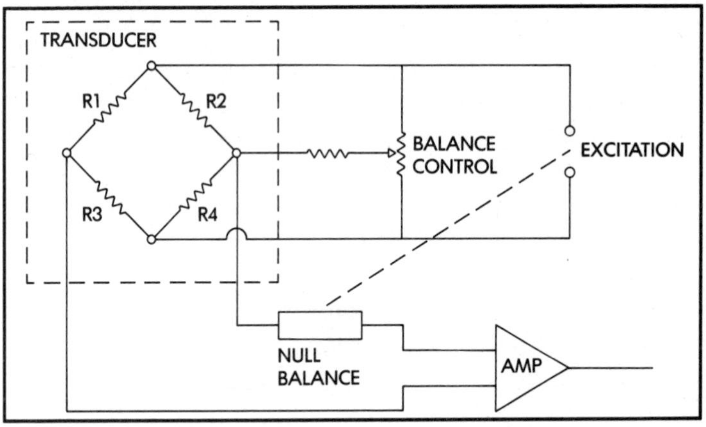

Fig. 4.8.8 Schematic of a Wheatstone bridge.

The resistive bridge is known as a Wheatstone bridge. It consists of four precision resistors configured as shown in Figure 4.8.8

The resistors used in an in-line transducer are called strain gages. They are high precision resistors made in a variety of alloys for different applications. They are made very thin so that any stretching or compressing will cause a change in resistance. When properly mounted, they act as an adding and subtracting electrical network that allows for compensation with temperature changes and other extraneous signals.

In-line transducers are available in a wide range of capacities and configurations. Most can be used directly with the DataMyte with no modification. The DataMyte supplies the signal conversion, data storage, and analysis by displaying the average, range, standard deviation, and other summaries.

For Further Reference

Grant, Eugene L., and Leavenworth, Richard S. *Statistical Quality Control*. 5th ed. New York: McGraw-Hill Company, 1980.

Juran, Joseph M., ed. *Quality Control Handbook*. 3d ed. New York: McGraw-Hill Book Company, 1979.

Juran, Joseph M., and Gryna, Frank M. *Quality Planning and Analysis*. New York: McGraw-Hill Book Company, 1970.

Mitutoyo Metrology Institute. *Fundamentals of Precision Measurement Textbook*. Tokyo: Mitutoyo Mfg. Co. LTD.

H.C. Charbonneau and Gordon Webster, *Industrial Quality Control,* New Jersey, Prentice-Hall, 1978.

A.R. Eagel, "A Method for Handling Errors in Testing and Measuring." *Industrial Quality Control,* pp. 10-14, March, 1954.

5. ACCEPTANCE SAMPLING

5.1 THEORY OF ACCEPTANCE SAMPLING

Acceptance sampling is the practice of inspecting a small quantity of the parts in a lot for conformance to specification. An assumption is then made whether to accept or reject the entire lot based on the findings of the sample. The justification for acceptance sampling is that it provides a cost savings over 100 percent inspection (see Section 5.4 for Dr. E. W. Deming's proof to the contrary). The cost savings are the result of less time needed to inspect a sample, and requirements for fewer inspectors. There is the additional expense and overhead required to design and administer the sampling plans, however. Other reasons for sampling include:

- *Greater Speed* — Data can be collected and summarized faster with sampling than 100% inspection. Scheduling and delivery may be improved as a result.
- *Minimized Handling* — By inspecting only a sample, fewer items are subjected to the possible damage which sometimes occurs in handling or measuring during the inspection process.
- *Greater Accuracy Handling* — The problem of inspector error due to monotony is minimized. With fewer items to inspect more time can be used to ensure completeness and accuracy.
- *Faster Corrective Action* — Lot rejection due to sampling tends to dramatize quality deficiencies and to speed up corrective action over 100% sorting.

The disadvantages of acceptance sampling are administrative costs, sampling risks, and the fact that decisions have to be made with less information than is provided with 100% inspection.

Acceptance sampling should be used when 100% inspection is causing errors due to monotony, for destructive testing, and when the cost of inspection is high in relation to the cost resulting from passing a defective.

Importance of a Random Sample

A random sample is one which was chosen by a process which was set up to give every item in the population an equal chance of being chosen. The concept of sampling is based on the idea that a sufficient quantity of items is chosen in a random fashion. The sample must contain all the characteristics of the total population. One statistical tool developed to help in selecting a random sample is *a random number table* (see Appendix Table A-7 for an example). Before using the table it is first necessary to assign a number to each unit in the population. Simply enter any column or line and select the sequence of numbers as they occur. For example, if we require five samples, and choose to enter the table at line 21, we would get the numbers 26, 20, 46, 66, 36 (Table A-7). These are the corresponding numbers you would select from the population. Further information on random number tables can be found in various statistical textbooks.

Risks Associated With Sampling

In sampling, certain inherent risks are involved which must be addressed and understood.These risks can be broken down into the following two types:

- *The Producer's Risk* (also referred to as α Risk) can be understood easiest when thought of as the probability that a good lot will be rejected by the sampling plan. The quantified risk must be defined prior to adopting a given sampling plan. The risk is stated in conjunction with a numerical definition of good quality such as AQL (acceptable quality level). The sampling plan should have a Producer's Risk which is equal to or better than the AQL.
- *The Consumer's Risk* (also referred to as the β Risk) is the risk that a bad lot will be accepted by the sampling plan. The consumer's risk is generally stated in conjunction with a numerical definition of bad quality such as LTPD (lot tolerance percent defective).

Estimating Sampling Risks

The estimation of the *Producer's Risk* of a sampling plan includes the following steps:

- Plot an OC curve for the sampling plan in question. OC curves are described in the following section.

- Find the percent defective in the process when it is running at capability.
- It may be necessary to estimate it, but if greater accuracy is desired a process capability study should be done.
- Find the process capability percentage on the OC curve and follow it up to determine the probability of acceptance.
- Subtract this probability of acceptance from 1.0. This number is the producer's risk for the sampling plan.

To estimate the *Consumer's Risk* proceed as follows:

- Plot the OC curve for the sampling plan in question.
- Find the percent defective which the consumer wants to reject. This may be understood to be the worst case quality which the customer will accept.
- Find this value on the horizontal scale of the OC curve. Follow it up to determine the probability of acceptance. This number will be your risk of accepting bad quality material.

5.2 OC CURVES

Operating Characteristic Curves — The OC curve is a means of quantifying the producer's and consumer's risk. The OC curve for an attributes plan is a graph of the percent defective in a lot versus the probability that the sampling plan will accept the lot. The probability must be stated for all values of "P" (percent defective) since "P" is unknown. An assumption is made that an infinite number of lots will be produced.

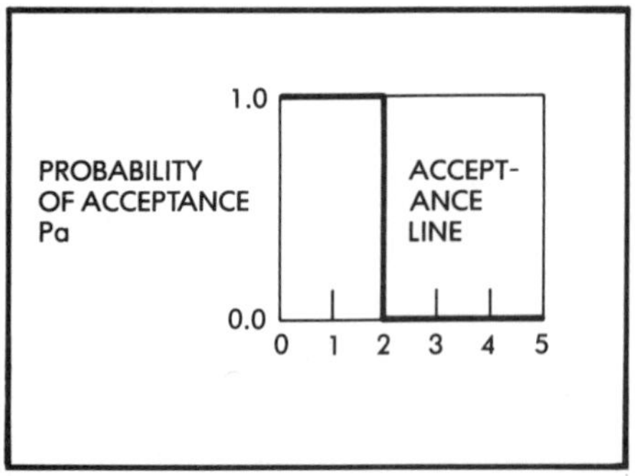

Fig. 5.2.1. Optimum sampling plan performance.

It is characteristic of sampling plans that the probability of acceptance is high as long as product quality is good, but becomes less as product quality becomes poorer. An example of an optimum OC curve is shown in Figure 5.2.1. Let us assume that we desire to accept all lots less than 2% defective and reject all lots greater than 2% defective. All lots less than 2% defective have a probability of acceptance of 1.0 (certainty) and all lots greater than 2% defective have a probability of acceptance of 0%. However, in

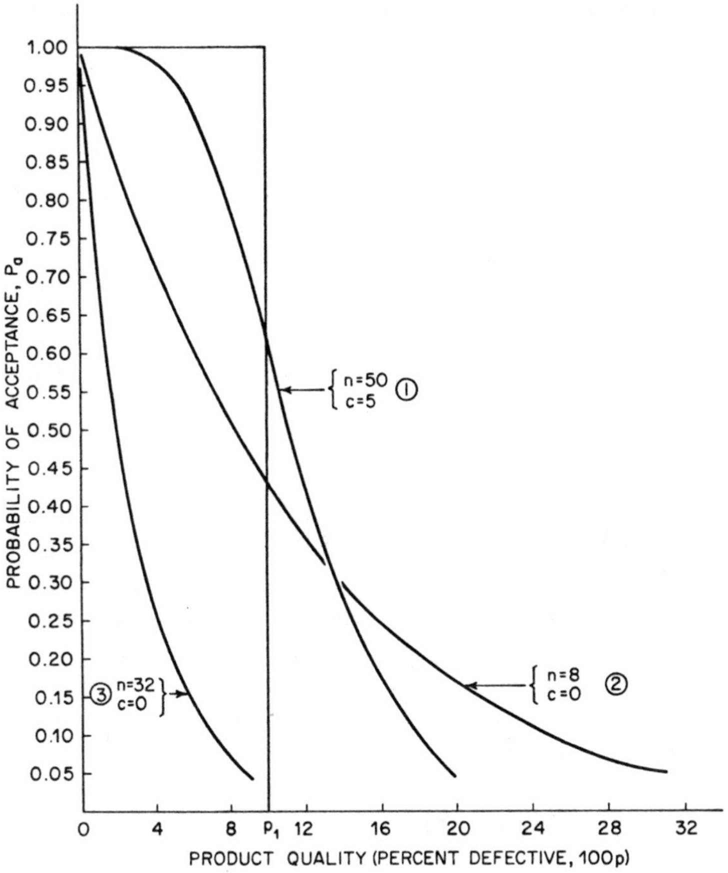

Fig. 5.2.2. How OC curves are affected by the parameters of a sampling plan. Reproduced with permission from J.M. Juran, "Quality Control Handbook," 3d ed., 1979, McGraw-Hill Book Company.

reality, there are no sampling plans which are perfect. There will always be some chance that a good lot will be rejected or a bad lot will be accepted. The one major goal in developing a sampling plan should be to make the acceptance of good lots more likely than the acceptance of bad lots.

The shape of the OC curve can be affected greatly by the parameters of the sampling plan. Figure 5.2.2 illustrates this by showing the curve for perfect discrimination as well as the curves for the other sampling plans. As the sample size approaches the lot size and an appropriate accept number (C) is used, the OC curve approaches the perfect curve P1. With an accept number of zero, the resultant OC curve will be exponential in shape or concave upward as in curves 2 and 3. Increasing the acceptance number tends to push up the OC curve for low values of P (percent defective) as in curve 1. Increasing both the accept number and sample size at the same time (curve 1) gives a curve which most closely resembles the perfect discriminator curve of P1.

Constructing OC Curves

Construct an OC curve by determining the probability of acceptance for various values of P (percent defective in a lot). The probabilities of all values of P must be determined since P is unknown. There are three distributions which may be used to find the probability of acceptance. They are the *Poisson, hypergeometric,* and the *binomial.* Probably the easiest one to use is the Poisson distribution if all assumptions are met for its use.

Some assumptions which must be met are as follows:

- Sample size must be 16 or greater.
- Lot size must be at least 10 times greater than the sample size.
- Percent defective is less than 0.01.

Many tools exist which can aid in calculating and plotting the OC curves. One such tool is shown in Figure 5.2.3. The following steps are required to plot the OC curve for a single sampling plan.

- Set up a table like the one shown in Table 5.2.1 for various values of P (percent defective). Express "P" as a decimal. The "P" value range should cover both good and bad product.
- Complete the second column of the table by multiplying each of the "P" values in column 1 by "n" (sample size).
- Find the probability of acceptance (Pa) by using the table of curves in Figure 5.2.3.

Sampling Plan n = 200, c = 10		
P	nP	Pa
.01	2	0.99999
.02	4	0.997
.03	6	0.96
.04	8	0.81
.05	10	0.69
.06	12	0.35
.07	14	0.28
.08	16	0.08
.09	18	0.02
.10	20	0.01

Table 5.2.1. Calculations for plotting an OC curve.

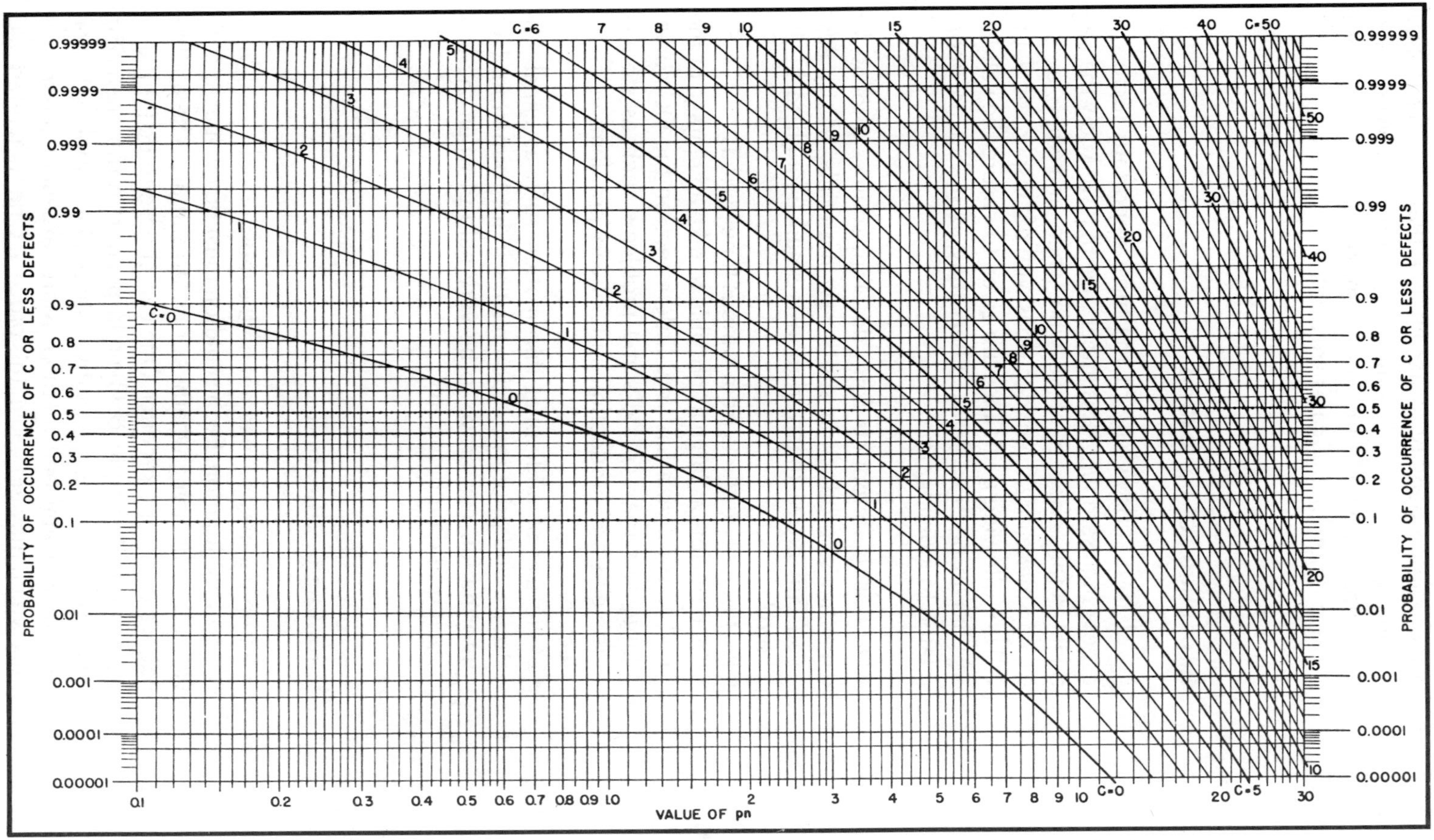

Fig. 5.2.3. Cumulative probability curves of the Poisson distribution. Reproduced with permission from Harold F. Dodge and Harry G. Romig, "Sampling Inspection Tables, Single and Double Sampling," 2d ed., 1959, John Wiley & Sons, Inc. (A modification of a chart given by F. Thorndike in "The Bell System Technical Journal, Oct. 1926). These curves serve as a generalized set of OC curves for single sampling plans when the Poisson distribution is applicable.

- Plot the probability of acceptance (Pa) for each corresponding value of "P" as shown in Figure 5.2.2. When comparing a number of OC curves, make sure the same vertical and horizontal scales are used.

Inspection Lot Formation

Lot formation is one of the most important factors in acceptance sampling. It is imperative that we know the pertinent details about a lot (i.e. who, when, and what), before we can make intelligent decisions with the inspection data.

The following guidelines are given to ensure the validity of your inspection data. Others may exist, but are more related to individual processes.

- Do not mix products from different sources (process or machines, production shifts, raw materials, etc.) unless you can prove that variation is small enough to be ignored.
- Do not mix products from various time periods.
- Keep the lots as large as possible to take advantage of the fact that lot size has very little effect on the OC curve. Large lots may create some problems such as storage problems and production and delivery problems when rejected.
- Make use of additional information such as capability studies and prior inspection results in lot formation. This information can prove to be very helpful when the lots are few and far between.

Sampling Justification

Sampling may or may not be the most effective solution for a given situation. Each situation must be evaluated individually in deciding whether or not to sample. Three alternatives exist for a product. One can choose to do (1) 100% inspection, (2) sample, or (3) no inspection. A thorough cost analysis of all three alternatives should be completed prior to adopting any one method. Many excellent references exist which may aid you in this process. One such reference is *Quality Planning and Analysis,* by Joseph Juran and Frank Gryna.

5.3 SAMPLING PLANS

A sampling plan basically consists of a sample size and the acceptance or rejection criteria. The required number of samples are taken from a lot or batch and the decision criteria for acceptance or rejection are applied to the results of the inspection. All samples must be taken randomly because they are supposed to be representative of the lot. As the lot size has essentially no effect on the probability of acceptance, many sampling plans do not include lot sizes.

Sampling plans are used to minimize the cost of inspection and should be carefully studied and chosen to adequately fill the needs of both the consumer and the producer and not chosen merely for convenience. But the plan should be easy to understand and administer as overly complicated plans are often ignored, misinterpreted or result in poor information. No sampling plan ensures that only good lots will be accepted and that all bad lots will be rejected. The OC curve for the sampling plan will be helpful in recognizing inherent sampling risks.

Parameters Affecting Sampling Plans

Sampling plans are of two general types: lot-by-lot inspection plans, and continuous process plans. These two are the most often used types but there are other plans which can be used for special inspection problems.

Lot-by-lot sampling plans are used whenever product can be broken into distinct homogeneous lots. The lot size is the quantity of units in the lot. The sample size is a specified number of samples taken from the lot for purposes of inspection subject to acceptance or rejection. The sample plan will specify the criteria for acceptance or rejection. Many plans allow for single, double, or multiple sampling choices.

Continuous process plans involve product that is produced in a continuous stream and cannot easily be broken into separate lots. Initially, product is inspected 100% until some consecutive number of good units are found between successive bad units. When the required number of defect-free units are found, inspection proceeds on a sampling basis until a specified number of defects appear. When this happens 100% inspection again goes into effect and the cycle begins again.

There are three types of continuous process plans. The plan described above is known as the CSP-1 plan. The CSP-2 plan is different in that it allows a single defect to be found and doesn't return to 100% inspection unless another defect is found in the next given number of samples. The CSP-3 plan differs in that an inspection period, i.e., a production shift, is incorporated into the plan.

The U.S. Department of Defense document H107 contains prerequisites for sampling plans for continuous production. The process must produce homogeneous products, be capable of 100% inspection and the inspection procedure must be fairly simple. The product has to move such that it can flow past an inspection station.

Classifying Sampling Plans According to: AQL, LTPD, and AOQL

Sampling plans are classified according to three quality indexes: AQL, LTPD and AOQL.

AQL Plan — Acceptance Quality Level is defined by MIL-STD-105D as "the maximum percent defective (or the maximum number of defects per hundred units) that for purposes of sampling inspection can be considered satisfactory as a process average" (*MIL-STD-105D*, 1963). AQL plans favor the producer as they give a high assurance of probable acceptance. They do not take into account the other side, which is the product that will be rejected, or the consumer's risk.

LTPD Plans — Lot Tolerance Percent Defective is defined in the Dodge-Romig tables as "an allowable percentage defective; a figure which may be considered as the borderline of distinction between a satisfactory lot and an unsatisfactory lot (*Dodge, H.F., and Romig, H.G.*, 1959). When chosen, these plans tend to favor the consumer as they decrease the risk of accepting a lot equal to or below the lower quality limits. As AQL plans do not tell anything about the product that will be rejected, LTPD plans do not tell anything about the product that will be accepted. In order to obtain this information it is necessary to refer to the OC curve of the plan.

AOQL Plans — Average Outgoing Quality Limit is a sampling plan which is to be used only when product can be 100% inspected. The AOQL plan assumes that the average quality over many lots of outgoing product will not exceed the AOQL after rejected lots have been 100% inspected and all defects replaced with non-defective units. Thus some lots will be accepted based on the sample and rejected lots will be accepted only after they contain 100% good product. Beware of returning bad lots to the producer for 100% inspection as you have no control over whether they will actually do it.

Types of Sampling Plans

Sampling plans are either attribute plans or variable plans. An attribute plan is one in which each sample is inspected and classified as defective or non-defective. The lot is accepted or rejected based on the number of defects found compared with the acceptance number from the plan. A variable plan takes a measurement of each sample and a statistic such as an average, is calculated and compared with the acceptance limit of the plan, indicating whether the process is in or out of control. Attribute plans are often used for lot-by-lot production and variable plans for continuous process production. Chapter 2 describes ways of analyzing variable and attribute data.

One of the most widely used attribute plans is MIL-STD-105D, which uses the AQL as its quality index. This plan favors the consumer because the probability of accepting material at the specified AQL level is high. The plan includes three general inspection levels: I, II and III. Level I for lots with high inspection cost, level II for normal and level III for low inspection cost. These levels are also used during switching procedures. Another group of special inspection levels is included to be used for destructive testing. The plan also includes switching procedures to tighten or reduce inspection levels and should be used in order to obtain the maximum benefits of the plan. Different tables are used for single, double or multiple sampling plans.

MIL-STD-414 is an example of a variables plan and uses the AQL as its quality index. This plan requires that the distribution of individual measurements be known and that the process is stable. It allows for the choice of three measures of variability: average range, known standard deviation, and estimated standard deviation. The plan provides five inspection levels with level IV considered normal. Two acceptance procedures are offered, Form 1 and Form 2, with Form 2 being preferred. A variables plan offers an advantage over an attributes plan in that the sample size is smaller.

Single, Double, and Multiple Sampling

Many sampling plans offer a choice of single, double, or multiple sampling. In single sampling plans, a random sample of n items is drawn from the lot. If the number of defectives is less than or equal to the acceptance number, c, the lot is accepted. If not, it's rejected. In double sampling plans, a smaller initial sample is drawn and a decision to accept or reject is made if the number of defectives is either quite large or quite small. A second sample is taken if the first is inconclusive. Since it is only necessary to draw second samples in borderline cases, the average number of pieces inspected per lot is fewer than with single sampling. In multiple sampling, one or more still smaller samples are taken until a decision is finally reached. This process may result in fewer inspections but is more complex to administer. Figure 5.3.1 diagrams a multiple sample plan (*Juran,* 1979, p. 24-5).

Double or single plans simply stop at levels A or B in the diagram respectively. In double or multiple sampling plans, the probability of acceptance is more difficult to calculate. It is also more difficult to calculate for a variables type plan. In the case of the most frequently used plans such as MIL-STD-105A, Dodge-Romig and Bowker and Goodes, OC curves are given selectively for single, double and multiple

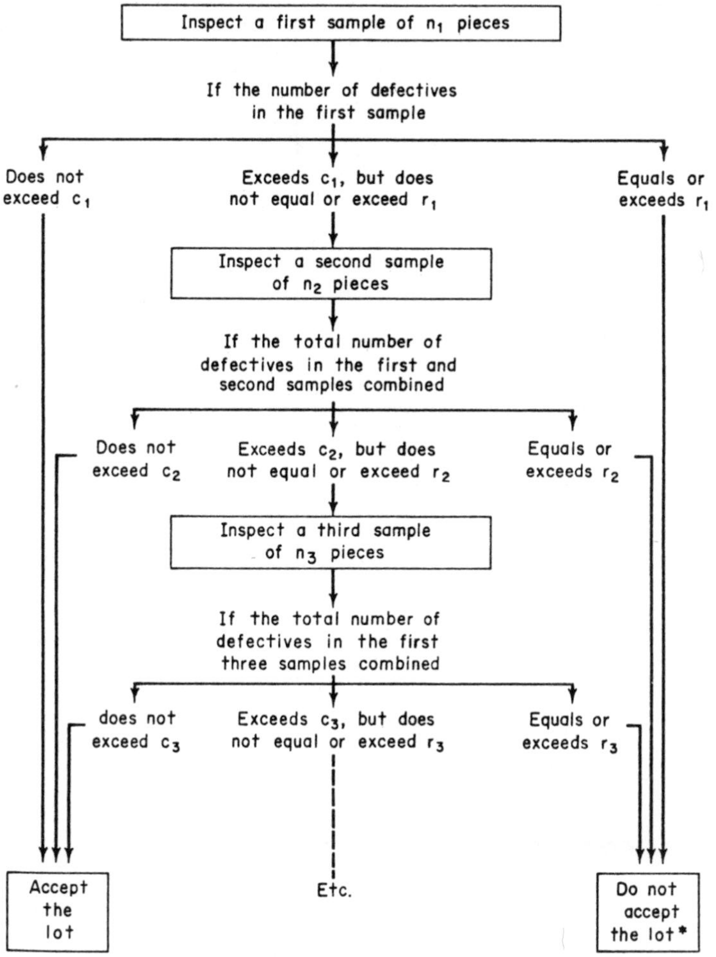

Fig. 5.3.1. Flow diagram for multiple sampling. The asterisk means that fully inspecting the lot may be necessary at this point. Reproduced with permission from J. M. Juran, "Quality Control Handbook," 3d ed., 1979, McGraw-Hill Book Company.

plans. Care should be used in drawing conclusions from published OC curves because they may not be plotted on comparable scales. However, in general, it is possible to derive single, double or multiple sampling schemes with OC curves. (*Western Electric*, 1956, p.242, *Juran*, 1979, p.24-1 and 24-24, and *Juran/Gryna*, 1970, p.418).

Table 5.3.1 summarizes comparative advantages and disadvantages of single, double and multiple sampling. In cases where the cost of inspection per part is high, the reduction in number of pieces may justify multiple sampling despite higher administrative costs. On the other hand, single sampling is preferred if minimally trained operators are used or other costs are high.

Feature	Single sampling	Double Sampling	Multiple sampling
Acceptability to producer	Psychologically poor to give only one chance of passing the lot	Psychologically adequate	Psychologically open to criticism as being indecisive
Number of pieces inspected per lot	Generally greatest	Usually (but not always) 10 to 50% less than single sampling	Generally (but not always) less than doubling sampling by amounts of the order of 30%
Administration cost* in training, personnel, records, drawing and identify samples, etc.	Lowest	Greater than single sample	Greatest
Information about prevailing level of quality in each lot	Most	Less than single sample	Least

*This is not to be confused with total cost of inspection, which includes administration cost of the plan.

Table 5.3.1. Comparative advantages and disadvantages of single, double, and multiple sampling. Reproduced with permission from J. M. Juran, "Quality Control Handbook," 3d ed., 1979, McGraw-Hill Book Company.

Characteristics of Effective Sampling Plans

Good acceptance sampling plans have several characteristics. They are listed below and elaborated in following subsections (*Juran/Gryna* , p.418).

- The quality index (AQL, ADQL, etc.) is chosen to reflect real needs of the consumer and producer. In concept, the AQL should not call for a higher quality than actually required. It should represent a balance between the cost of achieving higher quality and the cost of permitting a lower level. In practice it is a compromise between vendor capability and buyer requirements.
- Sampling risks are realistically shared between producer and consumer according to quantitative terms. Sampling tables can be used to match required producer's risk with consumer's risk. If tables don't work, special sampling plans can easily be devised. Producer's risk is defined broadly as the probability or risk of a "normal" product being rejected by inspection. Consumer's risk is that of

accepting product when the lot quality is relatively poor (The *Statistical Quality Control Handbook*, by Western Electric Co. Inc., 1956, discusses these concepts in detail).

- The total inspection costs are minimized. A complex set of costs can only be approximated because the primary and secondary costs depend on agreed upon procedures.
- Ancillary knowledge such as process capability, vendor data, etc., are built into the plan. Sampling data (either past or present) is only one source of information concerning probable acceptability. For example:

1) Vendors test data, operator's measurements, automatic machine records (these can be validated through the concept of decision audits and used to further understanding).
2) Scientific and/or engineering knowledge pertinent to the process.
3) Separately acquired data on process or machine capability. For example, the standard deviation.

There are no general procedures for defining how such data is used to alter published sampling tables. However, where specific knowledge exits, it may well improve or simplify the plan.

- The plan is sufficiently flexible to reflect pertinent changes. Flexibility is a definite asset. MIL-STD-105D has been noted as an example of a very flexible plan (*Juran/Gryna,* 1970, p. 425).
- Measurements taken are exact and repeatable. Any quality measuring process loses credibility if it is not repeatible. Measuring tools must often be specially designed to ensure ease of use and accuracy of measurement. Automatic recording of data and conversion of data to computer format further reduces likelihood of error and greatly speeds up the process.
- Measurement data becomes a data base for both short and long-run process control. Modern computer technology makes it relatively easy to catalog and store process and audit data. If collected data is converted to computer format and transmitted to a larger computer with an appropriate software, archival record storage is not difficult.

- The plan is simple to explain and easy to administer. Some plans have gone some distance to achieve ease of understanding, but at the time of this writing, much remains to be done. Modern computer technology has much to offer in this regard.

Sampling Bias

When sample selection is left to human choice, human biases can inadvertently intrude. For example:

- Sampling from the same location in all containers.
- Selecting only samples that appear to be defective or acceptable.
- Only picking samples that are easily accessible.

There is a classic story of an inspector who always picked samples from the four corners of each tray and the knowing production operator who carefully placed perfect product in each corner. Structured sampling plans assume randomness. To avoid distortions from biases, sampling must be planned. Once a plan is chosen, it must be policed to ensure that actual sampling occurs according to plan (*Juran*, 1979, p.24-7, and *Juran/Gryna* , 1970, p.434).

Sampling Plans Based on Prior Quality Data

Conventional sampling plans assume that the frequency distribution of sampling lots follow classical probabilities of occurrence. In short, they ignore any previous knowledge gained on the past quality sampling. If this knowledge could be rationally applied to future sampling processes, it should reduce sample sizes and thus inspection costs. This is called the "*Bayesian*" approach after the Bayes Theorem (*Juran*, 1979, p.24-33). A Bayesian plan generally requires a smaller sample than does a conventional plan with equivalent risk factors. But this is not always true because the assumption that prior distributions can be applied to present sampling practice is not always valid. Oliver and Springer have developed "*Bayesian Sampling Plans*" that provide sample size and acceptance criteria for single and double sampling plans, (*AIIE Technical Papers*, 1972, p.443). They do so by incorporating data on the quality of previous lots into the sampling tables. The methodology is straightforward:

- Collect quality data on previous lot sizes of N and sample n. Calculate the fraction defective p in each sample.
- Calculate the average fraction defective p, and the standard deviation of fraction defective using the basic formulas.
- Define the values for AQL, LTPD and the corresponding producer's and consumer's risks.
- Read the plan from the tables.

Juran and Gryna, in their book, *Quality Planning and Analysis*, page 435, illustrate that this technique does indeed result in smaller sample sizes. There is considerable literature available on this subject (see references at the end of this chapter). Hald provides an extensive analysis of sampling plans based upon prior product quality distributions (*Technometrics*, 1980, pp. 275-340). He also questions the assumption of transference of past data to present situations.

5.4 MINIMIZING TOTAL COST OF INSPECTION AND REPAIR

An entirely different perspective on incoming lot inspection is obtained if one views the goal to be minimizing the total cost of incoming parts inspection, plus the costs of repairing and testing assemblies that fail because of defective parts being incorporated into these assemblies. Dr. W. Edwards Deming offers some simple mathematical proofs to show that the least-cost method of production is either no incoming inspection or 100 percent inspection (*Deming, W.E.*, 1982, Chapter 13).

To illustrate this point some suppositions need to be made:

- Initially, a single incoming part will be considered. (The method can be extended readily to multiple parts.)

- Every assembly produced is functionally tested.
- If the incoming part is defective, and goes into an assembly, the assembly will fail its test. (If the part is not defective, by definition, the assembly will pass its test.)

To examine this premise mathematically we need a few definitions:

p — The average fraction defective in the incoming part receipts (say for one day).
k^1 — The cost to inspect one incoming part.
k^2 — The cost to fix and retest an assembly that had a defective part.
k^1/k^2 — The "breakeven" percentage point.

Now consider two cases:

Case 1 — The worst lot of incoming parts will have a fraction defective (p) less than k^1/k^2:

$$p < k^1/k^2$$

The least cost solution is zero inspection.

Case 2 — The best lot of incoming parts will have a fraction defective (p) greater than k^1/k^2

$$p > k^1/k^2$$

The least cost solution is 100 percent inspection.

See Figure 5.4.1a and b for a graphical representation of these cases. The proof for these rules is quite simple. Let:

i — A randomly selected part from an incoming lot.
k — Cost to test a part drawn from supply S and continue testing until a non-defective part is identified.
k^1 — The cost to inspect one incoming part.
k^2 — The cost to fix and retest an assembly that had a defective part.
x_i — 1 if defective and 0 if not defective.

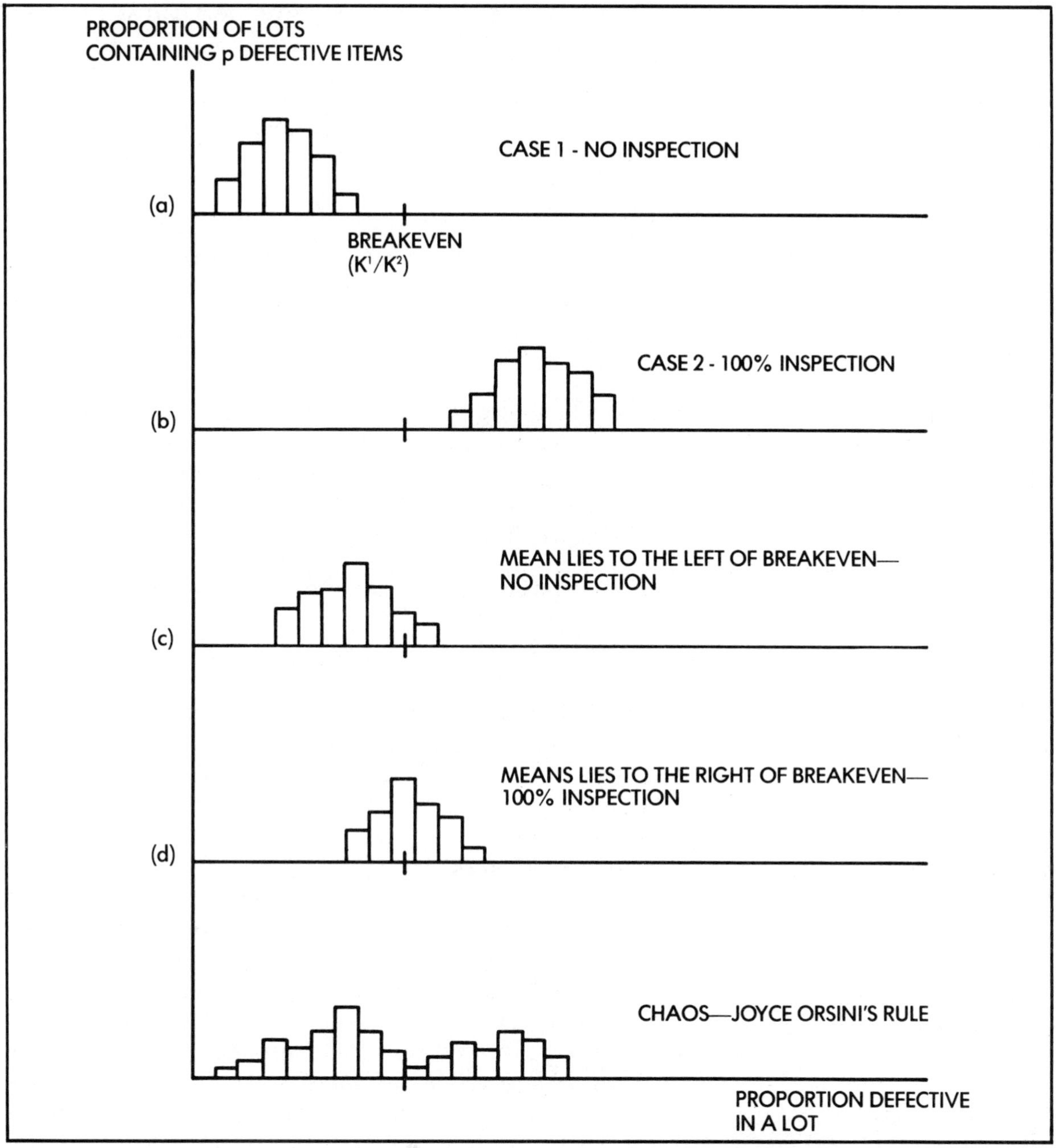

Fig. 5.4.1 Illustration of how either 100% inspection or no inspection is the least cost method.

If p = Average x_i, then the cost to inspect part $i(c^1)$ is:

$$c^1 = k^1 + kx_i$$

The cost to repair the assembly (c^2) is:

$$c^2 = x_i(k^2 + k)$$

Note that c^1 and c^2 cannot both have values. If one is not zero, the other must be zero.

$$\text{The total cost } c = c^1 + c^2$$

Note that at the break even point where $p = k^1/k^2$, the total cost c is the same whether the part is inspected or not. Further, if $p < k^1/k^2$ no inspection will always give the lower total cost and if $p > k^1/k^2$, 100 percent inspection will always give the lesser total cost.

Several conclusions can be drawn from this analysis:

- To treat a clear case 1 as a case 2 situation (test every part) will maximize the overall cost, as will the inverse.
- In cases where defective parts are binomally distributed around a mean p, the same case rules apply even though the distribution of defective parts straddles the break even point (Figure 5.4.2c and d).
- One must be sure, for a Case 1 decision, that p will be less than break even. This requires that the purchaser or the vendor keep the production process for the incoming part under statistical control — As a minimum, test small samples from every lot.
- If there is no clean grouping, the process is said to be in chaos (Figure 5.4.3e). In this case, and assuming that the break even point is greater than 0.002, Joyce Orsini's rule may be used (see last reference in chapter): take a random sample of 200 parts from a lot. If there is no defective part in the sample, accept the remainder as is. If one or more defective parts are found, replace them and inspect the rest of the lot.
- In the event of work being done to a semi-finished part, analysis shows that the same case 1 and case 2 rules apply where k^2 is now the average loss from downgrading or scrapping finished product that fails.

Comparing the Deming method with standard acceptance plans such as the Dodge - Romig tables and Military Standard 105d lead to some surprising conclusions. For example, the theory behind the Dodge-Romig tables is said to be to minimize the cost of inspection to achieve a prescribed level of quality or percentage of acceptable parts rather than minimizing the total cost.

Anscombe says "It is time to realize what the problem really is, and solve that problem as well as we can instead of inventing a substitute problem that can be solved exactly but is irrelevant." (*Journal of the American Statistical Association*, 1958, pp. 702-719)

It is argued that, in many circumstances, prescribing an acceptance plan will cost considerably more in total than 100 percent inspection. It is argued further that if the process producing the parts were in good statistical control, tests of samples would provide no useful information.

For Further Reference

Government Printing Office, *Sampling Procedures and Tables for Inspection by Attributes, MIL-STD-105D.* Washington, D.C.: Government Printing Office, 1963.

Grant, Eugene L., and Leavenworth, Richard S. *Statistical Quality Control.* 5th ed. New York: McGraw-Hill Book Company, 1980.

Hald, A. "The Compound Hypergeometric Distribution and A System of Single Sampling Inspection Plans Based on Prior Distributions and Costs." *Technometrics* (1960) 2: 275-340.

Juran, Joseph M., ed. *Quality Control Handbook.* 3d ed. New York: McGraw-Hill Book Company, 1979.

Juran, Joseph M., and Gryna, Frank M. *Quality Planning and Analysis.* New York: McGraw-Hill Book Company, 1970.

Oliver, Larry R., and Springer, Melvin D., "A General Set of Bayesian Attribute Acceptance Plans." *American Institute of Industrial Engineers. 1972 Technical Papers.*

Schafer, R.E. "Bayesian Operating Characteristic Curves for Reliability and Quality Sampling Plans." *Industrial Quality Control* (1967) 14:118-122.

Schafer, R.E. "Bayes Single Sampling Plans for Attributes Based on the Posterior Risk." *Naval Research Logistical Quarterly* (1967) 14:81-88.

Western Electric Co., Inc. *Statistical Quality Control Handbook.* 2 ed. Easton: Mack Printing Company, 1956.

Deming, W. Edwards *Quality, Productivity, and Competitive Position,* 1982, Massachusetts Institute of Technology, Chapter 13.

Ascombe, Francis J., "Rectifying Inspection of a Continuous Output." *Journal of the American Statistical Association,* Vol. 53, 1958: pp. 702-719.

Joyce Orsini, "Simple rule to reduce total cost of inspection and correction of product in state of chaos," dissertation for the doctorate, Graduate School of Business Administration, New York University, 1982. Obtainable for University Microfilms, Ann Arbor, 48106.

6. JUST-IN-TIME & TOTAL QUALITY CONTROL

INTRODUCTION

This chapter will help to acquaint the reader with currently popular manufacturing management practices used to improve quality and productivity. People who use SPC should become familiar with just-in-time (JIT) and total quality control (TQC) concepts because they provide a framework for addressing quality issues on a plant level.

With SPC, the task of reducing variation in a process soon takes us beyond the process itself. Concerns about proper machine maintenance, adjustment and operation turn into other concerns like simpler methods, better raw material uniformity and more efficient parts handling. Further improvement in quality and productivity soon becomes an environmental issue; that is, SPC can document a need for improvement in just about any manufacturing environment, but there are some environments where the actual improvement can occur faster than others. This chapter is a look at those types of environments.

JIT and TQC practices can optimize the use of SPC. That JIT and TQC differ in methods has more to do with the broad nature of manufacturing itself and how people with different cultural backgrounds (the Japanese with JIT for instance) discover methods that work.

6.1 JUST-IN-TIME MANUFACTURING

There are many articles and books on the subject of JIT. The most notable source for the information found in this section is "Japanese Manufacturing Techniques, Nine Hidden Lessons in Simplicity," by Richard J. Schonberger (Macmillan Publishing Co., Inc., 1982).

Just-in-Time is a manufacturing strategy that is intended to increase profit and competitive position. It is not simply a way to reduce inventories, or force suppliers to deliver goods "just in time" for their use in manufacturing. JIT is based on the idea that a company should buy or produce only what is needed and only when it is needed.

JIT aims at the timely delivery of materials and tools to each work station, and the many benefits that occur from working toward this goal. Some of the quality and productivity benefits are:

- Workers become responsible for making defect-free parts, resulting in much less scrap, rework, material waste and wasted effort.
- More awareness of the sources of delay and error.
- Higher levels of worker motivation.
- Creates a fertile environment for plant-wide quality improvement.
- Greater productivity and lower cost — which fuels a continuous quality effort.

JIT was developed in Japan to improve companies that did repetitive manufacturing, which is capital and labor intensive in both Japan and the United States. JIT is a radical departure from traditional U.S.-style manufacturing with its shop-oriented plant layout, large inventories, elaborate material handling and computer controlled production management systems. Instead of focusing on factory automation and elaborate control systems, JIT aims at simplifying and streamlining the flow of goods and labor.

JIT and Quality

JIT manufacturing represents a commitment to quality. In a sense, a company using JIT bets its whole manufacturing process on the quality of its goods. If there are no defects the process runs smoothly, but if there are defects the process grinds to a halt. A defect becomes a disease from which the whole body suffers, therefore defects become highly visible and are dealt with. This is unlike traditional batch-mode production methods, where a certain level of defects is assumed as unavoidable, and in order to keep the process running, batches of parts are made so that there are always enough good ones around.

By reducing inventories and switching away from batch-mode production, producing defect-free parts becomes much more important. A part with a defect becomes a break in a chain that can cause work stoppage all the way along the production process. With batch-mode production, a bad part simply gets thrown into a scrap pile, and production does not stop because a worker can simply pick another piece from the bin.

Not coincidentally, JIT practices apply wherever SPC can be used to improve quality. JIT requires each worker to fully inspect a piece before handing it to the next worker. Every worker must know what quality looks like at every work station, and feel responsible for it. The feeling of responsibility is not a dictated feeling either. It is a personal motivation continually reinforced by relationships with other production workers in the plant.

Although it is difficult to apply in principle, an ideal JIT practice is to have each worker physically hand his finished piece to the next worker in line. This tends to create a strong feeling of pride, social responsibility and teamwork. Each worker knows that the next worker depends on that piece being made well and on time in order to do his work. This motivation is lost in the case of a worker simply putting the piece in a finished parts bin, and the bin is moved by conveyor or lift-truck to some unknown destination on the other side of the plant.

JIT Practices

The JIT commitment to quality is part of a central goal of reducing waste and therefore the cost of manufacturing. JIT can be started in a plant by following these practices:

- Cutting lot sizes
- Cutting setup times
- Total quality control
- Implementing a pull system
- Organizing the plant for continuous flow manufacturing
- Withdrawing buffer inventories
- Simplifying buying practices

Each of these practices will be described briefly. The biggest misunderstanding about JIT is that it should start with one's vendors — reducing carrying costs by forcing vendors to deliver just in time. Although JIT does take on that appearance, as a strategy it should start at the other end of the plant, in the final assembly area, and work backward.

Cutting Lot Sizes

Lot sizes are usually determined by the cost and time it takes to set up a machine and the carrying cost for the batch of parts. As machine tools become more performance oriented and more expensive, larger lot sizes occur. The negative ramifications of large lots are not examined as closely as machine setup and inventory carrying costs:

- Large lot sizes hide defects.
- They create waste.

- They create a "hurry up and wait" mentality where a fast machine produces a lot of parts that sit around and wait for the next manufacturing stage.
- They require elaborate shop floor control and material handling to schedule and move the parts to and from the machining center.

Many of the costs associated with large lots are assumed to be fixed. Cutting lot sizes may create more costs initially because it forces us to confront these fixed costs, such as setup times, production scheduling and material handling. But effort put into simplifying and streamlining the operation eventually can create many benefits, not the least of which is a more flexible manufacturing operation capable of responding faster to market demand.

With a lot size of one, an ideal with JIT, an order to ship is all the documentation necessary. Successive manufacturing stages are positioned right next to each other. The material is handled one piece at a time station to station. Set up time is reduced to seconds and work is apportioned so that each step takes an equal amount of time. A lot of teamwork occurs because each worker knows that work will halt and quotas will not be met if there are defective parts or problems at any one station.

A lot size of one is impractical in most instances, but the goal of reducing lot sizes is not. Reducing lot sizes exposes quality problems and sources of delay. It is easier to trace a problem to the time it occurred and the circumstances behind it. It forces us to think of ways to create efficiencies between manufacturing steps rather than relying on the internal efficiencies of some high speed machine tool to make up the difference in waste and carrying costs.

Cutting Setup Times

Machine setup times must be cut in order to justify cutting lot sizes. Japanese companies expend a lot of effort in cutting the setup times of machinery to the point of making special fixtures and conveyors for dies and jigs, and drilling teams of workers from neighboring machines to join in and set up a particularly cumbersome machine when needed.

When setup times are no longer viewed as fixed, a whole new type of plant engineering can take place, that of developing manufacturing systems with minimal setup that are responsive to more instantaneous demand. A lot of the setup time caused by the machine being a general purpose machine tool is engineered out. The resulting more dedicated machinery can produce better quality in smaller lot sizes.

Total Quality Control

Total quality control will be elaborated on later in this chapter. Total quality control allows JIT manufacturing to function smoothly. JIT and TQC are self-perpetuating in that JIT exposes defects and TQC serves to eliminate them, which allows lotless production to continue.

Implementing a Pull System

Most manufacturing systems are push systems. Work piles up, or cues up in front of each machine with the idea that this guarantees continuous production. Work begins at the next station when there is a large enough quantity of unfinished parts to be worked on. To smooth over the whole production process, buffer inventories and safety stocks are put in front of machines that operate faster than others, so they won't be idle.

A pull system is production that is responsive to final assembly, which in turn is geared to customer orders. Rather than pushing materials through a factory, a part is made when that part is needed at the next stage in the process. Parts are thus delivered just in time to the next station. The Japanese Kanban (card) system is a shop order system where a station needing a quantity of parts places a card at the previous station to signal the production of those parts. Idle labor is not so much a concern with a pull system. Productivity eventually increases as management and workers divide up the work more equitably and the system smooths itself.

Organizing the Plant for Continuous Flow Manufacturing

Just-in-time manufacturing requires an abandonment of the job-shop layout of a plant in favor of a cellular layout. In a cellular layout, successive stages of a production cycle are physically situated right next to each other — a punch press next to a grinding/deburring station next to a drill press and so on. The idea is that it is much more important to have workers on the same part work next to each other and understand successive steps in the making of the part than to group like machinery in separate shops. A cellular layout removes much of the need for material handling apparatus such as fork lifts going between stations. With reduced buffer inventories between stations, the floor space occupied by the layout is much less also.

Withdrawing Buffer Inventories

To expose sources of problems, Japanese managers use an offensive strategy of actually removing buffer stock between machinery. This stimulates activity to remove sources of delay, potential quality problems, and leads to a continual perfection of the process. Once the process smooths out in operation, the managers remove a bit more buffer again to expose the workers to other problems.

Simplifying Buying Practices

Buying practices for JIT are aimed at dock to assembly line movement of parts rather than dock to inventory. Arrangements are made for more frequent deliveries of less parts, without a lot of the formal paperwork. The vendor is made more responsive to the needs of the plant and coached to develop his own resources so that he can play the role profitably. Long-term relationships and quality are stressed rather than competing for a low bid.

6.2 TOTAL QUALITY CONTROL

Total quality control was definitively described in the book "Total Quality Control" by Armand V. Feigenbaum (McGraw-Hill Inc., 1961). TQC has also become a catchall phrase for quality practices in Japan that are part of JIT manufacturing. TQC is an expansive subject, and only a few definitions and concepts will be dealt with here.

Total quality control is a management system for an entire organization, not just the manufacturing area, according to Fiegenbaum. It is a system of integrated controls which ensure customer quality satisfaction and economical costs of quality. It includes engineering, purchasing, financial administration, marketing and manufacturing. Fundamental to the concept is that quality must be designed and built into a product. The idea that quality can be inspected into a product is rejected. Defect prevention is emphasized rather than defect detection.

TQC is a systems approach that recognizes both the advantages and inherent flaws of the division of effort required in an organization. It seeks to complement this with quality improvement through an integration of effort. The characteristics of TQC are that it has a point of view of continuous improvement and it requires the thorough identification and documentation of tasks and responsibilities. As a result, TQC becomes a foundation for ongoing organizational quality control and provides for the systematic engineering of order of magnitude improvements in quality.

Cost of Quality

TQC requires an understanding of the costs of quality. Cost of quality has been elevated in a total quality control system to a financial control on a par with labor costs and material costs. The cost of quality is more than just the cost of scrap. It includes the costs of control and the costs of failure.

The costs of failure are divided into internal failures and external failures. Internal failure costs include:

- Scrap
- Rework
- Engineering changes
- Idle time

External failure costs include:

- Market research
- Technical support
- Warranty repairs
- Lost business

There is debate as to whether some expenses, such as technical support and marketing, are a cost of quality. Technical support is aimed at increasing customer satisfaction and thus at lowering external failure costs. Marketing is aimed at establishing market expectations for a product. Market research helps to identify the specifications a product needs to be successful. Both marketing functions would tend to reduce product failures if successful. At the same time, product failures, and their resulting quality costs, would occur despite good engineering and manufacturing if the product specifications did not match the

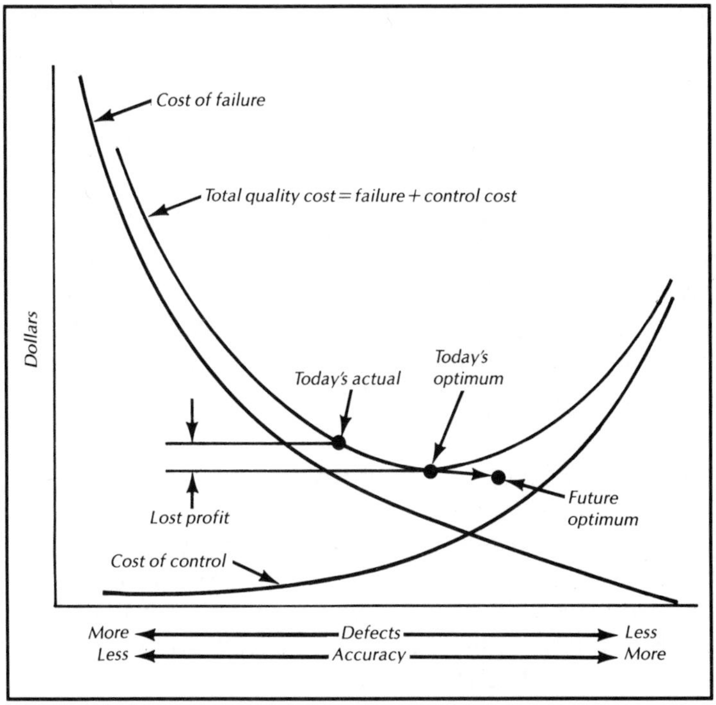

Fig. 6.2.1 Cost of quality curve.

needs and expectations of the customers.

The costs of control can be divided into prevention costs and appraisal costs. Prevention costs are the costs of preventing failures from happening in the first place and include:

- Design reviews
- Specifications reviews
- Quality training
- Preventive maintenance

Appraisal costs are the costs of determining whether specifications are being met and include:

- Prototype process development
- Data collection
- Inspection
- Quality control
- Test and inspection equipment

Total quality costs can be graphed as shown in Figure 6.2.1. For each company there is an optimum cost of quality, where failure cost is least but control costs are not so excessive as to make quality control unprofitable.

An analysis of cost of quality can be quite illuminating to a company. The cost of quality can amount to as much as 40 percent of production cost and 20 percent of sales. If a

$50 million a year company has a cost of quality of 15 percent of sales, that's $7.5 million a year being spent. If that cost of quality could be reduced to 3 percent, or $1.5 million, that's a $6 million savings every year.

More important than how much is spent is where it is spent. A company that is spending most on failure costs could certainly afford more control costs. A company who spends an inordinant amount on engineering specification reviews, and changes may need be able to justify an investment in a CAD/CAM (computer-aided design/computer-aided manufacturing) system to help design more quality into its products.

Japanese Total Quality Control

The Japanese took Feigenbaum's statement "The burden of quality proof rests ... with the makers of the part," to heart. Their efforts to simplify production systems also tends to decrease the amount of systems documentation, staffing specialization and controls for quality, but increases the dependence on the worker. The following are some TQC practices from Japan (Schonberger, 1982):

Responsibility for quality is placed in the hands of the production department — Workers are required to know what quality looks like, and to ensure quality piece by piece. Quality problems are addressed at the lowest level, with quality control staff serving in an advisory role.

Statistical process control — Workers use SPC to discover ways to reduce variability.

A habit of continuous improvement — TQC is seen as a dynamic rather than a static system. There is no such thing as "acceptable quality levels," rather, there is instilled in each worker the desire to think of ways to improve quality and productivity and to help implement them.

Measurable standards for quality — Visible indicators of quality are placed at each process and throughout the plant. Charts are kept and displayed and gaging and inspection equipment are made highly conspicuous.

Vendor inspections — Quality inspections by customers to their vendors take on the form of a military inspection, with a list of demerits and a timetable.

Insistence on compliance — Management must continually make everyone aware of the quality expectations and how they can be achieved. Compliance must be strict in that no product can be shipped that does not pass all criteria.

Line stop — Workers are given the authority to stop a production line in order to solve a quality problem.

Correcting one's own errors — Rather than have a separate rework line, rework must be done by the same worker who produced it.

Project-by-project improvement — Workers meet and develop a list of projects and activities for quality and productivity improvement. These promote teamwork and lead to improvements faster than what one worker or an isolated staff could accomplish alone.

6.3 START SMALL, MAKE A SUCCESS OUT OF SPC

Most people need to be convinced on their home turf that statistical process control, or SPC, is worth it. The skeptical ones might say "Isn't SPC another of those Japanese business practices, like lifetime employment, morning calisthenics, company songs and quality circles? Must we try all of them?"

Some attitudes can be well justified and dead wrong at the same time. It's true, over the last five years we've sent plenty of people to Japan to study their business practices. After a few weeks (sometimes months) of saki, geisha houses and other forms of hospitality, they come back with all sorts of theories. It's enough to make you a little wary. The problem with this viewpoint is that it just isn't true about SPC. First of all, its pioneers are a pair of Americans, W.A. Shewhart and W.E. Deming. Although it seemed discredited in the 1950s and '60s, when American industry had little competition for its products, SPC is *the* management tool to achieve and maintain product quality. William Conway, former chairman of Nashua Corporation of Massachusetts called Dr. Deming's methods the third wave of the industrial revolution, the first wave being the mechanization of English textile plants in the 18th century, and the second wave being the introduction of mass production by Henry Ford.

Strong testimonies notwithstanding, there are some definite probems with SPC and they have to do with that dark fearsome beast called implementation. When you read about Dr. Deming's management philosophies, and study SPC as it is currently practiced in Japan, you find out how rigorous a practice it can be. Some of the conditions deemed necessary for SPC to work are:

- Educating management on the philosophy of SPC.
- Training management and hourly workers in simple statistics and using control charts. Sometimes basic mathematics must be taught first.
- Retooling fixtures and inspection systems to measure variability. Reducing or eliminating final inspection is an eventual goal.
- Dedicating workers, process engineers, and management to the task of process improvement based on statistical techniques. This can involve restructuring jobs, work standards, and even wage contingencies.
- Accepting the results — which can affect product deliveries, inventory, tooling, machinery purchase, and the whole manufacturing process.

As they say, strong medicine can sometimes kill the patient. What perhaps ought to be whispered in back of the call to get started is: "You can start small." Most of the examples you read and are mentioned here involve American companies that have really just gotten started. They didn't send all their personnel to statistics boot camp. They assigned responsibilities to a small group, usually the quality or process engineering group. For fear of choking, they didn't swallow the whole retooling bag either. What they did do is pinpoint one or two processes that could stand improvement, and they gave SPC a try.

Edgewood Tool and Manufacturing Co. of Taylor, Michigan, is one example. They had a problem with misformed parts on hood hinges for Ford light trucks. The problem was traced back to the blanking stage. One critical dimension — the distance from the edge of a pierced hole to the edge of the part — was monitored using a control chart. They found that parts variation increased whenever the operator loaded a new coil onto the machine. The solution was an inexpensive gaging block which made loading and positioning the coil a more precise operation.

The significance of Edgewood Tool's use of statistical process control is not so much that they were able to solve a problem, and decrease scrap, rework and inspection, but that they did it by monitoring only one characteristic. They needed only a few trained personnel to achieve results.

A bumper supplier for Ford Motor Company had a similar experience. The supplier used SPC to monitor a plating bath. By determining the capability of the plating bath, and working on one characteristic — bath temperature — they realized a 25 percent energy savings on that part of the process. Once again, a limited application paid off in both real terms, and in an increased awareness of the power of SPC.

Ford, in its efforts to encourage their suppliers to implement SPC, offers these suggestions:

- Start with a pilot program
- Select just a few characteristics
- Train the group involved in statistics
- Adopt gaging for variability
- Document your results
- Create management awareness

One more suggestion is to look into purchasing a hand-held data collector/quality control computer. It will offer a lot of help in collecting data and making statistical sense out of it — areas that newcomers to SPC can have quite a few problems with. But more on the hardware later. First, let's expand on Ford's suggested methodology.

Choosing a Pilot Program

The chief criteria for a pilot program should be its visibility and its potential for success. There is an advantage in selecting a new operation for these reasons. A new operation may also have newer machinery, and people more inclined to do things differently. If an older process is used, select one that needs improvement, and where improvement can be measured. As many variables as possible should be isolated, so that the results of your work will be dramatic.

Select a Few Characteristics

There is a tendency for newcomers to try to monitor as many characteristics as possible. ITT Hancock, a supplier of front door hinges for Ford, had this problem. Their quality control manager and supervisor attended a 5-day seminar on statistics conducted by the Ford Suppliers Institute, and came away determined to implement a program. Their initial approach was to try to control 28 characteristics that contributed to a hinge torque problem. They found that they could make little headway. After 3 months, they cut the number of characteristics to 12 and then to 5 for on-going control.

One of ITT Hancock group's conclusions was, "... an SPC program will generate the earliest results and enthusiastic local support when only few characteristics are selected for a first application." Their tangible gains were a 10 percent reduction of machine downtime, a 15 percent reduction of labor for rework, a 10 percent scrap reduction, and improved relations with Ford. But they also learned a bit about implementing SPC by the experiences of their own operation.

Training in Statistics

Training should include some of the prime decision makers involved in your pilot program. That would normally include the QC manager, production manager and supervisors, and plant manager. Since, according to Dr. Deming, management is responsible for 85 percent of quality problems, upper management training is needed to provide the rationale for change when change is required.

Those directly responsible for the pilot program, including the production engineer, QC auditor, and machine operators, should receive some training also. The training would include how to make and keep control charts, and how to correctly interpret results. This will help eliminate the common pitfalls of making corrective adjustments too soon in a process.

If you are an automotive supplier, excellent training can be obtained through the Ford Suppliers Institute seminars. Unfortunately, most other industries have not developed extensive training resources. Hiring a statistical consultant to help with the program is one solution.

Adopt gaging for Variability

Part of the selection process for the pilot program must involve choosing characteristics that can be measured easily, and to which you can apply statistical techniques. The aim of SPC is to reduce variability, regardless of engineering specifications. This means that gaging and fixturing must be capable of measuring any significant deviation from the nominal. GO/NO-GO gages and other pass-fail types of fixtures will not do.

It is in the accuracy of measurement devices where the power of statistics in identifying problems lives or dies. It is here where you should take advantage of some of the latest measurement technology. Since it is necessary to collect data systematically and render it meaningful with the least amount of error, the best system would be one that ties measuring devices directly to data collection equipment. Gages with readouts still require you to copy down readings. They invite transcription errors and a lot of intermediate paperwork. The ability to handle the data collection dictates to a large extent the number of characteristics you can control. You can imagine how bogged down in paperwork an ambitious SPC program can get.

Document Your Results

The primary document used is the control chart. It takes some training to read them properly, but, once understood, they are what the people who run the process use to get the process in control. Once in control, histograms and capability studies can be used to predict whether design tolerances can be met.

Histograms and capability studies are documents that managers will find valuable. With them you can estimate the percentage of defective parts. How much scrap or rework is expected will determine your inspection load. You can also use the histograms to minimize the cost of production. Presuming that scrap is more costly than rework, cost can be minimized by shifting the mean of your parts distribution away from the scrap end, and accepting just a bit more rework.

Create Management Awareness

The final suggestion is the most important. The selling aspect of SPC pilot programs cannot be overemphasized. You must create management awareness by making a success story. Most companies have plenty of experience with the problem-ridden periods of a process startup. One strong point right off the bat is that SPC is a morale builder. Workers feel that they gain a controlling influence over the process. Most companies using SPC find that the workers become the best advocates of it. That's why the publicity about the program should flow upward to management and to other areas of your company that could use SPC.

A well documented SPC program provides the kind of statistics and charts that managers can understand, and can translate into dollars. Pontiac Division of General Motors, for example, boasts that their implementation of SPC in one plant cut the cost of their engine production by 30 percent in 18 months.

Choosing a System

There are a number of computer-aided SPC systems on the market today. Most require a desktop computer and software to perform analysis. They depend on the manual input of data, which usually makes results slower than you would want. The DataMyte 1500 Stand Alone System solves that problem and provides a turnkey system from start to finish.

What the DataMyte Statistician does is quickly collect and process data, providing control charts, capability studies, and histograms simply by connecting it to a printer. No other equipment is required to generate graphs and reports. One QC auditor can perform both the data collecting and reports generation. The system will also interface with a mainframe computer or a desktop computer such as the IBM PC or Hewlett-Packard Series 200 Model 16 for data storage and more sophisticated analysis.

Such a system can manage your data collecting and do the statistics for you, leaving you free to concentrate on analysis and problem solving. You can build a bit more potential for success into your pilot program. It also provides a systematic approach to data gathering that you can literally carry over to other manufacturing processes.

Conclusions

To repeat, American companies have so far achieved quite a bit of success using SPC. This is in spite of most of them being in their infancy - limited to one or two processes and a small group of people. In many ways, success is assured by this approach, because any negative ramifications will never be more than that involved with the trials of improving a single process.

Using a pilot program makes the learning process easier, and it cuts through the hierarchy of job responsibilities, making production of a part the main goal, and process control a unified endeavor. Using current technology right at the start, and by promoting the success to others in your organization, a pilot program can spearhead the greater usage of SPC, and the revitalization of quality control in your company.

For Further Reference

Crosby, Philip B., *Quality is Free*. New York: Mentor, 1979.

Deming, W. Edwards, *Quality, Productivity, and Competitive Position*. Massachusettes: MIT, Center for Advanced Engineering Study, 1982.

Feigenbaum, Armand V., *Total Quality Control*, 3rd edition. New York: McGraw-Hill Book Company, 1983.

Kume, Hitoshi, "Business Management and Quality Cost: The Japanese View." *Quality Progress*, May 1985.

Schonberger, Richard J., *Japanese Manufacturing Techniques, Nine Hidden Lessons in Simplicity*. New York: The Free Press, 1982.

Taguchi, Genichi, *Introduction to Off-Line Quality Control*. Japan: Central Japan Quality Control Association, 1979.

PART II Applications

NOTE: The applications are listed by industry. To find applications of various gages and measuring devices, consult the index, or the reference notes in Chapter 17.

7. AEROSPACE AND DEFENSE INDUSTRIES

CASE 7-1 AIRCRAFT PARTS MANUFACTURER

Improved System Supplies Statistical Proof of Quality

A major sub-contractor to both commercial and military air frame manufacturers needed a way to increase the amount of data collected on the shop floor while not increasing their current staff size. The subcontractor was required to produce statistical proof of quality for its products.

Problem Definition

The one key area this company was particularly interested in was that of gaps, mismatches and interfaces between components of an assembly. The existing method of collecting data was to have an auditor use a feeler gage or some other dimensional measurement device. The measurement was then recorded on a worksheet, and from there, keypunched into a computer.

This method had some serious drawbacks. The time and labor involved in collecting and handling the data was very extensive. In some instances, because of the physical dimensions of the sub-assembly, it would take two people to collect the data — one to measure and another to record it. Also, this same data had to be handled several times, first by reading and recording, then by keypunching. The risk of transcription errors was too great.

Solution

See Chapter 17 for a description of the 516 gap gage.

To help solve these problems, the company considered a means of automatically collecting data. They chose a DataMyte Statistician and a 516 gap gage. This greatly simplified the data collection process and eliminated the repetitive handling of raw data.

In one instance, where it normally took forty-five minutes to collect measurements, they were able to complete the same operation in less than fifteen minutes. At the conclusion of the collection process, they were able to get immediate statistical summaries on the DataMyte display by connecting it to a printer.

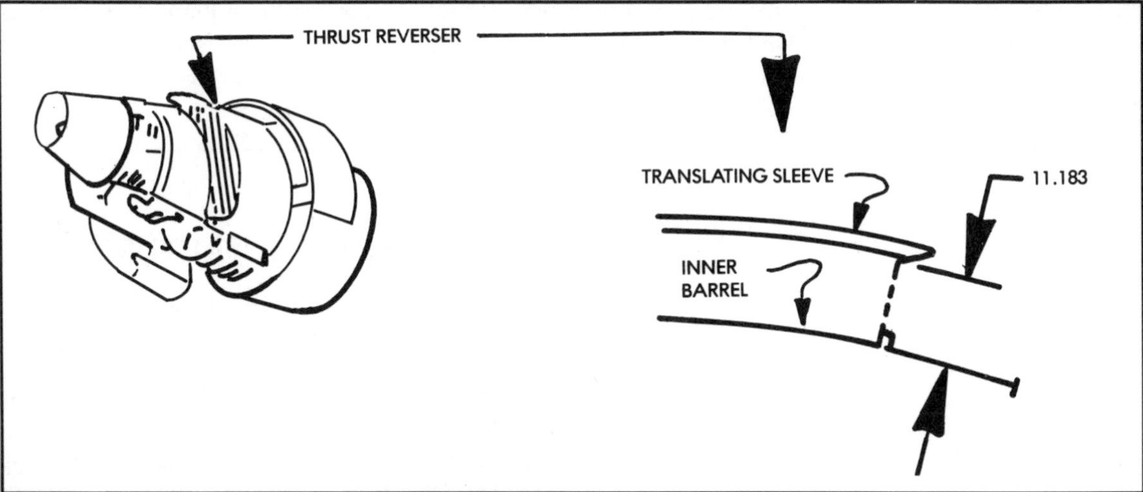

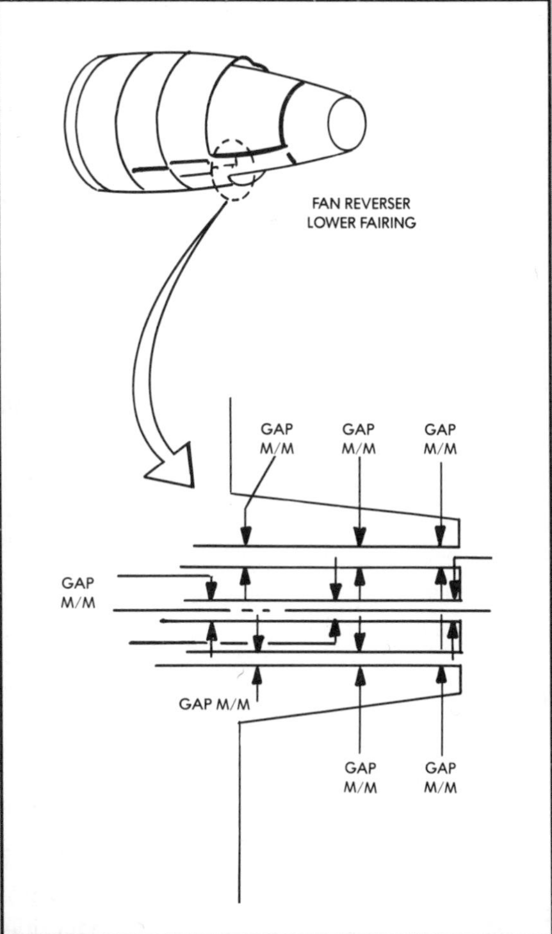

Fig. 7.1.1 Fan reverser exit area.
Fig. 7.1.2 Fan reverser lower fairing.

Operation

What follows is a brief description of how measurements were made using the DataMyte and 516 gap gage. In the fan reverser exit area is a critical gap between the inner barrel and the translating sleeve. (Figure 7.1.1). The 516 gage is required to read a gap of 11.183 $\pm$.200 mm. Having a resolution of 0.05 mm, the gage is able to discriminate measurement within this tolerance. When connected to the DataMyte, the gage sends an analog signal that varies as the gage jaws are separated. The DataMyte samples this signal, and using a peak detection program, records the maximum jaw separation at the moment of measurement.

The fan reverser lower fairing represents a different type of measurement (Figure 7.1.2). Both a gap and mismatch (flushness) reading are required. The flushness end of the tool is opposite the gap fingers. With flushness, the DataMyte will record the maximum travel of the flushness rod and compensate for any offset to obtain the desired range. It can be set up to read either deviation from nominal or the absolute mismatch.

In both of these examples, the engineering limits were preloaded into the DataMyte, along with prompts, the number of items to be measured, and the number of samples to be taken. The engineering limits are used for automatic limit checking during data collection. If a gap or flushness reading is taken that exceeds the tolerance, the DataMyte beeps, thereby alerting the auditor. The prompts are used to guide the auditor from checkpoint to checkpoint, providing the consistency required for critical tolerance checking.

CASE 7-2 AIRCRAFT MANUFACTURER

Improved Methods of Defect Recording Increases Inspection Accuracy, Reduces Bottlenecks

An aircraft manufacturer implemented a method of data collection that was faster and reduced errors. The manufacturer needed data on defects found in the aircraft cockpit area. Manual data collection was too slow, and information was not always recorded in proper format. This also made data processing and reporting slow.

Problem

After a helicopter sub-assembly was completed, the quality auditor inspected it. The inspection data was recorded along with an inspection code, part code, part number, station, operation number, and a description of the quality problem observed.

Their previous data gathering methods had several problems besides being slow. One problem was that a defect description had to be coded in a format that the mainframe computer could analyze. The defect data also had to be downloaded to the mainframe for historical analysis. It was decided that since there were only 50 to 75 descriptive words used to document all defects, if the inspector could be forced to use only the select description words, this could help eliminate errors in the computer system.

Another problem was that errors in inspection reports had to be edited and keypunched back into the system. This slowed the identification of defects and the production of sub-assemblies.

Solution

Descriptive words were chosen for each sub-assembly. The information was coded into bar code labels. A chart of bar codes were produced for each sub-assembly. The chart followed all the sub-assemblies around until completion. A handheld data collector was loaded with the needed information for each sub-assembly. The proper information was loaded from a computer database directly to the data collector. The inspector was then prompted for the required information.

Information was entered using a bar code pen. Information for a prompt was recorded, and then the inspector was prompted for defect information. Only a few select words were needed to describe the defect. This forced the quality inspector to follow a prescribed format.

The major benefits of this program were:

- All information was recorded.
- The errors in recorded data were drastically reduced.
- Descriptions of defects were in a more consistent format.
- Information could be sent directly to the computer for processing.
- Keypunching time was reduced.
- If errors did appear in recorded data, the quality control inspector could use the data collector to edit the data at the assembly site.
- Edited data then could be sent back to the computer file for updating.

The equipment selected for this application was the DataMyte 1005 with bar code. The only other equipment needed was a cable linking the DataMyte to the computer, and a slight modification to existing computer programs.

See Chapter 16 for a description of attributes data collectors.

Time was saved in three major areas:

- Data recording time.
- Proper format followed, less errors.
- Data could be edited in a timely manner.

CASE 7-3 AEROSPACE SUBCONTRACTOR

CNC-Mounted Gaging System Dramatically Reduces Inspection Time

A major aerospace subassembly subcontractor required precise measurements on master models for three-dimensional wing molds. The size of a model was 13 x 26 feet, with up to 26 inches of contour. Measurements had to be taken at 579 points along the master model and deviations from specifications recorded.

Problem

Handwritten methods of measurement and recording took up to 25 hours on a master model. The time directly affected their ability to make corrections to the model. The measurements and deviation analysis process had to be repeated after each series of corrections. A tremendous cost savings, and a more competitive service could be obtained by automating the data collection process.

Because a CNC machine did the work, current data collection methods were slower than the actual machining process. If a data collection system could be adapted which would follow the CNC pattern, this would provide an effective solution.

Solution

The solution was to mount an electronic digital indicator on the CNC machine. The indicator was then connected to a DataMyte 1558 data collector. The CNC machine positioned the indicator and a reading was recorded in the DataMyte.

With this system they were able to collect all the data in six and one-half hours, and have an immediate report detailing all 579 points. This advanced correction time by a full day, a considerable cost savings. The CNC machine was certified before data collection, and rechecked afterward. There was only a 0.0006 inch deviation from nominal.

See Chapter 16 for a description of the 1558 data collector.

The 1558 data collector provides enough storage and data analysis capability for this application as well as for other applications at the company. The unit is also used to measure installed rivet height and flushness and gap measurements between matching component panels.

CASE 7-4 ELECTRONIC DEFENSE SYSTEMS CONTRACTOR

Company Reduces Scrap Costs 10-15 Percent And Improves Government Reporting

A large defense contractor was already documenting their inspection when it saw a need to implement SPC. The company believed that SPC could reduce costs and make them more profitable in the face of increasing cost control pressure. The result of their efforts was a million dollars saved in the past year.

Problem

Although they were collecting the data, their methods were too slow to respond to process changes. The result was an unacceptably high scrap rate in their PC board assembly operation.

When they introduced control charting in the assembly area, it proved ineffective for two reasons:

- The analysis was too slow to do any good.
- The workers didn't keep them current.

The workers obviously had not been "sold" on their value. They found them time-consuming and annoying.

The assembly area had low production volumes of many different types of parts. All of the parts were tracked by part number. The manufacturer had to have some way to keep the jobs separate.

Solution

The quality improvement plan had several key goals:

- Streamline the data collection effort.
- Get analysis in time to prevent scrap.
- Maintain flexibility for short-run low volume production.

The task force did not feel that re-educating workers in SPC would be as effective as simply making it less time-consuming, so that a few auditors could do as much data collection as all the assembly workers.

For their incoming inspection area, where they measured small parts such as metal plates and rivets, they installed a DataMyte 750 fixed station data collector. Using micrometers and calipers, inspectors could record readings at the touch of a button. All of the data was traceable by time, date and part number.

For the assembly area they used handheld data collectors, which could keep track of all the part numbers and instantly produce charts. Data from the data collectors was also archived on an IBM PC running FAN software. Not only was the data available in a single format for government reporting, but the data could be transferred back to the data collectors so the operators could compare the current run to a previous run.

In-process inspection of the PC boards was also streamlined using a DataMyte 769 attributes data collector. Using bar code entry, visual inspection could be made and Pareto diagrams and p-charts produced on the video display terminal.

See Chapter 16 for a description of these data collectors.

Overall, the company estimates it is saving 25% in labor costs using the DataMyte system. Scrap rate was reduced by 10 to 15% because of the shorter time between collecting and analyzing data.

CASE 7-5 AEROSPACE CONTRACTOR

Attribute Data Collection to Meet Military Specifications

A large manufacturer of instruments for aerospace and process industry applications uses precision fabricated and machined metal components in their products. The manufacturer buys some components, but does its own precision machining on proprietary components. The manufacturer builds its electronic assemblies to military workmanship requirements. Most new military programs require the parts to be built to specification WS6536 Rev E. The specification includes extensive data collection on all electrical and electronic assemblies involving soldering.

Problem

The manufacturer had to conduct 100% visual inspection of all soldered connections and assemblies. Any defects found had to be documented and recorded for future reference. The manufacturer had to calculate defect rates for the printed wiring assemblies (PWA), a percentage of defects for each PWA and a daily rate of defects. This required individual records for each PWA as well as a summary of daily production.

The manufacturer had divided the defects into three types: printed wiring board (PWB), component and part, and solder joint. The manufacturer divided the defective parts into two groups: rework and repair. From the different types of categories and two groups, the manufacturer had 77 total defects.

Solution

The company purchased DataMyte Model 769 data collectors to help collect data. The 769 data collector has a bar

DATA COLLECTION SHEETS FOR WS 6536 DATA
DATE -- 01/14/87

INSPECTOR

ASSEMBLY NO.

ASSEMBLY NORM NO

SOLDER NORM NO.

JOB NO.

SERIAL NO.

ATTRIBUTES

A02.1	A11.1	A14.1
A16.1	B17.1	B22.1
B23.1	B25.2	B30.2
B36.1	B55.1	C57.1
C60.1	C64.2	C77.2

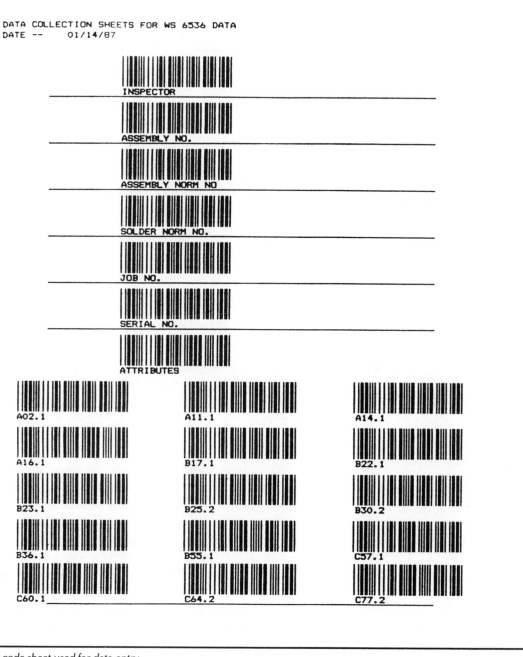

Fig. 7.5.1 Bar code sheet used for data entry.

code wand for bar code entry, which makes data entry faster than typing it into a computer. Figure 7.5.1 is an example of bar code sheet used for data entry. The manufacturer liked the ability of the 769 to sort data by defect type, by product type, by date or by any other characteristic of the data collected. This allowed the company to look at the data that affected its processes the most.

The 769 displays its charts on a video monitor, which gives operators immediate feedback on the quality of parts they are building. Transfer of data to a computer is done with the DataMyte 769 Software program. The data can then be presented to government inspectors, to satisfy the requirements of specification WS6536 Rev E. From the computer, the data can be used in a spreadsheet or data base program.

See Chapter 16 for a description of attributes data collectors.

Because of the quantity of data the company had to collect, the DataMyte 769 paid for itself within a few months.

CASE 7-6 MISSILE PARTS MANUFACTURER

Company Gets 20 Percent Productivity Improvement While Controlling Scrap

A missile parts manufacturer automated the tracking of trends on a low volume job and provided more time for their operators to do machine maintenance and adjustment.

Problem

The Department of Defense required the company to document 25 critical dimensions on each missile part. Although each machine operator produced only one or two parts per hour, there was still not enough time to take measurements and properly analyze the process.

Fifteen of the less critical dimensions were checked with go/no go gages. The ten most critical dimensions were measured by hand and the operators plotted control charts. The documentation effort overall was costing them 30 percent in reduced production. In addition, each scrapped part cost $900 - 1200.

Solution

Because of the small sample size, $\bar{x}$ & R charts would not be sensitive to process changes. The plant elected to use moving average and range charts.

DataMyte 862 data collectors were set up for moving average and range charts, and programmed with the following trend rules:

See Chapter 16 for a description of the 862 data collector.

- 1 point out of 3 sigma
- 2 consecutive points between 2 & 3 sigma
- 7 points up or down
- 7 points above or below the mean

If an operation was out of control for any of these reasons, the DataMyte would beep and display a warning. The operator would then have to enter a code into the DataMyte describing the change he made to the process.

Operators now had time to decide if a new tool or machine adjustment was required. The operator also knew when he had to involve an area supervisor.

Overall, the use of this system reduced documentation time from 30% of each hour in production down to 10%. The system also helped predict tool life, and reduced the incidence of scrap.

CASE 7-7 DEFENSE MANUFACTURER

Low Tolerance Measurements Require Control Charting and Histograms

A manufacturer of several different types of casings used for bullets and other defense related items was experiencing a significant increase in the number of pieces being scrapped. Since scrap costs are a critical factor in determining the winner of a defense contract, this manufacturer needed to improve their statistical quality control program.

Problem Definition

During the prodution of minute metal casings, conventional methods such as manual gaging and charting were being used to monitor case length and diameter. The results from these observations clearly indicated that a significant increase of piece scrapping had occurred. While these conventional methods indicated a serious problem existed, they were not able to pinpoint the causes for the problem. This was due in large part to the vast amount of data that required manual processing.

Solution

The first step was to decrease data turn-around time. By generating reports sooner, they felt they could reduce the time it took to remedy assignable causes of variation. This could be done by:

- Automating the data collection process.
- Eliminating manual charting of the statistical data.
- Monitoring several phases of the production process, not just the "finished product."

Based on their analysis they chose a DataMyte 1508 data collector, a micrometer, and a caliper. In this arrangement, the DataMyte would provide a data collection capability that could be used to generate all necessary charts and capability reports. The caliper and micrometer provided automatic data capture.

See Chapter 16 for a description of hand-held data collectors.

Areas of the process that were to be monitored included the case length, case diameter, and metal thickness. The caliper was used for measuring the case length and diameter, and the micrometer for metal thickness.

Within a short time, a large percentage of the scrap costs were eliminated and rework time was decreased by nearly one-half. Benefits realized by using the DataMyte 1508 included:

- No requirements for an increase in manpower. The manufacturer's inspectors already responsible for manual data collection could easily handle all data collection activities.
- There was a substantial reduction in the time required for processing data for reports and charts.
- Personnel freed from the task of manual charting of data were able to become more actively involved in the problem-solving processes that could lead to further reductions in scrap and rework.

Operation

The information that follows provides an overall description of how the DataMyte 1508 was used by the manufacturer. The first step taken was to perform a capability study for all three areas of measurement. According to specifications, the three areas should be as follows (Figure 7.7.1):

- Case length: .615 inches (±0.005 inches)
- Case diameter: .225 inches (±0.005 inches)
- Metal thickness: 0.09 inches (±0.015 inches)

Once the setup information was entered, the operator entered the Data Collect mode and the matrix was filled with the data collected by the inspector. After taking the samples on 75 cases, a capability report was generated for each item. See

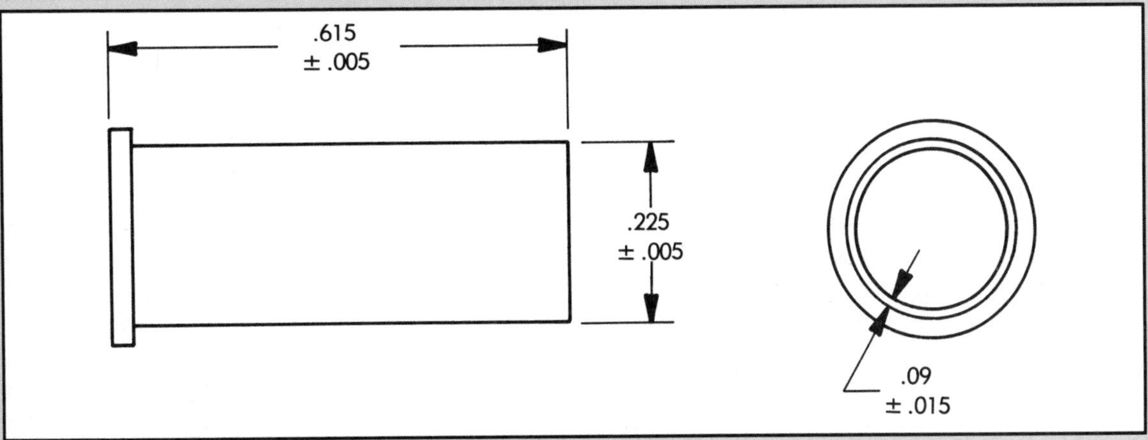

Fig. 7.7.1 Example of bullet casing.

Figure 7.7.2. The 3-sigma tolerances for each item was discovered to be within the specification limits, and therefore the process was considered in control. However, this did not reflect why the increase in scrap costs was occurring. Since it was determined that the process was "in control," it was clear that an $\bar{x}$ & R chart method could be used to indicate trends; hopefully depicting when the process changed from a point of "in control" to "out of control." At that point an asssignable cause of variation could be noted, remedied, and the increased scrap costs minimized.

The capability matrix was kept intact (in the event a study was necessary at a later date). A new matrix to be used for $\bar{x}$ & R charting was then created.

Upon entering the Data Collect mode of operation, the part number was entered for the matrix ID, the date entered, the operator's name or employee number entered. The notes contained in-

Fig. 7.7.2 Capability report.

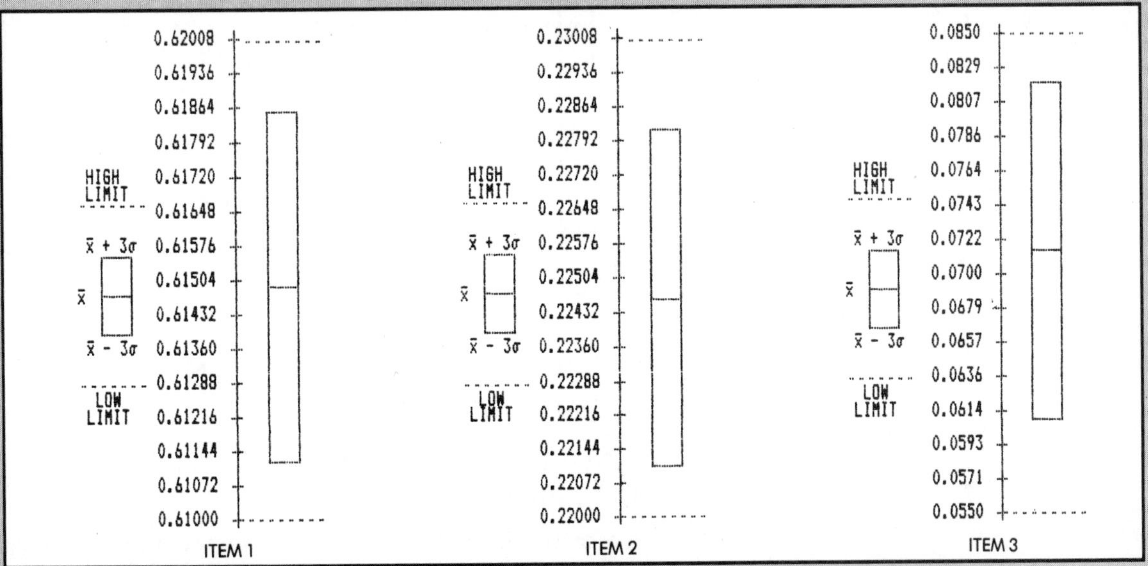

formation depicting the shift number, machine number, and lunch time for that particular shift.

The lunch time was an important factor. It was thought that machine "down time" during this period could lead to an assignable cause of variation. During this period, the machine was shut off to conserve energy. The sample sets of five were taken once an hour and a chart was generated once a day at the end of the second shift.

The first chart was printed after the first shift on the second day; thus, having 24 points of $\bar{x}$ & R chart data (Figure 7.7.3). At that point, the older data would be replaced once the 30 point limit had been reached; all charts from that point would contain the 30 most recent points of history.

A histogram was printed once a day to allow the operator to see the process dispersion. See Figure 7.7.4. These histograms were printed at random intervals. They were not used to indicate trends, but to visually indicate to the operator how closely those measurements were resembling a normal bell curve of distribution. Any time a trend was noted on the $\bar{x}$ and R charts, histograms would be used to depict the data graphically; thus providing another look at the dispersion.

With this concept of $\bar{x}$ & R charting, along with the periodic histograms, the process variation was maintained at a minimum. Trends could be identified almost immediately, and assignable causes of variation identified sooner. The end result was that the amount of scrap was significantly reduced. It should be noted that a minimum of manpower was needed to perform all of the statistical data collection.

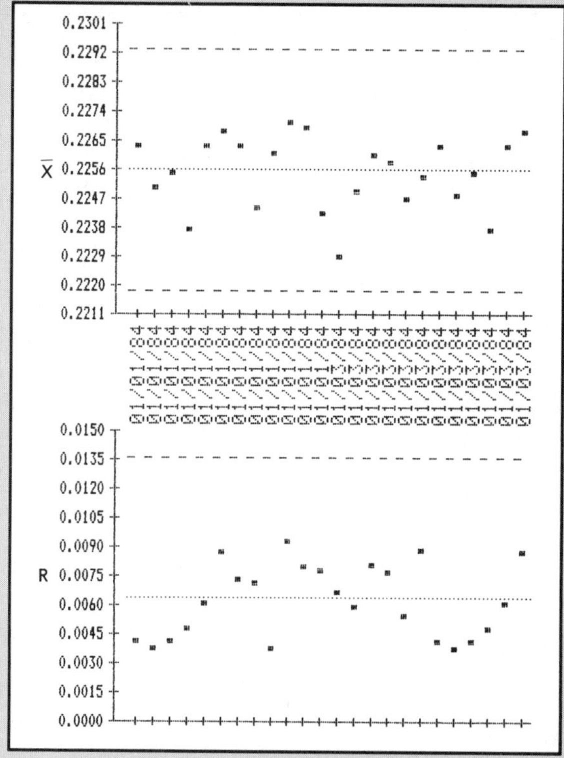

Fig. 7.7.3 x & R Chart

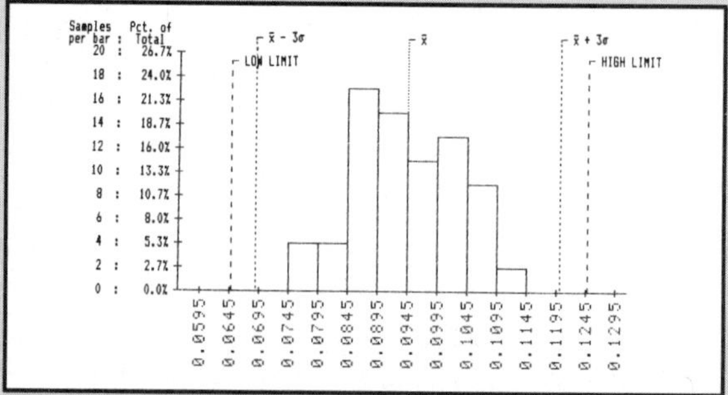

Fig. 7.7.4 Histogram

CASE 7-8 MAJOR GOVERNMENT SUBCONTRACTOR

Inspection Department Joins Apollo Work Station Network, Improves Response Time

A major defense subcontractor selected the DataMyte system to control manufacturing processes. By linking the

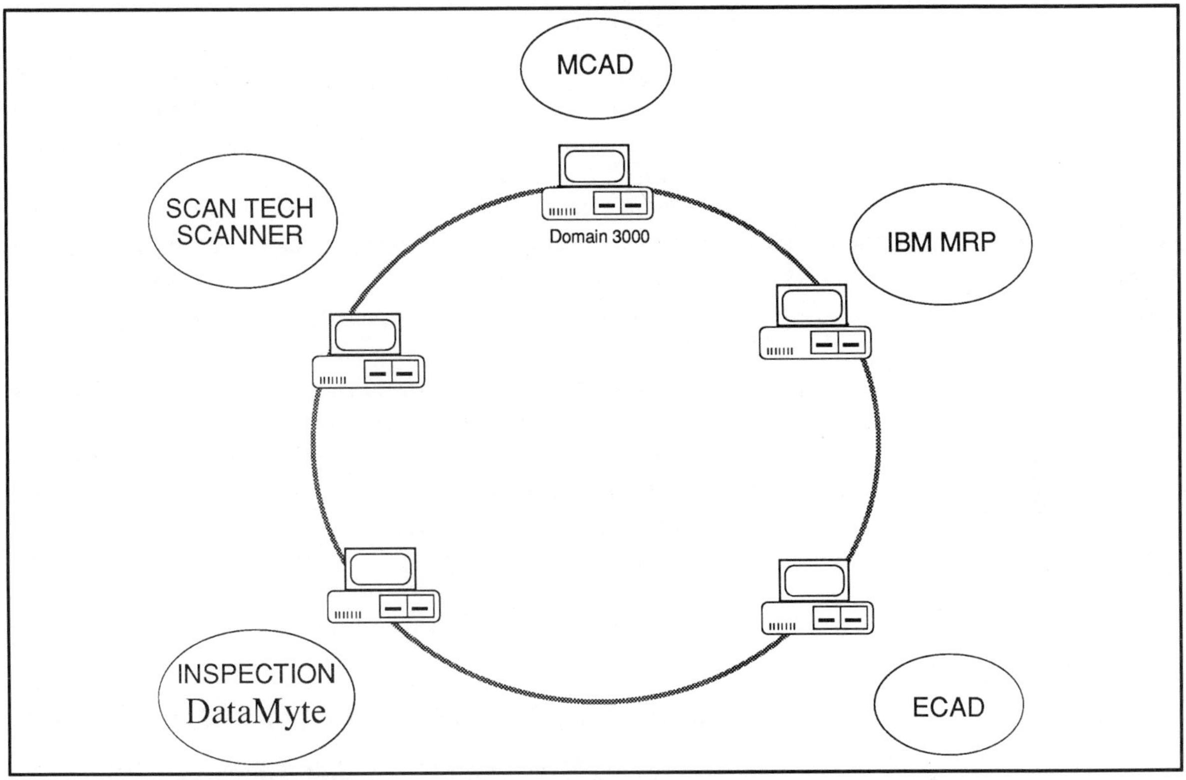

Fig. 7.8.1 Apollo network configuration.

DataMyte system to their Apollo multi-tasking personal work stations, they dramatically improved response time and reduced scrap rework.

Problem

This company was looking towards the factory of the future in manufacturing information systems. The goal was to produce a true paper-free environment shared by quality control, manufacturing, engineering, and administration.

The company selected the Apollo DOMAIN System network as its principal architecture. See Figure 7.8.1 Each Domain workstation is a node on a ring, serving as gateways to an IBM mainframe running an MRP program, mechanical drafting, computer aided design, a scanner for supplier documentation, and other manufacturing data bases.

The biggest problem with the new system was that quality control engineers were still required to manually record data which had to be keypunched later into the Apollo network.

See Chapter 22 for a description of the Apollo System.

Solution

As part of a joint effort with Apollo, DataMyte provided a system to automate the quality control inspection process and provide an interface to Apollo work station (Figure 7.8.1).

See Chapter 18 for a description of FAN software.

DataMyte FAN software was installed on an Apollo DOMAIN 3000 work station, which had an IBM PC compatible co-processor option. Data from individual DataMyte data collectors could then be uploaded into FAN software and made available to anyone on the network.

Although the initial objective was to automate the data collection task, it was quickly discovered that DataMytes used for on-line operator-based process monitoring allowed rapid analysis of the data and reduced the response time for correction action.

Scrap and rework was reduced substantially. In fact, payback calculations presented to upper management revealed a ten month return on a $150,000 investment.

CASE 7-9 MUNITIONS COMPANY

Company Uses Data Collection Systems for Highly Secretive Manufacturing Documentation

A privately run operation for the Department of Energy manufactures cruise missile fuses. The company is subject to all the intense security restrictions around a munitions manufacturer. It has been required by new military specifications to provide SPC data ensuring the quality of these high precision component parts. Due to the defense nature of the product, the highest possible quality must be maintained to ensure workability in the war environment.

Problem

The major problem being experienced by this company was in the method of data collection, and in the error rate experienced in their data collection. The company is a highly secretive operation, in which outsiders are not allowed anywhere near the manufacturing areas.

The major reason for their interest in automated data collection was in the reduction of error rate, and the reduction of time consumed in SPC data collection. The high precision parts that they manufacture run in very small dimensional checks. These checks require special gaging and use of such things as column gages to allow precise measurements on all of their close tolerances.

The customer has been taking these readings manually and utilizing tally sheets to control the information flow. However they found that the error rate in a manual data collection system was in excess of 18%, which is way above their goals for quality product. Therefore, the data was erroneous enough to be almost ineffective in their uses. The data also would not at that point match the military specifications they had for quality.

Solution

The customer evaluated types of data collectors for several years. They chose the DataMyte 750 family, 2003, and 769 for applications within their operations due to the ease of use and capabilities of the units. DataMyte helped the company design specialized systems with special gages for each of the applications according to drawings that they supplied.

See Chapter 16 for a description of data collectors.

The majority of the fixed station applications used DataMyte 762 data collectors with multiple types of gaging interfaces, and DataMyte 769 data collectors for attribute fixed station data collection. In addition, 2003 units were utilized as auditing fixtures for the floor inspectors to ensure that data received was within specifications.

The company signed a licensing agreement for DataMyte FAN II software which allowed them to store and analyze data.

One of the major problems with military auditing procedures is that the military will not check any data for long periods of time, and then will require data that may be six or seven months out of date. One of the major software features for the company was the fact that you can specify starting and ending dates for data retrieval, which allows them to provide the charting immediately for analysis by GAO inspectors.

CASE 7-10 MUNITIONS MANUFACTURER

Company Automates Data Collection to Meet U.S. Government SPC Contractual Requirements Included With MIL-Q 9858A

A munitions manufacturer needed to monitor eleven critical dimensions involved in the production of grenades.

Problem

The contract required SPC data on the total production run of over 25,000,000 pieces. Without finding an economical approach to this challenge the company could possibly lose the contract.

Solution

See Chapter 16 for a description of the 761 data collector.

Special analog gaging was used to send data automatically to a DataMyte 761 data collector. Gage stations were developed and placed in three strategic locations on the factory floor. This enabled one inspector per shift to harvest the parts on a periodic basis and collect the needed data.

Each critical dimension could be individually monitored on the video display terminal. The graphs generated allowed for rapid interpretation of trend analysis information so potential problems could be anticipated before the occurrence.

The data was then transferred to an IBM PC for archiving and easy retrieval. The additional feature of the date and time stamping of the data collected especially impressed the auditing group. Due to tremendous numbers involved it was obvious this challenge could never have been met economically and competitively without automated data collection.

As a result, this contract was satisfied and the government is offering additional business to this supplier.

CASE 7-11 HELICOPTER COMPANY

Company Uses SPS Sensor I Torque Wrench to Solve Graphite Composite Material Assembly Problems

On graphite composite material components used for helicopter blades, a major aircraft manufacturer was experiencing assembly problems where these parts were bolted together.

Problem

Graphite composite parts were being crushed and their reliability being put into dispute when tightening bolts through them under conventional torque control.

This was leading to a high rejection level of very expensive parts.

Solution

The SPS Sensor I Wrench was used to tighten the bolts to torque while in the JCS mode. If a yield of the joint was detected before the required torque value was reached the operator stopped, knowing if he went further he would destroy the components. This resulted in a considerable component cost saving. By tying the wrench to the DataMyte 2003 data collector, the company stored the torque data along with serial number, time and date, making documentation easier.

See Chapter 17 for the SPS Sensor I Wrench.

8. AUTOMOTIVE SUPPLIERS

CASE 8-1 SMALL ENGINE MANUFACTURER

Corporate-Wide Quality Commitment Spurs Many Applications For Automated SPC

A large manufacturer, primarily known for its small engines, has improved its ability to use SPC by installing new systems for measurement and data analysis. Although the company is family-owned and thought of as rather conservative, more innovative methods were being advanced for the following reasons:

- Their existing SPC program depended on handwritten methods for data gathering and record keeping. These methods could not cope with the volume of data.
- Several of their customers were demanding better documentation of their SPC efforts.
- Searching for improved methods was always part of their corporate commitment to quality.

Problem

The company had metalworking applications in their foundry, key and fastener plant, engine assembly plant and die casting plants. They were interested in a system for SPC that had these characteristics:

- The system would collect and process data faster and more accurately than handwritten methods.
- At the user level, it must be adaptable to a variety of gaging and fixturing needs.
- At the system level, it must have a great deal of uniformity and upward compatibility.

The company realized that there may not be a single supplier that could help implement all the SPC applications. Many applications required in-line gages and automatic triggering of the data collection system. Other applications required full operator involvement in measurement and data analysis.

Solution

Because of the volume of engines and parts being produced by the company, and the massive amount of data required to perform SPC, the company purchased a DataMyte FAN® (Factory Area Network), knowing the system could pay for itself in less than six months in labor savings alone. Being completely modular, the FAN® system could be used in a great variety of individual applications (see *Operation*), and be expanded to handle a virtually unlimited amount of data. The system also provided complete analytical capability at the operator level, where day to day quality problems were expected to be solved.

See Chapter 15 for a description of the FAN system.

The FAN® system consisted of DataMyte 750 data collectors at machining and assembly stations, a DataTruck® to harvest accumulated data, DataMyte 2000s, 1500s and 1000s for roving auditors checking both variables and attributes data, and software for their IBM PC computers.

Operation

What follows are descriptions of several gaging applications used at the company to collect data for SPC.

Foundry — DataMyte 750s are used with digital indicators to measure critical dimensions on flywheels. Six dimensions, including overall thickness, and height from the vein down certain key position slots, were all previously checked by hand. Using a 750 and a multiplexer for Fowler Ultra-Digit indicators, all six dimensions can be measured and recorded in one 750. Control charts for each characteristic are displayed on a monitor with the press of a button.

Key and fastener plant — The plant that produces raw keys (without individual grooves) for automobiles needed a faster method of maintaining process control. Two thousand keys were produced each hour. A fixture which resembled a steering wheel lock is used to measure overall length, thickness and fit. Two Federal Maxum dial indicators attached to the fixture were used to display the measurements, but the gages had to be read and the data recorded by hand. See Figure 8.1.1.

A DataMyte model 754 was interfaced directly to the Maxum gages, so that readings on the gage are recorded with the press of a button. The DataMyte compares each reading to specifications and beeps audibly if any reading is out of specification. Control charts are displayed on a monitor, so an immediate indication of the statistical state of the process is available. Readings are now easier to record, and therefore the operators are able to maintain a sampling rate more in keeping with the speed of the process.

The tap-ream-grinding operation at the plant required a completely automated approach to data collection. Ten unmanned machining centers each had a carousel-type part handling system. See Figure 8.1.2. The carousel would bring a part to each of the eight stations, were it would be drilled, shaped, redrilled, a keyway cut, and finally put into a test fixture. The test fixture had several LVDT indicators, which would come down on the part at the same time and display readings on ten column gages. A DataMyte model 751 uses its auto-scan feature to input each of the ten column gage readings in sequence. The process can then be monitored by displaying histograms and control charts for each dimension on the CRT monitor. Accumulated readings are unloaded from the 751 into a DataTruck and then transmitted to an IBM PC for archiving and long term analysis.

For incoming inspection, DataMyte 2000 data collectors are used with calipers and micrometers. Auditors check bins of small parts, such as fasteners, springs and bar stock. Individual parts are compared to specs, and a histogram is printed out to

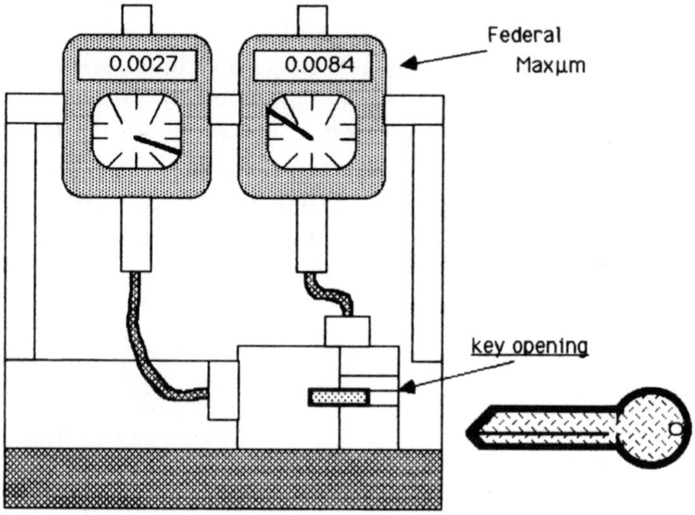

Fig. 8.1.1 DataMyte used with key checking fixture.

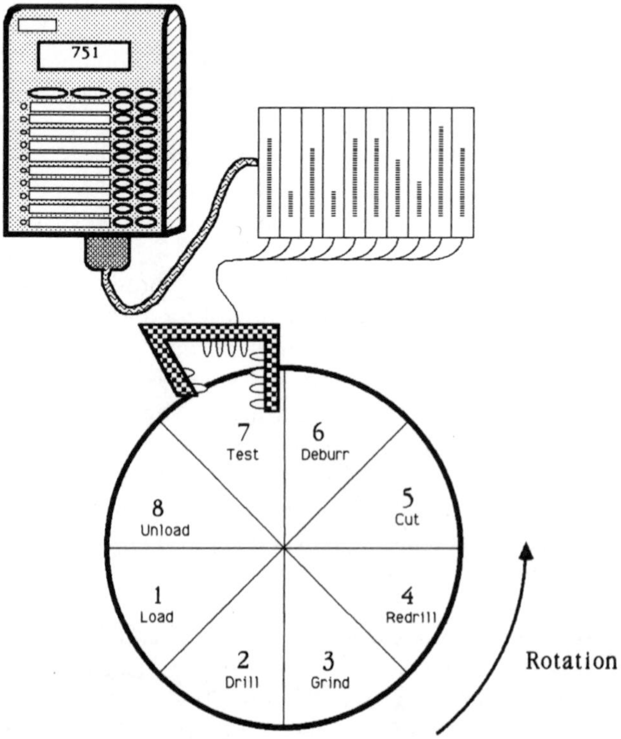

Fig. 8.1.2 Automatic machining fixture, including an operatorless checking station.

judge the acceptability of a lot. The DataMyte 2000 is also used by a roving auditor to check parts coming off low volume processes.

Engine plant — DataMyte 1500s and 753s are used to audit fastener torque at the engine assembly plant. A DataMyte 1500 is used by a roving auditor to check breakaway torque on the assembly line, using a handheld wrench. A DataMyte 753 is tied in-line with a nut runner. Each nut runner has a torque transducer mounted in-line with its spindle. The transducer is then tied to a 753 which uses its counting feature to record every tenth reading while fasteners are being tightened down.

DataMyte 751s are used in the machining area of the assembly plant to check variability in milling and boring operations in their crankshaft, piston rod and camshaft lines. Both two-cycle and four-cycle engines are manufactured and assembled at the plant, and the DataMytes allow instant recognition of problems on the continuous high volume processes.

Die casting plants — The company's two die casting plants are using DataMyte 2000s for rough overall measurements. The DataMytes allow them to measure dimensions as well as process variables such as pressure and temperature. A contact temperature probe is used to check mold cavity temperature, and they are realizing a tremendous savings in scrap by controlling just this aspect of the process.

CASE 8-2 AUTO STEERING GEARS

Company Integrates Data Collectors With Programmable Controllers in Flexible Machining Cell

A major supplier of automotive steering gear mechanisms needed a highly integrated manufacturing process to reduce labor costs and improve quality. By setting up a closed loop system, using in-line gaging, data collection and statistical feedback to their cell controllers, the company became the highest quality, lowest cost supplier.

Problem

A highly regarded supplier to the major auto makers and a leader in automation techniques needed to improve both quality and productivity. The objective of the company project was to produce the highest quality steering gear at the lowest possible cost. This would require incredibly high volume processing, the use of statistical process control, and minimal labor.

Solution

The company set out to design a turnkey, totally automated manufacturing cell. They used both Marposs and Sylvac in-line measuring devices to gage the process. These gages were connected to DataMyte model 762 data collectors.

See Chapter 16 for a description of the 762 data collector.

Using a skip counting feature, the data collector would skip a set number of readings, record five, skip some, and record five more. This provided the statistical sampling scheme. The data collector automatically calculated average and ranges and displayed $\bar{x}$ & R charts on a video display terminal.

At the same time, the data was automatically transmitted from the data collector to a programmable controller. The PLC was used to make corrective action on process parameters. Because statistical analysis was being used, overcorrection problems were avoided.

A simple ladder logic program was written for the PLC to interpret and make corrections based on the statistical sampling.

The benefits gained integrating data collection with closed loop control were enormous. It provided instantaneous response to out of control trends, and became a key part of a start-of-the-art cell that helps retain the company's favorable position as an automotive supplier.

CASE 8-3 PISTON MANUFACTURER

New SPC Charting Methods Create Time Savings and Operator Enthusiasm

A large piston manufacturer had each operator running two different machine tools, and a need for statistical process control. To keep productivity up and to ensure quality at the same time, the company adopted automated gaging and control charting.

Problem

Handwritten methods of control charting were not keeping up with production demands or the need to recognize process changes and take corrective action. Each operator had to measure three or four characteristics on pistons at regular intervals. With two machines to maintain, the operators could not effectively do SPC.

Solution

The company investigated the possibility of automating SPC by installing a single DataMyte 751 at a work station.

The data collector interfaced with a cradle gage through Series E column gages. The operator did their measurement checks, only now the data was logged automatically. A control chart was displayed on the video display terminal at the press of a button.

The operator response was immediately positive. They got the impression that management believed enough in SPC to supply a system for them to do it more effectively. Management also found that a quick look at the video display kept them in touch with what was going on.

See Chapter 16 for data collectors and Chapter 17 for column gages.

The company has since implemented the system at 25 gaging stations. The result has been better control of the processes, more quality characteristics could be monitored, and documentation that they could supply to their customers.

CASE 8-4 METAL FABRICATING SHOP

Data Collection System Saves 15 - 18 Minutes Per Hour At Each Machine

A medium size metal fabricating shop specializing in stamped parts for the automotive industry wished to find a rapid way to implement SPC at the machine level.

The company wanted operator involvement to the extent that operators must be able to view and interpret control charts so trends could be spotted. Being able to spot individual in or out of control points was not sufficient. Control charts could also identify poor setup procedures and excessive tool wear.

Problem

Hand calculated control charts were drastically lowering productivity. Operators were becoming discouraged with the time and arithmetic involved. A method for automating data collection and control charting had to be implemented.

A system had to meet certain plant criteria:

- Factory hardened to withstand mist of oil
- Multiple gage inputs
- Easy to use
- Low cost

- Able to interface with either a personal computer or mainframe

Solution

A DataMyte FAN® system was purchased and placed at all presses. Operators could now pick up a part and record three to five dimensions automatically by pressing a button on a caliper, micrometer or dial indicator. Data was recorded in one minute rather than two and a half minutes the old way. Overall, the DataMyte system saved 15 to 18 minutes per hour at each station, counting the time saved for recording five characteristics and entering the data into a calculator to get summaries. Operators knew immediately after measuring how each dimension was set up and whether a change was necessary.

See Chapter 15 for a description of the FAN system.

The DataTruck was used to harvest data periodically from each 750 in the shop. The data was then transmitted to a computer for longterm storage. This eliminated the need for cabinets full of two and three year old control charts, since their customers requested they retain full documentation.

After transmitting the previous day's data, each DataMyte 750 could then be reprogrammed by the computer or DataTruck for a new job or part number. Workers were very pleased with the system and felt it had enhanced their jobs while giving them time to control their own process. After six months, scrap rates fell and dollars were saved.

CASE 8-5 TIRE COMPANY

Tire Tread Width Monitored

A tire manufacturer needed to control the width of tread in a cutting application. They needed to automate the entire operation, including the actual cutting, measurement of the tread width, collection of data, and report generation.

Problem

Handwritten data collection and computation did not work. By the time operators got the results, they already produced a lot of bad products which had to be scrapped. Operators were over-adjusting the cutting operation because valid statistical evidence was not available in time.

Solution

The solution was to automatically measure tread width by mounting a laser micrometer behind the slicing blades. This accurately measured the product on the fly. They then interfaced a DataMyte 750 to the RS-232C port on the laser micrometer which sends a dimensional reading to the 750 every few seconds. The data is captured and stored by the 750 in subgroups. By using a CRT connected to the DataMyte, the operator can view a continuously updated $\bar{x}$ & R chart, and make adjustments to the process as required. If the chart did not indicate a problem, the process was left to run.

See Chapter 16 on data collectors and Chapter 17 for laser micrometers.

All the data from the laser micrometer was stored in the DataMyte's memory. The quality manager could then come to the machine, connect a DataTruck to the 750, transfer all of the new information that was collected, and take the DataTruck back to his IBM PC. He could then transfer the data to the PC, merge it with existing data files, and generate ongoing management reports.

CASE 8-6 SPARK PLUG MANUFACTURER

Use of Resistance Transducer and DataMyte Reduces Variability

A world leader in the manufacturer of spark plugs had determined that traditional methods for checking resistance during the manufacture of resistor spark plugs were not effective. Spark plugs are an integral part of any gasoline engine. If a plug does not fire, the cylinder in question goes through 720 degrees of wasted movement. Much depended on the high quality of this company's product.

Problem Definition

In the past, spark plugs produced by this manufacturer had exhibited a relatively high level of variability in resistance. In fact, it was estimated that 1% of production was being rejected as unsuitable due to resistance values that were out of specification. The problem was due in large part to the process used to determine the resistance of a resistor spark plug; this process involved the formation of a resistor within the plug. During the process, a special powder was carefully dropped into the ceramic shell that is the insulator for the plug. This powder was then fused under pressure and at high temperature to form the resistor. For the process to be effective, it was necessary for the powder to be dropped, tamped (compacted), and heated. Furthermore, all steps of the process required a high degree of accuracy and repeatability.

For several years the process was monitored by traditional methods; that is, by measuring the resistance of the completed plug with a multimeter. Essentially, all that was being done was a simple "GO" or "NO GO" evaluation. (Either the plug was good or it wasn't.) The data accumulated during this process did little to indicate the capability of the process or if it was being operated in a consistant manner.

To compound the problem, it was known that if the resistance couldn't be maintained within a range of from 2,500 to 12,000 ohms, radio and TV interference as well as ignition problems could occur when the plugs were used in an engine.

Solution

The manufacturer had defined the known problems and areas of concern, and began to investigate the best way to implement improvements. Several solutions were considered, ranging from acquiring new production equipment to performing 100% inspection. Cost for these choices were prohibitive, however. They determined that prerequisites for the overall program must include:

- A method that did not require the need for new production equipment or additional manpower.
- Equipment that was portable.
- Equipment that could interface with existing computing equipment and peripherals such as printers.
- Equipment that would allow all necessary $\bar{x}$ & R charts and capability reports to be generated on an "as needed" basis.

Based on their analysis, they decided to use a DataMyte 1506 handheld data collector connected to a specially developed resistance transducer. This equipment arrangement provided a data collection and analysis capability that was portable, user friendly, and could be used to produce all necessary charts.

Once the equipment was installed, the manufacturer's quality control personnel used the special transducer to measure and record the resistances of the production spark plugs. Data was fed directly into the DataMyte 1506 for analysis. From the DataMyte, the data could in turn be fed into the computing system for further analysis or dumped to a printer. When the data was plotted on $\bar{x}$ & R charts, the magnitude and source of any variation in resistance was identified.

See Chapter 16 for a description of the 1506 data collector.

The first control charts generated indicated that the resistance powder dropping process was out of statistical control. Analysis of the process indicated that the mechanism controlling the flow of resistance powder was operating in an inconsistant manner. Further, it was found to have a great deal of variability in the volume of powder deposited over a relatively short interval of time. Once the problem had been isolated using the DataMyte, changes were implemented in the dropping mechanism to reduce the variability.

Operation

The information that follows provides a brief description of how the DataMyte 1506 with transducer were used by the spark plug manufacturer. Early on, because of the relatively simple operation of the DataMyte, it was felt that the best way to implement an SQC program in the firing furnace area was to involve the operators themselves. They had the ability to measure and record the resistance data and they were in the best position to be able to take action on their results. To facilitate the collection of data, the furnace operators took production samples to a centrally located SQC area, where a resistance checking fixture was located. Each operator followed a simple procedure for recording the resistance measurements.

The fusing furnace's line number was used as the matrix number in the DataMyte. During production, the plugs were set in furnace racks of 60 plugs (122 rows by five deep). The matrix was therefore set up in a 12 item by five item sample matrix. The operators generally took a tray of 60 plugs once or twice each hour over to the SQC area, where they used the DataMyte and transducer to measure and record the resistance of the samples. Several times a day, the DataMyte was connected to a printer and the $\bar{x}$ & R charts for each resistance station were plotted.

Within several weeks of the start of the program, all the operators were taking sample measurements and recording the resistance of their production. $\bar{x}$ & R charts became routinely used.

CASE 8-7 GLASS MANUFACTURER

Current Automobile Designs Demand Tighter Tolerances

A large manufacturer of glass used in automobiles needed to maintain closer tolerances. Tolerances became a concern when the automobile industry, using more sophisticated design methods, began to measure the drag coefficient of cars. A significant increase in scrap and rework had resulted in their attempts to produce higher quality windshields and by using conventional quality control equipment.

Problem

The problem had to do specifically with holding tolerance with off-form measurement of curved glass. A 0.200 tolerance was no longer sufficient, and the auto maker had eliminated the large windshield moldings to reduce drag. Their current procedures could not maintain the tolerance because of the variables involved in the glass bending process. The glass forming process required precise controls over humidity, line speed, and quench time (first stage of cooling). The bending bar can remain in contact with the glass for only a certain amount of time. Vacuum can only be applied for a certain time period also. If a piece of glass explodes during quenching, the next several pieces could become scrap because of broken glass on the conveyor belt system.

Lack of control was compounded by the fact that little statistical analysis was performed on raw data being collected. This was simply a result of the limitation of the inspection equipment being used and the fact that not enough personnel were available to manually collect and analyze data.

Solution

A group of management personnel was organized to evaluate the needs of the process control system. Several conclusions were reached about data collection needs:

Little or no variability due to measurement devices, or to

differences in methods from inspector to inspector, could be tolerated.

- The data collection system must be easy to use. Training must be kept to a minimum.
- Statistical information must be available immediately to the inspectors.

The solution seemed to lie in a combination of automatic data collection, precise gaging and fixturing. They chose a DataMyte 1506 handheld data collector because it could interface with a gap gage for data collection, and then be connected to their computer to produce capability graphs and control charts. The 516 gap gage was selected because it was precise enough for their measurement needs, and could be modified easily to work with a new fixture design.

See Chapter 16 for data collectors and Chapter 17 for the gap gage.

The modification of the gap gage was the first step. A local machine shop was contracted to modify the gage fingers with a positive locating pin that would fit in a glass checking fixture. Figure 8.7.1 shows the positive pin locators and the SQC analysis system.

The checking fixtures were then designed with slots at the measurement points for the gage locating pin. Operator variability was virtually eliminated with this scheme because the gage mated positively with the fixture. As long as the glass was fixed in position in the fixture with no variation in positioning, the gage measurements would reflect the variability of the glass alone.

The DataMyte could also be programmed with prompt messages, indicating the check point location, and specification limits to instantly alert the operator to bad pieces. This further increased the validity of the data.

By using automatic data collection and well designed fixturing, statistically meaningful data could be obtained. The positive locating pins had reduced operator variability and increased the ease of measurement. This eliminated the need for an extensive operator variability study, and allowed the inspectors to concentrate fully on data gathering and process control.

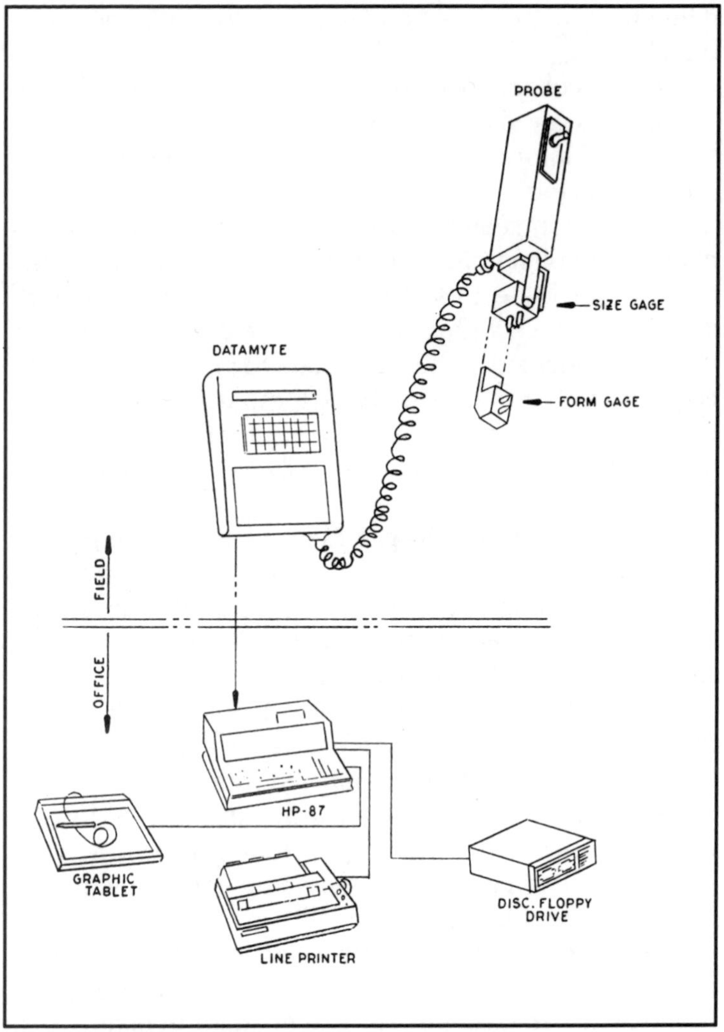

Fig. 8.7.1 Positive pin locators and SQC system.

CASE 8-8 ENGINE BEARINGS MANUFACTURER

Use of DataMyte Reduces Scrap From 5% to Less Than 0.5%

A large manufacturer of engine bearings needed to reduce its scrap costs and to produce parts that were more consistently acceptable to its customers. This company produces thousands of engine bearings a day and is a major supplier to the automotive industry.

The cost of quality in this company has been exceedingly large, and they faced stiff pricing competition in the marketplace. Maintaining precise, capable dimensions would allow them to satisfy their demanding customers and provide a significant cost savings due to reduced scrap.

Problem

One particular dimension in the production of these engine bearings that was a tremendous cause for concern was "split-line height". See Figure 8.8.1. This dimension had a critical tolerance of 15 tenths, but in production it would range as high as 30 tenths. Such variations caused this dimension alone to account for over five percent of all engine bearing defects. Auditors were attempting to control the variations in split-line height, but the time required to process the data manually was so great that many bad parts were being produced.

Solution

The solution to this problem was to have the auditors use a DataMyte 1500 to collect and analyze the data. Each machine was assigned a matrix in the DataMyte's memory. The auditors measured split-line height using their existing gage fixtures and manually entered the readings into the DataMyte. Statistical information was calculated immediately and capability charts were provided to the operators

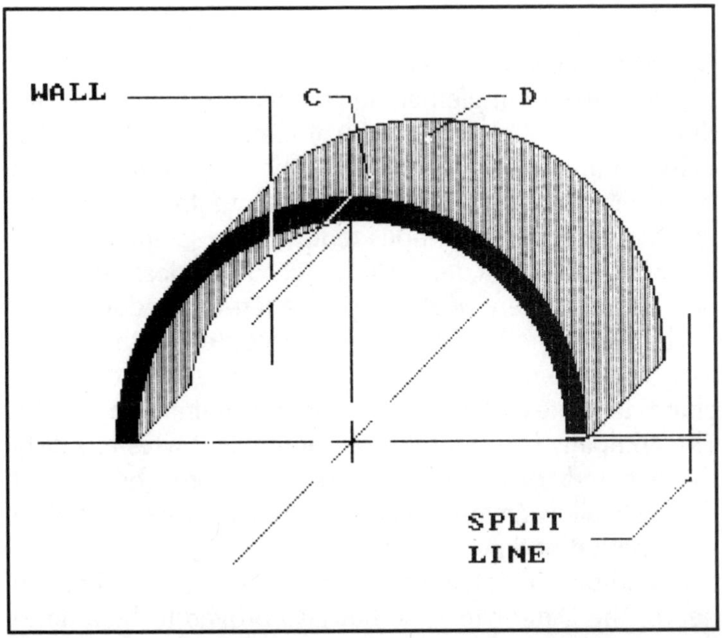

Fig. 8.8.1 Critical dimensions on the bearing cross section.

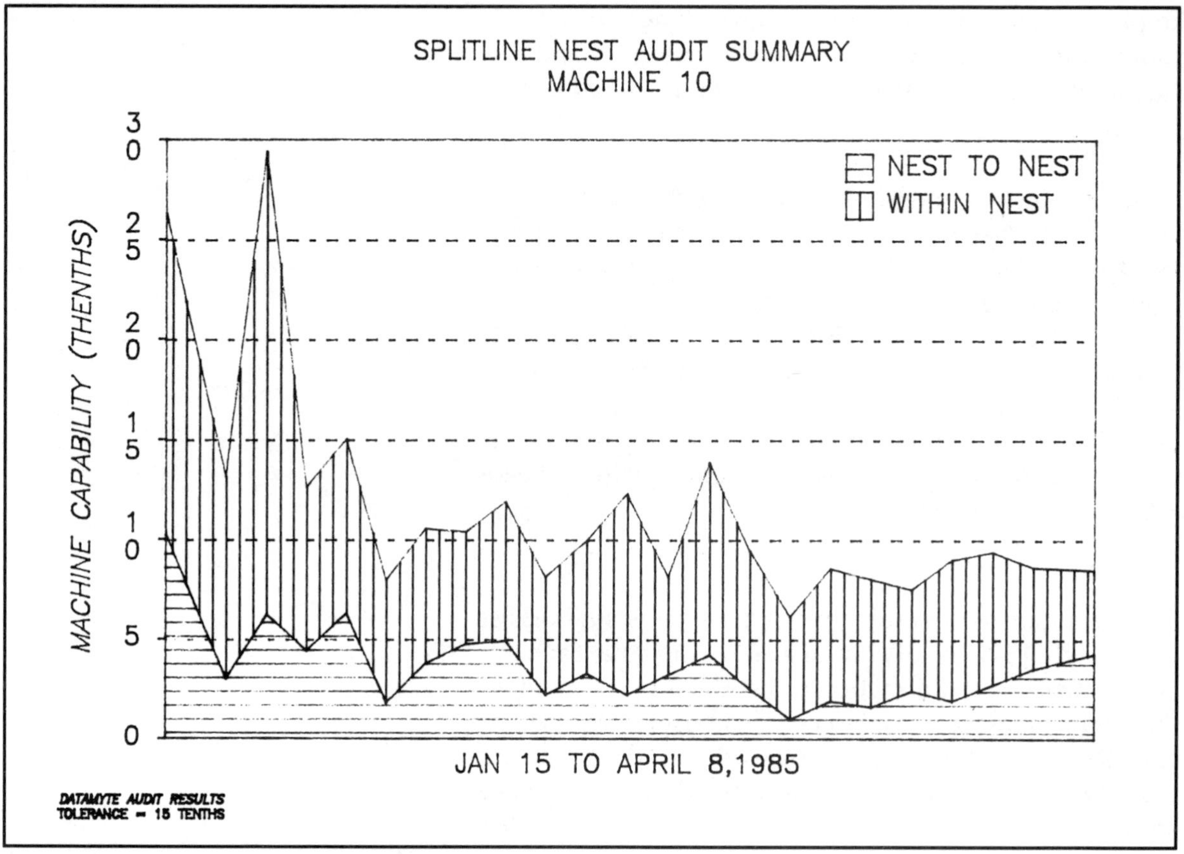

Fig. 8.8.2 Chart showing reduction in split-line height variability.

so that they could adjust their machines. The results of the DataMyte program were dramatic. See Figure 8.8.2. Within a few weeks of implementation, split-line height was reduced to well below the critical tolerance of 15 tenths. With continued use of the DataMyte, this dimension is being maintained below a level of 10 tenths. Along with this has come a tremendous reduction in scrapped material. Split-line height defects now account for less than one-half of one percent of all scrap — a ten-fold reduction.

The DataMyte has been readily accepted by the operators. They are now asking the auditors to check their machines to make certain that they are maintaining capability. The company has had to order more DataMytes to satisfy the demands of the auditors and operators who are not willing to allow anyone to borrow the DataMyte for even a short period of time.

In addition to solving real-time factory data collection needs, the DataMyte 1500 has also proved to be a timesaver for management. Information in the DataMyte is transferred directly into the supervisor's IBM PC-XT. Using the utility software program supplied by DataMyte, the supervisor is able to take the data and put it into a "DIF" format on his hard disk. This "DIF" file is then read directly by his spreadsheet program for instant analysis.

See Chapter 16 for data collectors and Chapter 18 for software.

CASE 8-9 TRUCK ENGINE MANUFACTURER

Torque Data Collection Time Decreased Three Fold

A large manufacturer of truck engines wished to increase the productivity of their torque auditors and obtain information faster for analyzing fastener clamp load. Auditors were using electronic torque wrenches, but were forced to write all information down, walk over to a personal computer, keypunch the information, and wait for analysis.

Problem

The company wanted a way to eliminate the double and triple handling of data and the associated delays. Company management felt that the time delay made problems hard to track down. However, they wanted to retain some of the features of the system, namely, immediate identification of a bad fastener, and archiving of the data onto a computer system. Also, a range of torque wrenches, from 50 to 350 lb. ft. had to be accommodated.

Solution

The company found that simply by upgrading some of the equipment they could retain all of the features of the present system and enhance performance as well. The new equipment consisted of a DataMyte 1556 data collector, printer and cables for their exisiting electronic torque wrenches.

See Chapter 17 for torque wrenches.

The DataMyte provided these features:

- Connection to a variety of wrenches, including in-line torque transducers.
- Direct recording of torque values. Auditors would no longer have to record them by hand.
- Immediate identification of bad fasteners. When an auditor took a reading the DataMyte would compare it to

preset specifications and emit an audible signal if it was not within spec. The DataMyte also compared subgroups of readings to preset control limits and would alert the auditor if the last subgroup was out of control.

- Graphic analysis, in the form of capability studies and control charts, obtained by connecting the DataMyte to a printer.
- Full communications with their existing computer system, for the archiving of data.

The company now uses one DataMyte to monitor 140 different fasteners. An auditor can check 99 engines without having to reprogam the unit. Breakaway torque is monitored by checking fasteners with handheld wrenches. Peak torque is monitored by connecting the DataMyte to an in-line transducer mounted on a nut runner.

The company notes that the speed of data collection has improved three fold. Data analysis was reduced from four hours to thirty minutes. The performance in improvement allows rapid changes of tight or loose bolts, reducing the possibility of failures in the field.

Analysis is obtained in a number of ways. Data accumulated by the auditor in the DataMyte was printed out on the printer in the form of a capability report (see Figure 8.9.1). The report plots twelve types of fasteners on one axis, which allows quick identification of problems. Data is also transmitted to the office personal computer and transmitted over a phone modem to the company headquarters 500 miles away, where it is stored by the mainframe computer.

CASE 8-10 BENCH SEAT MANUFACTURER

Company Monitors Torque Tools to Meet Federal Guidelines and JIT Schedule

A bench seat manufacturer that produces for a truck and bus final assembly plant needed to improve their fastener torque monitoring to meet federal guidelines. By using a DataMyte 2003 handheld data collector with in-line torque transducers they established an ongoing program for maintaining proper torque.

Problem

Federal guidelines required a certain torque on bolts used to fasten bench seats, because some of these seats would be on school buses and buses used for public transit. The company had recently failed to meet these guidelines.

Fig. 8.9.1 Capability report on fastener torque.

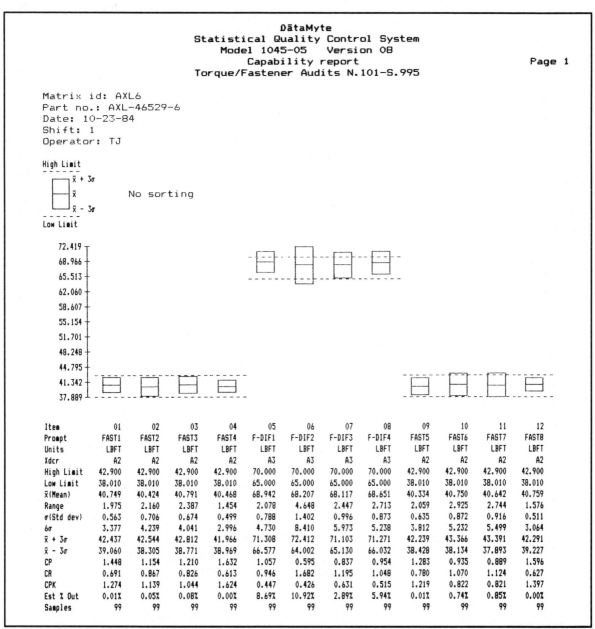

DātaMyte
Statistical Quality Control System
Model 1045-05 Version 08
Capability report **Page 1**
Torque/Fastener Audits N.101-S.995

Matrix id: AXL6
Part no.: AXL-46529-6
Date: 10-23-84
Shift: 1
Operator: TJ

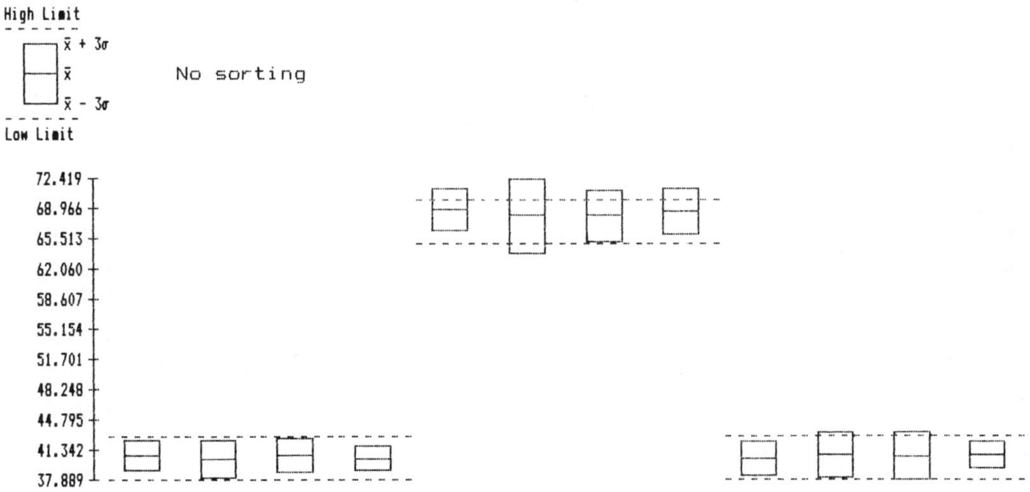

Item	01	02	03	04	05	06	07	08	09	10	11	12
Prompt	FAST1	FAST2	FAST3	FAST4	F-DIF1	F-DIF2	F-DIF3	F-DIF4	FAST5	FAST6	FAST7	FAST8
Units	LBFT	LBFT	LBFT	LBFT	LBFT	LBFT	LBFT	LBFT	LBFT	LBFT	LBFT	LBFT
Xdcr	A2	A2	A2	A2	A3	A3	A3	A3	A2	A2	A2	A2
High Limit	42.900	42.900	42.900	42.900	70.000	70.000	70.000	70.000	42.900	42.900	42.900	42.900
Low Limit	38.010	38.010	38.010	38.010	65.000	65.000	65.000	65.000	38.010	38.010	38.010	38.010
x̄(Mean)	40.749	40.424	40.791	40.468	68.942	68.207	68.117	68.651	40.334	40.750	40.642	40.759
Range	1.975	2.160	2.387	1.454	2.078	4.648	2.447	2.713	2.059	2.925	2.744	1.576
σ(Std dev)	0.563	0.706	0.674	0.499	0.788	1.402	0.996	0.873	0.635	0.872	0.916	0.511
6σ	3.377	4.239	4.041	2.996	4.730	8.410	5.973	5.238	3.812	5.232	5.499	3.064
x̄ + 3σ	42.437	42.544	42.812	41.966	71.308	72.412	71.103	71.271	42.239	43.366	43.391	42.291
x̄ - 3σ	39.060	38.305	38.771	38.969	66.577	64.002	65.130	66.032	38.428	38.134	37.893	39.227
CP	1.448	1.154	1.210	1.632	1.057	0.595	0.837	0.954	1.283	0.935	0.889	1.596
CR	0.691	0.867	0.826	0.613	0.946	1.682	1.195	1.048	0.780	1.070	1.124	0.627
CPK	1.274	1.139	1.044	1.624	0.447	0.426	0.631	0.515	1.219	0.822	0.821	1.397
Est % Out	0.01%	0.05%	0.08%	0.00%	8.69%	10.92%	2.89%	5.94%	0.01%	0.74%	0.85%	0.00%
Samples	99	99	99	99	99	99	99	99	99	99	99	99

It seems that the powered torque tools used to fasten the seat bolts either over or undertightened the bolts. Overtightening could stress the joints and cause fatigue, and undertightening did not achieve the required clamping force.

In addition, the truck and bus assembly plant was adopting a just-in-time (JIT) production system that required on-time delivery of defect free parts. The company was strategically located about thirty miles away from the assembly plant, and felt confident with a better SPC program for torque they could meet both delivery and reliability requirements.

Solution

The company was using Ingersol Rand torque drivers. The key to ensuring consistent torque on the fasteners was to be able to read the torque as the tool was running down the bolts on the seats. To read the torque they installed in-line torque transducers between the Ingersol Rand drivers and the sockets. The transducers provided a signal which could be interpreted by a DataMyte 2003 handheld data collector.

See Chapter 16 for 2003 data collector and Chapter 17 for torque tools.

The DataMyte 2003 was then used to continuously audit the tools. The auditor would go from station to station, connect the 2003 to the torque tool, and do a capability study. The study would compare a sample of readings against the specifications.

The DataMyte 2003 displayed the study results on its LCD (see Figure 8.10.1). Once capability was verified, the auditor could proceed to the next station. A tool could be adjusted immediately if the results indicated it was not meeting specifications.

They also did visual inspection of defects on finished bench seats with the DataMyte 2003. They would record a defect, its location, bench seat type and other notes. The data collector would display a Pareto chart showing the frequency of defects in rank order by type. See Figure 8.10.2. They would then construct p-charts and continuously monitor the most frequent defects.

The establishment of this program led to improved torque capability, their meeting federal guidelines, and on-time delivery to their customer.

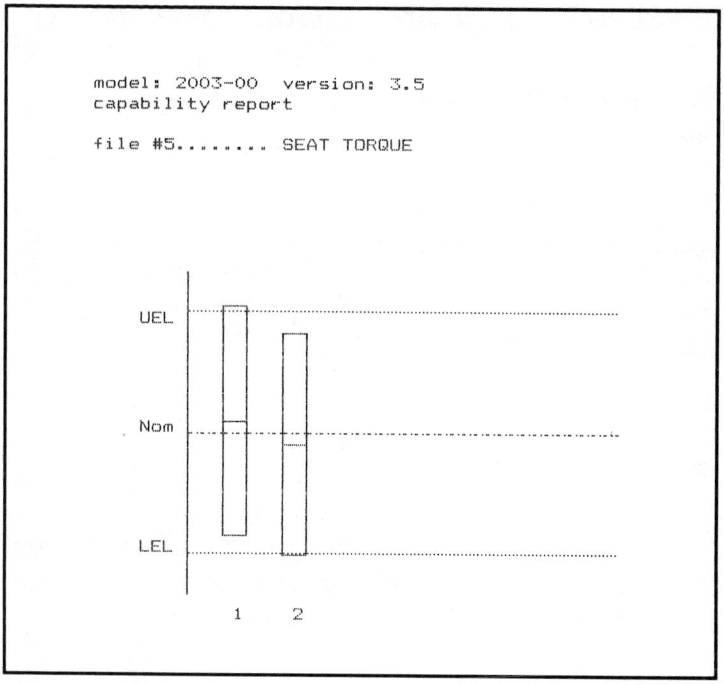

Fig. 8.10.1 Example of a capability graph used to check the torque tools.

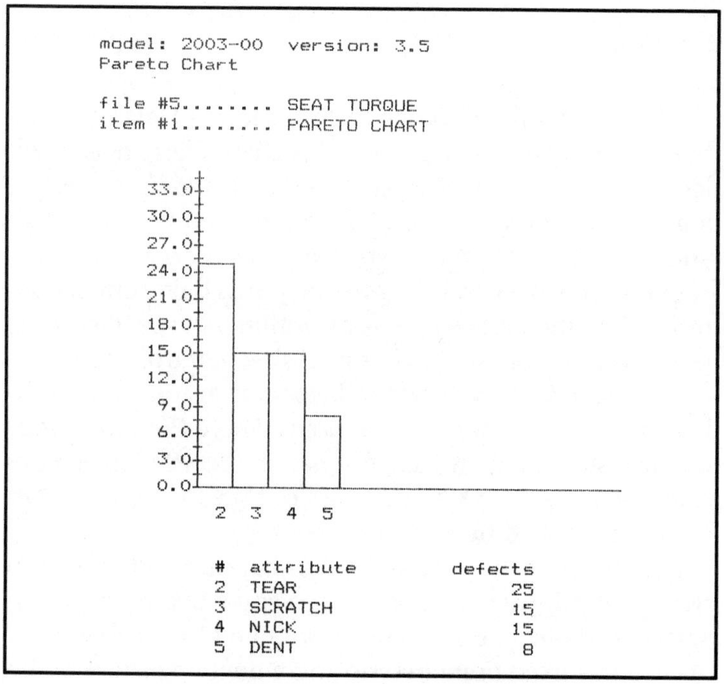

Fig. 8.10.2 Example of a Pareto chart used to analyze the results of visual inspection.

CASE 8-11 STEERING GEAR COMPANY

Automated Data Collection Speeds SPC Problem Solving

Shortly before the holiday break the number four O.D. grinder in department 62 developed a serious form problem. The spherical form of many of the cages being sent to the assembly line were very much oversized. Cages with this condition will not assemble.

Problem

Using the traditional electronic gage assigned to the job, the operator was able to tell that his parts were running on the high limit, but still within part specification.

Solution

At this point the floor inspector used the DataMyte system to produce an $\bar{x}$ & R chart. This chart relies on data collected from a series of parts. The data is then grouped on a graph line with a set of high and low limits. These high and low limits are called upper and lower control limits.

In this case the chart showed the job as being out of control. While the parts were failing within part specifications, they were out of the newly established control limits.

The DataMyte enabled the inspector to track the problem backwards in time to the point where the form problem first started. Statistical information recorded over a period of time had created a history of how the number four O.D. grinder had been running.

The DataMyte 761 was used in this application. For more information see Chapter 16.

Prior to using the DataMyte, number four had been torn down twice by machine repairmen and worked on by jobsetters and engineers. No one could find the problem.

Having a fixed point in time and a definite history of the problem enabled plant four repairmen to trace the form problem to a malfunctioning dresser motor.

The data collection system has enabled the plant to increase quality, without adding to the operator's workload.

CASE 8-12 AUTOMOTIVE BATTERY SUPPLIER

Real-Time Math Capability Helps Company Monitor Battery Performance

A leading manufacturer of automotive batteries not only needed to collect the data but apply some formulas to obtain the final analysis. Without the use of a DataMyte Model 762 the task could not be accomplished in a timely manner.

Problem Definition

To meet the specified power requirements for the batteries it is necessary to maintain control of how much electrolytic material is being applied to the individual plates which make up the cells. This task is complicated by the fact that the material is applied wet.

At the time this was strictly a laboratory procedure. The results were provided at the convenience of the lab, not manufacturing.

Solution

They found that the mathematical capabilities of the DataMyte 762 data collector could help calculate and chart electrolyte. Model 762 was pre-programmed with the necessary formulas and placed on the factory floor. The operators then periodically removed an individual plate already filled with wet paste. This plate was weighed and the results automatically transmitted to the Model 762. The DataMyte stored the results in item 1. It then proceeded to subtract off from this reading a constant value equal to the weight of the plate. Now stored in item 2 was a net value equal to the paste only. The operator then took the plate with paste and placed it in a moisture balance. The amount of moisture was established and this value was automatically sent to the Model 762 and stored as item 3. The DataMyte then subtracted this value from 100% and stored the value in item 4 identified as percent solids. Then without any direction the Model 762 multiplied item 2 by item 4 and arrived at the needed value of "dry electrolyte" applied to the individual plate.

See Chapter 16 for a description of the DataMyte 762 data collector.

Control charts were generated by the DataMyte and put up on the video display terminal for immediate review.

They could now predict the expected performance that the battery would provide.

In addition, the raw data was available so problems could be traced back. When the lab provided results there was always confusion regarding whether the paste was being applied incorrectly or was of the wrong consistency.

As a result, production levels are better than ever since the rework has been reduced so dramatically. The operators also have benefited in they now control their own destiny.

CASE 8-13 BUSHINGS MANUFACTURER

DataMyte Data Collectors Reduce Inspection Time

A manufacturer of metal and rubber bushings and sleeves for the automotive market needed to reduce the amount of time they spend doing inspection. They choose to automate their data collection by using a DataMyte 762.

Problem

The company needed to measure the O.D. and length under the flange to the end of the outer shell of a suspension bushing. They needed a way to cut down inspection time without sacrificing quality or their contract with an automotive manufacturer.

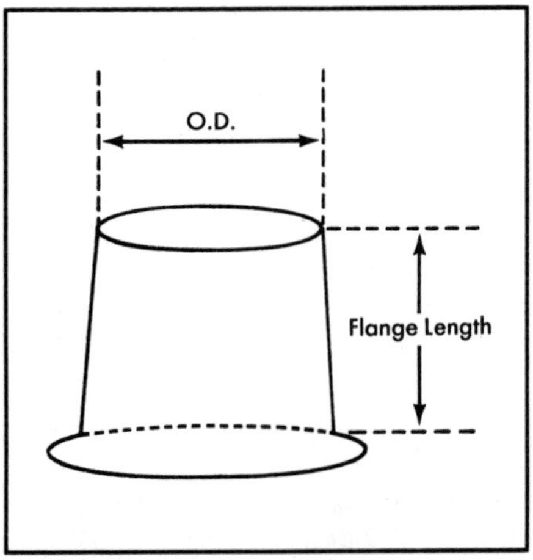

Fig. 8.13.1 Bushing measurements.

Solution

The company found that by having a DataMyte 762 at each press, inspection time was cut drastically. The company will not need to add an additional inspector and they they will be able to supply the necessary reports to keep their contract with the automotive manufacturer.

CASE 8-14 WINDSHIELD MANUFACTURER

Data Collection System Pays for Itself Within Nine Months

A manufacturer of windshields was collecting data manually on 30 lines. Data collection was too time consuming and costly.

Problem

The company needed a way to speed up data collection. With 30 lines to collect data on, much of their day was spent collecting and analyzing data.

Solution

The company found that a DataMyte 762 on each line dramatically reduced the time spent collecting data. They use their data collectors to measure the depth of bend for their windshields. See Figure 8.14.1. The company calculates that the data collection system will pay for itself within nine months.

See Chapter 16 for a description of the 762 data collector.

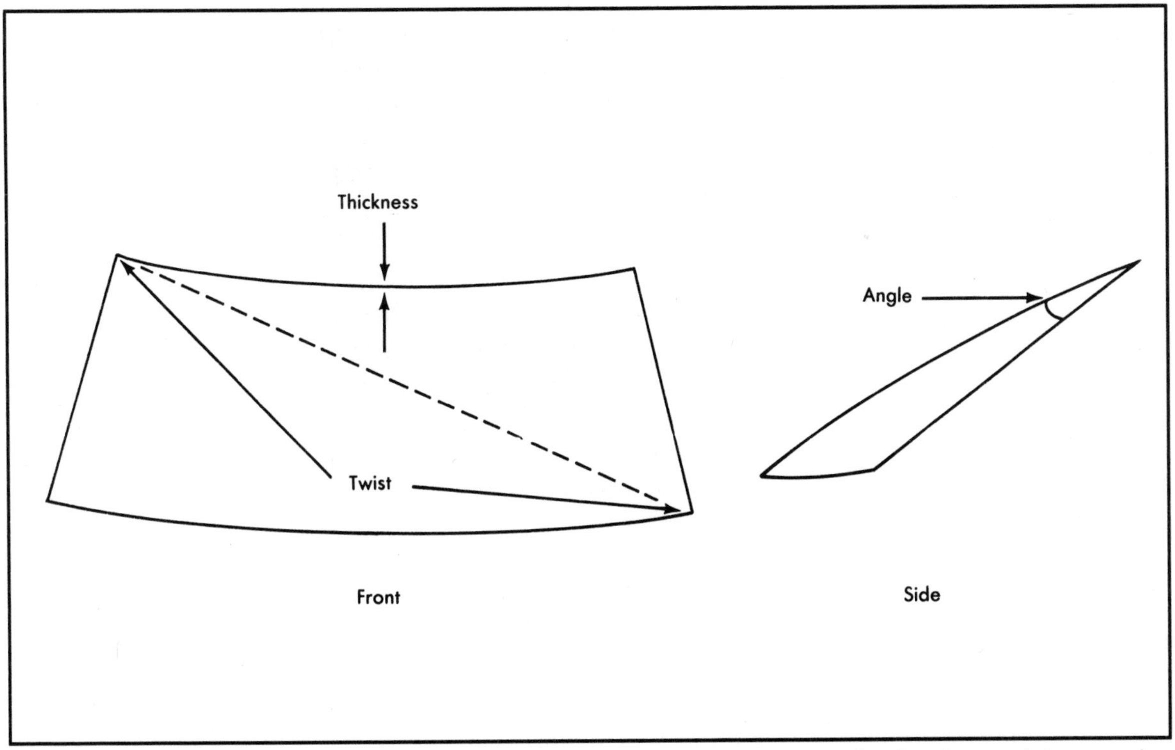

Fig. 8.14.1 Quality characteristics on a glass windshield.

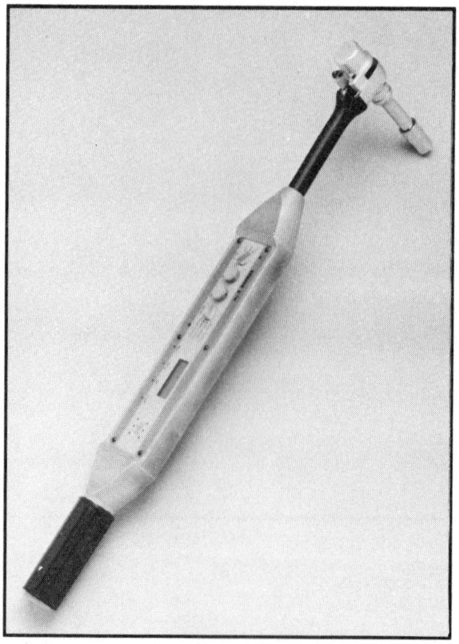

Fig. 8.15.1 SPS Sensor I Torque Wrench

See Chapter 16 for the 2000 data collector and Chapter 17 for the SPS Torque Wrench.

CASE 8-15 AUTO COMPONENT MANUFACTURER

Company Uses SPS Sensor I Torque Wrench To Monitor Bolt Breakage

An automotive component manufacturer has been trying to control scrap costs through bolt breakages. While their product was a high performance unit, increased competition forced the company to examine all areas of its manufacturing process. The company looked for an affordable and reliable way to automatically reduce bolt breakages.

Problem

To attain high equipment performance, the assembly torques on ten hold down bolts had been raised several times. While this had not caused product failures, it had resulted in periodic bolt failures at the time of assembly. On some lots this resulted in scrap and rework of 10 percent of the products.

Solution

The company used an SPS Sensor I Torque Wrench (Figure 8.15.1) to tighten fasteners to the recommended torque, and used a DataMyte 2000 to automatically record the torque/angle readings. The result was the elimination of bolt breakages. Repair was significantly reduced and scrap was virtually eliminated, with a cost savings of 10 percent.

9. ELECTRONICS AND COMPUTER INDUSTRIES

CASE 9-1 SEMI-CONDUCTOR MANUFACTURER

Better Control Leads to 15 Percent Scrap Reduction in Chip Cutting Operation

A consistently uniform, high quality silicon wafer is critical to a top quality finished product as well as keeping production costs to a minimum. By paying close attention to the early stages of production of a semiconductor this manufacturer has been able to remain a leader in this field.

Problem

The company was using SPC and was searching for a more efficient way of collecting data for controlling seven very similar processes.

The process involved the cutting of silicon wafers used in the production of semi-conductors. In order to avoid problems downline and reduce internal failures it was necessary to control wafer thickness to very tight specifications (± 7.5 mils). Additionally, silicon bar stock being very expensive, scrap reduction was also a goal.

The two operators working the seven cutting saws were having difficulty keeping accurate charts on all saws simultaneously.

Solution

The solution was to automate control charting with a system that allowed the two operators to quickly record data and review the results for all seven saws, randomly as the processes dictate.

See Chapter 16 for the 762 data collector.

The DataMyte 762 data collector with data grouping capability was the system chosen to solve this problem. Because thickness was the only dimension tracked at each saw and all data was collected at one inspection area the 762 provided the capacity and flexibility required.

The grouping feature was of particular importance to the working of this system. It permitted each operator to enter data for a given saw in any sequence. This way if one saw was shut down for a blade change, or any reason, data collection could continue without disrupting the collection routine. Likewise, it was not necessary to have one operator wait for the other to complete a subgroup before moving to the next saw.

By giving the operators the flexibility of random data entry and immediate feedback of variability of the cutting process significant efficiencies were gained. Freed from the task of manual recording and charting of data operators could concentrate on solving problems, adjusting the process and predicting blade change intervals. This translated into a 15% decrease in failure and scrap.

The DataMyte 762 was set up for seven items each corresponding to a saw. Specification and control limits were set up for each item and edited as needed for product changes. Each item was assigned as a separate group so operators could easily move from item to item as the collection tasks required. After collecting the thickness data with a hand micrometer operators review $\bar{x}$ & R charts and make necessary adjustments. Capability studies are also run for each saw.

CASE 9-2 COMPUTER COMPONENTS MANUFACTURER

FAN® System Helps Achieve Suppliers Requirement to Furnish Statistical Charts Before Shipment of the Order

A major computer manufacturer isolated a few critical components of their mainframe computer system that were being supplied by outside vendors. This firm decided, however, to minimize their supplier base and require the use of statistical process control by the remaining suppliers. A company that could furnish proof of their commitment to SPC would then continue to supply these critical components, if they were awarded the contract.

One company who supplied computer components, and was recognized as a quality leader in their field, was one step ahead of its customer base. Their management was quick to realize the benefits of SPC and implemented a manual SPC program with its workforce. This included SPC training, and control charts maintained at each machine by the operator. Some benefits were already starting to occur — such as being able to tell the major computer manufacturer that SPC was already in place.

Problem

There was one looming question. This customer wanted statistical charts on machined parts sent prior to the shipment, not with the parts. The problem was how to produce these charts rapidly, efficiently and neatly. The customer's intent was to verify statistically that the parts were good. Upon approval they could be shipped. If the current method of manual charting was maintained, it would cause delays in the shipping (approvals had to be given).

The supplier had a desktop computer that could be linked through a modem to the customer's computer, but the real delay would be in the keypunching of data into the computer. With the amount of machines running, and the volume of data, keypunching data into the PC took about two hours a day. This was after a verification step which included manually calculating the $\bar{x}$ & R values for each point on a chart. Total time, including verification, was about four hours per day.

Solution

A system which could automatically collect data, electronically transfer the data to the computer, which could then transmit the data through a modem to the customer was seen as one solution. This would be tantamount to a local area network (LAN). Placing a computer terminal at each location where data collection was required was expensive. The total cost of a LAN, including terminals, cable, and environmental protection, was estimated at $36,000.

See Chapter 15 for a description of FAN.

Another possible solution surfaced when a manager, glancing through a leading magazine, found that there were dedicated SPC devices on the market. After looking into several of these devices, and receiving demonstrations, the organization purchased the DataMyte FAN® (Factory Area Network) system.

Justification for the system, as spelled out by the company, included the following:

- Devices manufactured by DataMyte were proven to withstand severe factory environments. (This was learned by speaking with a couple of organizations that were using DataMyte equipment locally.)
- The FAN® system provided real-time feedback to the operator. (After all, operators had all been trained on SPC. Now they could have the tools to apply this knowledge efficiently and learn with it).

- The ability to capture data from more than one gage, and not be required to use one brand of gaging. (Several different brands of gaging were currently in use.)
- Each 750 station provided the capacity to store data on 10 characteristics.
- Data could be transmitted to the computer without having the computer "poll" each terminal.
- Data collection routines could be stored on floppy disk and sent electronically to the DataMyte.
- The cost of the system was approximately $7,500.

Along with the data collectors (DataMyte 750s), the organization purchased FAN® software for the IBM PC. The operators would now collect data and receive feedback immediately while measuring the parts. If an out of engineering limit reading was taken, the DataMyte 750 gave an audible warning so that the operator could remove this "bad part" from the lot. Each operator was assigned the responsibility to send his collected data to the PC at various intervals. All of this data was accumulated, then transmitted to the customer's PC. Verification for shipment now took less than one hour after all the pieces of a production run were complete.

Using the FAN® software in another capacity, the company organization stored the data for all their production runs on floppy disk. This allowed them to maintain data files without filling up filing cabinets full of paper. Anytime a hardcopy report was required, the data was retrieved off a floppy disk and formatted into a report.

CASE 9-3 ELECTRONIC CONNECTOR MANUFACTURER

Single Format System Improves Pin Dimension Checking

A large manufacturer of electronic connectors, including gold-plated pins, recognized the need for initiating a statistical program for monitoring their manufacturing processes. Areas critical to this manufacturer were the size of the pins themselves and the plating thickness on the pins. To remain competitive in their particular market, this manufacturer needed to implement an SQC program as soon as possible.

Problem Definition

Current measurement techniques used by this manufacturer involved "eyeballing" measurements with mechanical gages; this included the length, diameter, and head diameter of the pins and measurement of the plating thickness by using an x-ray florescent device that transmitted data directly to an Apple II computer. Because this manufacturer was using traditional methods for measurements, no statistical analysis was being performed on the data. This was also due in part to the fact that the Apple II computer was only dedicated to retrieving and storing data generated by the x-ray device.

The manufacturer had several plants, and each was experiencing failure problems with their connectors. While they knew that a serious problem existed, they were not able to pinpoint the causes for the problem. This was due in large part to the vast amount of data that required manual processing.

Solution

The manufacturer determined that prerequisites for the overall program must include:

- The ability to perform statistical calculations on the data coming from the x-ray florescent machine.
- Eliminating the need for 100% inspection of the sizing of the pins, yet obtaining a significant increase in the quality of their products.
- Eliminating manual charting of the statistical data.
- Monitoring several phases of the production process, not just the "finished product."

See Chapter 16 for data collectors and Chapter 17 for calipers.

Based on their analysis, they chose a DataMyte 1508 handheld data collector along with an electronic caliper. The DataMyte would provide the data collection and analysis capability and could also be used to generate the necessary charts and capability reports. Further, the DataMyte would be able to retrieve the x-ray data from the Apple II computer and then perform statistical calculations on that data.

By using a DataMyte as part of the overall SPC program, the manufacturer was able to eliminate manual charting and reduce data turn-around time. Areas of the process that were to be monitored included pin length, pin diameter, and head diameter.

Operation

The information that follows provides an overall description of how the DataMyte 1508 was used by the manufacturer. The critical area of concern with respect to plating thickness was on shaft "B", as this is where the connection to other devices takes place once the pins have been imbedded in the connector. It was determined that two matrices would be set up to monitor the measurements statistically.

The first matrix would be dedicated to the pin measurements. This included four items: A = length; B = head diameter; C = "A" shaft diameter; and D = "B" shaft diameter. (See Figure 9.3.1.) A history file would be used to keep track of x̄ & R chart values for each item. The first matrix was set up as follows:

HISTORY = YES (for x̄ & R history)
ITEMS = 4 (one for each area to be monitored)
SAMPLES = 10
CELL SIZE = 6
HORZ/VERT = H
PROMPTS = YES

The associated prompts were set up as follows:

ITEM 1 = LENGTH
ITEM 2 = HD DIAM (head diameter)
ITEM 3 = A DIAM (A shaft diameter)
ITEM 4 = B DIAM (B shaft diameter)

Limits were established as follows:

LIMITS = YES (the limits were defined as:)
ITEM 1 (Lo = 20.0mm, Hi = 20.6mm)
ITEM 2 (Lo = 3.25mm, Hi = 3.75mm)
ITEM 3 (Lo = 2.25mm, Hi = 2.75mm)
ITEM 4 (Lo = 1.25mm, Hi = 1.75mm)

CTRL LIMITS = NO (No control limits were entered at first. When sufficient data was collected, the DataMyte would calculate the limits itself.)

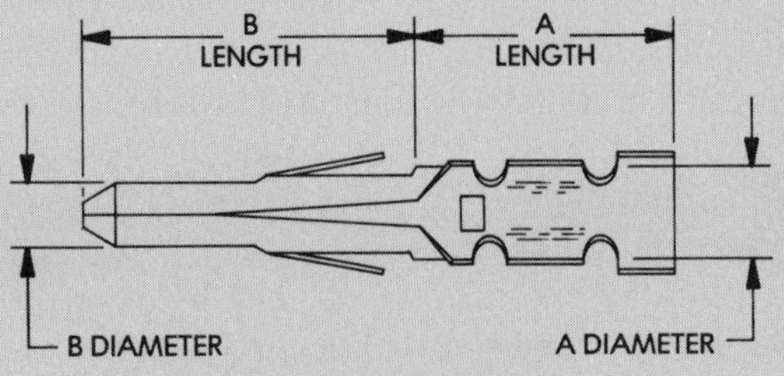

Fig.9.3.1 Pin dimensions

The XDCR table was set up for C1 to designate the Model 544-1 digital caliper. Therefore, C1 was entered as the alphanumeric code during setup of the matrix.

Once the setup information was entered, the operator entered the Data Collect mode and keyed in the following:

MATRIX ID = A6B (part number)
DATE = (as required)
OPERATOR = (initials of the inspector)
NOTE 1 = 0B (designates part name)
NOTE 2 = CON (designates part name)
NOTE 3 = PINS (designates part name)

Once the DataMyte had accumulated sufficient x̄ & R history, charts could be generated daily and process control could be maintained accordingly.

The second matrix was set up to handle the data received from the Apple II computer, which received its data from the X-ray florescent device. The Apple II was configured to communicate with the DataMyte via an RS232-C serial interface card. The DataMyte, which was connected to the Apple II computer with a cable, was then put into Remote Control mode.

The second matrix consisted of one item and 10 samples. An IH command was used to set up a history matrix. After completion of the setup, the DataMyte was placed in the Data Collect mode.

Once the data collection process was completed, data resident in the Apple II computer was downloaded to the DataMyte. Upon receiving the specified amount of data, the DataMyte exited Remote Control mode. After sufficient history had been created, the DataMyte was connected to an electronic printer where the $\bar{x}$ & R charts of the x-ray data were dumped.

With the SPC program in place as described in the previous paragraphs, the connector pin manufacturing process could be statistically monitored, with all of the critical measurement areas covered. All that was required at this time was to periodically clear the data in the matrices and change the date in the Data Collect mode.

As can be seen from this operational process, the DataMyte was able to accommodate automatic data capture while eliminating mechanical, "eyeballing" gages. It was also able to statistically summarize and analyze data from extremely sophisticated electronic testing equipment.

CASE 9-4 DISK DRIVE MANUFACTURER

Control Charts Help Predict Tool Maintenance

A major disk drive manufacturer attaches terminal connectors to wire leads in motors and brakes of machinery used to produce disk drives. The connectors are attached with a crimping tool after the wire insulation is stripped.

Problem

If an inspector could determine when a crimping tool was starting to go bad, instead of finding out after it had already gone bad, he could have the tool rebuilt before useless wire leads were produced. The QC engineer was using SPC to determine when the crimping tool needed to be rebuilt (see Figure 9.4.1). He would take crimp height measurements with a micrometer and plot them on an $\bar{x}$ & R chart.

After the tool was rebuilt, the engineer noticed that the crimp heights were still out of control, so he constructed a histogram (Figure 9.4.2). The histogram showed that the distribution was skewed to the high side. This was already suspected because the points on the $\bar{x}$ & R charts were moving up and down together. He concluded that the tool only allowed the variation in crimp height to be biased one way and the natural distribution would be skewed.

Closer examination of the crimp height measurements (Figure 9.4.1) showed that the measurements did not have enough precision. The engineer was trying to make decisions on data calculated to 0.0001 inch and the readings were only accurate to 0.001 inch.

****
* CAPABILITY STUDY *
****

FORM NO. 2462D

PROCESS CONTROL CHART (X & R)

ASSEMBLY Crimp Contact Pin PART NO. 51905809 REV 1

MFG. MGR. Dick Weller MFG. ENG. Larry Hanke Q.C. ENG. Ken Fastner

CHARACTERISTIC Crimp Height SPECIFICATION .052±.002

1	525	52	053	051	.050	.051	052	052	052	52	52	051	051	053	053	050	050	050	.052	051
2	53	53	056	051	.050	.051	052	52	52	52	52	051	051	052	053	050	050	050	052	051
3	53	525	055	051	.050	.050	051	052	52	53	052	051	052	053	053	050	051	050	053	051
4	53	0525	052	052	.050	.051	052	051	52	052	052	051	052	053	052	050	050	050	052	050
5	525	053	053	051	.050	.051	052	052	53	52	052	051	051	052	052	050	050	050	052	051
TOTAL	.264	.263	.269	.256	.250	.254	259	259	261	261	260	.254	257	263	.263	250	.251	250	.261	254
MEAN - X	.0528	.0526	.0538	.0512	.050	.0508	0518	0518	.0522	.0522	.052	.051	0514	.0526	.0526	.050	.0502	050	.0522	.0508
RANGE - R	.0005	.001	.004	001	.0000	001	.001	001	001	001	000	000	001	001	001	000	001	000	001	001
EMPLOYEE NO																				
DATE	7/11	7/18	7/25	7/26	8/1	8/4	8/15	9/20	9/21	9/22	9/23	9/24	10/3	10/4	11/17	11/18	11/28	12/11	12/13	1/9
TIME	11:05																			

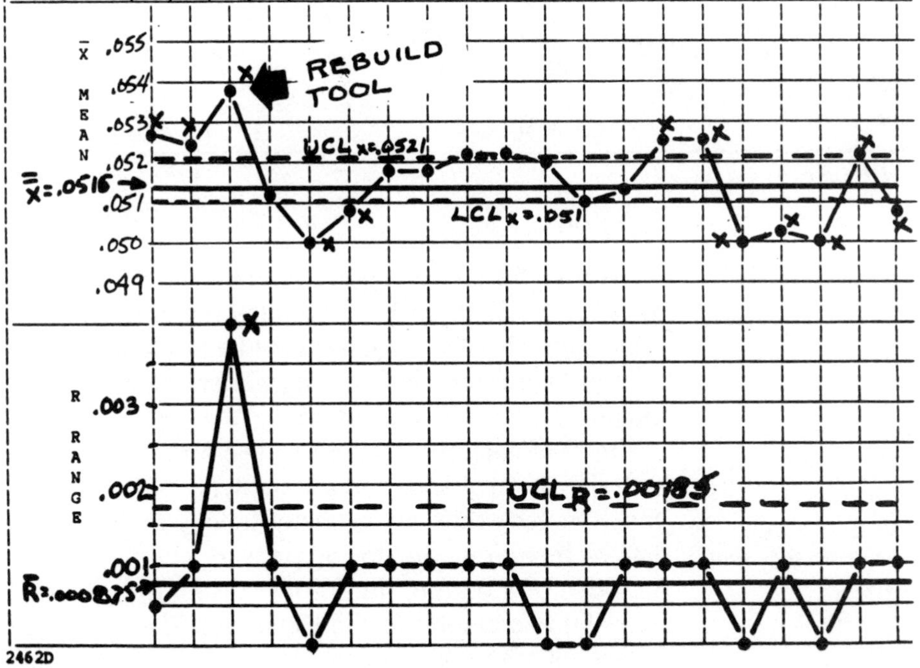

2462D

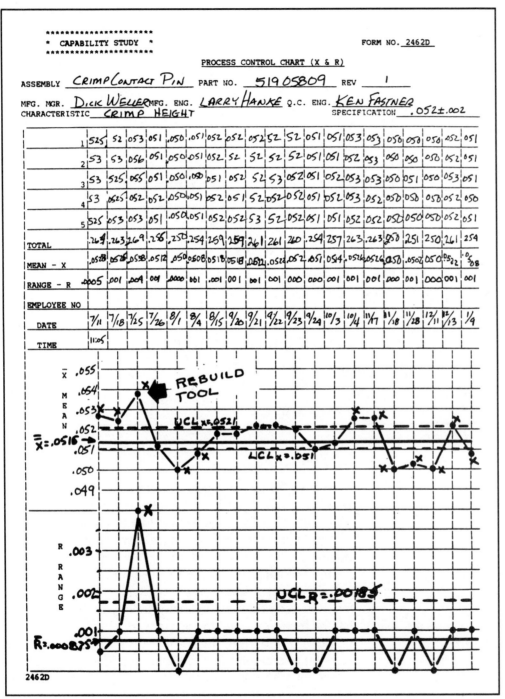

Fig. 9.4.1 Crimp height control chart

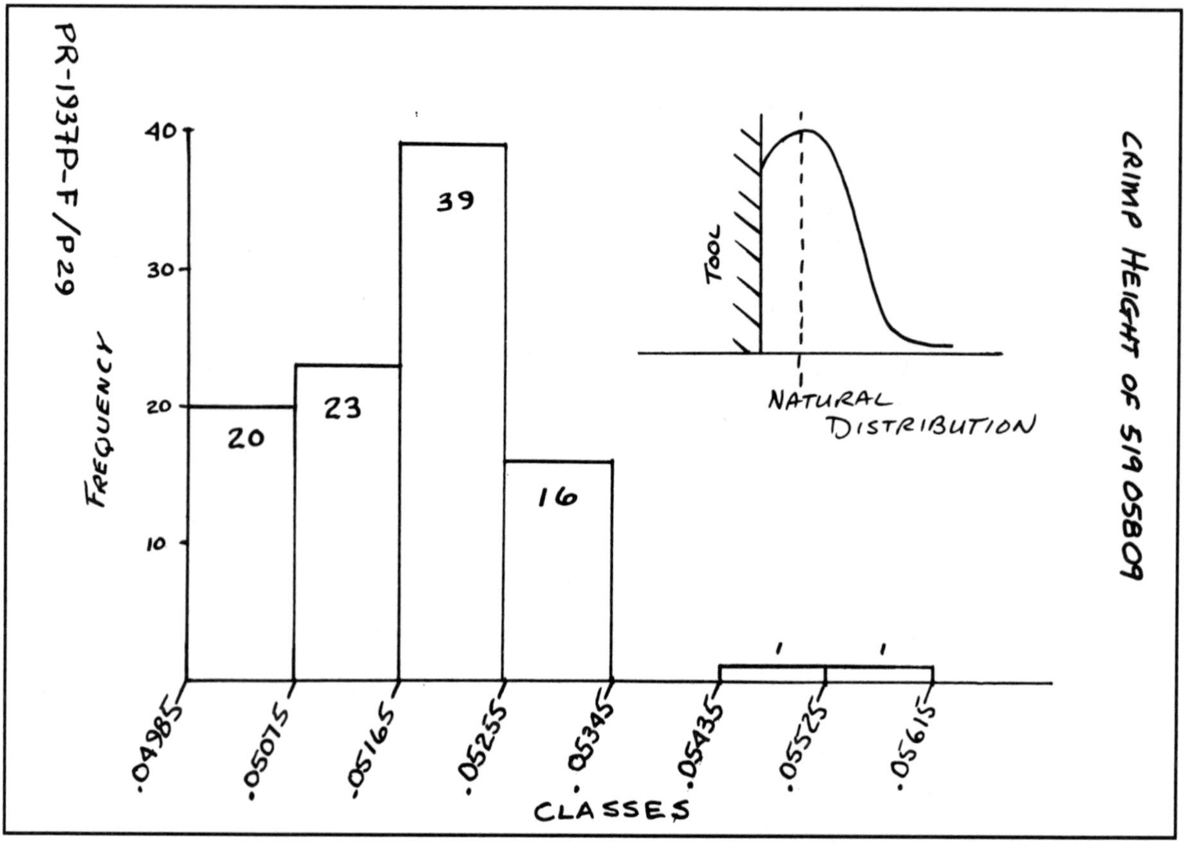

Fig. 9.4.2 Histogram of crimp heights.

See Chapter 16 for data collectors and Chapter 17 for micrometers.

Solution

Because the specification called for the crimp height to be 0.052 $\pm$ 0.002 inches, the micrometer had to be read more carefully. The engineer could either train his people how to take more accurate measurements or use an automatic data collection system.

The manufacturer decided to use a digital micrometer with special anvil ends and a DataMyte 1507 to collect the data. On each shift, an inspector trained in SPC collected data by measuring the first 50 parts for crimp height. With the push of a button, the inspector sent a digital reading from the micrometer to the DataMyte. The DataMyte recorded all of the digits necessary for the control charts. At the end of the third shift, the inspector connected the DataMyte to an IBM PC to transfer and store the data on a floppy disk. After the data was transferred, the inspector cleared the data from the DataMyte so it was ready for the next day's data collection.

The third-shift inspector generated the $\bar{x}$ & R control charts for analysis. With the charts, the inspectors discovered that a downward trend in the $\bar{x}$ chart indicates possible tool wear. Even though the readings are within the control limits, the inspectors have the crimping tool rebuilt, to prevent bad parts from being produced.

The cost savings associated with the DataMyte system justified the purchase in only 2-1/2 months.

CASE 9-5 DISK DRIVE MANUFACTURER

Both Variables and Attributes Data Collection Used to Verify Disk Drives.

A world leader in the manufacturing, design, and implementation of large computer disk drives needed to reduce scrap and rework. ANSI standards had to be met. However, the cost of 100 percent inspection was just too expensive.

The base material for the magnetic storage media was developed into round disks, with very critical inside and outside diameter dimensions. Any discrepancy outside of engineering or ANSI specs caused the disks to fail and damage the drive system in which they were placed.

Problem

Implementing statistical quality control on the critical dimensions would help minimize the scrap and rework. There still had to be a method, however, when performing first article inspection, to screen rejects until the process is "in control". During the initial inspection, all disks would be monitored so that no rejects (those that exceeded limits) could pass through the system. Once the process was in control, then sampling could be used. The parts to be inspected are shown in Figure 9.5.1.

Three outside diameter measurements were taken to identify any out-of-roundness conditions. The ID was also measured at three separate locations for the same reason. The data would then be fed to the mainframe computer system for processing and report generation. The inspection procedure shown in Figure 9.5.2 was developed for data collection. All measurements were taken with a 6 inch caliper that was mounted on a special extension arm fixture. See Figure 9.5.3.

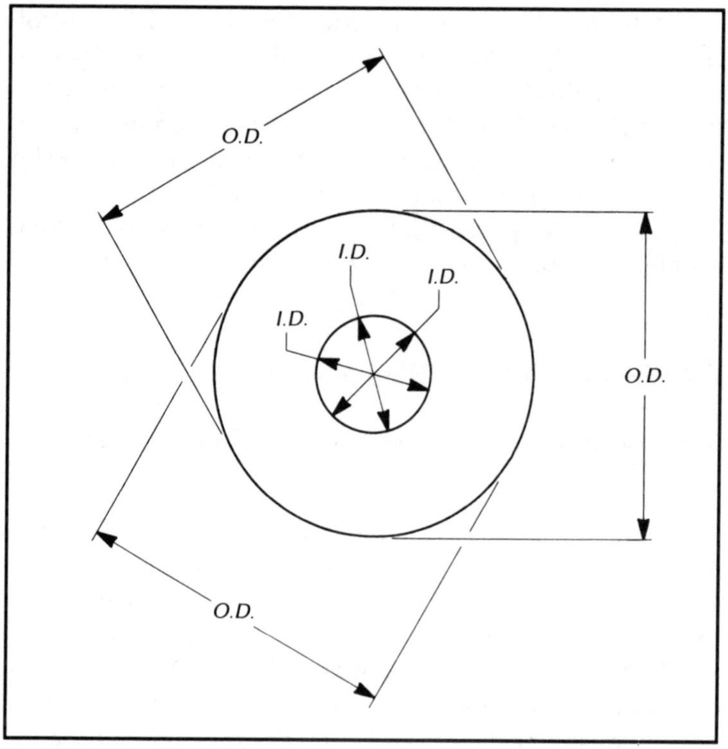

Fig. 9.5.1 Three sets of inner and outer diameters were measured on a disk to check out of roundness.

Fig. 9.5.2 Sample inspection form used.

Batch # ____________ Quantity ____________

Outside Diameter Measurement 1: ____________

Outside Diameter Measurement 2: ____________

Outside Diameter Measurement 3: ____________

$\overline{X}$ = ____________ R = ____________

Inside Diameter Measurement 1: ____________

Inside Diameter Measurement 2: ____________

Inside Diameter Measurement 3: ____________

$\overline{X}$ = ____________ R = ____________

Pass ☐ Fail ☐

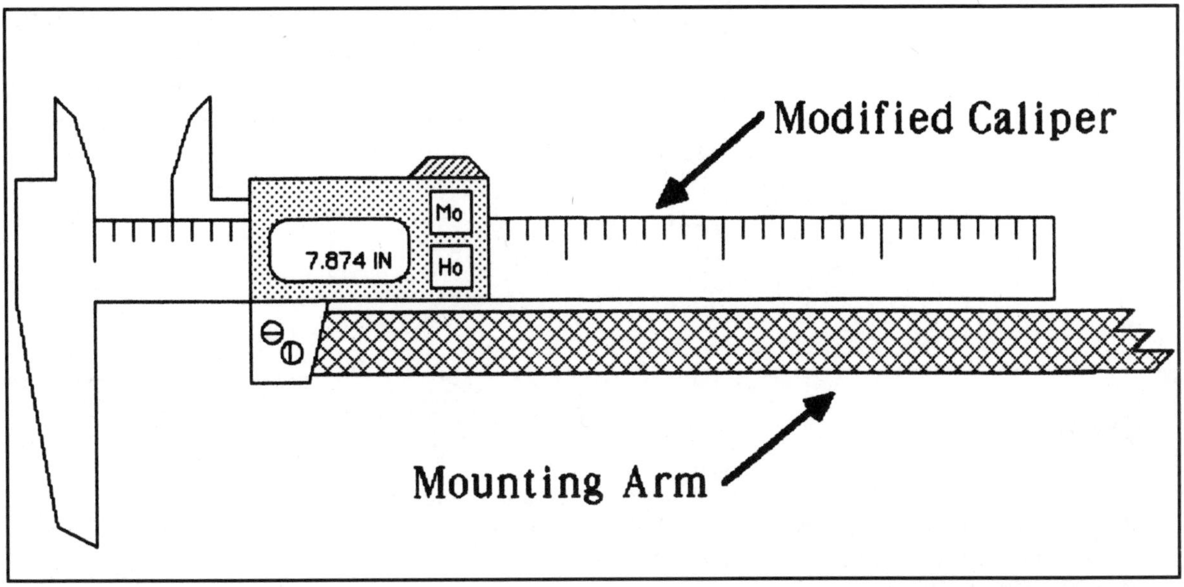

Fig. 9.5.3 Caliper modified with extension arm to measure disk diameters.

Along with variables data on the ID and OD measurements, attribute data collection was also important. Any excessive scratches, dirt or nicks in the raw material could cause failure of the disk when the magnetic storage medium was placed upon it. At that point in the process, visual inspection of the disks was needed. Without some way to collect and analyze the data the inspection process would provide no basis for eliminating common problems.

Solution

Two handheld data collectors were adopted for use, the DataMyte 1558 for variables data collection and the DataMyte 1005 for attributes data collection. The 1558 was used with an electronic caliper to take diameter measurements. The operator was warned instantly of any out-of-limits condition. Accumulated data was transmitted to the mainframe computer for analysis.

See Chapter 16 for a description of handheld data collectors.

By using the DataMyte 1558, manual data collection errors were eliminated. What previously took an inspector an average of five to six hours of inspection per day was now condensed to one hour. This time included inspection of the disks and manual calculation of the $\bar{x}$ & R values, which the DataMyte performed "on the fly". This also allowed them to get the process in control much more quickly.

Using the 1005 for attribute data collection reduced the turnaround of inspection reports from three days to six hours. This not only led to faster inspection of disks, but allowed criteria for visual examinations, such as what is a scratch or what is a nick, to be more easily defined and maintained.

Operation

What follows is a brief explanation of how a DataMyte 1558 and a caliper was used to implement variable data collection, and how the 1005 was used for attributes.

The 1558 matrix was set as follows:

Items = 6 (3 ID measurements, 3 OD measurements)
Samples = 50 (to get process into control)
Horiz/Vert = H horizontal (one disk inspected at a time)
Eng limits = CR (yes, they were to be used)
Prompts = CR (yes, one for each measurement)
Transducers = CR (yes, a C1 code for the caliper was used)

The nice feature about the DataMyte in this application was its ability to warn the operator for an out-of-limits condition, thereby making it very easy to screen rejects. The information for engineering limits was set as previously indicated. Separate matrices were used for the different models they were inspecting. The transducer table was set for C1 and C2 (caliper) and because the special fixture was used in conjunction with the caliper, the offset column was set to the specified amount, depending on the model of the disk being inspected. C1 was set for the larger models and C2 set for the smaller models.

As for attribute data collection, the DataMyte 1005 was set up with the following prompt loop:

Date, operator
(batch no., Qty insp., Qty rej., (defect codes))

Note that defect codes were nested as a prompt, allowing the operator to enter multiple readings for this prompt before going back to batch number. Also note that date and operator needed to be entered only once for a data collection cycle because the following prompts are also nested. The prompts for this routine show up as follows:

Date, operator, batch no, qty insp, qty rej, defect code, defect code, defect code .....

After the last defect code was entered, the next prompt shown would be "batch no."

Each possible defect (scratches, dents, grooves, dirt, etc...) was assigned a separate two digit code and these codes were written on the DataMyte 1005 note pad. An inspector would just enter them accordingly. The software residing in the computer would then sort the codes and indicate problem areas to the engineers and inspection team. Management reports were also generated to indicate defects per pre-determined quantity of disks inspected (usually defects per 100). It used to take three days for manual inspection of the disks, the accumulation of all the data, inputting into the computer, and waiting for the reports to be generated. Now it takes six hours. Attribute data collection was now efficient and practical.

CASE 9-6 COMPUTER MANUFACTURER

Torque Auditing Helps Monitor Incoming Inspection

A large manufacturer of desk-top computers was experiencing problems related to the quality of products being supplied by some of their subcontractors. It seemed that certain subcontractors were failing to adequately test their parts and assemblies prior to shipment to the manufacturer. Costs associated with incoming inspections, rework, and customer relations were soaring.

As a leader in the area of desk-top computers, this manufacturer knew that problems related to untested parts and assemblies were hurting their reputation. To regain control of the situation, the manufacturer decided to implement a program that included the use of DataMyte 1503 data collectors to handle the inspection of various incoming parts and assemblies.

Problem Definition

Many of the major assemblies that make up a desk-top computer consist of printed circuit boards that have critical fasteners attached to them. It was found that if these fasteners were not properly torqued prior to shipment, the printed circuit boards could easily crack.

Furthermore, many of the subassemblies had dimensions that were considered critical to the overall computer design. If the dimensions for these subassemblies were allowed to vary significantly, supply voltages could be shorted. This in turn would lead to a complete power failure in the computer.

Solution

A method was needed to monitor the torque on fasteners as they arrived from suppliers and monitor the spacing between these assemblies as they are assembled into the computer.

Hard copy results were needed immediately after data collection. They considered manually taking the measurements, charting the readings, and submitting data to their data processing department for reports and copies. They also considered automating the process with an intelligent data collector. It was determined that the best solution would be to connect DataMyte 1503 data collectors to either a torque wrench or a gap measurement device. Using

See Chapter 16 for data collectors and Chapter 17 for torque tools.

these arrangements, the manufacturer was able to verify fastener torque and critical dimensions at the incoming inspection level.

In addition to being able to measure torque and check critical dimensions, other benefits realized by using the DataMyte 1503 data collector included:

- The ability to have the DataMyte generate capability reports and charts on demand.
- A significant cost reduction due to a decrease in rework.
- A significant reduction in data acquisition time.
- The manufacturer did not have to purchase any additional computing or test equipment since the DataMyte was capable of being interfaced to the existing hardware.

Operation

The information that follows provides a description of how the DataMyte 1503 was used by the manufacturer to meet their requirement for being able to perform torque and critical dimension measurements.

One matrix of the DataMyte was established to deal with the problem of fastener torque. This matrix was set up to measure six of the fasteners. See Figure 9.6.1. Since suppliers usually submitted these assemblies in lots of 50 the sample size was also set to 50. Overall, this matrix was set up as follows:

ITEMS = 6 (one for each of the six fasteners)
SAMPLES = 50
CELL SIZE = 6 (this represents the default value)
HORZ/VERT = H (horizontal, as only one assembly at a time would be tested)
PROMPTS = YES

Prompt values were established as follows:

ITEM 1 = LTF (left top fastener)
ITEM 2 = LBF (left bottom fastener)
ITEM 3 = LCF (left center fastener)
ITEM 4 = TCF (top center fastener)
ITEM 5 = RCF (right center fastener)
ITEM 6 = RSF (right side fastener)

Limits were established as follows for each of the items:

LO = 30.0 in/lbs
HI = 38.5 in/lbs

For this matrix, the same transducer was used for each item. To keep it simple, A1 was used as the alphanumeric code for the torque wrench. After the setup information was entered, the DataMyte Data Collect mode was entered. The Matrix ID was set up with the supplier identification codes. In this case, seven-character codes were assigned as follows:

Supplier A = 1A36B11
Supplier B = 2A36B11
Supplier C = 3A36B11
Supplier D = 4A36B11

The date and operator identification entries were completed as required. The three note spaces were left blank. Once the data was collected for a particular supplier, a report was generated. The matrix would then be cleared of all its data and a new batch of subassemblies tested. When the new batch was tested, the new supplier code was entered into the Matrix ID entry column. The date and operator identification were also re-entered as required.

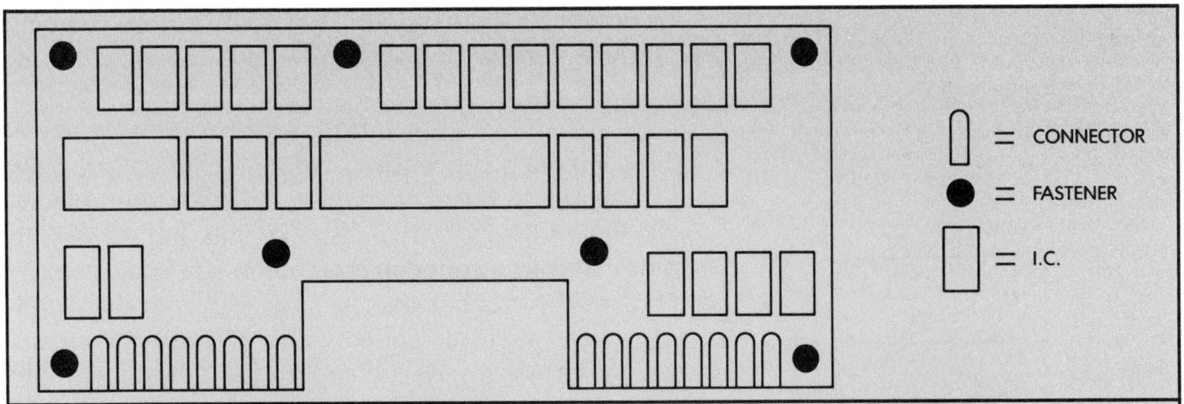

Fig. 9.6.1 PC board torque checks.

To accomodate testing of the critical gap measurements, a second matrix was set up as follows:

ITEMS = 3 (one for each area of the gap to be tested)
SAMPLES = 10
CELL SIZE = 6 (this represents the default value)
HORZ/VERT = H
PROMPTS = YES

Prompt values were established as follows:

ITEM 1 = TOP
ITEM 2 = MIDDLE
ITEM 3 = BOTTOM

Limits were established as follows for each of the items:

LO = 7.0
HI = 9.5

For this matrix, the same transducer was used for each measurement. The code used was G1 for gap gage.

When entering the Data Collect mode, the matrix ID was set up to reflect the shift number (i.e., shift 1, shift 2, or shift 3). The date and operator identifications were entered as required. The three note spaces contained the following:

NOTE 1 = SUBA
NOTE 2 = SPEC
NOTE 3 = TEST

The note entries were used to help identify the area of measurement on the final product. The shift number was also important as it helped to identify the particular shift when the improper installation took place.

With the above matrices in place and being used, the manufacturer was able to meet the requirements for measuring fastener torque and for making the critical gap measurements.

CASE 9-7 PROCESS CONTROLLER MANUFACTURER

Company Reduces Variability on Circuit Board Pick and Place Machine

A manufacturer of process controllers and valves for the petrochemical industry needed to reduce PC board failures. By automating data collection at their circuit pick and place operation, they found they could control variablity and reduce defects.

Problem

The company's concern was with their automated pick-and-place circuit board assembler and solderer. It has six control heads loaded with belts of circuits and resistors to be automatically inserted in the appropriate spot on a circuit board. The problem they had was with critical pressure points when the head, loaded with the resistor or circuit, comes down and inserts the appropriate component into the circuit board. The critical variable was the pressure from the head on the circuit board. The pressure fluctuated too much, and needed to be monitored constantly. The old way was to shut the machine down and manually check the pressure with a gage.

Solution

See Chapter 16 for data collectors and Chapter 18 for FAN II software.

The solution was to hook up an electronic gage via an RS-232 output to a DataMyte 762 data collector. This allowed them to read each of the six heads individually and to make the appropriate adjustments on-line without stopping the process. Additionally, DataMyte FAN II software allowed the data to be exported into the data base file for their post process analysis.

10. FOOD, COSMETICS, AND HEALTH CARE INDUSTRIES

CASE 10-1 PROCESSED MEAT COMPANY

Packaged Meats Company Improves Margins With Better SPC Program

A major food processing company is the largest in the United States specializing in sliced meats and processed foods, turkey products and seasonings. The company has its own seasoning plant and it also has its own plastics facilities for making the wrapping and packages. By automating its data collection process and by using SPC they reduced scrap by 5 to 10 percent and reduced labor by even more.

Problem

The company had been using manual SPC methods to keep track of the weights, thicknesses and temperatures of some of their processed meats and bologna. The food processor needed real-time, or near real-time data analysis in order to reduce scrap and waste. Charting by hand took too much time and the charts ended up almost useless because they were too messy and dirty.

The data also had to be keypunched into a computer so the company could archive the data. The archived data was for their own use as well as for meeting government regulations and presenting to inspectors.

Solution

See Chapter 16 for data collectors and Chapter 17 for weigh scales.

The employees collected data from an electronic weigh scale, which had RS-232C output, a caliper and a temperature probe, which also had RS-232C output. Using a DataMyte 750 data collector they could record the readings automatically. DataMyte 750 models with Cusum charting capabilities were installed at each operator station. The CuSum charting gave the employees a faster reaction to changes in the data than the $\bar{x}$ & R chart did. After collecting the data, the employees transferred the data to an IBM PC with the FAN II software program. Current data could readily be presented to government inspectors. The FAN II software program also allowed the employees to bring data back from the computer and load it into the DataMyte 750 the next time the product is run. This gives an instant comparison to previous runs.

The company's time lag between collecting data and seeing control charts was practically eliminated. This helped reduce their scrap and waste by about five to ten percent—helpful in a low margin industry, such as the food industry. Manpower requirements were reduced by about 20% because one day per five day work week had been devoted to recording, keypunching and calculating the charts.

CASE 10-2 FROZEN DINNER COMPANY

Statistical Sampling Reduces Variability in Frozen Breakfast Portions

A well-known company in the food industry was introducing a new line of frozen breakfast entrees. The automated cooking and packaging line could produce several varieties of meals, including eggs, sausages and hash browns, or pancakes and sausages, at the rate of two meals per second.

Problem

An automatic sensor on the packaging line kicked out any meals that were underweight before they were boxed and frozen. The trouble was, there was no good way to automatically check for overweight meals. The company was concerned about not putting too much of any one item in each meal, but checking the gross weight of the meal did not supply criteria for adjusting the egg, sausage and hash brown portions.

Company managers decided that statistical sampling of the weights of portions going into the meal would provide data to control the process. The speed of the packaging line required an efficient method of gathering and analyzing data, however. Since the line was automated to a fairly high degree, the company felt that a labor-intensive SPC activity would not be suitable.

Solution

The SPC system that would be most effective needed to record and analyze weights automatically. The results of statistical sampling must be made visible to workers, who could then respond with solutions such as adjusting the process. The company selected a digital weigh scale with RS-232 output, a DataMyte 750 and a CRT monitor. The DataMyte would record weights and plot $\bar{x}$ & R charts on the CRT. The chart could be updated for each subgroup, allowing instantaneous verification of the process.

See Chapter 16 for a description of the 750 data collector.

It was soon discovered that of the three items being plotted, the egg making process had a lot of variability and contributed most to the problem of overweight meals. The eggs were supplied already cracked and in barrels. They were fed into a machine that scrambled them and then dumped them into a bin. The bin metered the eggs into the dinner trays. A control chart of the egg weights found that the amount metered into each meal varied according to how many eggs were in the bin. The bin metering mechanism was rebuilt to reduce the influence.

SPC resulted in a savings on the usage of eggs in this line. As the variability in the process was reduced, the frequency of sampling could be reduced also. This further justified their assumption that dedicating extra labor to the SPC task was unwise.

The company has now purchased additional DataMyte 750s and monitors for each shift. Each shift has a separate line setup, and a different type of frozen meal is produced. Having a easy to use, standardized system for SPC allows workers from each shift and managers to talk about the breakfast making process in the same terms.

CASE 10-3 COSMETICS COMPANY

Company Automates SPC In Plastic Molding Operation

A leading producer of cosmetic products needed to control the plastic molding operation in their container manufacturing area. Fifteen inspectors were being utilized, but their responsibility had deteriorated to sorting good and bad product. Scrap and rework had become an accepted part of the process.

Problem Definition

The company recognized that to remedy the condition it would be necessary to involve the operators in quality improvement. They felt that for their SPC program to work they needed to give the operators the tools that went hand in hand with the responsibility. Only in this manner could the operators continue to perform their present job while handling the SPC data collection task. In addition to these challenges, there were some FDA regulations to be considered. Inspection personnel were needed to collect the data in sufficient detail to meet these requirements.

Solution

It was decided that only by employing automatic data collection techniques could they accomplish their goals.

- Each work station was equipped with a DataMyte model 752 data collector, display terminal and digital gages.
- Operators could now produce their own real-time control charts. This included date and time stamping of data to meet the FDA regulations.
- A DataTruck was employed to harvest data from the factory floor and transport it to the QC department.
- An IBM PC was purchased for archiving and report generation.

Data collection and quality are now the operators responsibility. As a result, productivity has reached new levels earning corporate recognition in this world wide organization. Scrap is almost a forgotten entity and the inspection force has been reduced to zero in this area.

See Chapter 16 for a description of the 752 and DataTruck data collectors.

The success in this area is really only the first phase. The next project targeted for SPC is the container filling area where cost savings approaching a million dollars per year are possible.

CASE 10-4 PERSONAL CARE PRODUCTS COMPANY

Company Uses Digitizing Tablet and Data Collector to Audit Diaper Product

A large consumer products company, manufacturing many types of foods and toiletry articles, began a corporate wide SPC program to help cut costs and improve quality. The company retained Dr. W. Edwards Deming as a consultant to develop a top-down management commitment.

Problem

The company was looking for better ways to automate data collection, and also looking for specialty gages to fit their needs.

In one division the company was interested in measuring the critical dimensions on a new adult diaper. Because of the nature of the product, they needed to hold close tolerances to ensure the comfort and wear of the product.

A major problem with the diapers is that they are not designed to lay flat on a surface and measured. In the past all measurements were done with a ruler and written down. Control charts were done by hand. This proved to be extremely tedious, time consuming and inaccurate.

Solution

Company engineers thought that a digitizing tablet could simplify the measurement process. A digitizing tablet is a flat table on which the process engineer could tape the diaper down onto the surface. By using a light pen he could mark the xy coordinate reference point. Each time the light pen is moved to a different portion of the diaper the tablet automatically references back to the original xy position, and takes its measurements in relation to the original coordinate.

See Chapter 16 for a description of the 2003 data collector.

The digital signals from the tablet were fed directly into a DataMyte 2003 data collector. The engineer set up a matrix in the DataMyte for each of the dimensional characteristics. The DataMyte made the subtraction and calculation steps for each coordinate in relation to the reference point, and calculated the between coordinate dimensions.

The company found a 75 percent labor savings by using

the digitizing tablet and DataMyte 2003 compared to the previous data collection method.

CASE 10-5 PERSONAL CARE PRODUCTS COMPANY

Manufacturer Streamlines Incoming Inspection, Fill Weight and Torque Monitoring

The quality department of a major manufacturer of cosmetics and other personal care products faced the task of efficiently monitoring data being collected in different areas of the plant. Monitoring was needed to insure that increased production schedules and product quality could be maintained and improved.

Problem

In incoming inspection the company faced the need to monitor numerous vendor product containers. The characteristics to be monitored were:

- Cap and bottle neck diameters,
- Container (internal and external) dimensions,
- Part thicknesses.

The containers are made from various materials including glass, plastic and metal. The monitoring of these and other dimensions were critical to product quality. Lack of adherence to proper dimensional requirements caused such problems as:

- Improper package sealing,
- Package unattractiveness,
- Proper application of the product became difficult or impossible.

The company previously collected data using various dimensional gages. Samples were collected from the incoming lots and data recorded by a staff of quality technicians. Later the data would be manually calculated, and the results would determine if the lot was to be accepted or rejected. The technician would complete a chart recording the past history of the particular part. What was needed was a means of streamlining this data collection process while eliminating the volume of paper which was being produced by the manual system.

Streamlining the collection and processing of data would result in the following benefits:

- Shorten the time needed from which the product was received at the shipping dock and ready for release to the plant floor,
- Reduce the time and expense of incoming inspection,
- Provide a comprehensive source of archived data to aid in analyzing problems in vendor parts.

Solution

See Chapter 15 for a description of the FAN system.

The company streamlined the incoming inspection area, and achieved the above mentioned goals by implementing a DataMyte FAN system. The system was composed of DataMyte 752s, several different types of electronic gaging equipment (including electronic calipers, digital indicators and a horizontal axis measuring device), DataMyte FAN software and Lotus 1-2-3 software.

Once a particular lot was received in the shipping area, samples were gathered and taken to the measurement lab for evaluation. At the same time, a DataMyte 750 would be uploaded with the various part numbers and part specifications required for the technician to gather the data. The technician would then take the DataMyte and measure the parts with electronic gages.

See Chapter 18 for a description of DataMyte software.

During the measuring process, the DataMyte would notify the technician of out of spec conditions, at which time the technician could further review the situation using the DataMyte screen. Once the data had been collected, he would then return the DataMyte 750 to the PC, where the data would be processed using the FAN software and Lotus software. Lotus software allowed the Quality Department to customize its reports and charts to meet its particular incoming inspection needs. The application software streamlined the data collection process, but also enabled them to produce customized reports that not only aided in the accept/reject decisions for incoming parts, but also allowed a complete data base history to be maintained in an efficient manner.

Fill Weight and Removal Torque Monitoring

Once the vendor's containers were released to the plant floor, a new challenge was faced of monitoring a dozen different fill lines.

The product containers being filled ranged from 1 oz. to 12 oz. and required removal torque between 12 to 25 in.lb., depending upon the particular package being monitored. Removal torque is the force required to remove the lid from a jar. The task of monitoring these two characteristics required the operator to sample each product line every half-hour. Manual sampling methods included:

- Establishment of a standard tear value for the amount of containers being used,
- Setting of the scale for the given tear value
- The weighing and manually recording of the weight of each sample, and
- Calculating the $\bar{x}$ & R, manually plotting the charts.

A similar process was then repeated for the monitoring of removal torque on each production line.

Although the manufacturer felt the implementation of SPC had been quite successful in monitoring both the fill weight and removal torque, it became quite apparent that the time the operator needed to produce the charts was overly burdensome. There was also no easy way for management to archive and review the past data.

Solution

The adoption of a full scale FAN system provided solutions for these applications also. Each product line was equipped with a 750 and monitor interfaced to an electronic weigh scale and a removal torque test unit with RS-232 output. The DataTruck was then used to set up part files on each of the product lines and to harvest data on a daily basis. The data was sent to an IBM PC equipped with FAN support software.

See Chapter 17 for weigh scale and torque testers.

The FAN system allowed the quality department to establish computerized files on each of the various parts being manufactured. When a part is scheduled, the file is loaded to the DataTruck and transported to the 750 data collector located on the line. The operator then monitors the production run with half-hour samplings. If adjustments or changes are needed, the operator indicates the nature of the adjustment or change by coding the $\bar{x}$ or R control point with a special decimal code. This code will then appear on all future $\bar{x}$ & R charts that the operator generates. The data is then harvested from the DataMyte and loaded into the PC for archival and report generation. The installed system created numerous new benefits which include:

- Decreased time the operator needed to spend in collecting and recording the $\bar{x}$ & R charts,
- Allowed the operator to easily review and analyze the process charting,
- Eliminated errors which were encountered in the manual system, and
- Provided management with an organized data base for use in evaluating product quality and machine productivity.

The information became useful in maintaining and improving product quality, and also became a valuable tool for the machine maintenance department in evaluating various machine repairs and for planning preventive maintenance.

CASE 10-6 PHARMACEUTICAL COMPANY

Company Improves Monitoring of Bottle Cap Opening Force

A large manufacturer of pharmaceutical products was faced with reducing its workforce and needed to make its existing workers more productive. The company uses SPC to monitor the production of their plastic containers as well as various aspects of their packaging line.

Problem

The company had been using a manual SPC system for the molding process of plastic containers. Their SPC problem solving activities were too slow to effectively help their molding process. They needed a faster response time so the workers could adjust their machines when necessary.

The company was also monitoring the fill weights of certain products on their packaging line. Other data they needed to keep track of included the amount of force necessary to "pop" the caps off bottles and the crush strength of the container.

The company wanted to keep track of attribute data in the final packaging end area to make sure the products were labeled and packaged correctly. All in all, the company had several requirements that it wanted for its SPC program, including ease of use.

Solution

The company purchased a DataMyte 762 data collector to use with various hand tools in both the packaging and container-making areas. The tools the company used for monitoring the container molding process included calipers, micrometers and optical comparators. Workers used force gages to test the force needed to uncap filled containers. They also used electronic weigh scales to monitor various fill weights of the containers. See Figure 10.6.1. Using the DataMyte FAN II software program and a DataTruck, the workers stored the data on an IBM PC. This gave them easy access to historical data to track improvement and to provide reports to government inspectors. The DataMyte 769 attribute data collector suited the company's need for attribute data collection. The workers found the 769 easy to use, with its bar code wand for data entry, and its ability to print its own bar codes.

The company arranged for DataMyte to train its workers to get the most from their DataMyte FAN system. After purchasing and using the FAN system, the company had decidedly increased the productivity of a shrinking workforce.

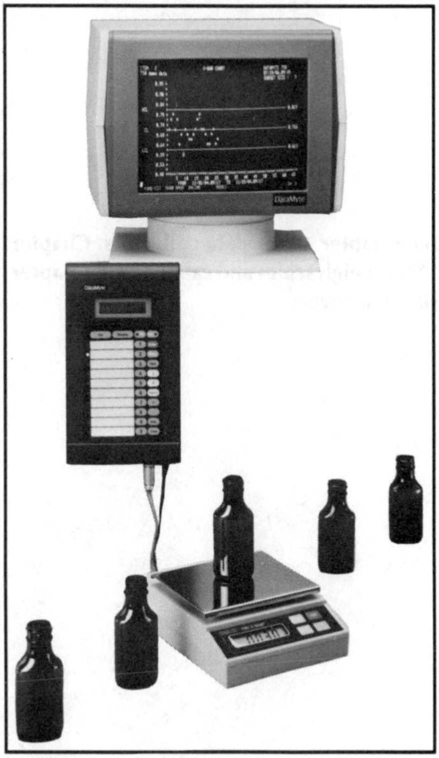

Fig. 10.6.1 Checking weights of pharmaceutical vials.

CASE 10-7 HEALTH CARE PRODUCTS MANUFACTURER

Company Expands SPC Operations

A major manufacturer of health care products successfully implemented a SPC program to monitor a medical gauze pad product.

Problem

With SPC successfully implemented, the manufacturer's interest in expanding operator duties not only included monitoring, but boxing and palletizing of the product as well. These new demands on the operator's time quickly showed a need for more efficient means of maintaining $\bar{x}$ & R charts.

Solution

The $\bar{x}$ & R charts were produced on 2-hour increments with five samples for each subgroup. The weight and length of the gauze pad are critical for the product to retain proper absorbency. The solution was to install a DataMyte FAN system consisting of DataMyte 750s with monitors and a DataTruck to harvest and archive the data using FAN Support Software on an IBM PC.

See Chapter 16 for data collectors, Chapter 17 for weigh scales and calipers and Chapter 18 for software.

The 750, interfaced to a scale and caliper, quickly increased the speed in which the operators were able to collect and produce $\bar{x}$ & R charts. When a point on a chart required action, the operator would note the change on the $\bar{x}$ & R charts using a set of established codes to illustrate the action which was taken to correct the processes at the particular point and time. This code will appear on all future $\bar{x}$ & R charts the operator generates.

The manufacturer was able to recoup the system cost with the operator time savings. The time required for machine shut down to perform the manual SPC chart was greatly reduced. This became a very important issue to the operator acceptance of the DataMyte system, since their compensation package was based on an incentive system. Management was also able to take advantage of being able to archive data collected by the DataTruck and FAN Support Software.

CASE 10-8 MEDICAL PACEMAKER COMPANY

Use of DataMyte 750s Provide "Front-End" Solution to QDM 1000

A large manufacturer of human heart pacemakers was interested in implementing an SPC program in order to remain competitive and hold its leadership in the marketplace. The company produces thousands of pacemakers per month and is a recognized leader in the industry. The cost of quality in this company has been large, and they are continually being monitored by the FDA to assure that their products are reliable. The ability to collect and analyze data and feed this into their mainframe computer would provide them with significant cost reductions in their manufacturing process.

Problem

Several areas in the plant were targeted for initial DataMyte applications. These included various receiving inspection areas where numerous dimensional measurements are taken. Analysis of the data was always too late to offer the opportunity for correction of the process, and many parts ended up being scrapped. Another area targeted for immediate SPC application was the machining operation. No checking of the material was being done during production; it was being left to inspectors to sort out the bad parts.

Solution

The solution to this problem was to have inspectors use DataMyte 750s to collect and analyze the data. The inspectors were given a DataMyte 750, monitor, electronic calipers and micrometers. They collected data in a fraction of the previous time and were able to analyze their results immediately.

In addition, some of the production machines were equipped with a DataMyte 750 and monitor. Operators are asked to collect data on their parts as they are produced. The operators required some additional training to fully realize the benefits of an SPC program.

Data from the DataMytes was entered into the company's mainframe computer system through the Hewlett Packard QDM 1000 to DataMyte interface option. The QDM package allows the company to archive vast amounts of data in an effective manner. Customized charts and reports are generated from the DataMyte data utilizing the powerful software options of the QDM 1000.

See Chapter 22 for a description of the H-P QDM 1000.

CASE 10-9 MEDICAL SYSTEMS MANUFACTURER

Laser Micrometer Interfaces with DataMyte

A medical systems manufacturer in the midwest required a more efficient reporting system for their assembly operation. The systems they made required rigorous process control to achieve high quality and faultless operation.

Problem Definition

See Chapter 17 for laser micrometers.

With the increased sophistication of checking devices on their assembly floor, some of which had data output capabilities, there was a need for more efficient data collection. The manufacturer required a large amount of critical data from their Tech Met Laser-micrometer, which had an RS-232C data output port. They considered several systems for capturing this data.

Solution

Rather than purchase a fixed station data recording device, such as a desktop computer, which was not really suitable for factory use, they purchased a DataMyte 1508 Stand Alone System. The system consists of a handheld data collector and printer. The data collector could be taken into the factory and connected to the laser micrometer. The data collector would accept and store the data, having 64K of memory. The DataMyte would then be simply connected to the printer to produce $\bar{x}$ & R charts. No other system or software was required. In addition, the data collector could be interfaced with a number of other checking devices, such as an electronic weigh scale, which they anticipated using in the future.

CASE 10-10 ORTHOPEDIC IMPLANTS COMPANY

Data Collectors Used to Ensure Quality of Hip and Joint Replacements

A company making orthopedic implants needed a more comprehensive inspection system to meet federal guidelines. They found that the use of data collectors for both dimensional and defect inspection provided the feedback they needed for manufacturing and the documentation to meet federal guidelines.

Problem

Federal guidelines are very stringent on these types of products. The company was required to document the dimensional characteristics, such as length, diameter and circumference, and also attributes. The attributes included the presence of scratches, nicks, blemishes and other defects. The reason for defects inspection is because the presence of defects can affect the outcome of the implant surgery if they harbored bacteria that could infect the joint.

Solution

The company decided that a standardized data collection system would help alert the manufacturing processes making the parts. The real-time analysis would allow them to make adjustments before an unacceptable amount of defects occurred.

DataMyte 762 data collection systems were used for recording and analyzing dimensional data. DataMyte 769 data collection systems were used for recording and analyzing defects. Operators at each inspection station were responsible for both dimensional and defects inspection. Both systems provided a standard documentation scheme as well as instant feedback on a video display terminal.

See Chapter 16 for a description of the 762 and 769 data collectors.

The results of their system implementation has been an increased vigilance by their operators on quality improvement as well as automatic documentation to meet federal guidelines.

CASE 10-11 PHARMACEUTICAL COMPANY

Company Automates Data Collection in Aseptic Packaging Line

A major pharmaceutical company wanted to automate data being collected with regard to the filling of plastic drug delivery pouches.

Problem

This is an aseptic process performed in a clean room environment. The process involves two sets of four filling machines. Each set of four is tied to a common conveyor that brings the pouches to a packaging operation. Because of the sterility requirements, the company wanted to minimize the amount of time personnel needed to be present in the room and also minimize the amount of equipment present. The measurements being tracked in this process are fill weight and the thickness of the seam on the plastic pouch.

Solution

The company chose a system consisting of two DataMyte 762 data collectors with monitors as well as scales and micrometers to collect the measurements.

The DataMyte 762 is able to handle a group of items (weight and thickness) for each of four different filling operations. This allows them to monitor each operation separately. An additional variable was the need to track production by lot number.

See Chapter 16 for a description of the 762 data collector.

This system decreased the time needed to collect and analyze the data, eliminated error which occurred in the manual system, and provided real time feedback for controlling the filling process.

CASE 10-12 PHARMACEUTICAL COMPANY

Automated Raw Materials and Packaging Lab System Increases Productivity Five-Fold

A major drug company was very concerned with productivity and felt that a tremendous profit could be obtained by improving their plant operations. By automating SPC data collection of variables and attributes data in their packaging and receiving areas, they improved productivity five-fold and paid for the system in about one month.

Problem

The raw materials and packaging department had to inspect 13 samples of every lot of approximately 70 different parts per month. Each sample had to be checked for weights, lengths, widths, volume capacity, neck length, neck OD, neck ID, bottle OD, cap opening/closing, and torque testing. The time it took to measure 13 samples per lot was 45 minutes to 1 hour 15 minutes. All of the statistics were kept by hand and documented on paper. They used a computer to summarize the data, and then the sample was either released to production, rejected, or put on hold. If a part was rejected, a raw materials card was generated and sent to purchasing. Purchasing, in turn, would contact the vendor for appropriate action to be taken.

The primary problem in the raw materials and packaging lab was the incredible amount of time needed to generate reports on incoming samples. When a shipment of raw material or incoming production material arrived, it took 10-14 days before the material was released to the production line. In conjunction with their just-in-time program, just starting to ramp up, if they could reduce the time the raw material sat prior to release to production, they could save money on payments to their vendors and speed up the packaging of their products. This was a just-in-time production goal.

Inspectors spend most of their time logging and documenting the necessary statistics for their incoming inspection, which allowed them to do only about four samples a day. The typical attributes report would classify the defects according to priority. They would reject a lot depending on the priority of the defect.

Solution

The company investigated ways of automating the inspection process. As a part of the productivity improvement they began using DataMyte data collectors. A DataMyte 862 data collector was used to check 10 critical dimensions. The data collector could interface with their caliper and weigh scale. They entered measurements from a ruler by using the keypad. A DataMyte 769 data collector allowed them to input all the possible visual defects on all their products, using bar code entry.

See Chapter 16 for data collectors, Chapter 17 for calipers and weigh scales and Chapter 18 for FAN II software.

The use of the data collectors cut data collection time per lot from a maximum of 1 hour 15 minutes to about 10 to 15 minutes. The time savings was quite substantial, but more importantly was the ability to store the data on DataMyte FAN II software. This allowed them to generate reports and approve incoming lots substantially faster. Additionally, when they tried to give performance reports to their suppliers of raw materials, it was extremely time consuming and many times did not get done. They had not been getting reports out on time for the last three quarters.

The payback on the data collectors for the raw materials and packaging lab took one month.

11. FURNITURE AND APPLIANCE INDUSTRIES

CASE 11-1 OFFICE FURNITURE SYSTEMS MANUFACTURER

Data Collection Decreases Variability in Attribute Inspection

A leading manufacturer of modular furniture systems for offices established an employee participation program for quality control in 1981. The program made the employees responsible for the quality of their own work. At the time, 4% of the work force participated in the program. The program has grown so that now the company has 65% of the workforce involved. Last year, the company conducted over 25,000 employee audits of finished products. In the past six years, productivity has risen about 70%, while the cost of quality has fallen 80%. DataMyte data collectors have contributed to this boost in the company's efficiency.

Problem

When the company started the quality contol program, it was primarily collecting attribute data, looking at the fit and finish of the finished products. However, because of the way the data was collected, not everyone collected data the same way. What one person might call a good product, someone else might not. The company needed a way to look at some of its processes with variables data, so that everyone was inspecting from the same perspective.

For example, one product that this affects is a shelf called a "flippy" in the trade. This is an enclosed shelf that mounts on a wall-like panel. The shelf has a front cover that flips up and slides over the top of the shelf. The shelf is made of laminations of particle board and plastic laminate. An edging material is applied to the edge of the shelf. The edging material is a fixed, consistent width. One of the defects the company inspected for was the fit of the edge to the shelf. Because the thickness of the shelf could vary, the edging material may or may not fit properly.

Solution

The company found that by tracking the thickness of the shelf during production, a more reliable product could be obtained. This involved using Mitutoyo calipers and micrometers to monitor each stage of the shelf lamination process. Employees had been using DataMyte 752s and 762s to measure dimensions of their products. The company has been introducing the DataMyte 862, to take advantage of the 862's ability to store data from many different parts at once.

See Chapter 16 for a description of the 862 and 769 data collectors.

By using numerical data from these data collectors, the company is able to do several things. It can monitor the performance of each operator and workstation. Adjustments can be made to ensure a consistent thickness for the product. The company can also monitor the process capability over time. This becomes important because of the variation in seasonal conditions: summers are more humid than winters, and the humidity affects the thickness of the pieces as they are assembled.

The DataMyte 769 is used in a final inspection area to collect attribute data with a bar code wand. The inspectors pull different pieces of the furniture system at random and assemble them. They then inspect the fit and finish of the assembled product.

CASE 11-2 RETAIL APPLIANCE COMPANY

Column Gage — DataMyte Linkup Provides Real-Time Operator Involvement

A leading retail appliance manufacturer needed a data collection and analysis system that was capable of interfacing directly with two different types of column gages. Up to ten of these column gages were tied into one fixture. In addition, the system had to be small enough that it would not crowd the operator's work station and still give the operator real time feedback for SPC.

The measurements were extremely precise. The system had to provide enough data to help produce a more consistantly dimensioned part as well as improve overall plant productivity. The company was also interested in maintaining all raw data to do further analysis, but was not interested in having filing cabinets full of paper. Paper records were considered essentially "worthless", since the information would never really be used by management in a timely manner.

Problem

The difficulty of managing data generated from 25 production lines and interfacing with (on an average) six column gages at one time seemed monumental. The company was doing the data collection in a very traditional manner and they were forced to:

- Manually collect data from their existing column gages.
- Write the data down on forms for each process that they were monitoring.
- Manually calculate the mean of the data.
- Manually plot the $\bar{x}$ value on a control chart at the process.
- Later attempt to accumulate the raw data and calculate manually the control limits for the process.

Needless to say, the problems in this system began to grow because of the amount of data that had to be collected on just a few production lines. The time that it took to evaluate the data was also considered prohibitive. In addition, the company had begun to install new electronic column gages that were being viewed as being more difficult to work with by the operators. This added to the problems of overall data collection and analysis.

Solution

It was decided that a FAN® (Factory Area Network) system, consisting of a DataMyte model 751 data collector, with a ten column gage interface and junction box, would be the best system for data collection. This particular system solved some cumbersome problems:

- Up to ten column gages could be interfaced to each DataMyte — the operator simply had to put a part in a fixture and hit a foot switch and all of the measurements from the columns were immediately recorded in the DataMyte — this eliminated the operators difficulty in reading the often difficult column gages. The operator no longer had to write down all of the information and do the calculations. The DataMyte immediately alerted the operator to parts out of specification.
- When the operator completed his last sample in the subgroup, the DataMyte told him if he was in or out of control. The appliance manufacturer went a step further and tied each DataMyte into a video display at the process. By doing so, the operator simply had to push a

button and his most recent 55 $\bar{x}$ points were displayed on a graph on the screen. At the same time, the operator also had the ability to look at a histogram of each characteristic being measured.

As a result of their success with the DataMyte FAN® system, real-time process control was established at each of the manufacturing processes in the plant. Because the DataMyte 751 maintains all the raw data collected at each process, the data could be harvested with a DataTruck twice each shift. Data was then transmitted to an IBM PC managed by the DataMyte FAN® Support Software package. The Software package is used to manage all of the manufacturing setups in the facility as well as generating hard copy $\bar{x}$ & R charts. Capability reports and histograms furnished by the FAN® system are used on a real-time basis by management to further reduce the variability of their processes.

See Chapter 15 for a description of the FAN system.

CASE 11-3 ELECTRIC METER MANUFACTURER

Interactive SPC Data System Boosts Machine Shop Production

A leading manufacturer of kilowatt-hour meters wanted to completely computerize their screw machine facility. Their goal was to develop a totally interactive system allowing operators to download new setups directly from the factory floor and send the reports back to the operations office. At the same time operators needed to generate their own graphic reports at the work station for statistical process control.

Problem

One of the problems was how to economically provide the hardware to support eleven operators and eighty screw machines. Each operator had to have complete access to the system to match the changing hourly and daily requirements. The system had to be easy to work with.

Solution

They decided the best approach would be supply each operator with his own work station data acquisition system. Available for easy access would be a DataMyte 750

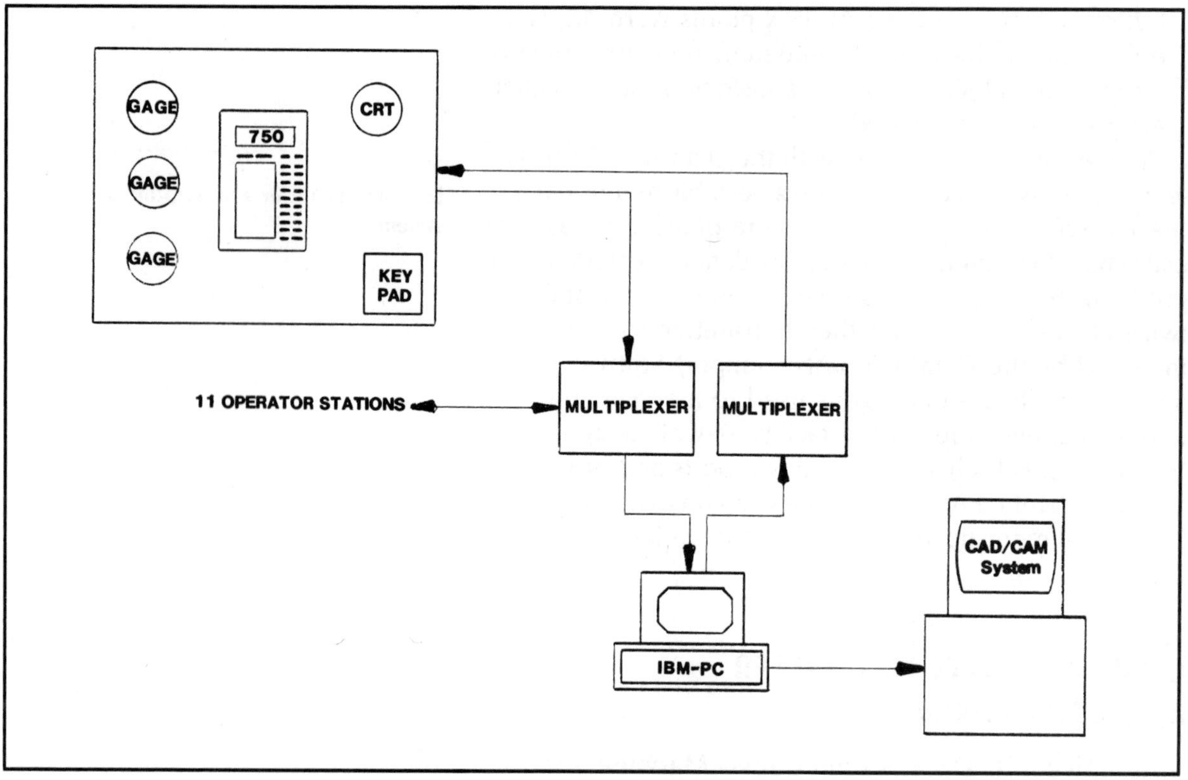

Fig. 11.3.1 Flowchart of communications network.

equipped with three gage ports and a monitor for immediate display of control charts. See Figure 11.3.1.

In addition, they equipped each location with a simple keypad for communication with a desktop computer. In this manner the operator could request the FAN® software to locate the desired part number and download to the 750 located at the work station. The operations department could also now poll the data collectors on the floor and harvest the information in the most timely fashion to plan production schedules.

See Chapter 15 for a description of the FAN system.

The implementation of the FAN® system has provided this company with one of the most advanced SPC facilities in the world today. They are enjoying the benefits of better quality, reduced defects, and haven't added one bit to the work load of the operators.

CASE 11-4 FLOOR SWEEPERS MANUFACTURER

Coordinate Measuring Machine — DataMyte Linkup Provides SQC Report Consistency

A world leader in the manufacturing of industrial floor sweepers needed a data collection and analysis device that was capable of analyzing the outputs from a coordinate measuring machine. They also wanted all statistical reports generated to be consistent in format. Since this manufacturer was already a user of DataMyte handheld data collectors, it was their desire to have data generated by their coordinate measuring device fed into the DataMyte for subsequent analysis and reporting. By using the DataMyte in this manner, the manufacturer was able to detect areas in the manufacturing process where machining costs could be reduced. The manufacturer was also able to achieve the desired consistency in report format.

Problem Definition

The process of analyzing data generated by the coordinate measuring device and generating reports was time consuming. It also did not fully meet their requirements for statistical process control (SPC). Before the DataMyte was implemented to handle the data analysis and reporting functions, the manufacturer was forced to:

1) Manually accumulate the measurements.
2) Load the data collected into the main computer memory.
3) Load in other applications programs that would in turn process and format the appropriate data.
4) Output the raw data collected to a printer.
5) Perform manual analysis of the raw data.

Because data analysis and reporting was so cumbersome, inspectors were spending far too much time collecting and analyzing data, and not enough time looking for ways to further their use of SQC.

Solution

It was decided that by simply feeding the output from the coordinate measuring device into the DataMyte, they could virtually eliminate steps 3 through 5 of their current data processing procedure. See Figure 11.4.1.

See Chapter 16 for a description of DataMyte data collectors.

Fig. 11.4.1 DataMyte and coordinate measuring machine.

Since the computing system in use had a serial RS-232-C interface, inputting data to the DataMyte was easy; only one cable was required to connect the two devices. Once connected, X values were transferred to the DataMyte, followed by the Y and Z values from the computer's memory. Once sufficient data was transferred, the DataMyte was used to generate the required capability studies, charts and graphs.

CASE 11-5 FLOOR SWEEPERS MANUFACTURER

Painting Operation Put in Statistical Control

A manufacturer of industrial floor sweepers required tighter control over painting operations. A new paint system was installed for higher accuracy and easier, less costly control over the process. Yet, how they would monitor the process was still a looming question.

Having already implemented DataMyte systems for torque control, incoming inspection and attribute data with significant success, they turned to DataMyte for an SPC solution on monitoring paint thickness.

Problem

Current methods and inspection procedures only called for visual inspection, and a minimum one mil thickness on all painted pieces. This was a very random, inconsistent inspection method because color variations made it impossible to detect problem areas. Weak paint on white pieces was easy to detect, but the blue/green areas were a different story — making it next to impossible to readily see thinly painted areas.

Solution

A DataMyte 1559 paint thickness auditing system was implemented for control of the paint area. See Figure 11.5.1. Ideally suited for a roving auditor, to randomly inspect pieces as they came out of the drying booth, the 1559 would allow for data collection and immediate report generation. Not only could they insure that at least one mil thickness was maintained, but they could also minimize excessive paint applications. This would lead to less paint runs and a far more consistent thickness for all painted articles.

See Chapter 16 for a description of the 1559 data collector.

With the stand-alone capabilities of the 1559, the paint personnel could immediately see how the process was operating. Corrections, adjustments and decisions could be made while the process was running. With limit checking capabilities, the auditor could insure that every inspected piece maintained and met the one mil thickness specs. An auditor could learn to use the 1559 in a matter of minutes for measuring paint thickness.

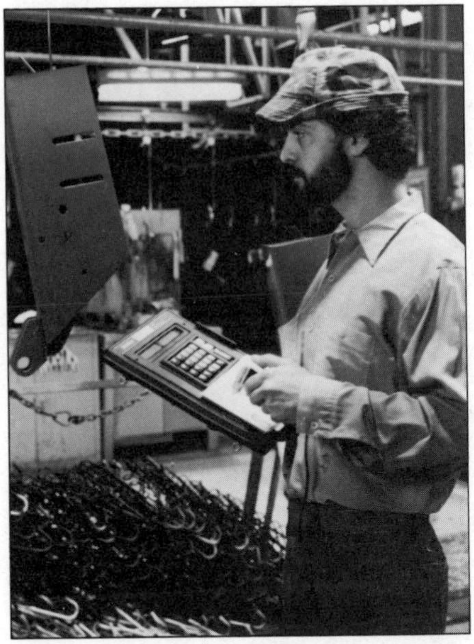

Fig. 11.5.1 Plant inspection using a DataMyte 1559.

When setting up a DataMyte matrix, all 99 items and 99 samples were used. This allowed the operator to take several random samples. At a later date, the QC team would decide on specific audit points and routes. They would then restructure the matrices for this purpose. Only low limit checking was used for the one mil thickness spec.

Histograms were generated at first in order to see the process variation. Then appropriate statistical analysis using $\bar{x}$ & R charts and capability studies would be implemented for different paint colors and pieces. Data would also be transferred to their IBM PC for further analysis and archive storage. A permanent QC data base on paint auditing would be maintained to help them analyze and reduce variability in the entire process.

CASE 11-6 GARAGE DOOR SYSTEMS MANUFACTURER

Manufacturer Saves Fourteen Hours Per Week in Documenting Their SPC

A manufacturer of transmitters, receivers and motor controls for garage door opening systems had a very labor intensive final assembly operation that made defect auditing difficult. Seventy to eighty percent of the parts for a remote control were inserted at the final assembly stage. Sometimes the wrong parts were used or the parts were not cut properly. The manufacturer had to monitor these and other defects in the assembly.

Sample PC boards that go into the transmitters and receivers were visually inspected and the defects recorded for these parts. To record this type of data and construct p-, c- and u-charts, the manufacturer used an attribute data collection system. The manufacturer monitors and records the characteristics of the remote controls in each department, as well as in the Insertion Room, before the control goes into the next stage.

Problem

One person in each manufacturing area was designated to collect the data by hand. This person collected and recorded the data on paper and then manually plotted the charts. The procedure required sixteen man-hours per week.

The company did not want to spend this much time collecting and charting the data. The manufacturer also thought the operators should have more immediate feedback about the jobs they were doing.

Solution

See Chapter 16 for data collectors and Chapter 18 for software.

The manufacturer obtained one DataMyte 1005 attribute data collector for each manufacturing area and eventually plans to have one DataMyte for each operator. With DataMyte's Attribute Software for the IBM-PC the manufacturer saves fourteen hours per week when generating charts. Instead of recording data on paper with a pencil, the operator keys the data into the DataMyte. The DataMyte stores the data in its memory until the operator downloads the data to the PC.

Data collection is more convenient and accurate because the operator does not need to write down the data on paper and later hand-calculate the data for his charts. The feedback is immediate; the operator does not have to wait a day or more to look at the charts that concern his or her operations.

CASE 11-7 STAMPING PLANT FOR TELEVISION FRAMES

Plant Obtains Squareness Calculations Automatically with New Data Collection System.

A stamping plant that supplies television frames for a popular American TV brand was being pressured by its customer to implement an SPC program and show evidence of it. The plant produces several thousand frames per day. Five to ten different sizes, both square and rectangular, are made each shift.

The existing SPC program required mostly handwritten methods of collecting data. The data was then keyed into a computer for statistical analysis and chart making. The plant felt that by upgrading their SPC program they could not only satisfy their customers request for SPC documentation, but also obtain tangible improvements in quality.

Problem

The customer demanded statistical control of the squareness of TV frames, as well as the overall dimensions. The stamping plant uses a fixture to check the frames. They measure the distance from a fixed reference point on one side of the frame and then the other and take the difference. By taking these measurements between the fixture and frame edge all the way around they could derive squareness.

All of the measurements had to be taken down by hand and subtracted one from the other before the squareness data could be plotted on a chart and input into a computer. Because of the volume of frames being produced, the time it took to collect the data became a burden. So did the time required to input the data into a computer.

Solution

The stamping plant decided to obtain equipment that would eliminate having to write measurements down by

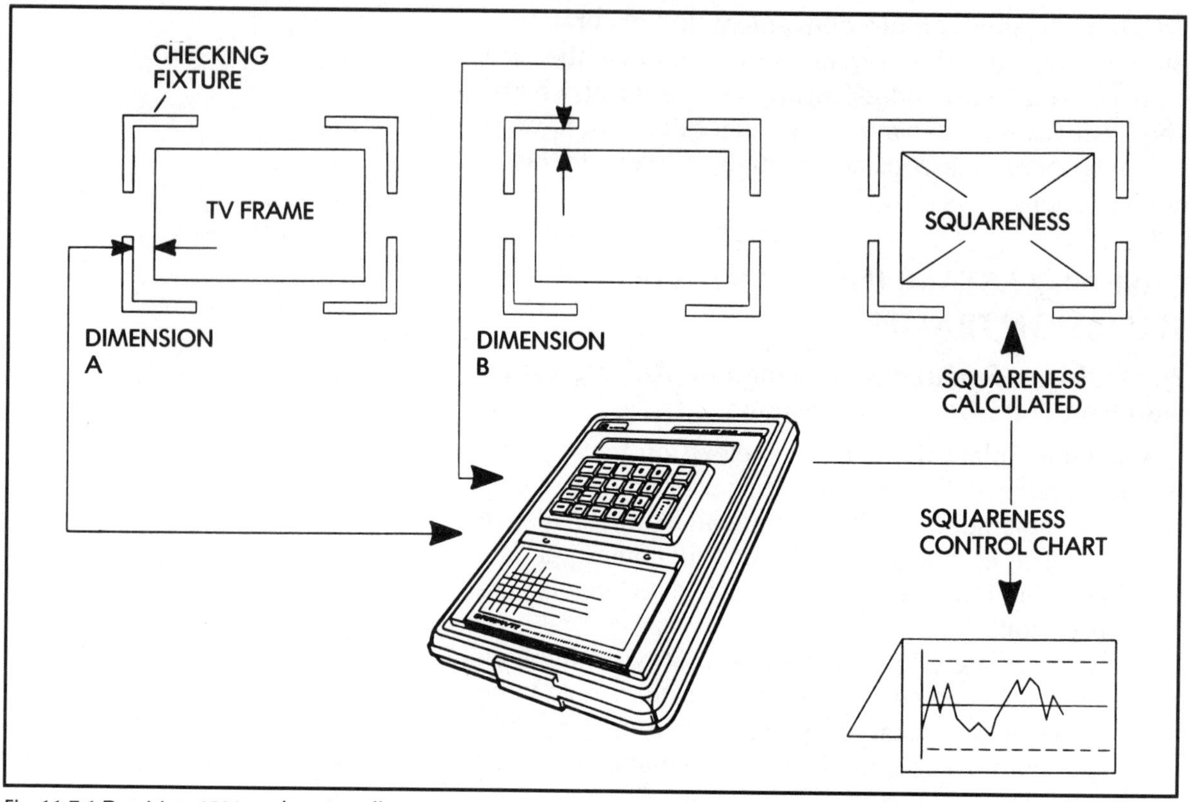

Fig. 11.7.1 DataMyte 1500 math option allows a squareness calculation to be derived from several linear measurements, and then plotted.

hand. They purchased the DataMyte 1556 and an electronic gap gage. Using the gap gage, they could quickly go around a fixture and take readings against the TV frame. In addition, the DataMyte 1556, with its math feature, would subtract one column of readings from another and save the result in a third column. Therefore, data on squareness was produced instantaneously. See Figure 11.7.1.

Used with their existing computer, a DataMyte software program allows them to set up the 1556 data collector for each type of frame, and program a prescribed sequence of measurements for the squareness calculation. The data collector is then used in the factory to record the data. At the end of the shift, the data is fed back to the computer. Charts are printed on both the overall dimensional and the squareness.

See Chapter 16 for a description of the 1556 data collector.

The DataMyte system provides a number of benefits, including a labor savings, reduction of error and complete documentation. The existing computer is used for long-term storage of data and for management reports. In the eyes of the customer, both the appearance of improved

SPC and the actual results of better quality products went hand-in-hand.

CASE 11-8 MICROWAVE MANUFACTURER

Company Monitors Material Flow Through Fabrication and Painting Areas

A manufacturer of microwave ovens requires verification of piece part counts in the fabrication and paint departments, particularly the more expensive parts.

This company, a world leader in microwave appliances, needs to continually monitor the fabrication and paint areas. Comparisons need to be made of the count shown on the container move tickets. A physical count is performed by the auditor, who records the results of such an audit. In addition, the auditor may be required to affix a label to the move ticket indicating that an audit has been performed and showing the results of that audit. This method needs to be refined in order to increase the accuracy of piece counts and the efficiency of final production.

Problem

During final production, there was a problem getting finished goods onto the production line on time from the fabrication and paint areas. Part of the problem was from an inadequate method of keeping track of these pieces as they went through the process. Current tracking systems were time consuming, results were not readily attainable to reflect changes in production scheduling, and individuals currently tracking the system were also performing other duties. They were actually adding delays into the system when they manually performed these audits while trying to keep pace with their current job functions. The proposed solution would attack these problem areas, and hopefully allow the efficiency of these areas to increase dramatically. Another problem, which directly related to this inefficiency, was that a definable methodology of performing these audits had never been established.

Solution

The first step was to define an audit format that an inspector or inspectors could follow in a prescribed sequence so that errors could be minimized. Results of this audit would need to be available within a very short period of time in order to facilitate accurate production scheduling. Since inventory is based on production completion, which is solely derived from the operator's time cards, it would be possible to obtain a comparison between quantities shown in inventory and those shown by the audit. Further comparisons could be made by using a daily or hourly computer print-out. Some definable comparisons would be: shop status by part, shop status by machine, labor recap by employee and machine hours recap. The audit format, which would be used by the inventory inspectors, is listed below:

1. Date
2. Shift
3. Machine
4. Operator
5. Work Order
6. Part
7. Operation
8. Description
9. Move ticket count
10. Audit count
11. Count type (hand or scale)
12. Percent error (calculated from move ticket count and audit count difference

During the audit, the percent error would not be calculated. This would be completed and shown by the computer — available on the computer print-out. Along with the instantly available computer print-outs showing the previously mentioned status reports, inventory records could be updated much more efficiently. Another factor would be the ability to have this audit performed by individuals other than the operators — so that they could concentrate on their specific job details, and not concern themselves with inventory control. This would also increase the overall efficiency.

See Chapter 16 for a description of the 1000 data collector.

A DataMyte 1000 was implemented for this audit function. Portability was a major factor in this function — and the DataMyte could certainly be used to audit various areas — taking into consideration its portability feature. Another feature of the DataMyte was its ability to easily interface to most computer systems so the data collected could be uploaded to the computer in order to generate the status reports and inventory results on a computer print-out. The actual set up of the DataMyte, once performed, would never have to be changed, just periodic clearing of the inputted data would be required, once the data was transferred to the computer system.

Operation

Set-up of the DataMyte was performed as follows:

Memory was cleared

Control 1 was set to: 02 21 11 (Prompt section of record, prompt loops and record 1.) This allows you to enter prompts.

The word "Date" was entered, then the word "shift was entered.

The next set of prompts was nested in order that they be repeated as often as required during the course of the audit. This nested loop would continually repeat itself. The date and shift would only be required to be entered once for each audit. To nest a loop you would first key in a left parenthesis. This is accomplished by keying, ctrl, left, beg.

A left parenthesis would then be displayed on the DataMyte display. This would then be entered by keying the enter key. Then each of the following prompts was keyed in as a separate entry:

Machine
Operator
Work order
Part
Operation
Description
Move ticket count
Audit count
Count type

After the last prompt was entered, a right parenthesis needed to be keyed in, in order to "nest" the prompt loop. This was accomplished by keying, ctrl, right, beg.

Now the DataMyte was set up with the appropriate prompt loop, and data collection for the audit could now begin. In order to collect data, ctrl 1 would be changed to the following:

15 21 11 — Data Section of record, with prompt loop, and record 1.

To start the audit, the clear key would be depressed. The first prompt (date) would appear on the left side of the display. The operator would simply key in the day's date. After hitting the enter key, the next prompt (shift) would appear on the display. After entering the shift number, the next prompt (machine #) would appear. This sequence of prompts would continue, until the last one appeared (count type). After keying in the count type and depressing the enter key, the prompt loop would go back to machine #. This occurs because this loop is "nested." It would not return to date because for a specific audit, the date and shift would only be required to be entered once.

At the completion of the audit the operator would key in 'ctrl, EOR.' This puts that audit into record one on the DataMyte. Additional audits could be set-up exactly the same way and put into other records.

For post processing, the DataMyte was connected to an IBM-PC desktop computer. The appropriate record number was selected on the DataMyte and transmitted to the PC. The software on the IBM was set up to accept this data and generate the print-outs for management and inventory control. Percent error was also calculated by the computer from the data that was transferred from the DataMyte. For audits following this days' collection, the only requirement was to clear the data out of the records. This was accomplished by keying 'ctrl, 1' and then keying 113355. The DataMyte was then ready to accept another audit with the prompt information still remaining in the DataMyte.

Now that an audit format has been established, results were attainable on an ongoing basis. Efficiency was dramatically increased because only one operator was needed to perform the audit and generate the reports. The reports were available within minutes after the audit, not hours, and decisions could be generated accordingly.

Inventory quantities could now be adjusted at anytime with a much higher degree of accuracy and dependability. Data processing time was now within reason, with emphasis on report generation. The reports indicated who completed the jobs, where and when the individual pieces were completed, and what area of final production there were available for.

12. GLASS, PLASTICS, PAPER AND CHEMICAL INDUSTRIES

CASE 12-1 GLASS MANUFACTURER

High Speed Process Controlled with Simple Fixturing

With the increase in the cost of manufacturing, a major glass producing company wanted to cut down on the amount of scrap and rework. They needed to hold closer tolerances on a flat glass surface. By solving a measurement problem, they increased the capability of their process and cut scrap by 85 percent.

Problem Definition

Glass rolled off the assembly line too fast to manually record data. The glass was large flat plate glass. 130 data points were needed to perform the initial capability study. The quality control department hoped that after the process was brought to a state of statistical control, they could eliminate some of the data points required. A fast data collection and data processing device was needed. It also had to be portable and record the data at the manufacturing site. The data capture had to be accurate. Another problem was they did not want to re-design all the checking fixtures. That would be cost prohibitive.

Solution

All the existing checking fixtures were used. A common vernier caliper was selected as the measuring instrument. The checking fixtures were machined with a 3 mm reference slot. 130 slots were machined for the initial capability study. Electronic vernier calipers were used because the information had to be collected and recorded as fast as possible. The result needed to be available at the process so decisions could be made on the spot. The caliper's data was automatically transferred to an electronic data collector. The data collector stored the data and processed it, too.

See Chapter 17 for descriptions of calipers.

Now the measurement problem was solved. With a single test fixture modification they could use an electronic caliper connected directly to the data collector for processing and long term storage. A printer was kept at the location for the printed results. Information could also be viewed on the display of the data collector.

Some of the unseen benefits of this program were:

- Data collection time was cut by 450%.
- Only 75 of the original data points were needed.
- Scrap was cut by 85%. CPK Index approached 2.00.
- Information could be off-loaded to a host computer for long term data storage and analysis.

The equipment selected to perform the capability study, and for long term process control was the DataMyte 1558 with 64K of usable data storage. No single brand of electronic verniers was selected because of the wide variety on the market today.

See Chapter 16 for a description of the 1558 data collector.

CASE 12-2 PLASTIC CONTAINER MANUFACTURER

Operator-Oriented System Provides Better Process Control

A plastic container manufacturer had to keep track of various measurements to ensure the quality of the finished product, such as plastic milk bottles. They were looking for a system the operators of injection molding machines could use without interfering too much with their main task of making bottles.

Problem

The manufacturer measures and compares to rigid specifications finished thread dimensions of bottle caps and tops of plastic bottles. The manufacturer also checks the weight of the plastic containers. They need to weigh the finished containers for two reasons:

- The high-density resin used to produce the bottles is expensive. The manufacturer weighs the finished product to make sure the proper amount of resin is used when the bottle is made.
- The manufacturer also weighs the containers before and after an appropriate liquid or powder is placed in the container. This insures that the containers hold the amounts of material that were specified.

The manufacturer measures the wall thickness and other dimensions of the containers to make sure that the bottle has been formed properly and is the proper size for its purpose.

Solution

See Chapter 15 for a description of the FAN system.

The DataMyte FAN® system was the best alternative for the manuacturer, who looked at several types of computerized and handheld data collection systems. They use DataMyte 762s to record the data from electronic digital micrometers, electronic weigh scales and electronic digital calipers. The operators will take measurements and record the data at their injection molding machines. Two types of micrometers are used by the manufacturer. The operators use flat micrometers to obtain the measurements to determine the volume of a container.

The manufacturer uses a DataTruck to collect the data whenever necessary from the 762s. They use an IBM PC to store data and FAN® software to manage and report the data.

CASE 12-3 PLASTICS MANUFACTURER

Expansion Plans Require Better SQC Program

A leader in the manufacturing of several types of plastic utensils, including plates, cups, forks, spoons, etc., wanted to expand their operations. To help accomplish this, they needed to refine their SQC program. Their goals were to improve product quality, to reduce scrap costs, and to enhance data turnaround time.

Problem Definition

The manufacturer was using manual charting methods to analyze and track the data gathered by its inspectors. Once the data was gathered, the inspectors would sit down with their calculators and manually plot $\bar{x}$ & R charts. This required each inspector to spend from four to six hours per day. Since the results of their analysis were generally not available for at least four hours (and often not even until the next shift), process conditions had already changed substantially and it was next to impossible for them to locate and remedy problem areas.

Solution

The SQC program enhancements were defined as follows:

- Perform data analysis automatically.
- Generate reports and charts on an "as needed" basis.
- Allow the inspectors to spend their time on the floor locating problem areas (and not involved in extensive data processing).

The equipment they chose to implement these improvements was a DataMyte 1508 handheld data collector. As a testament to the ease of use of the system, after seeing an audit sheet and a four minute explanation of how to load all of the information into the DataMyte, an inspector proceeded to load all this information into the DataMyte and was ready to go out on the shop floor and collect data in 10 minutes.

See Chapter 16 for a description of handheld data collectors.

Operation

The information that follows provides a brief description of how the DataMyte was used by the manufacturer. The unit was loaded with the prompts, limits, and matrix size required to simulate the exact audit sheet the manufacturer was currently using. See Figure 12.3.1. Each of the measurement areas from the audit sheet (12 in all) were loaded as items, with 20 samples of each being used for charting. Measurements on each item were performed three times each hour on every shift.

Since the unit was capable of generating histograms, the manufacturer decided to make use of them in their management reports. When needed, the inspector would print a histogram of current data in the matrix. These reports were then used to verify the natural dispersion of the processes. Management would then, in turn, base their decisions on how to minimize these dispersions; ultimately getting all areas to try and match the $\bar{x}$ values.

PROCESS INSPECTION

SUPERVISOR SIGNATURE

DATE: 2-29-84 TIME: am 7:30-->7:30 pm INSPECTOR: Chevre 1 SETUP: B

				LEFT CAVITY				RIGHT CAVITY			
Press 3c	Part 3c	Full Cycle	Cure Cycle	Cavity No.	Part Wt.	Mold Temp. (upper)	Mold Temp. (lower)	Cavity No.	Part Wt.	Mold Temp. (upper)	Mold Temp. (lower)
64	527	196	103	21	315	350	320	22	307	340	330
76	522	191	98	32	839	330	330	31	829	340	320
75	499	222	124	12	810	330	330	11	803	340	340
63	527	208	104	12	314	330	310	11	313	340	320
73	500	208	113	92	[illegible]	330	320	91	[illegible]	340	310
82	452	208	126	211	829	340	320	151	790	350	350
83	452	209	122	102	834	330	330	112	841	350	310
84	452	206	106	342	816	320	310	312	793	340	320
85	452	238	108	132	842	350	300	141	828	330	310
86	452	173	99	481	818	350	320	482	824	330	300

Fig. 12.3.1 Sample audit sheet.

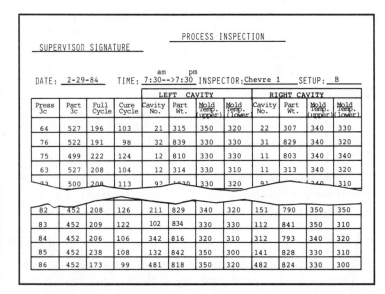

CASE 12-4 PLASTICS AND FIBERGLASS MANUFACTURER

Electronic Gap Gages Improve Tolerance Checking

A manufacturer/supplier of plastic and fiberglass piece parts needed a way to improve the overall quality of their products. The manufacturer is having too many of its parts returned. Quite often the reason stated for the return was that the part was out of tolerance.

After investigating the causes, the manufacturer determined that the methods being used to measure parts were not effective. Not only did they provide insufficient data for quality improvements, they did not address the problem of high scrap costs.

Problem Definition

In the past, the piece part products produced by this manufacturer had exhibited a relatively high level of variability in tolerance. The problem was due in large part to the process used to measure the tolerance.

The procedure involved placing the parts in a checking fixture and then measuring their size in relation to the fixture. This was done by inserting a tapered feeler gage between the part and the fixture. When this measurement method was repeated at several locations around the part, the size of the part could be determined.

The feeler gages being used had rules etched every 0.5 mm. Thus, the operator would insert the gage, read the rule line that was closest, and then estimate down to the closest 0.1 mm. This procedure was not accurate since parallax errors were being introduced by the operators.

Solution

See Chapter 16 for data collectors and Chapter 17 for the gap gage.

To facilitate their program, they purchased a DataMyte 1503 handheld data collector and a 516 flush and gap gauge. (See Figure 12.4.1.) This provided a data collection and analysis capability that was portable, user friendly, and could be used to produce all necessary charts. The gap gage had a useable range of 12.7 mm and a resolution of 0.05 mm.

Soon after implementing this system, they noticed that the variation from part to part had increased. Suspicions arose regarding the repeatability of the DataMyte and the

Fig. 12.4.1 Model 516 flushness and gap gage.

transducer being used. This prompted further investigation of the entire system. To begin with, several parts were checked by a number of different operators using the same checking fixture and the same tool. The variation was excessive. By placing one part in the fixture and having several operators check it, they greatly reduced variation (approximately 0.1 mm). Thus, they had proved that operator variability in using the tool was quite acceptable and a major improvement over their previous method of estimating to the nearest 0.1 mm.

The only thing left to check was the variability of the fixture. Using one operator, one part and one fixture, the operator was instructed to place the part in the fixture and check it. The same operator then removed the part and placed it back into the same fixture to check it again. This procedure was repeated several times. The results from the checks varied greatly, proving that the variation was a result of the variability in placing the part in the checking fixture. The solution was to redesign the checking fixture so that a more positive placement of the part was assured no matter who placed the part in the fixture.

CASE 12-5 PRESSURE MOLDED TEFLON PARTS

SPC Saves Pressure Molded Teflon Manufacturer Hours and Dollars With New Method of Control Charting

A manufacturer of pressure molded teflon parts was feeling pressure to implement Statistical Process Control (SPC). The 22 molding machines at its Michigan facility could produce over 150 teflon parts, from microwave oven inserts to coated piston rings. A time lag between sample inspections and the posting of the latest statistical information was a problem.

Problem

An inspector would spend several minutes at each process gathering dimensional readings using a vernier caliper or micrometer. After the inspector had completed the inspection route, he would calculate the statistical analysis for each controlled dimension. The calculation would then be posted on control charts in the quality control office. By that time, the latest inspection information could be hours old.

Solution

The company began posting control charts at the process where the machine operator could see each update. The inspector began using a DataMyte 1508 with calipers and micrometer to gage the part samples and make calculations. Those calculations were then plotted with a grease pencil on the plexiglass covering the control chart at that process. At the end of the inspection route, the inspector transferred the information into the history file of the DataMyte and began the inspection route over again.

See Chapter 16 for data collectors and Chapter 17 for micrometers and calipers.

After the inspector uses the DataMyte 1508 with calipers and micrometer to gage five samples, he uses the DataMyte summary mode to review the calculations for $\bar{x}$ & R. This information is plotted on the chart at the process with a grease pencil. At the end of the inspection route, the inspector transfers the $\bar{x}$ & R information to the DataMyte history file. At the end of each shift, the DataMyte is connected to an Epson printer, and control charts are printed.

These charts went to the quality control manager and copies were passed out to the machine operators at a meeting each morning before production began.

Since charts were updated more frequently and information was more readily available, operators could more closely control the process and avoid problems before bad parts were produced. The company said that in just a few months the new method of control charting paid for itself.

CASE 12-6 PEN MANUFACTURER

Controlling Ink Filling Process Brings Substantial Savings

A manufacturer of ball point pens needed better control of how much ink went into pen cartridges. Millions of cartridges were produced each year, so reducing variation in the amount of ink could potentially save an estimated $20,000 to $100,000 a year. The amount of ink directly affected the quality of the pen, also. Too much ink in a cartridge affects the mechanical performance of the pen. Too little ink depreciates the pen in the eyes of the customer.

Problem

The ink filling process could not be measured directly. Quality control inspectors weigh a dry cartridge, have it filled, and then weigh it again. The difference would be the weight of the ink. Monitoring these weights would presumably tell them how much ink was going into the cartridges.

To do this properly at the frequency required for producing process control charts involved a lot of work. Two separate measurements plus a subtraction step were needed for each result. Measuring and recording just the filled weights of the cartridges would not establish the amount of ink actually used because of the added variation of the dry cartridge weights. A working system would involve either a lot of manual labor or a type of automated data collection system that could also derive ink weights through a subtraction calculation.

Solution

The company purchased a DataMyte model 1558 data collection system. The DataMyte could interface with their

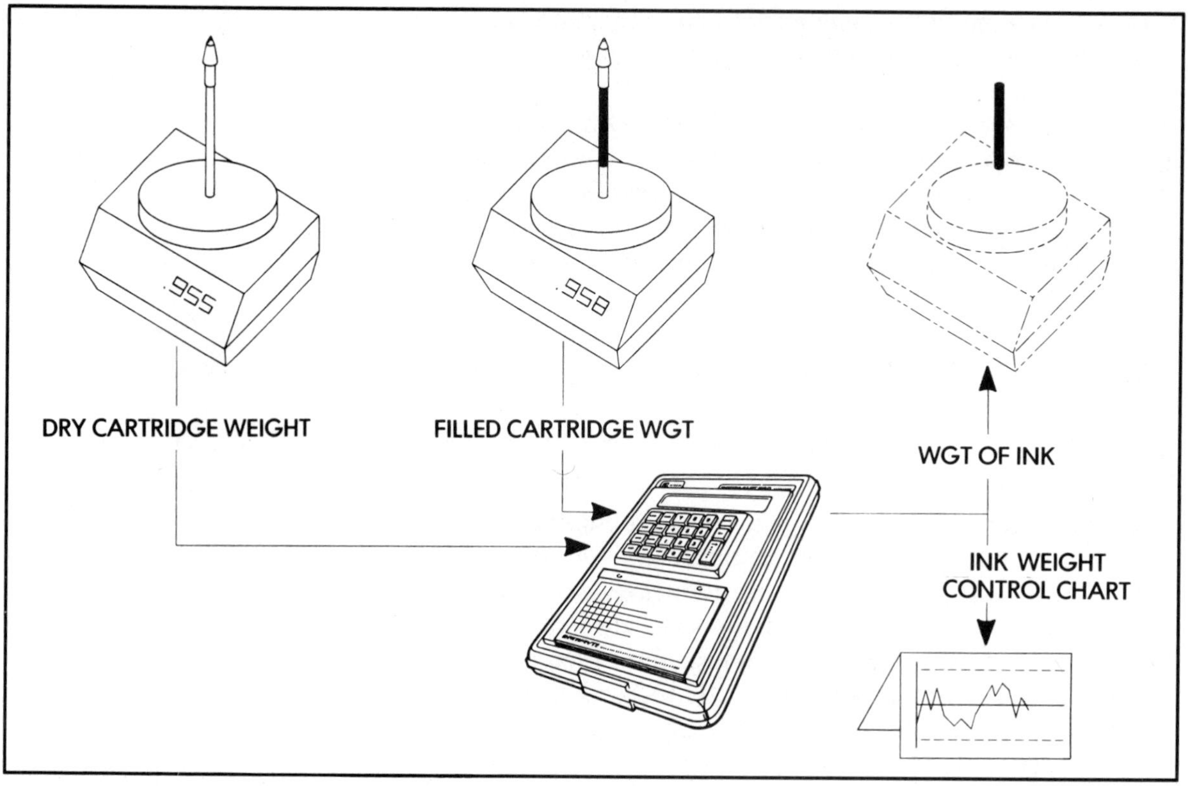

Fig. 12.6.1 DataMyte 1500 math option allows the ink weight to be derived and plotted.

See Chapter 16 for data collectors and Chapter 17 for weigh scales.

Mettler weigh scales to record weights directly—without error. In addition, the DataMyte had a math function, which can subtract one column of numbers from another and put the results in a third column. See Figure 12.6.1. The data in the third column, in this case the ink weights, could be printed out in the form of an $\bar{x}$ & R control chart or histogram.

Although two measurements were still necessary for each result, since the readings were input directly from the scale via an RS-232 cable, there was much less error. Less time was needed to record the measurements, and since the subtraction step was handled internally in the DataMyte, there was a substantial reduction in time and error overall in the data recording process.

Data processing was instantaneous. The DataMyte was simply connected to a printer to produce the control charts. Charts on cartridge dry weights were also available as an added benefit.

Overall, the DataMyte system provided a savings that would pay for its cost in an estimated two to three months.

Case 12-7 PAPER CAN MANUFACTURER

DataMyte 750s Provide Real-Time Statistical Analysis of Production. DataMyte 1000s Simplify Attributes Data Collection.

A large paper can manufacturing company has been looking at ways to implement statistical process control in its operations. One of the company's major customers was demanding that it supply evidence that its materials meet specifications. A committment was made by management to implement an SPC program in one of their southern plants in an effort to control costs and improve overall quality.

Problem

When manufacturing paper cans and lids used by various food and fruit juice companies, several factors caused problems. The plant was checking over 80 different attributes on each type of can during the manufacturing process. This data was all collected manually on preprinted forms. Much of the data was never even examined due to the tremendous amount of time required to sort through the stacks of paper that were generated. By the time any charts were analyzed, much of the product had already been shipped.

The problem that the company faced was that they had no way of effectively analyzing the attribute data they were collecting. In addition, they could not keep up with the control charting on key characteristics that was being required by their customers.

Solution

The solution to the problem involved the use of a DataMyte 750. Critical dimensions on the paper can were measured using a digital indicator mounted on a height stand. This data is currently entered using electronic digital gages that will input directly into the DataMyte 750. Cans are checked every hour at a specified inspection area which contains the gages, DataMyte 750, and monitor. All four production lines have their own inspection area. Control charts are generated immediately after data collection and any changes to the machines are made. Once a shift

See Chapter 16 for a description of the 750 data collector.

the data is downloaded to an IBM PC located in the QC office using a DataMyte DataTruck.

Attribute data is still being collected at each inspection area. A DataMyte 1000 is programmed with the correct prompt sequence to guide the inspectors through the attribute data collection. Data is collected for eight hours, and then the information is downloaded to the IBM PC and pareto analysis is done using the DataMyte Attribute Software program. Plans are to reduce the amount of control charting.

See Chapter 18 for a description of attribute software.

With the DataMyte data collectors, the company has solved a major collection and analysis problem in a critical area of their operation. They are now able to provide real-time analysis of their data as well as supply useful records to their customers. They have been able to improve their overall quality and to assure their customers that their materials are meeting specifications.

CASE 12-8 PRINTING COMPANY

Printer Collects Ten Times More Data

A supplier of corrugated packaging containers principally serving the food processing industry was committed to supplying the highest quality product to their customers.

The company's principal manufacturing processes included cutting, printing and wax coating operations. This company is one of the largest suppliers of this type of product with numerous manufacturing sites throughout the United States. Although the company would like to reduce manufacturing costs, their principal motivation to begin an SPC program was to demonstrate to their customers their commitment to quality. Their customers were not demanding documentation of conformance to specifications, nor were they mandating SPC techniques.

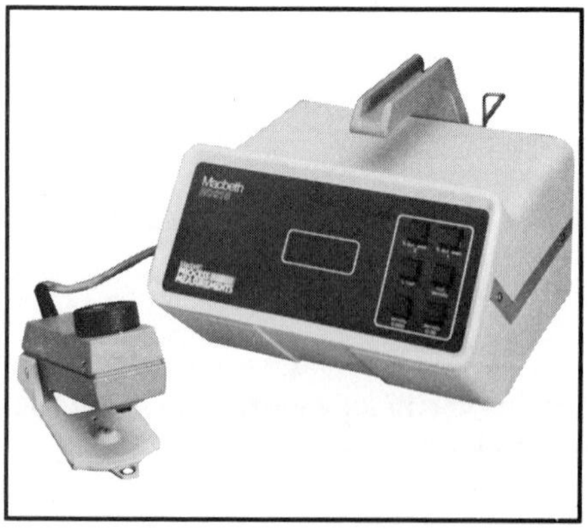

Fig. 12.8.1 MacBeth densitometer.

Problem

The biggest obstacle to this company was converting their existing inspector based quality control program to operator based data collection and analysis. Their primary target was the printing presses where they used MacBeth Densitometers to record color density and percent dot concentration. See Figure 12.8.1.

Time was a critical concern from two aspects. First, the operator was engaged in numerous activities on the press and could not be burdened with excessive data collection tasks. Second, responding to out of control conditions needed to be rapid to ensure consistency of finalized products.

Solution

The company elected to use the DataMyte 762 in conjunction with their MacBeth densitometers. By using the DataMyte, operators were capable of collecting up to ten times more data than in manual methods. Since graphs were generated immediately, corrective responses were implemented in process. Before using DataMyte data collectors, in-process corrections were rarely made due to the short cycle runs and lengthy calculation requirements for process control parameters.

See Chapter 16 for the 762 data collector and Chapter 17 for the densitometer.

Before using DataMytes, operators would depress the densitometer head and handle assembly to record a value. Before proceeding to the next value they would stop to record the data on a tally sheet and then proceed again. With DataMytes brought into the operation, the operator depresses the densitometer and upon releasing the head and handle assembly the reading is automatically recorded. At the end of each subgroup, an $\bar{x}$ & R chart appears automatically for each color on the product. At the end of a run, the operator unloads his data to the DataMyte FAN II software program and downloads his product file.

The operation on the printing presses was so successful, that this manufacturer expanded the use of DataMytes to the wax coating application where electronic balances measure the amount of wax applied and DataMytes monitor processes for control. Additional DataMytes are used in conjunction with micrometers to measure the thickness of raw materials. DataMyte 769s are used extensively for visual defect audits. Today, over 50% of all processes in this company are controlled using DataMyte products.

See Chapter 16 for the 769 attribute data collector.

CASE 12-9 MAIL SERVICE

Automatic Data Collection Zips Out Case Density Studies

The Eastern Region of a large mail-handling concern performed case density studies to determine how manual letter and flats diagrams should be designed. The diagrams minimize the distribution required in subsequent operations and arrange the case separation for maximum distribution efficiency. Performing this task manually was labor intensive and therefore very costly. Also, the chance for introducing errors into the data during transcription and key punching operations was high. In an effort to upgrade their capabilities and because of the high volume of mail passing through the Eastern Region on a daily basis, the mail service determined that they needed to implement an improved system as soon as possible.

Problem Definition

The Case Analysis System (CAS) required a daily 500 piece sample of ZIP codes. To ensure an accumulation of representative data for designing the case diagram, special sampling techniques were used. The procedure for sampling was performed as follows:

1) A 500 piece sample consisting of letters and flats was taken daily at each test point. This sample was actually divided up into five 100 piece sub-samples, which were taken at randomly selected hourly increments. The time intervals chosen for sampling were based upon the probability of mail availability during the hourly increment.

2) Next, the sample ZIP code data was recorded manually on a density sampling worksheet. Each worksheet could accomodate 250 ZIP codes for each operation, so two coding sheets were turned in. Note that this method required the manual counting and recording of the mail in these separations.

3) Finally, the collected data was converted into machine language for processing by the host computing system, which was located on the West Coast. This process involved transcription, keypunching, editing, and re-keypunching operations before the actual processing could begin.

Solution

The Eastern Region determined that the solution for reducing costs and for increasing the data turn-around time was to close the loop in their data collection/processing system by fully automating the procedure. Handheld microprocessor-based data entry terminals were used by the auditors for recording the ZIP code data. There were basically three advantages to automating the data collection/processing procedure:

1) The rapidity at which data can be recorded.

2) The immediate availability of the data in computer processible form.

3) The increased reliability of the data due to the elimination of transcription and keypunching operations.

Once the mail service had defined the known problems and areas of concern, they began to investigate the best way to implement their program. They determined that the program implemented must be able to:

- Perform data collection and analysis automatically.
- Interface with the various types of existing computing terminals that are used to access the central mainframe on the West Coast.
- Ensure the integrity of data. (This was necessary since the data was being sent via telephone transmission lines.)

Based on their analysis, they selected a DataMyte 1000 handheld data collector. The DataMyte 1000 provided a data collection and analysis capability that was portable, user friendly, and could be used to interface with all their existing computing terminals and mainframes. The DataMyte could be programmed to transmit using sophisticated communications protocol, providing error checking to ensure data integrity. The DataMyte was rugged and had proven reliability as a field terminal.

See Chapter 16 for a description of the 1000 and 2000 handheld data collectors.

By using the DataMyte 1000 for data collection, analysis, and reporting purposes, the mail service was able to improve their case density studies program. This unique system was able to speed up the whole procedure for performing case density studies. Further, because of the high degree of automation, the possibility for human error was greatly minimized. The savings in keypunching costs alone were substantial. The DataMyte, after just one use, saved the Eastern Region 144 manhours at $15.00 an hour, more than justifying its purchase in a single use.

Operation

The information that follows provides a brief description of how the DataMyte 1000 was used by the mail service.

The DataMyte 1000 was installed at the user's facilities, it was set to IN-Mode, Section of Record 5. The unit was configured with an entry counter feature that audibly alerted the operator when the 500 piece sample was completed. As each piece of mail was sampled, a five digit code was entered into the DataMyte's memory via the keyboard. Immediately following data collection, the DataMyte was linked to the central mainframe and the data was transmitted. At the mainframe, the data was written to a sample ZIP code file, where it accumulated until Case Analysis System (CAS) programs could analyze and collate the data. Once the data was processed by the CAS programs, it could be used to design a new case diagram, analyze an existing case diagram, or to generate ZIP code reports for further analysis.

CASE 12-10 PHOTOGRAPHIC EQUIPMENT MANUFACTURER

Latest Short-Term Payback Installation Eliminates Manual Setup Changes

A major photographic equipment manufacturer uses DataMyte data collectors throughout its corporation. When this manufacturer makes a capital equipment purchase, it assigns an industrial engineer to analyze the return on investment. The company's first DataMyte purchase was for the film capsule line. The engineering study compared the automated data collection, with real-time feedback, to the manual data collection the company had conducted previously. The study justified buying 40 more systems for the plant.

The manufacturer has since installed many more DataMyte systems throughout their plants. In all major system installations, in their tape, film, film cartridge and camera divisions, the manufacturer has documented a payback in less than six months.

The manufacturer's latest installation incorporated the DataMyte FANLINK network.

Problem

In many of the company's manufacturing processes, part changes on machines occur several times in one day. Each machine may be required to run hundreds of different parts each year. When this condition is multiplied by hundreds of machines in the department, data management becomes a severe problem. Consistency in part quality between runs is difficult to correlate.

Solution

As a result, this firm looked to hardwired networks to speed up the setup changes in the DataMytes between parts. Using a FANLINK network eliminates the problems described above. The network incorporates data collectors, line drivers, a host computer (in this application, an HP 1000) and customer developed software.

See Chapter 15 for a description of the FANLINK network.

The hardwired FANLINK network is a true two-way communication system. The host computer serves as an enormous data base of part setups. Literally thousands of electronic files are stored in the computer. Each file fully describes the various parts and process parameters. These electronic files are accessed by operators on-line through a menu selection in their DataMyte data collectors. When new part setups are required, operators keypunch in the desired part number, which signals the host computer to pick up the file resident in the data collector. Upon uploading the resident file from the data collector, all new data is filed with historical data archived in the host computer from previous runs. The archived data at the host computer can be accessed via a PC network by various departments within the company. The computer then sends the requested file to the data collector.

The individual requesting information from the host computer can call up a file by part number and review some or all of the historical data and perform post process analysis of the data in a variety of third party statistical software programs.

CASE 12-11 CHEMICAL PROCESS MAINTENANCE

Automatic Data Collection Improves Predictive Maintenance Program

A major chemical company uses reliability inspection data to maintain equipment in their inspection plants. Their program at first had impressive results, providing reports to maintenance, operating, engineering, and supervisory personnel on equipment that required maintenance. Problems developed, however, that were directly related to the use of conventional methods for making measurements, analyzing the data, and producing reports.

Problem Definition

Several times each day the company's inspectors would take vibration readings and make other general observations related to the various pieces of equipment in use. The data collected was then manually recorded on inspection sheets. Once the inspections were over, the inspectors would return to their offices and transcribe the data collected onto data spreadsheets. Finally, when the data was collated, the inspectors would begin the process of analyzing the data so that necessary capability reports and charts could be prepared. The problems involved with this process were numerous. Major drawbacks included:

- The use of conventional equipment for making the measurements.
- The time required to physically log and collate the data collected; it was taking the inspectors as much time to generate reports and charts as it was to inspect the equipment.
- The format of the reports themselves. The reports generated by the inspectors listed all equipment in use rather than just the equipment that required maintenance. This required users to spend a lot of time just interpreting the report data generated.
- The fact that many of the reports were handwritten by the inspectors; this caused some problems in just being able to read the report data.

Solution

The solution involved computerizing the tasks of data collection and report generation. To achieve this solution, the company chose a test site and equipment. The test site was a plant that had to perform over 900 equipment inspections per month. The equipment chosen was:

- A DataMyte 1000 handheld data collector.
- A Hewlett Packard 3000 minicomputer to store and analyze the data plus download the route information to the DataMyte.

- A data base program to produce the required routes and reports.

The DataMyte 1000 was selected because it provided a fast and efficient method of collecting and temporarily storing inspection data. See Figures 12.11.1 through 12.11.3. Furthermore, the DataMyte could interface with the HP 3000 computer through an RS-232C serial port. See Figure 12.11.4. Other reasons for the company's selection of the DataMyte were based on the following:

- The DataMyte was capable of being programmed to accept header, prompt, and previous data readings. Its 32 character display buffer provided for very intelligible messages.
- The DataMyte was capable of emulating the data collection sheets currently being used by the inspectors. In fact, its clipboard size and pad for note taking made it readily accepted.
- Use of the DataMyte did not require computer expertise or a departure from existing data collection disciplines.

Several system requirements were considered. A route may contain up to 50 pieces of equipment to be inspected, each with a different number of inspection points and different observations to be made. This required intelligible prompt messages in the data collector to guide an inspector through the route. A data base management system was chosen instead of a dedicated route program to provide the flexibility to add or change records as equipment was added or changed.

Since the whole system would be used and maintained by people without computer expertise, every effort was made to make the program easy to use. The prompt messages loaded into the DataMyte emulated the existing data collection sheets.

The benefits seen immediately from the pilot program were:

- Twice as much inspection data was collected without increasing personnel. In other words, productivity was doubled.
- Reports were more timely, comprehensive, and legible.
- The reports were more accurate since transcription errors were eliminated.

Development of the system took three months and 400 man hours. This included learning the existing system, the

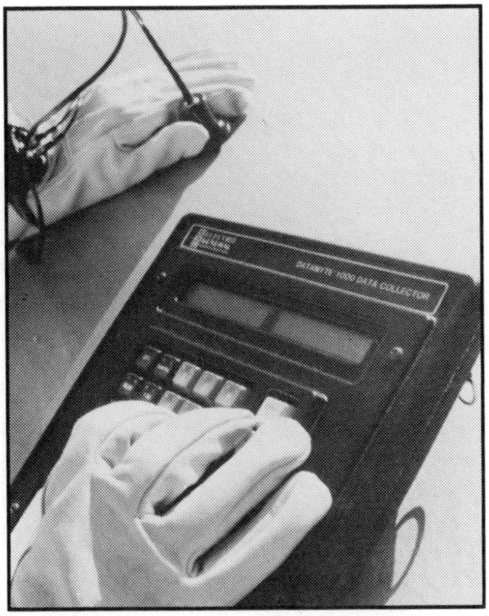

Fig. 12.11.1 Thickness testing.

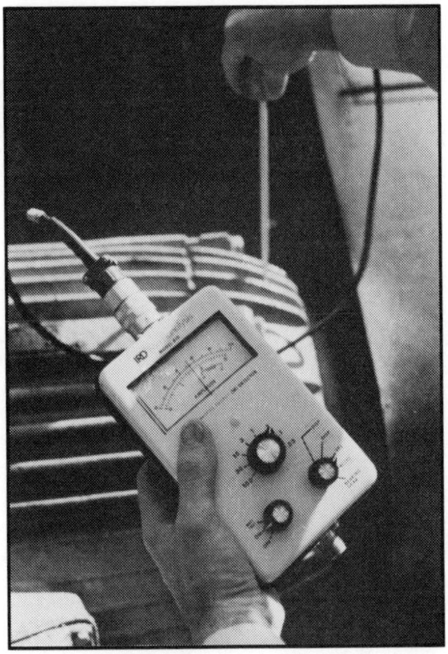

Fig. 12.11.2 Vibration testing.

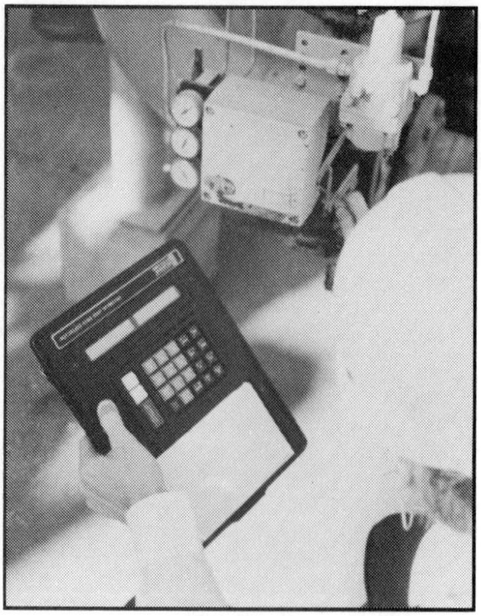

Fig. 12.11.3 Entering gage data.

Fig. 12.11.4 Transmitting data to a computer.

data base language, redesigning the data base program, and writing a download program for the DataMyte.

During the test phase, information was collected relative to the durability, ease of use and time savings of the DataMyte, all of which was positive.

Direct cost savings (labor savings) show a payback of approximately one year. Indirect cost savings through an improved predictive maintenance program could reach several hundred thousand dollars per year in their larger plants. The company felt that the principles and methods they developed would be applicable to not only chemical processing equipment maintenance but other types of industries as well. For this reason, the program was also adapted to run on the IBM PC and Fortune computers as well as the HP3000.

CASE 12-12 TEFLON SEAL MANUFACTURER

Company Automates Gaging Stations to Maintain Production Flexibility

A company manufacturing pressure molded teflon seals needed to expand its implementation of SPC.

Problem

The company had 30 different molding machines producing a wide variety of teflon parts. Operators were taking time to gather dimensional measurements with a vernier caliper or micrometer. After each subgroup was collected it would be manually averaged and plotted on an $\bar{x}$ & R control chart. Some operators are responsible for several machines and not all molding machines were in operation at any given time.

The company wanted to reduce the time involved in operator based collection as well as improve the accuracy and reliability of the charts.

Solution

The company set up their gaging stations to allow machine operators to take measurements faster, keep a number of control charts and have the most amount of time possible to maintain production on the molding machines. Each station used a DataMyte 862 data collector, video monitor and electronic micrometers and calipers.

The DataMyte 862 could handle a number of independent jobs in separate files. This allowed data collection and SPC on several machines by one operator, and the ability to start or stop data collection to match the production.

See Chapter 16 for a description of the 862 data collector.

CASE 12-13 PLASTIC BOTTLE MANUFACTURER

The DataMyte 862 Reduces Time Spent Collecting, Storing, and Reporting Measurements

A major manufacturer of plastic bottles for the beverage industry needed a way to reduce the labor intensive task of collecting, storing, and reporting measurements. The measurements help them to keep product quality up and are also required by the companies that they supply.

Problem

The company needed to keep track of several measurements:

- The weight of an empty container
- The volume from the weight of the container
- Concentricity studies on their containers (see figure 12.13.1)
- The wall thickness of the containers

Solution

The multi-file DataMyte 862 is able to record all of the measurements needed. The company expects to receive a payback in less than three months.

See Chapter 16 for a description of the 862 data collector.

CASE 12-14 INDUSTRIAL CERAMICS

Improved Monitoring of Die Wear Paid for Data Collection System in One Month

A manufacturer of industrial ceramics, including ceramic seals, ceramic ball bearings, and ceramic grinding wheels, faced tremendous pressures from off-shore competitors, both on quality and price. By improving the measurement and monitoring of dies they are reducing die change intervals and saving costs.

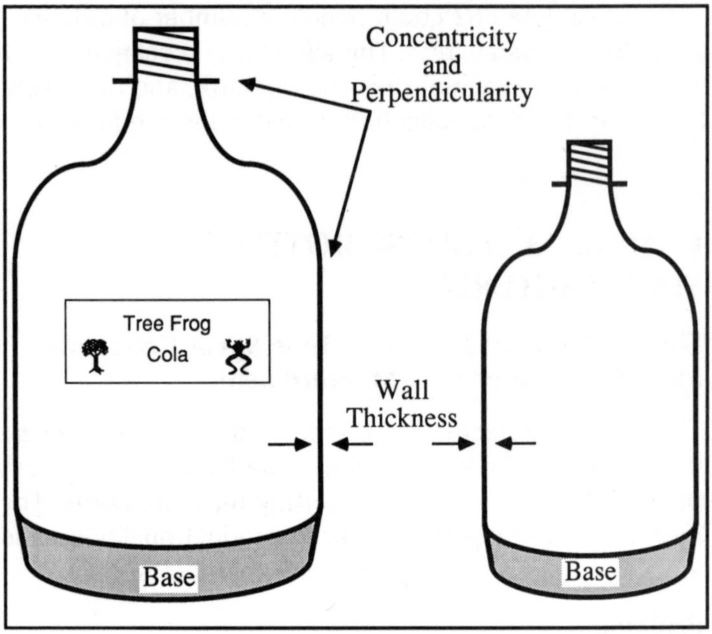

Fig. 12.13.1 Critical dimensions on a beverage bottle.

Problem

The most glaring problem was on the six to eight hundred ton press that takes powdered ceramic material and presses the material into a form. Each die costs up to $10,000. The previous method of predicting die change was with an arbitrary number of 1500 strikes of the press. After 1500 strikes, the $10,000 die was discarded.

Solution

See Chapter 16 for a description of the 762 data collector.

Utilizing the DataMyte 762 data collector along with calipers measuring wall thickness, ID, OD of the final product, they not only retained customer certification, but more importantly gained the ability to predict the change precisely. If they find they can go more than 1500 strikes of the press, they save money by not having to buy a new die so soon. If they find they have to replace a particular die before 1500 strikes of the press they save money by not making a bad product.

The payback on this system was less than one month due to the frequency of die changes and the ability to precisely predict die changes. In addition, for customers that required certification of specs on the products they ordered, the data was generated as the parts were being manufactured. This eliminated the task prior to shipment of generating a report of certification of process which was shipped with the product to the customer.

CASE 12-15 PLASTIC BOTTLE MANUFACTURER

Company Uses Data Collection to Check Bottle Forming Process

A large maker of plastic bottles used for motor oils found that they needed better process controls to meet the demands of the oil companies. By using DataMyte data collectors the company gained better control and quickly reduced scrap and rework costs.

Problem

The company needed to monitor critical characteristics in the blow molding of plastic bottles. They needed to make bottle neck diameter, thread diameter, height and thickness measurements. They were also checking weights to control the amount of plastic used. Other applications included attribute data such as bottle defects and label positioning.

Solution

After looking at several methods of automatically collecting the data, they determined that a combination of DataMyte 2000, 769, and 862 data collectors could work succesfully in their application. Using the DataMyte 2000 they would check bottle defects and thread diameter. The 2000 data collector was also used to audit the accuracy of their vision system for labels positioning. Rejected bottles were studied and causes were entered into the 2000. The DataMyte 2000 would then provide a Pareto chart listing the most frequent problems, which the company used to make adjustments to their label application machines.

See Chapter 16 for a description of these data collectors.

The largest cost savings came from using a DataMyte 862 data collector to monitor weights and volumes. The data collector produced control charts helping them better control the amount of high density resin used in the blow molding machines. The data collector also tracked trends and alerted them in advance of a process problem.

13. METALWORKING AND MACHINERY INDUSTRIES

CASE 13-1 ALUMINUM EXTRUSION AND FABRICATION MANUFACTURER

Use of Handheld Data Collectors Cuts Scrap, Speeds Up Reaction Time, and Verifies Process Capability

An aluminum extrusion and fabrication manufacturer was practicing SPC by collecting data and plotting charts manually. Manual data collection and charting caused their reaction time to be too slow. Therefore, they had a lot of scrap. The company decided to try automating data collection to increase their speed.

Problem

The manufacturer was measuring several different parts in two areas of the plant. They needed a fast and accurate method to collect data and plot charts.

Solution

See Chapter 16 for a description of the 762 data collector.

Since the manufacturer already had an SPC program, they felt they could automate it successfully by using data collectors. Six DataMyte 762 data collectors were selected to be used at operator stations.

In the fabrication area, data is collected on piercing, sawing, CNC milling, and downstream assembly operations. The DataMyte 762 is used with a multiplexer interfaced to specially constructed digital indicators, a micrometer and caliper at each cell.

In the extrusion areas, the data collectors are used for monitoring critical features during "stretching" operations to provide dimensional certification. Characteristics are also monitored on mill and drill operations in this department. The data collectors are used with micrometers and calipers. See Figure 13.1.1.

Previously, parts were dimensionally certified using a CNC machine. DataMytes were able to significantly reduce verification time on parts. More accuracy has been obtained with DataMytes, and faster reaction time has led to a reduction in scrap.

Fig. 13.1.1 Calipers and data collector for checking stretching operations.

CASE 13-2 MACHINING COMPANY

Use of Handheld Data Collectors Cuts Scrap by 31%

A machining company was having many problems collecting data manually in their milling and shaping areas. The process was too slow. DataMyte data collectors helped them improve response time and cut their scrap by 31%.

Problem

In the milling area, there were two operators, one responsible for each line of 18 machines. In the shaper area, there was one operator running one line of 18 machines.

In either department, the operator was responsible for bringing parts from each machine hourly to the central gaging station.

The problem with doing this manually was that data collection took too much time and the operator lost productive time charting data rather than running the machine. All data was calculated by hand for control charting and then keypunched again into the computer for capability studies and monthly reports.

Fig. 13.2.1 Multi-part gaging station using a DataMyte 2003 data collector.

Solution

The DataMyte 2003 data collector was selected in each area because of its multipart capability.

In the milling area, 36 part setup files were stored in the data collector. The DataMyte 2003 is used with a Mitutoyo MUX-10 and interfaced to a Mitutoyo caliper and Mitutoyo 543-423 indicator. See Figure 13.2.1. Every hour the operator pulls four parts from each machine, takes them to the data collector and measures the parts for overall height and tooth width. On-screen graphs provide real time feedback on process control.

See Chapter 16 for a description of the 2003 data collector.

In the shaper area, 18 part setup files are stored in the DataMyte 2003. The data collector is used with a MUX-10 and three Mitutoyo micrometers. Each hour the operator pulls two parts per machine, and uses the micrometers to check pitch diameter. On-screen graphs provide instant feedback using $\bar{x}$ & R charts.

In both departments, hard copy reports are generated weekly off the DataMyte 2003.

A scrap reduction of 31% was realized because the use of DataMyte data collectors provided for faster reaction time to problems. More accuracy was achieved also using automated data collection. Staffing in the SPC department was reduced by 75% by going to automated data collection.

CASE 13-3 SPECIALTY STEEL MANUFACTURER

Combining Data From DataMyte 769 and Lotus 1-2-3

A manufacturer of specialty steel was having problems correlating ultrasonic testing results with production records in order to spot trends and take corrective action. The company is a manufacturer of specialty steel and steel alloys. The highly competitive nature of the world steel industry as well as the high cost of materials involved required that problems with billet quality be tracked back to the source as efficiently as possible.

Problem

Due to the amount of data needed to track billets through melting, casting, cooling and testing, collecting it manually proved cumbersome. The company needed to record furnace numbers, ingot location, billet size, surface condition, operator names, sonic testing equipment used, and sonic test data including type of defect, its location in the rod and severity. Collecting this information on paper and keypunching into Lotus 1-2-3 for correlation with data on furnace temperature was not acceptable.

Solution

The solution was to provide a system that eliminated the need for keypunching by allowing operators to collect the required data efficiently and download to Lotus 1-2-3. Once collected, it could be readily available to quality personnel for production analysis. The system that solved this problem was the DataMyte 769 and support software.

At the end of a shift, data recorded in the 769 is downloaded to Lotus 1-2-3 and combined with furnace temperature data. The capacities of the 769 to accept data on

200 different attributes, interface with software such as Lotus 1-2-3 and dBase III and prompt operators for entries made the data collector an ideal solution.

The DataMyte 769 has allowed this company to collect the type and quantity of data needed to better understand their production process. It is now possible to pinpoint the cause of quality problems as well as provide data to customers on specific products. In addition, data is now available to help determine the costs associated with specific failures.

Choice fields are set up in the data collector for furnace numbers, ingot location, billet size, surface condition, operator names and sonic testing equipment. Attribute fields are used for type of defect, its location in the rod and its severity. Quantity fields are also used for entry of data recorded on shop sheets at the end of a shift. Bar codes are then printed from the 769 support software program for all specifiers and attributes to be used for data entry. When the shift is over, data from the 769 is transferred to Lotus 1-2-3 and combined with furnace temperatures and data from other sources.

The DataMyte 769 data collection system has permitted this company to combine information from different sources permitting meaningful analysis of relationships among different processes in terms of final product quality. The company has built a data base of quality and production data that can be used to track defect causes and improve quality and productivity.

See Chapter 16 for a description of the 769 data collector.

CASE 13-4 HYDRAULIC VALVE MANUFACTURER

Valve Manufacturer Produces Charts to Send With Parts Shipments Using New System

A hydraulic valve manufacturer had a problem: Although they had a totally automated line using programmable controllers making automatic adjustments, they were producing marginal parts barely in specifications. Due to the fact that each piece was measured in-line, the grinder would make constant adjustments creating tremendous variability. The plant needed a way to monitor process performance statistically and record traceable data for reporting.

Problem

Every valve which came down the track would be gauged with in-line transducers. Data would then be sent to a programmable controller which evaluated the information and send a signal to the machine to make an adjustment. By reacting to each part being made the programmable controller was overadjusting the machine and adding variability.

Solution

A programmable controller was equipped with an RS-232C interface which would allow it to send data to the DataMyte 762 data collector. Although each piece was inspected for multiple characteristics, the DataMyte "skip counting" function allowed a recording of every hundredth piece, which was five times per hour. Automatically after each subgroup the DataMyte would update its $\bar{x}$ & R chart through its graph logging feature. This allowed supervisors to see how the process was running. It became clear that many erratic adjustments were made when the machine should have continued to run. This created a large variation in the process and a low or poor CPK value. The CPK was the main index in which the manufacturer's quality was decided by their customers.

Once a day, data in the DataMyte 762 was transferred to a DataTruck and sent to a PC using the DataMyte FAN II software. Long-term analysis could then be made. This eliminated the need for a final inspection step of taking 50 pieces out of a box and running a capability or CPK analysis (histogram) to be sent with each shipment, saving 4-5 man-hours per week. The payback on the system was considered to be 7 months.

See Chapter 16 for data collectors and Chapter 18 for FAN software.

CASE 13-5 HYDRAULICS MANUFACTURER

Fifty Percent Labor Savings Gained With New Data Collection System

A leading manufacturer of tube fittings for hydraulic and pneumatic applications required that all SPC data be instantly available to their customers for liability reasons. This division of a billion-dollar corporation is extremely concerned with quality control, since the forces involved in hydraulics and pneumatics can lead to many liability problems if the product should fail. In order to ensure the best product, the company insisted that all SPC data be instantly available to their QC manager as well as to any current and potential customer.

Problem

Instant data collection was hindered by the fact that the QC manager required this data from two separate plants, located thirteen miles apart. The two plants consisted of 160 separate machining operations, with SPC being conducted at each machining operation. The SPC program collected both variable and attribute data in large amounts, and this data was being keypunched into an IBM AT. In order to make an automated system work, they needed a data collector with networking capabilities for instant data reports, and the system had to be economically feasible.

Solution

In order to meet the economic needs and greatly reduce the time spent on an SPC program, DataMyte recommended a 2003 data collector capable of recording both attribute and variable data electronically. Since the 2003 also has 512K memory, the unit could be shared among several machining operations. This would reduce both the number of data collectors and gages required to handle both plants.

Using a networking system designed in the plant, the customer was able to hardwire all of the units to the IBM AT through the use of short haul modems. Used in conjunction with the DataMyte FAN II software, this system allows the QC manager to collect data from various operations without leaving his office. Data could then be sent by modem to the requesting source, whether within their corporation or from one of their customers.

See Chapter 16 for a description of the 2003 data collector.

By using a single DataMyte 2003 to cover four separate operations, the customer saved over $135,000 in gages alone that would normally have been required to accomplish this task. In addition, the customer estimates that 50% labor savings has been achieved over a manual SPC program. By networking the 2003s together, the customer is able to provide instant data whenever it was requested. Because of the abilities of the units, only 40 of the 2003s were required to handle 160 machining operations.

CASE 13-6 SCREW MANUFACTURER

FAN System Helps Solve Plant-Wide Scrap Problem

A medium size screw products manufacturer wished to reduce scrap by improving quality on their multiple spindle screw machines. They elected to use SPC techniques.

Problem

Six to eight dimensions were critical to the part. All had to be held to ±.0002 inches. Operators were having to maintain a minimum of six $\bar{x}$ & R charts by hand. Productivity was cut drastically as a result. Yet, at 1000-2000 pieces per hour, scrap could add up very quickly.

The company determined they needed a faster way to get information to the operator. They considered computerized data collection as a possible solution. The company then set certain criteria for evaluating new equipment for SPC.

Solution

Much of the success the company had in solving their problem was due to their careful evaluation of needs. With fifty machines turning out a high volume, they realized that scrap could not be reduced without close control. The machine operators were the key players. An improved SPC program must focus on the operators, providing them with a way to input data and get results quickly. This would help them make good decisions, react faster, and ultimately reduce scrap.

Equipment for their SPC program had to have these features:

- It must be rugged, built for continuous usage in oily, dirty environments.
- In order to gain operator acceptance, it must be simple to use.
- It must have immediate, clear graphic display of process information right at the machine.
- It must be low-cost, to be economical for fifty machines.

The company decided to install a DataMyte FAN® system, consisting of these components:

- DataMyte 750 data collectors, one for each operator station. The model 750-12 was chosen, having inputs for up

to three gages and capacity for up to 2500 readings. Different gages were needed to measure the various dimensions. A 2500-reading memory capacity was needed to store multiple samples of up to eight dimensions.
- Electronic micrometers, bore gages and dial indicators.
- Video monitors for each station.
- A DataTruck to harvest accumulated data from each 750 on a route basis.
- FAN software for their IBM PC, to archive data and do management reporting.

This system satisfied all their criteria, increasing the speed of data collection and analysis, increasing worker productivity with regards to SPC, improving data management and thereby reducing scrap on a plant-wide basis.

In addition, they found that operator training was made easier. All data was recorded in the same manner. Charts on the video monitors provided analysis in uniform fashion. Gage reading and recording error was virtually eliminated, which was especially important when working to such tight tolerances.

All data was recorded and archived in the same format. This allowed management to do cross comparisons on their machinery. Using Pareto analysis, the least capable machine was identified for troubleshooting. Jobs that demanded higher precision were shifted to machines that proved to be the most capable at holding tolerances. In this way, management and workers together helped reduce scrap significantly and boost productivity at the same time.

See Chapter 15 for a description of the FAN system.

Operation

What follows is a brief description of SPC activities using the FAN® system. Each half hour, an operator would sample one piece per spindle and examine six to eight dimensions. The DataMyte 750 at the machine was connected to a micrometer, bore gage, and dial indicator simultaneously, with the micrometer being used to check most of the dimensions. The operator would then touch the $\bar{x}$ key to display the $\bar{x}$ chart, and the R key to display the R chart. When using manual methods, it took 30 to 35 minutes to make a decision. Now decisions took less than ten minutes. Out of control points were flagged with a big "0" on the video monitor. Two times each day, a supervisor came by and dumped accumulated data from the 750 into the DataTruck. The DataTruck was then connected to the IBM PC, and all the data was put on disk for permanent storage.

CASE 13-7 RIVET AND FASTENER COMPANY

FAN® System Boosts Operator Effectiveness in SPC Program.

A manufacturer of rivets, bolts, pins and threaded fasteners has an SPC program in place to monitor their manufacturing processes. The operators take measurements, collect the data, calculate averages and ranges for the subgroups and plot $\bar{x}$ & R charts. One of the critical measurements is the shoulder diameter on an expensive rivet. The diameter must be between 0.5851 and 0.5858 inches.

Problem

The manufacturer wanted to institute an automated SPC system because the operators did not like to collect the data by hand and then spend time plotting the data points on the control charts. The data collection and calculations were viewed as an additional chore instead of an integral part of the manufacturing task; the operator's part in the SPC program was directed too much towards the data collection and control charting. The operators work with more than one machine, so they cannot devote all of their time to monitoring a single part.

The operator had to plot the calculated data points on a paper chart that quickly became soiled and oily because the operator had to handle it every time a data point needed to be added. With charts that were hard to read and plot points on, long-term data storage was out of the question.

Solution

The operators now use electronic digital micrometers and calipers to take measurements. The data is automatically collected by DataMyte 750s. A DataMyte CRT is connected to each 750; all the operator has do is press a button on the 750 to see a control chart. An operator does not have to worry about getting the 750 dirty because the 750 is made to withstand the factory environment, having a sealed membrane keypad and hardened plastic shell.

See Chapter 16 for data collectors and Chapter 18 for FAN software.

Operators are glad to use the DataMyte FAN® system because it has made their jobs easier. Data collection is a less cumbersome task and they have more time to analyze the control charts — and work on the other machines. The manufacturer is also using the FAN® software instead of oily paper charts to archive the data and track the operations over time.

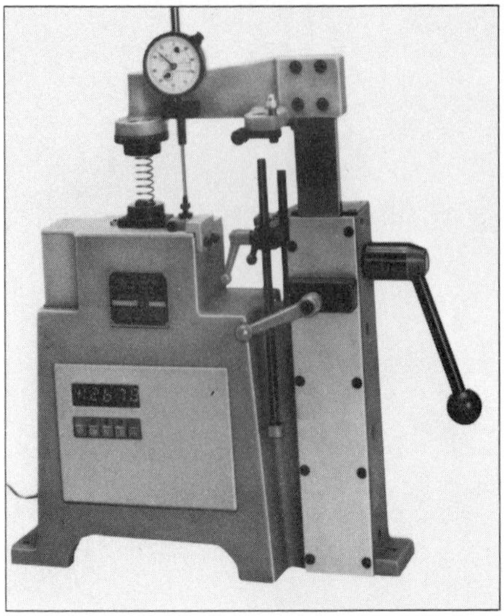

Fig. 13.8.1 Carlson Spring Tester.

CASE 13-8 INDUSTRIAL SPRING MANUFACTURER

FAN System Increases Capability of SPC Program

"How springy are your springs? A little squishy? Too stiff?" These are the questions that a manufacturer of industrial springs faced. The need for ultra-high precision springs in consumer products, missiles, computers, automobiles, electronic instruments and a host of other applications were growing rapidly. To get the answers to the questions his customers were asking, this manufacturer turned to a Carlson Electronic Digital Spring Tester. See Figure 13.8.1

The tester can be used on either extension or compression springs. Extension springs are loaded by pulling them apart, while compression springs are loaded by pushing them together. See Figure 13.8.2.

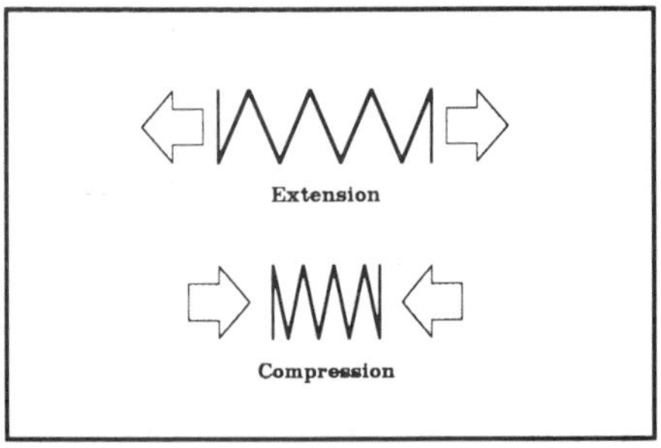

Fig. 13.8.2 Spring test characteristics.

Problem

The manufacturer was doing manual charting at the time of introduction to the DataMyte system. The major problem areas with the manual method were:

- Time consuming,
- Error prone,
- Charts existed on only one piece of paper.

The manager was not able to observe the process without picking up the operator's charts, which also meant that the chart had to be photocopied and returned at once.

Solution

Since the operators were paid by the hour, it was felt that paying for testing and analysis was a better buy than paying for pencil and paper math errors. The DataMyte 750 with a DataTruck offered some very real advantages.

- Instantaneous data recording. The RS-232 output of the

spring tester was transmitted directly to the DataMyte 750. No stopping to read the gage and write the value.

- Error free. The data was transmitted directly to the DataMyte 750, which calculated average, sigma, and range automatically.
- Management reports were available at any time. The DataTruck could pick up a copy of all the data in up to twenty 750s and generate statistical reports to a monitor or printer.
- Setup information could be saved in the DataTruck or by FAN® software. No more rummaging around file drawers looking for the chart for the current part. The setup could be down loaded with or without data. The operator could either start a new chart or pick up where he left off.

See Chapter 15 for the FAN system and Chapter 17 for the spring tester.

CASE 13-9 MACHINE SHOP

Shop Finds Faster Data Input Improves SPC Program

A small machine shop has had SPC implemented for three years. All the gaging, data collection and report generation was performed manually by the machine operators. The QC manager would periodically audit the operators by taking samples, manually inputting the data into a portable lap computer and generate statistical graphs for filing.

Many SPC benefits have materialized over the three years, such as a 35 percent reduction in scrap, 80 percent reduction in rework, and every process having a CP index of two or greater.

Problem

The problem that needed to be addressed was how to increase productivity. If they could eliminate manual data collection they could increase the productivity of their operators.

The solution was to find a data collection device that each operator could have at his machine. The device should also produce reports in real-time and have the ability to interface to a computer for storage and analysis.

Some electronic gages could be purchased, but the budget did not allow for a total revamping of their gaging. Therefore, whatever device was implemented, keyboard input of data was a requirement of the system.

Solution

A DataMyte FAN® system was purchased for the following reasons:

- The fixed station data collectors could tie into gages, or accept keyboard input.
- Real-time statistical graphs were available for the operators, which would allow for even better control of the process.
- When the Q.C. manager wanted to audit the operators, he could now use a DataTruck to harvest data from the operators' data collectors.
- An IBM PC was purchased for more efficient data report generation and its ability to run FAN® software.
- When the budget allowed for more sophisticated electronic gaging, DataMytes had the flexibility to connect to several different types and brands of gages. This way, a logical choice of gaging solutions for each process could be addressed.

Each 750 was set up differently, depending on the process at each location. SPC benefits now included increased productivity from the workforce, without all the errors associated with manual data collection/report generation. Instead of hard copy filing, which ate up file cabinet space, the data was stored on floppy disk and could be easily recalled at any time via part number. If changes were required in data collection routines, these changes could be done electronically from the DataTruck or the IBM PC. If customers wanted to see the SPC program at this organization, one trip out onto the shop floor would convince them of an efficient, results orientated system.

See Chapter 15 for a description of the FAN system.

CASE 13-10 TURBINE MANUFACTURER

Micrometer and Calipers Used for Critical Measurements on Stator Bars and Field Slot Widths

A large steam turbine-generator manufacturer determined that their present methods for taking critical measurements were too slow and costly. This manufacturer, a very large and well-respected leader in its field, recognized that those areas must be brought under control.

Problem Definition

The problem involved the measurement of the stator bars down the length of a generator (from 100 to 400 feet). These measurements were critical since they were needed to determine the amount of insulation tape required for wrapping around the bars. (If not enough tape was used, a voltage breakdown condition could result; if too much tape was used, clearance problems could be encountered.) To compound the problems inherent with such measurements, consider that seven measurements were required per bar and that anywhere from 36 to 72 bars could be used in a generator.

A similar problem was encountered when measuring field slot widths. Once again, the amount of insulation to be used was the critical factor to be determined by the measurements. The number of measurements required for the field slot widths was also staggering; there could be an average of seven measurements in each layer, with six to eight layers per slot, and up to 30 total slots.

Once all the measurements were taken (for both the stator bars and the field slot widths), the data was keypunched and then fed into a minicomputer to determine the correct amount of insulation. As can be expected, keypunching alone required a lot of time.

Solution

The company recognized that efficient data collection was necessary and began to plan some program improvements. They determined that the program implemented must be able to:

- Significantly reduce data acquisition time.
- Eliminate the time and costs involved in keypunching the measurements.
- Determine the inherent capability of the machining processes by identifying, isolating, and controlling key parameters that affect critical dimensions.

The equipment selected was the DataMyte 1507 handheld data collector, interfaced to a digital micrometer and caliper for input. The DataMyte 1507 could record the measurement in an organized, machine-readable form. Further, the data could be sent directly from the DataMyte to the minicomputer without the need for keypunching.

See Chapter 16 for a description of the 1500 data collector.

CASE 13-11 TURBINE MANUFACTURER

Production Bottleneck Eliminated Through Improved Data Collection and Analysis

A leading gas turbine-generator manufacturer determined that their present method of taking critical measurements on their gas turbine nozzles was too slow, costly, and inefficient. The company was open to new solutions, and recognized that those areas could be brought under control by implementing a statistical quality control (SQC) program.

Problem Definition

Each turbine required measuring critical gaps between air foils on their gas nozzles. Controlling this gap dimension ensures the correct amount of air flow through the nozzle; a very critical parameter in the operation of a gas turbine generator.

A large number of critical measurements were required. Depending on the size the particular nozzle, there could be either five or six dimensions per gap, and from 36 to 64 gaps per nozzle. This meant that there could be anywhere from 180 to 384 discrete measurements required for any particular nozzle, and the manufacturer was producing about six nozzles per week.

Once all the measurements were taken, the data was keypunched and then fed into a computer so that air flow through the nozzle could be calculated. As can be expected, keypunching alone required a lot of time. Further, if the data was not keypunched and fed into the computer on a timely basis to determine air flow, the overall manufacturing process would be slowed or even stopped altogether. This resulted because the next step in the overall manufacturing process required that the nozzles be mounted in special fixtures; however, they could not be mounted until the air flow had been calculated.

Solution

The production department sought a way to take the data processing department out of the manufacturing process. They determined that the new program must be able to:

- Reduce data acquisition time.
- Eliminate the time and costs involved in keypunching the measurements.
- Ensure that the production process was not slowed down or stopped.

Based on their analysis, they chose a DataMyte 1005 handheld data collector to help record measurements. The DataMyte could capture the necessary data in an organized, machine-readable form. Further, the data could be sent directly from the DataMyte to the computer without the need for keypunching.

See Chapter 16 for a description of the 1005 data collector.

To facilitate the data collection process, prompts were downloaded from the computer to aid the operators on the floor in collecting the necessary data. The program written to download the prompts for the operators was simple and straightforward. It also prevented the need for the operators to learn any new setup procedures; they could simply concentrate on collecting the data.

From a productivity standpoint, the DataMyte reduced from days down to minutes the time required for recording data, and for keypunching the measurements. The cost savings realized by not having to handle the same set of data twice (i.e., keypunching) was justification alone for the cost of the DataMyte. But the real benefit was that the backlog due to gap checking the nozzles at a fixed station disappeared. Production proceeded in a much smoother, more efficient manner.

CASE 13-12 BRASS MILLING OPERATION

Automatic Data Entry Speeds Statistical Reporting.

A large Midwestern brass company had been looking at ways to implement statistical process control on its operations. Many of the company's customers were demanding that the company supply evidence that its materials meet specifications. A commitment was made by management to implement SPC throughout their plant in an effort to control costs and improve overall quality.

Problem

One particular area that had been a continual concern for the company was its rolling mill operation. In this

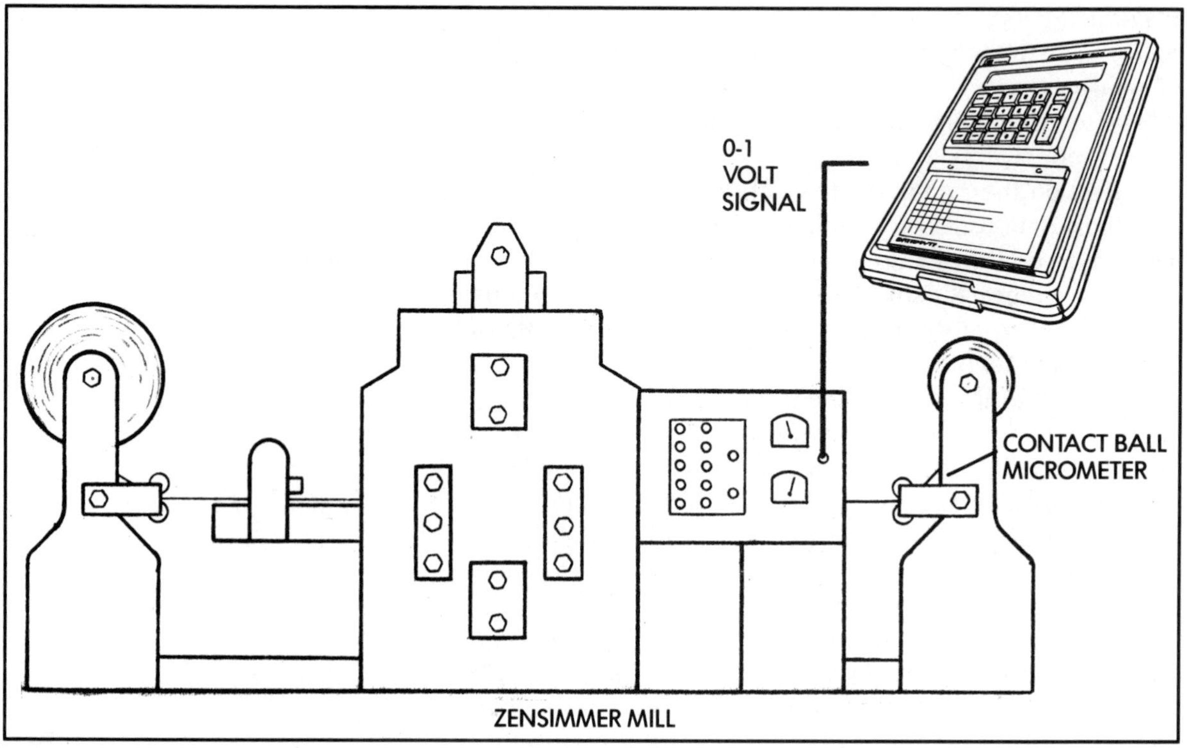

Fig. 13.12.1 DataMyte 1500 connected to Z-Mill.

process, rolls of brass plate are reduced in thickness. Large, 1000-5000 foot rolls are compressed from 60 gage thickness to as low as 8 gage utilizing a Z-Mill. The gage thickness is measured by a contact ball micrometer mounted on the Z-Mill. Output from this measuring device is directed to a large, free-standing control panel located 20 feet away. Operators watch the output from the micrometer on a needle gage in the control panel and adjust the Z-Mill as needed. The problem that the company faced was that they had no way of effectively monitoring how consistent the final gage of the brass roll was. Their only permanent record was a strip chart recording of the controller's meter, and this was almost useless since it was usually over 15 feet long and often illegible. It was not possible to identify areas in the roll that fell outside specifications, and so no corrective actions could be taken.

Solution

The solution to the problem involved the use of an analog DataMyte 1500. See Figure 13.12.1. The company's engineers provided a 0-1 volt output signal that was tied into the DataMyte's analog input port. They used the controller's linear metering capability to trigger thickness readings at specified length increments along the full length of the brass roll. In this manner, equally spaced thickness readings could be stored in the DataMyte.

Each brass roll in the plant is uniquely identified by its heat treat number. Therefore, each roll (heat treat number) is assigned a matrix in the DataMyte 1500. As the operators load the brass rolls into the Z-Mill, they pull up the correct matrix in the DataMyte. As the roll is processed through the Z-Mill, thickness readings are recorded directly into the DataMyte. Once roll processing is completed, statistical information is immediately available. Capability reports are generated and made a part of the permanent record. In addition, they produce run charts of the data which are used to indicate areas of the roll that fall outside specification limits. These areas are cut out of the roll and reprocessed.

With the DataMyte, the company has solved a major collection and analysis problem in a critical area of their operations. They are now able to provide real-time analysis of their data as well as supply useful records to their customers. They have been able to improve their overall quality and to assure their customers that their materials are meeting specifications.

See Chapter 16 for a description of the 1500 data collector.

CASE 13-13 STEEL MILL

Pyrometer and Handheld Data Collector Measures Bar Stock Temperature

To eliminate scrap and rework, a large steel manufacturer needed a fast, accurate, and easy-to-use method of measuring the temperature of hot bar stock as it emerged from the furnaces. Since molten steel is too hot to be safely measured by traditional methods, the manufacturer needed a solution to their problem that was based on state-of-the-art technology. By implementing a statistical process control (SPC) program that included the use of a DataMyte 1506 data collector configured with an optical pyrometer, the manufacturer was able to solve the problem.

Problem Definition

The problem involved measuring the temperature of hot bar stock as it emerged from the furnaces. Any manual method posed an extreme safety hazard to the inspector. Furthermore, a fixed station pyrometer did not offer the mobility necessary to follow the hot steel through its various forming and shaping stages. Without knowing the temperature of the bar stock, statistical process control was limited. This, in turn, resulted in unnecessary scrap and rework.

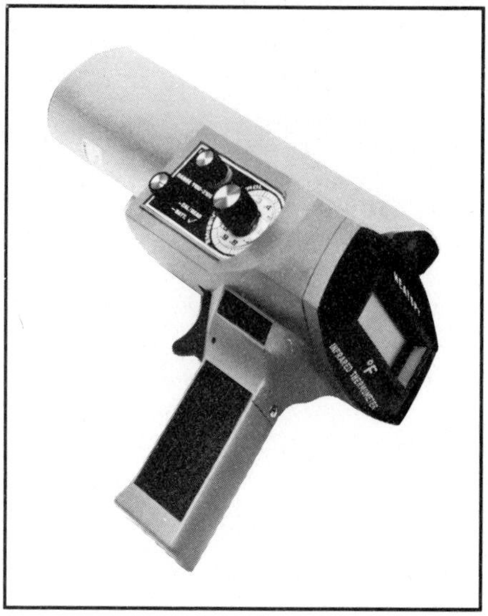

Fig. 13.13.1 Optical pyrometer.

Solution

They determined that what was needed must be able to:

- Allow the temperature of the bar stock to be measured without posing any safety hazards to the inspectors.
- Accurately measure the temperature of the molten steel.
- Measure temperatures at various locations during the forming and shaping stages.
- Analyze and collate raw data as it was input by the inspectors.
- Interface with the manufacturer's main computing system (in this case, an HP3000 mainframe).
- Generate $\bar{x}$ & R charts, capability reports, and histograms on an "as needed" basis.

In addition to the above requirements, the manufacturer did not want the system installed to require additional manpower or the use of expensive lab-type equipment.

Based on their analysis, they chose a DataMyte 1506 and a handheld optical pyrometer. See Figure 13.13.1. The optical pyrometer, which is a lightweight, handheld device that measures heat via infra-red reflections from the hot metal, allowed the manufacturer to safely and accurately measure the hot steel at a distance (in this case from 10 to 30 feet). The DataMyte 1506, which was attached directly to the pyrometer, received analog signals from the pyrometer, digitized the signals, and then stored the data into cell memory.

See Chapter 16 for a description of the 1500 data collector.

The operator could then go to the shop office, connect the DataMyte to its printer, and print out the basic $\bar{x}$ & R charts. The data was also transmitted through an interface cable to a terminal, and on to the mill's central HP3000 for further analysis and permanent storage.

CASE 13-14 CYLINDRICAL CONNECTORS

Manufacturer Reduces Scrap Costs With Improved Monitoring and Data Collection

This cylindrical connectors manufacturer needed to reduce its scrap costs so it could increase its competitive edge. The firm was an industry leader but several smaller firms were producing similar products and providing stiff competition. A reduction in waste and scrap costs would let this world-wide supplier of connectors trim its pricing and maintain its level of competition in the industry.

Problem

With several machines producing the same connectors, it was very difficult to pinpoint specific areas where excess waste was generated. Since dimensions were extremely critical on each connector, it was necessary to scrap a connector if its dimensions exceeded specifications. Each machine and machine operator were responsible for maintaining dimensions within specifications.

Solution

Each machine/machine operator combination needed to be monitored independently. A costly option would be to install a fixed station system to monitor each system and the connectors it produced. A better option for this manufacturer was one system which could monitor all the machines and correlate the accumulated data to each machine. Since the company used micrometers and calipers for measurement of critical dimensions, it needed a portable collection process which could collect data from such mechanical devices.

The company found the DataMyte Statistician an excellent tool for its needs. It could interface directly with micrometers and calipers so it would eliminate one step in the data collection process and use the gage itself for automatic data capture. The DataMyte could be set up to identify the data collected from each machine.

See Chapter 16 for data collectors and Chapter 17 for calipers and micrometers.

One operator and one DataMyte/caliper combination can now monitor each machine independently, determine which machine and operator are having difficulty in producing quality products, identify possible solutions to the problem and help keep scrap to an absolute minimum.

Operation

One specific part would demonstrate the efficiency of the DataMyte system for this firm. Figure 13.14.1 identifies this connector and the dimensions to be audited.

There were 12 machines producing these parts, so 12 matrices were set up in the DataMyte to independently monitor each machine. There were 4 critical dimensons to be measured so each matrix would contain 4 items. For $\bar{x}$ & R charting, 10 samples of each item was to be used. The DataMyte was set up as follows. Keep in mind that each matrix would be set up identically.

History = yes
Items = 4
X & R hist = yes
Samples = 10 Horz/Vert = H
Prompts = yes

Item 01 = OS-SHELL
Item 02 = IS-SHELL
Item 03 = FLANGE
Item 04 = R-ID

Limits = yes
Item 01 = HI .930 LO .934
Item 02 = HI .893 LO .895
Item 03 = HI .057 LO .067
Item 04 = HI .695 LO .698

CTRL Limits = no (not known at this time)

XDCS = yes
(The code for the caliper is C1, used for all items)
Item 01 = C1
Item 02 = C1
Item 03 = C1
Item 04 = C1

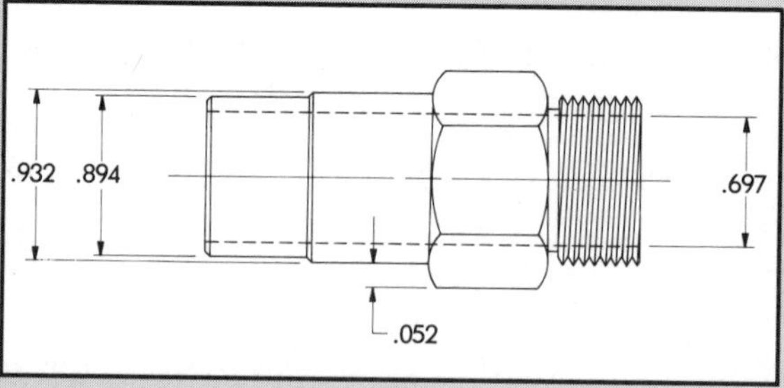

Fig. 13.14.1 Example connector.

After setting up each matrix, 12 total (one for each machine), the Data Collect mode was entered for the first matrix.

Matrix ID = MACH #1 (machine #1)
(this would change, of course, in order that each machine be identified by its own number in each matrix)
Date = (filled in accordingly)
Operator = (filled in accordingly)
Note 1 = NOT USED
Note 2 = NOT USED
Note 3 = NOT USED

Each machine was monitored, with the respective parts coming out of each machine being sampled 3 times per hour. The corresponding data was then transferred to the history file, and an $\bar{x}$ & R chart generated for each item on each machine. Four items per 12 machines translate into 48 $\bar{x}$ & R charts being produced by the DataMyte. At a point, when sufficient data had been collected, control limits were calculated. With each measurement being taken by the DataMyte, it would be easy to see where each machine was in respect to the control limits.

CASE 13-15 WELDING ELECTRODES MANUFACTURER

Better SPC Techniques Help Reduce Scrap

A large Eastern manufacturer of welding electrodes was experiencing difficulty in controlling some critical parameters on its product. The coating on a welding electrode is critical to the integrity of the weld since it is this coating which controls the gasseous envelope that forms around the welding arc. If the coating on the welding electrode is not properly deposited, gas bubbles and slag can become entrapped inside the weld, adversely affecting the integrity of the welded joint.

Problem

Two critical parameters needed to be controlled in order to reduce the amount of scrap being produced by this process. The first parameter was the concentricity of the coating. If the coating was not deposited concentrically to the rod, the arc could burn through, resulting in a faulty weld. This parameter had to be checked when the coating was in a newly deposited, semi-soft condition since there was no practical way to determine concentricity after the coating was baked hard. Also, by identifying defective rods prior to baking, the wire could be cleaned and recycled and the cost of baking a defective rod eliminated. The second parameter was the overall thickness of the coating, which was measured after the rod was baked.

Solution

The company contacted DataMyte for two reasons. First, they were interested in decreasing their scrap rate by more effectively controlling the process. Secondly, they wanted to institute a less time-consuming method of producing control charts and other statistical r(ports which would be provided to their customers.

DataMyte provided a two-fold solution to the problem. Measuring the overall coating thickness on a hard-baked rod was accomplished with a caliper and the DataMyte 750. Monitoring the concentricity of the coating was a more difficult application. Prior to installing the DataMyte system the concentricity was measured by placing the rod in a knife-edged jig and turning the rod until the jig contacted the bare metal. A dial indicator was then placed against the coating as the rod was rotated. The operator observed the high and low readings, subtracted the two and entered the difference. The DataMyte solution was to install a digital indicator which transmitted readings directly to a version of the 750 designed for total-indicator runout (TIR) measurement. This 750 records the high and low readings, subtracts the two automatically, and plots the difference on a control chart or histogram.

See Chapter 16 for a description of the 861 data collector.

By installing a DataMyte system, the company was able to have the operator closely control his process and reduce the amount of scrap produced. The time spent in recording readings taken on his samples was cut in half, giving him more time to monitor his process.

CASE 13-16 WIRE ROPE MANUFACTURER

Handheld Data Collector Aids Machine Tool Selection

Buyers of machine tools face a difficult task when evaluating machinery to be used in their plant. Machines can be purchased from a number of international sources; machines that do basically the same thing. A single machine can cost $100,000 or more, and it must operate profitably for a number of years. As age works against the machine tool, more often than not, higher quality and tighter tolerances are demanded of it.

Faced with many choices, but only a few right ones, industrial engineers at a large cable company are using sophisticated methods for machine tool evaluation. To increase the confidence level of a purchase, the company conducted a process capability study at the machine tool maker's shop, using electronic gaging and a portable data collection system.

Problem

The company continually needs to evaluate new machinery for its plants. The machines include extruders, cablers and braiders, all available from a number of sources. To select a tool they use a test production run, and look for the least natural variation in a machine. They employ the methodology of statistical process control (SPC) to find proof that a machine is stable during a production run. This requires measuring critical characteristic continuously during the run and analyzing the data.

Solution

Compared to conducting a capability study in one's own plant, a machine tool evaluation requires using equipment that can be carried around. Still, the equipment must provide accurate repeatable analysis, so that test runs on similar machines in different locations can be compared. The company had been using hand micrometers and handwritten methods of recording data. They have since adopted the use of a handheld data collection system.

The data collection system, made by DataMyte Corporation, consists of a DataMyte 1758 handheld statistical computer, an Epson printer, and gages having data output capabilities. Gage readings are automatically recorded in the DataMyte, allowing an engineer to concentrate on taking accurate readings without having to stop to record them. Data from gages that cannot be interfaced are entered on the built-in keyboard.

See Chapter 16 for a description of the 1758 data collector.

Up to ninety-nine characteristics can be monitored, with ninety-nine samples for each characteristic. Several of these 99 by 99 matrices can be stored in the DataMyte, forming a battery of machine tests which can later be transmitted to a computer for archiving.

When connected to the Epson printer, the DataMyte provides instant hardcopy results. The test run documentation, can include a real-time analysis of operating level, dispersion, trends and required adjustments ($\bar{x}$ & R chart), and a graph showing the distribution of all data for each characteristic such as Cp, CpK and estimated percent out of specification and histogram (capability report).

When evaluating a machine such as a cabler, which makes braided cable wire, several characteristics are monitored. The diameter of the cable coming off the machine is sampled continuously, with least variation the criterion. To do this, a LaserMike optical micrometer is positioned in-line with the machine. An RS-232C output cable connects the LaserMike to the DataMyte, and readings are recorded at various intervals.

Another characteristic is the lay of the wire, which is the distance between braids. This is measured by hand, using a Fowler Max-Cal caliper, which transmits the readings to the DataMyte. A tension meter is used to measure letoff tension, which is being maintained at each wire spool feeding the cabler. Other characteristics are uniform flyer rpm, taken directly from the machine readout, and bearing temperature. Bearing temperature is expected to rise from a cold state and then level off. The readings can be taken with a handheld pyrometer, and plotted in the form of an $\bar{x}$ & R chart.

The company finds an evaluation against a criterion, such as least normal variation, easier with the use of direct connect gaging and a handheld statistical computer. The large amount of data needed for a capability study is obtained more quickly with no loss of accuracy. Getting hardcopy results instantly gives the evaluation engineer the opportunity to share results with the machine tool maker. Evaluations are more fair.

CASE 13-17 FOUNDRY OPERATION

Company Uses Attribute Data Collector for Scrap Reporting

A foundry dealing in small-to medium-size castings wanted the ability to categorize the scrap that was being produced in their plant. They also wanted the ability to detect which part, what casting and which cavity of a particular mold the scrap came from. The system had to be used on the floor in an extremely hostile environment and be easy enough to use by non-technical people.

Problem

The major problem they were experiencing was an extremely high scrap rate and they had no way of determining where the scrap was coming from or when the scrap was actually cast. By automating the system they hoped to document all the casting parameters, including the part number, cavity, cast date, and the number of defects on any one casting.

Solution

The approach they decided to take was to use a DataMyte 769 data collection system. This system would provide the ability to collect all the required information, give real-time feedback to floor supervisors and also long-term data storage on the computer.

With the large amount of information that was processed every day they determined their best solution for software would be to use one of the popular data base programs available on the market and use that for archiving purposes.

See Chapter 16 for a description of the 769 data collector.

Over the course of a three month period they were able to reduce their scrap by 30% with the use of this system.

CASE 13-18 PRESSURE VALVE MANUFACTURER

A manufacturer of complex pressure valve assemblies wanted to perform an outgoing audit to ensure proper assembly of various valves. The way they were currently doing it was slow and not very efficient. A lot of errors showed up in the data that were errors due to data collection and not real assembly errors. They couldn't distinguish between assembly errors and operator recording errors.

Problem

This particular plant manufactured approximately 200 different valve assemblies. The need for this system was two-fold. One for internal defect analysis and also to provide a report that could be supplied to the customer on an outgoing audit basis.

Solution

To help collect and analyze the large amount of data, they started using a DataMyte 2000 data collector. Each inspection procedure was recorded in the DataMyte and stored under a file which referred to the actual part number. A directory of all the files was printed out so that the final inspector could call up the appropriate file, perform the required set of inspection points and then print the information out for hard copy. The reports were attached to the shipment and sent out with the proper valve assemblies.

See Chapter 16 for a description of the 2000 data collector.

By automating the final inspection sequence they were able to catch defective assemblies before they left the manufacturing facility.

CASE 13-19 STEEL COMPANY

Company Controls Costs By Holding Tolerances to Two Percent of Nominal

A steel company wanted to improve the methods used to collect and chart the measurements being used to control the rolling process in production of steel beams. By automating the analysis of steel beam dimensions, the company could avoid "giving away" too much steel.

Problem

As steel beams are produced, a one-foot section is cut from an end and used to calculate the footweight. This involves taking dimensional measurements from the flanges and web of the beam section, averaging them out and multiplying this result by a known density factor. The calculations are made separately for the flange length, flange thickness and web thickness. The individual results are then added up to produce a footweight, the weight of a one-foot section of a steel beam. Due to the number of measurements and the calculations involved, the company wanted to automate this function, which would allow them to react more quickly to size variations. Specifications call for the finished beam to fall within ±2% of expected footweight. The company attempted to stay within ±2% of tolerance.

Solution

A DataMyte 2000 was chosen to solve this problem. The measurements and attendant calculations needed to generate footweights needed a file consisting of 12 items, which the 2000 could handle. The footnote capability also allowed them to record the heat number (lot no.) and tag it to the measurement data for identification. The DataMyte 2000 could also store the file setups for many different footweights, since the rolling mill operators may produce many different beam sizes in one shift or in one week. Because of the concern for staying within +0-2% of nominal size, an additional item was added to each file to look at the final footweight calculation as a percentage of nominal (100%).

See Chapter 16 for a description of the 2000 data collector.

By being able to easily calculate footweights, the company was able to get this value produced on a constant basis. Knowing quickly what the mill is producing allows the operators to control the process to stay close to 2% over nominal and avoiding undersize beams as well as beams significantly larger than +2%.

The dollar savings are projected to be significant if beams can be held to +2% over nominal. They can thus avoid "giving away" one or two percent or more of their production.

14. TRANSPORTATION INDUSTRY

CASE 14-1 STAMPING PLANT

Critical Dimensions Checked on Vehicle Vent Windows

An automotive stamping plant that provides metal stampings and fabricated parts to their assembly division found that manual methods for data acquisition were too slow and, more importantly, unreliable. It was critical that the vent windows be uniform in nature. This manufacturer soon determined that what they really needed was to enhance their data acquisition capabilities.

Problem Definition

In the stamping process, vent windows go through seven different operations, starting with the initial stamping operator to final inspection and shipment. At each stage of the process, data must be gathered on critical characteristics of the metal frame, such as length, width, contour, and sweep. A checking fixture with marked measurement points was used. See Figure 14.1.1. The measurements would then be recorded on a sheet of paper. After recording a number of measurements, the data would then be sent to another department where it would be analyzed (provided, of course, that there was enough time to perform the analysis). The problem faced by this manufacturer was directly related to the sheer number of measurements that had to be made and the time required to process the raw data into usable chart form.

Solution

Rather than cut back on the characteristics which were measured, which they felt they could not do, they looked at ways to speed up data collection. They determined that the program implemented must be able to:

- Allow data to be collected automatically.
- Create information files.
- Process the data collected.
- Generate charts and reports.
- Reduce the number of man-hours required to collect, analyze, and process the data.

Based on their analysis, they chose 1503 Statisticians and gap gages. The DataMyte provided a data collection capability that was portable, user friendly, and could be used to produce the necessary charts and reports whenever they were needed.

Once the DataMyte was implemented as part of the SPC program, the manufacturer's roving auditors were able to automatically capture data with an electronic gap gage at each step of the vent window manufacturing process. Immediately following data collection, statistical summaries were displayed on the LCD display. When desired, the auditors could simply connect the DataMyte to an electronic printer and generate the required charts and capability reports.

Use of the DataMyte in this application had several positive consequences. First and foremost, it increased the validity, and therefore the believability of the data. Since data was captured automatically with a transducerized measurement probe and stored in DataMyte's solid state memory, transcription errors were completely eliminated. There was always a rush when data was collected manually and sometimes an auditor would massage the data to avoid the paperwork generated when a lot of units were out of spec. This problem was also been eliminated, thereby increasing data validity. Secondly, the data being captured by the DataMyte is now being utilized fully. Prior to using a DataMyte, the data was seldom analyzed. This was due to the sheer volume generated and the lack of staff to manually summarize it.

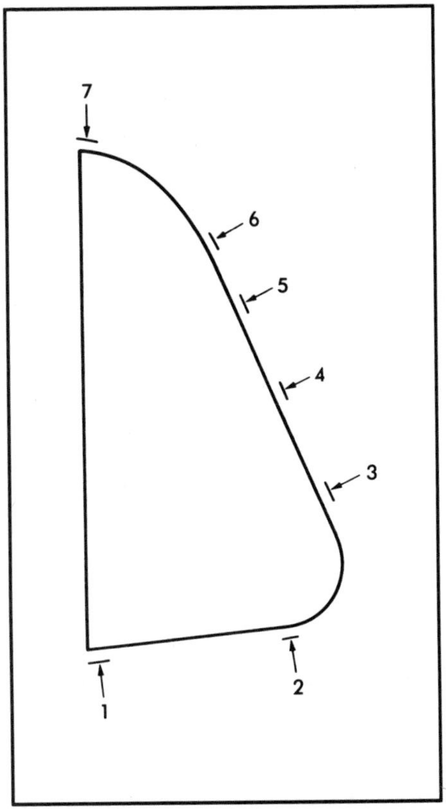

Fig. 14.1.1 Vent window check points.

See Chapter 16 for a description of the 1500 data collector
See Chapter 17 for gap gages

CASE 14-2 FINAL ASSEMBLY

Margin and Flush Checks Made During Final Assembly

A leading automobile manufacturer needed a data collection and analysis device that was capable of performing critical margin and flushness measurements at several locations on the perimeter of the hood, fenders, doors, quarter panels, deck lid, cowl and package tray.

Problem Definition

To form the body of the finished vehicle, a number of sheet metal parts and assemblies must be joined together during assembly. Each part is subject to dimensional variations which affect the outcome of the final assembly. This is also true of the process used to join the parts. To eliminate the necessity of selectively mating parts for fit during assembly, the dimensional variation of the sheet metal parts must be controlled during the stamping process.

Assuming that there is a minimum of piece-to-piece variation in the sheet metal parts, the "build-up" process, in which the assembly of those parts takes place, is controlled by measuring their fit after assembly. The measurements performed are critical to the overall process of producing an automobile.

Solution

The company chose a model 516 margin and flushness probe, used in conjunction with the DataMyte 1503 hand-held data collector. One end of the probe had a set of fingers, that when inserted in a gap and separated, would measure the distance (see Figure 14.2.1). Both curved and straight margins could be measured. The other end of the probe had a shoe and movable rod to measure flushness (see Figure 14.2.2)

Using the DataMyte and probe, the inspectors could take a series of measurements on each vehicle in a sample group. The measurements were taken at predetermined check points on the finished vehicle. Margin and flushness were recorded at several locations on the perimeter of the

Fig. 14.2.1 Model 516 gage used to check gaps.

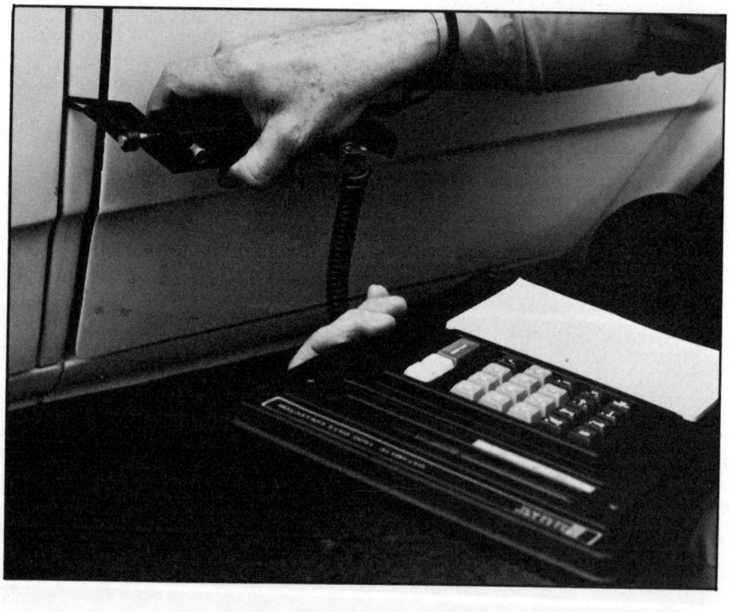

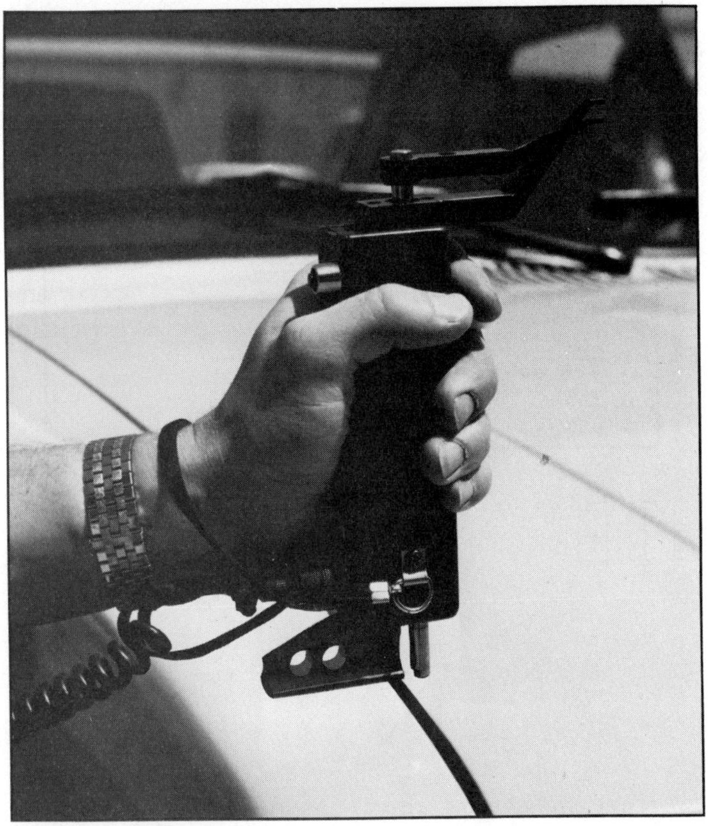

Fig. 14.2.2 Model 516 gage used to check flushness.

hood, fenders, doors, quarter panel, deck lid, cowl and package tray.

Several unit samples (typically 25 to 30 per inspection) were taken twice each shift. As the measurements were made with the margin and flushness probe, the data was fed directly into the DataMyte. When the inspection was complete, the DataMyte was connected to a desktop computer (in this case a Hewlett-Packard system) and the data transferred.

Once the data was transferred to the computer, it was analyzed by using the Electronic Dimensional Audit System (EDAS) programs supplied by DataMyte Corporation. Once the data was analyzed, a capability analysis report was generated. See Figure 14.2.3. This report was reviewed immediately by the plant's Quality Control and Process Engineering personnel to determine the overall operating conditions of the assembly process. If a problem condition in the fit of any body panel was identified, the quality control function responsible for that part was immediately notified and a corrective action initiated.

See Chapter 16 for data collectors, Chapter 17 for gap gages and Chapter 18 for software

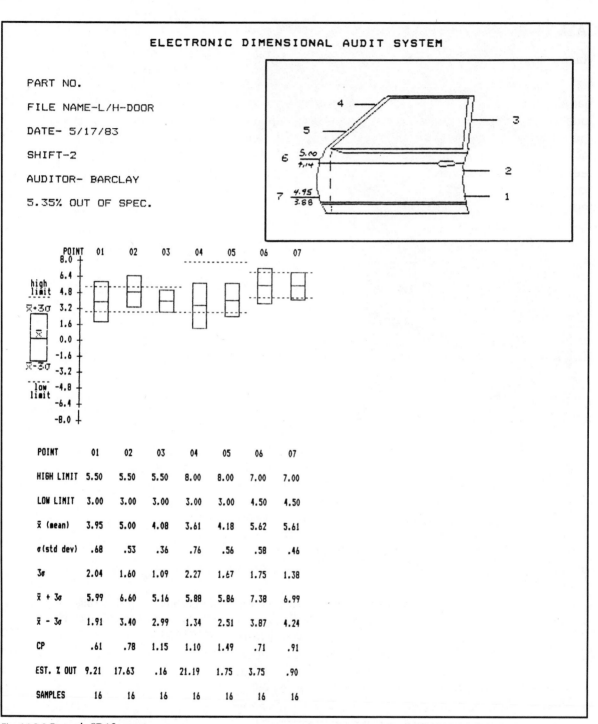

ELECTRONIC DIMENSIONAL AUDIT SYSTEM

PART NO.

FILE NAME-L/H-DOOR

DATE- 5/17/83

SHIFT-2

AUDITOR- BARCLAY

5.35% OUT OF SPEC.

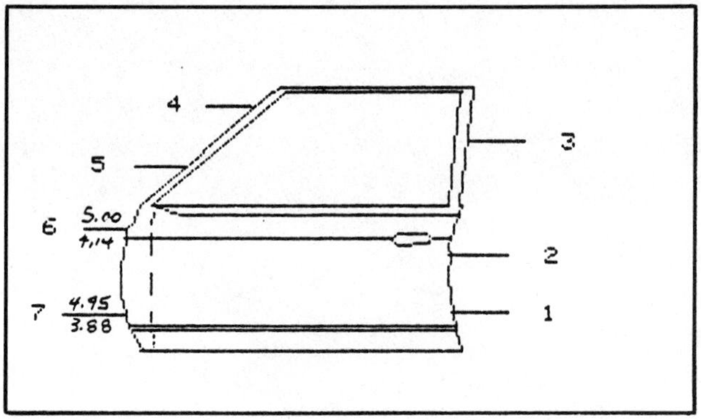

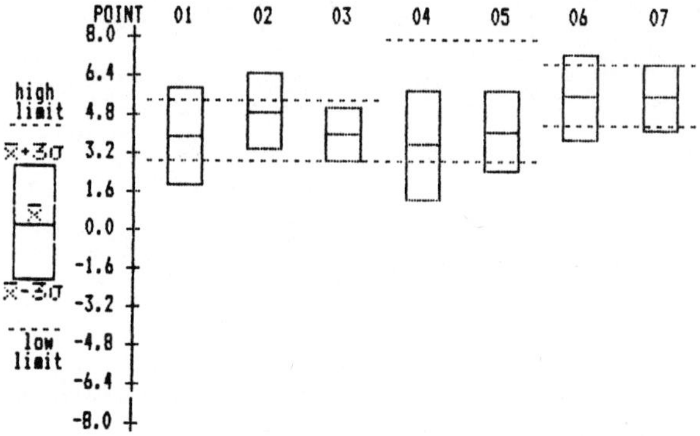

POINT	01	02	03	04	05	06	07
HIGH LIMIT	5.50	5.50	5.50	8.00	8.00	7.00	7.00
LOW LIMIT	3.00	3.00	3.00	3.00	3.00	4.50	4.50
$\bar{x}$ (mean)	3.95	5.00	4.08	3.61	4.18	5.62	5.61
σ(std dev)	.68	.53	.36	.76	.56	.58	.46
3σ	2.04	1.60	1.09	2.27	1.67	1.75	1.38
$\bar{x} + 3\sigma$	5.99	6.60	5.16	5.88	5.86	7.38	6.99
$\bar{x} - 3\sigma$	1.91	3.40	2.99	1.34	2.51	3.87	4.24
CP	.61	.78	1.15	1.10	1.49	.71	.91
EST. % OUT	9.21	17.63	.16	21.19	1.75	3.75	.90
SAMPLES	16	16	16	16	16	16	16

Fig. 14.2.3 Example EDAS report.

CASE 14-3 BODY ASSEMBLY

Magnetic Stripe Readers Speed Attribute Data Entry

The body assembly division of a leading automobile manufacturer recently implemented the largest attribute auditing program ever undertaken within the company. The program was costly to implement; however, the payback period was relatively short and savings have already been realized. The previous attribute program used by the manufacturer consisted of manual data collection and limited statistical processing. The company realized that to remain competitive, it needed to enhance its overall statistical quality program as soon as possible. They felt that by upgrading their attribute auditing program they could significantly cut costs. To this end, the company developed their own user software programs that were compatible with IBM mainframes and DataMyte 1000 series data collectors.

Problem

With their previous attribute audit program, inspectors would make hash marks on a grid sheet to represent imperfection data. The grid sheets were then tabulated each day after they had been collected. Reports generated as a result of grid sheet analysis were not available until the following day. Obviously, this process was too cumbersome and time consuming.

Solution

The manufacturer had two active car assembly lines. Each line assembled different model full-size cars. On one assembly line, a single IBM 8140 mainframe was used to interface up to 14 IBM 3646 magnetic scanner control units. The magnetic scanners would dump data into the Repair Audit Program (RAP) that was stored in main memory of the IBM 8140. The RAP program, which was responsible for tracking obvious imperfections, permitted the manufacturer to catch and repair imperfections before the automobile was moved into the final assembly area.

Nine DPX protocol converter boxes and nine DataMyte handheld data collectors were also used on this assembly line. See Figure 14.3.1. The DataMytes were used to dump asynchronous data information into the DPX boxes each hour (or whenever 1,500 entries had been received by a

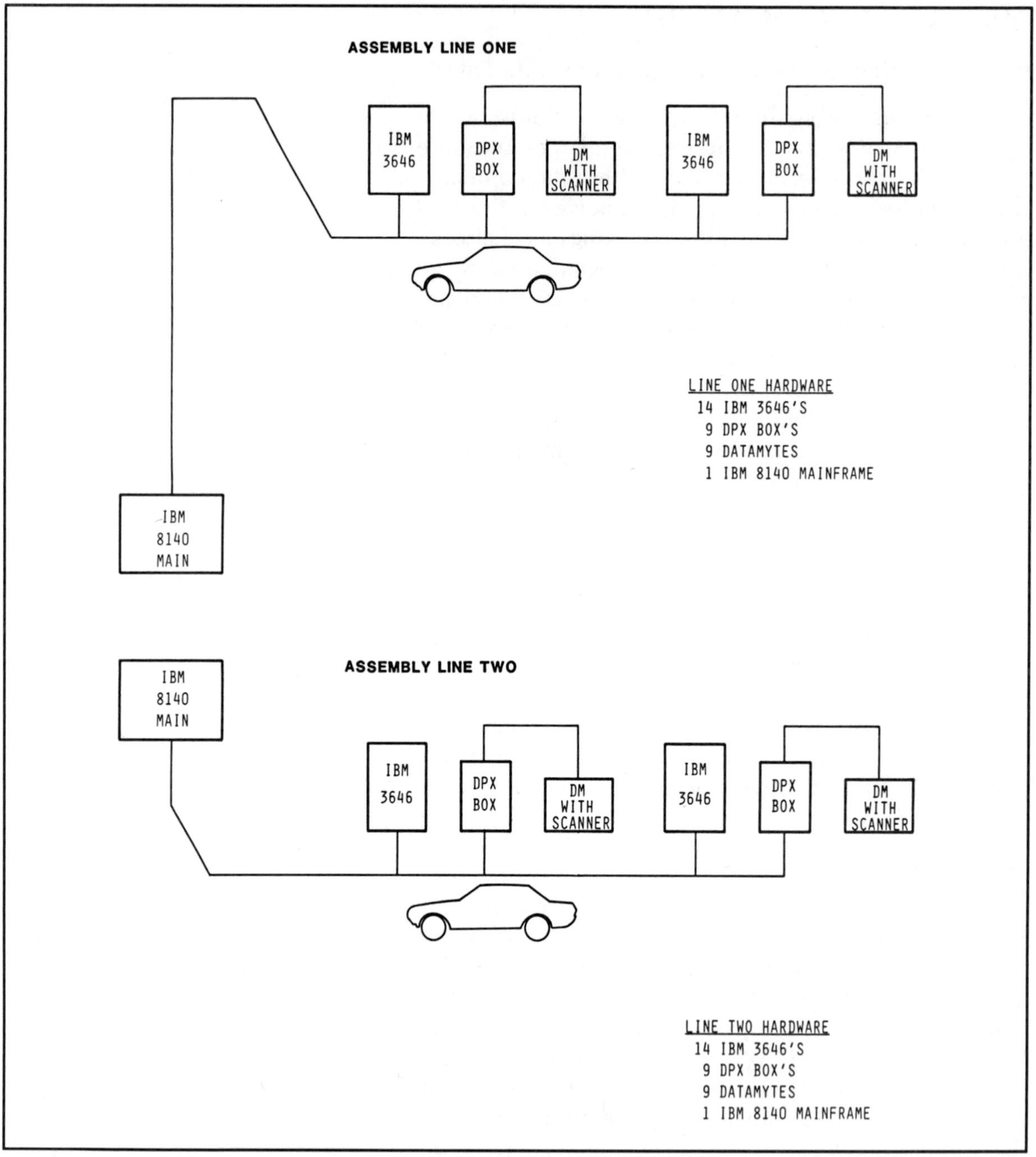

Fig. 14.3.1 Data collection system configuration.

DataMyte). The DPX boxes would then convert the data to make it compatible with Synchronous Data Link Communications (SDLC) protocol, and transfer the data to the IBM mainframe. The mainframe would then process the data by using the Critical Audit program (CAD). This program has the capability to track the smallest imperfection and to control a process.

See Chapter 16 for a description of data collectors.

Operational Characteristics

The following is a brief description of how the attribute system operates. As an automobile traveled down the assembly line, it would pass an IBM 3646 station. An auditor using a magnetic scanner was positioned at this station. Using the magnetic scanner, the auditor would gather data from a body plate, search for obvious imperfections, and then record the data.

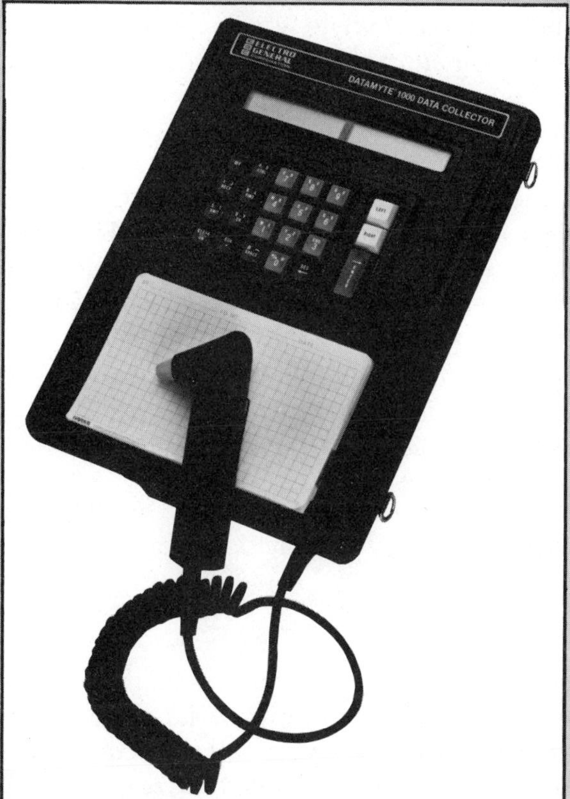

Fig. 14.3.2 DataMyte and mag scanner.

Next, the automobile would pass a DPX station where it underwent a more critical inspection. At this station the auditor was equipped with a magnetic scanner that was connected directly to a DataMyte data collector. See Figure 14.3.2.

During this inspection the auditor would input data via the magnetic scanner from plexiglass boards. These boards had many magnetic tapes, which consisted of imperfection locations and information related to the types and quantities of imperfections. A prompt loop in the DataMyte was set up to distinguish between such items as panel or location, type of imperfection, and quantities or counts.

The DataMyte was set up to accumulate the following information:

Headers: Identification
Shift
Stations
Hour
Style
Prompts: Panel
Type
Count

Once all attribute data was gathered, the following types of charts would be printed for further analysis:

- Trend charts (consisting of historical data)
- Pareto charts (reflecting the frequency of occurrences)
  Histograms
- Control charts (depicting trend analysis)

- RAP summary (a report showing the accumulation imperfection totals imperfection type)

CASE 14-4 PAINT AUDITING

Comprehensive Paint Auditing System

A major automobile manufacturer set a division objective to significantly reduce the number of paint (surface) defects on its new automobiles. This manufacturer established a goal of no more than 1.1 defects per automobile. It was important to reduce the defects for two reasons: (1) fewer defects would mean less corrosion problems over the life of the automobile, and (2) fewer defects would improve customer perception of their automobiles.

Problem Definition

Existing methods for collecting and analyzing paint (surface) defect data was a cumbersome and time consuming process that did not meet the requirements for statistical process control (SPC) as defined by this automobile manufacturer. Before the DataMyte was implemented to handle data collection and analysis functions, the manufacturer was forced to:

- Manually accumulate defect information. Six auditors were assigned at each plant, five who would collect data, one at each station in the paint process. See Fig. 14.4.1. The number of cars sampled per hour was determined by the line speed. If the line speed was less than 50, 20% per hour were sampled, or a minimum of 10.
- Each would record the data collected on tally sheets, and turn the sheets in to the sixth person.
- The sixth person would then manually assemble, collate, and plot the results.
- Daily totals were used for plant reports. Weekly totals were used for reports sent to division headquarters.

Solution

Once the manufacturer had implemented the manual system, they began to look for ways to automate the system. Considerations were: 1) what data collection system to use; and 2) what computer system to use.

The DataMyte 1000 was chosen for data collection for the following reasons: 1) their present coding scheme could be used without modification; 2) data input was easy and straightforward; 3) protocol selection on the DataMyte

1000 made the computer interface simple, and; 4) durability. Consideration for computer systems were: 1) stand alone desktop microcomputers, 2) the mainframe at each plant; or 3) the central office timeshare system. The plant mainframes were selected for three reasons: 1) the data processing department agreed to prioritize writing software for the project; 2) the mainframes at each plant were identical; and 3) the mainframes were already communicating with the central office timeshare system. This made the weekly reports to the Division easily transferable at minimum cost.

See Chapter 16 for a description of the 1000 data collectors

By implementing an automated system, the manufacturer was able to significantly reduce the number of paint defects per automobile and meet division objectives.

Another benefit was a reduction in the manpower required to collect the data. Soon after the system was installed, it was determined that three auditors could now do the job that had previously been done by six. The three auditors were responsible for transmitting their own data to the computer and generating needed reports. As a result of the labor savings alone, the equipment and initial programming costs were recovered in less than three months.

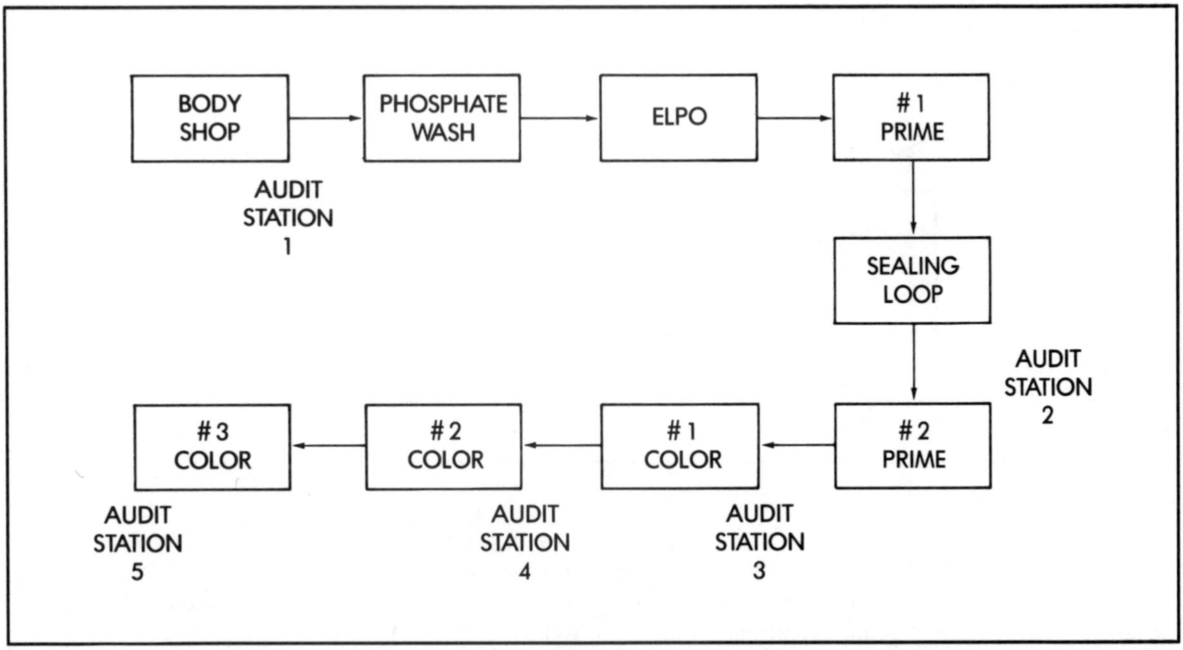

Fig. 14.4.1 Paint audit stations.

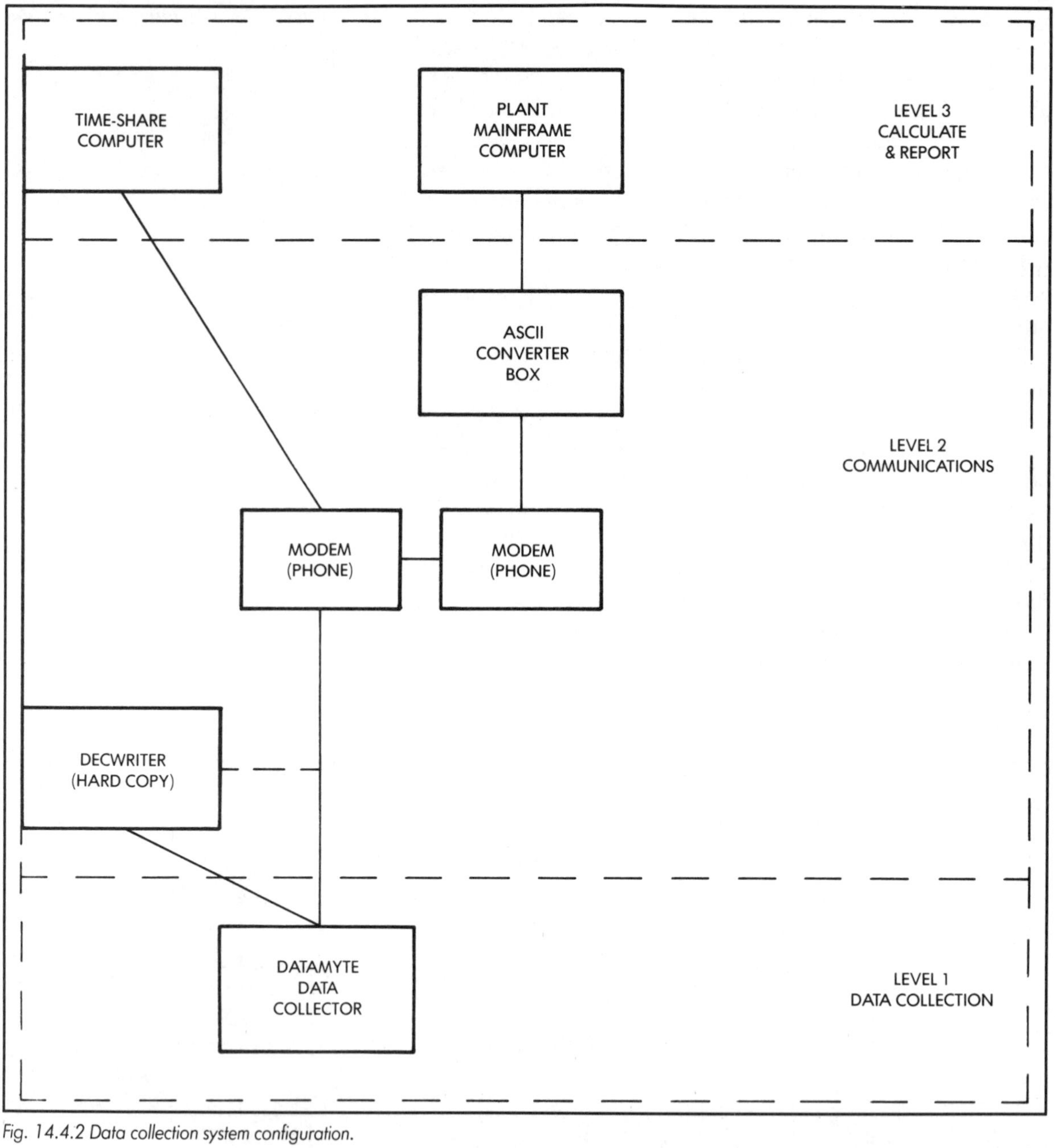

Fig. 14.4.2 Data collection system configuration.

Operation

The information that follows provides a brief description of how the DataMyte 1000 data collectors were used to reduce the number of paint defects. A pilot project was started at one of the manufacturer's plants near their division headquarters. System requirements for the plant were established as follows (Figure 14.4.2):

- Six DataMyte 1000 data collectors
- One DECwriter III printer
- One modem
- One protocol converter
- Applications software as required

The terminal, modem, and protocol converter were located near the paint area. Once the equipment was installed, the DataMyte 1000 was set up to store eight hours of data prior to transferring the information to the host computing system. This allowed each auditor the option of transferring data at the end of each hour, every four hours, or at the end of the shift.

Of primary importance was the ability of the equipment to not only pinpoint the most frequently occuring defects, but also the location of each defect. To this end, the coding scheme was created to record both panels and defects. Panels were coded alphabetically as follows:

A = left front hood
B = left front quarter panel
C = left front door
(etc.)

Defects were coded numerically as follows:

1 = dent
2 = run
3 = scratch
(etc.)

The plant was given the option of using either keyboard entry or bar code entry. (A bar code wand is a standard option available on the DataMyte 1000.) When the bar code entry was used, a menu sheet was created that listed all possible panels and defects with the appropriate bar code label for each. This sheet was installed on the note pad of the DataMyte 1000. When the keyboard entry was used, a list of all panels and defects was written on the note pad. This list was helpful at the beginning but soon became unnecessary because the auditors had memorized the coding scheme.

During data collection, the auditors moved around the automobile starting at the left front. See below. They recorded all observed defects and their appropriate panel locations. This was done while the cars were actually moving along the assembly line; line speed was not affected.

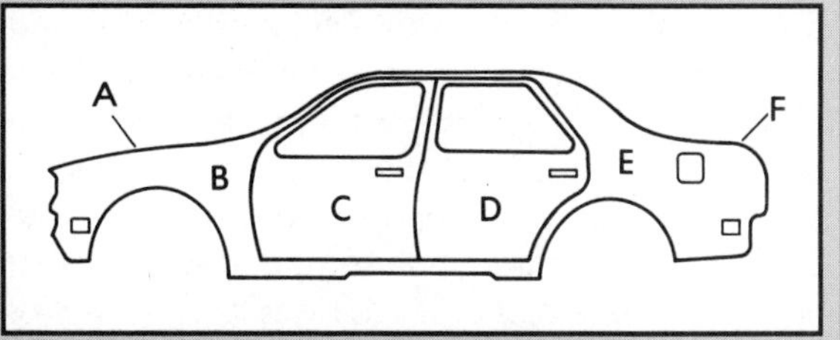

Data Analysis and Presentation

Following the Pareto principle, the following information was of interest:

1) The first, second, and third highest occurring defect for each hour, each day, and for each week. See Figure 14.4.3.
2) The first, second, and third highest problem panel (also for each hour, day, and week.)
3) The first, second, and third highest occurring combination of panel/defect (again for each hour, day, and week).

Daily Report

HOUR	1	2	3	4	TOTAL
1ST HIGH DEFECT	6/3	2/6	1/6	2/11	2/21
2ND HIGH DEFECT	15/3	1/3	2/3	1/5	1/16
3RD HIGH DEFECT	1/2	3/3	3/1	6/5	6/10
1ST HIGH PANEL	D/2	H/4	Y/4	L/5	H/10
2ND HIGH PANEL	G/2	M/4	J/2	D/4	L/10
3RD HIGH PANEL	H/2	D/3	L/2	F/4	D/9
1ST HIGH DEFECT/PANEL	L-6/2	H-2/4	Y-1/4	F-2/4	H-2/6
2ND HIGH DEFECT/PANEL	B-1/1	B-3/2	J-1/2	L-2/4	Y-1/4
3RD HIGH DEFECT/PANEL	H-1/1	B-1/1	H-2/1	D-6/4	F-2/4
AVERAGE DEFECT/CAR	6.5	9.6	7.5	13	9
HIGH DEFECTS/CAR	19	19	9	15	19
LOW DEFECTS/CAR	2	0	6	11	0
NUMBER OF AUDITS	4	3	2	2	11

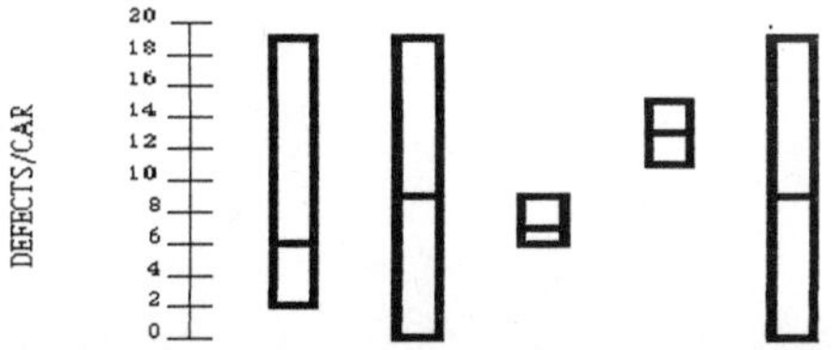

Fig. 14.4.3 Example of daily report.

A matrix was generated which clearly illustrated all possible combinations of panels and defects. The frequency of occurrence appeared in each cell of the matrix.

Four-by-eight foot charts were created and placed in the paint department. Hourly, daily, and weekly points were plotted on these charts so that all employees could see how they were doing on an ongoing basis. This immediate feedback provided a positive reinforcement for everyone involved in the process. Within three months, the average defect per car was one half of what it was at the onset of the project. Since then, the average defect per car has continued to decline.

Once the pilot project was proven successful, a regional implementation schedule was developed. A central plant in each region was selected as a training sight and a three-day training session scheduled. The training group consisted of representatives from DataMyte Corporation, division headquarters and central office data processing. A training manual was written and presented at the three-day session. Data was actually collected, transmitted to the computer and reports generated during the training session. Participants then returned to their respective plants and with the aid of the training manuals and their "hands-on" experience, trained their auditors.

Case 14-5 PAINT AUDITING

Computerized Paint Audit System Creates Graphic Reports

The U.S. manufacturing facility of a Japanese automobile manufacturer wanted to put their entire paint audit program onto a computer system. Computerizing the program would provide both graphic reports and faster turnaround of the data. Summarized data could be used to alert the front end of the paint line of the current status of defects occurring at the end of the paint line. With the information, adjustments could be made immediately to correct the problem.

Problem

One of the first problems they had to overcome was the large amount of data that had to be collected over a relatively short period of time. The data was composed of:

COLOR
BODY STYLE
PANEL
SPRAYBOOTH
DEFECT TYPE

The intent was to have one inspector on each side of the vehicle recording defects. Unfortunately, the line speed was such that the operator would soon lag behind and therefore was not able to perform a thorough inspection. They began a search for a data collector that would allow fast data entry and still offer the portability required in a large paint department.

Solution

They settled on the DataMyte 1005 with the bar code option because bar code entry would provide the fastest means of inputting the data. The DataMyte was programmed with nested prompts. Nested prompts allowed them to input the body style, color, spraybooth, and panel codes followed by any number of defect codes for each panel. Using the nested prompt feature they could jump to any level of the prompt loop at any time. The programmed loop looked like this:

See Chapter 16 for a description of attributes data collectors.

(body style (color (spraybooth (panel (defect)))))

A series of bar codes was generated for each of the categories listed above. The bar codes were simply three digit numbers, with a human readable description printed below each code.

The bar codes were produced at a high density so that they would all fit on a single card. This saved the inspector additional time that would otherwise be spent flipping from card to card.

To complete the system they needed a post processing software package that could break down the data into specific categories of concern and graphically represent the results. They chose the IBM PC because of its popularity and general compatability.

The finished program supplied them with the necessary information to break down the defects according to:

% of first run
Total number of defects
Average defects/vehicle
Total dirt defects
Average dirt/unit
Average mottle defects
Top three defects

and distributions of defects based on:
Color
Side of vehicle
Spraybooth
etc.

The implementation of this system resulted in a reduction of manpower in repair of defects, reduced warranty costs, reduced man-hours in repair of defects, reduced man-hours in data analysis, and better customer perception of their products.

CASE 14-6 CAR BODY PLANT

Adding SQC to Incoming Inspection Eliminates Faulty Moldings

A car body plant in Detroit discovered a great deal of variability in the linear dimensions of window channel moldings produced by outside suppliers. The plant manufactures decorative trim moldings, sunroofs and other trim parts for use in many of the car company's auto and truck assembly plants. These moldings have a significant effect on the appearance of a vehicle. For many years the plant and suppliers checked the linear dimension of incoming moldings in the traditional manner, but this was not effective in culling out all faulty moldings prior to installation.

Problem

During the assembly of sunroofs, there were problems with the channel moldings that formed the protective edge of the sunroof. These moldings, produced by outside suppliers, exhibited a high degree of variability in length. When the molding was too long, there was an unsightly gap on the edge of the sunroof. When moldings were too short, there was a gap where adjacent moldings came together.

Both the plant and the supplier inspected the molding dimensions in the traditional manner, using a "GO" or "NO GO" checking fixture, but it was not possible to check each molding prior to installation on the glass. As a result, it was a normal daily occurrence to have sunroofs rejected for rework because of problems with channel moldings. An additional hourly person was often employed on a full time basis just to inspect and rework the sunroofs after they were assembled because of moldings being too short or too long.

This situation existed in the plant for several years and there seemed to be no clear cut method to monitor and accurately control the length of these channel moldings from vendors. The costs of this problem were considered excessive.

Solution

Several solutions, ranging from changing vendors to 100% incoming inspection, were considered. The practical solution appeared to be the proper utilization of Statistical Quality Control (SQC) procedures for incoming inspection. It was hoped that this approach could demonstrate to suppliers that some of their production procedures were not in statistical control. A planned program was developed and implemented utilizing available plant personnel.

Quality control personnel used DataMyte 1503 Statisticians and 514 gages in a checking fixture to measure and record deviations in lengths on incoming channel moldings.

See Chapter 16 for data collectors and Chapter 17 for the 514 gap gage.

The first control charts indicated that the length dimension from vendors was out of statistical control in several cases. The vendor's quality control personnel were called in and most were surprised by the findings. Most felt that their production could control the linear dimension. Soon, some of the vendors began to monitor their length dimension with their own DataMytes. As a result, their moldings became less variable and began to center on a nominal value. This reduced scrap and rework for the body plant, as well as reduced the need for continued incoming inspection.

The implementation of SQC procedures during incoming inspection at the body plant has contributed to an improvement in the overall quality of channel moldings used in the assembly of sunroofs. The sunroof assembly department has not been forced to rework a sunroof due to faulty channel moldings since shortly after the SQC program was initiated.

Operation

Because of the relatively simple operation of the DataMyte, it was decided that the best way to implement an SQC system in incoming inspection was to involve the hourly inspection workers. They had the ability to plot and monitor control charts as well as act on the information produced by the charts. An hourly employee was trained in SQC calculations and control chart plotting and then he helped train other hourly workers.

Incoming inspection personnel take samples out of every shipping container. These samples are placed on the checking fixture and measured with a 514 gage for linear dimension. The data are collected by a DataMyte 1503. Each inspector follows instructions kept by the DataMyte to record these measurements. The DataMyte is set up in a 1 item by 10 sample matrix.

The inspectors generally take 10 moldings out of each shipping container. Then, with the DataMyte in the SUMMARY mode, the $\bar{x}$ & 6 Sigma values are read and plotted on the control chart for the particular supplier and part number.

CASE 14-7 STAMPING PLANT

Manufacturer Cuts Waste in Bar Stock Blanking Stage

An automotive stamping plant that specializes in the manufacture of decorative trim moldings found that traditional methods of checking linear dimensions was causing excessive scrap and rework. Since the moldings have an impact on the appearance of a car or truck, the company felt they contributed to the overall image, good or bad, of the entire corporation. The ability to manufacture moldings of high quality was therefore very important.

In their efforts to improve the overall quality of their trim moldings, this manufacturer decided to improve their statistical quality control (SQC) program. As byproducts of improving the SQC program, the manufacturer also wanted to be able to increase productivity and to increase customer awareness of their manufacturing capabilities.

Problem Definition

In the past, moldings produced by this manufacturer had exhibited a higher level of variability than what was considered acceptable. One process that was very critical to the ultimate quality of the moldings involved the cutting of metal bar stock to a specific length. This process, which needed to be performed often, required a high degree of accuracy. This cut was accomplished on a rolling mill during an initial forming process. For many years, this dimension was monitored in the traditional manner by using a "GO" or "NO GO" checking fixture. If the linear dimension couldn't be maintained within a tolerance of plus or minus 1.5 mm, problems would arise during later production processes.

As a result of not having a clear-cut method to monitor and accurately control the length of the trim blanks, and since traditional measuring methods were being used, it was considered a normal occurrence to have a basket of parts (1,500 to 6,000 pieces) returned each day for rework or disposal as scrap. In fact, an additional hourly person was often employed on a full time basis just to rework the materials that had been cut too long. The short pieces normally had to be scrapped. It was sometimes even necessary to have a mill in operation just to rework the defective oversize parts. Actual cost figures for rework and other expenses resulting from their problems were not available; however, the company did consider them to be excessive. It was thought that this situation had existed for fifteen to twenty years.

Solution

Several solutions were considered, ranging from acquiring new rolling mills, to increasing the production by using outside vendors. It was felt that tightening the engineering specifications would not solve the problem because of the inability to maintain the existing tolerances. A more practical solution seemed to be the proper utilization of statistical quality control procedures.

A planned program was developed and implemented using available plant personnel. They purchased a DataMyte 1503 Statistician and a 514 Gap Gage to measure and record deviation from nominal cut lengths. The data was plotted on $\bar{x}$ & R and sigma charts to identify the source and magnitude of variation.

See Chapter 16 for data collectors and Chapter 17 for the 514 gap gage.

The first control charts generated indicated that the cut-off process on the rolling mills was out of statistical control. Further analysis indicated that there were at least two assignable causes for this variability.

First, the operators were "tweaking" the length setting on the mills. That is, they would make a length adjustment whenever they had a sample that did not check as a "GO" on the checking fixture. To counteract this problem, the operators were instructed to change the cut-off setting only when it was indicated by the control chart.

Second, the mechanically actuated cut-off blades on the mills were not operating in a consistent manner. Due to wear, the setting would drift over a period of time. The company made plans to replace these blades with pneumatic cut-off blades that would not drift.

Shortly after implementing the SQC program using the DataMytes, the length dimension became less variable and began to center on a nominal value. This helped reduce scrap. Instead of receiving a daily basket of parts for rework or scrapping, the rolling mill department had returned only one basket of materials during the first six months (this basket was later discovered to have been from a mill whose operator had neglected to keep a control chart for his machine that day). Other benefits realized by using the DataMyte included:

- An increase in the production rate, due in part to the decreased operator time spent on inspection and machine adjustments.
- Increases in linear dimension performance that included: a decrease in variability (6 sigma in control and $\bar{x}$ in control); achieving a capability ratio of less than .75; and a return to processes centered on nominal values.
- Increases in productivity gains that included: reduced machine downtime, reduced labor for sorting out defects, reduced need for inspections, elimination of extra labor for rework, almost complete elimination of scrap, and improved relations and image with customers.

The use of DataMytes in the rolling mill area of the plant will be expanded in the near future so that each operator will have his own unit to enable more frequent sampling. The success at this company illustrates the role hourly workers can play in helping to build quality products in any manufacturing environment.

Operation

The information that follows provides a brief description of how the DataMyte 1503 and Model 514 gages were used by the manufacturer.

Early on, because of the relatively simple operation of the DataMyte, it was felt that the best way to implement an SQC system in the rolling mill area was to involve the operators themselves. It was believed that they had the ability to plot and monitor control charts and that they were also in the best position to act on the information that the charts were capable of giving them.

An hourly employee was chosen to become knowledgable in SQC calculations and control chart plotting. She, in turn, helped train the operators. It was felt that with the training coming from another hourly worker, additional credibility would be given to the project by the operators.

To facilitate the collection of data, the mill operators took production samples to a centrally located SQC area, where a linear measuring fixture was located. Using the DataMyte 1503 and Model 514 gages, each operator followed a simple procedure for recording the linear measurements.

The rolling mill's machine numbers were used as the matrix numbers in the DataMyte; it was set up for a 1 item by 10 item sample matrix. The operators generally took 10 moldings once or twice each day over to the SPC area, where they used the

DataMyte and gage to record the lengths of the samples. Then, with the DataMyte operating in the SUMMARY mode, the $\bar{x}$ and 6 sigma values were read and then plotted on the control chart for the mill.

Within a short period of time, all the operators were taking sample measurements of their productions and were routinely calculating $\bar{x}$ and 6 sigma values for plotting on their individual control charts.

CASE 14-8 AUTO MANUFACTURER

Dynamic Torque Measurement Reduces Rework

A large automobile manufacturer needed a method for measuring dynamic torque. As an auditing procedure, this manufacturer had monitored static torque for some time; however, they felt by auditing dynamic torque they would be able to better analyze the fastening process, and reduce rework.

Problem Definition

The problem faced by this manufacturer involved the measurement of dynamic torque. Their engineers felt that by auditing dynamic torque, they would be able to more fully understand what happened to a fastener as it was being torqued down. Dynamic torque measurement could capture data related to the fastener itself, the tool being used, and the force being applied by the operator.

The problem involved not having a versatile method of hooking up a tool to the data collector that would allow dynamic torque to be measured.

Solution

It was determined that the best solution would be to place in-line torque transducers on the assembly tools and set a DataMyte 1505 data collector to read the peak torque signal generated. See Figure 14.8.1. In addition to being able to measure dynamic torque, other benefits realized by using the DataMyte 1505 included:

See Chapter 16 for data collectors and Chapter 17 for torque tools.

- A significant reduction in data acquisition time.
- Elimination of the time and costs involved in keypunching the measurements.
- The ability to have charts and capability reports generated on demand.

Fig. 14.8.1 In-line torque transducer mounted on a torque tool.

- Added flexibility. The DataMytes could be used to measure both static and dynamic torque on a variety of fasteners.

By using the DataMyte 1505 for data collection purposes, the manufacturer was able to implement a program that provided them with the ability to perform dynamic torque measurements.

The DataMyte was flexible and handheld, which provided advantages over most torque data collection devices. The air stall tools they used required no special settings, other than the installation of in-line transducers.

Operation

The information that follows provides a brief description of how the DataMyte 1505 was used by the manufacturer.

The DataMyte 1505 was set up to read as many items (characteristics or control points) and samples as were deemed necessary. A common matrix setup consisted of 50 samples; each sample representing a car wheel (for example). For each sample (car wheel) there were five items (five lug bolts). The DataMyte 1505 was connected to an in-line transducer via a common Bendix connector.

The DataMyte XCDR table was set for P (peak algorithm), 0 dwell time, 0 rej %, and 0 sample time. The readings were then taken automatically. As the tool reached peak torque, it stalled out, sending a torque value via the transducer to the DataMyte, where the value was stored in memory.

Once all necessary data was collected, the DataMyte was connected to an electronic printer and the stored data printed. When necessary, the data could also be dumped to a graphics printer or sent to the host computing system for further analysis.

CASE 14-9 ASSEMBLY PLANTS

Comprehensive Audit Program Spans Fourteen Plants

A major auto manufacturer embarked on an ambitious program to consolidate torque auditing in fourteen of its assembly plants. The manufacturer felt for a variety of reasons that torque audit data collection, analysis, and interpretation was too important to be left as an independent plant function. The knowledge to be gained by combining this data would surpass what individual plant programs could hope to attain, and since this knowledge should be shared equally, consolidating the program would be more efficient.

Problem Definition

Torque audit data in an auto assembly plant is of basically two types:

- Data on fasteners whose tightness is mandated by the government to be checked, and records kept. They are called delta fasteners and would be such things as seat belt fasteners, motor mounts, and front end fasteners. They were checked twice a shift.
- Data on fasteners whose tightness must be verified as part of the company's history of warranty claims. They would be such things as valve cover gasket fasteners, alternator bracket fasteners, etc. They were checked once a shift.

All of these fasteners were required to be audited through centralized guidelines, even though the responsibility of administering the audit rested on each individual plant. It was considered both inefficient and impractical to continue with existing methods since the plants were essentially duplicating each other's tasks with little or no benefit from information transference.

Solution

The solution involved some sort of computerization of this program. A breakdown of the information and tasks that could be computerized is:

- Data on the type fastener to be checked, its location, number, frequency of check, and nominal torque value. This would come from company headquarters and would be disseminated to the plants.
- A route program that would take the data on the fasteners and develop audit routes for each inspector.
- The data collection. Electronic torque wrenches and DataMytes were already being used to some extent by the company for auditing static torque, and this method was considered the most likely one to adopt on a large scale.
- Detecting and flagging bad fasteners on the spot, so that repair could be initiated.
- Compiling audit data into reports that could be used to monitor the capability of the fastening process.

Static torque was checked in the audits, as opposed to dynamic torque. Dynamic torque is the torque recorded while installing a fastener, whereas static torque is the breakaway value. The reason for choosing static torque rather than dynamic torque was that the company wanted to know the integrity of a fastener after relaxation had occurred.

Various types of computer systems were considered, from individual plant configuration, to a one, centralized computer, with links to each plant. The latter route was chosen. The equipment to be used consisted of a Honeywell mainframe at company headquarters, a Victor 9000 desktop computer with modem, serial interface, and printer at each plant, and an average of ten DataMytes for each of the fourteen plants. Also included were electronic torque wrenches in all the size ranges needed.

About ten people in each plant, with supervisory help, were included in the program. Each inspector obtained one week of training from DataMyte Corp. on usage of the DataMytes, proper techniques for measuring static torque, and interfacing with the desktop and mainframe computers. A software program was developed for the Honeywell computer which would interface through the Victor 9000 computers directly to the DataMytes used in each plant. The Honeywell system could then program each DataMyte for its intended audit route, and receive data back at the completion of the route.

Within a year all plant personnel had been trained and the system developed to operating level.

Although results from such a large program are hard to measure in terms of the impact on the fastening process, both a cost and time savings are apparent after only a year and a half of work. The company feels it has developed a model program which other companies both large and small could benefit from learning about.

Operation

What follows is a brief description of how the program operated at the torque auditing level. Each inspector would begin by dialing the central computer and connecting the Victor 9000 and DataMyte to it. Through menu selections the inspector chooses to download a specific route to the DataMyte. The download would consist of between 4 and 8 hours of checks, each fastener having a separate identification and locator on the assembly line.

The inspector would then take the DataMyte and choose torque wrenches and sockets in the proper size ranges for the fasteners on the route. The prompt message appearing on this DataMyte would tell the inspector which size wrench to use for a given fastener.

Each type of fastener is sampled five times in a route. Usually five of one type were checked and then five of the next. At the bottom of each column of five in DataMyte memory appeared a label space. This is used to record the line rotation number. The line rotation number allowed the inspector to track any "out of control" reading to the group of vehicles that the readings were taken from.

After five of the same type readings are recorded and the line rotation number entered, the DataMyte would automatically determine whether the group was in or out of control and display an 'IN' or 'OUT' on the LCD display. The calculation is based on upper and lower $\bar{x}$ and upper range control limits downloaded into the DataMyte from the Honeywell system. This allows immediate problem tracking.

Care was taken in designing audit routes to prevent an overlap of inspectors. This helps reduce variability due to different inspectors and measuring tools. The route also assigned as many of one type of fastener to one inspector as possible. This helped reduce the number of torque wrenches each inspector had to carry around.

When an inspector completed the route, they would connect the DataMyte to the desktop computer, dial up the Honeywell computer, and transmit the data. They then ran reports on the data, with hard copy printouts obtained right away for analysis. Daily, periodic and statistical reports were used by the inspectors to verify the process, and the data in the main computer was then available for higher level statistical analysis and as a permanent record.

CASE 14-10 OUTBOARD MARINE ENGINE MANUFACTURER

Capability Studies Improve Head Cover Torque Reliability

A midwestern marine engine manufacturer was using handheld dial indicator type torque wrenches to set final torque on the six fasteners holding cylinder head covers. This was a time consuming process, but these fasteners were critical to the operation of the engine. Although air driven nut runners were used to run down the nuts prior to their final torque, the requirements of virtual 100 percent compliance to specifications seemed to preclude their use for final torque setting.

Problem

Air driven, torque-controlled nut runners were available, and the quality control manager felt that significant savings could be realized by using them for final torque setting. The problem seemed to be with how to make sure torque specifications were being met. The solution seemed to lie in implementing a statistical monitoring program to ensure

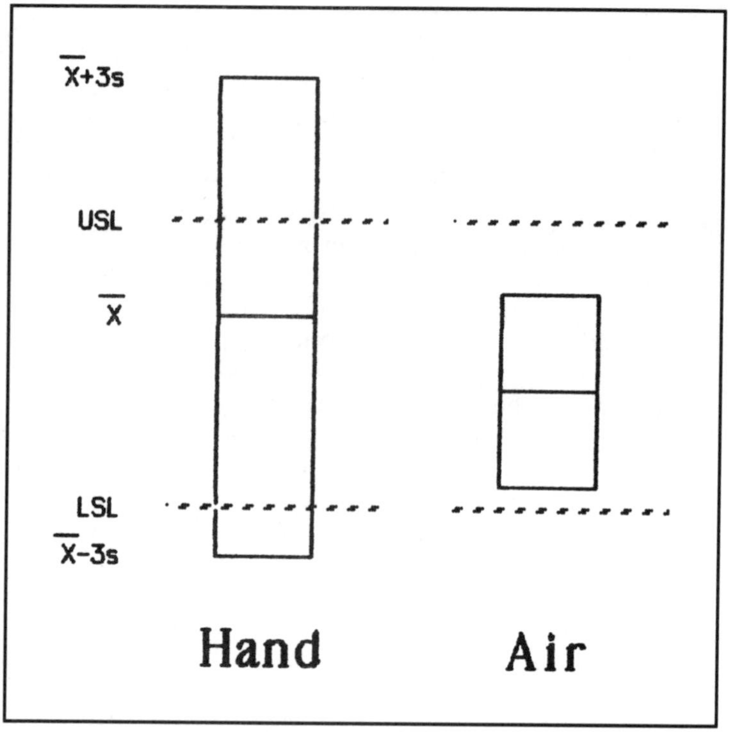

Fig. 14.10.1 Distribution of torque measurements made by hand as compared to those made by a torque controlled nutrunner.

the highest quality was maintained at the highest confidence level.

Solution

A two part program was proposed. First, capability studies would be performed to establish the capability of both hand torqueing and air driving the six critical fasteners. These studies were to be performed with static or breakaway type torque checks. Secondly, if as expected the air driver was more capable than hand torqueing, a monitoring system based on dynamic torque would ensure continuing adherence to specifications.

The capability study, performed with the DataMyte 1556, showed that the air gun was far more capable than torqueing by hand. See Figure 14.10.1. The study also showed a strong tendency of the manual method to overtorque the fasteners.

See Chapter 16 for a description of the 1556 data collector

The second part of the program was the daily monitoring of the air driver. Five samples were taken daily from an in-line torque transducer. These readings were recorded as the fastener was torqued. The gun appeared to have more variation than expected. An alert operator noticed that although the cadmium plated fasteners were purchased to the same specification, some batches were bright and shiny and some were dull and blackened. The operator also observed that there was a consistent 10 percent variation between torque readings that was dependent on fastener finish.

Having determined that a large part of the variability in the process was caused by raw materials, the Q.C. manager alerted engineering, purchasing, and incoming inspection to the problem. A close examination of the fasteners showed that both types met the specification as written! At this point engineering issued tighter specifications to ensure uniform fastener procurement.

CASE 14-11 AUTOMATIC TRANSMISSION PLANT

Freight Checking System Provides Dependible Tracking of Shipments

A major auto manufacturer had developed some innovative methods for ensuring proper shipments of transmissions to its many assembly plants throughout the U.S. They found that the usage of bar code tags and DataMyte handheld data collectors provided better materials tracking at shipping time. The DataMyte used had a special freight checking program that checked a serial number against lists of serial numbers downloaded into its memory.

Problem

One plant produced about ten different model 4-speed transmissions used as standard or optional equipment on a variety of cars and trucks. The transmissions were mounted on special pallets prior to shipping. The pallets were metal with plastic forms shaped to hold six transmissions, with their drive shafts facing in, and the bell housings out. The housings were stamped with the model and serial number. The pallets were stacked three high in the loading area.

A shipping transaction would involve having a forklift load a semitrailer with these pallets according to the particular order from an assembly plant. A person would then have to physically count and verify the number and types of transmissions being shipped. Problems occurred when the wrong models or too many of one model were mistakenly put on a truck, or there was a miscount. Coordinating shipments and keeping accurate records required better methods.

Solution

Part of the solution was to institute a system of bar coding each transmission. The tags were affixed to the bell housings, and included the model and serial number information. The tags were used to track parts requirements throughout the transmission assembly operation, and then used for shipping identification. The Code 39 tags were printed in large rolls with the required serial number range.

Since order processing was computerized, it seemed logical to develop a computerized method of shipping verification also. The company contacted DataMyte Corporation, who developed a DataMyte 1000 series data collector which would perform the verification. The DataMyte 1000 with attached bar code wand could read the tag on a transmission, and check the tag data against lists of parts numbers. It was also capable of screening out bad transmissions, because it would check against a list of bad serial numbers if one were loaded. The counts of various models and serial numbers were then fed back to a computer, and very accurate shipping papers produced. Since the DataMyte had room for several separate records in memory, a number of shipments could be verified without having to reprogram the DataMyte.

See Chapter 16 for a description of the 1000 data collectors

Operation

The freight checking program of the DataMyte worked like this. Lists would be downloaded to it from a computer. Each list would correspond to a different model transmission. In this case ten lists were needed. The lists had this information:

Broadcast code (model number), of 3 digits, 2 letters and a space
Low serial number limit, of 8 digits
High serial number limit, of 8 digits
Planned count
Actual count

For example:

619CJ
0156
0444
0036
0000

The entire code, as read on a tag, would be 15 alphanumeric digits.

As a shipment was being made, the freight checker, with the DataMyte, would move between the pallets of transmissions and wand each tag. If the serial number on the tag was within a range included in memory, the data on the tag was recorded in the data section of memory, and a count was recorded in another section. Counts were tallied for each list. When the desired count was reached the word 'DONE' appeared on the display.

If the broadcast code read off of a tag did not match those of any of the lists in memory, the DataMyte would beep four times, display "CODE", and the data would not be recorded. If the serial number on the tag is not within the range of those in memory, the DataMyte would beep four times, display "SN RANGE", and the data would not be recorded.

A list of bad part numbers could also be downloaded. These could include units with a known or suspected problem that required rework. The DataMyte could then help prevent the inadvertant shipping of transmissions that might be sitting in the loading area and had not been reworked. A 16-character message could be loaded into the DataMyte, such as "HOLD FOR REWORK", which would be displayed if a tag having a bad number was read. The checker had the choice then of accepting the tag data into memory (with an asterisk appended to it) or rejecting the data.

When the freight checker had finished verifying the shipment (when "DONE" appeared on the DataMyte display), the DataMyte was connected to an IBM PC computer. The tag data was then transmitted back to the computer, which prints out the data right on the shipping papers. The data would consist of the number of each model included in the shipment, and the serial number ranges.

CASE 14-12 AUTOMOTIVE GLASS DIVISION

Division Maintains Quality and Delivery Schedules with Automated Attributes Inspection

Divisions of major automotive manufacturers are moving toward just-in-time production, with their assembly plants as customers. By using in-process atributes inspection systems, and auto glass division maintained close control over quality, which kept their production on schedule.

Problem

Glass inspection requires detailed visual inspection and rapid attributes analysis to provide advance warning of process problems. The company needed a way to turn the inspection functions into a better feedback mechanism. The existing inspectors made accept and reject decisions, but provided no statistical analysis for preventive quality control.

Solution

The company decided to install a data base-like attributes system out in the factory floor. They chose the DataMyte 769 attributes system because it had fast bar code entry and built-in software for Pareto and defects analysis.

See Chapter 16 for a description of the 769 data collector.

Before each product was shipped, operators identified the part number, job number, and defects if they found any. The Pareto and percent defectives charts produced by the DataMyte gave the feedback to make production corrections on the fly.

CASE 14-13 ENGINE PLANT

Plant Automates SPC on Crank Shaft Cam TIR

The engine plant of a major automotive company acquired control charting on critical crank shaft dimensions. By using DataMyte 761 fixed station data collectors, they improved measurement accuracy and could do trend analysis automatically.

Problem

The dimensions on the crank shafts included two readings per cam, a taper reading and a total indicator reading (TIR). The TIR reading involved an operator rotating the shaft in a fixture, and using his own judgement to determine the high and low spots. The operator would then have to write down both high and low readings and subtract the two to get the TIR.

Solution

See Chapter 16 for a description of the DataMyte 761 data collector.

Using a DataMyte 761 data collector, they could use a single instrument to record all readings. For the TIR reading, the operator had to simply rotate the part in the fixture once in the fixture and the DataMyte would read and calculate TIR at all five points. See figure 14.13.1. In addition, runs and trends were tracked, and the operator was alerted to them and asked for an assignable cause. Data collection time was reduced by a factor of ten.

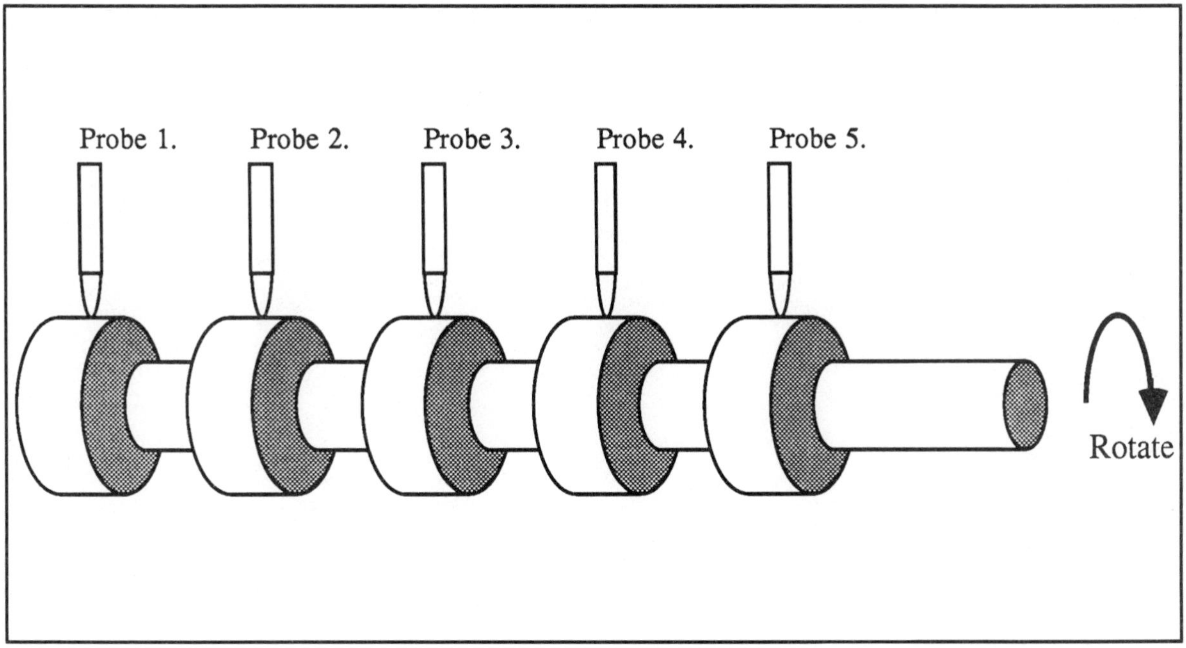

Fig. 14.13.1 Automatic TIR calculation.

Part III Products

15. COMPUTERIZED DATA COLLECTION FOR SPC

INTRODUCTION

The DataMyte FAN® (Factory Area Network) system is a totally new concept for statistical quality control. It makes SPC work on a plant-wide scale. Data collection is rapid, accurate and automatic (see Figure 15.0.1). The analysis is in "real time", "on line" rather than later. At each point in the process:

- Operators enter their own data.
- Readings are stored.
- Statistical computations are made.
- Analysis is immediate, giving operators the ability to control the process.

The FAN® system consists of:

- Gaging with electronic output (see Chapter 17)
- Data collectors (see Chapter 16)
- Special software for computers (see Chapter 18)
- Training (see Chapter 20)

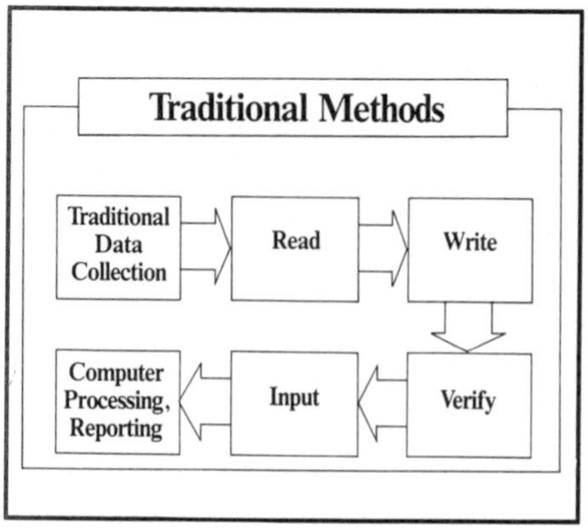

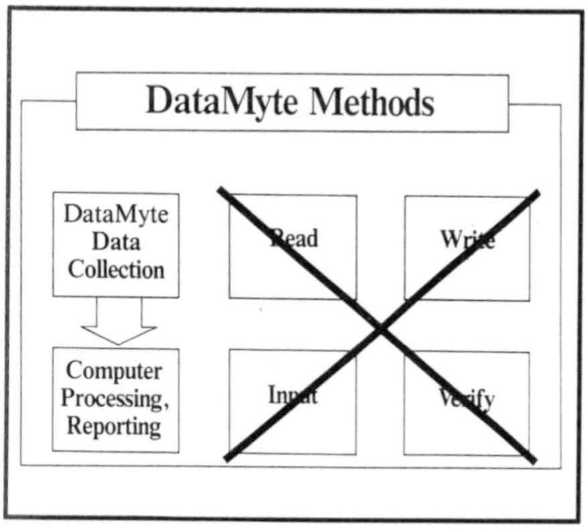

Fig. 15.0.1 Traditional handwritten methods of data collection compared to DataMyte methods.

At each operator station, gages are used to measure process characteristics. Data collectors are used to record the data. The data collectors provide operators with control charts and other analysis to help them monitor the process. See Figure 15.0.2. Data that accumulates at each station is periodically picked up and transmitted to an IBM PC or other type of computer. At the computer, the data can be archived and analyzed further.

The FAN system enables communication between workers and management. The FAN system can be an "unwired" network, using a DataTruck® handheld data collector. Once a day, or as often as needed, the DataTruck can be taken on a route, stopping at each operator station in the plant (see Figure 15.0.3). The DataTruck plugs into and "harvests" the data from each data collector. It stores the data from each data collector in a special file. It can also program a data collector for a new operation. Up to twenty data collectors can be serviced in this way on a single route. At the end of the route, the DataTruck is connected to the IBM computer, and all the data is transmitted to the computer, where it can be stored on floppy diskettes.

This is one type of FAN system. The FAN system can include both fixed station data collectors dedicated to monitoring one part or process, and handheld data collectors for roving auditors who monitor many parts. A fixed station fully-wired FAN system can also be installed. This is called FANLINK™.

This chapter describes the FAN system, and introduces DataMyte products that are part of it. The system is quite simple. It shares these concepts with SPC itself:

- Fast and error free data collection
- Worker responsibility for data collection
- Top-down and bottom-up communications

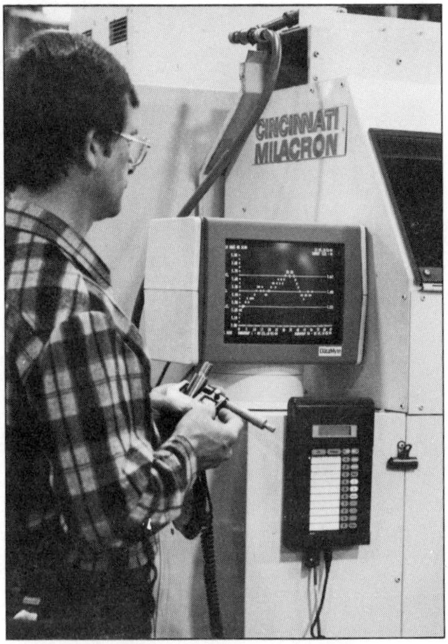

Fig. 15.0.2 DataMyte 750 data collector and video monitor used at a machine tool.

15.1 GAGING FOR SPC

A New Generation of Gages

The gaging industry has been revolutionized by microelectronics. Mechanical dial indicators are being overrun

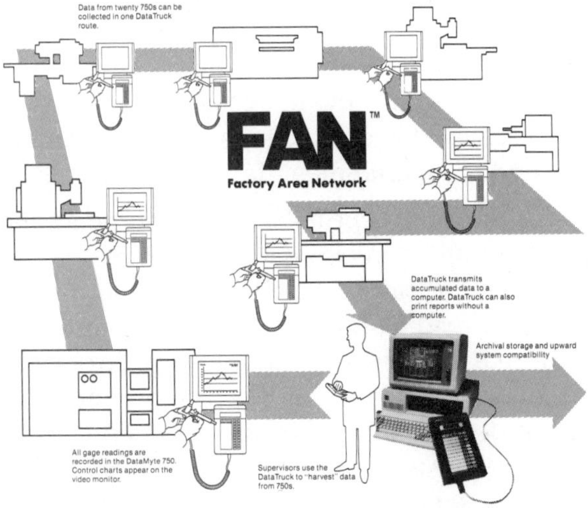

Fig. 15.0.3 A QC supervisor uses a DataTruck data collector to "harvest" data from data collectors in the plant. At the end of his route, the DataTruck connects to a computer to store the data.

by digital indicators. The hottest selling calipers and micrometers have computers on a chip, with LCD readouts, better resolution, functions such as maxumim hold, inch/millimeter conversion, and displays within displays.

A trip to any trade show that exhibits metrology will convince you that technology sells. Handheld gages seem to be going the way of watches and pocket calculators. They have more functional ability, in smaller packages, for lower prices. Fixed station instruments have all taken on the ubiquitous "system" tag. They have many features all of which cannot possibly be used in a given application.

Although it may not always be apparent, what gaging manufacturers are attempting to do with electronics is make measurement easier. By that we mean the act of measurement, or quantifying data, will be more reliable, repeatable, and efficient.

Since gaging is vital to statistical process control, let's consider what the new generation of gages has brought to SPC. Rather than reviewing specific gage features we should try to identify the characteristics a gage should have. We can then look at how a gage becomes part of an effective data collection system for SPC.

Gage Characteristics for SPC

The gage produces variables data — SPC requires resolution to detect minute changes in a process. The higher the resolution of a gage the better as long as other criteria are served as well. In general, go/no-go gages do not provide the kind of measurement data needed for SPC.

The gage promotes repeatability and reproduceability (R & R) — SPC requires precision. If a person uses the gage to measure the same part repeatedly, the person should obtain the same reading reliably. Similarly, another person should be able to reproduce those results. Error caused by R & R reduces confidence in the data and our ability to make good decisions. The human engineering put into a gage, such as how it must be held, how a part needs to be positioned in it for a measurement, and how much training is required to operate it, must evidence a concern for R & R.

The gage is efficient — SPC requires lots of data. This calls for a gage that produces data fast and can be used over and over again reliably.

The gage supports the analytical effort — SPC is concerned with groups of data. A gage is essentially a serial device. It produces one piece of data at a time. A gage must support data collection by providing data in a uniform format, so it can be recorded and grouped.

Of course, not all of the enhancements of electronic gaging support data collection for SPC. In fact, there is one feature that makes many of the others nonessential. That feature is electronic data output.

A gage that does not have electronic data output still has to be read, no matter if it has LCD digits, columns of lights, mechanical pointers, a large display or a small display. If it has to be read by someone it becomes subject to human error. Any gage can be read wrong and the reading interpreted wrong and written down wrong. Electronic output to a data collector solves this problem.

A gage with electronic output speeds both measurement and data processing. The person taking the measurement can concentrate on getting a good reading. The data collector can convert the serial stream of numbers coming from the gaging into groups of measurements for analysis.

Many of the new generation of gages now have electronic output. See chapter 17 for details. The gages can be connected to a data collector which records and analyzes the data. Several somewhat standard gage outputs have been developed, such as serial BCD, serial ASCII, serial binary, and of course RS-232C. Some column gages and metrology displays have analog outputs at standard voltage levels.

Converting Versus Replacing Gaging

Companies that use SPC need to have gaging for variables data. Gaging for SPC is an investment, either in the cost of converting existing gaging and fixturing or replacing existing gages with newer ones. Since most of the cost of the original gaging is in the special fixturing needed for an application, there is a temptation to either convert existing gages and fixturing, or not do it at all. But in many cases, thanks to the new generation of gages, it can be less expensive to simply replace gages than convert them.

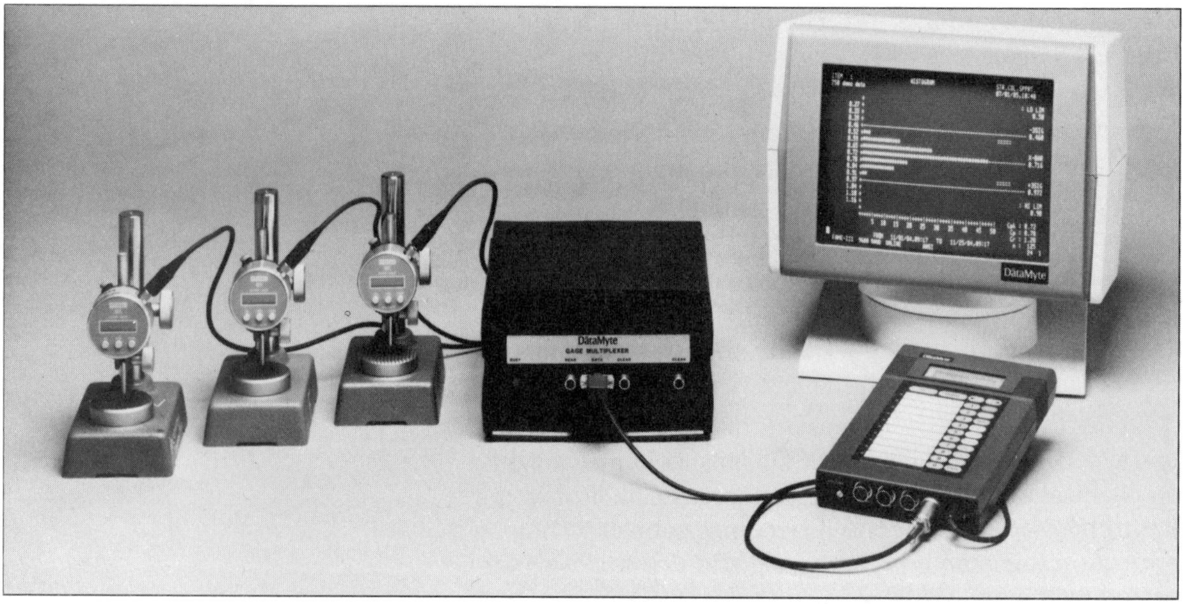

Fig. 15.1.1 Digital indicators having electronic data output.

Fig. 15.1.2 Electronic column gages are an alternative to air gages.

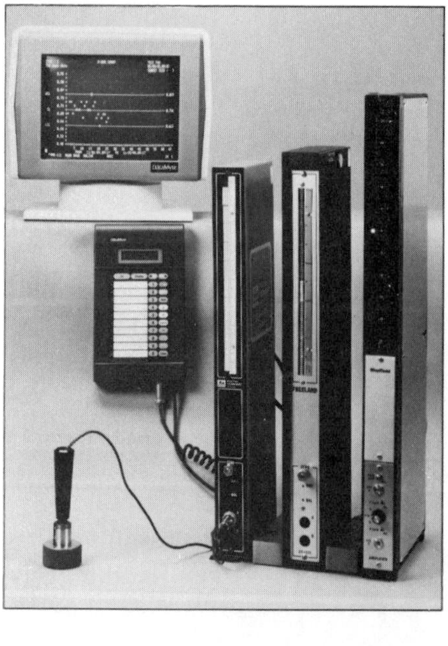

For example, a test fixture has sixteen mechanical dial indicators. To convert these dial indicators into ones with electronic output, an LVDT conversion package could be added. However, it may be less expensive to simply buy some of the popular LCD readout digital indicators which are designed to be a direct replacement (see Figure 15.1.1). The digital indicators already have digital output, use less power, and can be easily used in any similar fixtures in the plant.

Another example would be an air gage fixture. Air gages have high resolution, and air-actuated columns provide good readout, but they do not adapt well to electronic output. To convert air gages, a pressure transducer and custom circuitry is necessary. As alternatives, the air gages could be replaced with electronic columns or high resolution digital indicators such as the Federal Maxum indicator (see Figures 15.1.2 and 15.1.3).

Very often, if cost is the only criteria, completely replacing existing gaging with new gaging is cheaper in the long run. Whether converting or replacing, it is important to get a gaging system with good repeatability and reproduceability, with adaptability to fixturing, and with electronic output that is compatible with a data collector.

As a final example, several companies are using their CNC machines for measuring as well as machining (see Chapter 7, Case 7-3). By mounting a digital indicator on the

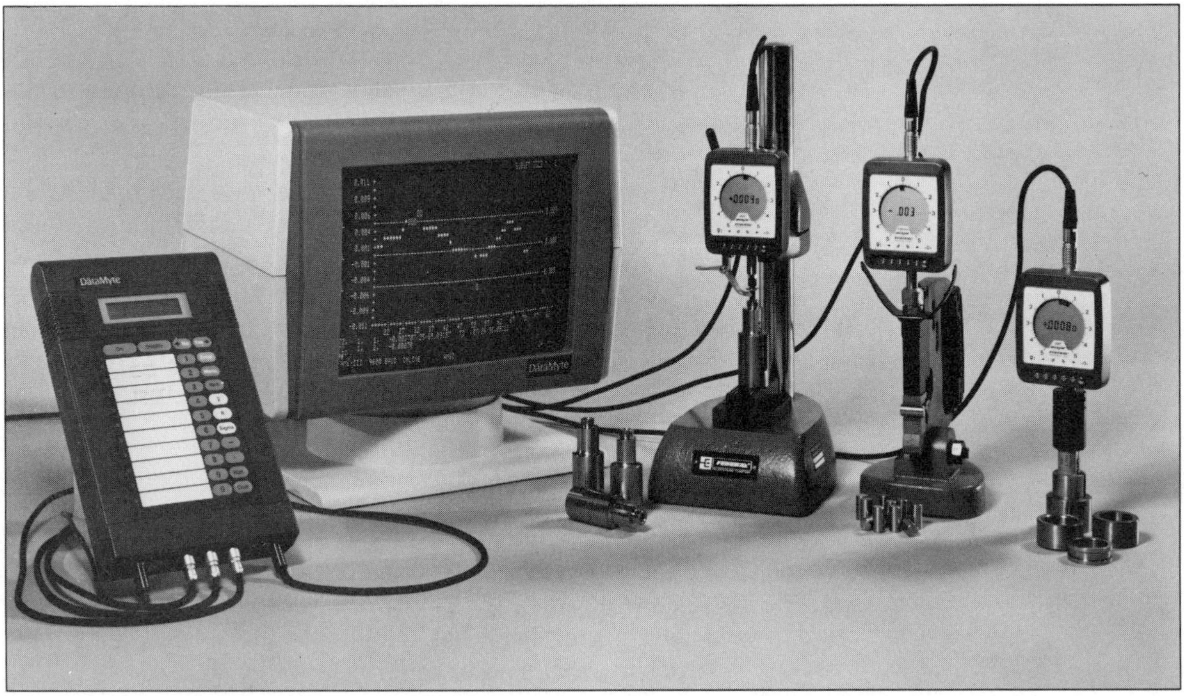

Fig. 15.1.3 Federal Maxum indicators are an alternative to air gages.

machine spindle and connecting it to a data collector, they take point measurements on aircraft wing molds. This eliminates the need for a separate coordinate measuring machine. The same program that machines the model can be used to check it, resulting in a considerable savings in equipment and labor.

A Gage Buying Philosophy

Several companies with active SPC programs have adopted gage buying philosophies that link gaging to data collection. The main points of one such philosophy are:

- Measurement that requires operator intervention should be handled with a gage that has electronic output, so the data can be sent automatically to a data collection device.
- Since it is also important that the operator see that measurement took place, the gages themselves should have digital readout.
- Ideally, gaging should be operator independent. An operator should simply place a part into a fixture, press a button or flip a switch, and remove the part. The data should be recorded automatically, although the operator should still have a readout to verify the activity.

- At a higher level, gaging should not even be done by an operator. If the application warrants it, 100 percent on-line gaging should be used. This can be done with fixturing that uses air actuated, spring return gages or with vision systems.
- At the highest level, gages should feed data back to the process in such a way that automatic adjustments to the process are possible. This would be a closed-loop control system, where data collection and analysis are integrated into the process itself. This type of system usually represents a large investment and a complete conversion to a computer integrated type of manufacturing.

From Gage to Data Collector

Starting with SPC as an operator intensive activity, and moving to where gaging is more in-line, we find that data collection systems are broken up and defined as subsystems whereby:

- The gaging itself has minimal "smarts," but does have data output, and in some cases a digital readout.
- A data collection device is used at the source to record data in computer-readable form and provide feedback to the operator (or a process controller).
- Standard SPC software is used to perform analysis and produce reports.

Separating a data collection system into subsystems allows us to better identify what type of specialization belongs where. For example, it would be redundant to purchase multi-function gages that have statistical software built in, when several gages are needed at a test station, and the statistical software is already in the data collector. In this case, a gage with data output is all that is necessary.

DataMyte concentrates some "smarts" — that is, SPC software designed for machine operators — in the data collectors themselves. This provides several advantages.

- Operators need feedback at the process, more than what any one gage can give them. This includes prompting an operator for what gage to use and what dimensions to measure.
- A data collector can compare each gage reading against reasonable limits, part specifications, and subgroups against control limits and alert the operator when something is wrong.
- A data collector can do math operations on several gage inputs at once, and plot charts on derived variables such

as total indicator readings (TIR), minimums and maximums.

Where the process is largely unattended, data could be recorded at the process, but analysis could occur off-sight, typically on a desktop computer in the QC office. Or, a handheld data collector with SPC software could be used at the process on a periodic basis.

From Data Collector to Computer

A data collector is a vital link to the third subsystem, which is computer software for SPC. Although most of the actual SPC work is done at the process, most of the decisions that effect the process occur at the plant level. Good decisions require good data. A data collection system for SPC that can feed information to management serves to focus management resources on the big problems (the Pareto principle). SPC software on a computer provides a common language for discussing problems that occur at each process, and is a tool for estimating capability, scrap and rework, and cost of quality.

But the weakest link in all computer software is manual data entry. If the data has to be entered through the computer keyboard, most likely the SPC software will not be used. It becomes too labor intensive, and the data is subject to keypunching error. The answer, of course, is having a data collection system that can communicate directly with the computer and store data files which can be analyzed by SPC software.

DataMyte has desktop computer software as part of its data collection systems, and maintains an open architecture to its systems. Many commercial software vendors have developed interfaces to DataMyte equipment (see Chapter 19). This allows SPC users to choose among many valuable analysis and reporting features, and to maintain SPC data bases on a variety of different computers.

15.2 FAN® AT THE OPERATOR LEVEL

Fixed Station Data Collection Systems

The DataMyte 750 family of data collectors are for fixed station usage. The data collectors add these capabilities to gaging used at the process:

- Memory
- Statistical reporting

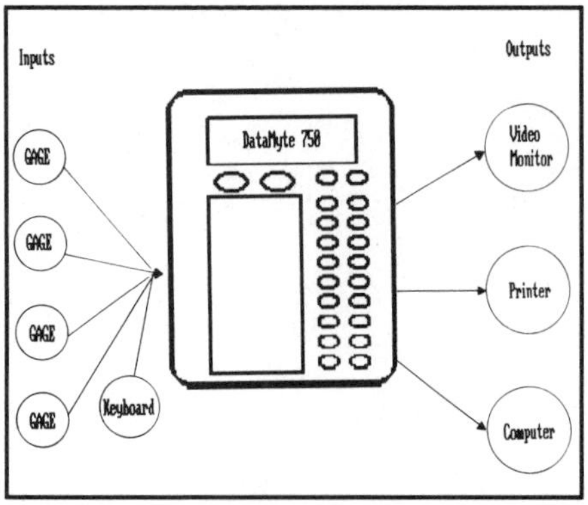

Fig. 15.2.1 Inputs and outputs of a DataMyte 750.

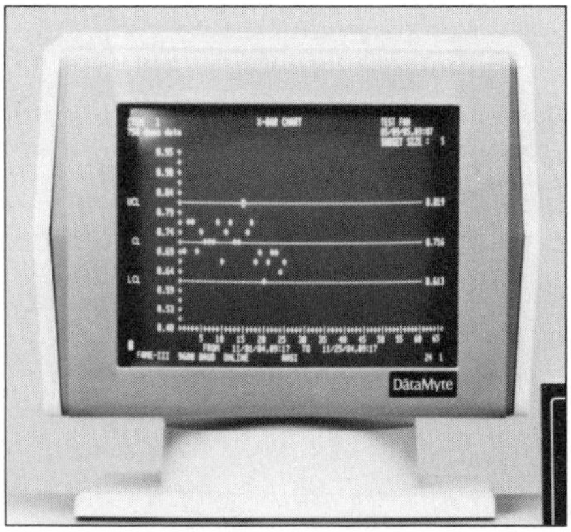

Fig. 15.2.2 Control chart on a video monitor.

- Direct computer interface

At each station throughout a plant, operators can use gaging with electronic output to record measurements in the data collector (see Figure 15.2.1). Up to ten different characteristics can be monitored at any one time. Measurement is fast, resolution is maintained, and the data is automatically placed in subgroups logged with the time and date it was taken.

The data collector connects to many different gages, as described in Chapter 17. The keypad on the unit can also be used to enter data. The operator can enter process specifications and the data collector will alert the operator if any reading is outside of specifications. Process control limits, and reasonable limits (gage range) can also be entered. If a subgroup of data is outside the process control limits, the operator is alerted immediately.

Producing Control Charts

Control charts are created in a 750 family data collector by first specifying the size of the subgroup. The operator then records data in these subgroups, and each subgroup becomes a point on a chart. For an $\bar{x}$ & R chart, the data collector calculates the average and range of each subgroup and plots them. If more than twenty subgroups have been recorded, the 750 can calculate the control limits and include them on the chart.

The data collector displays control charts on a video monitor, or can print them on a printer. See Figures 15.2.2 and 15.2.3. The operator simply presses the $\bar{x}$ button for a $\bar{x}$ chart, or similarly the R button, sigma button and histogram button for those charts.

For process monitoring, a video monitor has two advantages over printed charts:

- A monitor is more visible. It serves as a constant reminder. Paper charts can be soiled, torn, lost, or filed away and not used.
- A monitor can be updated instantly with each new subgroup.

Although paper control charts provide good permanent records, they are not the most efficient vehicle for data. Control chart data must be keypunched into a computer for the data to be made available for other types of analysis. The data collector stores data in computer readable format right at the process. So, in addition to producing control charts, the data collector provides for high speed communications.

The Smarts for Spotting Trends

A data collector won't tell you what went wrong, or why it went wrong, but it can help you spot it sooner. Once you establish the rules for spotting trends, some data collector models will display warning signals when a trend occurs.

There are four rules you can set up:

- 2 points greater than 2.0 sigma.
- 7 points on one side of x-bar.
- 3 points greater than 1.0 sigma.
- 7 points ascending or descending.

The underlined numbers can be changed to anything from 0 to 9 (0.0 to 9.9 for sigma). For example, changing the first rule to "3 points greater than 1.0 sigma", means that if there are already 2 subgroups on one side of 1 sigma away from a control chart centerline, a third subgroup will trigger a trend alert message.

The operator is then asked for an assignable cause number before he or she can continue collecting data.

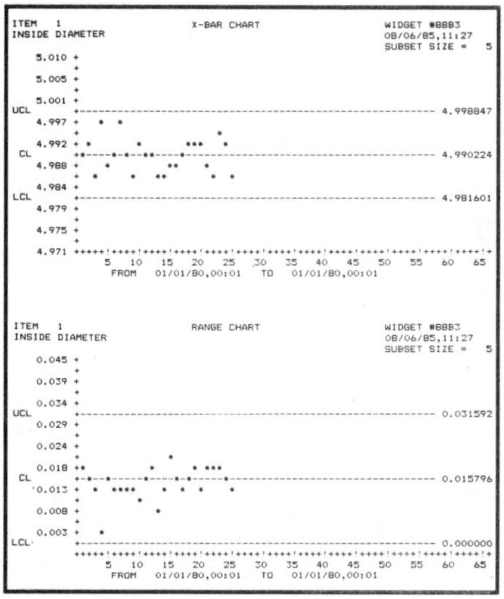

Fig. 15.2.3 Printed control chart.

Math and TIR Capabiltiy

Some 750 models have math capabilities for addition, subtraction, multiplication, division and functions such as minimum, maximum and range of several inputs. The math can be performed on gage inputs, existing readings and constants. An example of use would be finding the weight of a liquid in a container. The container can be weighed dry and then filled. The data collector will subtract the two automatically and plot a control chart on the liquid weight.

The range function can be used to find the difference between the highest and lowest of several inputs. An example would be checking the flatness of a surface along several points by placing it in a fixture that has several column gage indicators. The data collector will read all of the column gage inputs, calculate the range, and plot the range on a control chart.

The total indicator reading (TIR) capability allows a data collector to calculate the minimum, maximum or difference from a series of readings from one gage. An example of use would be to check ovality with a bore gage, where the gage is inserted and rotated in the bore. The data collector finds and calculates the difference between the

Fig. 15.2.4 Roving auditor uses DataMyte handheld data collector to check part dimensions.

Fig. 15.2.3 Roving auditor checks torque.

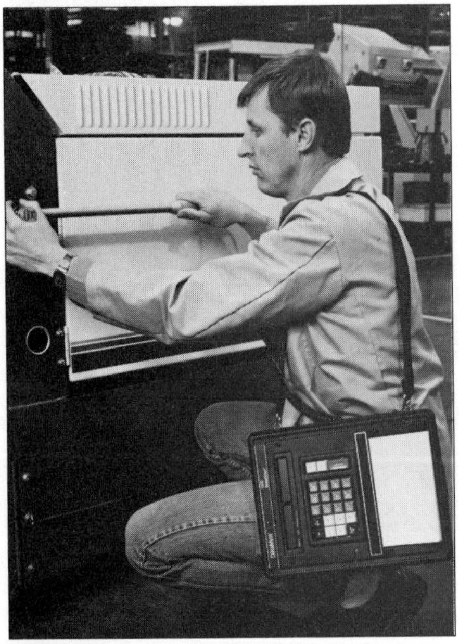

maximum and minimum and plots it on a control chart. Another example would be to check runout on a wheel, where the wheel is placed in a fixture and rotated against a digital indicator.

Handheld Data Collection Systems

There are several DataMyte handheld systems:

- 2000 series for both variables and attributes data
- 1700 and 1500 series for variables data
- 1000 series for attributes data

The usages of handheld data collectors include:

- Having a single person audit many processes (see Figure 15.2.4).
- Collecting data on moving assembly lines (torque, fit of mating parts, coating thickness, etc.), as in Figure 15.2.5.
- Making periodic capability studies both in-plant and off-site.

The 2000, 1700 and 1500 series data collectors can produce $\bar{x}$ & R charts, sigma charts, histograms and capability reports by connecting to a printer. The data collectors can also transmit the data to a desktop computer, where the data can be analyzed by an SPC software program.

DataMyte handheld systems have more memory capacity and more flexibility than a fixed station data collector. They can audit many different parts and processes. Typically, an auditor will set up a route consisting of dozens of parts, each with several characteristics. The data collector then guides the auditor through the route, prompting for the proper part measurement, and signalling when a measurement is out of specification, or when a subgroup is out of control. Many types of handheld gages and RS-232C devices can connect to the data collector for direct gage input.

When used with SPC software on a desktop computer, data collection routes can be set up and saved on floppy disk, then downloaded to the data collector when needed. At the end of a route, all the data can be transmitted to the computer and archived. DataMyte FAN computer software supports this activity as well as the activities of fixed station data collectors.

For attributes data, either the DataMyte 2000 or 1000 can be used. Attribute descriptions can be programmed into the DataMyte or printed on bar codes. When using bar codes, each part number and defect type are put onto a palette and carried along with the data collector. The part numbers and defects are then recorded in the data collector with a bar code pen, making data entry fast and error-free. See Figures 15.2.6 and 15.2.7.

A desktop computer such as an IBM PC and attributes software is used with the data collector. DataMyte attributes software will take the data from a data collector, summarizes occurrences of defects, and produce Pareto charts, or p, np, c, and u-charts. The user can build a data base, edit data, and create setups and routes to download to the data collector.

Fig.15.2.6 Defects auditing using a DataMyte 1000.

15.3 FAN® AT THE NETWORK LEVEL

There are two basic Factory Area Network configurations:

- An "unwired" system, using a DataTruck data collector as the go-between.
- A wired network, using FANLINK.

A factory can also have a blended system, where both configurations are present. The type of configuration depends entirely on the needs of the factory.

Networking With a DataTruck®

The DataTruck data collector provides for periodic batch-mode data collection. A data collection route is set up, and once a day or more often, the DataTruck is brought to each data collector in the plant (up to twenty can be accommodated), connected with a short cable, and the data from a data collector is transmitted to the DataTruck. Transmission takes about ten seconds. The DataTruck has a large memory in which the data is filed. At the end of the route, the DataTruck is connected to a desktop computer using FAN software, and all the data is then transmitted to the computer.

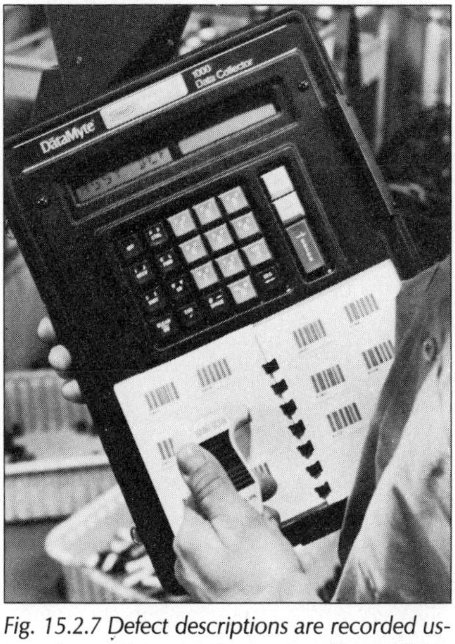

Fig. 15.2.7 Defect descriptions are recorded using a bar code pen and pre-printed bar codes.

The sequence can work in reverse also. See Figure 15.3.1. The computer can be used to set up each data collector in the plant, and the setup files transmitted to them via the DataTruck. Setup files and data files are the same thing in effect, because the setup information goes with each transaction that occurs. There are two options for the data that resides in a data collector, taking all the data in memory, or taking only what was recorded since the last transmission. The second option can reduce communications overhead.

The advantages of the "unwired" network are numerous:

- The cost of wiring (and re-wiring as things change) is saved.
- There is no "downtime" to the network. Data collectors function independently.
- Daily or periodic archiving onto a central computer is usually as frequent as is necessary.
- The more personal touch of a supervisor stopping by with a DataTruck reinforces the SPC activity.

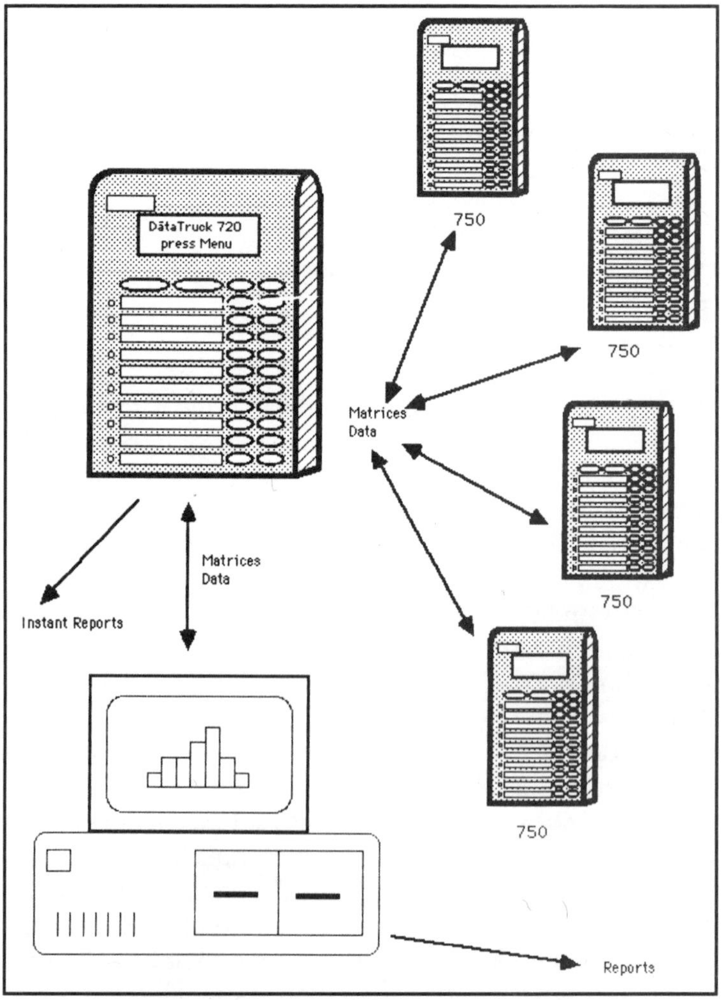

Fig. 15.3.1 The DataTruck serves as the network link between a computer and data collectors located in the plant.

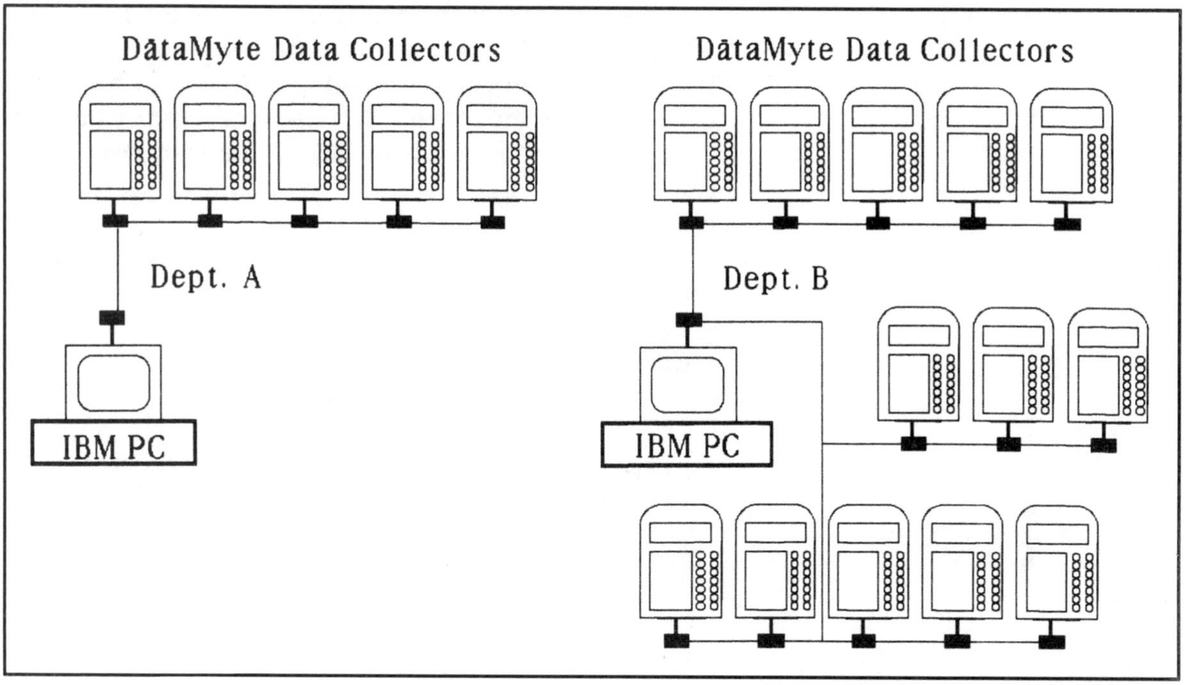

Fig. 15.3.2 Two examples of a wired FANLINK system.

FANLINK®

FANLINK puts the FAN system on-line and hardwired directly to an IBM PC/AT computer. This allows the IBM, using FAN software, to set up any DataMyte data collector (or DataMyte 2000) in the network, or call up and request data files from them. FANLINK can create a cell-level or department-level communications network to facilitate faster changeover of data collectors for different jobs, and closer supervision of problem processes. See Figure 15.3.2.

FANLINK provides the best alternative to a DataTruck in the FAN system. It is practical for groups of machines or departments that require more frequent information interchange than what a DataTruck can offer. Rather than the once or twice a day data harvest, the wired FANLINK allows a person at the IBM PC to access a 750 or 2000 station at any time.

Using Easy-to-install cable and FANLINK adaptors you can connect approximately thirty data collectors to the FANLINK computer. Total cable distance can be up to one mile.

In the network, each data collector is assigned a unique address. The FANLINK software package will be able to send setup information to a unique data collector or request a copy of the data that has been collected by the data collector. This can be a manually initiated request or data can be collected automatically by the FANLINK software package.

For more information on computerized data collection, see

- Chapter 16 for data collectors
- Chapter 17 for gages
- Chapter 18 and 19 for software
- Chapter 20 for training
- Chapter 21 for Allen-Bradley Quality Management
- Chapter 22 for Factory Automation

16. DATAMYTE DATA COLLECTORS

16.1 FIXED STATION DATA COLLECTORS

INTRODUCTION

The chapter contains model by model descriptions of DataMyte data collectors.

The DataMyte Fixed Station Data Collectors are the building blocks for the FAN® (Factory Area Network) system. They provide memory storage, feedback for Operator SPC and full communications for management reporting. Fixed station data collectors positioned throughout your plant can communicate with an IBM PC by using a DataTruck. The DataTruck is a unique data collector and is featured on page 16-38 and described also in Chapter 15. The DataTruck, together with the DataMyte FAN II Software program, provide two-way communications, supporting both SPC efforts at the operator level and management-level reporting.

There are two types of fixed-station data collectors:

- Data Collectors for Variables Data: The data collectors used for variable data produce $\bar{x}$ & R charts, $\bar{x}$ & sigma charts and histograms. The several models of variable data collectors all collect data from assorted electronic gages. Each time a subgroup (set of samples) of data is collected, the data collector can automatically display the desired control chart on the DataMyte monitor. The charts are sent directly to a video monitor or printer. These data collectors take their data directly from electronic gages.
- Data Collectors for Attributes Data: This data collector produces Pareto and percent-defectives charts. The charts are sent directly to a video monitor or printer. The operator enters the data using a bar code wand and a set of bar codes produced by the data collector.

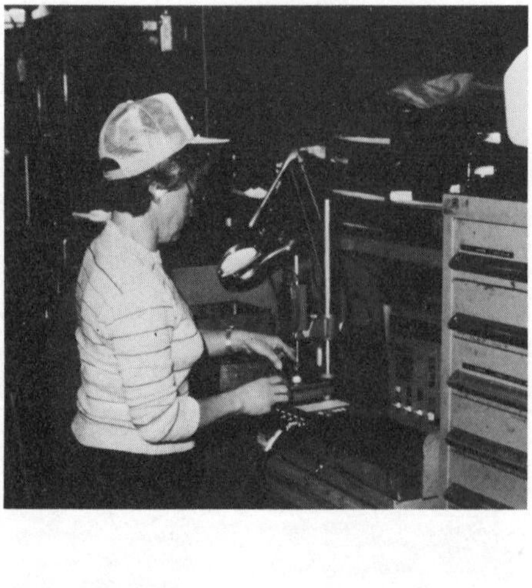

Fixed-Station Variables Data Collectors

The DataMyte 750 family of data collectors are for real-time operator SPC at the process. They make SPC easier, faster and error-free. Machine operators get better data, in more useable form, much faster than they could with paper and pencil. With a single keypress, an operator can display a control chart on a monitor — some models automatically display charts when a subgroup of data has been collected. Each control chart has control limits, and points out of control are clearly marked. During data collection, the data collector alerts the operator to readings that are out of specification and subgroups that are out of control.

The data collectors are designed to connect to gages that people checking parts at a station would normally use. A handheld data collector like the DataMyte 2000 is for a roving auditor using mostly handheld gages. See Chapter 17 for the gages that can be used with these data collectors.

The fixed-station data collectors are made for machine operators and production workers. They are extremely easy to use, providing the maximum output with the fewest keypresses, whereas a DataMyte 2000 is more sophisticated, and designed more for a full-time QC auditor.

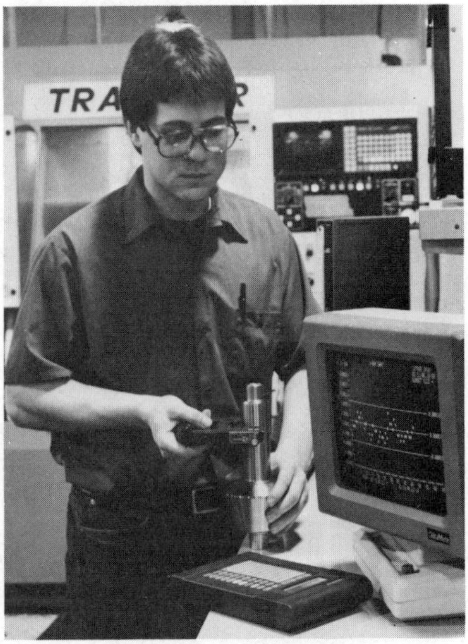

The fixed-station data collectors can be used for multi-part or single part applications. The 860 model data collectors can track several characteristics of over 15 parts. The 760 model data collectors are designed for processes or machines that produce one type of part.

The fixed-station data collectors will alert operators when trends are occurring. Once you have established the rules for treating successive data subgroups, the data collector will display warning signs when a trend occurs.

The fixed-station data collectors will automatically display charts. The data collector will automatically add new points to a control chart as new subgroups are recorded. Each individual measurement is also displayed, and if the data is out of specification, a message appears.

The fixed-station data collectors are low-cost. Because they are single purpose rather than general purpose like a DataMyte 2000, the fixed station data collectors have less memory. This makes them inexpensive enough to be stationed throughout a plant, wherever SPC is required.

862 Data Collector

The DataMyte 862 data collector is designed for any factory that has groups of automated or semi-automated machinery maintained by a single setup and inspection person. The data collector works especially well at gaging stations that handle a number of parts, or where there is a frequent changeover of parts.

The 862 has three gage channels — record data from one channel at a time or from all three with a press of the footswitch. Many types of gages are compatible with the 862 data collector. See Chapter 17 for details. You can connect up to three DataMyte Gage Multiplexers to record readings from up to 24 digital indicators.

For examples of use, see pp. 7-11, 10-17, 11-3, 12-20, 12-21 and 12-23.

The DataMyte 862 data collector has several special features for statistical process control, including:

- Trend alert — to let the operator know when a trend has occurred.
- Assignable causes — to show when a change in the process, or other factor occurred.
- Individuals, moving average and range charts.

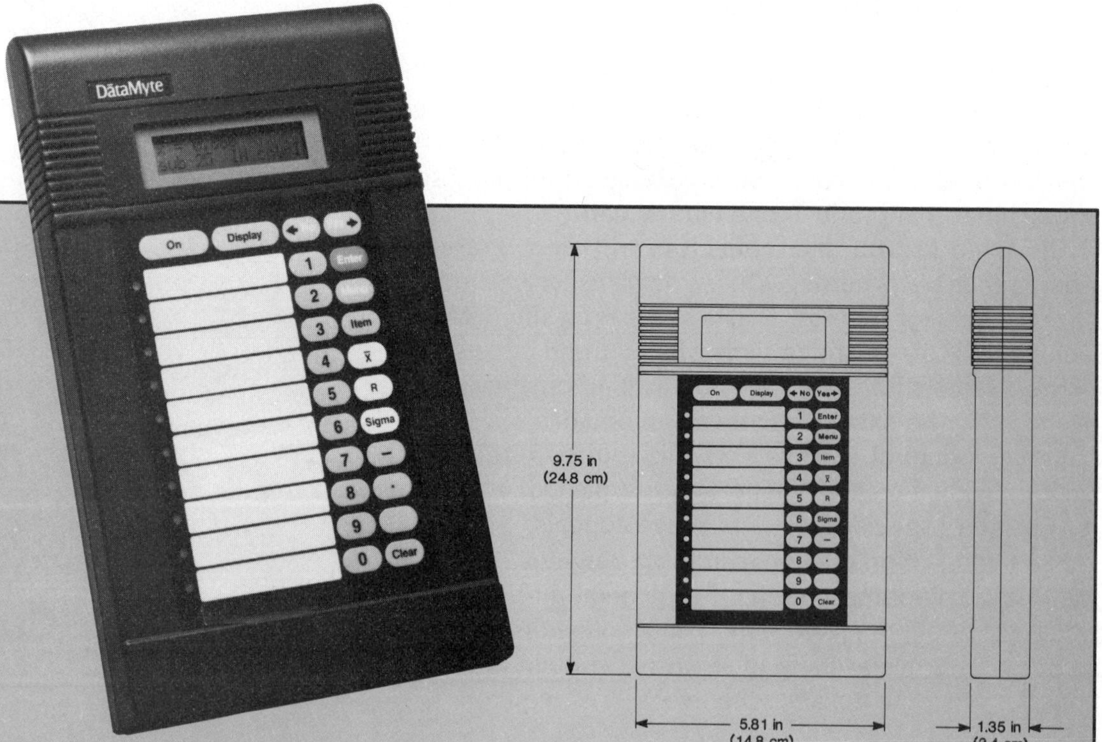

Special Features

- Three digital/RS-232C gage ports
- Multiplexer available to expand the gage connections to 24 gages. Up to three different types of multiplexed gages can be used.
- Math capability for adding, subtracting, multiplying and dividing readings
- Selectable number of characteristics (10 per file)
- Record up to 10,000 readings
- Tracks more than one type of part at once, without changing the setup
- Automatic scanning and recording of gage inputs
- Automatic control charting
- Directory indicates files and memory available
- Trend alert feature lets operator know when a trend has occurred
- Assignable cause, machine and operator codes
- Codes appear on printed reports; assignable cause codes also appear on control charts displayed on the monitor.

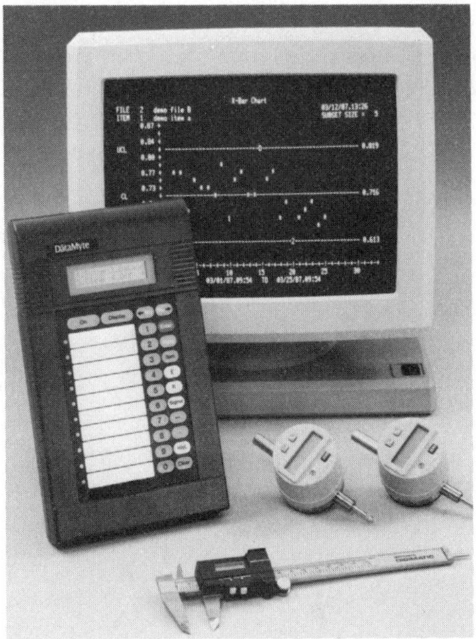

Other Features

- Interfaces with FAN software
- Easy, menu-driven operation
- Automatic time/date recording with each subgroup
- 24 tactile membrane keys
- Two-line by 16-character LCD display
- Selectable RS-232C transmission rates
- Nicad battery operated, with AC charger/adaptor
- Unit turns off after eight minutes non-use
- Rugged ABS plastic case, oil and water resistant
- Weights about 2 lb. (0.9 kg)

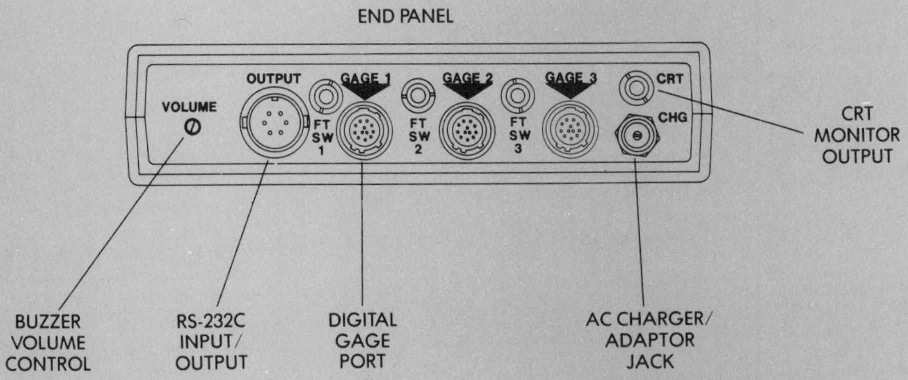

An x̄ & R report. All of the data collectors that record variables data can print a chart like this one. An assignable cause report (not shown) is also printed with this report.

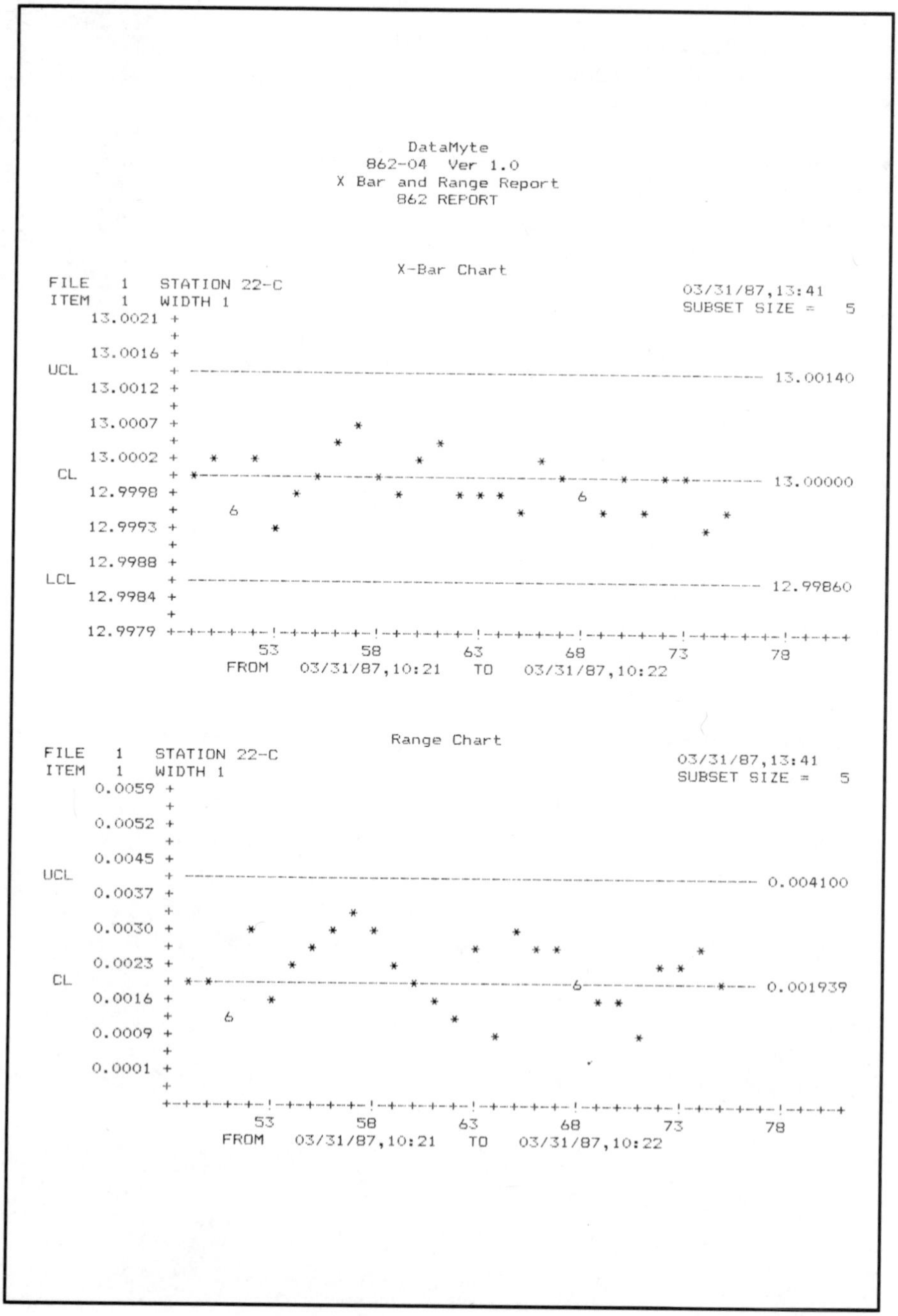

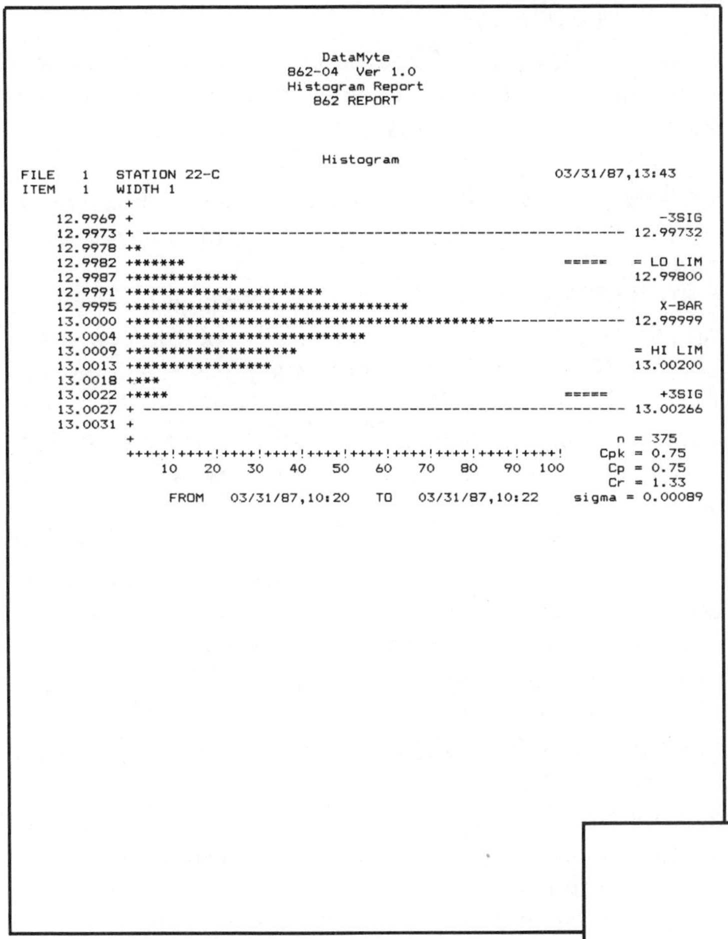

A histogram printed directly from the DataMyte 862 data collector. The histogram report contains as much or as little data as you want to include for one item.

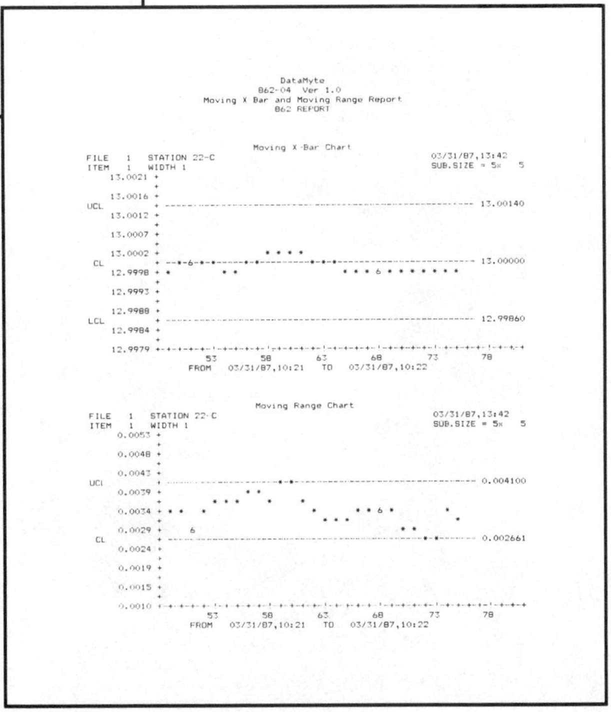

A moving $\bar{x}$ & R report printed directly from the DataMyte 862 data collector. You can define how many subgroups (up to nine) are to be combined into each data point.

861 Data Collector

Like the DataMyte 862 data collector, the DataMyte 861 data collector is designed for any factory that has groups of automated or semi-automated machinery maintained by a single setup and inspection person. The data collector works especially well at gaging stations that handle a number of parts, or where there is a frequent changeover of parts.

The 861, though, is used with up to 10 high-level analog output gages. These gages are typically column gages (see chapter 17 for details). Use the column gages in a test fixture to record several measurements of a single part at once. Readings for all gages connected to the data collector can be recorded at the same time by pressing the footswitch.

The 861 data collector has total indicator reading (TIR) capablility. This means you can record the minimum, maximum or ranges of values of a part rotated in a fixture. Additional capablity lets you record the minimum, maximum or range of values from several gages for parallelness or other applications. Other special features include:

- Trend alert — to let the operator know when a trend has occured.
- Assignable causes — to show when a change in the process, or any other factor, has occured that may have affected the data.
- Individuals, moving average and range charts.

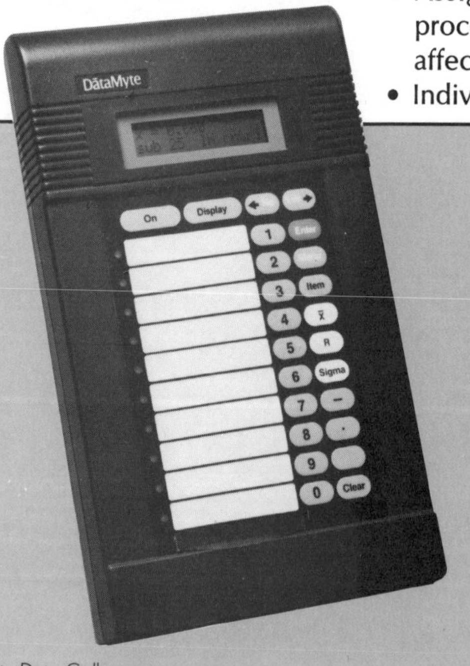

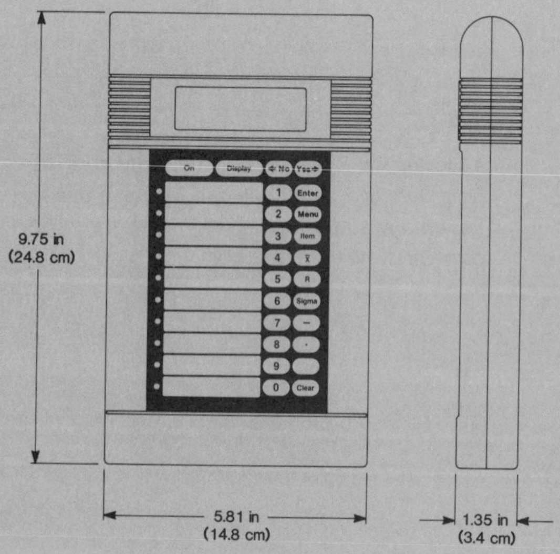

Special Features

- Connects with up to 10 high-level analog gages (such as column gages)
- Math capablity for adding, subtracting, multiplying and dividing readings
- Selectable number of characteristics (10 per file)
- Record up to 10,000 readings
- Tracks more than one type of part at once, without changing the setup
- Automatic scanning and recording of gage inputs
- Automatic control charting
- Directory indicates files and memory available
- Trend alert feature lets operator know when a trend has occurred
- Assignable cause, machine and operator codes
- Codes appear on printed reports; assignable cause codes also appear on control charts displayed on the monitor

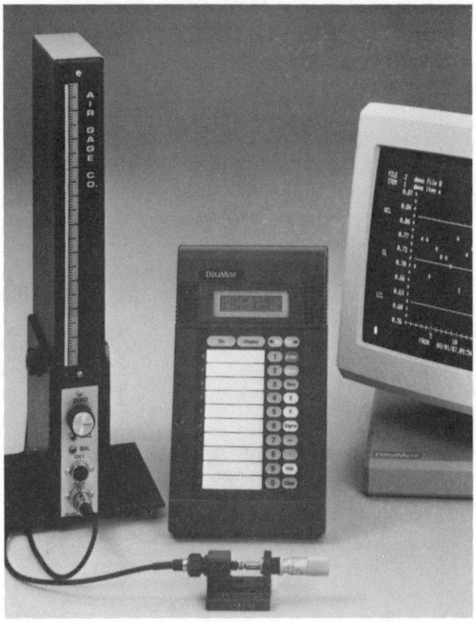

Other Features

- Interfaces with FAN software
- Easy, menu-driven operation
- Automatic time/date recording with each subgroup
- 24 tactile membrane keys
- Two-line by 16-character LCD display
- Selectable RS-232C transmission rates
- Nicad battery operated, with AC charger/adaptor
- Unit turns off after eight minutes one-use
- Rugged ABS plastic case, oil and water resistant
- Weighs about 2 lb. (0.9 kg)

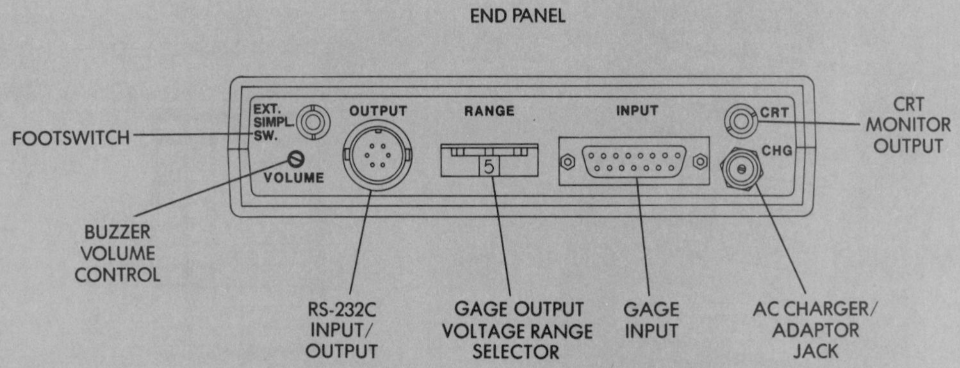

DātaMyte

762 Data Collector

The DataMyte 762 data collector connects to sophisticated measuring systems such as the Fowler Ultra-Cal II, Sylvac and Trimos gages, as well as other gages that use the same output technology. The 762 adds memory, real-time statistical analysis and management reporting to such applications as bore gaging, vertical measurement, micrometer heads, and groove and recess gaging.

The 762, in combination with the DataMyte video monitor, has a programmable trend-alert feature to let the operator know that a trend in the process has just occurred. Program the 762 to show that several readings in a row, outside of the desired limits, have just been recorded. The operator enters an assignable cause, which appears on all charts and reports, before continuing to collect data.

For examples of use, see pp. 7-17, 8-5, 8-23, 8-24, 8-25, 9-2, 9-18, 10-5, 10-8, 10-11, 10-15, 10-16, 12-4, 12-13, 12-22, 13-2 and 13-7.

Use the 762 skip-counting feature to take readings from fully automated manufacturing lines. Set the 762 to skip a certain number of readings before recording the next subgroup of data. This is quite frequently used in weigh-scale operations.

Three footswitch receptacles control the Sylvac and Trimos/Ultra-Cal II channels. The digital gage port accepts readings from micrometers, calipers, linear gages, height gages and many other RS-232 gages and devices, including weigh scales, laser micrometers, metrology display systems and the DataMyte multiplexer (for up to 8 digital indicators). See Chapter 17 for gages.

Like other fixed-station data collectors, the 762 displays complete x̄-bar and R charts, x̄-bar and sigma charts and histograms on a video monitor or printer.

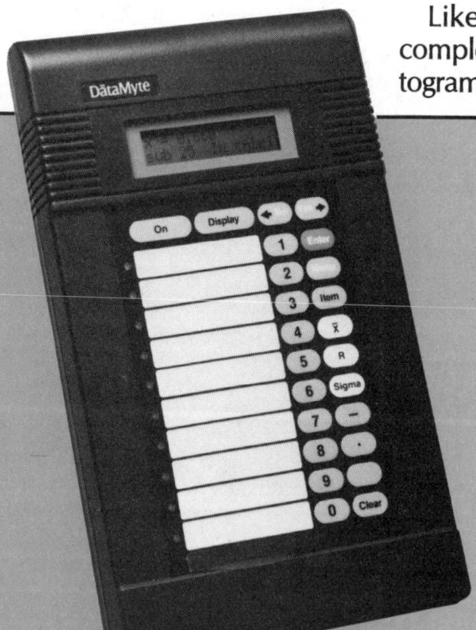

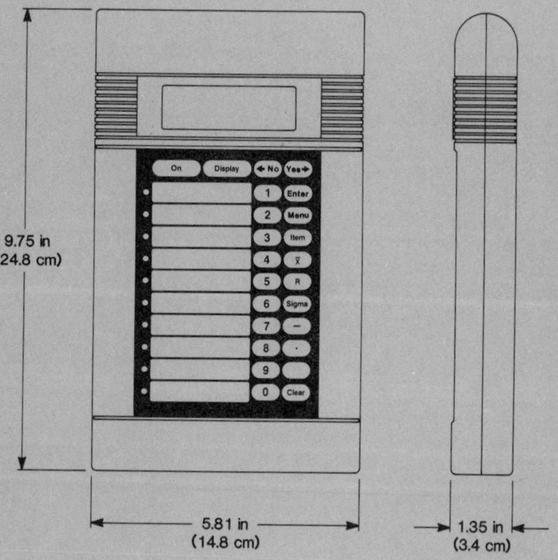

Special Features

- Automatic control charting
- Trend alert feature lets operator know when a trend has occurred
- Assignable cause, machine and operator codes
- Codes appear on printed reports; assignable cause codes appear on monitor, too
- Three digital/RS-232C gage ports
- Multiplexer available to expand the gage connections up to 24 gages
- Math option for adding, subtracting, multiplying and dividing readings
- Selectable number of characteristics, up to 10
- Automatic scanning and recording of gage inputs

Other Features

- Interfaces with FAN software
- Easy, menu-driven operation
- Displays charts on CRT and printer
- Ten items by 8 digits with plus and minus
- Automatic time/date recording with each subgroup
- 1000, 2500 and 4000 reading memory sizes
- 24 tactile membrane keys
- Two-line by 16-character LCD display
- Selectable RS-232C transmission rates
- Nicad battery operated, with AC charger/adaptor
- Unit turns off after eight minutes non-use
- Rugged ABS plastic case, oil and water resistant
- Weighs about 2 lb. (0.9 kg)

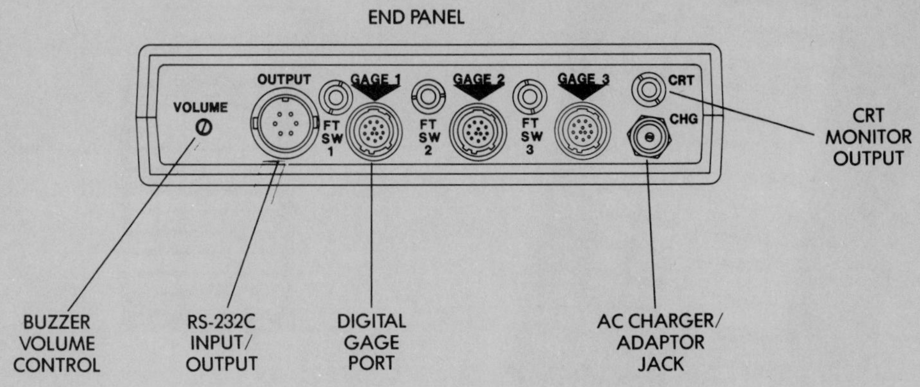

761 Data Collector

The DataMyte 761 data collector connects to column gages and analog displays. The 761 adds memory, real-time statistical analysis and management reporting to bore gage, snap gage and other column gage applications.

The 761, in combination with the DataMyte video monitor, has a programmable trend-alert feature to let the operator know that a trend in the process has just occurred. Program the 761 to show that several readings in a row, outside of the desired limits, have just been recorded. The oprator enters an assignable cause, which appears on all charts and reports, before continuing to collect data.

For examples of use, see pp. 7-18, 8-3, 8-6, 8-22, 11-4 and 14-30.

Three models are available, for interfacing one, five or 10 column gages. A junction box is included with the five and ten input 761s. Readings are recorded with a footswitch. An autoscan feature lets the 761 data collector record up to ten readings at once. A math and total indicator reading operation allows plotting control charts on min., max., differences and other indirect variables derived from up to 10 points.

Like other fixed station data collectors, the 761 displays complete x̄-bar and R charts, x̄-bar and sigma charts and histograms on a video monitor or printer. It communicates with the DataTruck, desktop computers and printers.

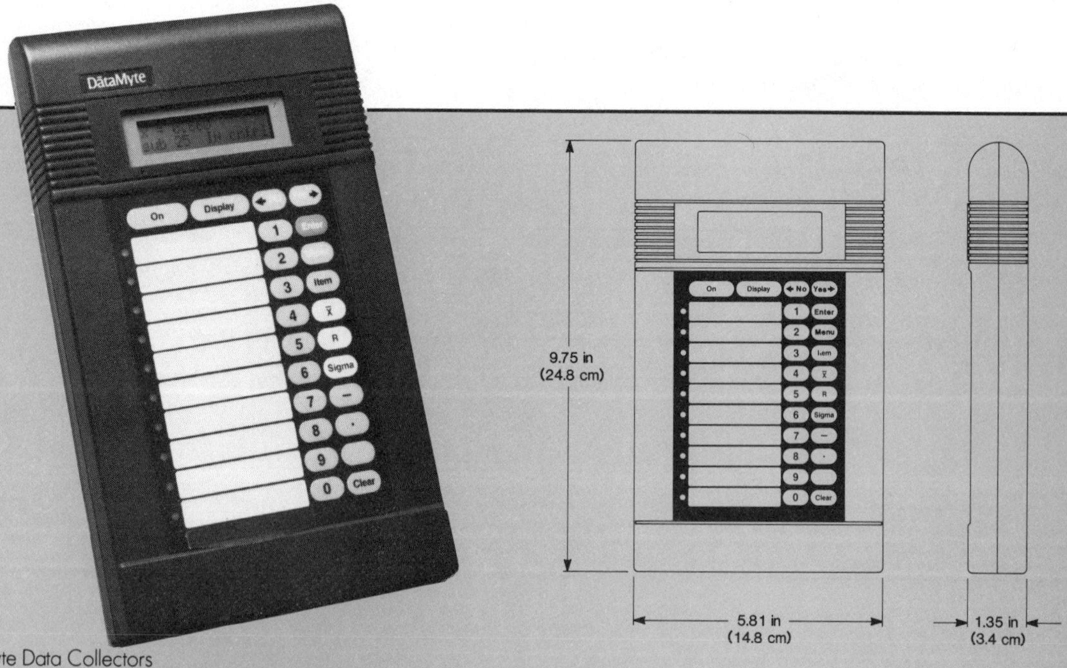

Special Features

- Automatic control charting
- Trend alert feature lets operator know when a trend has occured
- Assignable cause, machine and operator codes
- Codes appear on printed reports; assignable cause codes appear on monitor, too
- Connects with up to 10 analog gages (such as column gages)
- Math option for adding, subtracting, multiplying and dividing readings
- Selectable number of characteristics, up to 10
- Automatic scanning and recording of gage inputs

Other Features

- Interfaces with FAN software
- Easy, menu-driven operation
- Displays charts on CRT and printer
- Ten items by 8 digits with plus and minus
- Automatic time/date recording with each subgroup
- 1000, 2500, 4000 reading memory sizes
- 24 tactile membrane keys
- Two-line by 16-character LCD display
- Selectable RS-232C transmission rates
- Nicad battery operated, with AC charger/adaptor
- Unit turns off after eight minutes non-use
- Rugged ABS plastic case, oil and water resistant
- Weighs about 2 lb. (0.9 kg)

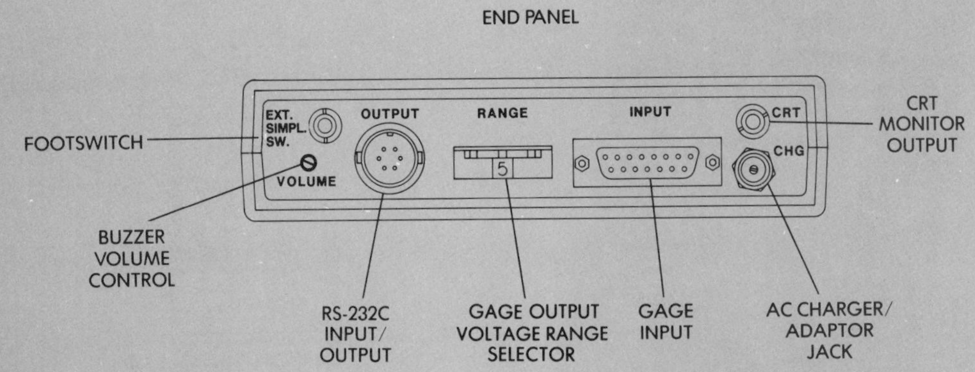

DataMyte

754 Data Collector

The DataMyte 754 connects exclusively to Federal Maxum™ gages. It adds memory, statistical reporting and direct computer interface to all Maxum gage applications, including:

- Bore gages
- Snap gages
- Bench comparators
- Thickness gages

Up to eight indicators can be connected at once. An auto-scanning feature records readings from all eight indicators with a single press of a footswitch. A special math option allows operations on inputs for finding min., max. and range.

Like all 750 models, the 754 displays complete $\bar{x}$ & R charts, $\bar{x}$ & s charts and histograms on a CRT monitor or printer. It communicates with the DataTruck, desktop computers, printers, and modems.

For an example of use, see pg. 8-3.

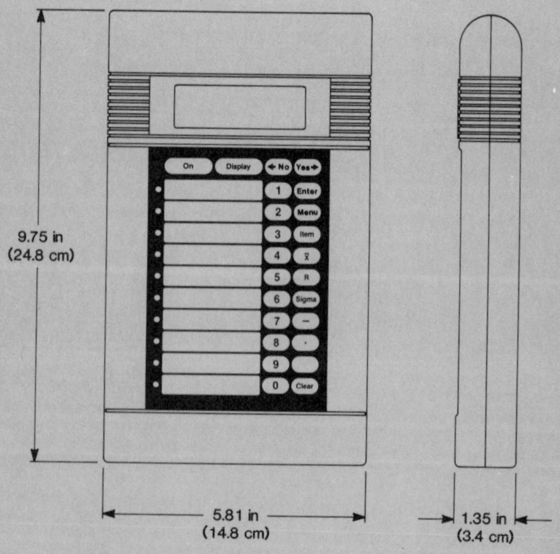

Special Features

- Connects to 4 or 8 Federal Maxum gages
- Autoscanning of all inputs
- Footswitch for taking readings
- Math option, to add, subtract, multiply, divide and find min., max., and range of a series of inputs.

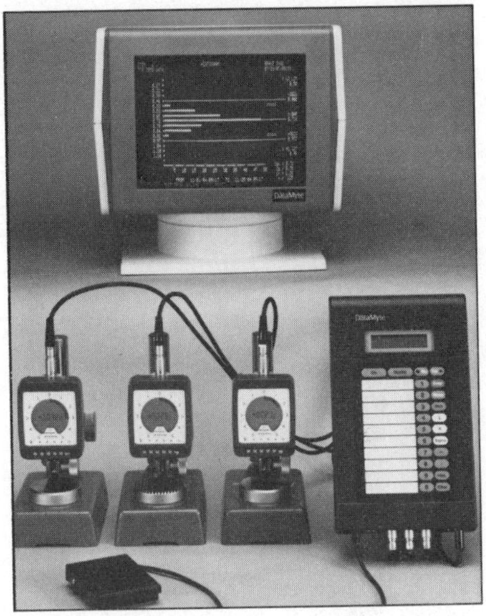

Other Features

- Interfaces with FAN software
- Easy, menu-driven operation
- Displays charts on CRT and printer
- Ten items by 8 digits with plus and minus
- Automatic time/date recording with each subgroup
- 1000, 2500 and 4000 reading memory sizes
- 24 tactile membrane keys
- Two-line by 16-character LCD display
- Selectable RS-232C transmission rates
- Nicad battery operated, with AC charger/adaptor
- Unit turns off after eight minutes non-use
- Rugged ABS plastic case, oil and water resistant
- Weighs about 2 lb. (0.9 kg)

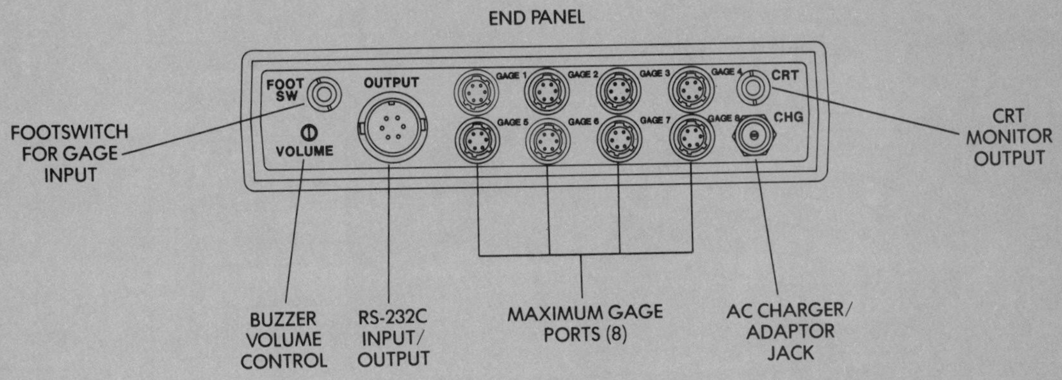

DātaMyte

753 Data Collector

The DataMyte 753 is a single channel data collector for low-level analog gages such as:

- Torque wrenches
- In-line torque transducers (for stall-type nutrunners)
- DataMyte 514 and 516 gap gages

Designed for production-line torque monitoring applications, it has a skip function for efficient unattended statistical sampling. Special software allows reading the peak torque (or gap). For sheet metal gap and flushness applications, a footswitch or gage sample switch lets you "back up" and retake a reading.

The 753 displays complete $\bar{x}$ & R charts, $\bar{x}$ & s charts and histograms on a CRT monitor or printer. It communicates with the DataTruck, desktop computers, printers, and modems.

For an example of use, see pg. 8-5.

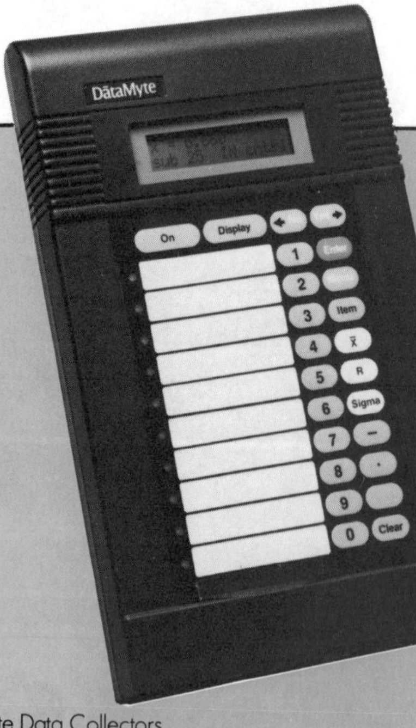

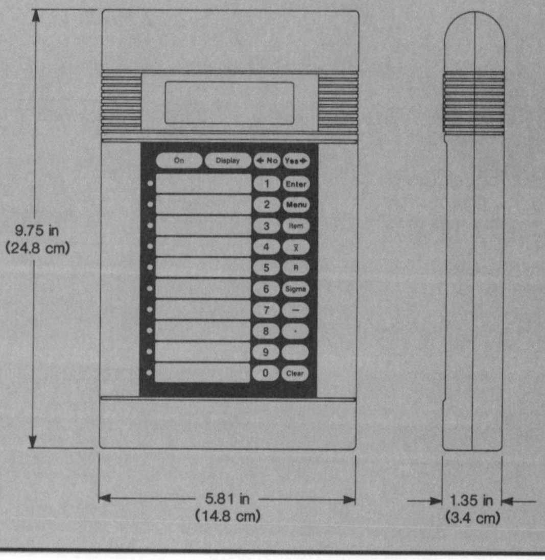

Special Features

- Analog gage port, for 2mV/1 or 0.8mV/1 input
- Peak algorithm
- Skip function to bypass a certain number of readings before recording next subgroup
- Math option for adding, subtracting, multiplying and dividing readings

Other Features

- Interfaces with FAN software
- Easy, menu-driven operation
- Displays charts on CRT and printer
- Ten items by 8 digits with plus and minus
- Automatic time/date recording with each subgroup
- 1000, 2500 and 4000 reading memory sizes
- 24 tactile membrane keys
- Two-line by 16-character LCD display
- Selectable RS-232C transmission rates
- Nicad battery operated, with AC charger/adaptor
- 16 hours continuous on time with battery only
- Unit turns off after eight minutes non-use
- Rugged ABS plastic case, oil and water resistant
- Weighs about 2 lb. (0.9 kg)

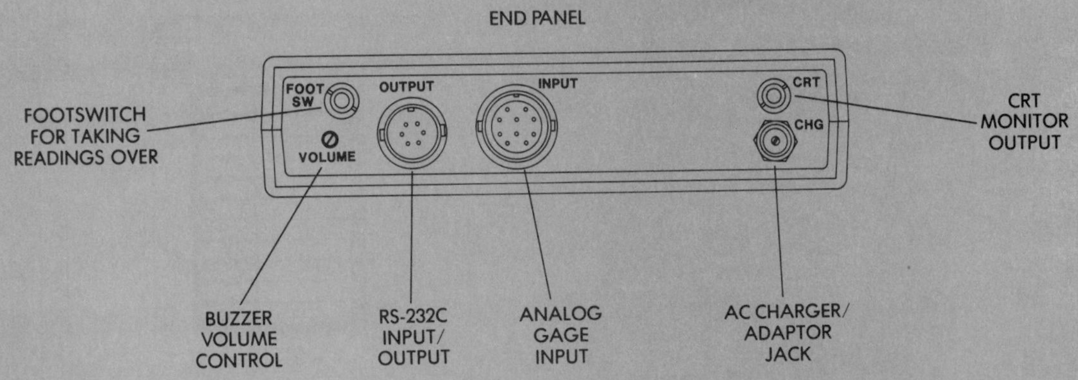

DātaMyte

750 Data Collector

The DataMyte 750 automatically captures data from micrometers, calipers and RS-232C devices, making it ideal for:

- Machine shops
- Metal stamping operations
- Die casting and forging
- Plastics extrusion and molding
- Weigh scale applications

A 750 can have up to three digital gages connected at once. Or, using a DataMyte multiplexer, it can record readings from up to 16 digital indicators. The 750 also accepts data from many fixed station RS-232C devices such as weigh scales and laser micrometers. See Chapter 17 for gages.

The 750 displays complete $\bar{x}$ & R charts, $\bar{x}$ & s charts and histograms on a CRT monitor or printer. A math option and a skip function facilitates in-line statistical sampling for many automated gaging and weighing/packaging applications.

For examples of use, see pp. 7-7, 8-3, 8-8, 8-9, 9-5, 10-2, 10-4, 10-9, 10-12, 10-13, 11-5, 12-11, 13-9, 13-11, 13-12, 13-14 and 13-23.

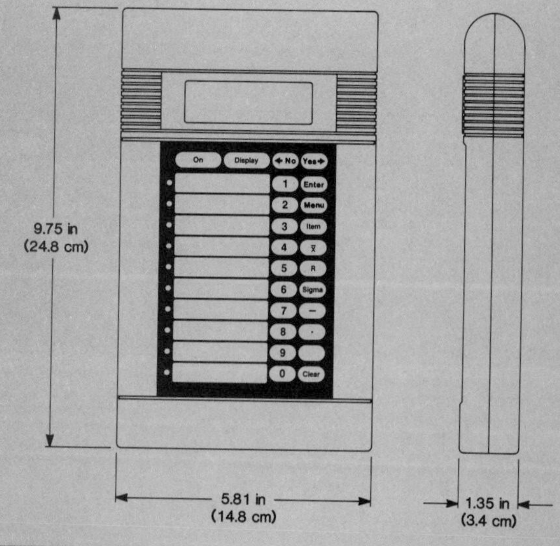

Special Features

- 3 digital/RS-232C gage ports

Other Features

- Interfaces with FAN software
- Easy, menu-driven operation
- Displays charts on CRT and printer
- Ten items by 8 digits with plus and minus
- Automatic time/date recording with each subgroup
- 1000 and 2500 reading memory sizes
- 24 tactile membrane keys
- Two-line by 16-character LCD display
- Selectable RS-232C transmission rates
- Nicad battery operated, with AC charger/adaptor
- 16 hours continuous on time with battery only
- Unit turns off after eight minutes non-use
- Rugged ABS plastic case, oil and water resistant
- Weighs about 2 lb. (0.9 kg)

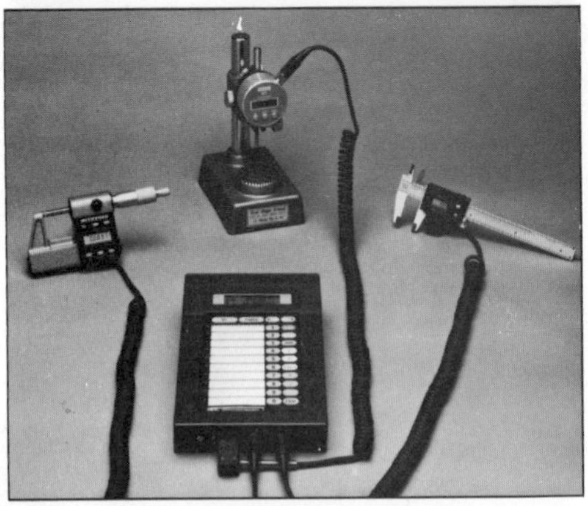

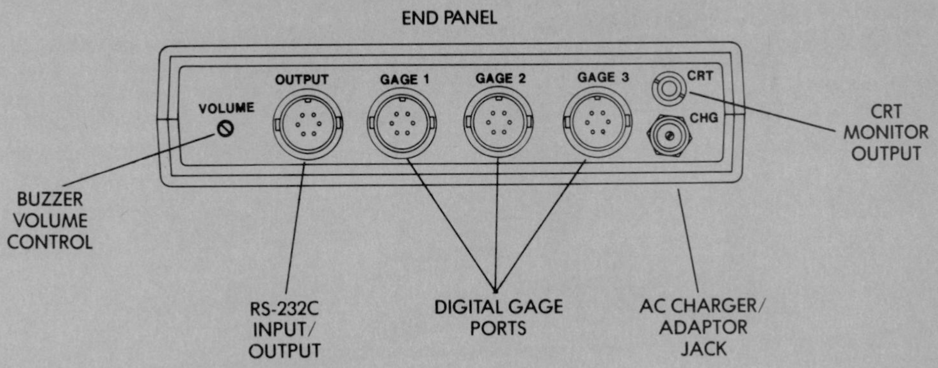

DataMyte

769 Fixed-Station Attributes Data Collector

For examples of use, see pp. 7-8, 7-17, 10-11, 10-15, 10-17, 11-3, 12-13, 12-23, 13-5 and 14-30.

The DataMyte 769 fixed-station attribute data collector is for real-time attribute analysis at the process. The DataMyte 769 works well in electronics, consumer goods, packaging, automobile, defense and other industries where attribute data collection is used.

Operators can quickly record defects with a bar code wand and look at Pareto and percent-defectives charts as they are working. The 769 simplifies any application where a product is counted, inspected for appearance or defects, or is graded, classified or tested for proper operation. The 769 is effective for:

- Scrap reporting
- Incoming inspection
- In-process inspection
- Final tests

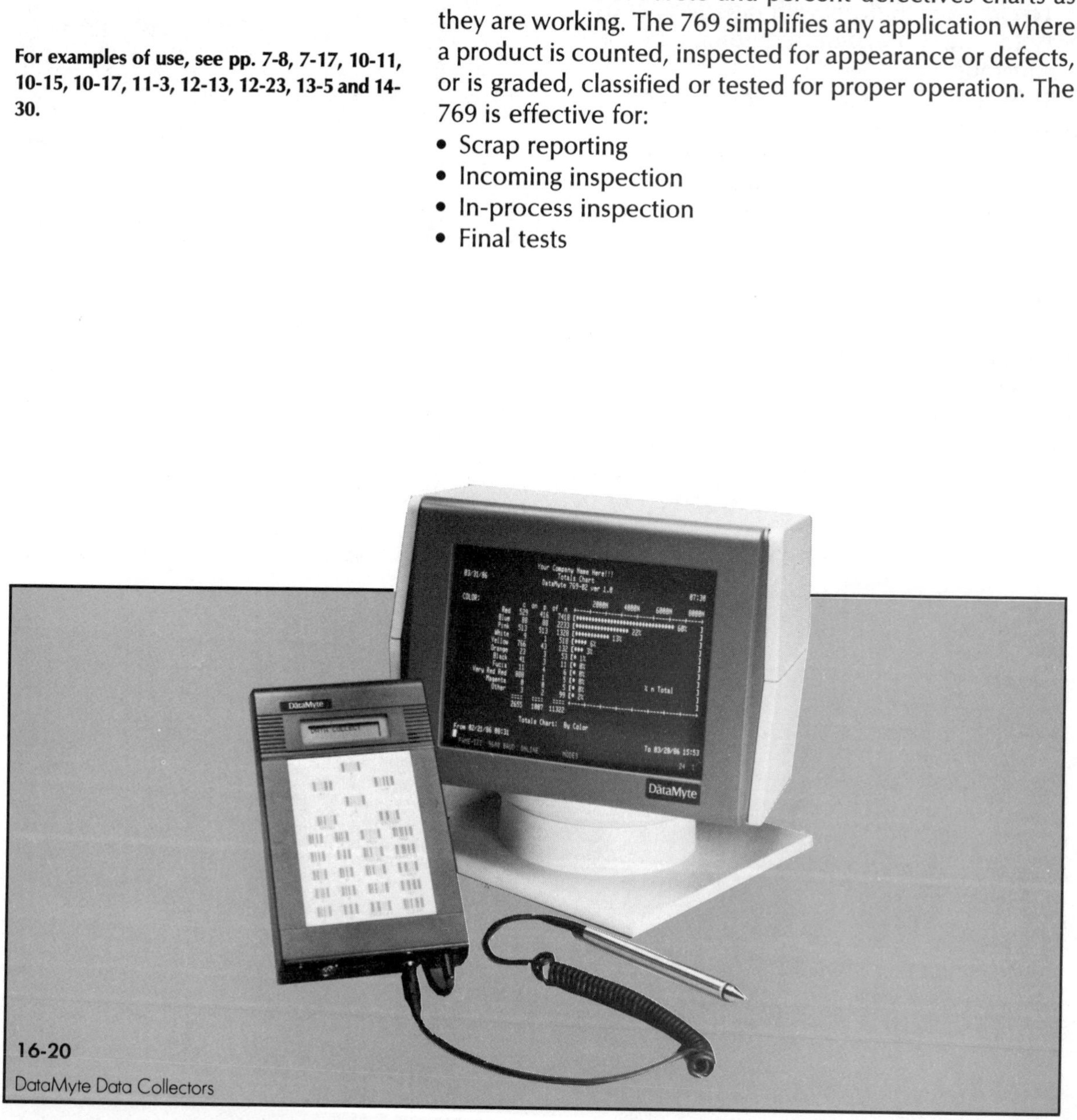

Special Features

- Bar code printing mode (using optional printer)
- Code 39 bar code input
- Reports menu for choosing types of data to appear on charts; these combination of charts are stored for future reference
- Print charts and data reports on optional printer

Other Features

- Software program is available which allows saving of data and setup information on an IBM PC
- 128K bytes memory for data
- Menu-driven operation, with all functions programmed through the bar code wand or optional computer program
- Date and time recorded with each data record
- Two-line by 16-character LCD display, with contrast switch
- Nicad battery operated, with AC charge/adaptor
- 16 hours continuous on time with battery only
- Unit turns off after programmable number of minutes
- Rugged ABS plastic case, oil and water-resistant
- Weighs about 2 lb. (0.9 kg)

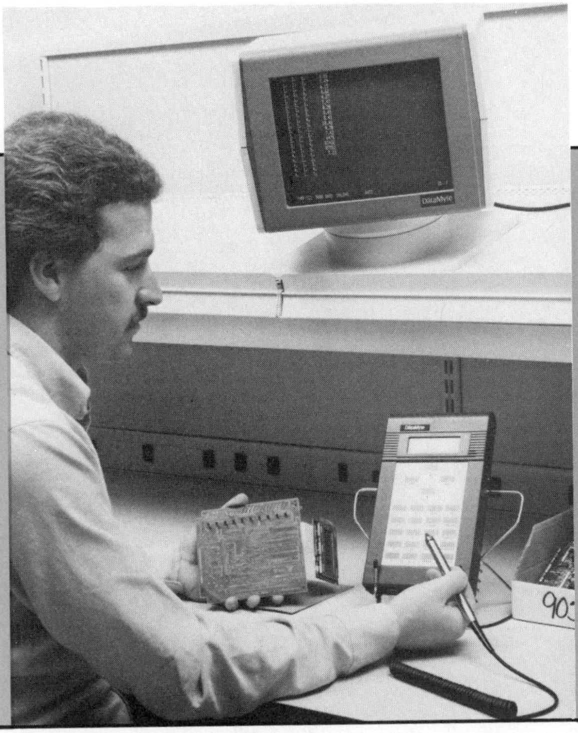

DātaMyte

769 Fixed-Station Attributes Data Collector

The DataMyte 769 fixed-station attribute data collector is for real-time attribute analysis at the process. The DataMyte 769 works well in electronics, consumer goods, packaging, automobile, defense and other industries where attribute data collection is used.

Operators can quickly record defects with a bar code wand and look at Pareto and control charts as they are working. Use the charts to look at the:

- Percentage of defective parts in a subgroup (p-chart)
- Number of defective parts in a subgroup (np-chart)
- Percentage of defects per part (c-chart)
- Number of defects per part (u-chart)

The same information can also be shown in a Pareto chart, which ranks the information presented.

The 769 simplifies any application where a product is counted, inspected for appearance or defects, or is graded, classified or tested for proper operation. The 769 is effective for:

- Scrap reporting
- Incoming inspection
- In-process inspection
- Final tests

Special Features

- User-definable subgroups
- Batching feature allows data collection in batches
- Code 39 bar code input
- Reports menu for choosing types of data to appear on charts; these combinations of charts are stored for future reference
- Print charts and data reports on optional printer

Other Features

- Software program allows saving of data and setup information on an IBM PC
- 512K bytes memory for data
- Menu-driven operation, with all functions programmed through the bar code wand, keypad or computer program
- Data and time recorded with each data record
- Two-line by 16-character LCD display, with contrast switch
- Nicad battery operated, with AC charger/adaptor
- 16 hours continuous on time with battery only
- Unit turns off after programmable number of minutes
- Rugged ABS plastic case, oil and water-resistant
- Weighs about 2 lb. (0.9 kg)

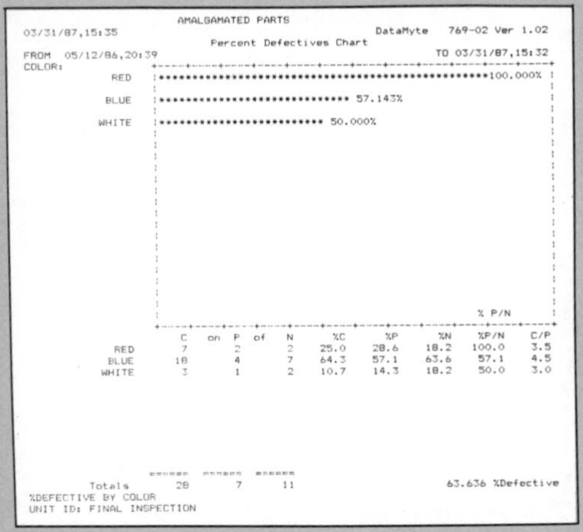

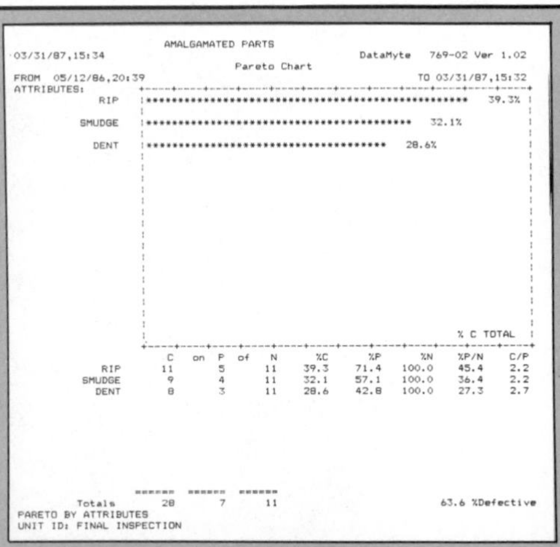

16.2 HANDHELD DATA COLLECTORS

This section contains model by model descriptions of DataMyte handheld data collectors.

The Ultimate Statistical Auditing System

The DataMyte 2000® is the most comprehensive SPC system available to a quality professional. In a single handheld unit it provides:

- Direct input for both digital and analog gages
- Direct bar code input
- Variables and attributes auditing
- Complete alphanumeric keyboard
- Statistical charting capability on its own 40-character by 8-line display
- Memory capacity for auditing virtually an unlimited number of characteristics

The DataMyte 2000 is modular, with interchangeable gage interface modules and program packs. From the time it is purchased, a 2000 can continue to grow as new applications demand statistical analysis. New gage interface modules can be inserted for specialized tasks. New program packs can equip the 2000 with the most advanced software offered by DataMyte for quality control applications. A 2000 will never be obsolete.

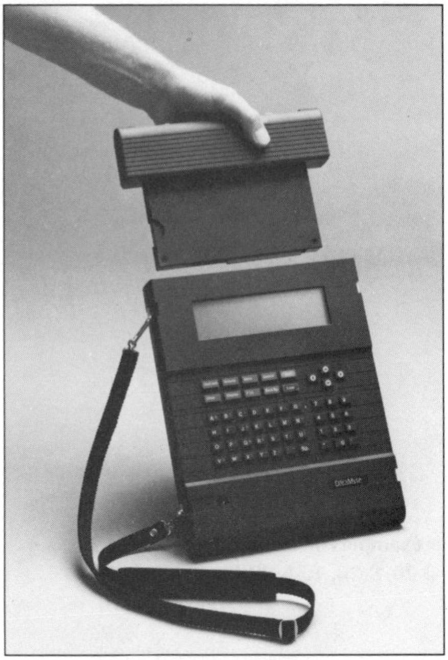

Replaceable gage modules (above) and program packs (below).

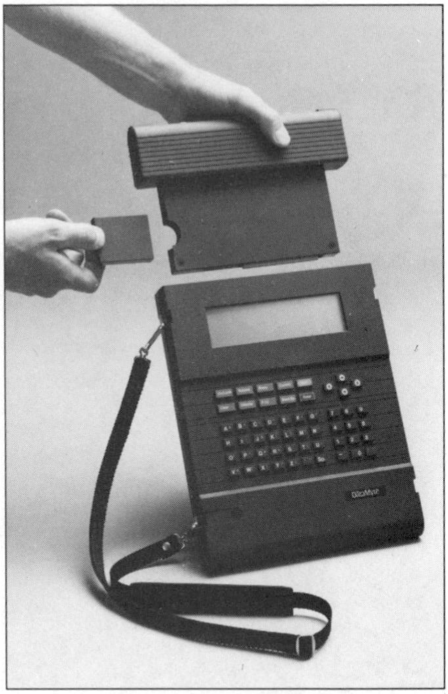

Total Quality Control With a 2000

The DataMyte 2000 is made for real-world decision making. In the hands of a quality professional, the 2000 is a powerful aid to total quality control activities. Alphanumeric footnotes can be linked with data from a gage, or points on a control chart. Part numbers, production counts and percentage defective can be tied together so that all of the details — both observed and measured — are part of an analysis. Practically anything that can be done on paper can be done faster and with less error on a 2000.

A 2000 accomplishes this with flexible memory and processing speed. Entries can be any length. Predefined operations can be executed with two keypresses. Reports and graphs contain both data analysis and alphanumeric notes. Audit routes and studies can be set up, and data gathered and analyzed without tying up desktop computers and other resources.

A Roving Link to the FAN® System

The DataMyte 2000 fulfills the role of a multi-task auditing tool in the FAN® (Factory Area Network) system. It can be used wherever process volumes do not require a fixed station data collector like the DataMyte 860. A 2000 can audit low volume processes, sequential operations, tasks on moving assembly lines, and do periodic capability studies and quality checks. It can be assigned to a continuous daily route preprogrammed by a computer, or be used to randomly log defects and other attributes wherever they are found.

Like the rest of the FAN system, the DataMyte 2000 is open-ended. It can be used as effectively in existing applications as it can in any new application that lies ahead. It will always be compatible with existing and future components of the FAN system.

2003 Data Collector

The DataMyte 2003 is a high-capacity data collection system that accepts direct input from both digital and analog gages. Digital gages include micrometers, calipers, digital indicators and many RS-232C devices. Analog gages include torque wrenches, in-line torque transducers, gap and flushness gages and column gages. See Chapter 17 for gages.

The 2003 has a 54-key keyboard that allows full alphanumeric input. The user can quickly enter footnotes to data, and execute user-defined function keys. The 8-line by 40-character display provides a complete status update during data collection, with statistical summaries and 80-column wide $\bar{x}$ & R charts, $\bar{x}$ & s charts and histograms. Graphs can be output to a dot matrix printer, and data transmitted to a desk top computer for archiving.

For examples of use, see pp. 7-17, 7-19, 8-3, 8-5, 8-20, 8-26, 10-6, 12-23, 13-4 and 13-8.

The 2003 is compatible with the DataMyte fixed-station data collectors and the DataMyte FAN II Software program. It has a terminal mode for sending and receiving large blocks of data. All functions of the 2003 can be programmed from a remote keyboard or computer program (such as FAN II Software), allowing routes to be set up and downloaded on a daily basis.

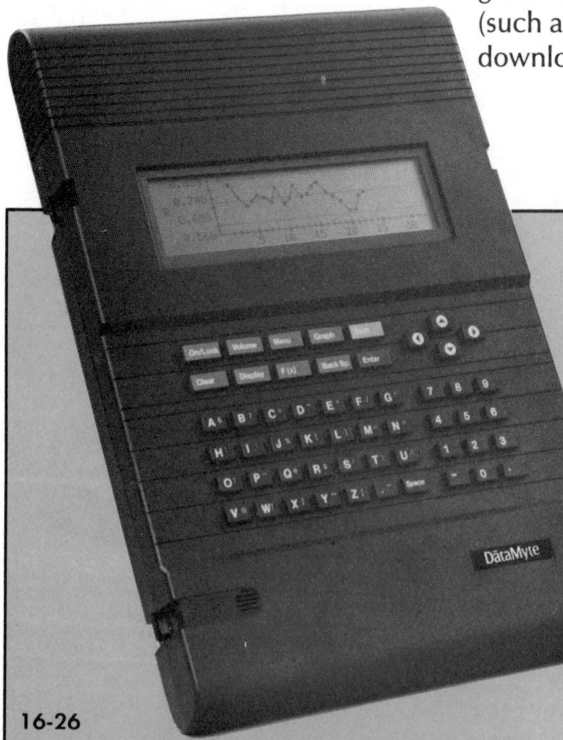

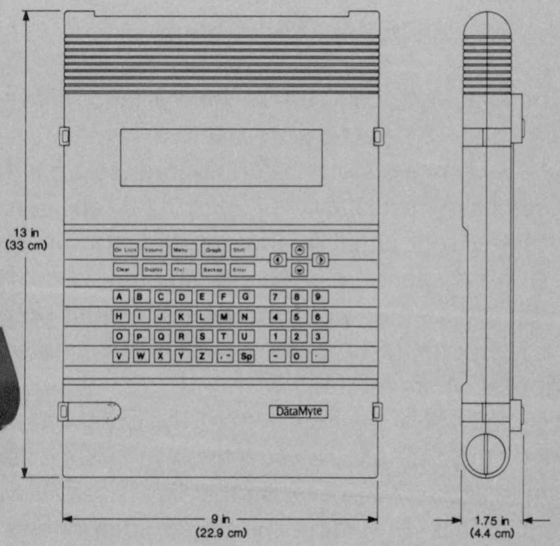

Special Features

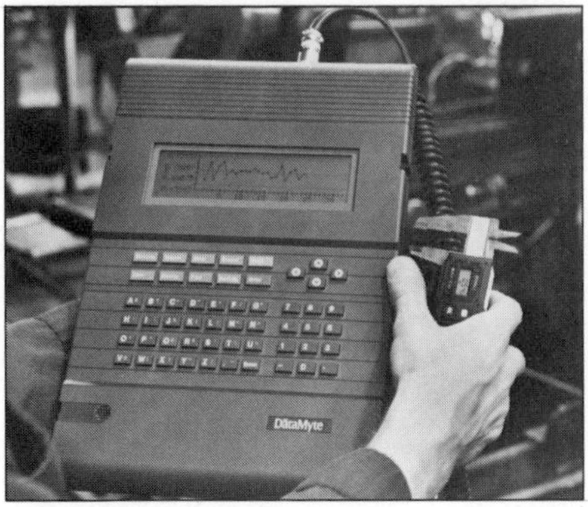

- 3 input ports, for digital gages, analog gages and bar code wand
- Control charts and histograms on unit display
- Alphanumeric footnotes
- Interchangeable program packs
- Math function for sums and differences of items
- 128K memory (256K numeric characters)
- Ten user-definable function keys

Other Features

- Interfaces with FAN software
- Menu driven with help screens and status displays
- Pull-down windows for selecting options
- User-definable headers for data collection
- Time/day/date labeling for subgroups
- Terminal mode
- RS-232C I/O port with fully selectable communications protocol
- Nicad battery powered, with removable battery pack
- Weighs about 4.2 lb. (0.9 kg)

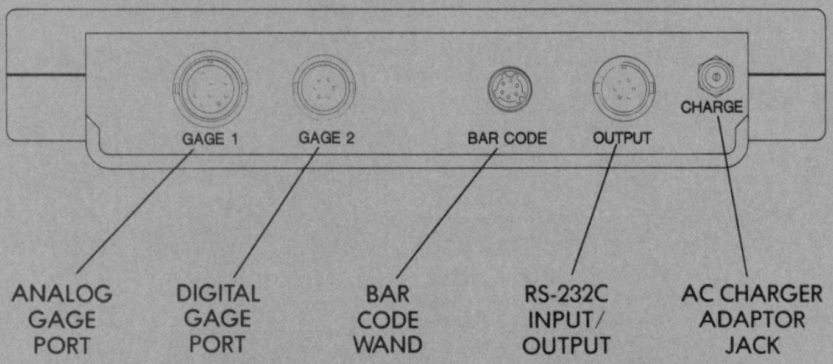

2005 Data Collector

The DataMyte 2005 is a high-capacity data collection system that accepts direct input from up to six digital gages. Digital gages include micrometers, calipers, digital indicators and many RS-232C devices. See Chapter 17 for gages.

The 2005 has a 54-key keyboard that allows full alphanumeric input. The user can quickly enter footnotes to data, and execute user-defined function keys. The 8-line by 40-character display provides a complete status update during data collection, with statistical summaries and 80-column wide $\bar{x}$ & R charts, $\bar{x}$ & s charts and histograms. Graphs can be output to a dot matrix printer, and data transmitted to a desk top computer for archiving.

The 2005 is compatible with the DataMyte fixed-station data collectors and the DataMyte FAN II Software program. It has a terminal mode for sending and receiving large blocks of data. All functions of the 2005 can be programmed from a remote keyboard or computer program (such as FAN II Software), allowing routes to be set up and downloaded on a daily basis.

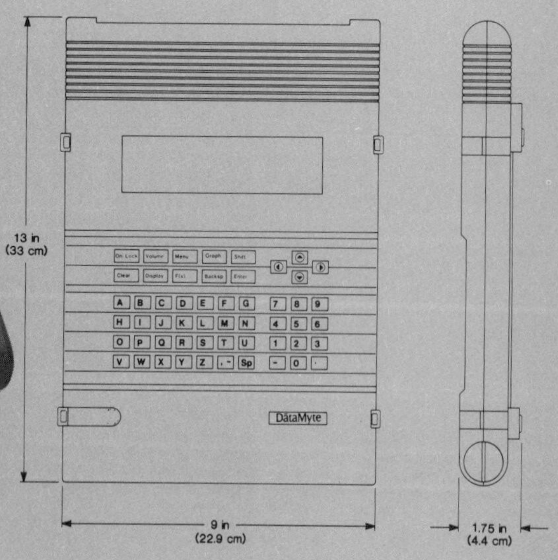

Special Features

- 6 input ports for digital gages
- Control charts and histograms on unit display
- Alphanumeric footnotes
- Interchangeable program packs
- Math function for sums and differences of items
- 128K memory (256K numeric characters)
- Ten user-definable function keys

Other Features

- Interfaces with FAN software
- Menu driven with help screens and status displays
- Pull-down windows for selecting options
- User-definable headers for data collection
- Time/day/date labeling for subgroups
- Terminal mode
- RS-232C I/O port with fully selectable communications protocol
- Nicad battery powered, with removable battery pack
- Weighs about 4.2 lb. (0.9 kg)

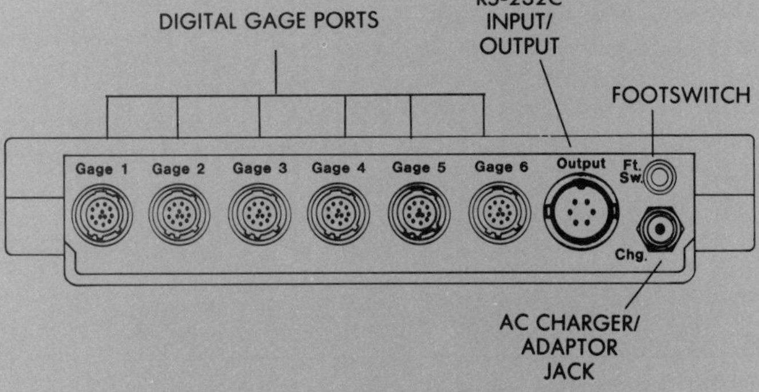

A p-chart printed directly from the DataMyte 2003 data collector.

page 1

model: 2003-00 version: 3.5
p Chart

13:58
04/08/87

file #6........ FENDERS
item #1........ DRIVER REAR

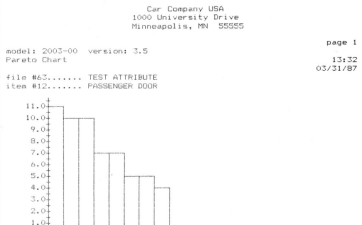

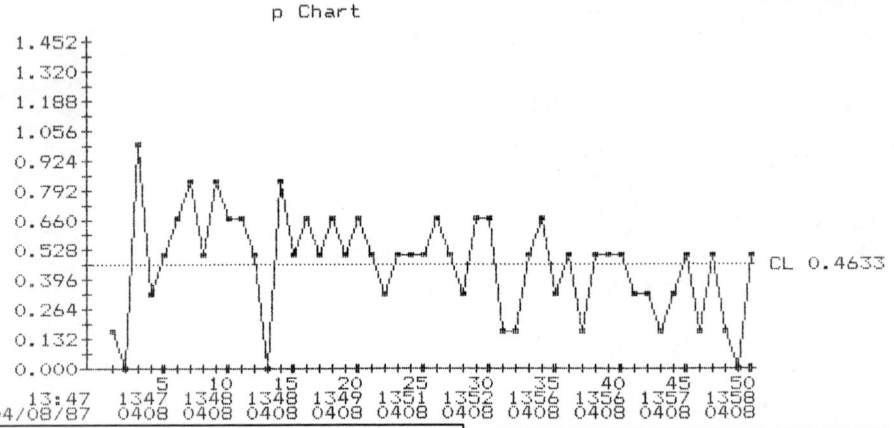

Car Company USA
1000 University Drive
Minneapolis, MN 55555

page 1

model: 2003-00 version: 3.5
Pareto Chart

13:32
03/31/87

file #63....... TEST ATTRIBUTE
item #12....... PASSENGER DOOR

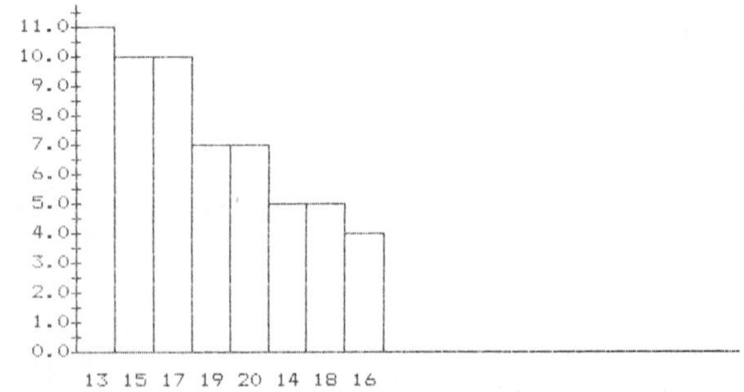

#	attribute	defects
13	DRIP	11
15	SMUDGE	10
17	WARPED	10
19	SCRATCH	7
20	RUN	7
14	WRINKLE	5
18	CHIP	5
16	DISCOLORED	4

start............. 09/23/86,14:04
stop.............. 09/23/86,14:35
samples........... 100
total defective... 20
total defects..... 59

A Pareto chart printed directly from the DataMyte 2003 data collector. The 2003 can collect attribute and variable data in the same file.

model: 2003-00 version: 3.5
histogram

page 1

13:18
04/08/87

file #3........ TRIAL FIXTURE
item #1........ A1

X-bar.......	12.54999	range.......	0.0046	sigma.......	0.00089
6 sigma.....	0.00534	X - 3s......	12.54732	X + 3s......	12.55266
low limit...	12.5480	high limit..	12.5520	nominal.....	12.5500
Cp..........	0.75	Cpk.........	0.75	Cr..........	1.33
min.........	12.5478	max.........	12.5524	samples.....	375

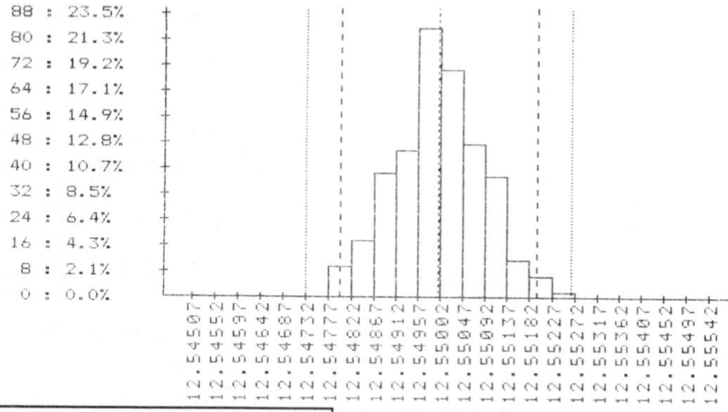

A histogram printed directly from the DataMyte 2003.

model: 2003-00 version: 3.5
capability report

file #3........ TRIAL FIXTURE

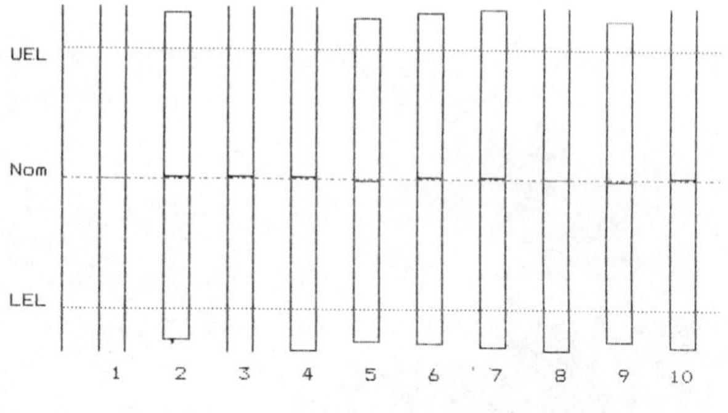

	1	2	3	4	5	6	7	8	9	10
ID	A1	A2	B1	B2	C1	C2	D1	D2	E1	E2
nominal.......	12.5500	12.5500	12.5500	12.5500	12.5500	12.5500	12.5500	12.5500	12.5500	12.5500
high limit....	12.5520	12.5520	12.5520	12.5520	12.5520	12.5520	12.5520	12.5520	12.5520	12.5520
low limit.....	12.5480	12.5480	12.5480	12.5480	12.5480	12.5480	12.5480	12.5480	12.5480	12.5480
X-bar.........	12.54999	12.55004	12.55004	12.55002	12.54998	12.55002	12.55002	12.55000	12.54997	12.55003
range.........	0.0046	0.0048	0.0046	0.0048	0.0047	0.0042	0.0048	0.0042	0.0043	0.0045
sigma.........	0.00089	0.00084	0.00091	0.00088	0.00083	0.00085	0.00086	0.00089	0.00083	0.00087
6 sigma.......	0.00534	0.00502	0.00547	0.00530	0.00497	0.00510	0.00518	0.00531	0.00495	0.00521
X + 3s........	12.55266	12.55255	12.55277	12.55267	12.55246	12.55256	12.55261	12.55266	12.55245	12.55264
X - 3s........	12.54732	12.54753	12.54731	12.54737	12.54749	12.54747	12.54742	12.54735	12.54750	12.54743
Cp............	0.75	0.80	0.73	0.75	0.81	0.78	0.77	0.75	0.81	0.77
Cr............	1.33	1.26	1.37	1.33	1.24	1.27	1.30	1.33	1.24	1.30
Cpk...........	0.75	0.78	0.72	0.75	0.80	0.78	0.77	0.75	0.80	0.76
samples.......	375	375	375	375	375	375	375	375	375	375

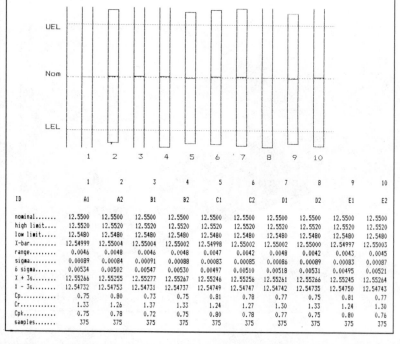

A capability report printed directly from the DataMyte 2003.

1700 AND 1500 SERIES DATA COLLECTORS

Two Basic Handheld Systems

By all outward appearances the DataMyte 1700 and 1500 are the same. They are rugged handheld data collection systems that interface to a huge variety of gages for direct input of data. They can print reports on a printer or communicate with a computer. They can audit virtually an unlimited number of parts and processes. They are made for a roving QC auditor — for applications where mobility and flexibility are needed.

The difference between a 1700 and a 1500 is that a 1700 saves all the data it takes to build an $\bar{x}$ & R chart. The data can then be used to print histograms and capability reports.

1556, 1558, 1756 and 1758 Data Collectors

For examples of use, see pp. 7-2, 7-6, 7-12, 8-3, 8-5, 8-11, 8-13, 8-15, 8-17, 9-6, 9-10, 9-13, 9-15, 10-14, 11-12, 12-3, 12-5, 12-6, 12-8, 12-9, 13-15, 13-18, 13-19, 13-20, 13-22, 13-25, 14-3, 14-4, 14-17, 14-19, 14-21 and 14-26.

The model 1556 and 1756 connect to analog gages such as torque wrenches, in-line torque transducers and gap and flushness gages. The 1558 and 1758 model connect to digital gages such as micrometers and calipers. All four models connect to many RS-232C devices such as digital indicators and weigh scales. See Chapter 17 for gages.

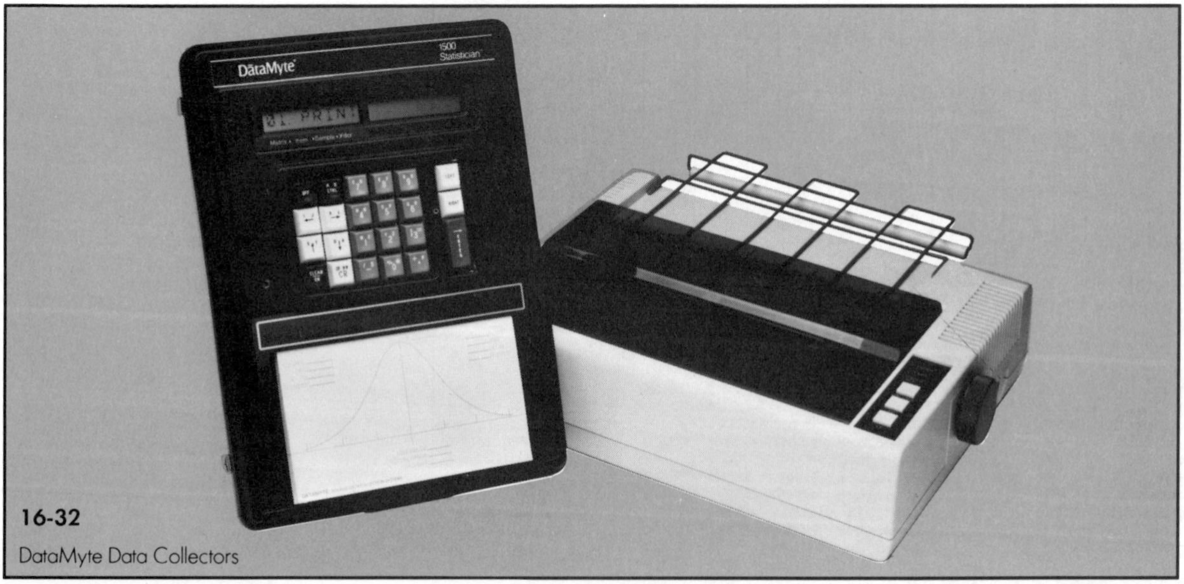

16-32
DataMyte Data Collectors

Special Features of 1556 and 1756

- Accepts readings from torque wrenches, gap and flushness gages, temperature probes, force gages and other analog transducers
- Special algorithms for reading peak and torque breakaway
- Internal resolution of 0.004 of full scale

Special Features of 1558 and 1758

- Accepts readings from calipers, micrometers, linear gages and other digital gages
- Resolution to 0.0001 in. (0.001 mm)

Other Features

- Calculates and prints $\bar{x}$ & R charts, $\bar{x}$ & s charts, histograms and capability studies
- Saves all $\bar{x}$ & R chart data
- Math feature for sum and difference of items and constants
- Alerts operator to item out of specifications and subgroups out of control
- Capacity for up to 40 ongoing control charts
- 64K character memory size
- Serial RS-232C I/O channel, with full parameter selection
- Remote control mode for download and upload of setups and data.
- Fully selectable communications protocol
- Nicad battery operated, with 14 hours continuous on time between chargings
- Weighs about 4.25 lb. (2.2 kg)

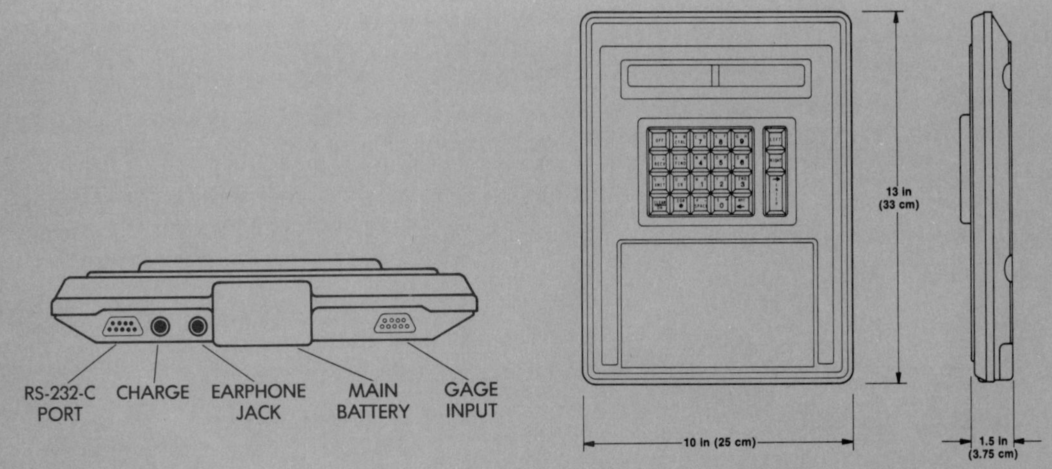

DataMyte

1559 Paint Thickness System

For an example of use, see pg. 11-9.

The Paint Thickness System combines a high resolution contact probe with the features of the 1500 series. The system measures the thickness of non-magnetic, non-conductive coatings such as paint, vitreous enamel, plastic, varnish, glass, epoxy, rubber, glass fiber and bitumen. The thicknesses of these coatings can be measured on curved or flat bases of mild steel, cast iron, magnetic stainless steel and galvanized steel.

Readings are automatically stored in memory simply by placing the probe on the surface. No keys need to be pressed on the DataMyte. Readings are compiled for histograms, $\bar{x}$ & R charts, $\bar{x}$ & sigma charts and capability reports which can be printed by connecting the DataMyte to its dot matrix printer.

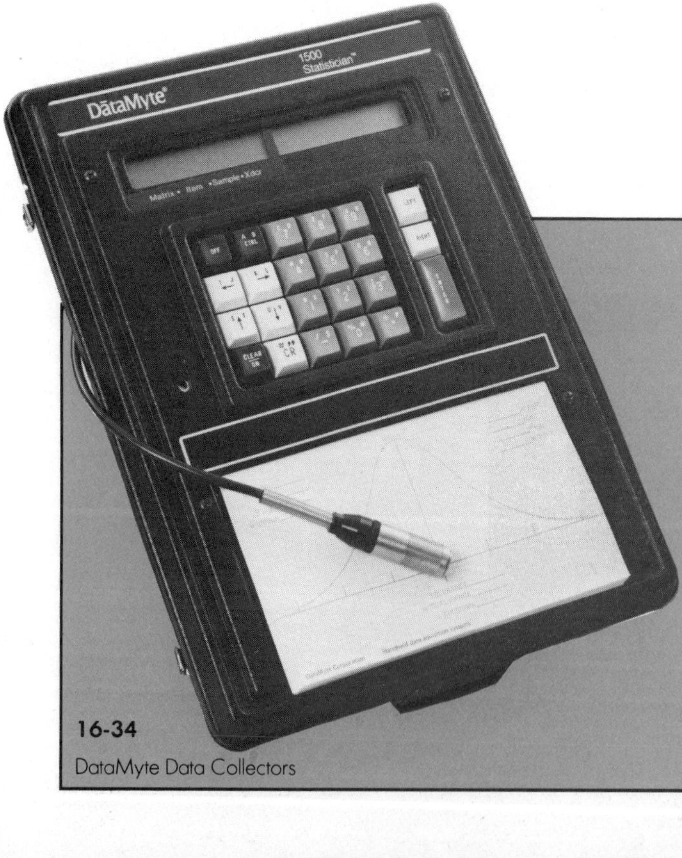

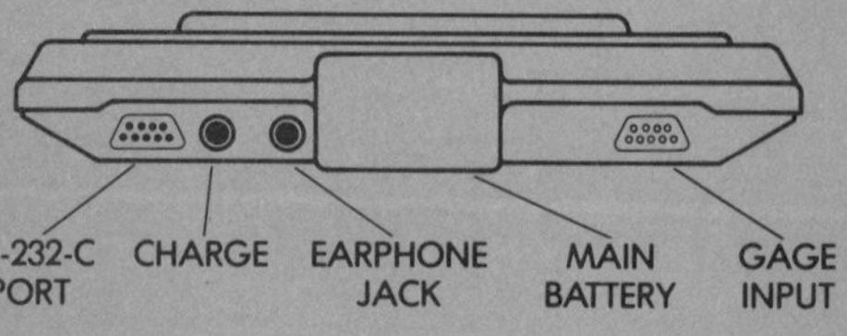

Special Features

- For coating thickness
- Math function for sums and differences
- Compares subgroups to control limits and displays IN CNTL or OUT CNTL as appropriate.

Other Features

- Resolution: 0.05 mils
- Accuracy: ±1% within ±3 mils of calibration point
- Range: 0 to 40 mil
- Stainless steel and aluminum probe body construction
- Fast, two-step calibration procedure.
- Algorithm automatically records the coating thickness upon probe contact.
- 64K character memory size.
- Serial RS-232C I/O channel.
- Fully selectable communications protocol.
- Fourteen hours continuous on time or 200 hours, stand-by between chargings. The 1559 has an internal standby battery as well as a removable main battery.
- Size: 13 x 10 x 1.5 inches (33 x 25 x 3.75 cm)
- Weight: 4.25 lb. (2.2 kg)

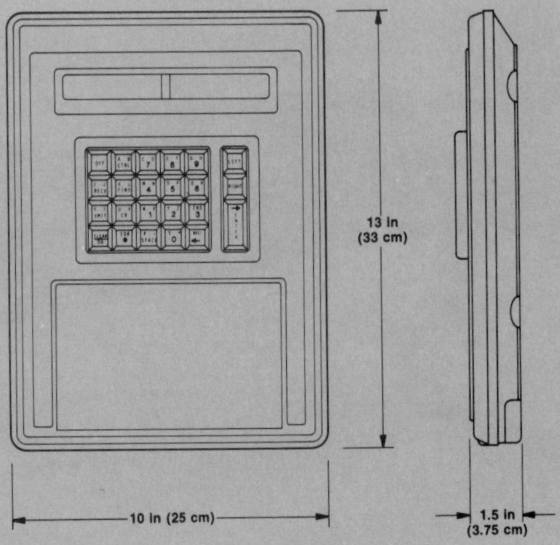

DātaMyte

HANDHELD ATTRIBUTE DATA COLLECTORS

1005 AND 1010 Data Collectors

The model 1005 and 1010 are ideal for attribute data collection. Externally they are similar to the more dedicated 1500 series, but internally they are quite different. Rather than having a matrix type memory suitable only for variables data collection, the memory is flexible, allowing up to 32 alphanumeric characters per entry. It can be configured to fit a given application, whether paint auditing, inventory cycle counting, preventive maintenance data collection, or magnetic stripe and bar code reading.

The handheld data collector comes in a selection of memory sizes, and has a 16-character LCD display, 23-key keypad, RS-232C port, and audible buzzer. There are many features worth noting in particular. It has a programmable clock, letting you automatically enter a clock time with each data entry. It has prompting, including nested prompts — loops within loops of prompt messages — that sequence data collection in a variety of ways. The devices it can interface with include serial RS-232C gages or fixed station equipment such as electronic balances; also, an optional bar code wand, IBM magnetic hand scanner and others. The 1010 can also be used for processing time study data. Use your own coding system to enter data. You can simply plug the 1010 into its dedicated printer, and the 1010 calculates and prints the time study reports all by itself.

For example of use, see pp. 7-5, 8-3, 9-13, 11-10, 11-14, 12-12, 12-15, 12-18, 13-17, 14-7, 14-10, 14-15 and 14-28.

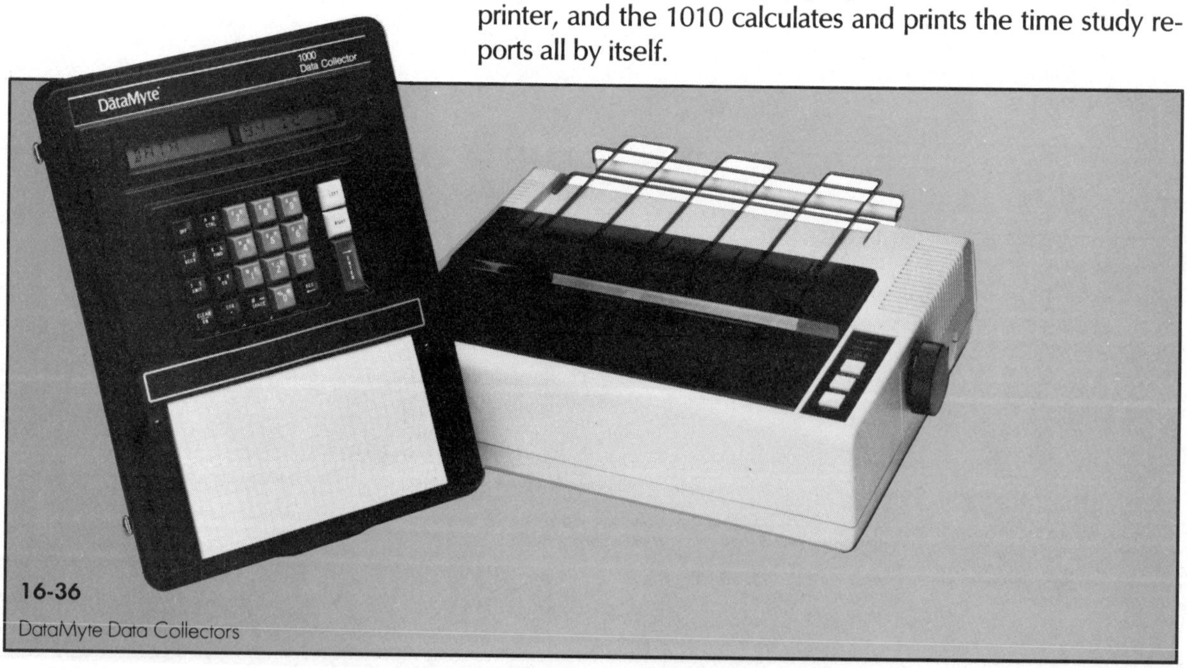

Distinguishing Features

- Full alphanumeric entry. Individual entries can be up to 32 characters wide.
- 16, 32, or 64K character memory size. Up to 8 separate records can be kept.
- Programmable headers, prompts, and parts list sections.
- Terminal mode for keyboard sign-on to a computer system.
- Clock, for military time, tenths, hundredths of a minute and thousandths of an hour.
- Serial RS-232C data input capability.
- Data logging, auto entry, and limit checking during data collection.
- Computer controlled downloading and uploading.
- Reports formatter for setting line lengths, etc.
- Weight — 4.25 lb. (2.2 kg)
- Operating Temp. — 32 to 122° F (0 to 50° C) for optimum battery performance.
- Main Battery — Rechargeable, removable, 12 to 18 hours of operation.
- Memory Retention — 15 hours without main battery, 200 hours with main battery.
- Keyboard — Alphanumeric (0-9, A-Z, some symbols).
- Input/Output — ASCII serial RS-232C port or 20 mA current loop.
- Transmission Rate — Selectable baud rates of 110, 150, 300, 600, 1200, 2400, or 4800.
- External control — Stop transmission, resume transmission, transmit next line (ACK), transmit last line (NAK).
- Display — 16-digit, 0.315 inch (0.8 cm) LCD.

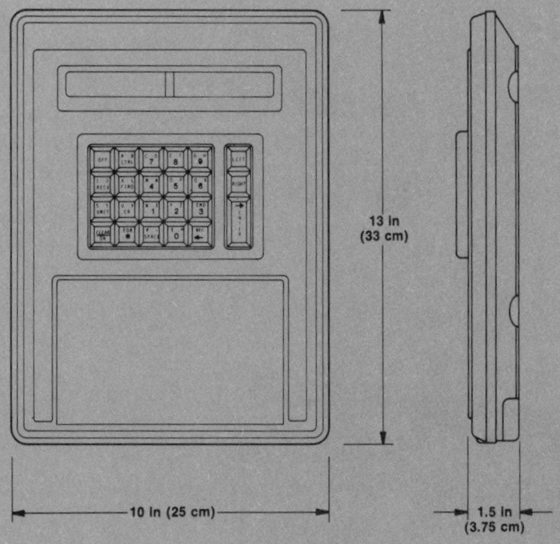

16.3 ACCESSORIES FOR DATAMYTE® DATA COLLECTORS

DataTruck® Data Collector

The DataTruck is used to harvest data from fixed-station data collectors located throughout a plant. It is the vital link in the unwired FAN® (Factory Area Network) system. The DataTruck can transfer setup information to a data collector as well as unload the memory contents of a data collector and transmit it to an IBM PC. See Chapter 15 for a description of the FAN system and how the DataTruck works within it.

Transfer of a file to and from a data collector takes about ten seconds.

For examples of use, see pp. 8-3, 8-8, 8-9, 10-5, 10-9, 10-12, 12-4, 12-12, 13-9, 13-12 and 13-14.

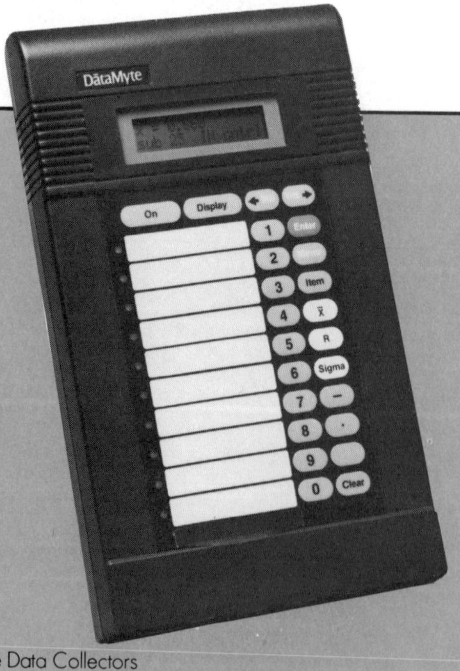

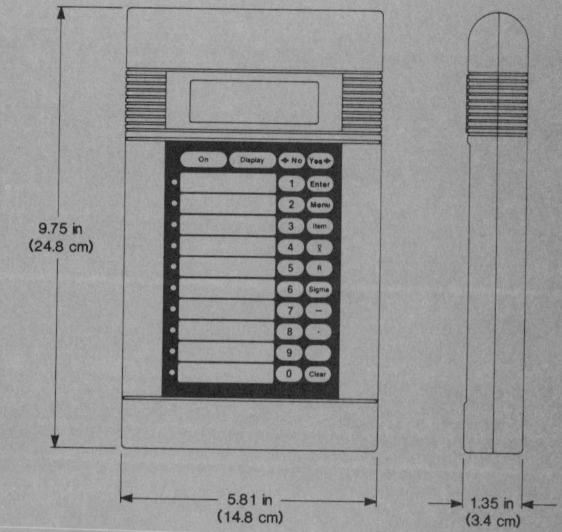

Special Features

- No gage port
- 50,000 reading capacity

Other Features

- Interfaces with FAN software
- Easy, menu-driven operation
- 24 tactile membrane keys
- Two-line by 16 character LCD display
- Selectable RS-232C transmission rates
- Nicad battery operated, with AC charger/adaptor
- 16 hours continuous on time using battery only
- Unit turns off after eight minutes non-use
- Rugged ABS plastic case, oil and water resistant
- Weighs about 2 lb. (0.9 kg)

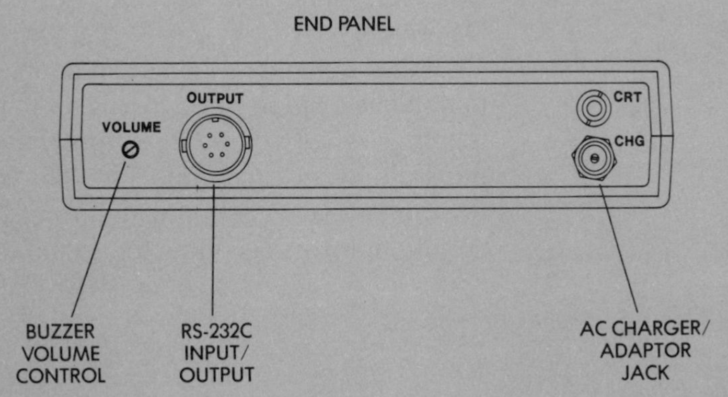

DataMyte Gage Multiplexer

The DataMyte Gage Mulitplexer is ideal for multiple-gage fixtures, where many measurements of one part of assembly are taken at the same time. When using a multiplexer, you place the part in the fixture and adjust the gages. Once the gages are put into place, record the readings from all the gages in the data collector by pressing the footswitch.

Each multiplexer can connect to eight gages. The multiplexer extends the gage capabilities of these DataMyte data collectors:

- 750
- 762
- 862
- 1556/1756
- 1558/1758
- 2003
- 2005

The multiplexer is available in four different models; one each for digital indicators from Fowler, Mitutoyo, Federal or Ono-Sokki. With the 762 or 862, you can connect other gages (with the Mitutoyo Digimatic format output) to the multiplexer. For instance, you might have several Mitutoyo digital indicators connected to a multiplexer, as well as a height gage and a bore gage.

Refer to the chart on the next page to see which multiplexer models can be used with a particular DataMyte data collector. All necessary interface cables are available from DataMyte.

All data collector models can connect to more than one multiplexer. Some need to "daisychain" the multiplexers together, while others have more than one input port that the multiplexer can connect to. Daisychaining means that the multiplexers are connected to each other, and one of the multiplexers is connected to the data collector.

For an example of use, see pg. 8-3.

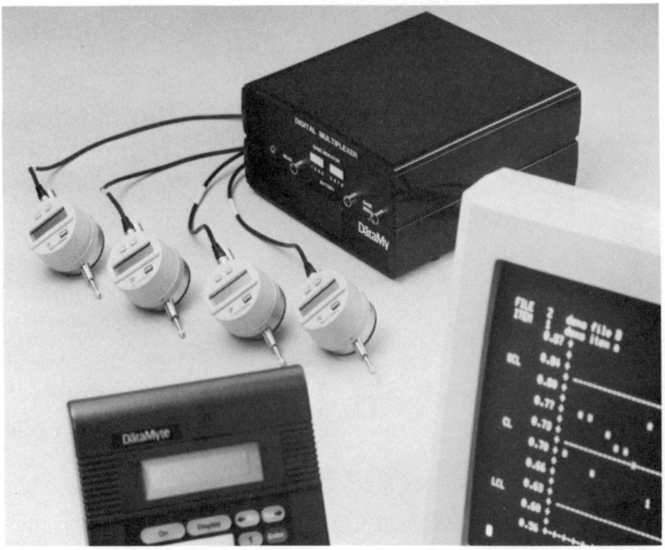

DataMyte Gage Multiplexer Model Numbers and Gage Compatibility

	Federal Maxμm	Fowler Ultra-Digit I or II	Mitutoyo Digimatic Indicators	Other gages with Mitutoyo Digimatic format output	Ono-Sokki
750		529-08	529-03		
762	529-09	529-08	529-07	529-07	529-10
862	529-09	529-08	529-07	529-07	529-10
1556/1756		529-06			
1558/1758		529-06	529-05		
2003		529-04	529-03		
2005	529-09	529-08	529-07	529-07	529-10

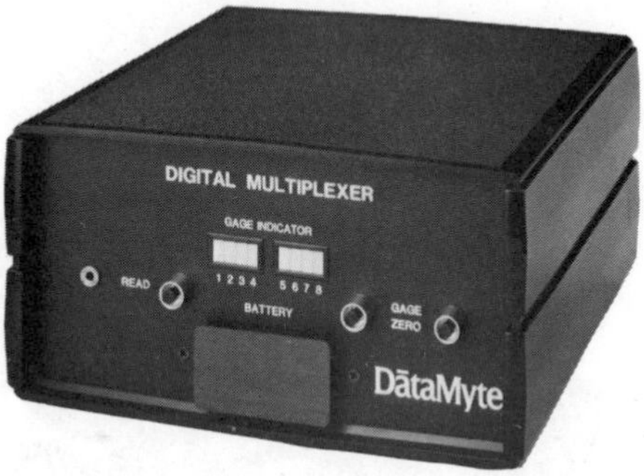

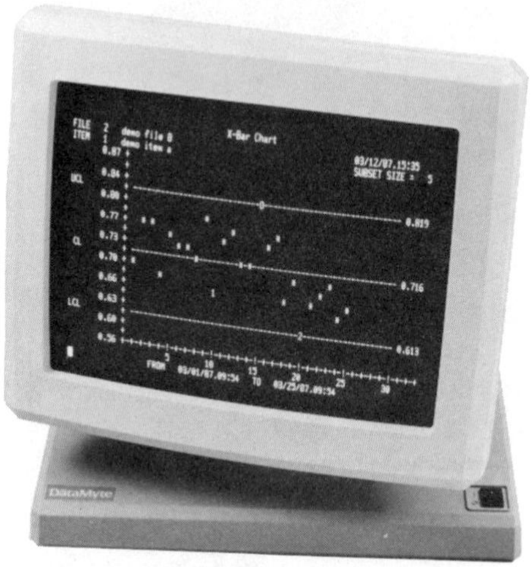

Video Monitor

The DataMyte Video Monitor is used with fixed-station data collectors to display control charts and histograms. It provides visible feedback for a machine operator at the gaging station. The monitor connects by cable to the data collector, and communicates at 9600 baud, so charts are quickly displayed.

The monitor has a 12-inch diagonal screen and uses the ANSI (American National Standards Institute) extended character set. The ANSI character set allows the monitor to display points that are part of a trend to blink continuously, if the data collector sending the chart has the trend alert feature.

Interface Cables

DataMyte has gage interface and communications cables for a large number of gaging and communications applications. An appropriate cable can be ordered from DataMyte to interface any of the gages featured in Chapter 17, as well as many other gages. Communications cables are available to interface DataMytes to a number of popular computer systems.

INTERFACE CABLE

High Speed Printers

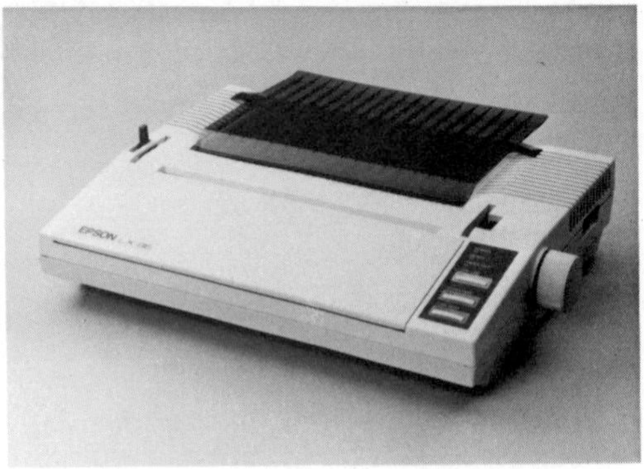

Two printers are available from DataMyte. One prints at 100 characters per second and the other at 160 characters per second. Both are configured for serial RS-232C communications. The printers can be used with any DataMyte data collector but they are required for obtaining graphic reports from the 1700, 1500, or 1000 series. An interface cable is included with each printer.

Battery Charger/Adaptor

The battery charger and adaptor is included with all DataMyte data collectors. There are both 110 and 220 volts AC models. The charger will bring a DataMyte up to charge in 14 to 16 hours. When connected to the DataMyte, the charger becomes an AC adaptor for fixed station operation. (The main battery must remain in the DataMyte during fixed station operation.)

Battery Charger for DataMyte 2000

The 2000 battery charger accessory will charge the 2000 battery pack while it is removed from the data collector. This lets you keep a spare battery pack charged all the time. The charger accessory plugs into the AC charger/adaptor.

17. GAGES

INTRODUCTION

This chapter features a sampling of current gaging that will interface with DataMyte data collectors. It is by no means a complete selection, but it is fairly representative of the types of measurement applications well suited to monitoring for SPC.

As shown in Table 17.0.1, most DataMyte data collectors will interface with more than one type of gage. Because there is no standard gage output format, no single data collector can interface with every gage. Use Table 17.0.1 to help select the DataMyte system for your gaging applications.

Some of the handheld gages — the gap gages and torque wrenches in particular — are offered exclusively by DataMyte. Other gages in the chapter are available from the manufacturer or distributor listed.

GAGE MODELS	DATAMYTE DATA COLLECTORS MODELS								
	750	753	754	761/ 861	762/ 862	1556	1558	2005	2003
Ametek Force Gage and Interface	•				•	•	•	•	•
Anilan Wizard Digital Readout	•				•			•	•
Autech Model 200 Diameter Measuring System	•				•			•	•
Bendix Cordax MPP-2 Coordinate Measuring Machine	•				•	•	•	•	•
Boeckler Microcode II Digital Readouts	•								•
Bottle Cap Torque/Force Tester	•				•			•	•
Brookfield Viscometer (Analog)				•			•		•
Carlson Spring Tester	•				•			•	•
Chatillon Digital Force Gage & Interface	•				•		•	•	•
Check•Line Coating Thickness Tester	•				•			•	•
Chicago Dial Indicator					•			•	
CMI International Model MR 300	•				•			•	•
Column Gages and Readouts				•					
Corning Model 155 pH/Ion Meter	•				•			•	•
DataMyte 514 Gap Gage		•				•			•
DataMyte 516 Gap Gage		•				•			•
Demco Contour and Outline Transducer		•				•			•
Dillon Force Gage	•				•			•	•
Federal Maxμm Digital Indicator			•		•			•	
Fischerscope Multi	•				•			•	•
Fowler Digitrix II Micrometer	•				•		•	•	•
Fowler Sylvac Measuring System					•			•	
Fowler Sylvac Ultra-Cal II Caliper					•			•	•
Fowler Trimos Mini Vertical					•			•	
Fowler Trimos Vertical Measuring System					•			•	
Fowler Ultra Cal II Groove & Recess Gage					•			•	•
Fowler Ultra-Digit I and II Indicators	•				•	•	•	•	•
Fowler Ultra-Height Digital Height Gage					•			•	•
Fryer Electronic Score Residual Gage	•				•		•	•	•
J.S. Research Gap and Contour Gage		•				•			•
Larson Spring Tester	•				•			•	•
LaserMike Optical Micrometer	•				•	•	•	•	•
Laseruler Vertical Bench Micrometer	•				•	•	•	•	•
Mauser Caliper					•			•	•
Mauser Digital Linear Scale					•			•	•
Mauser Height Gage					•			•	•
Mauser Indicator					•			•	•
Mauser Micrometer					•			•	•
Max-Cal Caliper (NSK)	•				•		•	•	•

Table 17.0.1. Gages and DataMyte models that interface with them.

GAGE MODELS	DATAMYTE DATA COLLECTORS MODELS								
	750	753	754	761/ 861	762/ 862	1556	1558	2005	2003
MBC MetraByte Digital Panel Meter	•				•			•	•
Mettler Weigh Scale	•				•	•	•	•	•
Micro-Derm MP 700D	•				•			•	•
Micro Dur Hardness Tester					•			•	
Micro-Vu MD-1 Metrology Computer	•				•	•	•	•	•
Mitutoyo Digimatic Holtest Gage	•				•			•	•
Mitutoyo Digi-Matic Height Gage	•				•		•	•	•
Mitutoyo Digi-Matic Indicator (543-162 & 543-135)	•				•		•	•	•
Mitutoyo Digi-Matic Indicator (543-425)	•				•		•	•	•
Mitutoyo Digi-matic Caliper	•				•		•	•	•
Mitutoyo Hardness Tester	•				•		•	•	•
Mitutoyo Micrometers (Series 293-311 & 293-711)	•				•		•	•	•
Mitutoyo MU-Gage (Ultrasonic Thickness)	•				•		•	•	•
Nanoscope Flaw Detector	•				•	•	•	•	•
Numerex BRN-18 Height Gage	•				•			•	•
Numerex DMM 624 Coordinate Measuring Machine	•				•			•	•
Ohaus Weigh Scale	•				•	•	•	•	•
Omega M 2110-2 Multi Meter	•				•			•	•
Ono Sokki EG Series Digital Linear Gage					•			•	
Orion Expandable Ion Analyzer									•
Quadra Check II Metrology Display	•				•			•	•
RD 918 MacBeth Densitometer	•				•			•	
Sartorious Weigh Scale	•				•	•	•	•	•
Scherr Tumico Series Caliper					•			•	•
Schleuniger-4M Pharmaceutical Hardness Tester	•				•			•	•
Sensor I Wrench	•				•	•	•	•	•
Series 500 Digital Hardness Tester	•				•		•	•	•
Sheffield Profilometer	•				•			•	•
Starrett 722 Caliper	•				•			•	•
Surfometer Measuring System	•				•			•	•
Sylvac Holmikes Bore Gage					•			•	•
Thor In-Line Torque Transducers		•				•			•
Torque Wrenches						•			•
UPA Technologies Caviderm CD-8	•				•			•	•
UTA Rotary Transducers		•			•				•
WACO Digital Enamel Rater	•				•			•	
Zygo Laser Telemetric System	•				•	•	•	•	•
#1792 Reflected Image Meter	•				•	•	•	•	•

17.1 HANDHELD GAGES

Max-Cal Caliper (NSK)

Fred V. Fowler Co., Inc.

Both a 6 and 8 inch caliper are available. They can read four types of measurements: inside, outside, step, and depth. All readings are displayed on its LCD display, which is independent of the data collector.

- Range: 150 mm (6 in.) or 200 mm (8 in.)
- Resolution: 0.001 mm (0.0001 in.)
- Accuracy: $\pm$0.03 mm ($\pm$0.011 in.)
- Quantization Error: 1 digit
- Operating Temp: 0 to 40° C (32 to 104° F)
- Storage Temp: −10 to 60° C (14 to 140° F)
- Battery: 2 × SR44 silver oxide
- Battery Life: 12 months normal use
- Interface cable
- Instructions

DataMyte models for gage:

- 750
- 762
- 862
- 2003
- 2005

ALL SPECIFICATIONS SUBJECT TO CHANGE WITHOUT NOTICE.

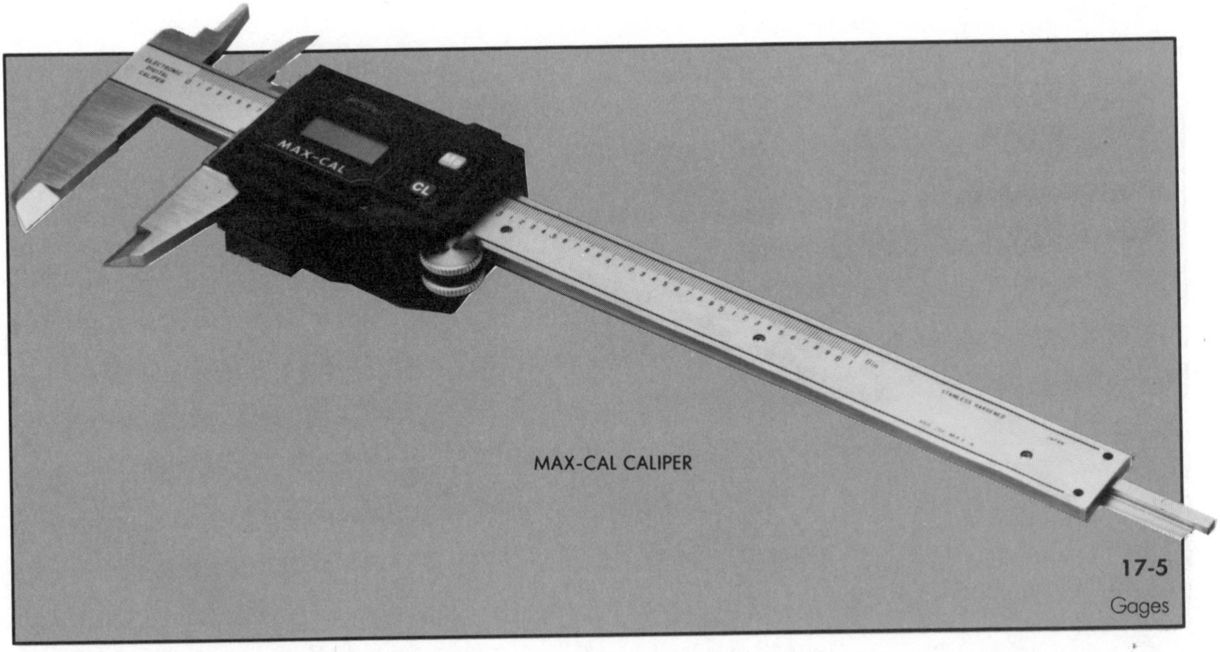

MAX-CAL CALIPER

DataMyte

Mitutoyo 293-311 & 293-711 Series Micrometers

MTI Corporation

Specifications

MODEL	311/711	312/712	313	314
RANGE	0 to 25mm 0 to 1 in.	25 to 50 mm 1 to 2 in.	50 to 75 mm 2 to 3 in.	75 to 100 mm 3 to 4 in.

DataMyte models for gage:
- 750
- 762
- 1558
- 862
- 2003
- 2005

Multiplexer for DataMyte:
- 529-07 (762, 862. 2005)

- Resolution: 0.001 mm (0.0001 in. or .00005 in.)
- Accuracy: ±1 mm
- Quantization Error: 1 digit
- Operating Temp: 0 to 40° C (32 to 104° F)
- Storage Temp: −10 to 60° C (14 to 140° F)
- Battery: 3 × U-5 alkaline magnesium AM-5 (LR-1)
- Battery Life: 500 hours continuous
- Interface cable
- Inch standard (metric standards available)
- Operating instructions
- Carrying case

For an example of use, see pg. 11-3.

ALL SPECIFICATIONS SUBJECT TO CHANGE WITHOUT NOTICE.

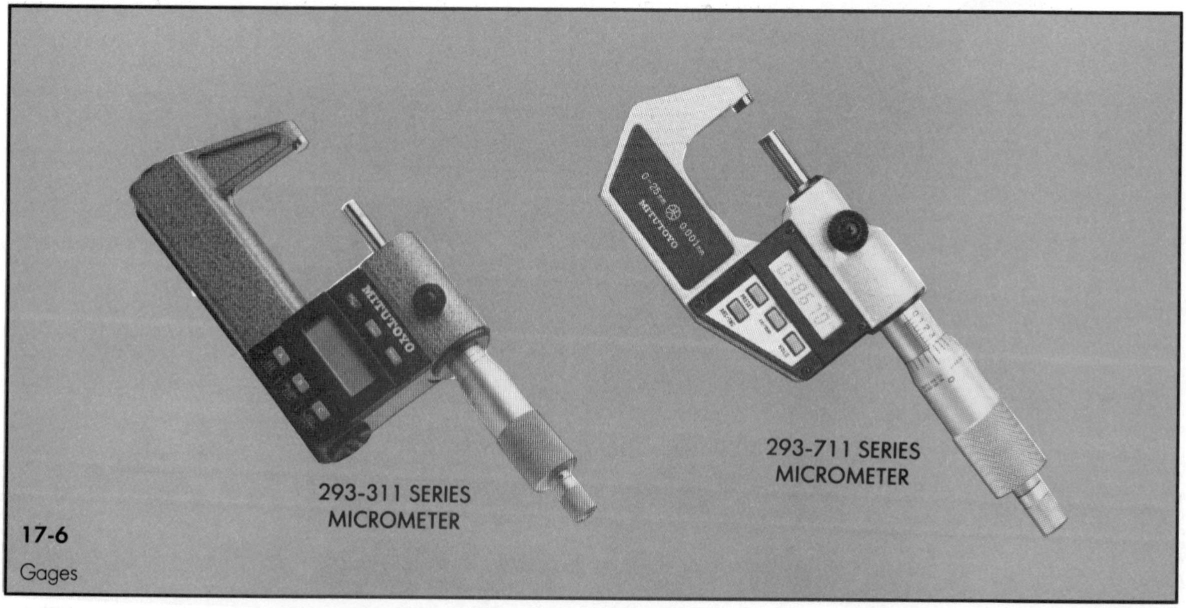

293-311 SERIES MICROMETER

293-711 SERIES MICROMETER

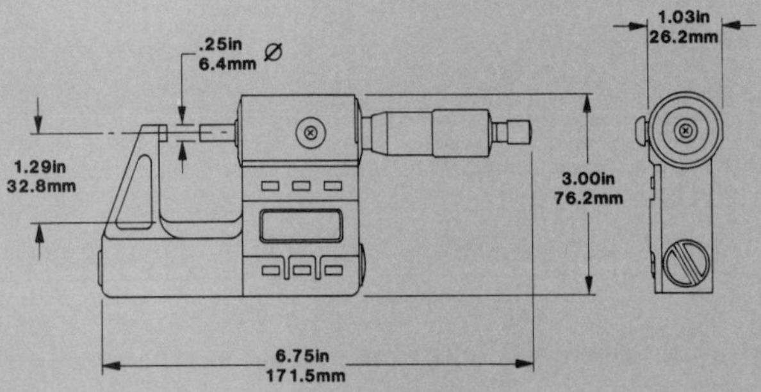

0 to 1 in.

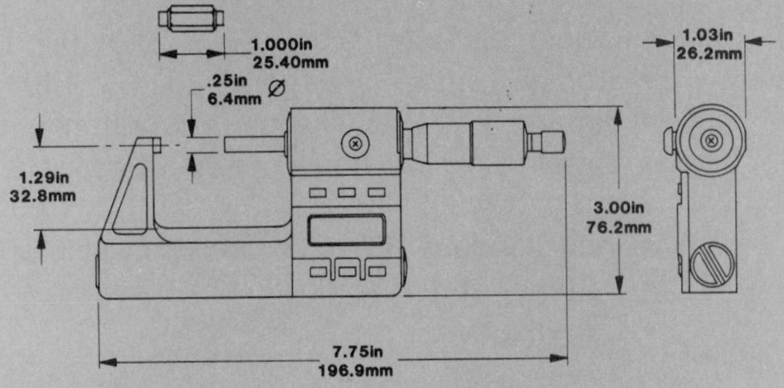

1 to 2 in.

2 to 3 in.

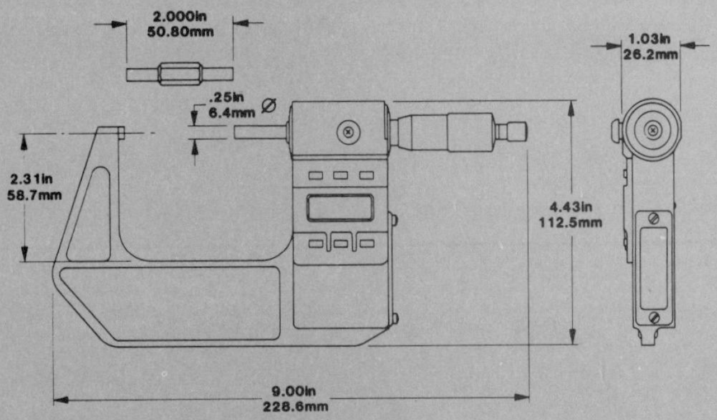

3 to 4 in.

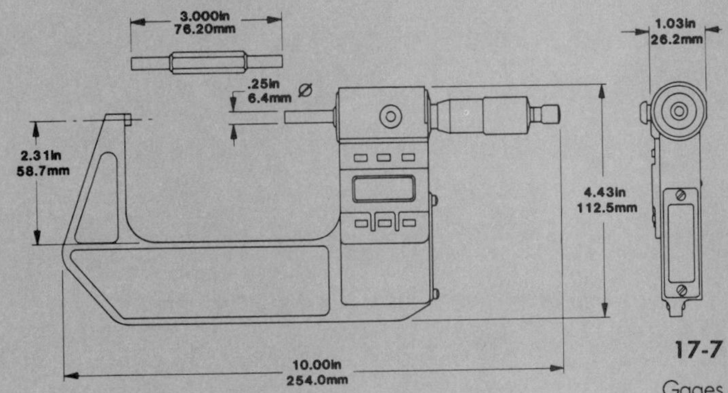

DataMyte

Fowler Digitrix II Micrometer
Fred V. Fowler Co., Inc.

Specifications

RANGE	0 to 25mm 0 to 1 in.	25 to 50 mm 1 to 2 in.	50 to 75 mm 2 to 3 in.	75 to 100 mm 3 to 4 in.

DataMyte models for gage:
- 750
- 762
- 1558
- 862
- 2003
- 2005

- Resolution: 0.001 mm (.00005 in.)
- Accuracy: 0.001 mm (0.0001 in.)
- Quantization Error: ± 1 digit
- Operating Temp: 0 to 40° C (32 to 104° F)
- Storage Temp: − 10 to 60° C (14 to 140° F)
- Battery: 3 × U-5 alkaline magnesium AM-5(LR-1)
- Battery Life: 500 hours continuous
- Interface cable
- Inch standard (metric standards available)
- Batteries and operating instructions
- Carrying case

ALL SPECIFICATIONS SUBJECT TO CHANGE WITHOUT NOTICE.

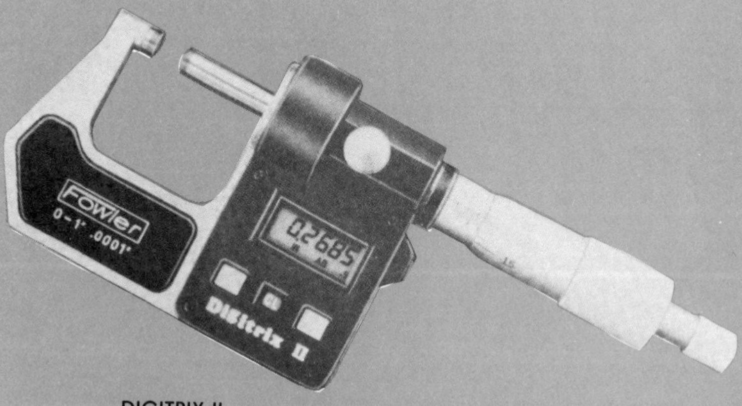

DIGITRIX II
MICROMETER

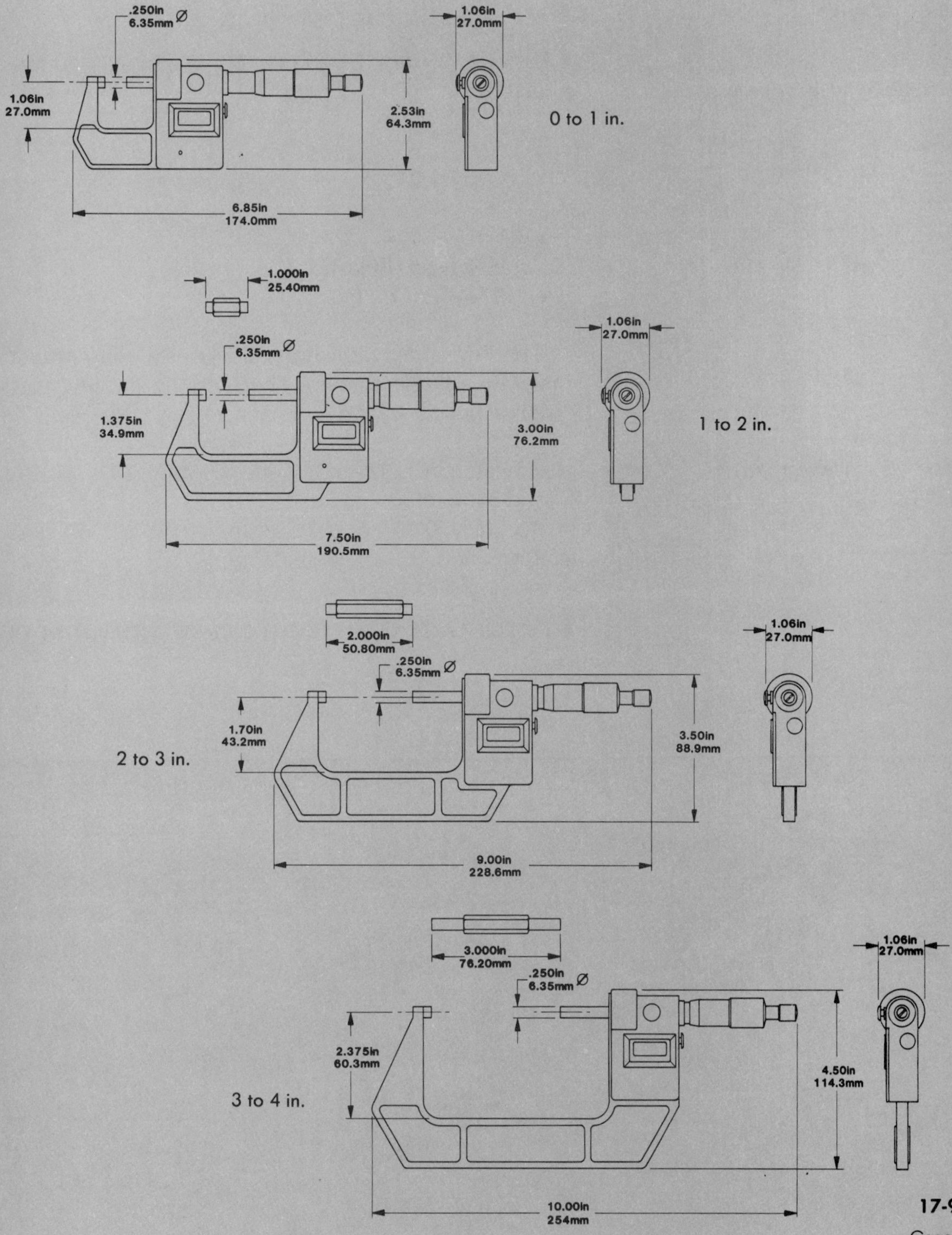

.250in
6.35mm Ø
1.06in
27.0mm
1.06in
27.0mm
2.53in
64.3mm
6.85in
174.0mm
0 to 1 in.
1.000in
25.40mm
.250in
6.35mm Ø
1.06in
27.0mm
1.375in
34.9mm
3.00in
76.2mm
7.50in
190.5mm
1 to 2 in.
2.000in
50.80mm
.250in
6.35mm Ø
1.06in
27.0mm
1.70in
43.2mm
3.50in
88.9mm
9.00in
228.6mm
2 to 3 in.
3.000in
76.20mm
.250in
6.35mm Ø
1.06in
27.0mm
2.375in
60.3mm
4.50in
114.3mm
10.00in
254mm
3 to 4 in.

DātaMyte

Mauser Micrometer

Precision Measuring Instruments

DataMyte models for gage:
- 762
- 862
- 2003
- 2005

- Range: 0-25 mm, 25-50 mm, 50-75 mm, 75-100 mm
- Resolution: 0.001 mm (.00005 in)

Fowler Sylvac Ultra-Cal II

Fred V. Fowler Co., Inc.

The Fowler Sylvac Ultra-Cal II uses a non-contact capacitative linear system. There are no moving parts to break down or wear out. Four size ranges are available.

DataMyte models for gage:
- 762
- 862
- 2003
- 2005

- Ranges: 6 in. (152 mm), 12 in. (305 mm), 20 in. (500 mm), and 32 in. (800 mm)
- Accuracy: 0.001 in. (0.025 mm)
- Resolution: 0.0005 in. (0.01 mm)

ALL SPECIFICATIONS SUBJECT TO CHANGE WITHOUT NOTICE.

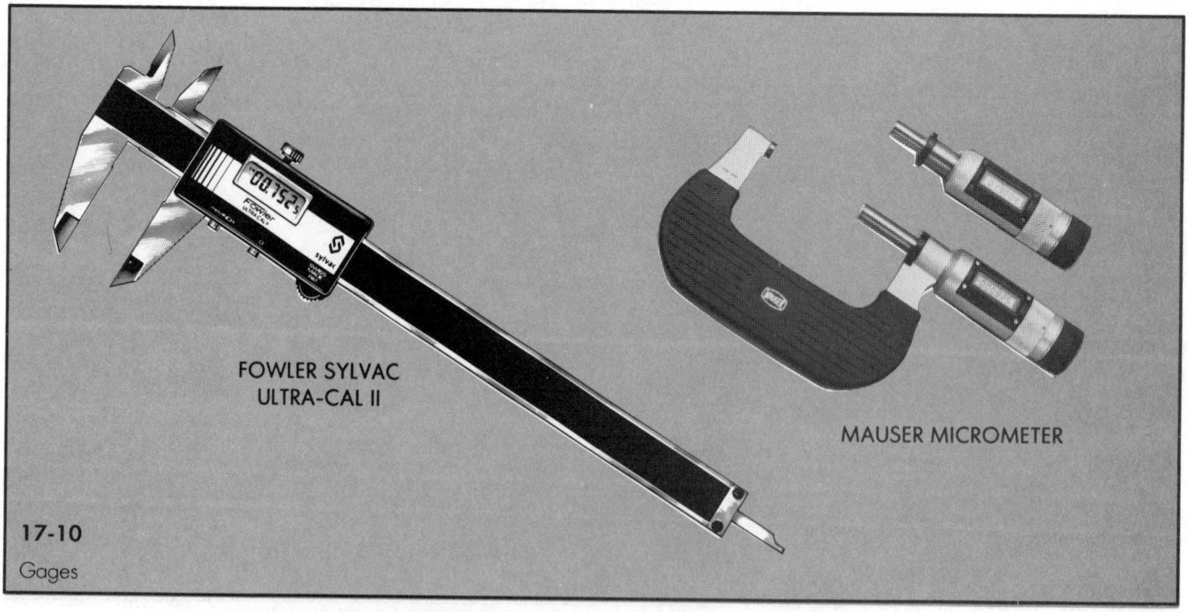

Mitutoyo Digi-Matic Caliper
MTI Corporation

- Range: 6 in. (152 mm), 8 in. (203 mm)
- Resolution: 0.0005 in. (0.01 mm)
- Accuracy: ±0.03 mm

DataMyte models for gage:
- 750
- 762
- 1558
- 862
- 2003
- 2005

Multiplexer for DataMyte:
- 529-07 (762, 862, 2005)

Scherr Tumico Group 10 Electronic Calipers
S-T Industries

Range:	6 in. (152 mm)	8 in. (203 mm)	12 in. (305 mm)	24 in. (610 mm)
Accuracy:	0.001 in. (0.025 mm)	0.001 in. (0.025 mm)	±0.001 in. (0.025 mm)	±0.001 in. (0.025 mm)
Resolution:	0.0005 in. (0.01 mm)	0.0005 in. (0.01 mm)	0.0005 in. (0.01 mm)	0.0005 in. (0.01 mm)

DataMyte models for gage:
- 762
- 862
- 2003
- 2005

ALL SPECIFICATIONS SUBJECT TO CHANGE WITHOUT NOTICE.

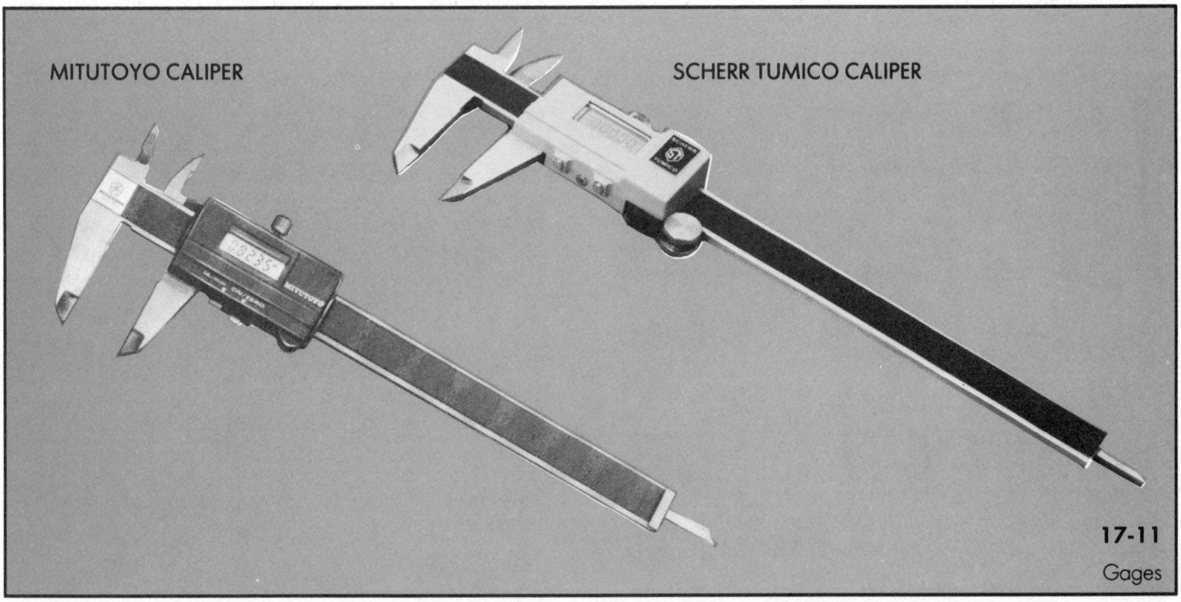

Mauser Caliper (NSK)
Precision Measuring Instruments

DataMyte models for gage:
- 762
- 862
- 2003
- 2005

- Range: From 150 to 1000 mm

Starrett 722 Caliper
L.S. Starrett Company

DataMyte models for gage:
- 750
- 762
- 862
- 2003
- 2005

- Accuracy ±0.025 mm (±0.001 in.)
- Range: 150 mm (0 to 6 in)

ALL SPECIFICATIONS SUBJECT TO CHANGE WITHOUT NOTICE.

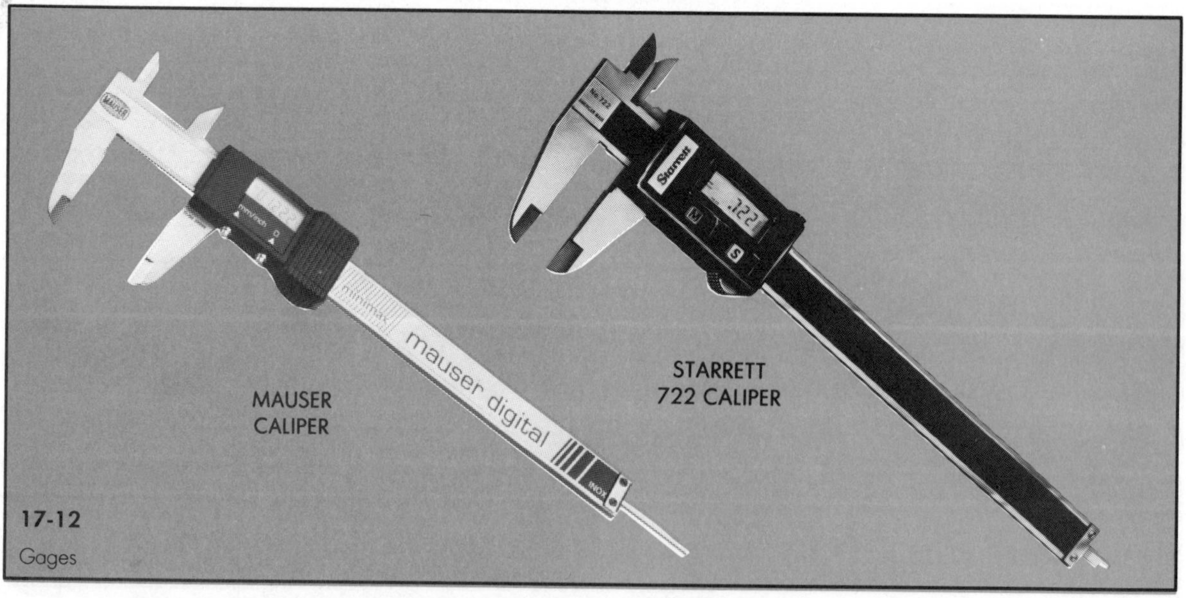

Fowler Ultra-Cal II Groove and Recess Gage
Fred V. Fowler Co., Inc.

- Internal Range: 1.378-8.030 in. (35-204 mm)
- Outside Range: 9.433 in. (240 mm)
- Resolution: 0.0005 in. (0.01 mm)

DataMyte models for gage:
- 762
- 862
- 2003
- 2005

J.S. Research Gap and Contour Gage
J.S. Research

- Range and resolution depends on gage and data collector used.

DataMyte models for gage:
- 753
- 1556
- 2003

Demco Contour and Outline Transducer
Demco Research and Development

- Range and resolution depends on gage and data collector used.

DataMyte models for gage:
- 753
- 1556
- 2003

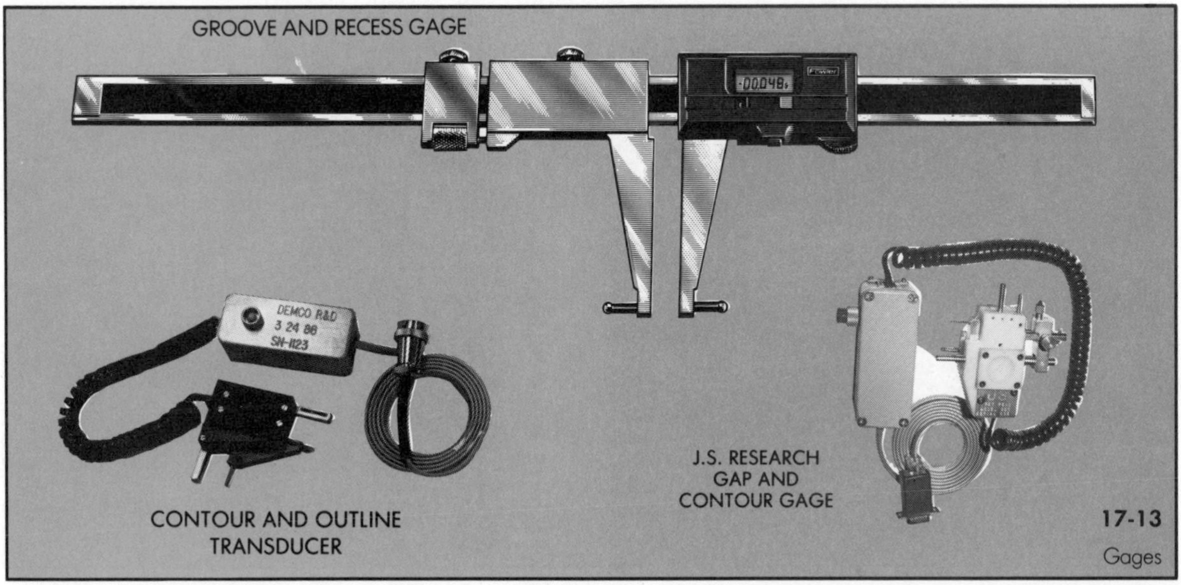

DātaMyte

514 Gap Gage
Available from DataMyte

The 514 Gap Gage is used to quickly measure and instantly record gap measurements between adjacent parts, parts in ring or margin fixtures, and any application where the amount of gap is critical to either the appearance or function of a product. This gage was designed for versatility. By substituting various easily fabricated fingers and attachments, the gage can be used to check depth, diameters, clearance in hard to reach areas, and other special types of measurements.

Several models are available, in different resolutions and with either gap fingers or a depth checking attachment.

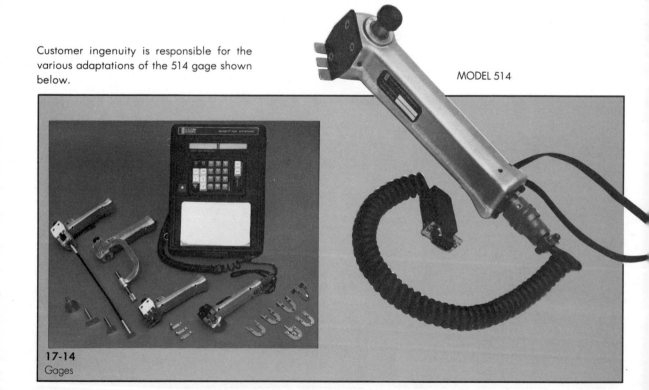

To order, select required range from specifications table and specify the corresponding model number.

DataMyte models for gage:
- 753
- 1556
- 2003

For examples of use, see pp. 14-3, 14-17, 14-19.

Customer ingenuity is responsible for the various adaptations of the 514 gage shown below.

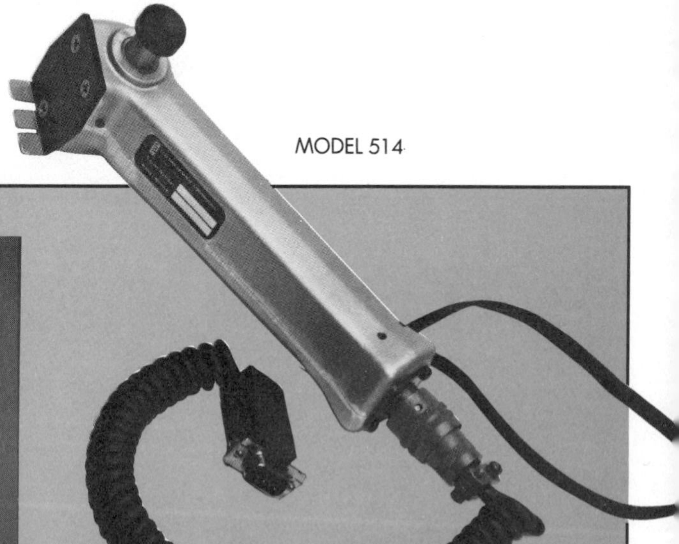

MODEL 514

Specifications

MODEL	514
RANGE	0.065 to 0.540 in.
RESOLUTION	0.002 in.
INACCURACY	±0.25%
NON-REPEATABILITY	0.1%
QUANTIZATION ERROR	±0.001 in.
WEIGHT	412g 14.5 oz.

* Call the DataMyte Sales Dept. for availability.

- Operating Temp: 0 to 50° C (32 to 122° F)
- Storage Temp: −30 to 70° C (−22 to 158° F)
- Battery: Powered from the DataMyte battery
- Battery Life: 12 hours minimum at 25° C
- Interface cable
- Built-in re-try switch
- Will measure in inches or millimeters

ALL SPECIFICATIONS SUBJECT TO CHANGE WITHOUT NOTICE.

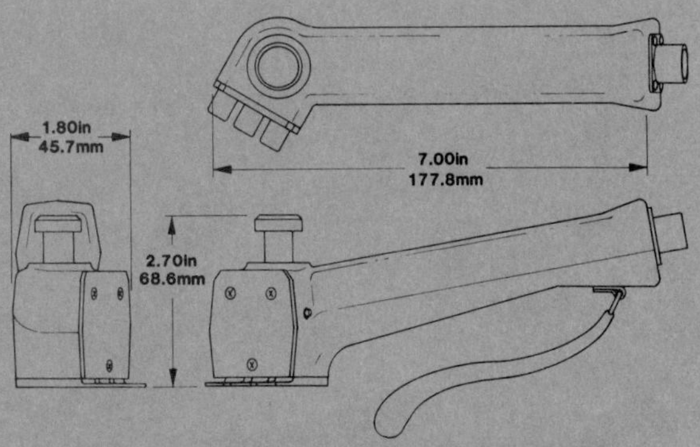

MODEL 514

516 Gap and Flushness Gage

Available from DataMyte

DataMyte models for gage:

- 753
- 1556
- 2003

For examples of use, see pp. 7-2, 8-13, 12-6, 14-4.

This gage enables fast dimensional audits between mating components. The 0.25 in. (6.35 mm) wide fingers allow measurements small radii gaps and hard to reach places. A single gage can be used instead of two because both gap and flushness readings can be made one after another.

Gap measurements are made by placing the upper edge of the fingers against one inner surface, and pulling the trigger until the movable finger contacts the opposite surface of the gap. The data collector automatically records the maximum separation. Flushness is measured using a movable rod and foot. The gage does not need to be perfectly perpendicular to take a reading because of the matching radius of the rod and foot.

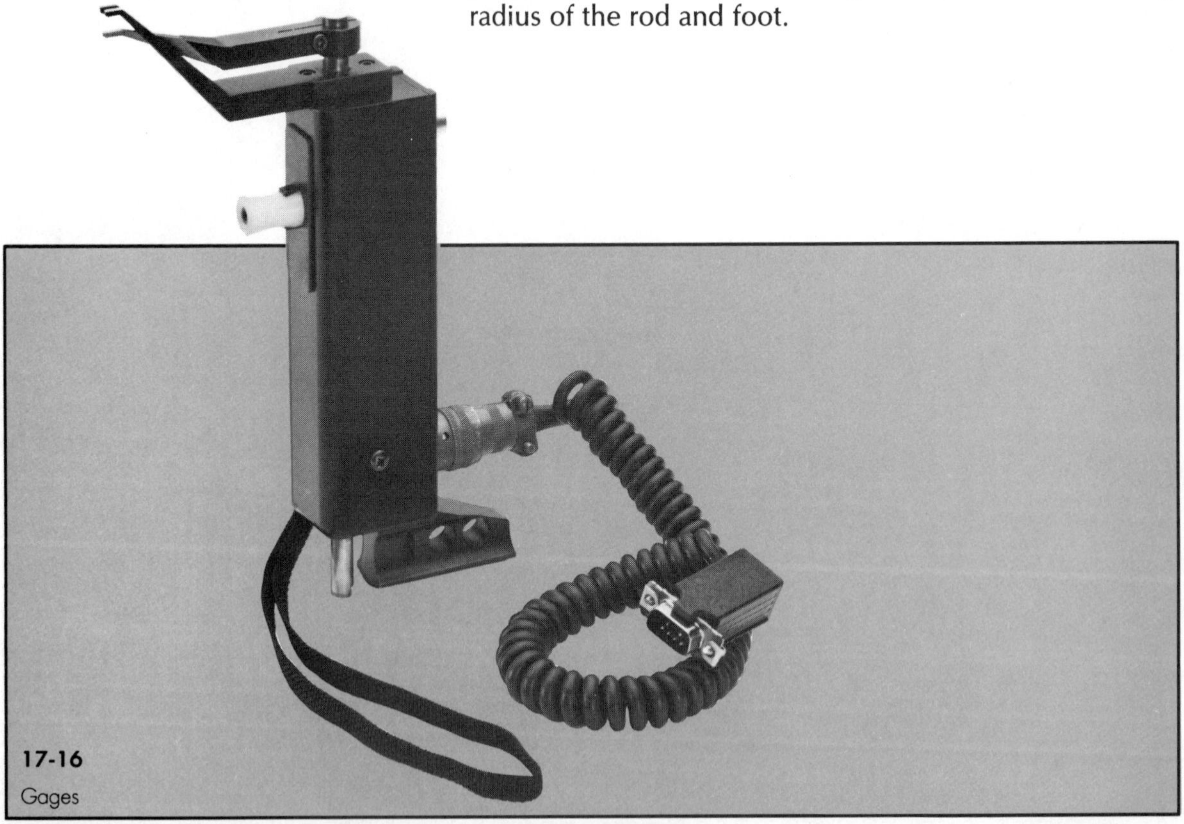

Specifications

- Model: 516
- Range: Gap = 2.54 to 14.48 mm (0.100 to 0.570 in.), Flushness = +6.35 mm to −5.72 mm (+0.250 to −0.225 in.)
- Resolution: 0.050 mm (0.002 in.)
- Inaccuracy: ±0.5%
- Non-repeatability: ±0.20%
- Quantization Error: ±0.025 mm (±0.001 in.)
- Operating Temp: 0 to 50° C (32 to 122° F)
- Storage Temp: −30 to 70° C (−22 to 158° F)
- Weight: 596 g (21 oz.)
- Battery: Powered by the DataMyte battery
- Battery Life: 12 hours minimum at 25° C
- Wrist strap
- Built-in re-try switch
- Will measure in inches or millimeters

ALL SPECIFICATIONS SUBJECT TO CHANGE WITHOUT NOTICE.

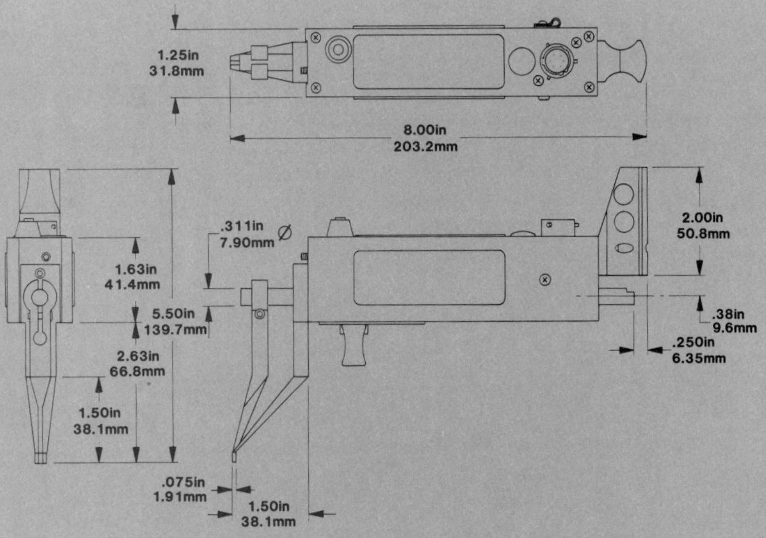

Chatillon Digital Force Gage & Interface
John Chatillon & Sons, Inc.

DataMyte models for gage:
- 750
- 762
- 862
- 2003
- 2005

- Accuracy: ±0.25% of full scale ± least significant digit

Dillon Force Gage
W.C. Dillon & Company, Inc.

DataMyte models for gage:
- 750
- 762
- 862
- 2003
- 2005

- Accuracy: ±0.1% of rated capacity ± least significant digit

ALL SPECIFICATIONS SUBJECT TO CHANGE WITHOUT NOTICE.

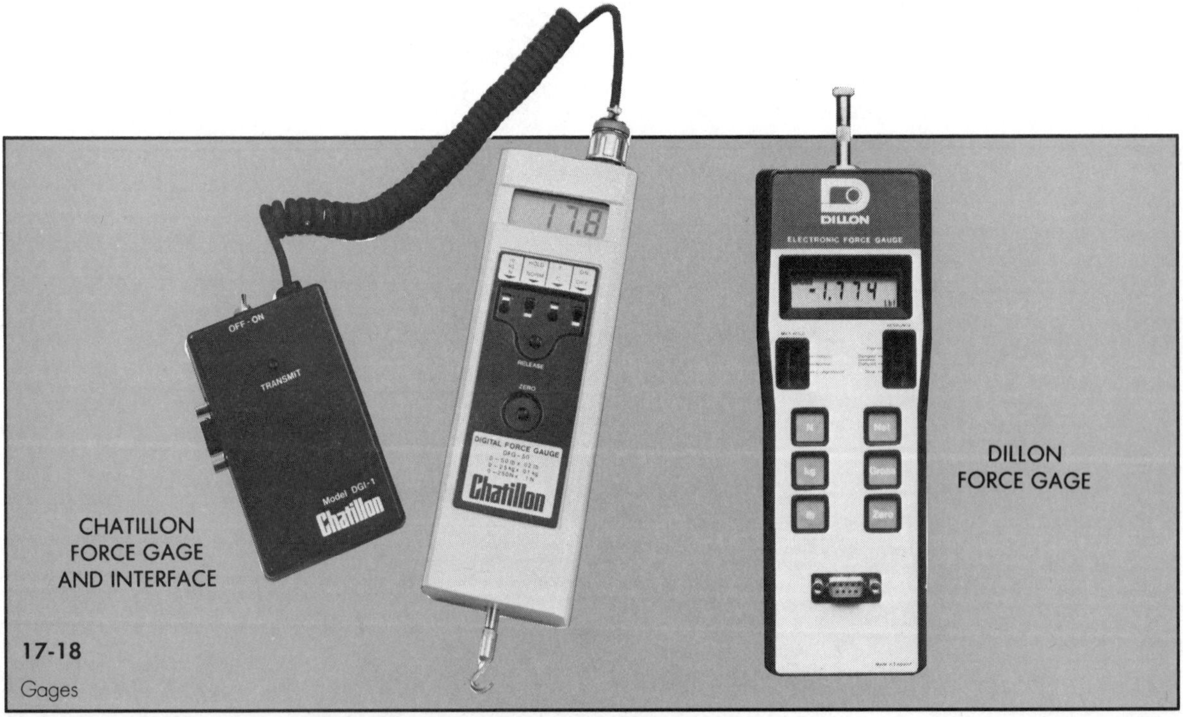

CHATILLON FORCE GAGE AND INTERFACE

DILLON FORCE GAGE

Ametek Force Gage

Hunter Spring Division

The Force Gage Interface connects the Ametek series of AccuForce™ II Force Gages to the data collector. There are three ranges of force gages available. With the gage you can audit opening and closing forces on automobile doors, forces needed for shift lever movement, breakaway forces on body trim parts, or forces required to open drawers.

DataMyte models for gage:

- 750
- 762
- 862
- 2003
- 2005

- Range: 1 lb. (4.4 N), 10 lb. (44 N), 100 lb. (445 N)
- Overload Range: To 150%
- Operating Temp: 10 to 38° C (50 to 100° F)
- Storage Temp: −30 to 60° C (−22 to 140° F)
- Weight: 0.5 kg (1.1 lb)
- Battery: Rechargeable nickel cadmium
- Format: Normal or inverse

ALL SPECIFICATIONS SUBJECT TO CHANGE WITHOUT NOTICE.

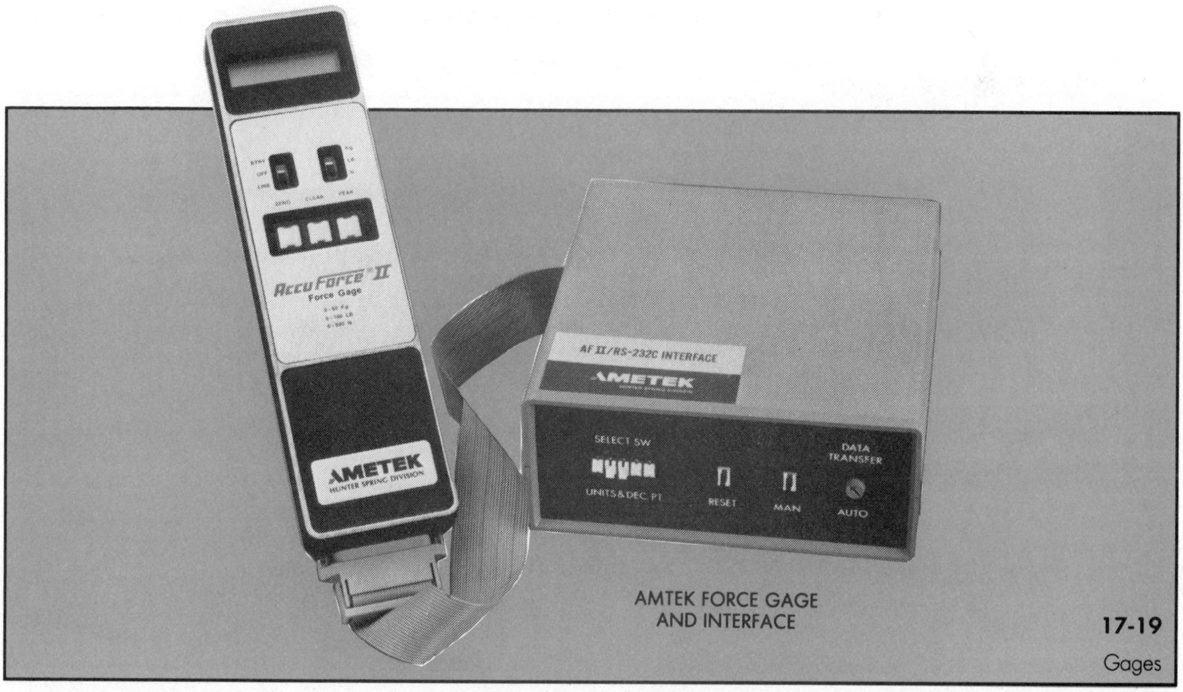

AMTEK FORCE GAGE
AND INTERFACE

DātaMyte

DataMyte models for gage:
- 754
- 762
- 862
- 2005

Multiplexer for DataMyte:
- 529-09 (762, 862, 2005)

Multiplexer Specifications
- For the 862 and 762 up to three multiplexers may be connected to the data collector to interface up to 24 gages.
- The 2005 may have up to six multiplexers connected to it (up to 48 gages).
- Indicator lights show which gage is being used.
- Manual or automatic gage sequencing.

17.2 FIXED STATION GAGING

Federal® Maxµm™ Digital Indicator

Federal Products Corporation

The Federal® Maxµm™ digital electronic indicator has only one moving part, is fully sealed against contaminants and is ruggedly constructed. Five basic models are available. The Maxµm™ is a versatile gage that can be used in many different fixtures:

- Bore gage
- Bench comparator
- Grinding gage
- Remote transducer
- Thickness gage
- I.D./O.D. comparator
- Snap gage

Range	0.01 in.	±0.002 in.	±0.04	±0.199 mm	±1.00 mm
Resolution:	0.0005 in.	0.0001 in.	0.0001 in.	0.001 mm	0.001 mm
Accuracy:	0.5%	0.05%	1.0%	0.5%	1.0%

ALL SPECIFICATIONS SUBJECT TO CHANGE WITHOUT NOTICE.

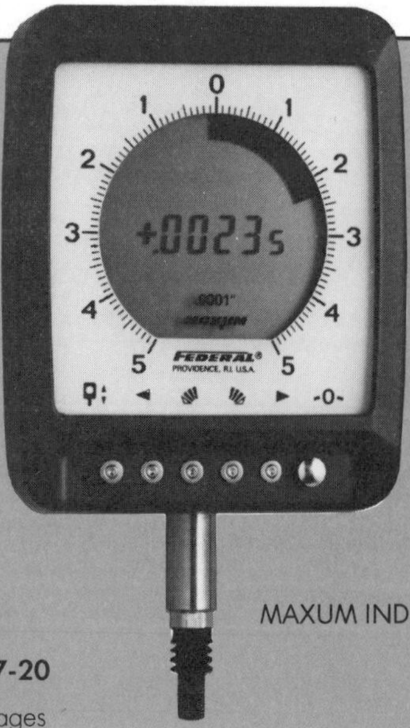

MAXUM INDICATOR

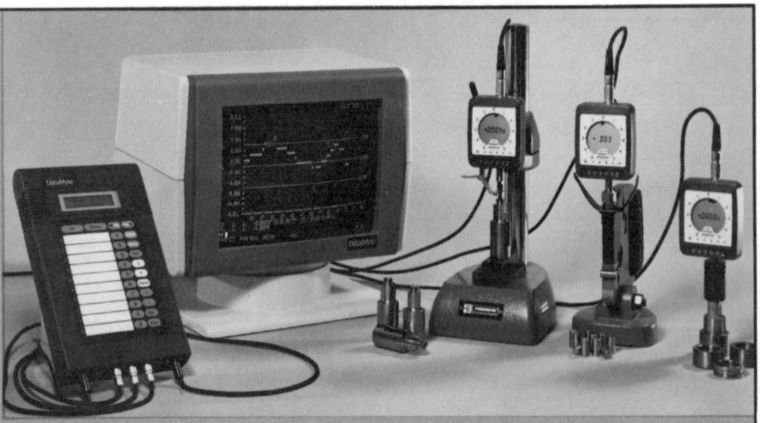

DATAMYTE 754 AND MAXUM

Fowler Ultra-Digit I and II Indicators

Fred V. Fowler Co., Inc.

The Ultra-Digit I and II indicators are both the same size as conventional dial indicators. They have a standard back-lug fitting for mounting on a stand.

- Range: 25 mm (1 in.)
- Resolution: Depends on kind of gage.
- Accuracy: AGD Group 2, for 1 in. range
- Quantization Error: ±1 digit
- Operating Temp: 0 to 40° C (32 to 104° F)
- Storage Temp: −10 to 60° C (14 to 140° F)
- Battery: Internal nickel cadmium
- Battery Life: 80 hours between charges

ALL SPECIFICATIONS SUBJECT TO CHANGE WITHOUT NOTICE.

DataMyte models for gage:

- 750
- 762
- 1556
- 1558
- 862
- 2003
- 2005

Multiplexer for DataMyte:

- 529-04 (750, 2003)
- 529-06 (1556, 1558)
- 529-08 (762, 862, 2005)

Multiplexer Specifications

- For the 750, 1500, 2003, one multiplexer interfaces up to 8 gages and several multiplexers can be combined to interface up to 48 gages.
- For the 762, and 862, up to three multiplexers may be connected to the data collector to interface up to 24 gages.
- The 2005 may have up to six multiplexers connected to it (up to 48 gages).
- Indicator lights show which gage is being read.
- Manual or automatic gage sequencing.

ULTRA-DIGIT INDICATOR

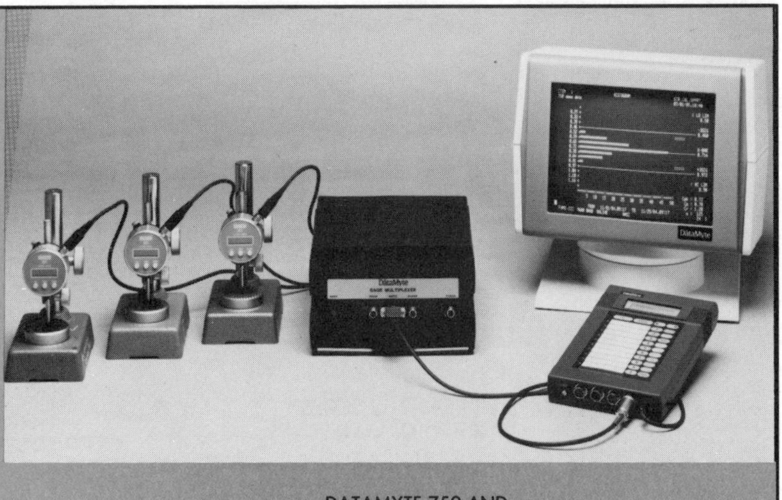

DATAMYTE 750 AND MULTIPLEXER

DātaMyte

DataMyte models for gage:

- 750
- 762
- 862
- 1558
- 2005
- 2003

Multiplexer for DataMyte:

- 529-03 (750, 2003)
- 529-05 (1558)
- 529-07 (762, 862, 2005)

Multiplexer Specifications

- For the 750, 1558, and 2003, one multiplexer interfaces up to 8 gages and several multiplexers can be combined to interface up to 48 gages.
- For the 762 and 862, up to three multiplexers may be connected to the data collector to interface up to 24 gages.
- Indicator lights show which gage is being read.
- Manual or automatic gage sequencing.
- The 2005 may have up to six multiplexers connected to it (up to 48 gages).

Mitutoyo Digi-Matic Indicator (543-162 & 543-135)

MTI Corporation

- Range: 13 mm (1/2 in.)
- Resolution: 0.001 mm (0.0001 in.)
- Accuracy: AGD Group 2

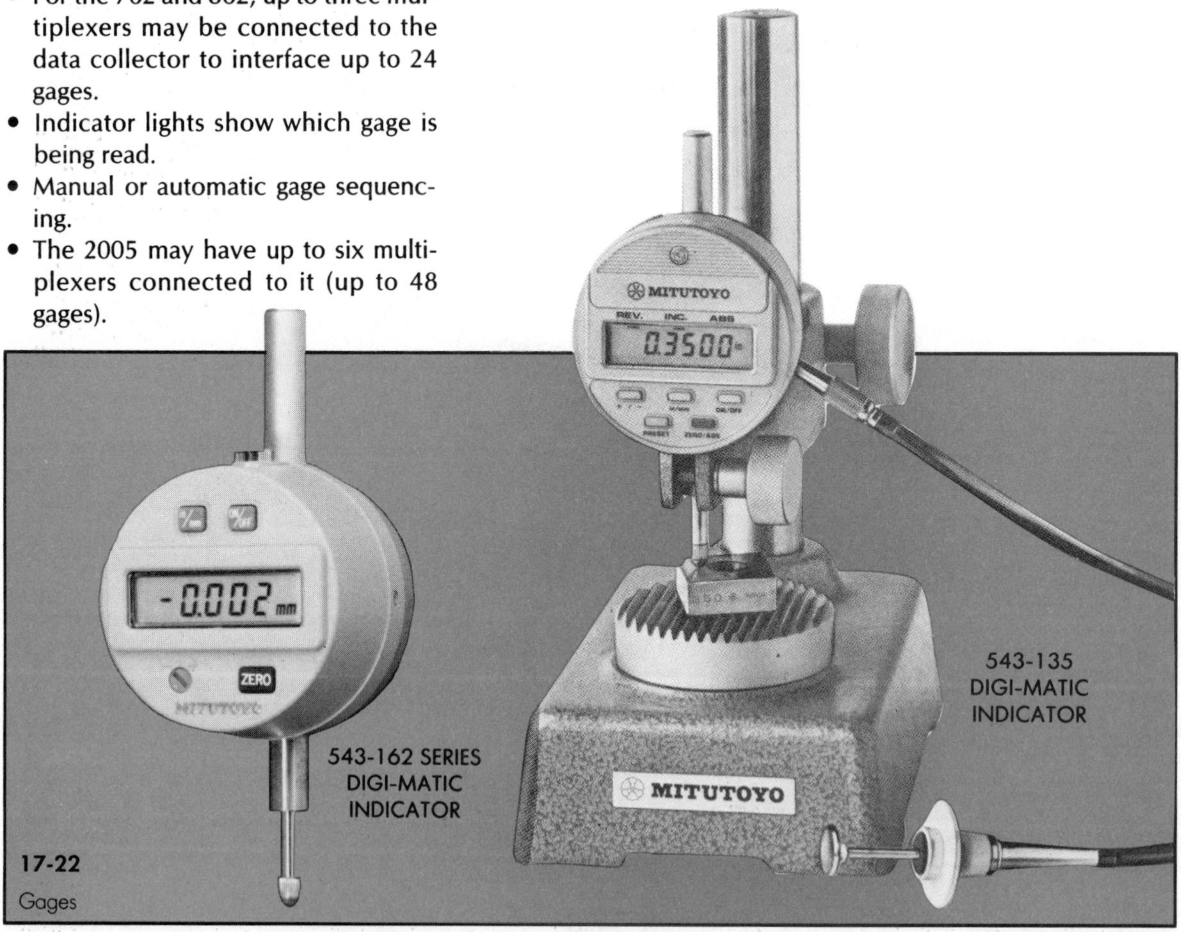

543-162 SERIES DIGI-MATIC INDICATOR

543-135 DIGI-MATIC INDICATOR

Mitutoyo Digi-Matic Indicator (543-425)
MTI Corporation

- Quantization Error: ± 1 digit
- Operating Temp: 0 to 40°C (32 to 104°F)
- Storage Temp: - 10 to 60°C (14 to 140°F)
- Battery: Ext. 110 VAC supply
- Zeroing at any point for comparative measurements
- Interface cable

Ono Sokki EG-233 Digital Linear Gage
Ono Sokki Co. Ltd.

- Range: 1.18 in. (30mm)
- Resolution: 0.00004 in. (1 micron)
- Accuracy: 0.00008 in. (2 microns)

ALL SPECIFICATIONS SUBJECT TO CHANGE WITHOUT NOTICE.

DataMyte models for gage:
- 750
- 762
- 862
- 1558
- 2003
- 2005

Multiplexer for DataMyte:
- 529-03 (750, 2003)
- 529-05 (1558)
- 529-07 (762, 862, 2005)

DataMyte models for gage:
- 762
- 862
- 2005

Multiplexer for DataMyte:
- 529-10 (762, 862, 2005)

Multiplexer Specifications
- For the 862 and 762 up to three multiplexers may be connected to the data collector to interface up to 24 gages.
- The 2005 may have up to six multiplexers connected to it (up to 48 gages).
- Indicator lights show which gage is being read.
- Manual or automatic gage sequencing.

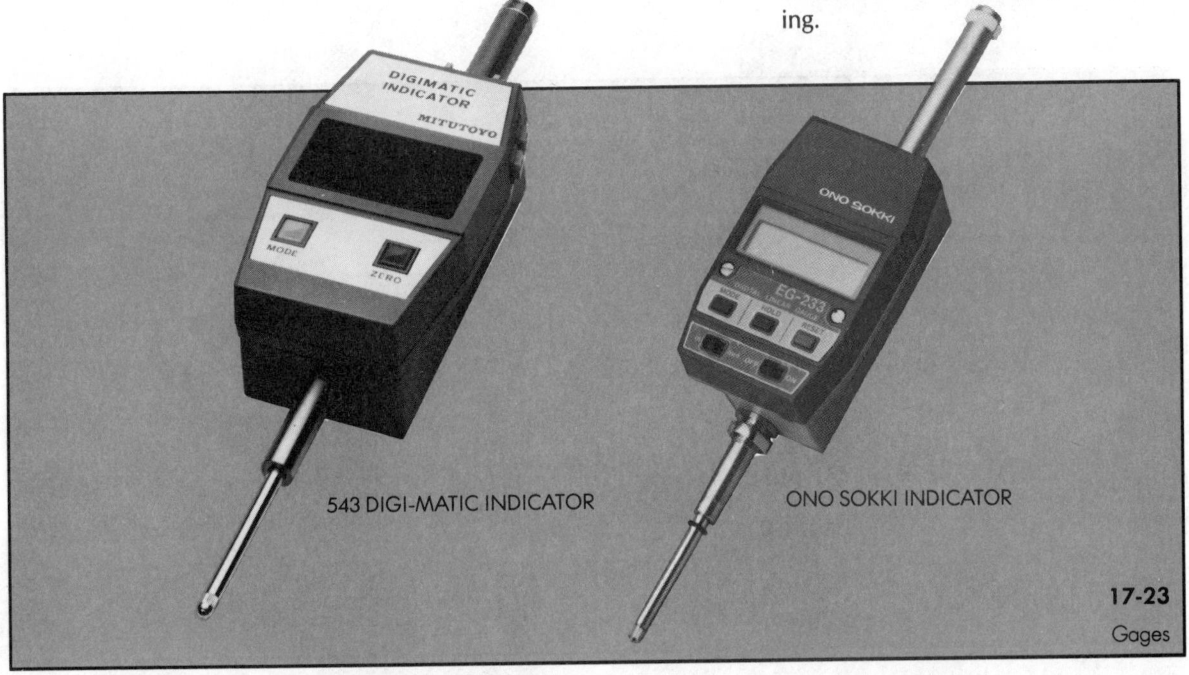

543 DIGI-MATIC INDICATOR

ONO SOKKI INDICATOR

DataMyte models for gage:
- 762
- 862
- 2003
- 2005

Mauser Indicator
Precision Measuring Instruments

- Various Ranges
- Resolution: 0.01 mm (0.0005 in.)

DataMyte models for gage:
- 762
- 862
- 2005

Chicago Dial Indicator
Chicago Dial Indicator Company

- Range: 1 in.
- Accuracy: ±0.0001

Also marketed as the Fowler Ultra-Digit III.

ALL SPECIFICATIONS SUBJECT TO CHANGE WITHOUT NOTICE.

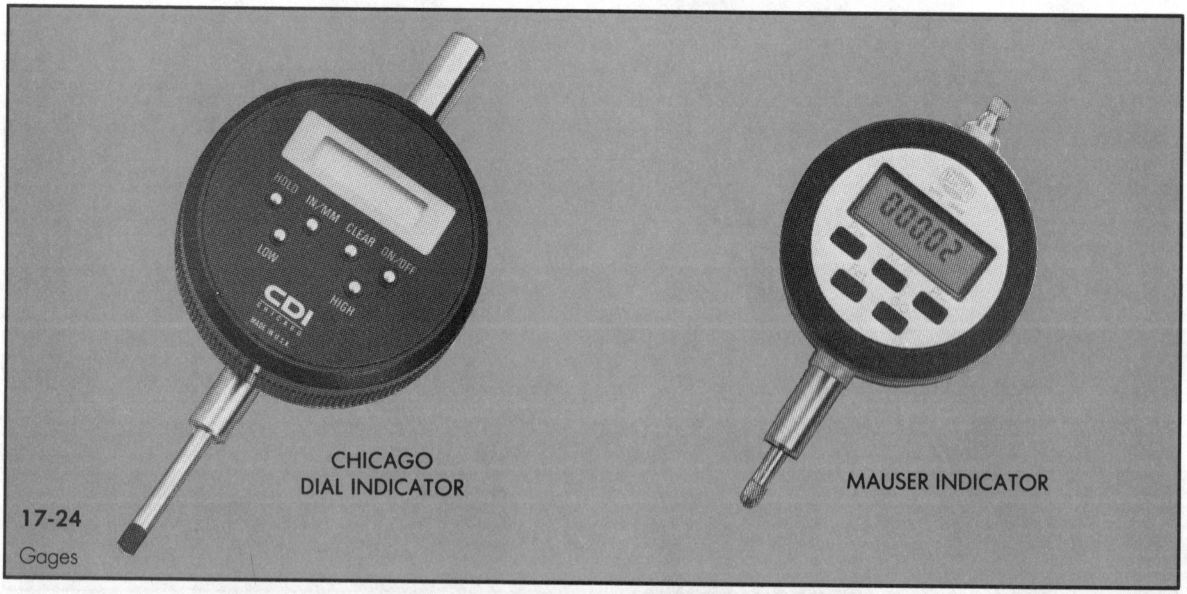

Sylvac Holmikes Bore Gage
Fred V. Fowler Co., Inc.

- Range: 6-204 mm (236-8.031 in.)
- Resolution: To 0.002mm (0.0001 in.)

DataMyte models for gage:
- 762
- 862
- 2003
- 2005

Mitutoyo Digimatic Holtest Gage
Series 468 with output
MTI Corporation

- Range: 6.925-304.8 mm (.275-12 in.)
- Resolution: 0.001 mm (0.0001 in.)

DataMyte models for gage:
- 750
- 762
- 862
- 2003
- 2005

Multiplexer for DataMyte:
- 529-07 (762, 862, 2005)

ALL SPECIFICATIONS SUBJECT TO CHANGE WITHOUT NOTICE.

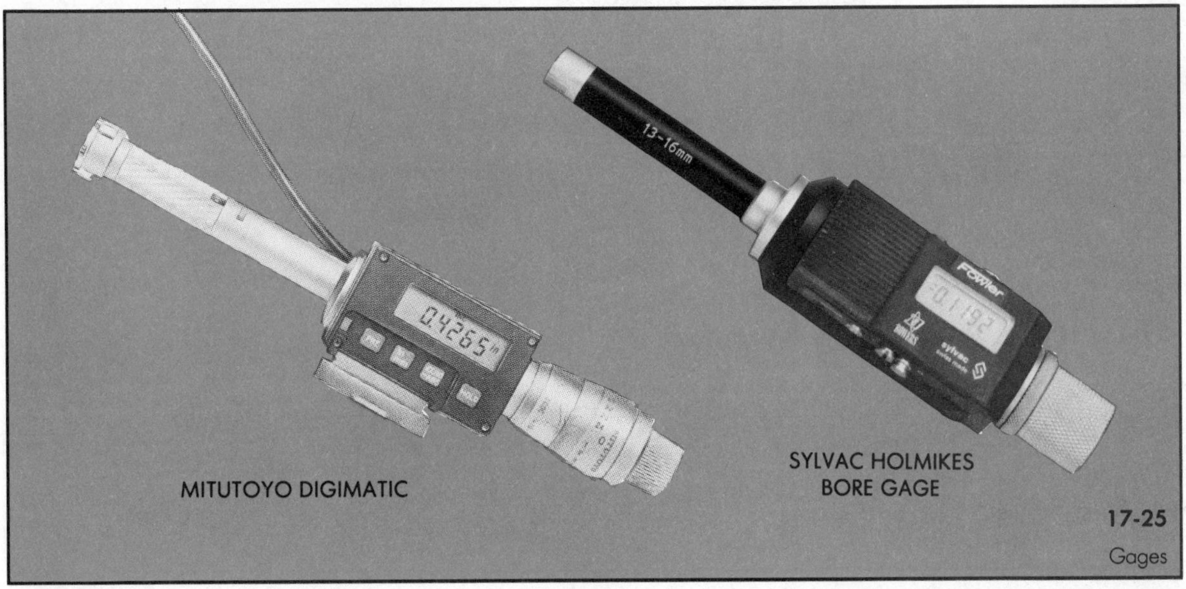

MITUTOYO DIGIMATIC

SYLVAC HOLMIKES BORE GAGE

DataMyte

DataMyte models for gage:
- 762
- 862
- 2003
- 2005

Fowler Ultra-Height Digital Height Gage
Fred V. Folwer Co.

- Range: 0 - 020.5 in. (0 - 521 mm)
- Resolution: 0.0005 in. (0.01 mm)
- Accuracy: ±0.001 in. (±0.025 mm)

DataMyte models for gage:
- 750
- 762
- 1558
- 862
- 2003
- 2005

Multiplexer for DataMyte:
- 529-07 (762, 862, 2005)

Mitutoyo Digi-Matic Height Gage, Series 192 Heavy-Duty Type
MTI Corporation

- Range: 12 in. (305 mm), 18 in. (457 mm), 24 in. (610 mm), 40 in. (1016 mm)
- Resolution: 0.0005 in. (0.01 mm)

ALL SPECIFICATIONS SUBJECT TO CHANGE WITHOUT NOTICE.

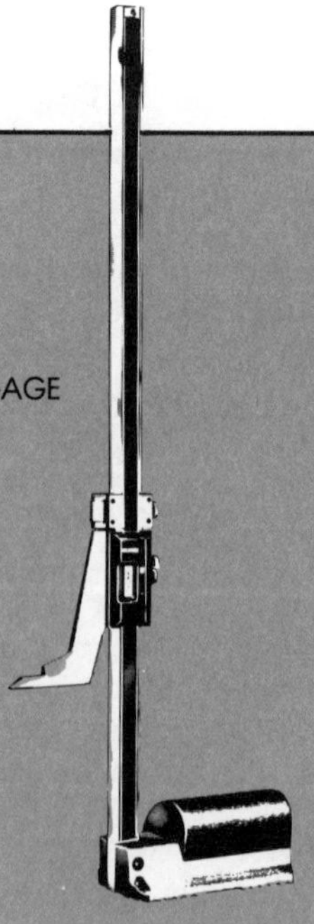

FOWLER HEIGHT GAGE

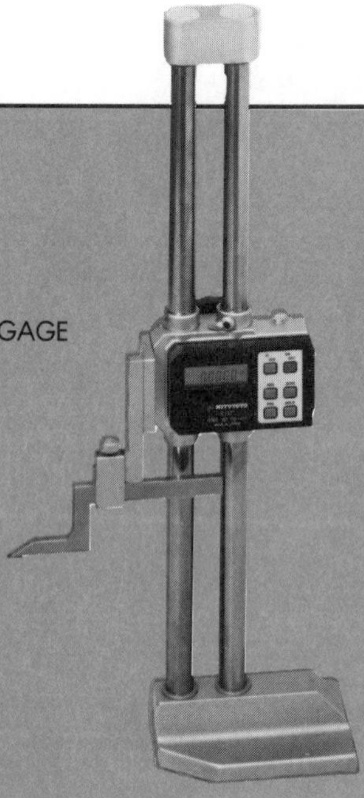

MITUTOYO HEIGHT GAGE

Mauser Height Gage
Precision Measuring Instruments, Inc.

- Various Ranges
- Resolution: 0.01 mm (.0005 in)

DataMyte models for gage:
- 762
- 862
- 2003
- 2005

Trimos Mini Vertical
Fred V. Fowler Co., Inc.

- Range 620 mm (0-24.4 in.)
- Resolution: 0.01 mm (0.0005 in.)

DataMyte models for gage:
- 762
- 862
- 2005

Numerex BRN-18 Height Gage
Numerex Corporation

- Resolution: 2µm (0.0001 in.)

DataMyte models for gage:
- 750
- 762
- 862
- 2003
- 2005

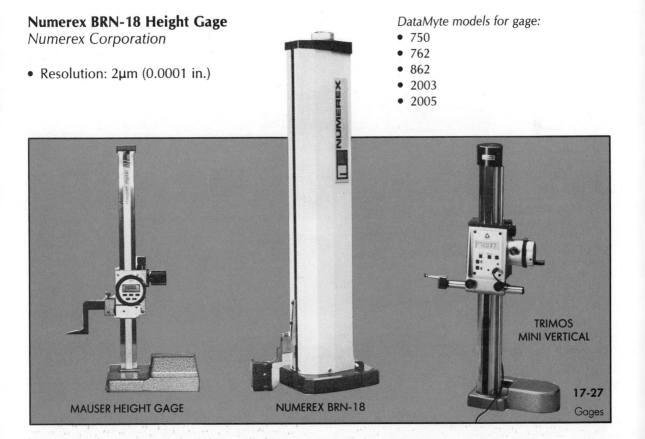

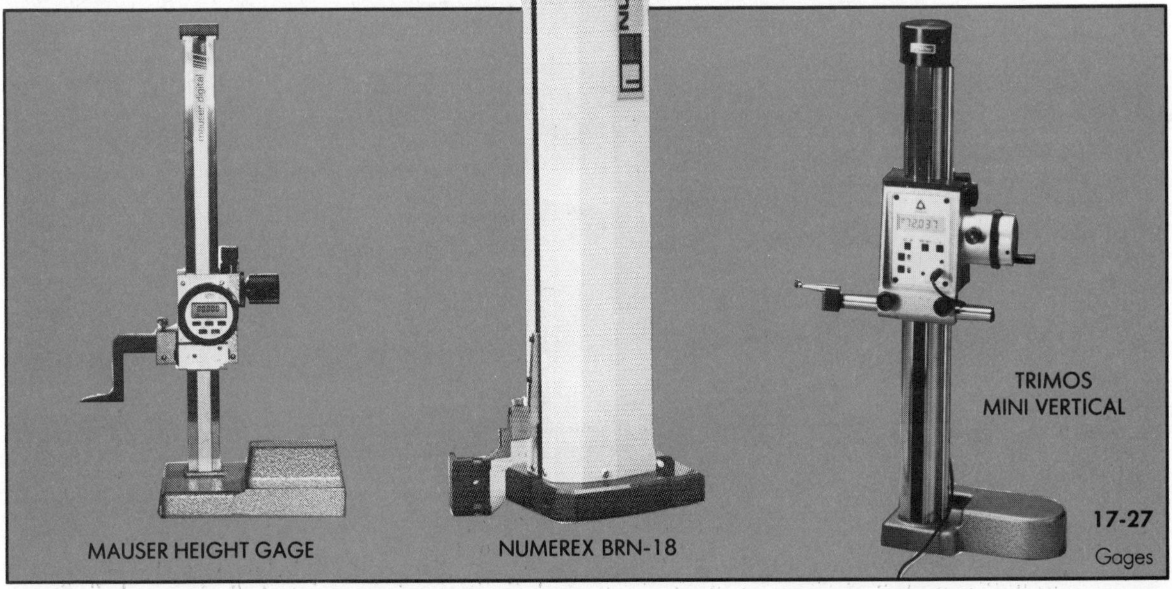

MAUSER HEIGHT GAGE
NUMEREX BRN-18
TRIMOS MINI VERTICAL

Fowler Sylvac Measuring System

Fred V. Fowler Co., Inc.

The Fowler Sylvac measuring system uses non-contact capacitive measuring probes for comparative and absolute measurements. The absolute measurement is the measured value corresponding to the mechanical position of the probe and this stays constant even after the power has been turned off.

DataMyte models for gage:

- 762
- 862
- 2005

Range:	0.4 in. (10 mm)	1 in. (25 mm)
Accuracy:	0.0004 in. (1 micron)	0.00006 (1.5 microns)
Resolution:	0.0001 in. (1 micron)	0.00001 in. (0.1 micron)

ALL SPECIFICATIONS SUBJECT TO CHANGE WITHOUT NOTICE.

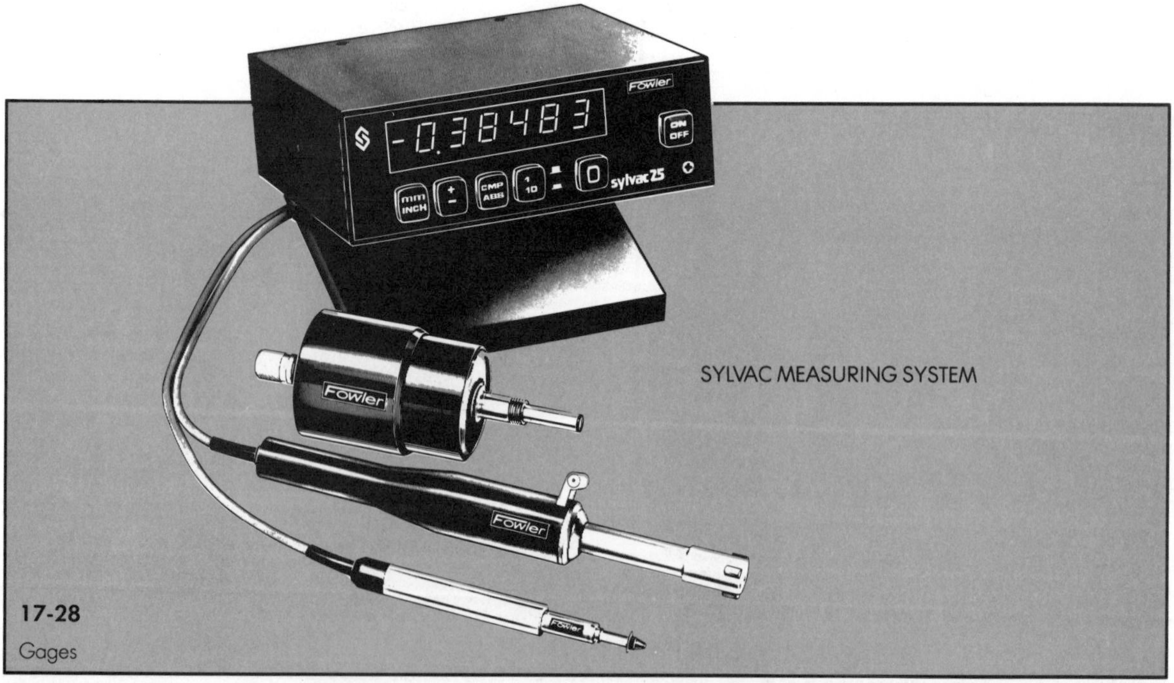

SYLVAC MEASURING SYSTEM

Fowler Trimos Computerized Vertical Measuring System Series

Fred V. Fowler Co., Inc.

The Trimos Computerized Vertical Measuring System is a multi-purpose measurement display that can automatically compute incremental measurements, compensate for probe diameters and convert from inch to metric values without rezeroing. The Fowler Trimos Computerized Vertical Measuring System Series has at least 37 applications, including:

- Height and depth
- Bore diameters
- Grooves and shafts
- Squareness and parallelism
- Flatness
- Normal and inverted surfaces

Range:	0.4 in. (10 mm)	1 in. (25 mm)
Accuracy:	0.00004 in. (1 micron)	0.00006 (1.5 microns)
Resolution:	0.0001 in. (1 micron)	0.00001 in. (0.1 micron)

DataMyte models for gage:
- 762
- 862
- 2005

ALL SPECIFICATIONS SUBJECT TO CHANGE WITHOUT NOTICE.

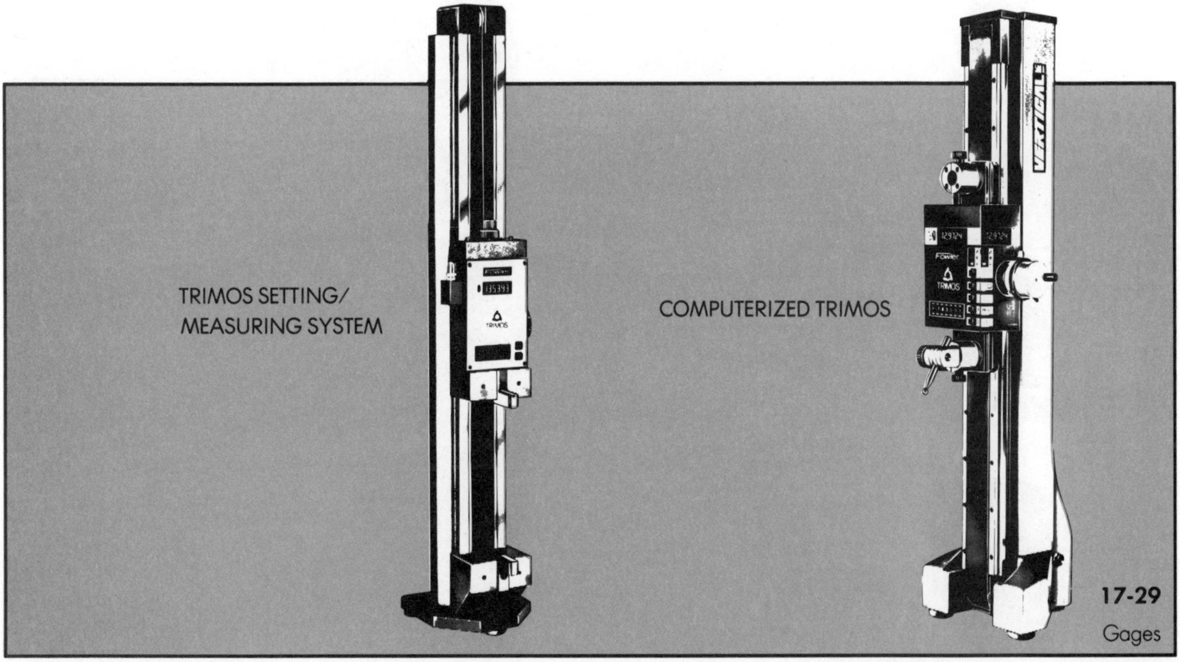

Zygo Laser Telemetric System
Zygo Corp.

Zygo 1201 series bench gages are noncontact systems for measuring diameters. The gage measures at high speed with a resolution of 0.00001 in. (0.0001 mm). Range is 0.01-2.00 in. (0.25 to 0.50 mm).

DataMyte models for gage:
- 750
- 762
- 1556
- 1558
- 862
- 2003
- 2005

LaserMike Optical Micrometer
Techmet Company

The series 83 LaserMike Optical Micrometer is a microprocessor based noncontact bench micrometer with a resolution of up to .00001 in. (0.0001 mm). The measurement range is 0.003 to 1.5 in (0.075 to 15 mm).

DataMyte models for gage:
- 750
- 762
- 1556
- 1558
- 862
- 2003
- 2005

ALL SPECIFICATIONS SUBJECT TO CHANGE WITHOUT NOTICE.

For examples of use, See pp. 8-9, 10-14.

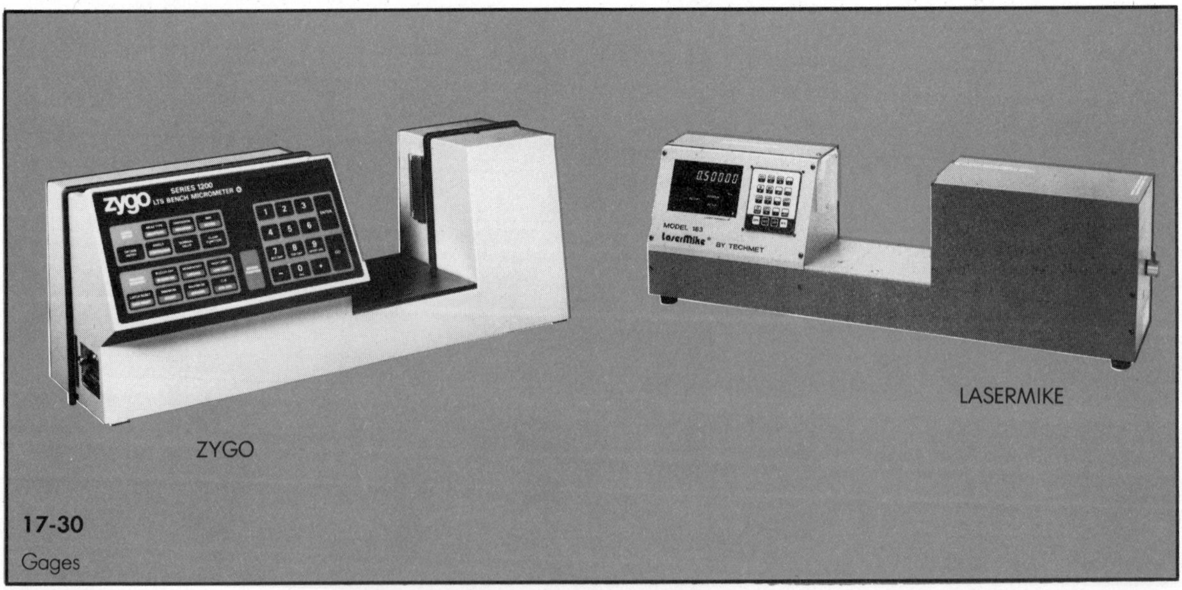

ZYGO

LASERMIKE

Laseruler Vertical Bench Micrometer

G.C.A. Corporation

- Range: 203mm (7.9 in)
- Resolution: 0.01µm (1 x 105-64)

DataMyte models for gage:

- 750
- 762
- 1556
- 1558
- 862
- 2003
- 2005

ALL SPECIFICATIONS SUBJECT TO CHANGE WITHOUT NOTICE.

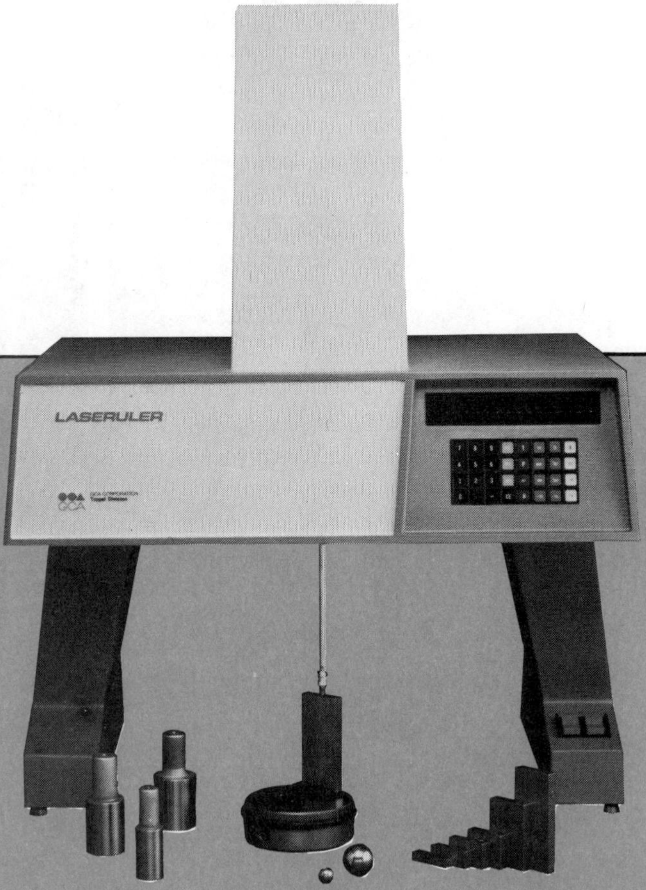

LASERULER

Column Gages and Readouts
Available from various sources.

The DataMyte 761 or 861 can interface with many different column gages. The DataMyte Junction Box allows up to 10 column gages to be connected to the 761 or 861 at once. Refer to Table 17.2.1 for the column gage manufacturer, model and DataMyte cable numbers.

For examples of use, see pp. 7-17, 8-7, 11-3.

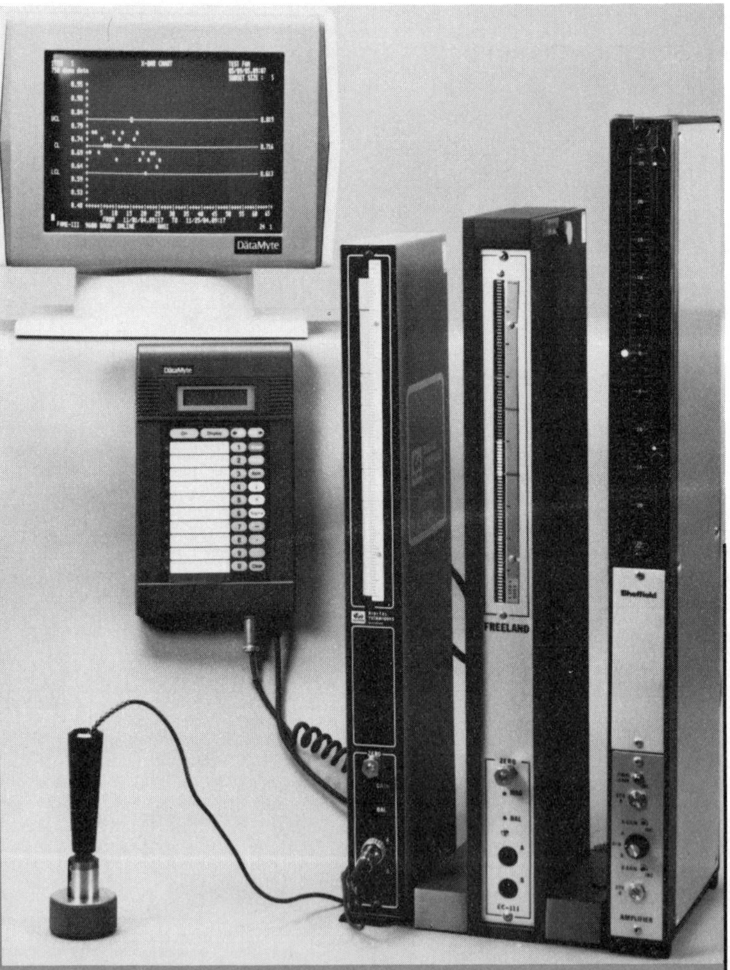

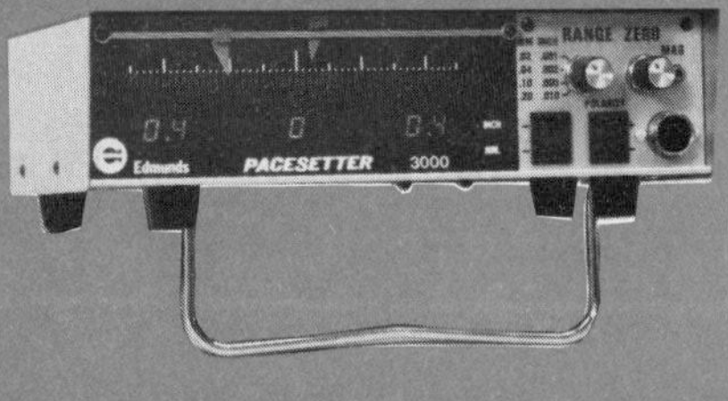

EDMUNDS PACESETTER

MANUFACTURER	GAGE MODEL	DATAMYTE	CABLE NO.
		TO 761 OR 861	TO JUNCTION BOX
Air Gage	Mini-Tron	90609	90601
Ames Mercer	122/122L	*	*
Bendix	BX	*	*
Bendix	BXT	*	*
Dearborn	Electronic Column	90609	90601
Digital Techniques	711G	90605	90604
Edmunds	Pacesetter 3000	90609	90601
Edmunds	Trendsetter	90594	90600
Etamic	CSZ	*	*
Freeland	EC110	90605	90604
Marposs	E4	90618	90619
Valmet Metem	250	90610	90611
Valmet Metem	520	90690	90691
Valmet Metem	551	90624	90625
MTI Instruments	MTI 1000	*	*
MTI Instruments	System 1000	*	*
Pre-Tec	2101	90669	90672
Pre-Tec	2701	90669	90672
Sensotec	BG-100	*	*
Sheffield	Electronic Column	90616	90617
Standard	Series 4000	90609	90601
Standard	Smart Column 8000	90614	90615
System E. Controls	System E	90622	90623

*Contact DataMyte Sales Department for cable number.

Table 17.2.1 Column gages that interface with the DataMyte model 761 or 861.

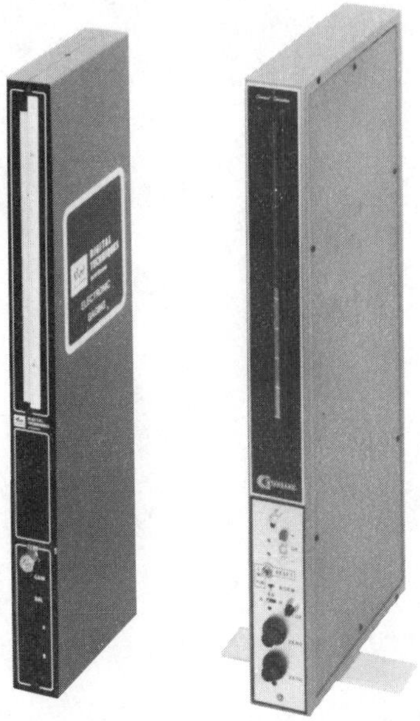

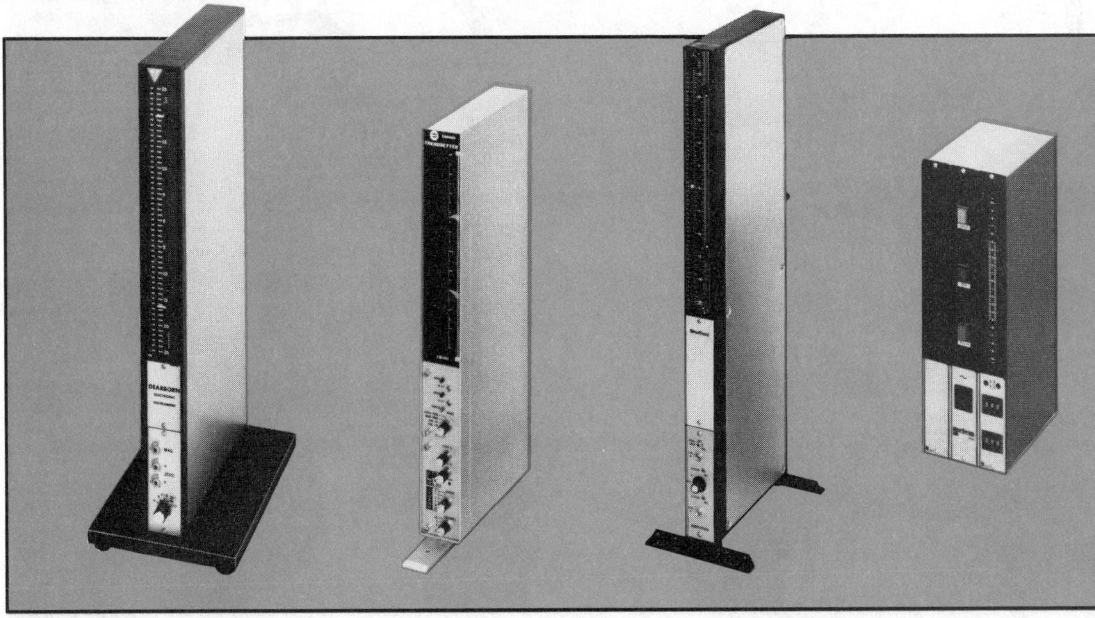

DataMyte

Quadra-Check II Metrology Display
Metronics Inc.

DataMyte models for gage:
- 750
- 762
- 862
- 2003
- 2005

The Quadra Check II (with QC 12V) is a digital readout for micrometer heads and optical comparators. The Quadra-Check II calculates radii, angles and distances, and has built-in RS-232 output.

Wizard Digital Readout
Anilam Electronics Corp.

DataMyte models for gage:
- 750
- 762
- 862
- 2003
- 2005

The Wizard Digital Readout is a digital readout for coordinate measuring machines that can transmit X, Y, and Z values to a DataMyte data collector.

Micro-Vu MD-1 Metrology Computer
Micro-Vu Corp.

DataMyte models for gage:
- 750
- 762
- 1556
- 1558
- 862
- 2003
- 2005

The MD-1 Metrology Computer interfaces with optical comparators and provides digital readout, calculation of radii, center of radius and polar coordinate, and transmits readings to a DataMyte data collector.

ALL SPECIFICATIONS SUBJECT TO CHANGE WITHOUT NOTICE.

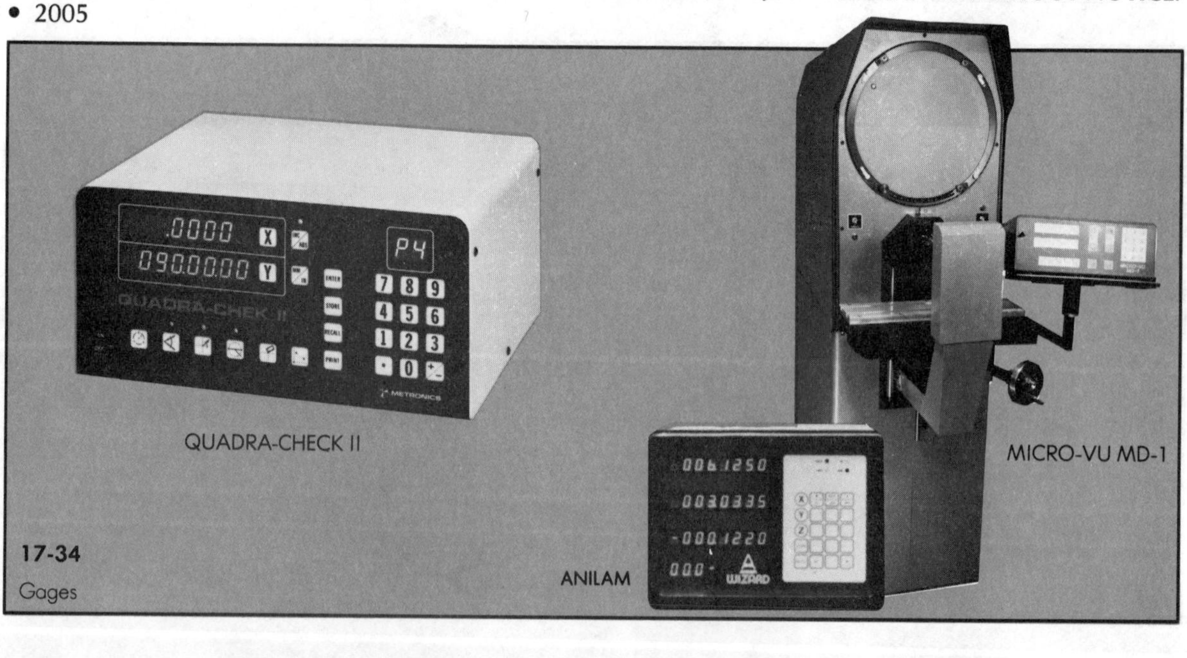

QUADRA-CHECK II

ANILAM

MICRO-VU MD-1

Autech Model 200 Diameter Measuring System
Autech Measurement Systems

- Various Ranges

DataMyte models for gage:
- 750
- 762
- 862
- 2003
- 2005

Numerex DMM 624 Coordinate Measuring Machine
Numerex Corporation

- Resolution: 2µm (0.0001 in.)

DataMyte models for gage:
- 750
- 762
- 862
- 2003
- 2005

See page 11-7, for an example of use.

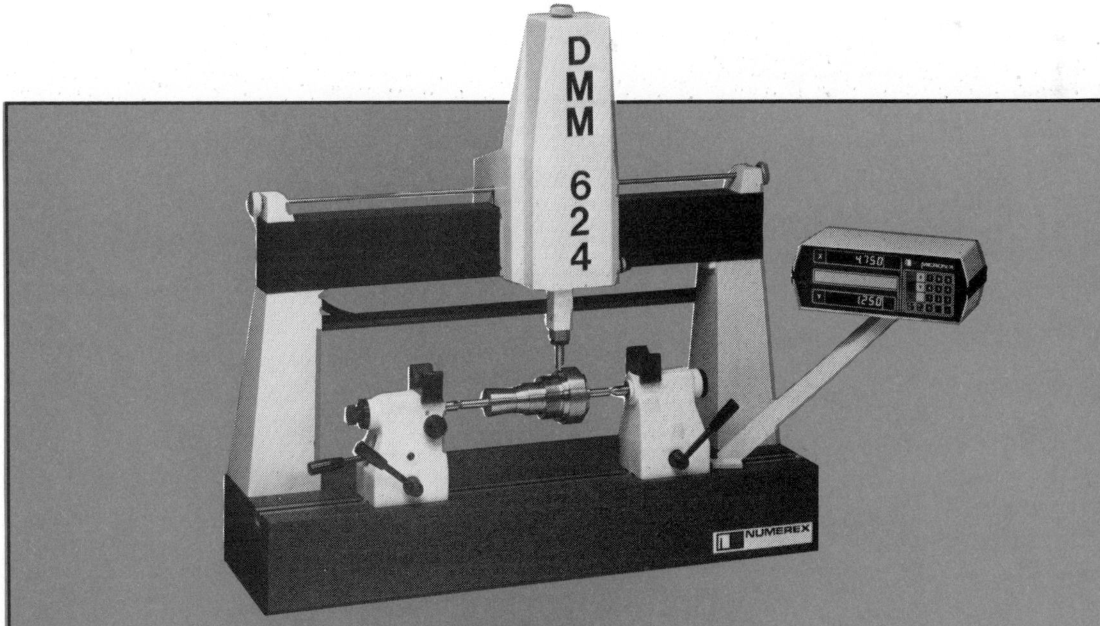

NUMEREX COORDINATE MEASURING MACHINE

DātaMyte

DataMyte model for gage:
- 2003

Boeckler Microcode II Digital Readouts
Boeckler Instruments

DataMyte models for gage:
- 750
- 762
- 1558
- 862
- 2003
- 2005

Bendix Cordax MPP-2 Coordinate Measuring Machine
Bendix Corporation

DataMyte models for gage:
- 750
- 762
- 862
- 2003
- 2005

Surfometer Digital Surface Roughness Measuring System
Precision Devices, Inc.

ALL SPECIFICATIONS SUBJECT TO CHANGE WITHOUT NOTICE.

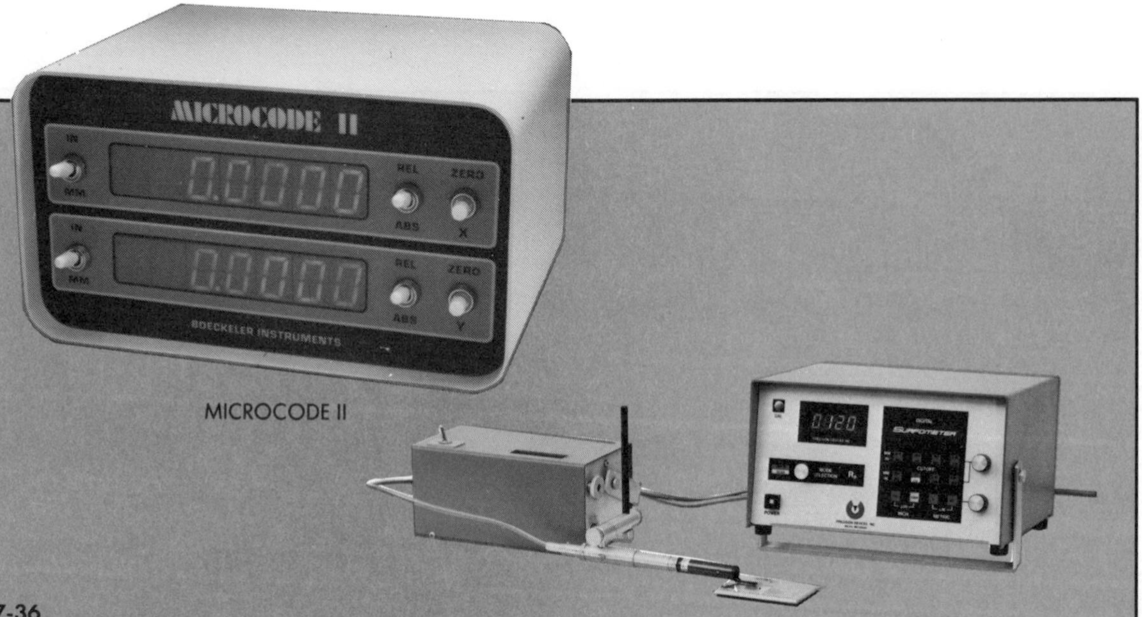

MICROCODE II

SURFOMETER

Profilometer™

Available from Sheffield Measurement Division

Profilometer systems measure the surface roughness of metals, plastics and most other solid materials. Average roughness Ra measured in microinches or micrometers. Readings are output to the DataMyte for control charts.

DataMyte models for gage:

- 750
- 762
- 862
- 2003
- 2005

ALL SPECIFICATIONS SUBJECT TO CHANGE WITHOUT NOTICE.

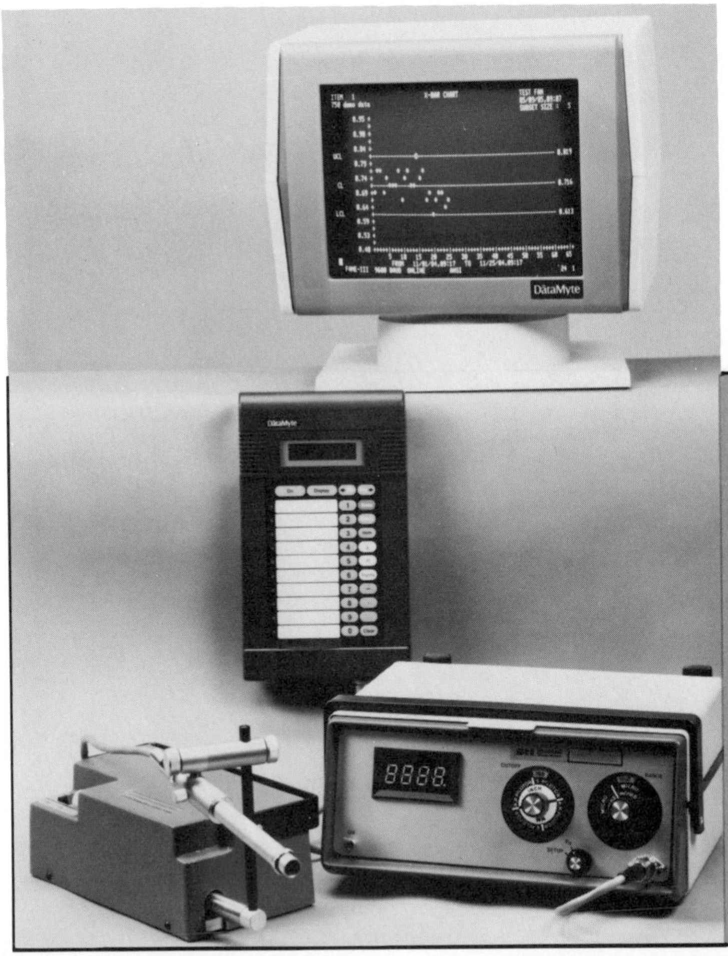

Carlson Spring Tester

Available from Carlson Co., Inc.

DataMyte models for gage:
- 750
- 762
- 862
- 2003
- 2005

The Carlson tester checks the loads and deflections of compression and extension springs. Accuracy is within 1 digit and is within 0.25 percent on any load. Up to 600 tests per hour can be made. A standard RS-232C port sends readings directly to the DataMyte.

Larson Spring Tester

Larson Systems,Inc.

DataMyte models for gage:
- 750
- 762
- 862
- 2003
- 2005

- Force Range: 0-1 lb. to 0-10,000 lbs.

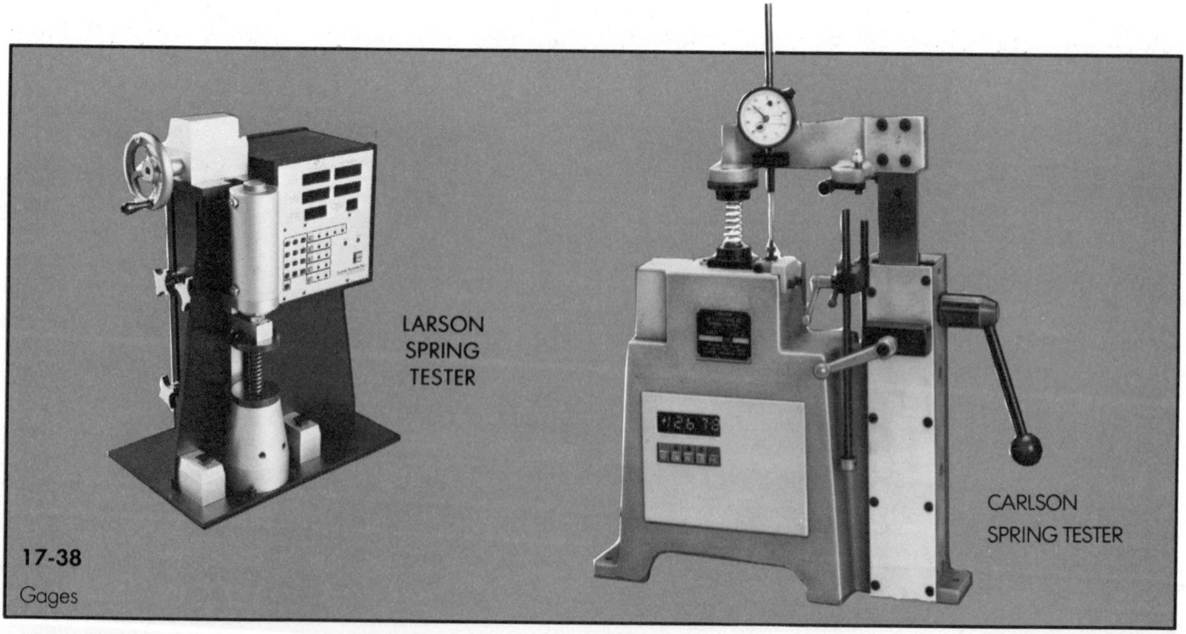

Electronic Balances

Mettler Instruments Corporation
Ohaus Scale Corporation
Sartorious (Brinkman Instruments Co.)

Three brands of electronic balances are listed here, but others are available that have RS-232 output compatible with DataMytes.

DataMytes allow the statistical sampling of weights, which is important in food and pharmaceuticals packaging and many other industries. Contact the DataMyte Sales Department for cables and DataMyte compatibility.

For examples of use, see pp. 10-2, 10-9.

DataMyte models for gage:

- 750
- 762
- 1556
- 1558
- 862
- 2003
- 2005

METTLER BALANCE

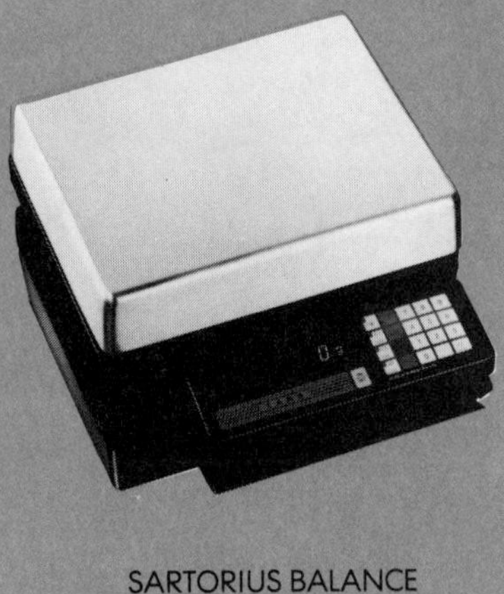

SARTORIUS BALANCE

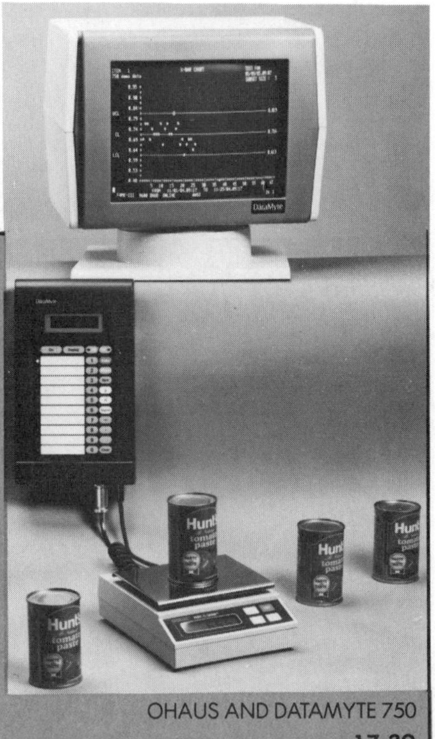

OHAUS AND DATAMYTE 750

DataMyte

DataMyte models for gage:

- 750
- 762
- 862
- 2003
- 2005

WACO Digital Enamel Rater
Wilkens-Anderson Company

Range: Low range 0-249.9 ma
High range 0-500 ma

DataMyte models for gage:

- 750
- 762
- 862
- 2003
- 2005

Fryer Electronic Score Residual Gage
Frank E. Fryer Company, Inc.

- Range: 50mm (2 in.)
- Resolution: 0.00015 in.

DataMyte models for gage:

- 750
- 762
- 1558
- 862
- 2003
- 2005

1792 Portable Distinctness of Reflected Image Meter
ATI Systems, Inc.

ALL SPECIFICATIONS SUBJECT TO CHANGE WITHOUT NOTICE.

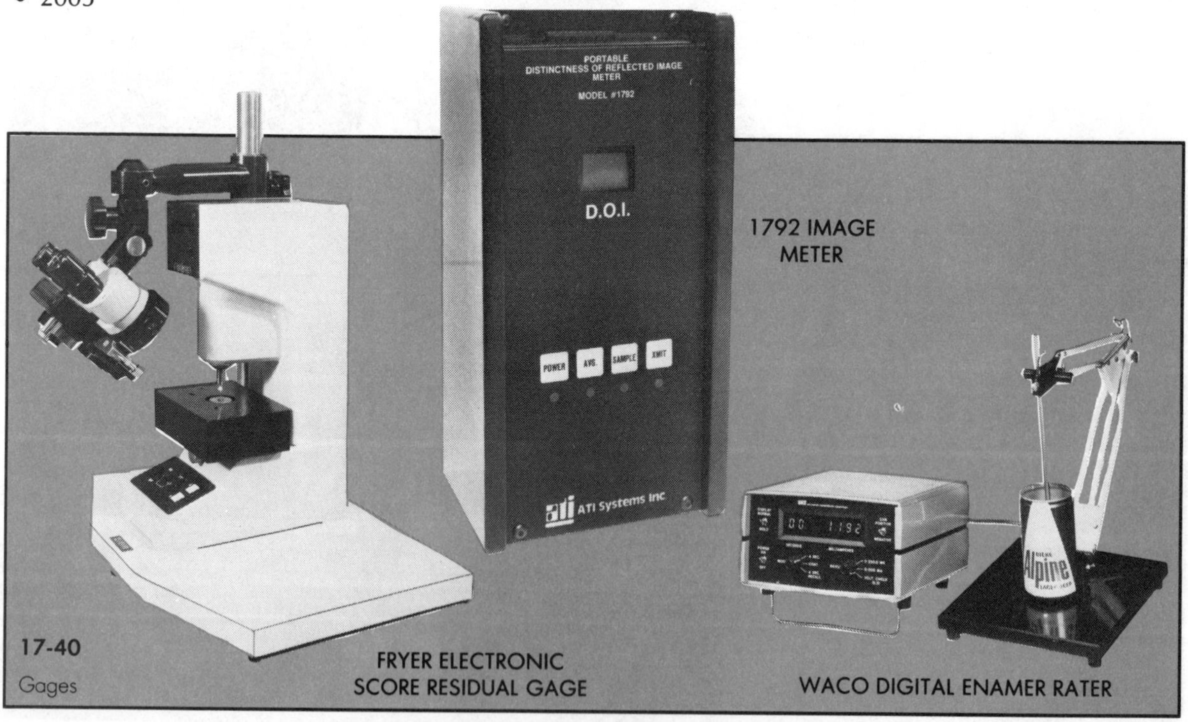

1792 IMAGE METER

FRYER ELECTRONIC SCORE RESIDUAL GAGE

WACO DIGITAL ENAMER RATER

RD 918 Macbeth Densitometer
Macbeth Process Measurements
For density only on pre 1987 production.

DataMyte models for gage:
- 750
- 762
- 862
- 2003
- 2005

Mauser Digital Linear Scale
Precision Measuring Instruments, Inc.

- Various Ranges
- Resolution: 0.01 mm (0.0005 in.)

DataMyte models for gage:
- 762
- 862
- 2003
- 2005

ALL SPECIFICATIONS SUBJECT TO CHANGE WITHOUT NOTICE.

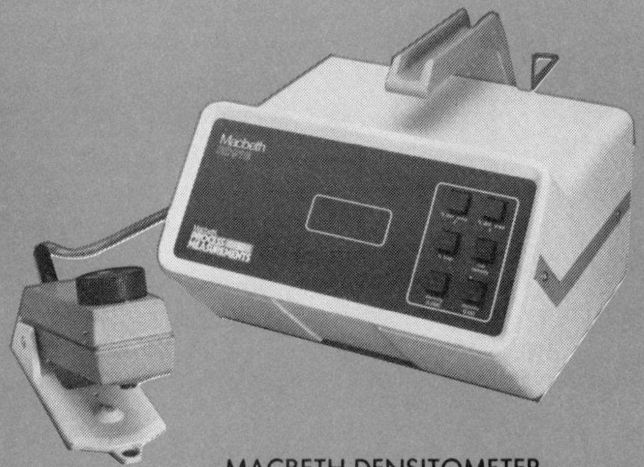

MACBETH DENSITOMETER

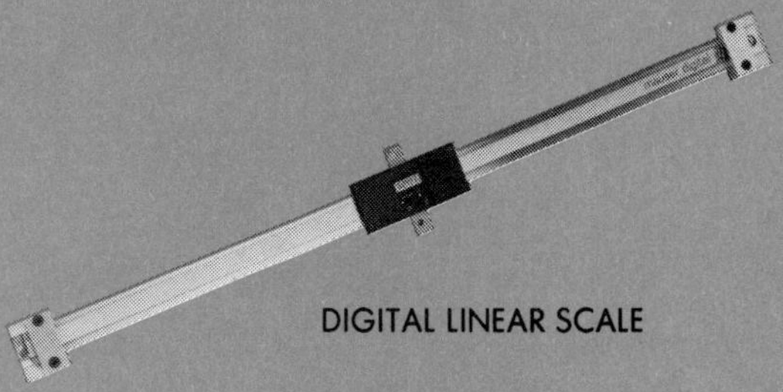

DIGITAL LINEAR SCALE

DataMyte models for gage:
- 750
- 762
- 862
- 2003
- 2005

Omega M2110-2 Multi Meter
Omega

DataMyte models for gage:
- 750
- 762
- 862
- 2003
- 2005

CMI International Model MR 300
CMI International

DataMyte models for gage:
- 750
- 762
- 862
- 2005

MBC MetraByte Digital Panel Meter
MetraByte Corporation

ALL SPECIFICATIONS SUBJECT TO CHANGE WITHOUT NOTICE.

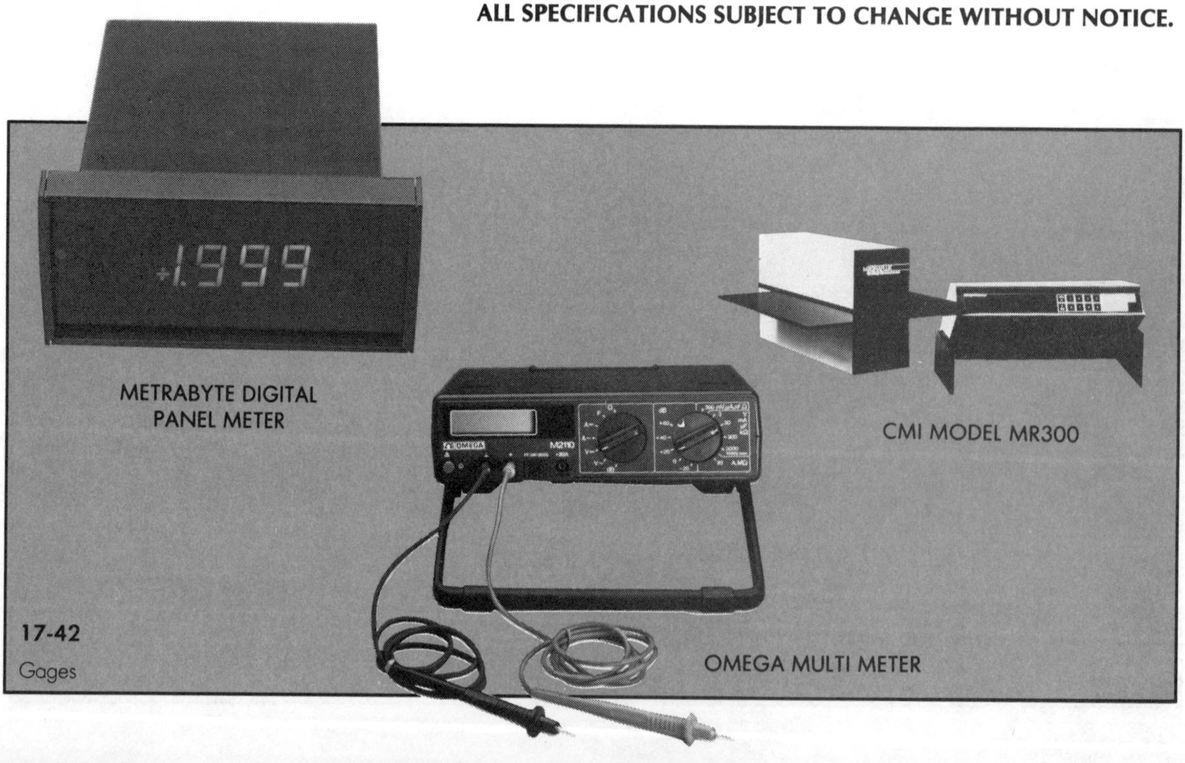

METRABYTE DIGITAL PANEL METER

CMI MODEL MR300

OMEGA MULTI METER

Series 500 Digital Hardness Tester
Page-Wilson Corporation

DataMyte models for gage:
- 750
- 762
- 1558
- 862
- 2003
- 2005

MicroDur Hardness Tester
Krautkramer Branson

DataMyte models for gage:
- 762
- 862
- 2005

Multiplexer for DataMyte:
- 529-07 (762, 862, 2005)

Mitutoyo Hardness Tester
MTI Corporation

DataMyte models for gage:
- 762
- 862
- 2005

Multiplexer for DataMyte:
- 529-07 (762, 862, 2005)

ALL SPECIFICATIONS SUBJECT TO CHANGE WITHOUT NOTICE.

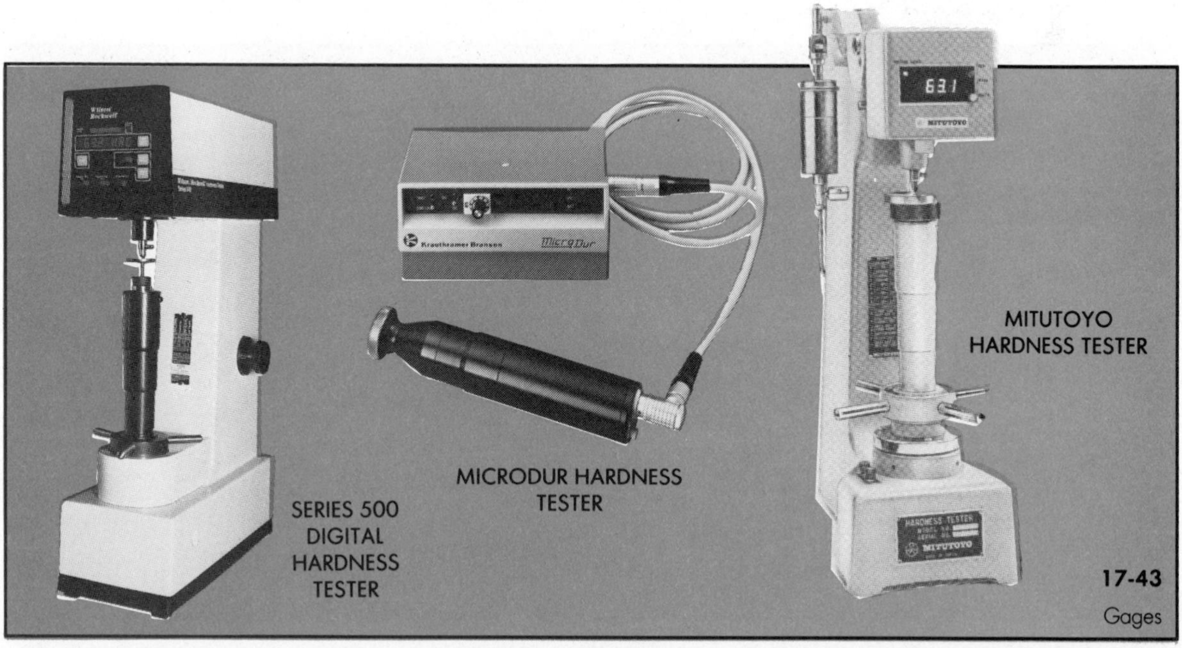

DātaMyte

DataMyte models for gage:
- 750
- 762
- 862
- 2003
- 2005

Schleuniger-4M Pharmaceutical Hardness Tester
Vector

DataMyte models for gage:
- 750
- 762
- 862
- 2003
- 2005

Multiplexer for DataMyte:
- 529-07 (762, 862, 2005)

Mitutoyo MU-Gage (Ultrasonic Thickness)
MTI Corporation

- Various Ranges
- Resolution: 0.0005 in.

DataMyte model for gage:
- 2003

Check•Line Coating Thickness Tester Model DAC-40S
ELECTROMATIC Equipment Co., Inc.

- Measuring range 0-1000 microhms
- Accuracy ±1%

ALL SPECIFICATIONS SUBJECT TO CHANGE WITHOUT NOTICE.

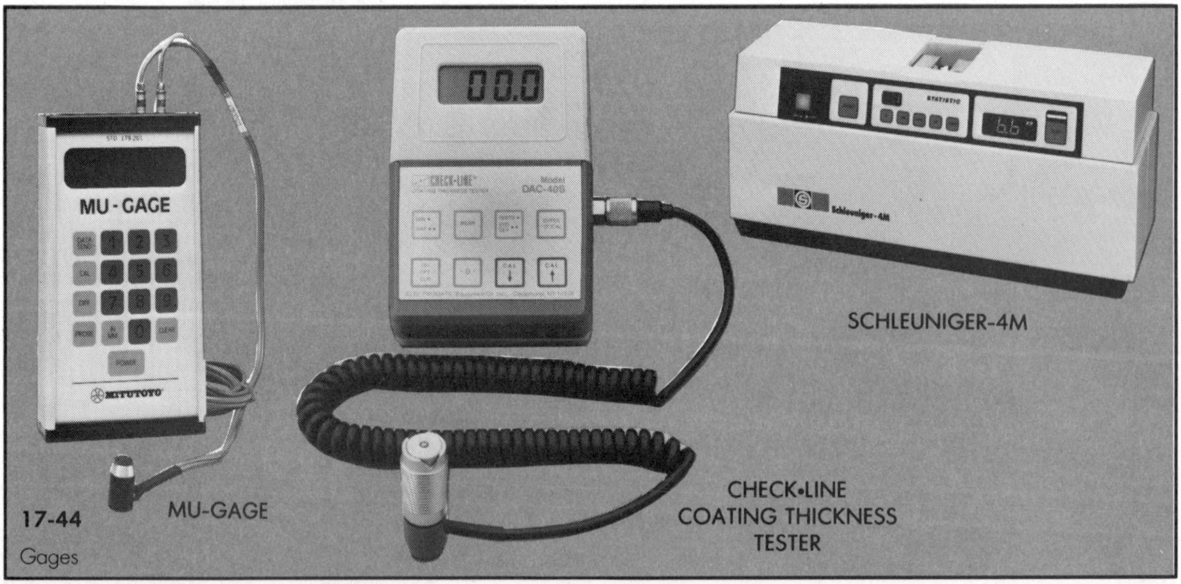

SCHLEUNIGER-4M

MU-GAGE

CHECK•LINE
COATING THICKNESS
TESTER

Corning Model 155 pH/ion Meter
Corning Glass Works

- Range: -2 to 14 pH
- Resolution: 0.001 pH

DataMyte models for gage:
- 750
- 762
- 862
- 2003
- 2005

Orion Model EA 940 Expandable Ion Analyzer
Orion Research Incorporated

- pH Range: -2,000 to 19,999
- pH Relative Accuracy: ±0.002 pH units

DataMyte model for gage:
- 2003

Fischerscope Multi
Fischer Technology, Inc.

ALL SPECIFICATIONS SUBJECT TO CHANGE WITHOUT NOTICE.

DataMyte models for gage:
- 750
- 762
- 862
- 2003
- 2005

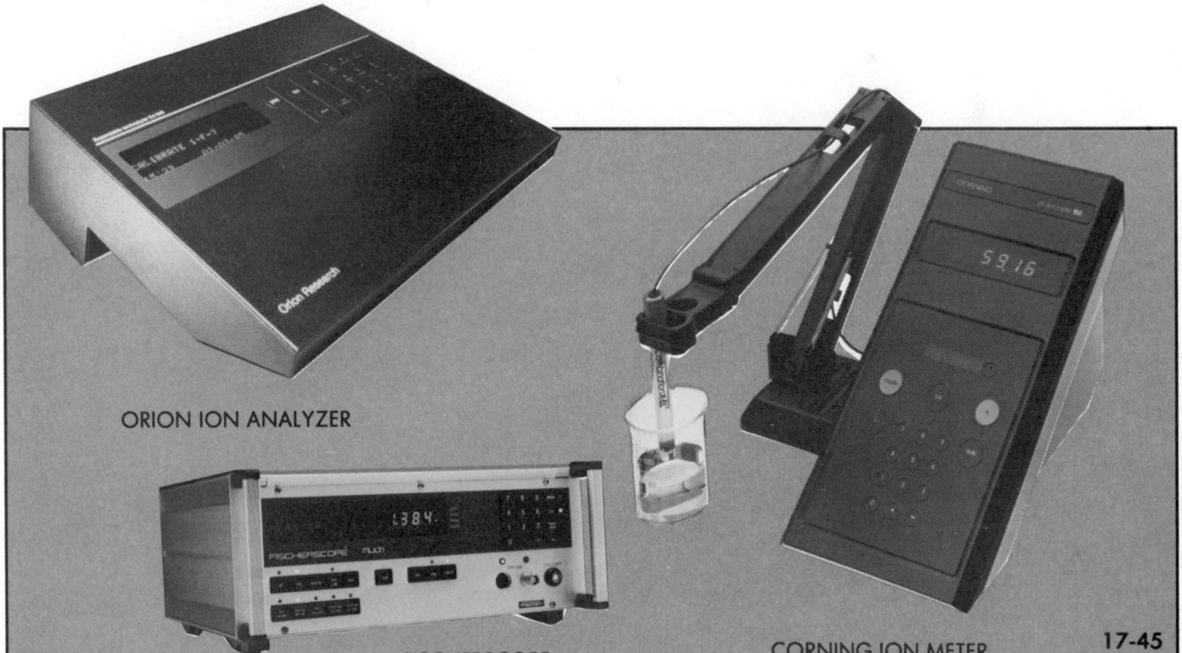

ORION ION ANALYZER

FISCHERSCOPE

CORNING ION METER

DataMyte

DataMyte models for gage:
- 750
- 762
- 1556
- 1558
- 862
- 2003
- 2005

Nanoscope Ultrasonic Flaw Detector
(with RS 232 upgrade)
Erdman Instruments, Inc.

- Range: From .012 to 1 in.

DataMyte models for gage:
- 750
- 762
- 862
- 2003
- 2005

Caviderm CD-8
UPA Technology, Inc.

- Resistance Range: 0-20000 microhoms

ALL SPECIFICATIONS SUBJECT TO CHANGE WITHOUT NOTICE

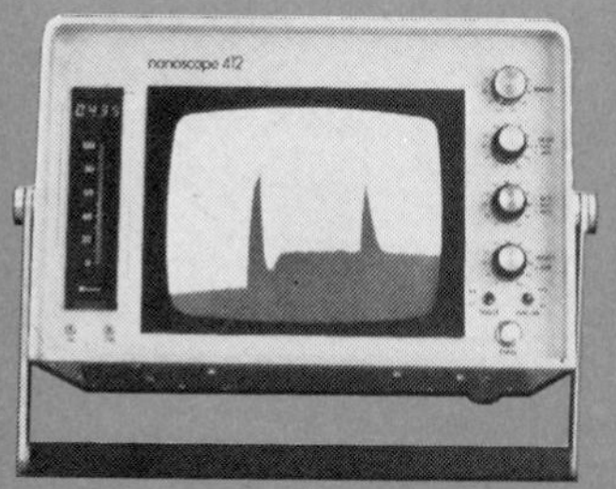

NANOSCOPE FLAW DETECTOR

CAVIDERM CD-8

Micro-Derm MP 700D
UPA Technology, Inc.

DataMyte models for gage:
- 750
- 762
- 862
- 2003
- 2005

Brookfield Viscometer (Analog)
Available from Brookfield Engineering Laboratories, Inc.

DataMyte models for gage:
- 761
- 861
- 2003

The digital viscometer measures the coefficient of viscosity (cp), which is a characteristic of liquid flow. Viscosity also affects coating and spraying characteristics of a liquid. This industrial rotational viscometer records cp values in the DataMyte.

ALL SPECIFICATIONS SUBJECT TO CHANGE WITHOUT NOTICE

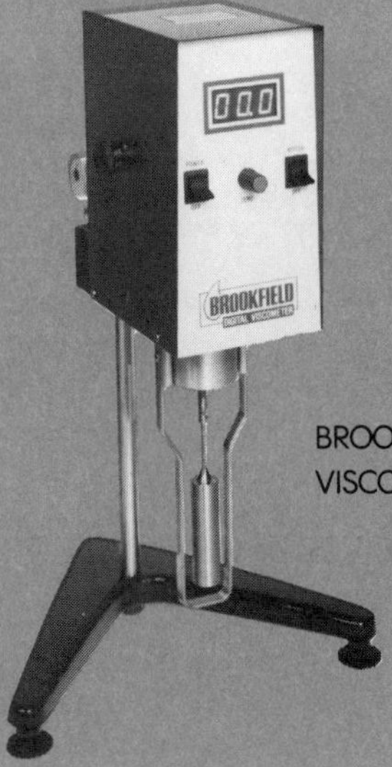

BROOKFIELD VISCOMETER

DātaMyte

17.3 GAGING FOR TORQUE MEASUREMENT

Available from DataMyte

DataMyte Torque Tools have been developed to meet the requirements of the industrial user. They are rugged but accurate tools suitable for assembly line auditing for critical fasteners subject to vibration or stress, such as heavy machinery and automobiles. When connected to the DataMyte, the torque tools can measure breakaway torque — the point at which a fastener begins to turn — with great accuracy.

The torque tools can be used with the DataMyte 1500 series and 2003. (See Table 17.0.1). The DataMyte 2003 can be used to audit fastners with either clockwise or counter clockwise rotation without the need to change setup parameters or cabling. To order, select required range from specifications table and specify the corresponding model number.

See page 8-18 for an example of use.

NOTE: Torque wrenches and drivers are not ratcheting tools. They must be used within their specified range.

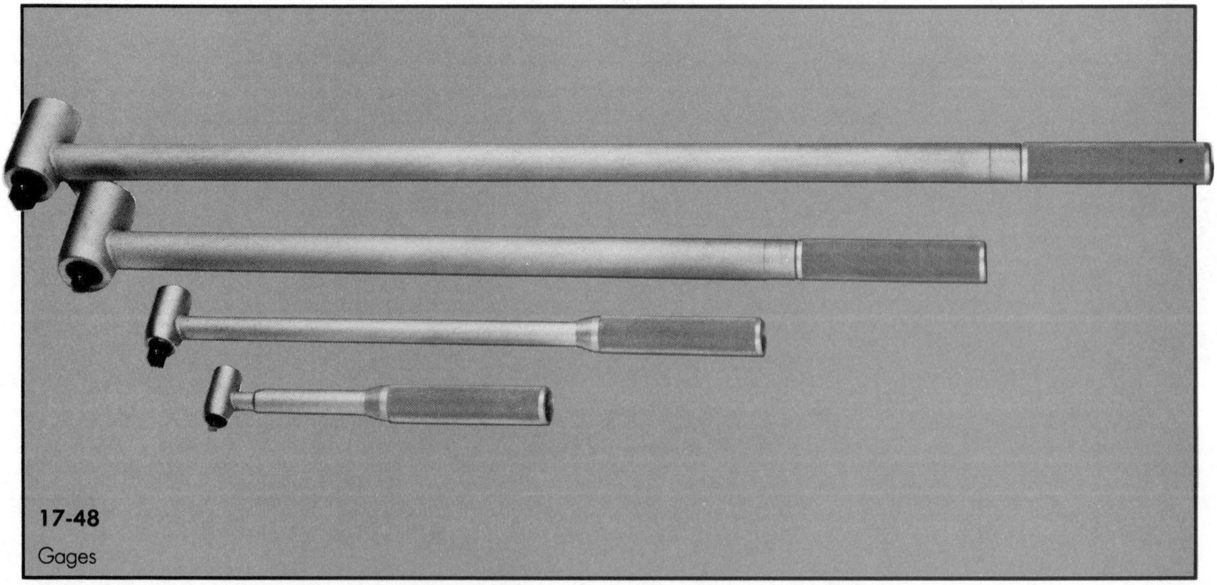

Specifications for Torque Wrenches

MODEL	518-01	518-02	518-03	518-04	518-05	518-06	518-07
RANGE	5.65 Nm 50 lb.-in.	11.3 Nm 100 lb.-in.	22.6 Nm 200 lb.-in.	67.8 Nm 50 lb.-ft.	136 Nm 100 lb.-ft.	271 Nm 200 lb.-ft.	475 Nm 350 lb.-ft.
RESOLUTION	0.02 Nm 0.2 lb.-in.	0.05 Nm 0.4 lb.-in.	0.09 Nm 0.8 lb.-in.	0.3 Nm 0.2 lb.-ft.	0.5 Nm 0.4 lb.-ft.	1.0 Nm 0.8 lb.-ft.	2.0 Nm 1.4 lb.-ft.
RESOLUTION FOR THE 2003	0.005 Nm 0.05 lb.-in.	0-.0125 Nm 0.1 lb.-in.	0.0225 Nm 0.2 lb.-in.	0.075 Nm 0.05 lb.-in.	0.125 Nm 0.1 lb.-in.	0.25 Nm 0.2 lb.-in.	0.5 Nm 0.35 lb.-in.
OVERLOAD RANGE	8 Nm 70 lb.-in.	16 Nm 140 lb.-in.	32 Nm 280 lb.-in.	95 Nm 70 lb.-ft.	190 Nm 140 lb.-ft.	380 Nm 280-lb.-ft.	665 Nm 490 lb.-ft.
QUANTIZATION ERROR	±0.01 Nm ±0.1 lb.-in.	±0.02 Nm ±0.2 lb.-in.	±0.05 Nm ±0.4 lb.-in.	±0.14 Nm ±0.1 lb.-ft.	±0.3 Nm ±0.2 lb.-ft.	±0.5 Nm ±0.4 lb.-ft.	±1.0 ±0.7 lb.-ft.
QUANTIZATION ERROR FOR THE 2003	±0.0025 Nm ±0.025 lb.-in.	±0.005 Nm ±0.05 lb.-in.	±0.0125 Nm ±0.1 lb.-in.	±0.035 Nm ±0.025 lb.-in.	±0.075 Nm ±0.05 lb.-in.	±0.125 Nm ±0.1 lb.-in.	±0.25 Nm ±0.175 lb.-in.
WEIGHT	0.5 Kg 1.1 lb.	0.5 Kg 1.1 lb.	0.5 Kg 1.1 lb.	0.5 Kg 1.1 lb.	1.0 Kg 2.2 lb.	3.9 Kg 8.5 lb.	5.0 Kg 11.0 lb.

- Inaccuracy: ±0.25%
- Non-repeatability: 0.1%
- Operating Temp: 0 to 50° C (32 to 122° F)
- Storage Temp: −30 to 70° C (−22 to 158° F)
- Battery: Powered from the DataMyte battery
- Battery Life: 12 hours minimum at 25° C

- Interface cable
- Certificate of calibration
- User's Guide

ALL SPECIFICATIONS SUBJECT TO CHANGE WITHOUT NOTICE.

DātaMyte

Torque Wrenches, Dimensions and Weights

PART NUMBER	SQUARE DRIVE	A	B	C	D	WEIGHT
518-01	¼ in.	1 in. (26 mm)	2.2 in. (56 mm)	11 in. (280 mm)	.75 in. (19 mm)	1.1 lb.
518-02	¼ in.	1 in. (26 mm)	2.2 in. (56 mm)	11 in. (280 mm)	.75 in. (19 mm)	1.1 lb.
518-03	¼ in.	1 in. (26 mm)	2.2 in. (56 mm)	11 in. (280 mm)	.75 in. (19 mm)	1.1 lb.
518-04	⅜ in.	1 in. (26 mm)	2.2 in. (56 mm)	11 in. (280 mm)	.75 in. (19 mm)	1.1 lb.
518-05	½ in.	1.25 in. (32 mm)	2.7 in. (67 mm)	20 in. (508 mm)	.75 in. (19 mm)	2.2 lb.
518-06	½ in.	2 in. (50 mm)	3.8 in. (97 mm)	30 in. (760 mm)	1.25 in. (32 mm)	8.5 lb.
518-07	¾ in.	2 in. (50 mm)	4.0 in. (102 mm)	40 in. (1.02 m)	1.25 in. (32 mm)	11 lb.

*Internal hex

ALL SPECIFICATIONS SUBJECT TO CHANGE WITHOUT NOTICE

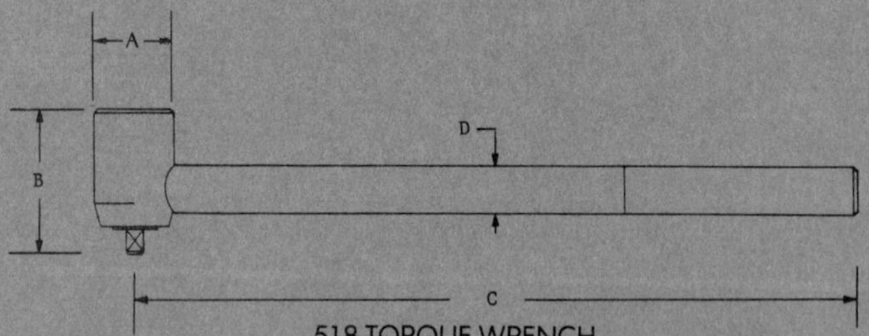

518 TORQUE WRENCH

In-Line Torque Transducers

In-line torque transducers are used with power tools to monitor dynamic torque while a fastener is being installed. DataMyte has several data collector models that interface with in-line torque transducers and have special peak algorithms to record torque.

For examples of use, see pp. 8-20, 13-7, 14-21.

Thor In-Line Torque Transducer

Stewart/Warner Corporation

- Ranges: 50 lb.-in. (5.6 Nm), 100 lb.-in. (11.3 Nm), 200 lb.-in. (22.6 Nm), 50 lb.-ft. (67.8 Nm), 100 lb.-ft. (136 Nm), 200 lb.-ft. (271 Nm)

DataMyte models for gage:

- 753
- 1556
- 2003

UTA Rotary Transducers*

Crane Electronic Limited

*GSE Rotating Socket Wrench Torque Sensors also work.

DataMyte models for gage:

- 753
- 1556
- 2003

ALL SPECIFICATIONS SUBJECT TO CHANGE WITHOUT NOTICE.

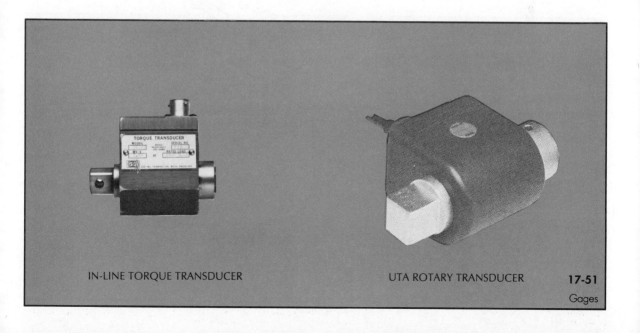

IN-LINE TORQUE TRANSDUCER

UTA ROTARY TRANSDUCER

Sensor I Wrench Model 125
SPS Technologies

- Range: 170 Nm (125 ft. lbs.)
- Resolution: 1°, 1 Nm (1 ft. lb.)

DataMyte models for gage:
- 750
- 1556
- 1558
- 2003

For examples of use, see pp. 7-18, 8-26.

Bottle Cap Torque/Force Tester
Torque Specialities Div., A.K.O., Inc.

- Torque Capacities: To 2,000 in. lbs.

DataMyte models for gage:
- 750
- 762
- 862
- 2003
- 2005

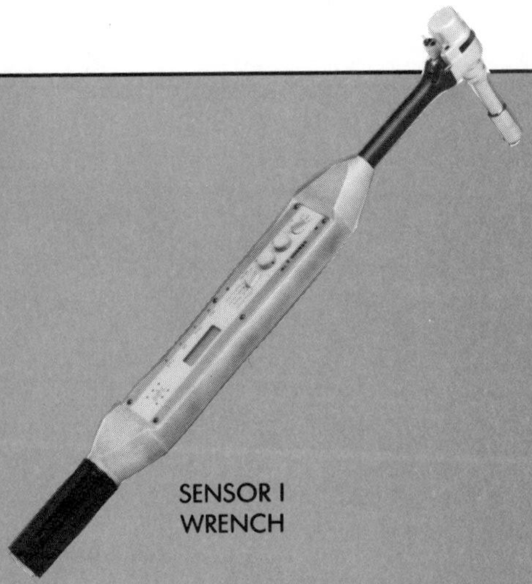

SENSOR I WRENCH

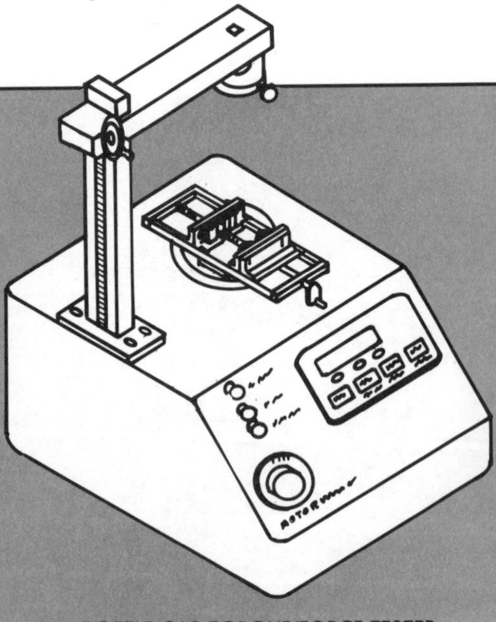

BOTTLE CAP TORQUE/FORCE TESTER

18. DATAMYTE SOFTWARE

18.1 FAN® II SOFTWARE PROGRAM FOR VARIABLES DATA

The FAN II Software program is an SPC data base that stores and analyzes SPC data collected by DataMyte data collectors in the Factory Area Network. The program has extensive editing and review capabilities that allow for fast setup of the data collectors and speedy data collection. Analysis of the data transforms it into control charts and histograms to give the user a graphic picture of a process under control. Better decisions can be made from control charts than from just looking at the original numeric data.

The user can send setup information to a DataMyte with the FAN II software program and later collect data from the DataMytes. The DataTruck, in conjunction with the FAN software program, lets the user treat a group of DataMytes as a route: the DataTruck can be loaded with setup information for a route and the DataMytes can all be set up just by connecting a cable from the DataTruck to each DataMyte in turn. Data is unloaded from a route in the same manner. The FANLINK network connects the FAN II software program to any DataMyte on the network and the most current data is available to any station linked to the network.

For examples of use, see pp. 7-7, 7-16, 7-17, 9-4, 10-2, 10-8, 10-9, 10-11, 10-12, 10-17, 11-5, 11-6, 12-4, 13-8, 13-9, 13-12, 13-13 **and** 13-14.

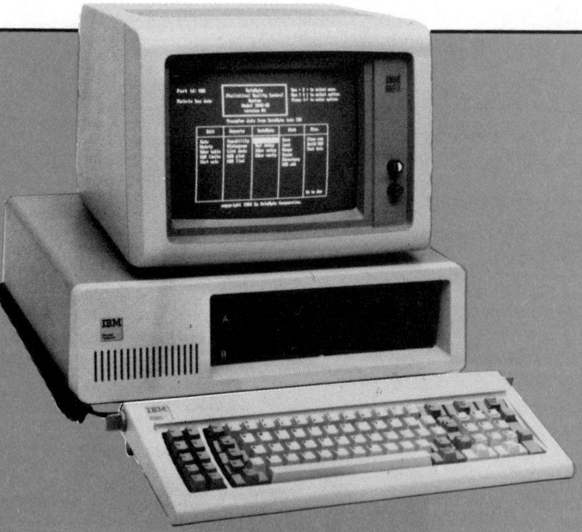

System Requirements

- IBM PC/XT, PC-AT or true compatible
- 256K memory
- Two disk drives
- Monitor (color optional)
- Asynchronous communications adapter
- Serial interface cable (available from DataMyte)

Charting

- $\bar{x}$ & R charts
- $\bar{x}$ & sigma charts
- Histograms
- Capability Reports
- CuSum charts
- Moving $\bar{x}$ & R charts
- Attribute Charts from DataMyte 2000 files
- Graphs may contain up to 50 subgroup points, plotted by date or subgroup numbers.
- Control limits can be entered or changed manually at any time, or calculated by the program.
- Control and engineering limits may be plotted on the charts.
- Graphs are displayed on computer systems with color/graphics option.

Communicating with DataMyte

- Edit setup and data files for downloading into DataMyte data collectors.

File Management

- Data is stored on floppy or hard disk.
- User specifies disk drive for data storage.
- Data files are organized by the Unit ID of the data collector.
- Spreadsheet-like editor for data files.
- Save, copy, delete or edit data files.
- "Export" data to Lotus 1-2-3 or dBase file formats.

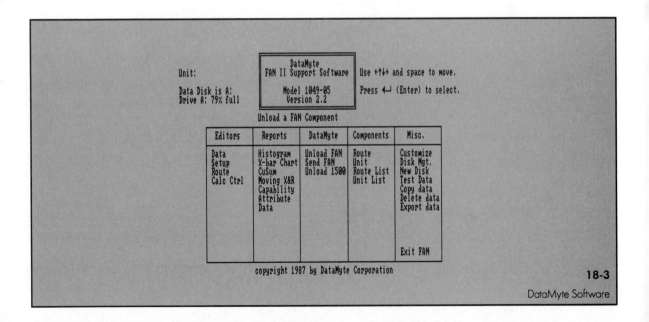

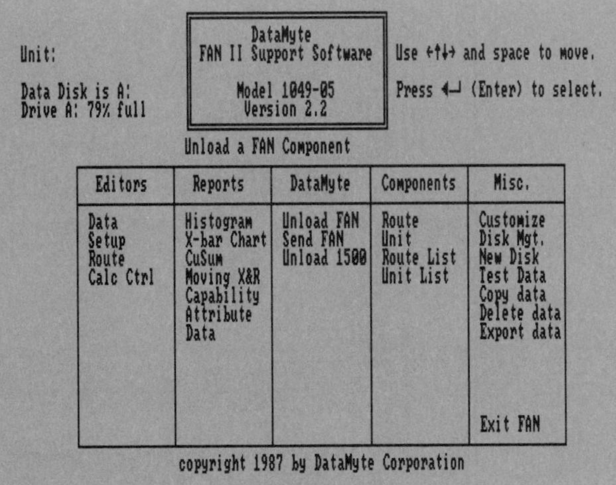

Reports from FAN® Software

$\bar{x}$ & R Reports — The FAN® II Software program $\bar{x}$ & R report can plot up to 50 subgroups of data, selected by date or number of subgroups to be plotted. The top of the chart gives the title of the report and the last line of the report heading is the custom heading, created by the user. The values of the limits and means (X double bar and R bar) are printed above the graphs.

The Unit ID, Item ID and parameters used in creating the graph are printed above the $\bar{x}$ & R charts. The user has the option of plotting X double bar, R bar, control limits and engineering limits on the chart. Control limits can be entered or changed manually at any time or the program can calculate them after 20 sets of data have been collected. The FAN II Software program prints an assignable cause, machine and operator code report, too. It can also print a data report with the chart. If the computer has a color or graphics monitor, the chart is displayed on the monitor before it is printed.

Sample $\bar{x}$ & R report, with assignable cause codes shown on the report.

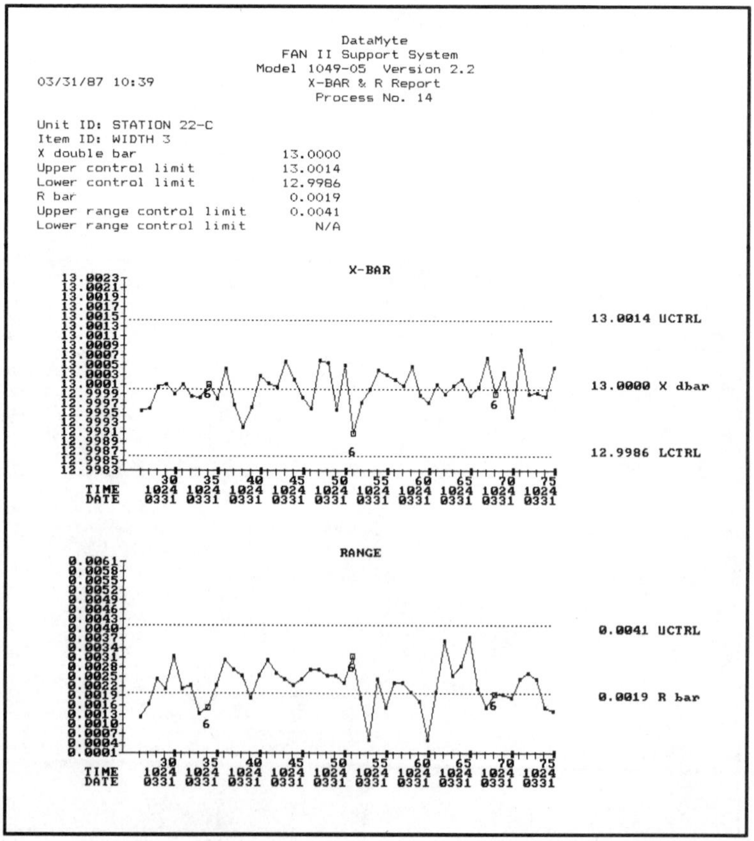

x̄ & s Report — The FAN® II Software Program x̄ & sigma chart can plot up to 50 subgroups of data, selectable by date or number of subgroups to be plotted. The top of the report has a five line heading that includes a custom report heading. The values of the limits and means (X double bar and s bar) are printed above the graphs. The control limits can be entered or changed manually at any time or the program can calculate them after 20 sets of data have been collected.

The user can choose to plot X double bar, s bar, control limits and engineering limits on the chart. The FAN II Software program prints an assignable cause, machine and operator code report, too. It can also print a data report on a separate sheet, when the x̄ & s report is printed. If the computer has a color or graphics monitor, the chart is displayed on the monitor before it is printed.

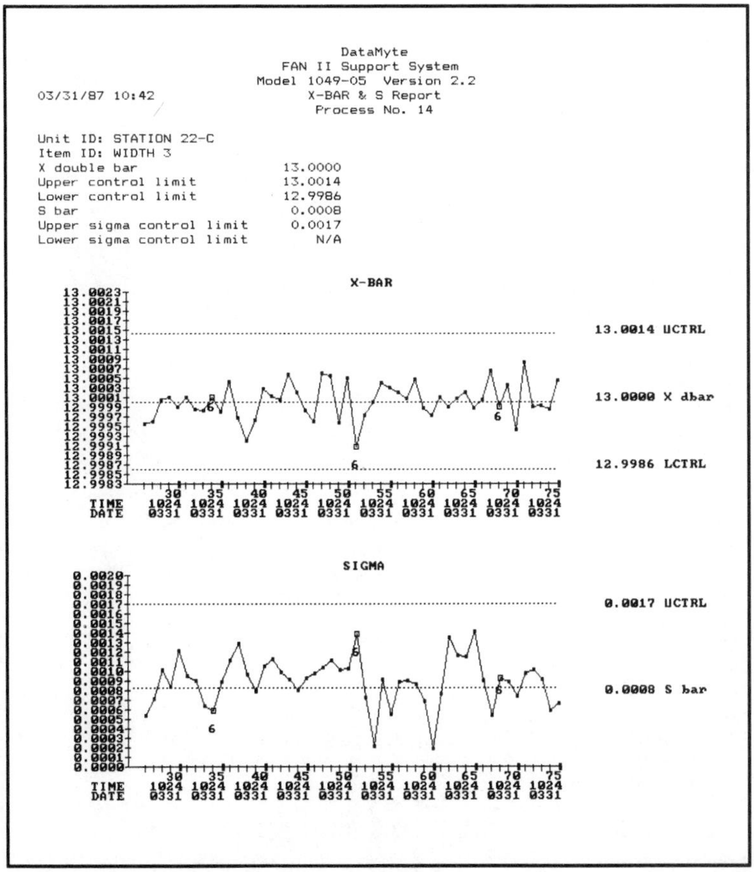

Sample x̄ & S report, with assignable cause codes shown on the report.

Histogram — The histogram report, a graph of the data distribution about the mean, contains a five line report heading which includes a custom report heading in the last line. Limits and the graph's numerical parameters, such as the number of samples on the graph, are located above the graph. The histogram report includes chi-square, skewness and kurtosis values.

The histogram has an adjustable scale (on the x-axis), and the range of data that each bar on the histogram represents is adjustable, too. The histogram's y-axis shows both the number of samples per bar and the percent of the total number of samples. The normal distribution curve and limits can be superimposed on the histogram.

Sample histogram report.

DataMyte
FAN II Support System
Model 1049-05 Version 2.2
03/31/87 10:46 Histogram Report
Process No. 14

Unit ID: STATION 22-C
Item ID: WIDTH 6

X bar (Mean).	13.0000	Sigma	0.0008	CP.	0.7846
Range	0.0042	6 Sigma . . .	0.0051	CR.	1.2746
Above high scale. .	0	X bar + 3 sig	13.0026	CPK	0.7784
Below low scale . .	0	X bar - 3 sig	12.9975	Est % Out . .	1.7810
Normal Population	NO	Crit. chi sq.	23.6848	Skewness	0.1163
Degrees of Freedom	14	Calc. chi sq.	35.5251	Kurtosis	2.4353
Samples 375 of	375	Beginning Date	03/31/87	Ending Date	03/31/87

Nominal: 13.0000

Limits:	Tolerance	X-bar	Range	Sigma	Reasonable
High	0.0020	13.0014	0.0041	0.0017	Null
Low	0.0020	12.9986	Null	Null	Null

.... X bar
.... X bar + 3 sigma
.... X bar - 3 sigma

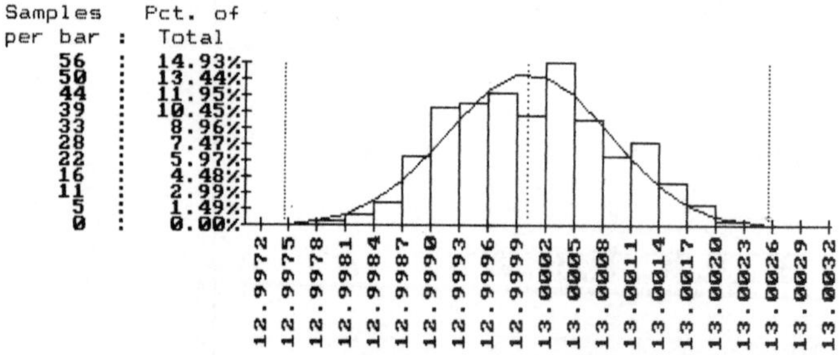

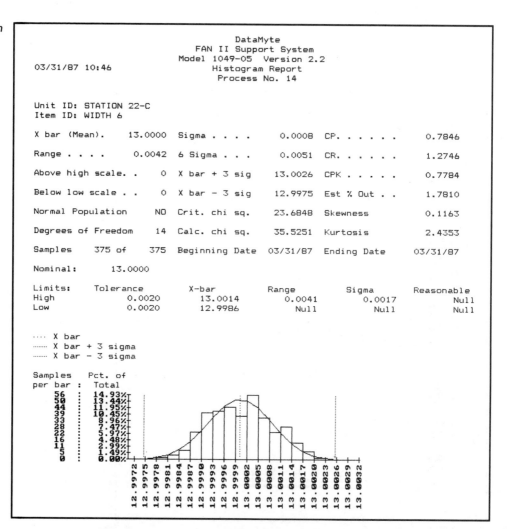

Cumulative Sum reports — The CuSum reports graph the accumulation of the sum of the difference of each subgroup's mean from the nominal value. Or, the sum of every subgroup's $\bar{x}$ − nominal. The graph is plotted either with the nominal as a reference line or with zero deviation as a reference. Below the graph, each subgroup's $\bar{x}$ and $\bar{x}$ − nominal is listed, along with the resulting CuSum. The user can choose the subgroups by date or choose the number of subgroups to plot. The top of the report contains a five line header that includes a custom title. The Unit ID and Item ID are printed right above the graph.

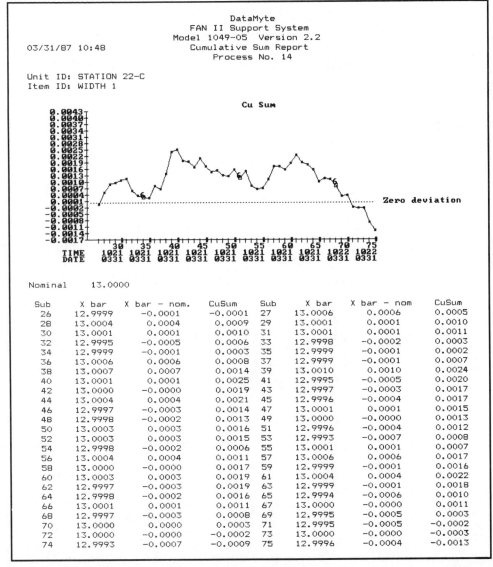

Sample cumulative sum report, with assignable cause codes shown.

DataMyte
FAN II Support System
Model 1049-05 Version 2.2
03/31/87 10:48 Cumulative Sum Report
Process No. 14

Unit ID: STATION 22-C
Item ID: WIDTH 1

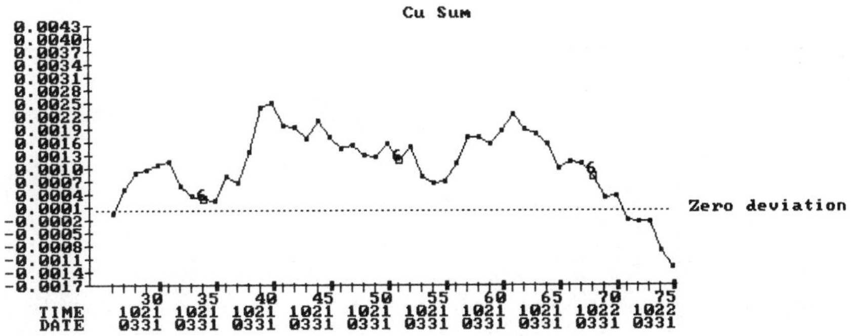

Nominal 13.0000

Sub	X bar	X bar − nom.	CuSum	Sub	X bar	X bar − nom	CuSum
26	12.9999	-0.0001	-0.0001	27	13.0006	0.0006	0.0005
28	13.0004	0.0004	0.0009	29	13.0001	0.0001	0.0010
30	13.0001	0.0001	0.0010	31	13.0001	0.0001	0.0011
32	12.9995	-0.0005	0.0006	33	12.9998	-0.0002	0.0003
34	12.9999	-0.0001	0.0003	35	12.9999	-0.0001	0.0002
36	13.0006	0.0006	0.0008	37	12.9999	-0.0001	0.0007
38	13.0007	0.0007	0.0014	39	13.0010	0.0010	0.0024
40	13.0001	0.0001	0.0025	41	12.9995	-0.0005	0.0020
42	13.0000	-0.0000	0.0019	43	12.9997	-0.0003	0.0017
44	13.0004	0.0004	0.0021	45	12.9996	-0.0004	0.0017
46	12.9997	-0.0003	0.0014	47	13.0001	0.0001	0.0015
48	12.9998	-0.0002	0.0013	49	13.0000	-0.0000	0.0013
50	13.0003	0.0003	0.0016	51	12.9996	-0.0004	0.0012
52	13.0003	0.0003	0.0015	53	12.9993	-0.0007	0.0008
54	12.9998	-0.0002	0.0006	55	13.0001	0.0001	0.0007
56	13.0004	0.0004	0.0011	57	13.0006	0.0006	0.0017
58	13.0000	-0.0000	0.0017	59	12.9999	-0.0001	0.0016
60	13.0003	0.0003	0.0019	61	13.0004	0.0004	0.0022
62	12.9997	-0.0003	0.0019	63	12.9999	-0.0001	0.0018
64	12.9998	-0.0002	0.0016	65	12.9994	-0.0006	0.0010
66	13.0001	0.0001	0.0011	67	13.0000	-0.0000	0.0011
68	12.9997	-0.0003	0.0008	69	12.9995	-0.0005	0.0003
70	13.0000	0.0000	0.0003	71	12.9995	-0.0005	-0.0002
72	13.0000	-0.0000	-0.0002	73	13.0000	-0.0000	-0.0003
74	12.9993	-0.0007	-0.0009	75	12.9996	-0.0004	-0.0013

Moving average and range reports — The moving average and range report combines more than one subgroup and treats the combination as a "new" subgroup. The averages of the new subgroups become the points on the moving average $\bar{x}$ chart. The range of the highest and lowest values within each new subgroup become the points on the moving range chart.

The FAN II Software program keeps a "rolling" combination of subgroups. You decide how many subgroups you want to combine into a "new" subgroup. After the program plots the first point, it drops the first subgroup in the new subgroup. Then it picks up the next one to make another new subgroup. The new plot is plotted. This continues for all the original subgroups you want in the chart.

The moving average and moving range report includes the moving $\bar{x}$, control and engineering limits. It also includes the Unit ID and Item ID for the data included in the chart.

Sample moving average and range report, with assignable cause codes shown on the report.

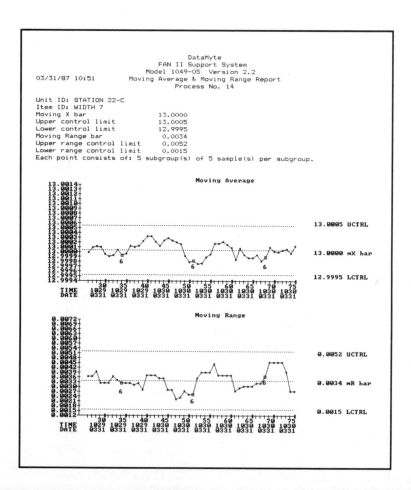

DataMyte
FAN II Support System
Model 1049-05 Version 2.2
03/31/87 10:51 Moving Average & Moving Range Report
Process No. 14

Unit ID: STATION 22-C
Item ID: WIDTH 7

Moving X bar	13.0000
Upper control limit	13.0005
Lower control limit	12.9995
Moving Range bar	0.0034
Upper range control limit	0.0052
Lower range control limit	0.0015

Each point consists of: 5 subgroup(s) of 5 sample(s) per subgroup.

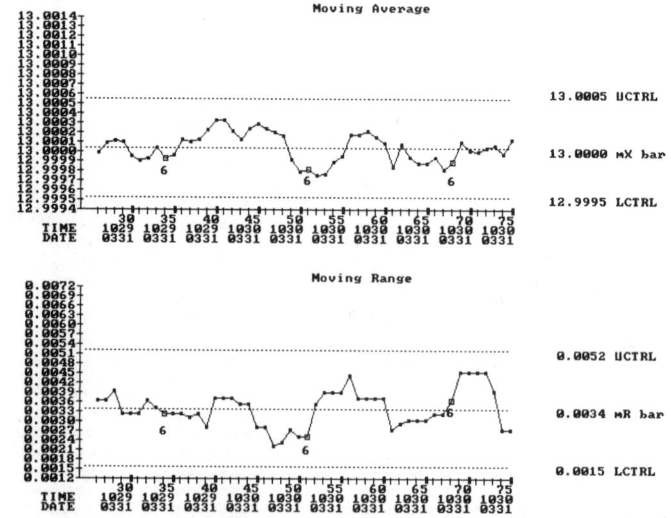

Capability Report — The capability report can help determine whether a process can meet specifications, or what percent of parts can be expected to be defective. The report helps you compare the capabilities of several items. The capability report can test for normality, and prints the upper and lower specifications, chi-square, kurtosis and skewness values.

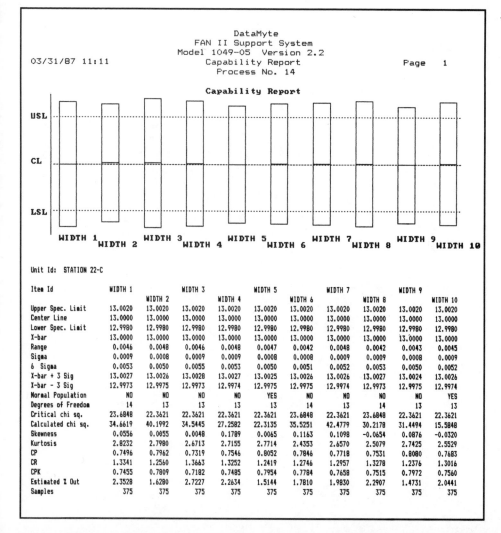

Sample capability report.

DataMyte
FAN II Support System
Model 1049-05 Version 2.2
03/31/87 11:11 Capability Report Page 1
Process No. 14

Capability Report

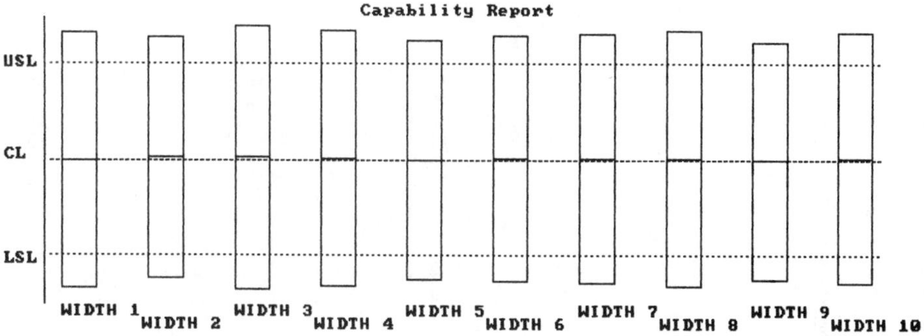

Unit Id: STATION 22-C

Item Id	WIDTH 1	WIDTH 2	WIDTH 3	WIDTH 4	WIDTH 5	WIDTH 6	WIDTH 7	WIDTH 8	WIDTH 9	WIDTH 10
Upper Spec. Limit	13.0020	13.0020	13.0020	13.0020	13.0020	13.0020	13.0020	13.0020	13.0020	13.0020
Center Line	13.0000	13.0000	13.0000	13.0000	13.0000	13.0000	13.0000	13.0000	13.0000	13.0000
Lower Spec. Limit	12.9980	12.9980	12.9980	12.9980	12.9980	12.9980	12.9980	12.9980	12.9980	12.9980
X-bar	13.0000	13.0000	13.0000	13.0000	13.0000	13.0000	13.0000	13.0000	13.0000	13.0000
Range	0.0046	0.0048	0.0046	0.0048	0.0047	0.0042	0.0048	0.0042	0.0043	0.0045
Sigma	0.0009	0.0008	0.0009	0.0009	0.0008	0.0008	0.0009	0.0009	0.0008	0.0009
6 Sigma	0.0053	0.0050	0.0055	0.0053	0.0050	0.0051	0.0052	0.0053	0.0050	0.0052
X-bar + 3 Sig	13.0027	13.0026	13.0028	13.0027	13.0025	13.0026	13.0026	13.0027	13.0024	13.0026
X-bar - 3 Sig	12.9973	12.9975	12.9973	12.9974	12.9975	12.9975	12.9974	12.9973	12.9975	12.9974
Normal Population	NO	NO	NO	NO	YES	NO	NO	NO	NO	YES
Degrees of Freedom	14	13	13	13	13	14	13	14	13	13
Critical chi sq.	23.6848	22.3621	22.3621	22.3621	22.3621	23.6848	22.3621	23.6848	22.3621	22.3621
Calculated chi sq.	34.6619	40.1992	34.5445	27.2582	22.3135	35.5251	42.4779	30.2178	31.4494	15.5848
Skewness	0.0556	0.0055	0.0048	0.1789	0.0065	0.1163	0.1098	-0.0654	0.0876	-0.0320
Kurtosis	2.8232	2.7980	2.6713	2.7155	2.7714	2.4353	2.6570	2.5079	2.7425	2.5529
CP	0.7496	0.7962	0.7319	0.7546	0.8052	0.7846	0.7718	0.7531	0.8080	0.7683
CR	1.3341	1.2560	1.3663	1.3252	1.2419	1.2746	1.2957	1.3278	1.2376	1.3016
CPK	0.7455	0.7809	0.7182	0.7485	0.7954	0.7784	0.7658	0.7515	0.7972	0.7560
Estimated % Out	2.3528	1.6280	2.7227	2.2634	1.5144	1.7810	1.9830	2.2907	1.4731	2.0441
Samples	375	375	375	375	375	375	375	375	375	375

Attribute Reports — The FAN II Software program will print attribute reports for attribute data collected with a DataMyte 2000 data collector. The program will print c-, u-, p-, np- and Pareto charts. The c-chart shows the number of defects of a single attribute per subgroup. The u-chart shows the percentage of defects in a subgroup. The p-chart shows the percentage of defective parts in a subgroup; and the np-chart shows the number of defective parts in a subgroup.

Sample attribute report, printed from a 2003 data file.

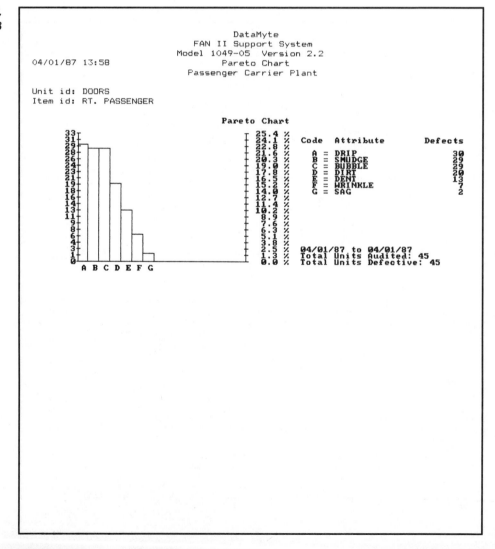

```
                              DataMyte
                        FAN II Support System
                    Model 1049-05   Version 2.2
04/01/87 13:58               Pareto Chart
                       Passenger Carrier Plant

Unit id: DOORS
Item id: RT. PASSENGER
```

Pareto Chart

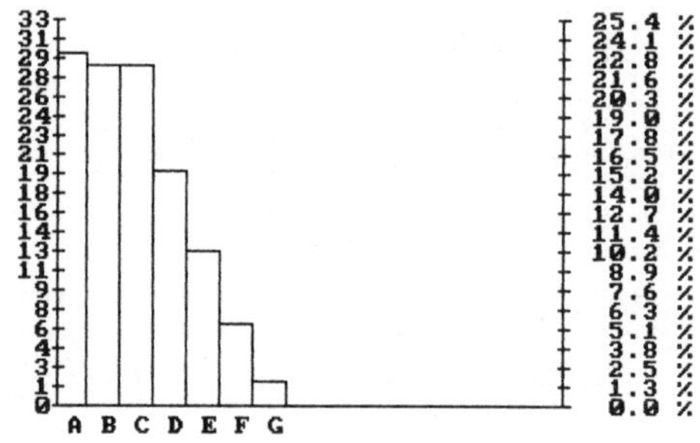

Code	Attribute	Defects
A =	DRIP	30
B =	SMUDGE	29
C =	BUBBLE	29
D =	DIRT	20
E =	DENT	13
F =	WRINKLE	7
G =	SAG	2

04/01/87 to 04/01/87
Total Units Audited: 45
Total Units Defective: 45

Data Reports — The data report prints the data samples, $\bar{x}$, R and sigma for each subgroup. The data report also includes assignable cause, machine and operator codes for each subgroup. The data report gives a short summary of the subgroups you included in the data report. The summary gives the number of samples in the data report, X double bar, range of the data and average sigma value.

Sample data report.

```
                                   DataMyte
                             FAN II Support System
                          Model 1049-05  Version 2.2
03/31/87 11:14                   Data Report                          Page 1
                                Process No. 14

Unit ID: STATION 22-C
Item ID: WIDTH 4

     1 03/31/87 10:25    000 000 000
                                 12.9983         13.0020         12.9983          13.0000
                                 13.0008
                   Mean of subgroup              12.9999   Range                  0.0037
                   Sigma                         0.0016
     2 03/31/87 10:25    000 000 000
                                 12.9996         13.0022         13.0014          13.0013
                                 13.0008
                   Mean of subgroup              13.0011   Range                  0.0026
                   Sigma                         0.0010
     3 03/31/87 10:25    000 000 000
                                 13.0008         12.9996         13.0002          12.9993
                                 12.9994
                   Mean of subgroup              12.9999   Range                  0.0015
                   Sigma                         0.0006
     4 03/31/87 10:25    000 000 000
                                 13.0007         13.0002         12.9990          12.9998
                                 12.9992
                   Mean of subgroup              12.9998   Range                  0.0017
                   Sigma                         0.0007
     5 03/31/87 10:25    000 000 000
                                 12.9992         13.0001         13.0007          13.0010
                                 13.0013
                   Mean of subgroup              13.0005   Range                  0.0021
                   Sigma                         0.0008
     6 03/31/87 10:25    000 000 000
                                 13.0006         13.0007         12.9995          13.0001
                                 12.9997
                   Mean of subgroup              13.0001   Range                  0.0012
                   Sigma                         0.0005
     7 03/31/87 10:25    000 000 000
                                 12.9996         13.0013         12.9995          13.0000
                                 13.0006
                   Mean of subgroup              13.0002   Range                  0.0018
                   Sigma                         0.0008

Summary of complete subgroups:
Number of samples                  35
X-bar mean                    13.0002
Data range                     0.0039
Sigma mean                     0.0009
```

DātaMyte

18.2 DATAMYTE ATTRIBUTE SOFTWARE PROGRAM

The DataMyte Attribute Software program analyzes and stores SPC attribute data that has been collected by DataMyte data collection systems. Data is changed into graphic form so better decisions can be made, rather than the QC manager having to rely just on numbers. This program lets the user send setup information to DataMyte 1005 and 1010 data collectors and unload data from these DataMytes directly from the computer.

The user can edit and look at prompt loops used in the DataMytes, edit and review collected data, format the data to be put into spreadsheets and data bases and back up data onto another disk. The program will also quickly and easily print bar code labels so data collection is more efficient, using a bar code wand.

18-12
DataMyte Software

System Requirements

- IBM PC or true compatible
- 256K memory
- Two disk drives
- Monitor (color optional)
- Asynchronous communications adapter
- Dot matrix parallel printer
- Serial interface cable (available from DataMyte)

Charting

- Pareto Charts
- p- and np- charts
- c-, c/100- and c/1000-charts
- u-charts
- Up to 50 subgroup points per chart
- Control limits are calculated by the program after 20 sets of data are collected

Communicating with DataMyte

- Edit prompt loops for data collection
- Print bar code labels for data collection

File Management

- Data is stored on floppy or hard disks
- User specifies disk drive for data storage
- Data files are organized by Audit ID, date and time of data collection
- Spreadsheet-like editor for data files
- Save, copy, delete or edit data files

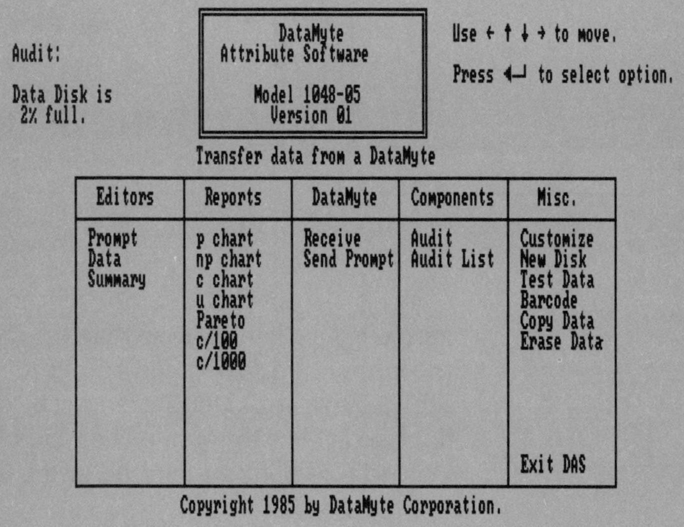

The DataMyte Attribute Software Program

Pareto Charts— The Pareto chart combines a bar graph that show the number and type of defects in an audit and a line showing the cumulative sum of the total number of defects. One chart shows one shift's worth of data.

The chart shows the number of defects as both a number and a percentage of the total defects. A table to the right of the graph gives the name of the attribute, the number of defects associated with that attribute and the code used on the graph identifying each defect.

The heading at the top of the report contains the users custom report heading and the Audit ID is displayed above the chart, too.

Sample Pareto chart.

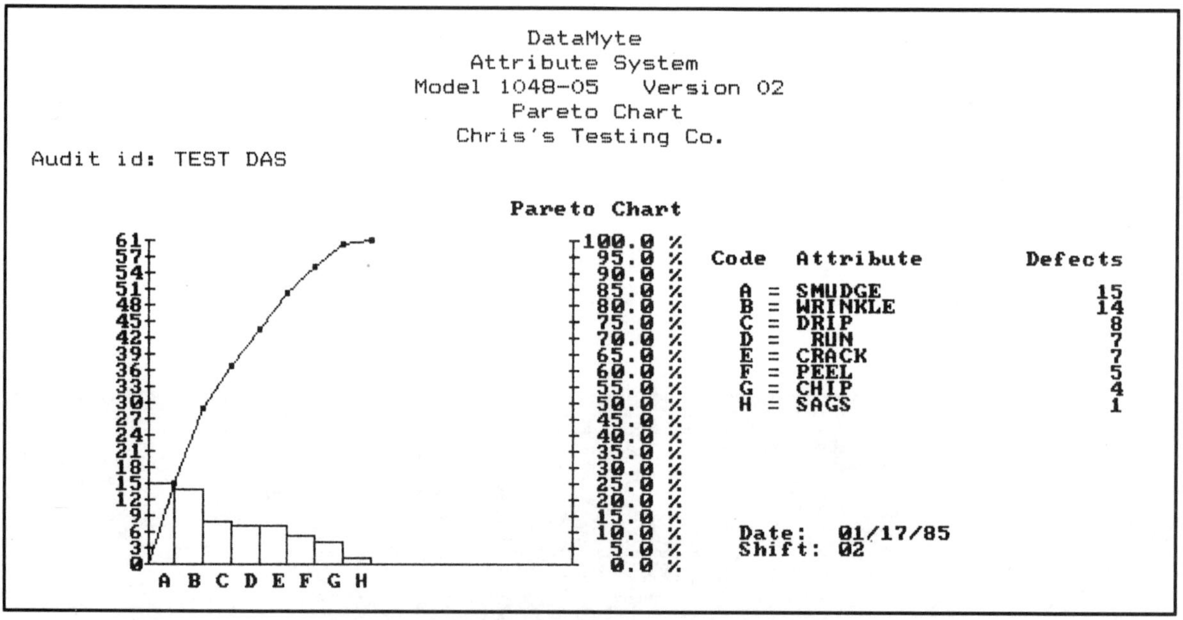

p-chart — A p-chart plots the percentage of parts found defective in a subgroup. DataMyte's p-chart displays p bar and the upper and lower control limits as percentages. The subgroups to be plotted are chosen by data and the Audit ID is displayed above the graph. The report has a five line heading that includes a line customized by the user.

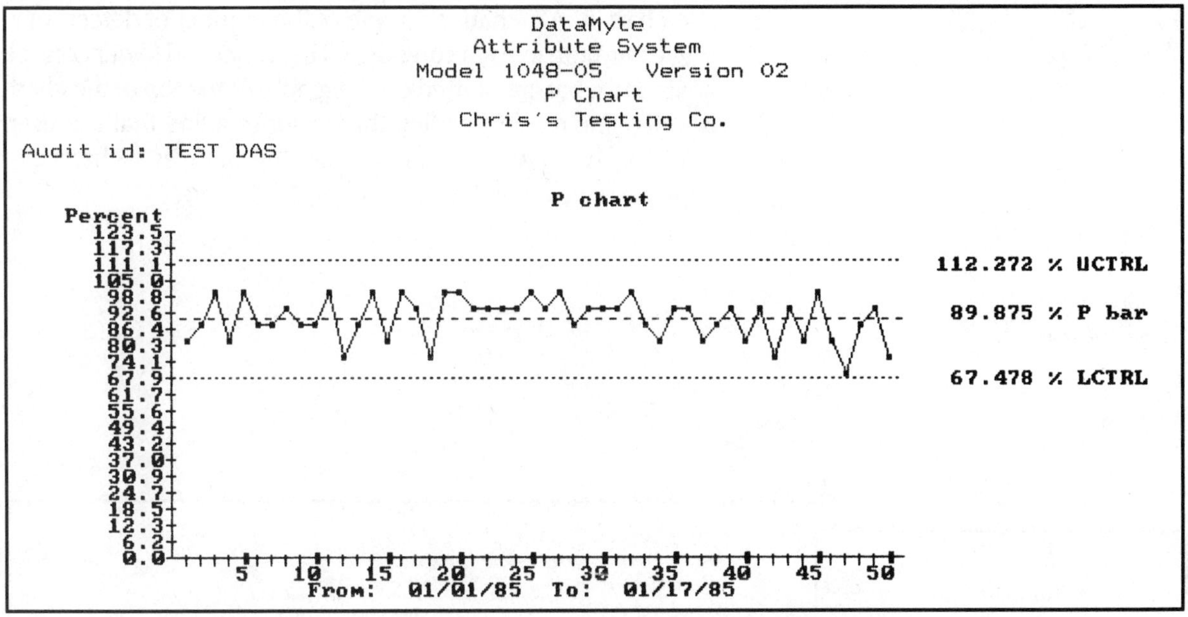

Sample p-chart.

np-chart — An np-chart is the same as a p-chart except the defects are plotted by number of defects instead of percentages. The DataMyte np-chart displays np bar and the upper and lower control limits. The plotted subgroups are chosen by date and the Audit ID is displayed above the graph. The report has a five line heading that includes a user-customized line.

Sample np-chart.

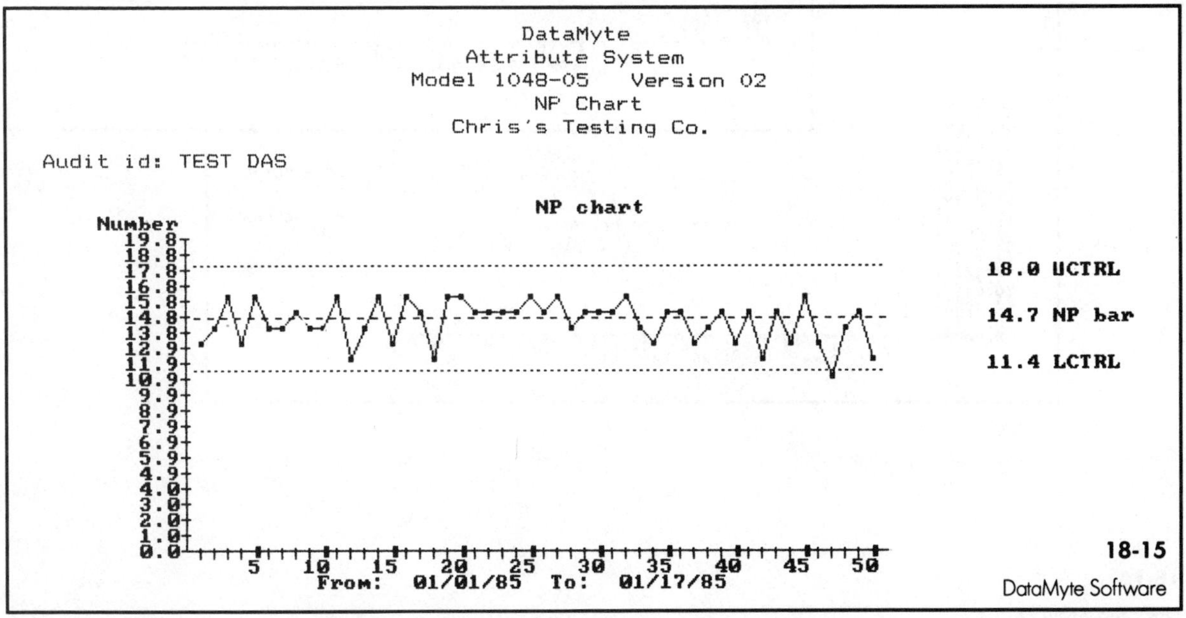

c-chart — A c-chart is a graph of the number of defects of a single attribute in each subgroup. The upper and lower control limits and c bar are plotted on the graph. At the top of the chart is a five-line report heading that includes a line that the user writes. c/100 and c/1000 charts are the same as c-charts except the data are plotted per 100 or 1000 parts.

Sample c-charts.

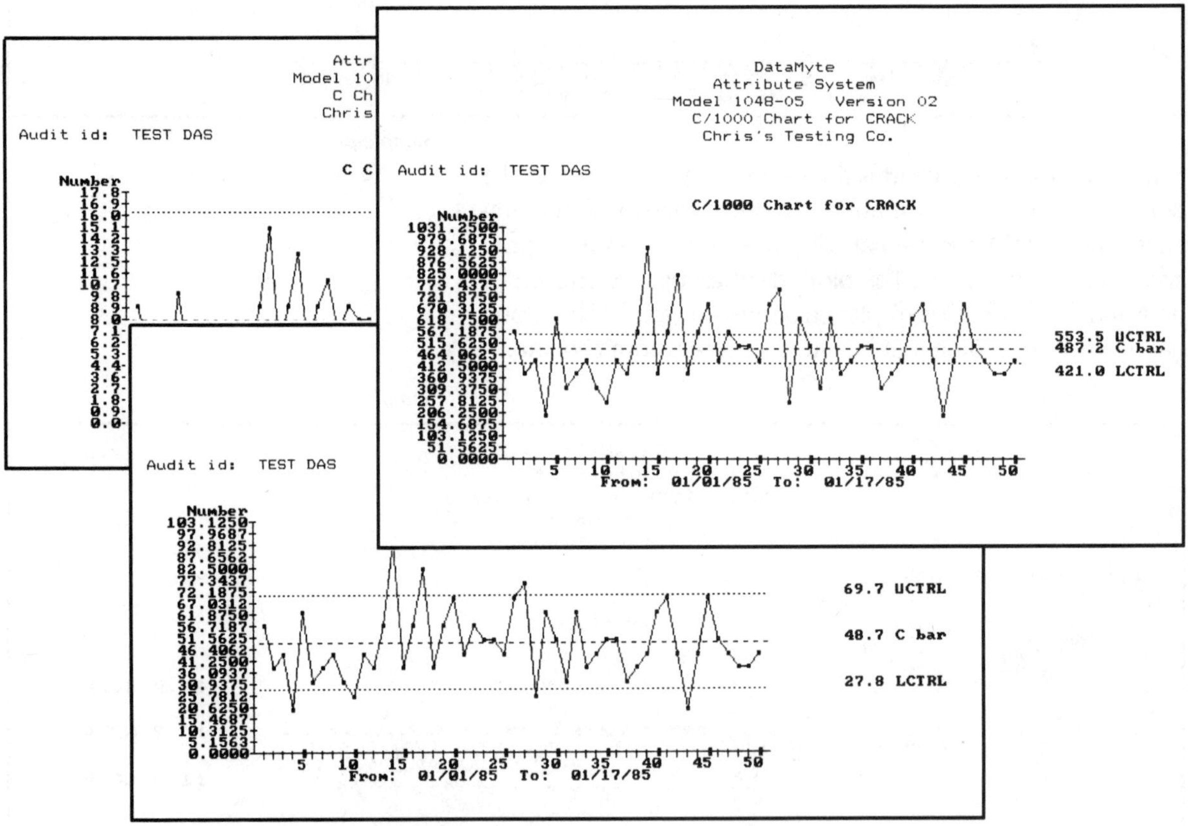

u-chart — A u-chart is a control chart of the percentage of defects in one subgroup to the total defects for an inspection. The u-chart shows u bar, the upper and lower control limits and the Audit ID. The report heading includes a line that the user customizes.

Sample u-chart.

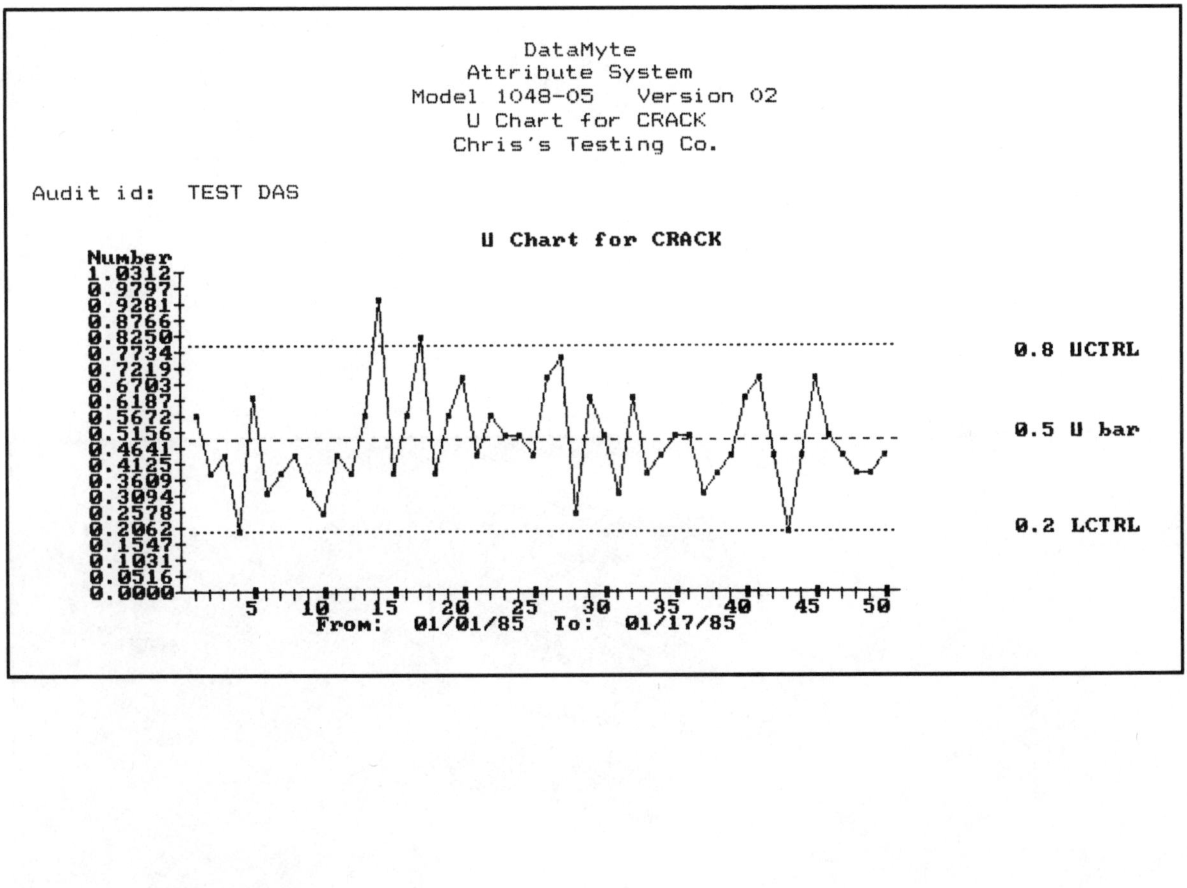

18.3 DATAMYTE UTILITY PROGRAMS

The DataMyte Utility Programs are software "tools" that will help the DataMyte user work with a computer. The programs are available for the IBM-PC and compatibles. The programs will:

- Transmit data from the DataMyte to the computer to save the data in a disk file,
- Print a report from the DataMyte by sending it through the computer to the computer's printer,
- Convert DataMyte data into files compatible with popular data management programs such as Lotus 1-2-3®,
- Print bar code labels,
- Allow the DataMyte to be used as a remote terminal and
- Send setup and other information to the DataMyte.

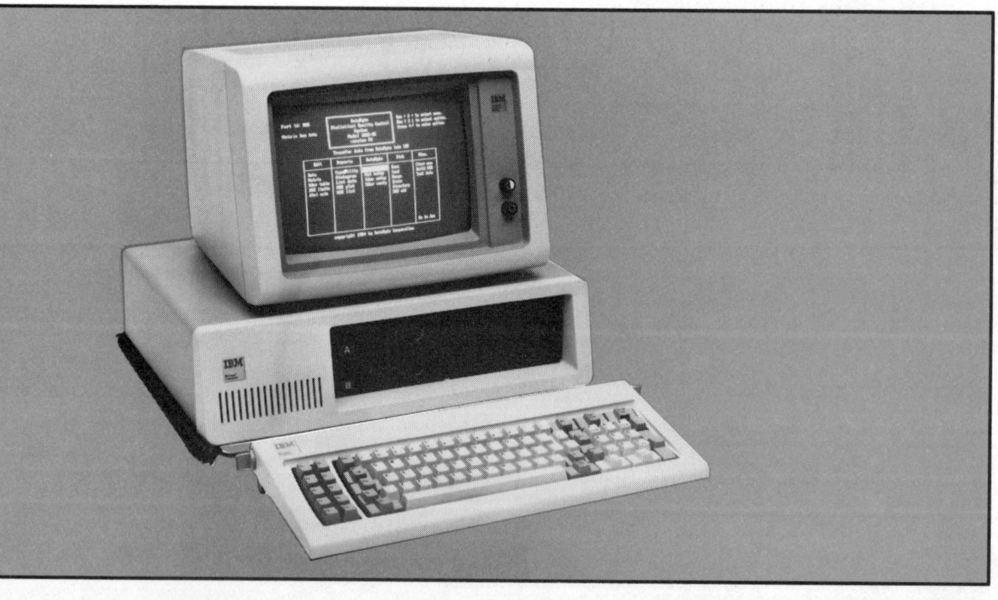

18.4 WORK MEASUREMENT SOFTWARE

DataMyte has two software disks for work measurement. The Time Study disk and the Work Sampling disk. Both of these disks work in conjunction with the DataMyte 1000 family of data collectors.

The Time Study disk uses four smaller programs to summarize both cyclic and continuous time studies for up to 100 elements and unlimited observations. The Time Study disk performs calculations required in time study data analysis and provides accurate and traceable documentation.

- The Time Study Check (TSC) program tallies the data and prints all observations to be deleted.
- The Time Study Extremes (TSE) program analyzes the highest and lowest readings for each element. This allows abnormally high or low extremes to be edited before printing any reports.
- Time Study Observations (TSO) is a basic worksheet program that essentially replaces the old clipboard form used in stopwatch studies.
- Time Study Summary (TSS1) prints the final time study summary, showing Normal/Occurrence, Normal/Cycle and Normal/Piece times.

```
              Time Study programs by DataMyte Corporation
                       Model 1031-04    version 06

                           Time Study Summary

Description ____________________________________________________________

Study Id: DRILL#1
Date: 03/06/84
Begin Time: 1519 (3:19 PM)

********** Deletions - time not used in summary ************************

                          1F,00144   0.13 ______________________________

                          4C,00262   0.06 ______________________________

                          2F,00507   0.11 ______________________________

                           H,00517   0.02 ______________________________

                          4F,00618   0.09 ______________________________

                     Time Deleted:   0.41

********** Summary *******************************************************
   obs      raw    rated   min   max     ave   rate nrm/cyc nrm/pce   nrm/occc

 0____________________________________________________________        0.1143
    14   1.6000   1.6000  0.06  0.20  0.1143 100.0   0.1143  0.0390

 1____________________________________________________________        0.0892
    13   1.1600   1.1600  0.04  0.16  0.0892 100.0   0.0829  0.0283

 2____________________________________________________________        0.0829
    14   1.1600   1.1600  0.05  0.15  0.0829 100.0   0.0829  0.0283

 3____________________________________________________________        0.0964
    14   1.3500   1.3500  0.04  0.29  0.0964 100.0   0.0964  0.0329

 4____________________________________________________________        0.0338
    13   0.4400   0.4400  0.01  0.08  0.0338 100.0   0.0314  0.0107


Totals                                         100.0   0.4079  0.1393
                                                       14 cyc  41 pcs

Fatigue at  15%                                        0.0612  0.0209
Totals                                                 0.4690  0.1602
```

```
              Work Sampling programs by DataMyte Corporation
                        Model 1031-04    version 06

                       Unrated Work Sampling Report

Description ___________________________________________________________

Errors...
   F09118O,     0126,    040129,
########## Cumulative percentages ####################################################
Activity> 1    2    3    4    5    6   7   8   9  10  11  12  13  14  15  16  17  18  19  20  21  22  23  24  Obs
Subject
  1    70.8  9.4  7.5    - 10.4  1.9   -   -   -   -   -   -   -   -   -   -   -   -   -   -   -   -   -   -  106

  2    53.8 10.4  7.5  0.9 27.4    -   -   -   -   -   -   -   -   -   -   -   -   -   -   -   -   -   -   -  106

  3    51.9  9.4  1.9  0.9 35.8    -   -   -   -   -   -   -   -   -   -   -   -   -   -   -   -   -   -   -  106

  4    54.3  5.7  2.9  1.0 36.2    -   -   -   -   -   -   -   -   -   -   -   -   -   -   -   -   -   -   -  105

  5    49.1    -    - 50.9    -    -   -   -   -   -   -   -   -   -   -   -   -   -   -   -   -   -   -   -  106

Total  56.0  7.0  4.0 10.8 21.9  0.4   -   -   -   -   -   -   -   -   -   -   -   -   -   -   -   -   -   -  529

High   58.1  8.1  4.8 12.1 23.7  0.6   -   -   -   -   -   -   -   -   -   -   -   -   -   -   -   -   -   -
Low    53.8  5.9  3.1  9.4 20.1  0.1   -   -   -   -   -   -   -   -   -   -   -   -   -   -   -   -   -   -

%Error  3.9 15.9 21.4 12.5  8.2 70.6   -   -   -   -   -   -   -   -   -   -   -   -   -   -   -   -   -   -
High, Low, %Error at 1.00 standard deviations.
```

- The Work Sampling program disk aids in the design and fixed interval and random interval work sampling and summarizes the work sampling data taken with the DataMyte. The types of reports generated are:
- Work Sampling Design WSD, which estimates the study and prints a random time schedule with times calculated not to interfere with breaks.
- Work Sampling Report (WSR), which summarizes cumulative data and prints percent activities for each subject. Both rated and unrated subjects can be entered. The composite rating for each subject, percent activities for the entire population and the specified confidence error for each activity are printed in each report. Up to 99 subjects, 24 activities and unlimited observations can be accommodated with the IBM-PC or HP-9816 software.

The Time Study and Work Sampling Software Package is available for:

- IBM-PC,
- HP-9816,
- Apple II, IIe, IIc and Macintosh,
- TRS-80 Model II and
- HP-85.

19. SPC SOFTWARE FROM OTHER SOURCES

INTRODUCTION

This chapter features software programs for SPC that are not available from DataMyte, but from other sources. The commercially available software packages listed here have all developed interfaces that allow their software to communicate with DataMyte data collectors.

There is not one SPC software program that would suit everyone's needs. Each company and industry requires unique SPC practices, some of which can be aided by computer-based SPC software. Many of these programs were developed first for a specific customer or industry and then offered commercially after they were found to be successful. Although all of the programs are comprehensive in offering both variables and attributes data analysis, each have distinct features, such as curve fitting or incoming inspection routines.

The descriptions that follow are very brief, listing only some of the capabilities, showing a few sample chart outputs, and describing the current hardware requirements. All specifications are subject to change. For more information on the software, contact the sources listed.

19.1 DESKTOP SOFTWARE

CAQE

C.A.Q.E.
102 Second Ave.
Warren, Pennsylvania 16365
Phone (814) 726-3707

The CAQE software program allows automatic or manual data input for up to 800 features into data base or indexed files. Each file allows up to 32 features. The data base allows up to six user-defined keys and time and date for sorting. Over 32,000 dimensions can be stored on floppy disks. Data can be transferred to other software applications through DIF files.

Charts include $\bar{x}$, sigma, histograms, p-, np-, c-, u-, and Pareto charts. Many statistics are available from the program, including skewness, kurtosis, variance, CPK and others. Analyze the data using t- and f-tests, chi-square, Poisson, binomial and normal distributions.

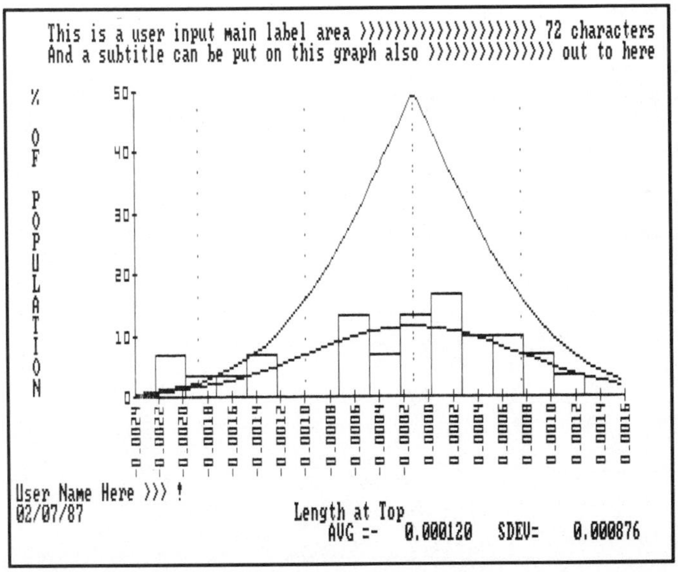

IBM PC Hardware Requirements:

- IBM PC, XT, AT or compatible
- Two disk drives
- 512K memory
- IBM Color Graphics (or equivalent)
- Color monitor
- RS-232 port
- IBM, Epson, Okidata, or compatible graphics printer
- Options supported include HP 7470/7475 plotter

Hewlett-Packard Hardware Requirements:

- HP 9000 series (200/300)
- Two disk drives
- 1Mbyte memory
- BASIC 2.1 (or later)
- HP printer or plotter

Program can Interface:

- DataMyte 750 series

Custom/QC

Stochos, Inc.
14 North College St.
Schenectady, New York 12305
Phone (518) 372-5426

Hardware Requirements:

- IBM PC, XT, AT or compatible
- Two disk drives
- 512K memory
- RS-232 port
- Options supported include color and monochrome graphics

Program can Interface:

- DataMyte 750
- DataMyte 1500

Custom/QC is an SPC software package featuring 16 control charts along with many other statistical tools for analyzing production data. It features configurable graphics output, keystroke macros for repetitive tasks and a capture device for receiving data from DataMyte data collectors.

The charts include $\bar{x}$ & R, $\bar{x}$ & sigma, moving average and moving range, histogram, cumulative sum & sigma, min/max, chi-square, t-square, Pareto, p-, np-, c- and u-charts. Statistics included with Custom/QC include CP, CPK, kurtosis, skewness mean square successive differences and others.

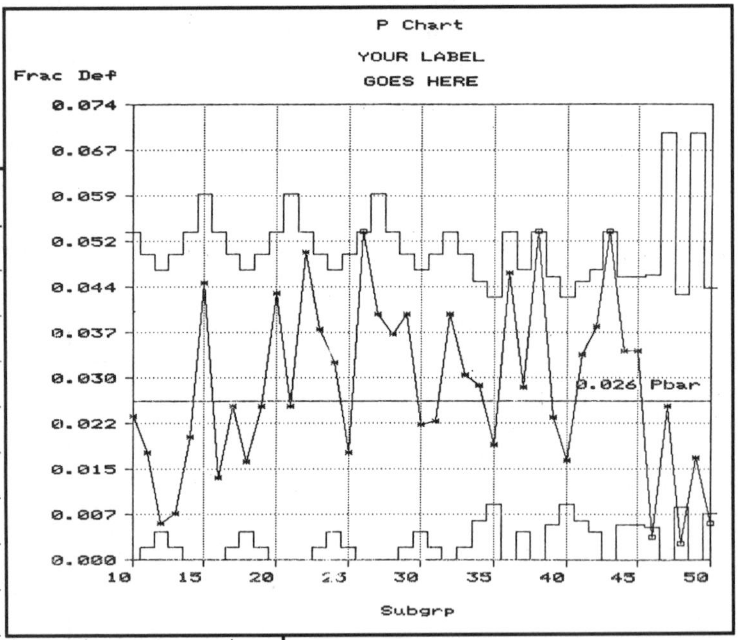

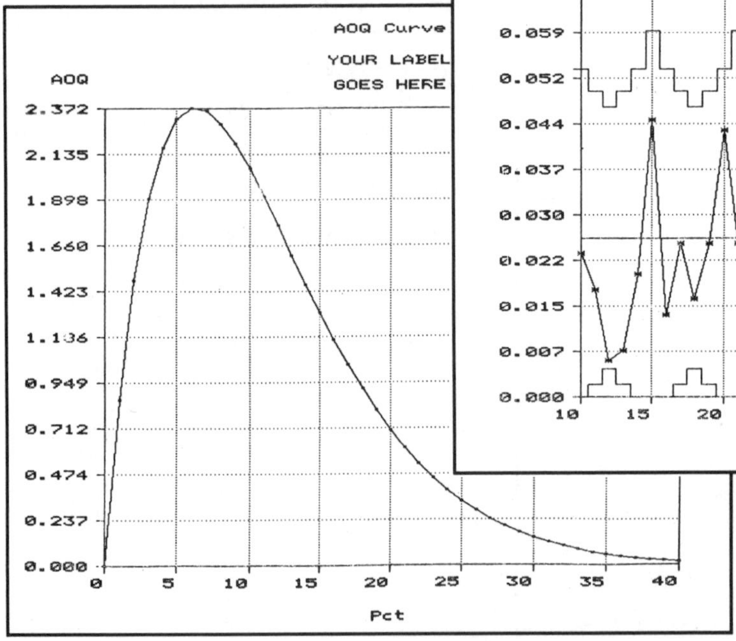

ECP StatMaster Statistical Process Control System

ECP, Inc.
12158 Globe Road
Livonia, Michigan 48150
Phone (313) 464-7900

ECP StatMaster is a statistical analysis system for both variables and attributes data. It features curve fitting routines and measures of skewness on histograms. Direct entry from a DataMyte and keyboard entry are supported. Data from a DataMyte 1000 can be transmitted and plotted on p-, np-, c-, and u-charts. User-definable keys enable data to be labeled with source machine numbers, shifts, operators, cavities, and other comments. Any date-time interval for part data can be selected for analysis. The program is menu driven with several features to guide data entry and analysis with a minimum number of keystrokes.

Besides interfacing DataMyte products, the program will accept readings directly from electronic columns and transducers. Parts are defined with up to 30 descripters, allowing quick search and editing. Besides $\bar{x}$ & R and sigma charts, the program provides scatter charts, median charts, individuals charts, trend analysis, and many others. Reported statistics include run sum tests and percentages in zones above and below chart centerline, as well as many others.

IBM Hardware Requirements:

- IBM PC, XT or AT
- 512K of memory
- Graphics board

Hewlett-Packard Hardware Requirements:

- HP 9000 series 200/300 computer
- 1Mb of memory
- Pascal 3.1
- RS-232 & IEEE-488
- HP 82906B Printer or HP 2225 ThinkJet Printer
- Similar software also available for HP 86.

Program can Interface:

- DataMyte 750 family
- DataMyte DataTruck
- DataMyte 1500 family
- DataMyte 1000 family

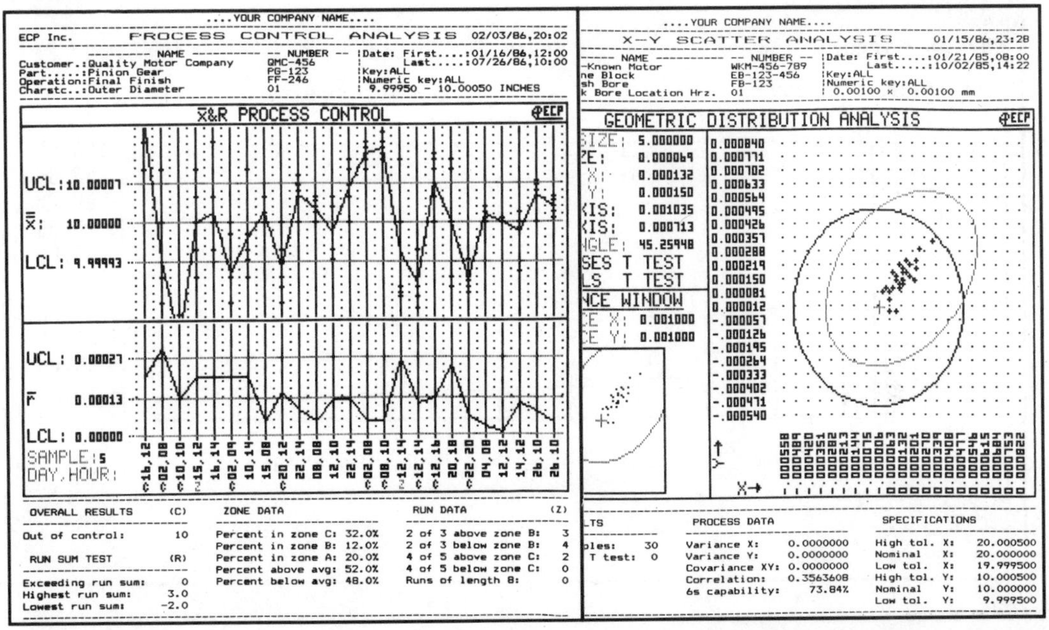

ESP-QC

Electronic Data Systems Corporation
P.O. Box 7019
803 West Big Beaver Road
Troy, Michigan 48007-7019
Phone (313) 244-2771

ESP-QC is a comprehensive set of routines that have the power to perform a wide range of statistical calculations, including:

- Descriptive statistics
- Histogram charting
- Pareto charting
- Variable control charts
- Attribute control charts
- Sampling plan analysis
- Measurement System analysis
- Capability analysis
- Bivariate data analysis
- Conformance to specifications

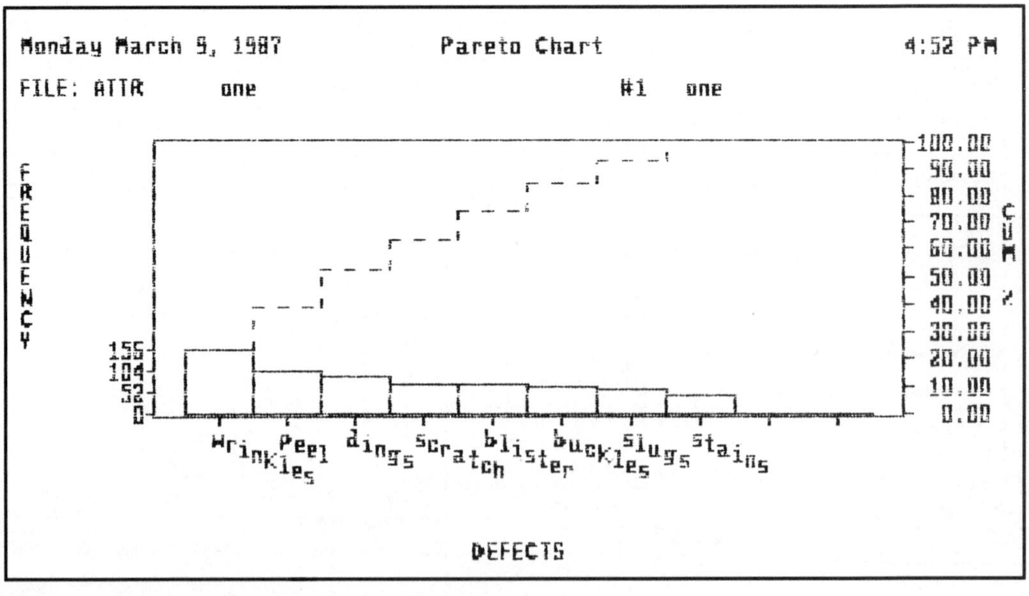

ESP-QC also provides the user with a graphics tool to visualize the part being analyzed. The results can be used to control processes, examine machine and employee performance, check gage variation, design effective sampling plans, and display the resulting information in the form of printouts and on-screen color graphics.

ESP-QC processes non-normal data using techniques proprietary to General Motors and Electronic Data Systems Corporation. Advanced routines provide accurate and timely means of tracking a process or product's level of conformance to specifications. Data sets are available to all routines in the program. The program guarantees automatic adherence to standard industry-wide SPC-related terminology.

Hardware Requirements:

- IBM PC, XT, AT or compatible
- Hard disk drive
- Math co-processor recommended
- 512K memory
- RS-232 port
- color graphics card
- Color or monochrome monitor
- Options include printers and HP plotters

Program can Interface:

- DataMyte 1000 family
- DataMyte 1500 family
- DataMyte 2000 family

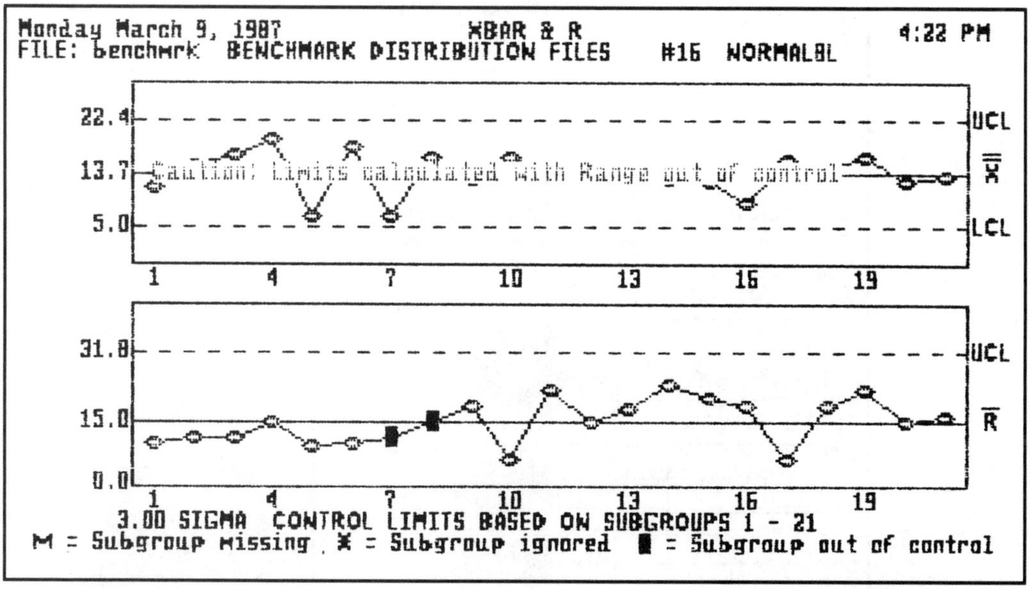

Genzlinger SPC

Genzlinger Associates, Inc.
Two Northfield Plaza, Suite 212
5700 Crooks Road
Troy, Michigan 48098
Phone (313) 879-7070

The Genzlinger Statistical Process Control system lets you enter from DataMyte 750s, the computer keyboard, portable pocket calculator, on-line gages or voice input. The program stores up to 99 characteristics per part and up to eight measurements per sample. The number of samples per characteristic is limited only by disk capacity. The DataMyte interface screen allows you to send part and characteristic data to a DataMyte data collector, print DataMyte reports and generate all of the Genzlinger charts and reports for analysis.

The charts generated by the program include x̄ & R charts with histogram, x̄ & sigma charts with histogram, data plot with x̄ and individual measurement histogram. Attribute charts include p-, np-, c- and u-charts. Data can be selected by date, time, and up to six user-defined categories. The program also interfaces with Lotus 1-2-3 and advanced statistical analysis packages.

Hardware Requirements:

- IBM PC,XT,AT or compatible
- Two disk drives
- 256K memory
- RS-232 port
- Color graphics
- Color or monochrome monitor
- Dot-matrix printer

Program can Interface:

- DataMyte 750 family

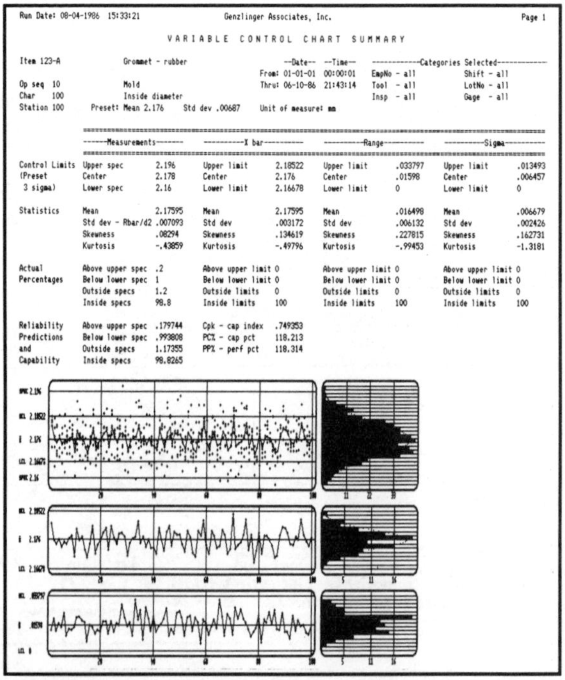

Run Date: 08-04-1986 15:33:21 Genzlinger Associates, Inc. Page 1

VARIABLE CONTROL CHART SUMMARY

Item 123-A Grommet - rubber
Op seq 10 Mold
Char 100 Inside diameter
Station 100 Preset: Mean 2.176 Std dev .00687 Unit of measure: mm

--Date-- --Time--
From: 01-01-01 00:00:01
Thru: 06-10-86 21:43:14

Categories Selected: EmpNo - all, Shift - all, Tool - all, LotNo - all, Insp - all, Gage - all

	Measurements		X bar		Range		Sigma	
Control Limits	Upper spec	2.196	Upper limit	2.18522	Upper limit	.033797	Upper limit	.013493
(Preset	Center	2.178	Center	2.176	Center	.01598	Center	.006457
3 sigma)	Lower spec	2.16	Lower limit	2.16678	Lower limit	0	Lower limit	0
Statistics	Mean	2.17595	Mean	2.17595	Mean	.016498	Mean	.006679
	Std dev - Rbar/d2	.007093	Std dev	.003172	Std dev	.006132	Std dev	.002426
	Skewness	.08294	Skewness	.134619	Skewness	.227815	Skewness	.162731
	Kurtosis	-.43859	Kurtosis	-.49796	Kurtosis	-.99453	Kurtosis	-1.3181
Actual	Above upper spec	.2	Above upper limit	0	Above upper limit	0	Above upper limit	0
Percentages	Below lower spec	1	Below lower limit	0	Below lower limit	0	Below lower limit	0
	Outside specs	1.2	Outside limits	0	Outside limits	0	Outside limits	0
	Inside specs	98.8	Inside limits	100	Inside limits	100	Inside limits	100
Reliability	Above upper spec	.179744	Cpk - cap index	.749353				
Predictions	Below lower spec	.993808	PC% - cap pct	118.213				
and	Outside specs	1.17355	PP% - perf pct	118.314				
Capability	Inside specs	98.8265						

MetriStat Lab System

MetriStat RealTime System
MetriStat Division, Business Systems Design, Inc.
1205 Wall Street
Oconomowoc, WI 53066
Phone (414) 569-9801

MetriStat is an integrated system of real-time data acquistiton and comprehensive analysis software featuring a relational data base and presentation quality control charting.

The RealTime System provides the operator with an instant run chart and histogram, capability study information, full population histogram, $\bar{x}$ & R charts, and other statistical results. Multiple gages and gaging stations can be suported by the Autoscan function that allows you to specify the sequence of gages.

The MetriStat Lab System allows both variable and attribute data to be entered, analyzed, stored long-term, and charted. The relational features allow manipulation of the data for multiple "views" of the data, by any combination of the following: date span, time span, operator, machine, or any user-defined variable. Notes can be added to clarify the situation occurring at the time the sample was taken.

Import/Export program transfers data into the data base from other programs.

Hardware Requirements:

- IBM PC or compatible
- 256K of memory
- Color monitor
- Graphics printer

Program can Interface:

- DataMyte 750 family
- DataMyte 760 family
- DataTruck

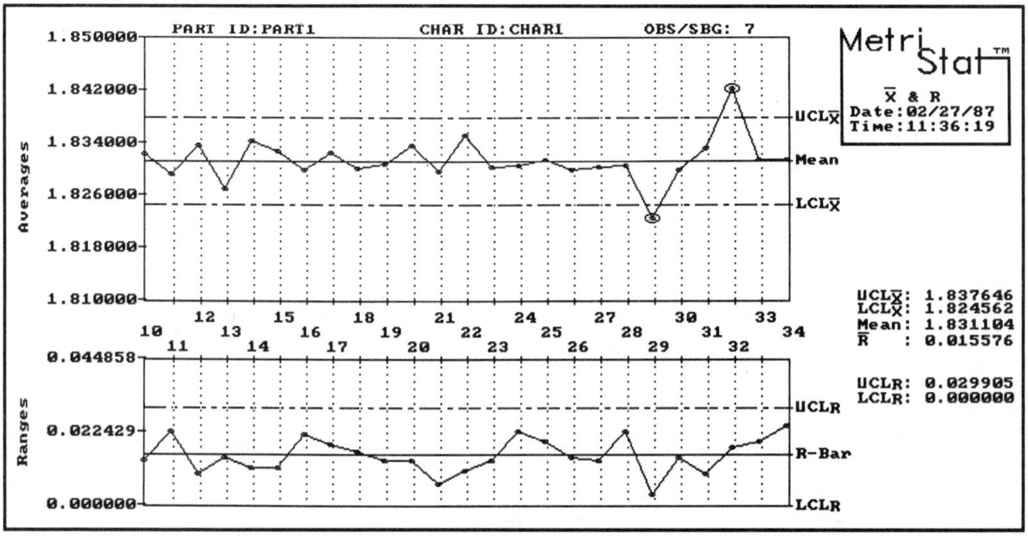

QA/S®

Paul Hertzler & Co., Inc.
221 North Main Street, Suite 200
Goshen, Indiana 46526
Phone (219) 533-0571

Hardware Requirements:

- IBM PC, XT, AT or compatible
- Hard disk drive
- IBM CGA, IBM EGA or Hercules graphics adapter
- RS-232 port
- Dot-matrix printer
- Options supported include multi-pen plotter (HP-GL compatible)

Program can Interface:

- DataMyte 750
- DataMyte 762
- DataMyte 1500
- DataMyte 2000
- DataTruck

QA/S® is a statistical process control program that permits entry from DataMyte data collectors or through the computer keyboard. Data may be retrieved by part, characteristic, date, time, Machine, Manpower, Method or Material. Data may be studied either as individuals or subgroups. Variables charts include $\bar{x}$ & R, $\bar{x}$ and moving range, tabulations, scatter diagrams, run sum, process capablility, paired sample and other kinds of analysis. The attributes module produces p-, np-, u-, c-, pie and Pareto charts, showing defects sorted by reason code.

Features of the program include context-sensitive help messages, pop-up data information windows and full cursor control.

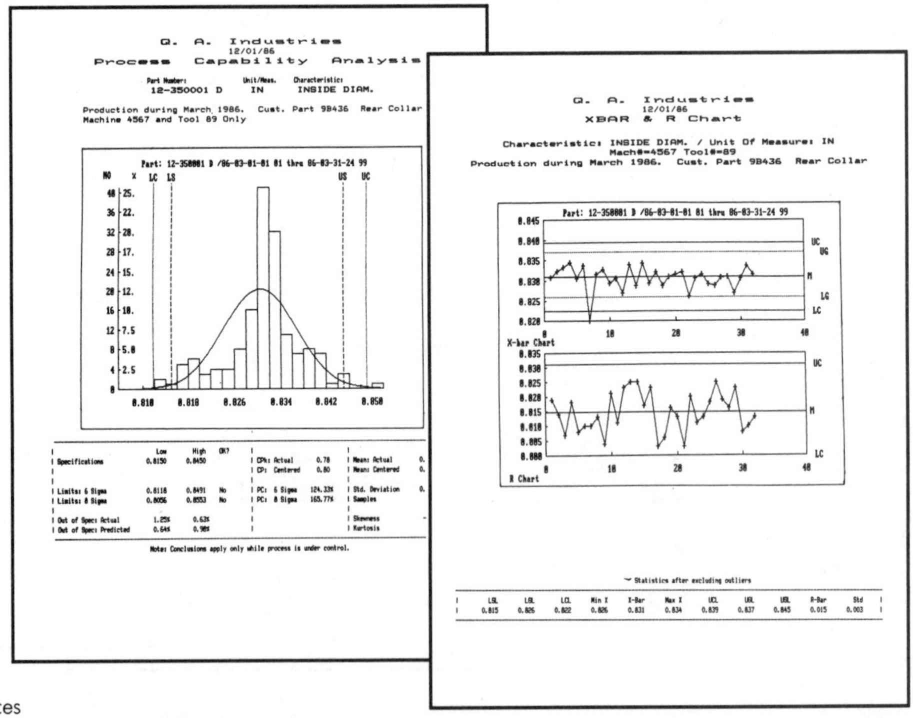

QC-CALC

Pro-Link Corporation
1214 Post Road
Fairfield, Connecticut 06457
Phone (203) 259-5008

QC-CALC lets you enter data through an RS-232 interface, or through its full-screen editor. QC-CALC can record data for 1250 dimensions and up to 5000 parts. Nominals, tolerances, feature and user labels, as well as other control parameters are stored and managed for each dimension. The program allows entry on non-variable (attribute) data for each observation input. Menu selections provide full data base extraction capability; data can be extracted based on date, record number sequence, attribute factors, or any combination of these.

The charts provided by QC-CALC include $\bar{x}$ & R, $\bar{x}$ & sigma, moving average and moving range, Pareto, p-, c-, and u-charts. The program also gives frequency distributions, distribution tests, regresssion and correlation, raw data plots and outlier analysis.

Hardware Requirements:

- IBM PC, XT, AT or compatible
- Hard disk drive
- 256K memory (320K with Hercules Adapter)
- IBM CGA, IBM EGA or Hercules HGC graphics adapter (or equivalent)
- Color monitor
- RS-232 port
- IBM or compatible graphics printer
- Options supported include HP Laser Jet or Think Jet Printer, pen plotter

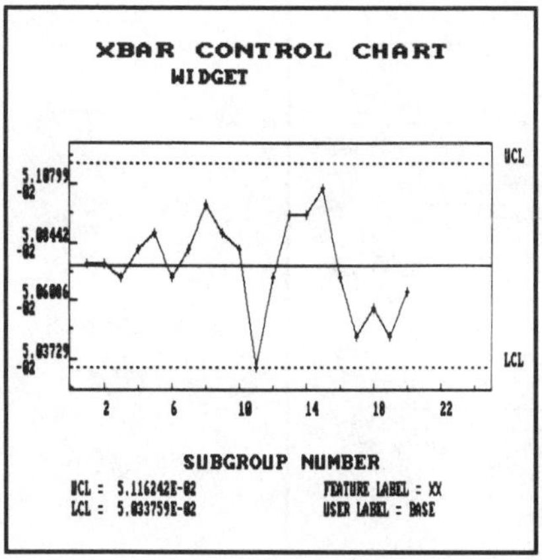

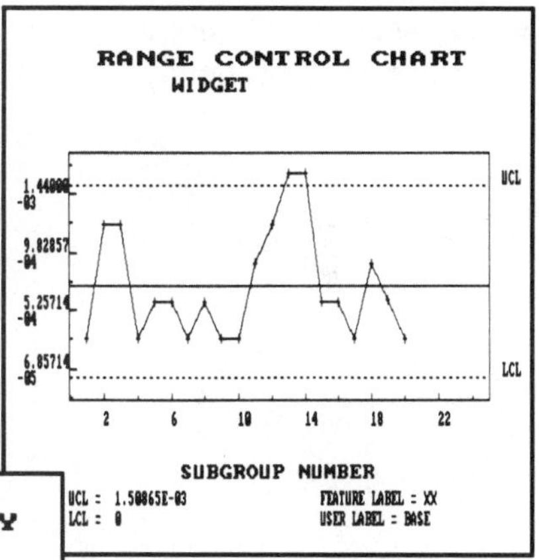

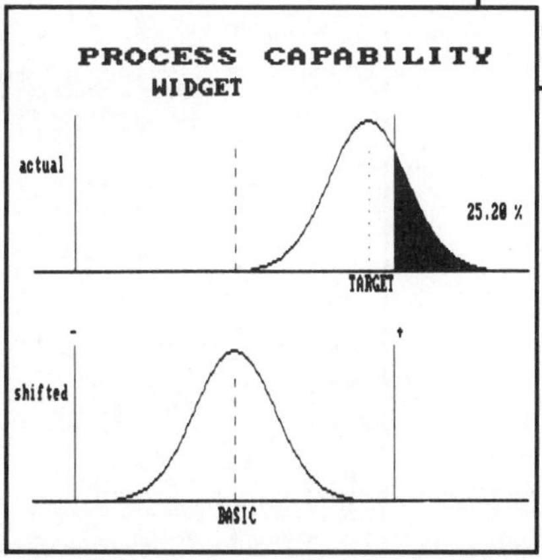

QScan System

ProScan, Inc.
13740 Research Q-2
Austin, Texas 78750
Phone (512) 250-1173

QScan is a PC-based expert system for dynamic statistical process control. It helps detect and explain process control problems and suggest corrective actions. QScan is an integrated set of configurable tools for managers, engineers and line operators. Engineers can use the program to design on-line data collection and analysis applications, to configure process control workstations with operator instructions and to diagnose the process. Line operators use the program to update control charts and to make process adjustments. They can use QScan to set up data collectors and download data for analysis.

QScan includes Shewhart, CuSum, GMA variables and attributes charts.

Hardware Requirements:

- IBM PC, XT, AT or compatible; IBM 3270 PC family
- Two disk drives
- 384K memory minimum, 640K memory desired
- RS-232 port
- Options supported include 8087 and 80287 math co-processors, PC Mouse, color graphics, graphics printers and plotters compatible with Lotus 1-2-3.

Program can Interface:

- DataMyte 750 family
- DataMyte 1000 family
- DataMyte 1500 family
- DataMyte 2000 family

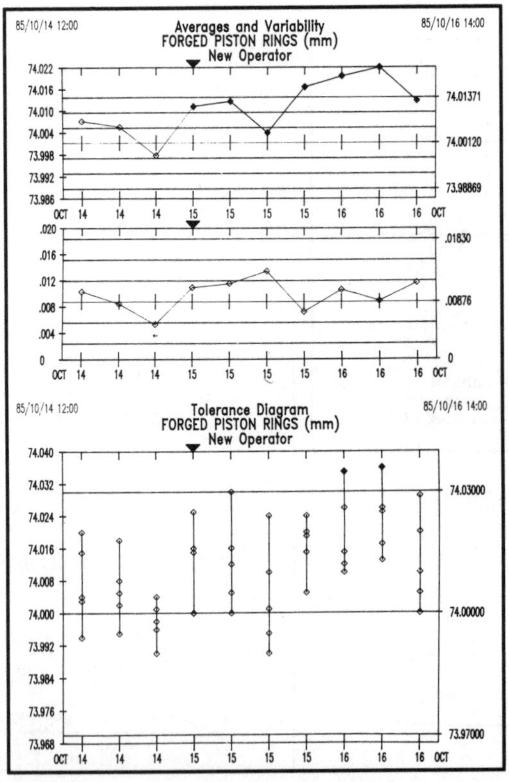

Quality Alert 2.5

Penton Software, Inc.
420 Lexington Ave.
Suite 2846
New York, New York 10017
Phone (800) 221-3414 or (212) 878-9600

Quality Alert 2.5 is a statistical quality control program that analyzes both variables and attributes data generated from samples selected from continuous processes. The program also analyzes process capability, features 11 types of control charts, and determines when quality deviations occur. Quality Alert produces numeric data, statistics, and graphics displays on a screen or graphics-capable printer.

The program communicates with DataMytes for variable data. File management includes storing, editing, merging and retrieving data. Variable charts include $\bar{x}$, range, s, moving average and moving range, histograms and cusum charts. Attribute charts include Pareto, p-, np-, u- and c-charts. The charts can be manually scaled.

Hardware Requirements:

- IBM PC, XT, AT and compatibles
- 128K of memory
- One or two disk drives
- DOS 2.0, 2.1, or 3.0 and 80-column display
- IBM printer with graphics, or Epson MX, RX, FX, and LQ series with Graftrax, Okidata, Toshiba 3 in 1 printers, plus graphics card.
- HP 7470 and 7475, Houston Inruments and Sweet P plotters (optional)

Program can Interface:

- DataMyte 750 family
- 1500 family

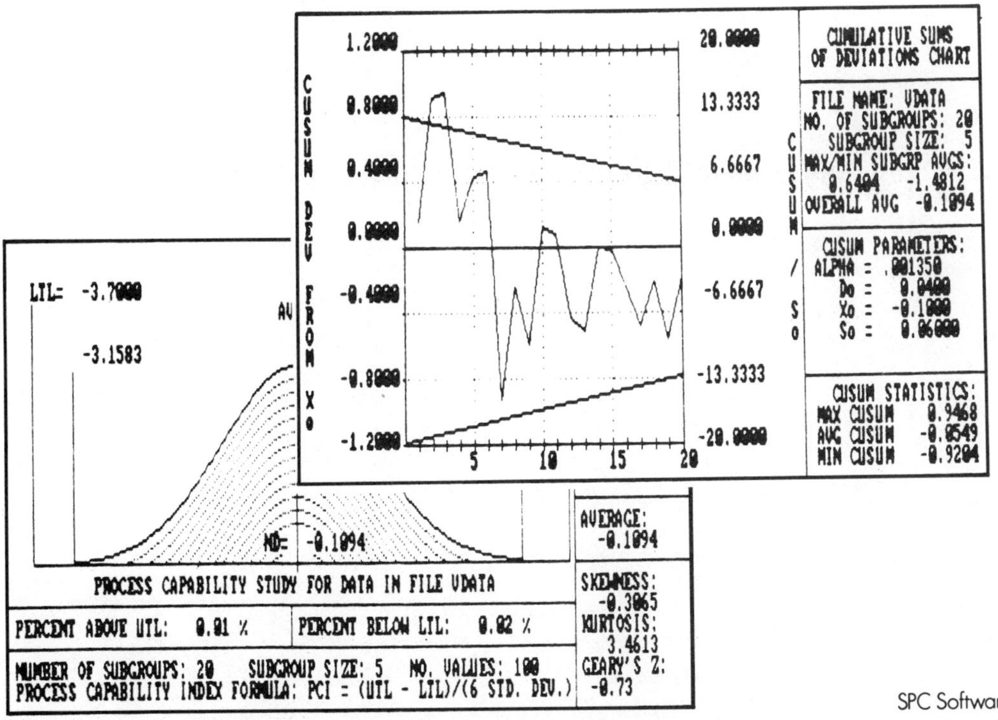

RS/1®

BBN Software Products Corporation
10 Fawcett Street
Cambridge/ Massachussetts 02238
Phone (617) 864-1780

Hardware Requirements:

- DEC MicroVAX, DEC MicroPCP-11; IBM PC/XT, IBM PC/AT
- Hard disk drive
- Memory depends on computer used
- Many printers and plotters

RS/1® has a full set of functions for reading and writing external data files. The ASCII files produced by DataMyte data collectors or the FAN II Software program may be easily read into one or more RS/1 tables for further analysis. In addition, the setup information for DataMyte data collectors may also be stored in RS/1 tables for downloading into DataMyte setup files.

The I/O functions of RS/1 are complemented by its ability to be temporarily interrupted while an external command or program is executed. This feature can be embedded into a procedure that automates the collection of data from DataMyte data collectors in a way that makes the intermediate data transfer steps completely transparent to the end user. As a result, the entire process of organizing and analyzing the data collected with the DataMyte data collector can be managed entirely within the RS/1 environment.

SPC DataLyzer

Stephen Computer Services, Inc.
34700 Grand River Avenue
Farmington, Michigan 48024
Phone (313) 478-1686

SPC DataLyzer has four software modules:

- Pac I for variables control charts takes data from a DataMyte 1500, 750 or the keyboard and produces $\bar{x}$ & R, $\bar{x}$ & S and individuals control charts.
- Pac II for attributes control charts takes data from a DataMyte 1000 and produces p-, np-, c-, n-, and Pareto charts.
- Pac III for capability studies takes data from DataMyte and produces a probability paper and histogram.
- Pac IV for gage repeatability and reproduceability produces performance/confidence curves for both attribute and variables gages.

Features of the programs include flagged runs and trends, stepped control limits (attributes), data curve fitting (capability) and auto scaling of graphs.

Hardware Requirements:

- Hewlett Packard HP 86 with 128K memory, or IBM PC, XT and AT with 384K of memory
- Printer, plotter or CRT for output

Program can Interface:

- DataMyte 750 family
- DataMyte 1000 family
- DataMyte 1500 family

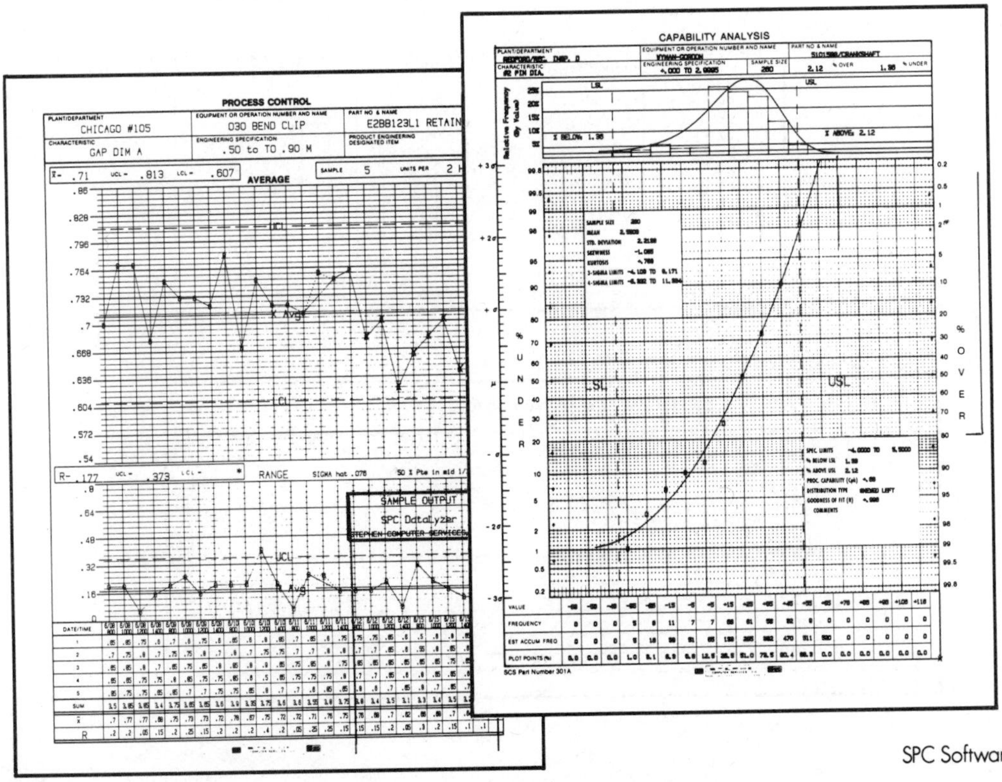

SPC1 +

Advanced Systems and Designs, Inc.
19853 W. Outer Drive, Suite 302
Dearborn, Michigan 48124
Phone (313) 278-5506

Hardware Requirements:

- IBM PC, XT, AT or compatible
- 384K of memory
- RS-232 port
- Options supported include color and monochrome graphics

Program can Interface:

- DataMyte 750
- DataMyte 760
- DataMyte 1500
- DataMyte 2000

SPC1 + is a statistical process control program that provides for dynamic memory allocation, unequal sampling sizes, extended pattern analysis on applicable charts, multiple control limit ranges, user-defined range of subgroups displayed on charts.

The variables charts include average and range, average and sigma, median and range, individuals with moving range, moving average and moving range, linear trend average and range and CuSum with masking. SPC1 + also calculates histograms and process capability, cumulative probability and descriptive statistics. The attribute charts include Pareto (by frequency or weighted value), p-, np-, c-, and u-charts.

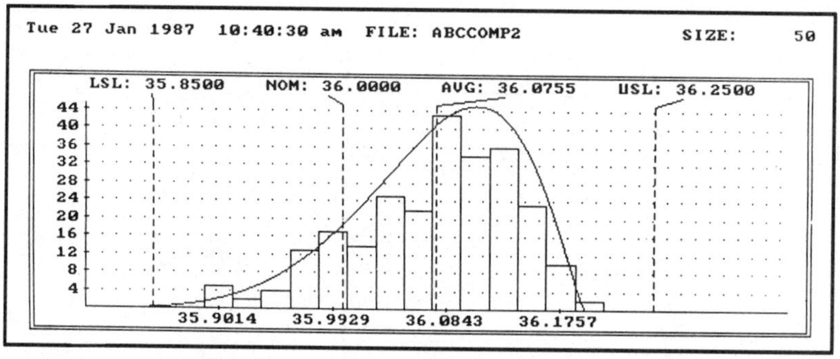

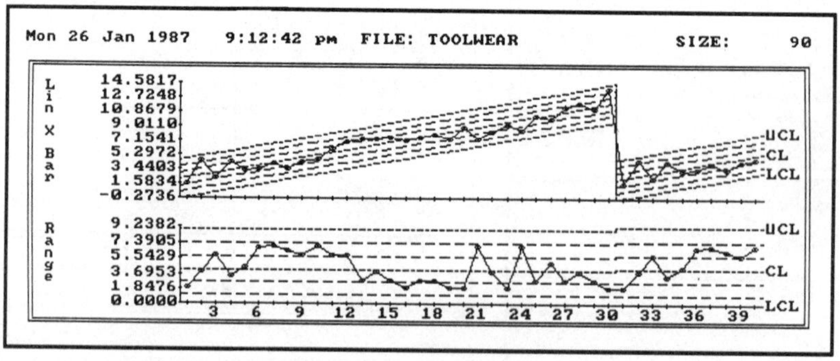

SPC Express

Major Micro Systems, Inc.
Distributed by Compuflex, Inc.
12355 Wormer Avenue
Detroit, Michigan 48239
Phone (313) 537-1226

SPC Express is a menu-driven software program written in compiled BASIC and Assembly language. The program takes data from a DataMyte, gages or keyboard and produces control charts for both variable and attribute data. On-screen graphics make extensive use of color to highlight control problems. Charts include $\bar{x}$ & R charts, individuals and moving range charts, p-, u-, n-, c-, and Pareto charts and histograms. Printed reports can be full page, one-third page or two pages, depending on the amount of detail desired.

File Management features include full-screen editing, browsing through any subgroup, and a built-in data protection system in case of power loss. Setup files can be downloaded to the DataMyte data collectors.

Hardware Requirements:

- IBM XT, AT, XT or compatible with 256K of memory
- Two floppy disk drives or floppy disk and hard disk
- Color or enhanced graphics adaptor card
- Epson or IBM graphics printers, HP ThinkJet, IBM Proprinter, IBM QuietWriter

Program can Interface:

- DataMyte 750
- DataMyte 762
- DataMyte 1000
- DataMyte 1500

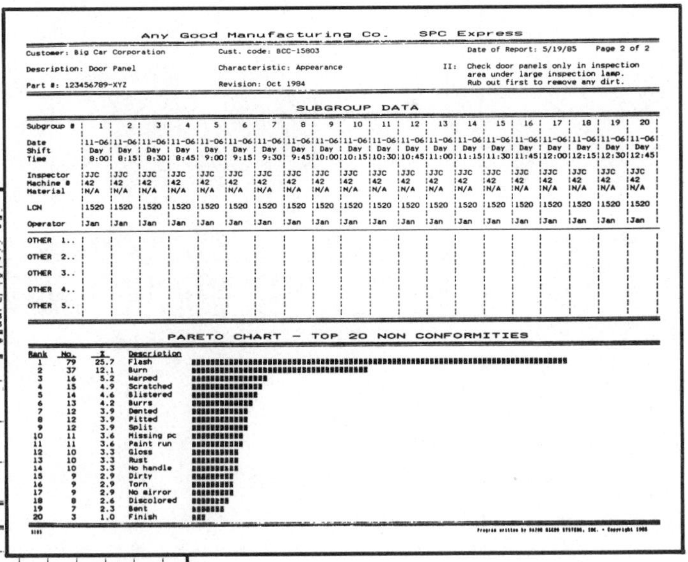

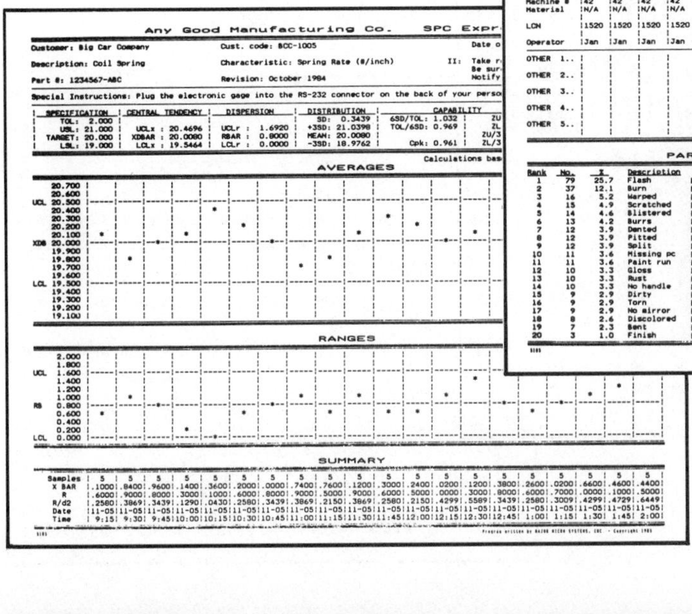

SPC TimeSaver

Zontec, Inc.
1329 E. Kemper Rd.
Cincinnati, Ohio 45246
Phone (800) 847-8100 or in Ohio (513) 671-0088

Hardware Requirements:

- IBM PC, XT, AT or compatible with 256K of memory
- Two floppy disk drives or floppy disk and hard disk
- PC-DOS 2.0 or higher
- Color graphic, black and white graphic or monochrome monitor
- Asynchronous communications adaptor

Program can Interface:

- DataMyte 1500 family
- DataMyte FAN System

SPC TimeSaver provides control charting, descriptive statistics, capability analysis, charting, charting of tool wear and Pareto charts in a single compiled BASIC program. The program has a single main menu, and provides complete control over data storage, calculation, analysis and display of control chart information. Three sets of control limits can be maintained on any set of samples. Samples can be withheld from calculations and then restored for data analysis.

Data from a DataMyte can be used in $\bar{x}$ & R, median and run charts, histograms and capability analysis. Up to 100 parts can be put on a control chart. Attribute charts include p-, np-, u-, c-, and Pareto charts. Control charts of shifting process averages can be used for tool wear analysis or detecting changes in efficiency over time.

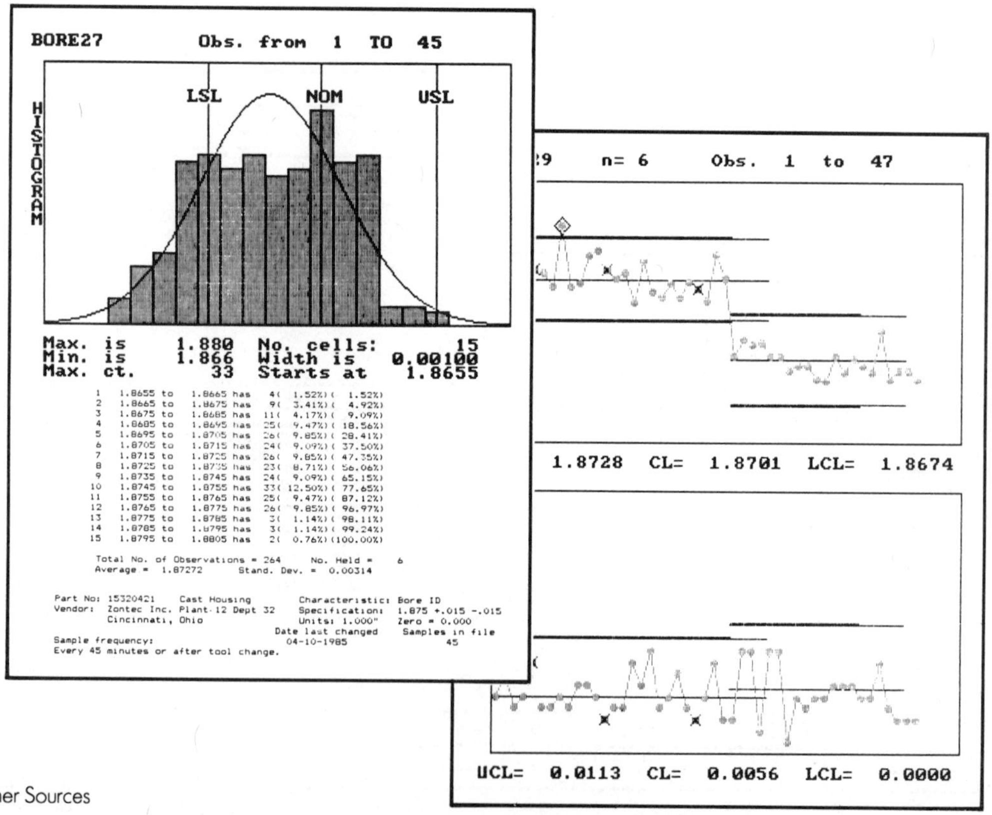

SQCpack

PQ Systems
470 Windsor Park Drive
P.O. Box 633
Dayton, Ohio 45459
Phone (800) 547-1565 or in Ohio (513) 435-9711

SQCpack includes variables and attributes charting, along with problem solving techniques in a compiled BASIC program. High resolution screen graphics are used to display charts, which can be dumped to a printer or HP plotter. The program will set up a DataMyte 1500 or 750. File sizes are unlimited, and can be edited on the screen.

Control charts include $\bar{x}$ & R, $\bar{x}$ & s, individuals, moving average and range charts, cumulative sum, and histogram capability analysis. Attributes charts include p-, np-, c-, and u-charts.

Hardware Requirements:

- IBM PC, AT or compatible, with 384K of memory
- Two floppy disk drives or floppy disk and hard disk
- IBM color graphics adaptor of equivalent
- Asynchronous communications adapter
- Various printers (IBM, Epson, Oki-data, C Itoh, Genuine and Prism) are supported
- HP plotter (HP 7470, HP 7475 or equivalent) is supported

Program can Interface:

- DataMyte 1500 family
- DataMyte 750 family

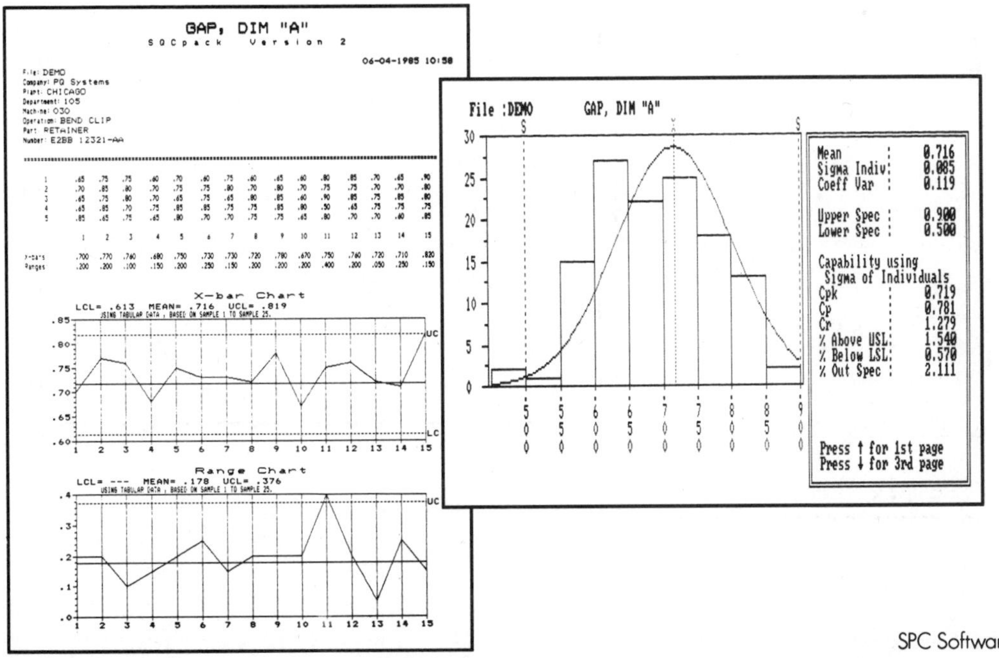

STATGRAPHICS

Statistical Graphics Corporation
Princeton Corporate Center
Five Independence Way
Princeton, NJ 08540
Phone (609) 924-9357

STATGRAPHICS is a menu-driven interactive data analysis and statistical graphics system. It includes procedures for Quality Control, Time Series Analysis, Sampling, Regression and Experimental Design. The program will import data from Lotus 1-2-3, dBase and DIF and ASCII file formats.

Hardware Requirements:

- IBM PC, XT, AT or compatible
- Two disk drives
- 512K of memory
- RS-232 port
- Graphics adaptor and compatible monitor
- Printer or plotter

Program can Interface:

- DataMyte 762

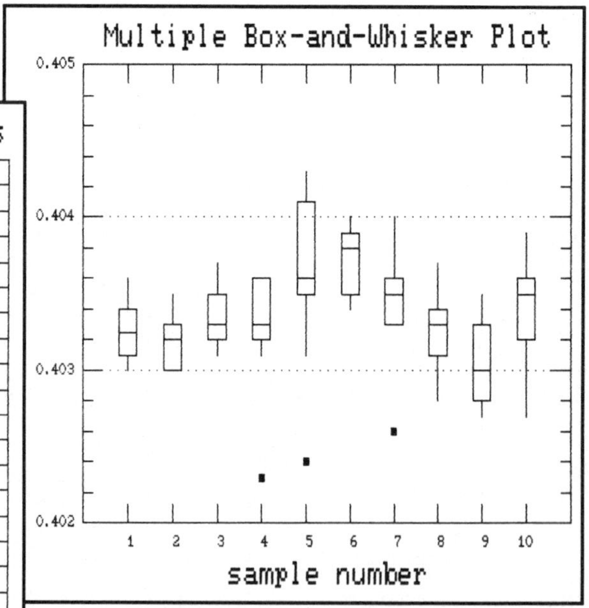

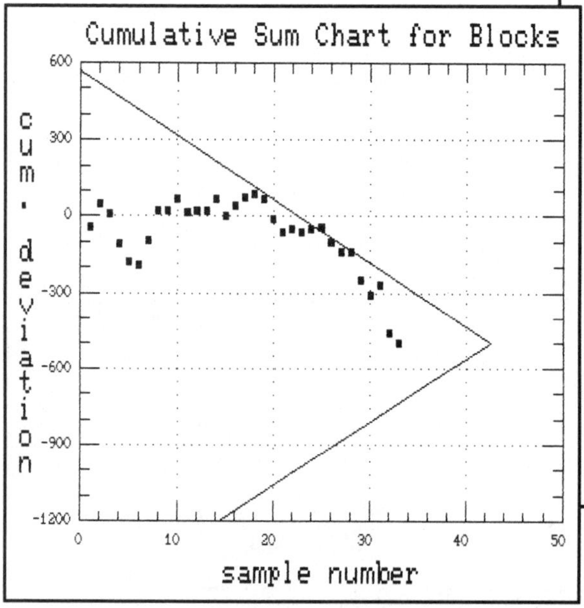

STATMAN:STATISTICAL MANAGEMENT 3.2

Interaction Research Institute, Inc.
4428 Rockcrest Drive
Fairfax, VA 22032
Phone (800) 782-8626

STATMAN offers x̄, R, median, individuals, p-, np-, c-, u-, and Pareto charts. Histograms, two-way regression, capability analysis, descriptive statistics, bar charts, fishbone, matrix and process flow techniques are also part of the STATMAN program. The charts can be printed and displayed, with up to six sets of control limits, which can be user-defined. The program is menu-driven, with "HELP" on each menu which describes features, options and steps. A "TEXT" facility can explain the logic of technique application and interpretation.

Hardware Requirements:

- IBM PC,XT,AT or compatible
- Two disk drives
- 256K of memory
- RS-232 port
- Options supported include color and monochrome graphics

Program can Interface:

- DataMyte 750
- DataMyte 1000
- DataMyte 1500
- DataMyte 2000

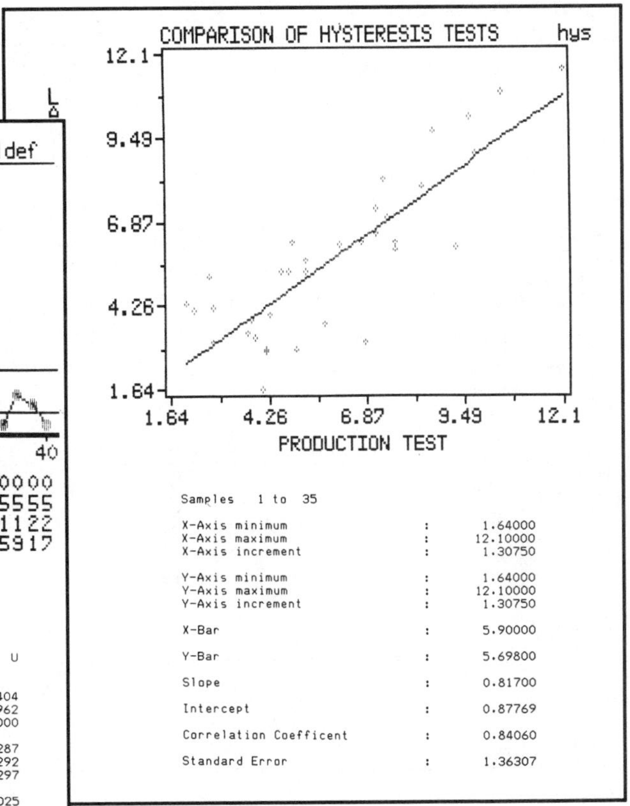

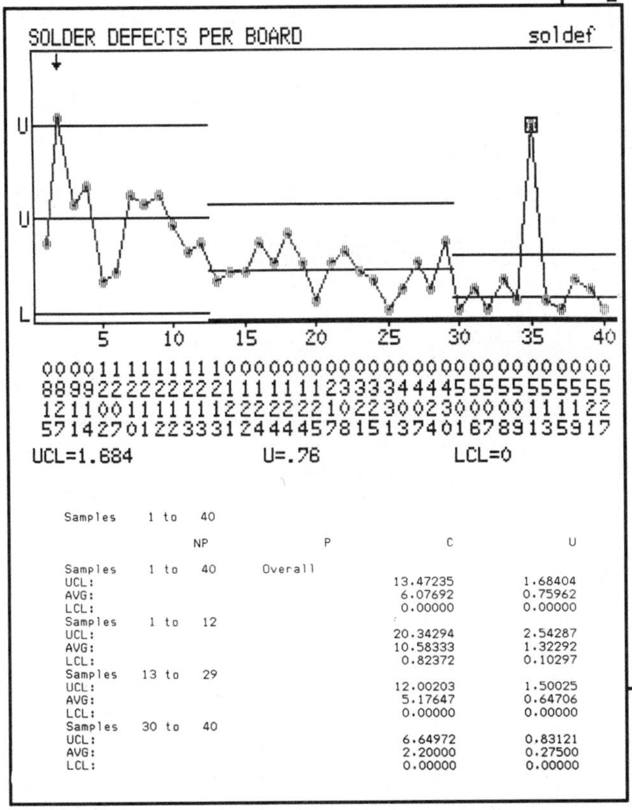

StatNET

Daedal Systems, Inc.
9951 Valley View Road
Minneapolis, Minnesota
Phone (612) 944-0072

StatNET provides a real-time link between the shop floor and management-level operator. Enter data into the program through the computer or with gages. Statistical testing includes checks for non-normal, trend and tolerance situations. The variables charts include $\bar{x}$, range, sigma, histograms, 3D histograms and regression analysis. The attributes charts include Pareto, p-, np-, u-, and c-charts.

Hardware Requirements:

- IBM AT or compatible (Management Level); IBM PC or compatible (Shop Floor Level)
- Network software
- Two disk drives
- 640K of memory
- RS-232 port
- Color monitor

Program can Interface:

- DataMyte 750
- DataMyte 1500
- DataMyte FAN system

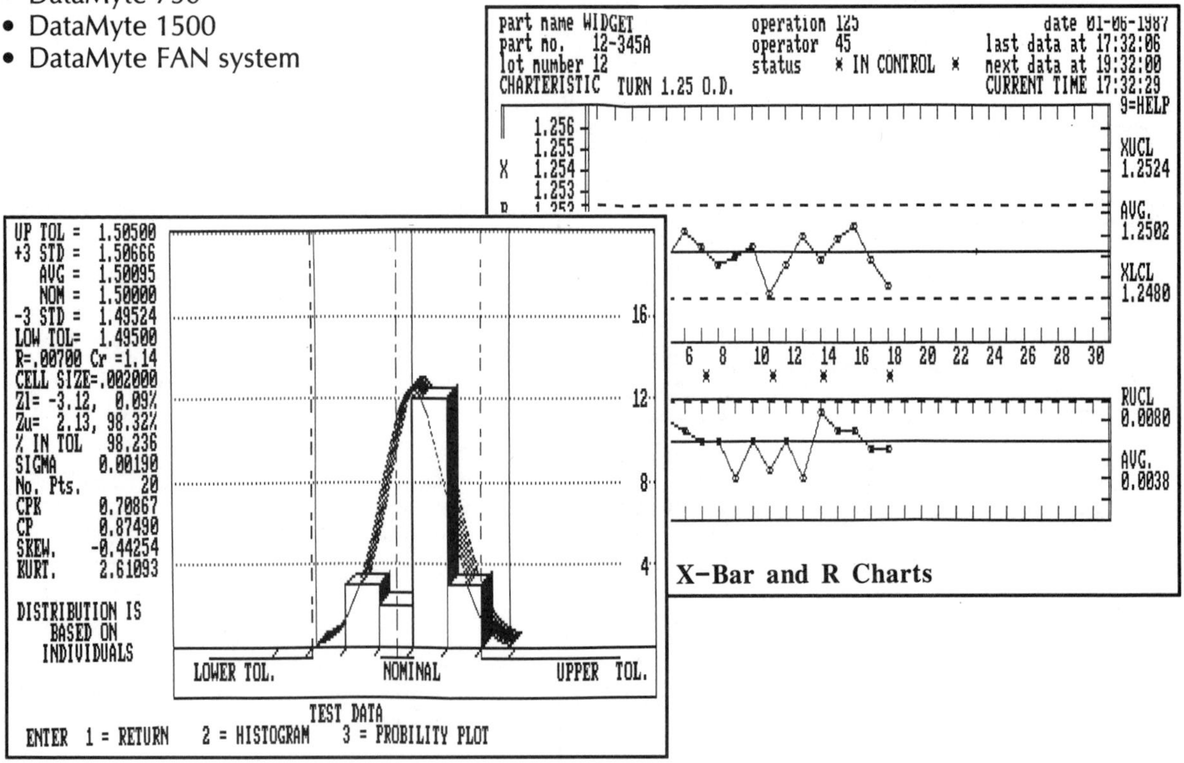

X–Bar and R Charts

xSTAT

Winstandley & Associates, Inc.
3950 Kettering Blvd.
Dayton, Ohio 45439
Phone (513) 299-5225

xSTAT, a statistical process control software and analysis system, features full communications to DataMyte data collectors. It performs data transfer trhough DataMyte 750s to an on-line IBM monitor, or in a batch dump mode, from DataMyte 1500 and 750s to an IBM PC. It provides $\bar{x}$ & R charts, individual and moving average charts, histogram, feature capability and normal probability. The xSTAT data base features a sorting routine to select specific data for analysis. Data can be exported to Lotus 1-2-3.

Hardware Requirements:

- IBM PC, XT, AT or compatible
- Two disk drives
- 384K memory
- RS-232 port
- Graphics capability
- Graphics printer
- Options include a color monitor and battery-powered clock

Program can Interface:

- DataMyte 750 family
- DataMyte 1500 family

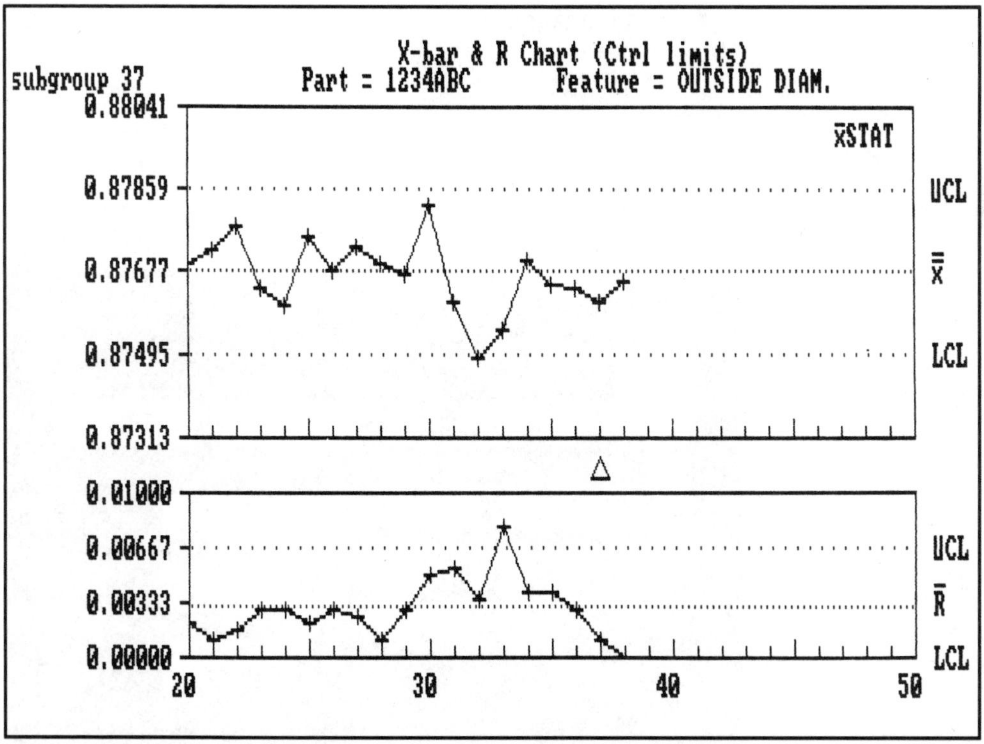

19.2 MINI AND MAINFRAME SOFTWARE

Real-time Quality Management/1000

Automated Technology Associates
7098 N. Shadeland Avenue
Indianapolis, Indiana 46220
Phone (317) 842-9488

RQM/1000 is intended to serve as a floor level complement to the Hewlett-Packard QDM/1000 system, allowing QDM to be dedicated to analytical and design activities. RQM/1000 allows factory floor systems to start with a few data collection stations and expand to several hundred through a logical growth path.

Hardware Requirements:

- HP 1000 RTE-6 or RTE-A operating systems
- Data acquisition supported on HQ series 200/300 systems

Program Interface:

- DataMyte 1500 Family

RQM/1000 provides these functions:

- Data acquisition support for DataMyte data collectors, CMMs and automated test equipment.
- Statistical analysis in real-time for $\bar{x}$ & R, $\bar{x}$ & s, p, np, c, u, individuals with moving R, moving average and range, histograms, Pareto charts and user add functions.
- Graphics analysis on any HP supported graphics device
- Data management

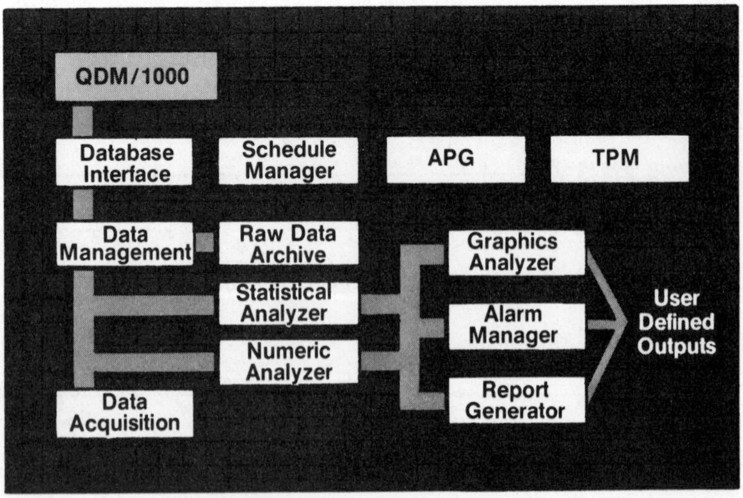

Real-time Quality Management

MANMAN/QUALITY

ASK Computer Systems, Inc.
730 Distel Drive
Los Altos, California 94022
Phone (415) 969-4422

The MANMAN/QUALITY program has a large number of statistical process control features, including both variables and attribute charting and descriptive statistics for the variables data. The variables charts include $\bar{x}$ & R, $\bar{x}$ & sigma, histograms, x and R, x and sigma (individual measurements in the sample and their range or standard deviation). The attributes data charts include p-, np-, u-, c-, and Pareto charts. Descriptive statistics include coefficient of variation, variance, standard deviation, skewness and kurtosis.

The MANMAN/QUALITY program provides standard system-supplied reports, such as vendor performance summary, material review board disposition summary, scrap summary and failure analysis by failure code. You can also generate user-defined reports to fit your reporting needs.

Hardware Requirements:

- HP 3000 Series
- DSG/3000 (optional) for high-resolution graphic reports

QMS PROGRAMS® Computer Software

John A. Keane and Associates
575 Ewing Street, Research Park
Princeton, New Jersey 08540
Phone (609) 924-7904

QMS PROGRAMS computer software allow DataMyte users to set DataMytes with prompts, limits and header information from the computer and download data from the DataMyte into the data base at 4800 baud.

The program integrates data from DataMyte with data from automatic test equipment, keyboard entry and other sources. The integrated database can provide on-line SPC and management summary reports on out of control conditions.

QMS PROGRAMS communicate along Ethernet, Baseway, DECnet and GM's MAP, and provide a bridge to MRP II systems such as NCA's Maxcim as well as providing a means to direct QMS PROGRAMS data into Datatrieve, RS-1, SAS or SPSS statistics and accounting packages. DataMyte users can interface to Digital Equipment Corporation's Micro PDP-11, and MicroVAX SP-11 through to VAX and VAX cluster systems and access graphics available from Tektronics and DEC's VT240 and VT125 Series terminals.

Hardware Requirements:

- DEC VAX
- DEC PDP-11

Program Can Interface:

- DataMyte 750 family
- DataMyte 1000 family
- DataMyte 1500 family

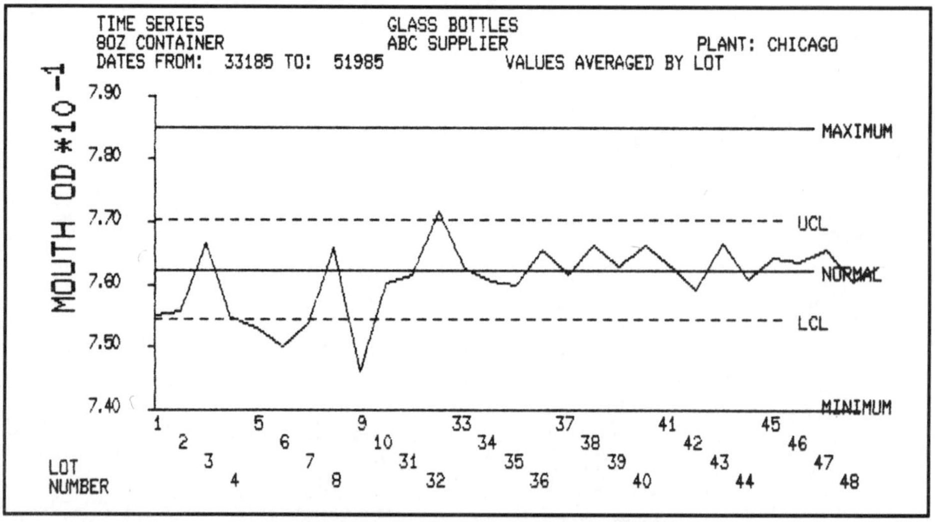

RS/1®

BBN Software Products Corporation
10 Fawcett Street
Cambridge/ Massachussetts 02238
Phone (617) 864-1780

RS/1 has a full set of functions for reading and writing external data files. The ASCII files produced by DataMyte data collectors or the FAN II Software program may be easily read into one or more RS/1 tables for further analysis. In addition, the setup information for DataMyte data collectors may also be stored in RS/1 tables for downloading into DataMyte setup files.

The I/O functions of RS/1 are complemented by its ability to be temporarily interrupted while an external command or program is executed. This feature can be embedded into a procedure that automates the collection of data from DataMyte data collectors in a way that makes the intermediate data transfer steps completely transparent to the end user. As a result, the entire process of organizing and analyzing the data collected with the DataMyte data collector can be managed entirely within the RS/1 environment.

Hardware Requirements:

- DEC VAX, DEC PDP-11; IBM 30xx, IBM 43xx, IBM RT PC
- Memory depends on computer used
- Many printers and plotters

SQC/3

Murphy Software Company
15301 Eleven Mile Road
Roseville, Michigan 48066
Phone (313) 445-2840

Hardware Requirements:

- IBM System/36 or System/38

System Can Interface:

- DataMyte 750 family
- DataMyte 1500 family

SQC/3 is a multi-user SPC software product for IBM System/36 and System/38 users. The program produces histograms, sample statistics, scatter plots and control charts in high-resolution color graphics. SQC/3 has a complete record keeping system; product specifications and current inspection results are available on demand. Detailed notes can be entered and reported in formats tailored to company requirements. Obsolete data can be stored off-line and recalled later.

SQC/3 is user-programmable and can be tailored to unique requirements of individual operators. A "PC Satellite" module allows selected portions of SQC/3 to run under MS-DOS providing remote independent operation plus overall system performance gains.

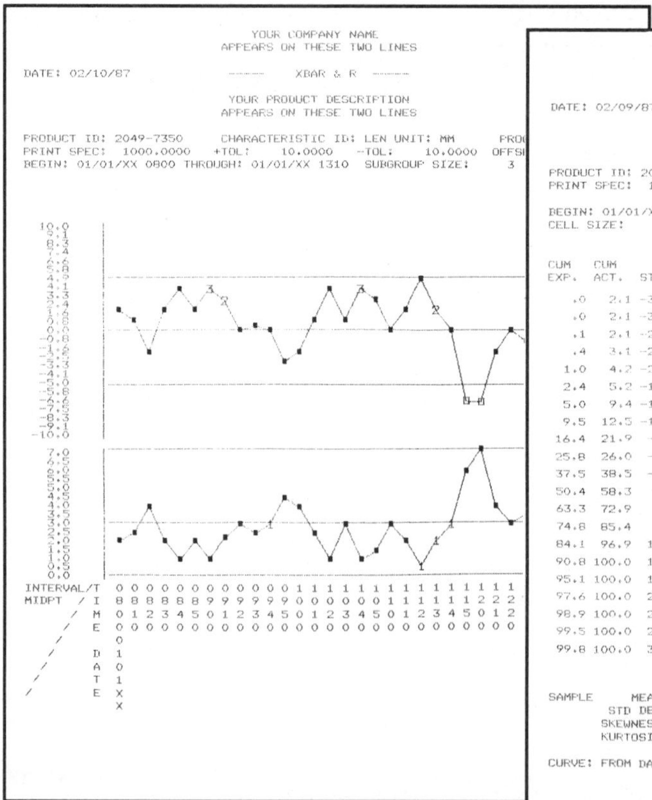

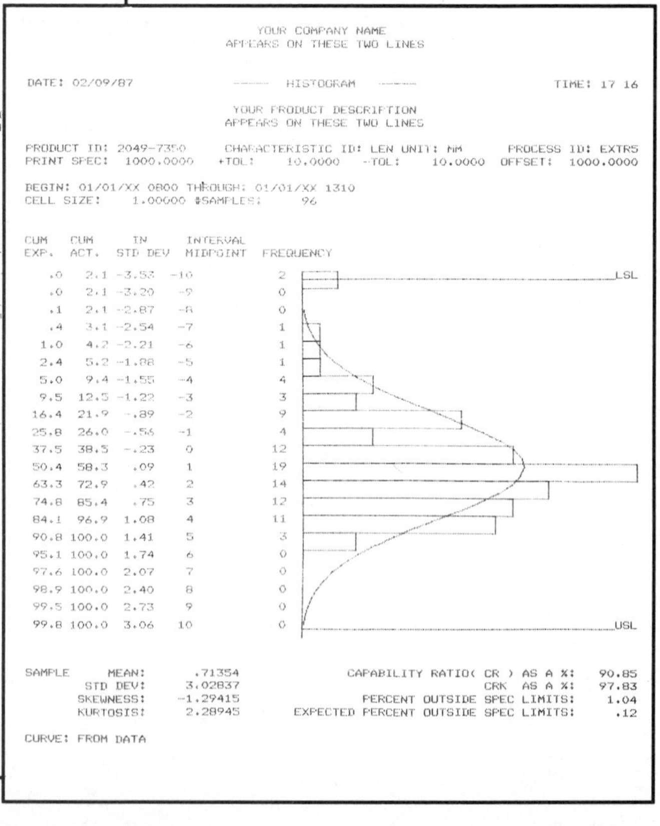

20. TRAINING

20.1 OVERVIEW OF DATAMYTE TRAINING

The goal of DataMyte training is to move your operators from a state of unfamiliarity with automatic data collection to being confident participants in the factory of the future. While DataMyte instructors are well versed in statistical theory, they do not teach statistics. They primarily answer the questions:

- How do I get started?
- What comes next?
- What does it all mean?

DataMyte training is based on a principle that is very similiar to the "pull system" of just-in-time manufacturing described in Chapter 6. In the pull system, the manufacturing process is driven by the exact requirements of each customer order. DataMyte training views each customer application as a special order and structures a training session that meets the particular needs of that application.

DataMyte customer training usually consists of three components: Application training, DataMyte product training and, if required, a review of required SPC knowledge and skills. The application training focuses on the successful operation of the DataMyte system in the customer's application. The product training session centers on complete coverage of the product training requirements for that application. If required, the SPC portion of the training is directed at providing the necessary SPC understanding required to complete the product training.

This structure provides a training experience that revolves around actual job requirements, not general theory or "nice to know" information. Figure 20.1.1 illustrates the "information pull" DataMyte training approach and the conventional "information push" approach. By starting with application needs, DataMyte training is designed for specific customer requirements.

Two key requirements of the DataMyte training system are:

- Accurately identifying application requirements prior to any training sessions, and
- The designation of any in-house DataMyte product specialist

Each DataMyte sales engineer is an application specialist who can identify a complete product/training/support sys-

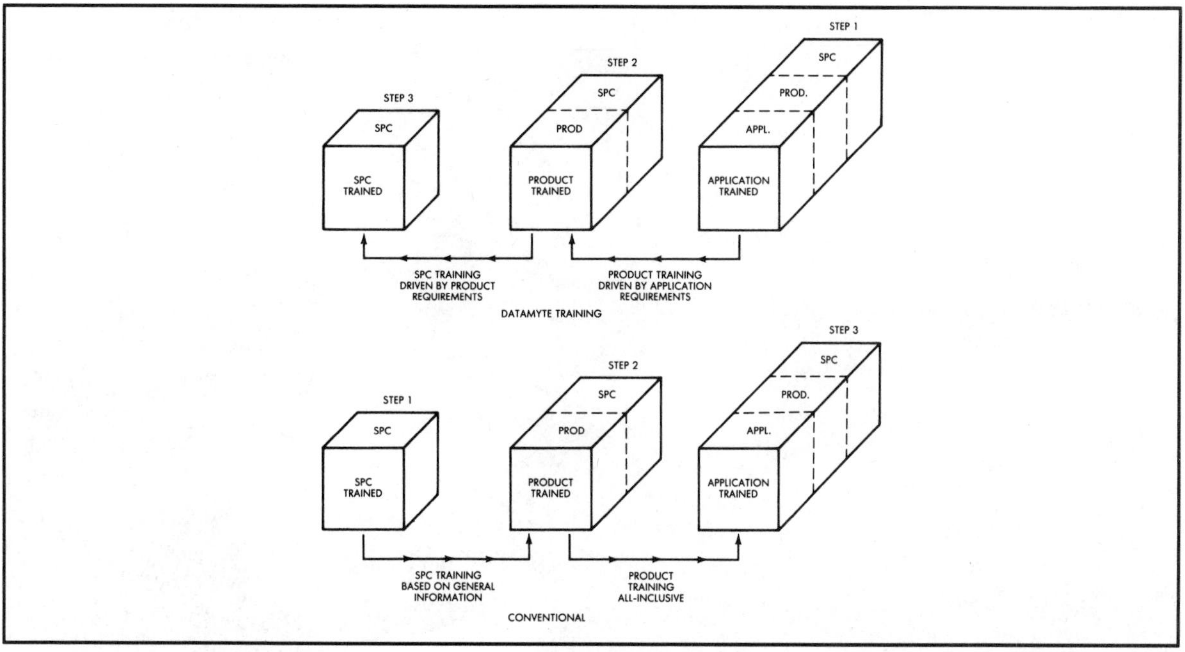

Fig. 20.1.1 The "information pull" DataMyte training approach.

tem proposal that provides a comprehensive solution to data collection problems. This proposal is the basis for DataMyte training. The in-house DataMyte product specialist is coached by DataMyte trainers to provide fast answers, troubleshooting and further applications to in-house DataMyte users. The DataMyte customer service group provides accessible technical support to the in-house DataMyte product specialist. Follow-up training costs may also be minimized by using the in-house specialist as an operator trainer using DataMyte training aids.

20.2 PRODUCT TRAINING

Fixed Station Data Collectors

DataMyte's fixed-station data collection systems are designed for operator's ease of use after a minimal amount of instruction. Each system typically includes a DataMyte data collector, gages, a video monitor and a printer. When getting started, the class participants learn how to connect the associated cables and complete the installation.

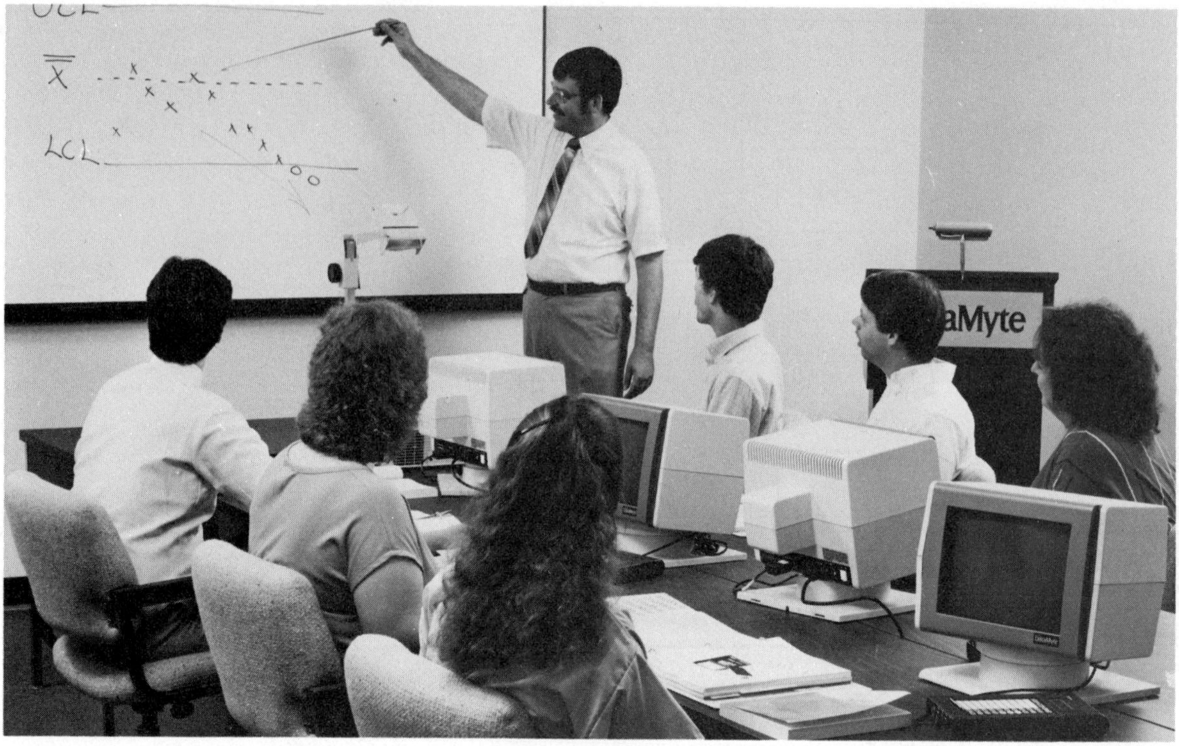

The DataMyte data collector is operated through choices made by the operator from menu selections provided on the front display of the unit. The training follows the organization of the menus which can be generalized into three categories:

- Setup (How do I start?)
- Data Collect and (What comes next?)
- Review (What does it all mean?)

The DataMyte data collectors need to be "set up" before they are used for data collection and this is the next topic in the training session. The setup routine allows the operator to program a file in the data collector by specifying how many critical dimensions will be measured and how many parts will be sampled before finishing a subgroup or updating the charts. The operator also learns how to label each characteristic, assign gages, enter engineering limits, control limits and gage reasonable limits.

Collecting data is after the setup routine and the operator spends time entering data, first manually through the alpha-numeric keypad and then with the gages they use in their application. Special features such as audible feedback (beep codes), reviewing raw data, editing data, entering assignable causes and interpreting trends are also discussed.

As data is being collected the participants become familiar with reviewing their data graphically on the video terminal either manually with the instant video keys or automatically at the end of a subgroup by setting a special menu selection. A printer can also be connected and "hard copy" reports are generated from selections off of the menu display. The operator can choose from:

- $\bar{x}$ & R charts
- $\bar{x}$ & sigma charts
- Histograms
- Data reports

Other subjects demonstrated include editing limits sets; clearing old data or all memory; calculating control limits; initiating the self-test; and setting up communications to the DataMyte DataTruck, IBM computers, and gages.

The DataTruck

The DataMyte DataTruck is designed as a convenience item for the "harvesting" of setups and data from data collectors found at multiple locations. Similar to the data collectors, the DataTruck has a menu-driven operating system for ease of use by the operator. The DataTruck transfers information to and from data collectors but doesn't collect data from gages.

The participants in the class learn about the DataTruck's method of storing data in files that are identified by a file name. The operator can read the file names by paging through a directory on the DataTruck's display.

The DataTruck has miscellaneous functions, such as checking to see how much memory is available; deleting files; initiating the self-test; and setting up communications to IBM computers.

DataMyte 2000 Roving Inspector Training

The training for the DataMyte 2000 data collector encompasses all aspects of the data collection problems seen by the inspector monitoring multiple processes: how to collect dimensional data (variables data); how to access a large variety of gage types (both analog and digital); how to collect visual defect data (attribute data) using manual input or the accompanying barcode reader and how to combine all the above together for a single process.

DataMyte's portable data collection systems are designed for storing multiple files and act as stand alone systems. All operations are contained within a single piece of equipment and are easily accessed through choices made by the inspector from menu selections provided on the large display built into the front of the unit. The training follows the organization of the menus which fall into three catagories:

- Setup (How do I start?)
- Data collect and (What comes next?)
- Review (What does it all mean?)

The setup routine allow the operator to program a file in the data collector by specifying how many critical dimensions will be measured and how many parts will be sampled before finishing a subgroup or updating the charts. The operator also learns how to label each characteristic, assign gages, input enginneering limits & control limits and gage reasonable limits.

Collecting data follows the setup routine and the operator spends time entering data, first manually through the fully alpha-numeric keypad and then through the specific gaging to be used for their application. Special features such as audible feedback (beep codes) an internal calculator, note pads, footnotes, reviewing raw data, editing data, reviewing statistics on individual subgroups or on a range of subgroups are also discussed.

As data is being collected the participants become familiar with reviewing their data graphically on the liquid crystal display of the unit with the instant graph key or through a special menu screen. A printer can also be connected and "hard copy" reports are generated from selections off the menu display. The operator can choose from: from:

- $\bar{x}$ & R charts
- $\bar{x}$ & Sigma charts
- Histograms
- Capability reports
- Summary reports and
- Data reports

Other subjects demonstrated are editing limits sets; clearing old data or all memory; calculating control limits; how to initiate the self-test; and how to set up communi-

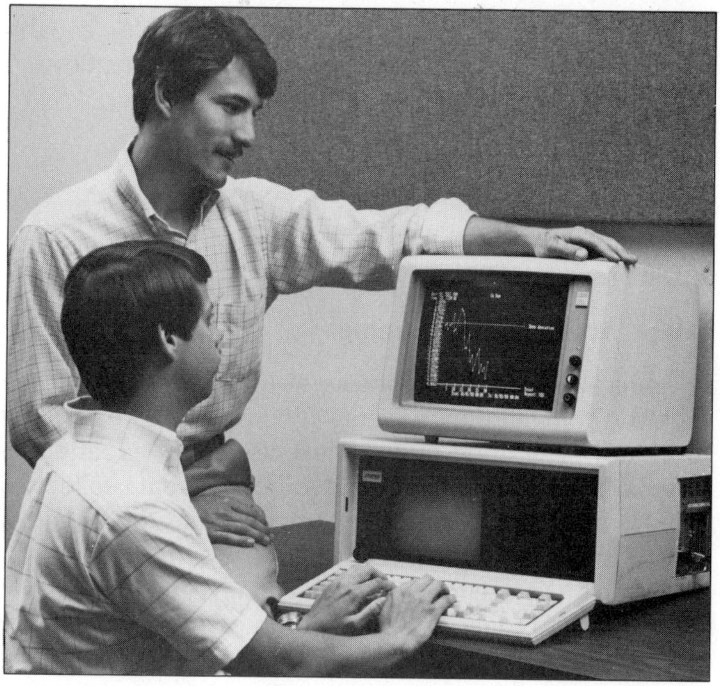

cations to IBM computers, other microprocessors, compatible printers and different gages.

FAN® II Software Program Training

The FAN II Software program operates through a main menu screen that is organized into five headings, each of which has several selections. The participants of the course will learn all of the options from the menu and interact with the status screens that show the operator all the information necessary to continue.

The course covers how the user can create setups; archive data; edit data; transfer setups and data to and from a DataMyte data collector or a DataTruck; view or print charts; export data; and to customize the FAN II Software program to the user's computer system.

Emphasis of the FAN II Software program training course is on the management of the data stored. The operators learn how to access different data drives; how the data is stored; how to copy data; how to calculate control limits; how to delete data; and how to make use of all the hardware in their computer such as a color graphics card. The

FAN II program has more sophisticated graphing capabilities as well. The charts and reports discussed include:

- $\bar{x}$ & R or $\bar{x}$ & Sigma charts
- Moving $\bar{x}$ & R or moving $\bar{x}$ & Sigma charts
- Histograms
- Cusum charts
- Capability reports and
- Data reports

20.3 Applications Training

Applications training consists of time spent out on the factory floor with the operators and inspectors, reaffirming all that they learned during their classroom experience. The participants are introduced to how the data collectors fit into their operations. Each participant has the opportunity to practice using the equipment under the supervision of a factory representative so that whatever assistance may be needed to make the installation a success is readily available.

21. ALLEN-BRADLEY QUALITY MANAGEMENT

INTRODUCTION

No other industrial automation supplier is better known for quality than Allen-Bradley. The word Quality at the base of the Allen-Bradley trademark summarizes a long-standing commitment (Figure 21.0.1).

From its beginning in 1903, as a pioneer in the field of industrial motor control, Allen-Bradley earned its reputation for quality from years of experience on the plant floor. Its founders, Lynde and Harry Bradley had a consuming dedication to quality, not just in regard to products, but in every part of the enterprise.

Fig. 21.0.1 Allen-Bradley trademark.

Today, Allen-Bradley is a Rockwell international company, and employs over 14,000 people in plants and sales offices in North America, Latin America, Europe, Australia and Asia. Its business is predominantly data acquisition, control and communication devices for industrial automation.

To help ensure the highest quality for all its customers in every one of its businesses throughout the world, Allen-Bradley has an ongoing quality program called the Total Quality Management System (TQMS).

Key to the TQMS philosophy is that quality achievement is a never-ending process and primarily a management responsibility. Through the application of scientific principles to real factory situations, Allen-Bradley has found that quality influences productivity, and can be measured objectively using statistical sampling and analysis.

As a result of TQMS, Allen-Bradley saved $80 million and received a $13 return for every dollar spent. In addition, the company's market share increased due to cost reductions and productivity improvements.

Allen-Bradley product offerings follow the TQMS philosophy. An integral part of Allen-Bradley industrial control and communication products is the concept of preventive quality control—the avoidance of nonconformities. In addition, these products produce data for statistical analysis and traceability.

Today, including the acquistion of DataMyte, Allen-Bradley has the broadest, deepest line of products and systems for quality management. It includes SPC modules for programmable controllers, industrial PCs and minicomputer systems for data analysis, automated quality systems for threaded fasteners, and programmable vision systems.

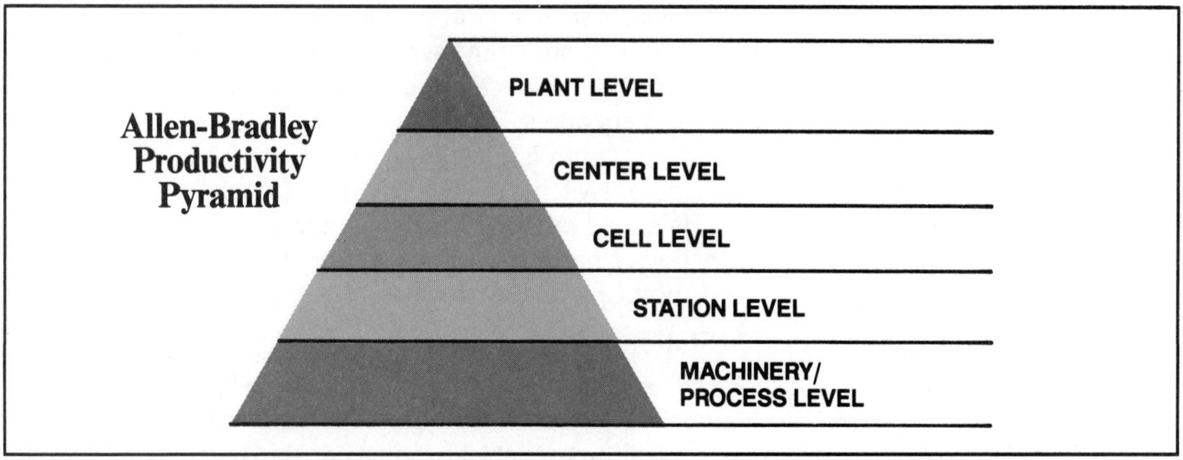

Fig. 21.1.1 Productivity Pyramid

Quality management products are part of the Allen-Bradley Productivity Pyramid, which is a blue-print for a fully integrated plant.

21.1 THE PRODUCTIVITY PYRAMID

The Allen-Bradley Productivity Pyramid is a master plan for increasing productivity and quality through the application of computer, control and communications technology. It provides the basis for plant-wide communications, permitting minute-by-minute management of information and the plant itself.

The Allen-Bradley Productivity Pyramid views a plant as five separate and distinct levels, each representing a different set of tasks requiring a different set of controls. See Figure 21.1.1. It's a systems approach to plant automation in which each control level builds on the information provided by the level below.

The ultimate goal is to weld each of these levels into a single, seamless automation system. Communications networks link all the plant levels from top to bottom, from computer mainframe to the most elementary production element. The result is a company controlled from the top down and informed from the bottom up.

Machinery/Process Level

The machinery/process level is the basic interface with production and process equipment on the plant floor. Here, sensing and control devices respond to upper level commands. At this level, the Allen-Bradley product line includes:

- Sensors such as limit switches, pressure and temperature controls, proximity switches, photoelectric controls, automatic identification including RF systems, bar codes, and encoders.
- Logic controls and indicators, including push buttons, selector switches, relays, low-cost programmable controllers, and intelligent panel systems.
- Power products such as motor starters, contactors, and motor protection devices.

Station Level

The station level converts input from lower levels to output commands based on direction from above. Allen-Bradley real-time control products at this level include an integrated family of programmable controllers, vision systems, intelligent motion control, intelligent I/O modules, and drive systems.

Cell or Supervisory Level

The cell level bridges the gap between data processing and plant floor control. It coordinates production flow among various stations and integrates them into an automated system. Products for this level include VISTA 2000 and other cell level control systems, advanced programmable controllers, color graphics systems, PC mangement systems, and distributed numerical control (DNC) systems, all linked through Allen-Bradley subnetworks. Cell level products also include the Allen-Bradley fastening systems which ensure manufacturers of consistent bolt, tension and joint quality.

Center Level

The center level integrates industrial computers and management computers. It schedules production and provides management with information by monitoring and supervising lower levels, managing programs and parameters, collecting information form cell level controllers, analyzing data, and reporting to higher-level computers.

Plant Level

The plant level provides overall planning and execution. This requires two-way communication between the mainframe computer and lower levels. Utilizing internationally accepted communications standards, including MAP, Allen-Bradley VistaMAP products provide for the integration of activities at upper pyramid levels.

A Standardization of Communication Links

Plantwide automation requires standardized communications links. The success of tomorrow's industrial plant will depend on its ability to gather, share and use data for effective planning and control.

The Productivity Pyramid provides a top to bottom blueprint for automating the gathering and sharing of production information. It creates a closed-loop real-time feedback system, which provides a wealth of information at low cost.

For several years, Allen-Bradley has been in the forefront of a cooperative effort to establish a standard, industry-wide data architecture. This effort has involved major companies and international standards organizations, and has resulted in the Manufacturing Automation Protocol (MAP) family of standards. MAP makes it possible to tie an entire plant together through standardized communications. It has been adopted by many companies representing many industries.

Allen-Bradley now offers a family of MAP-compatible communications networks and gateways to enable the linking of multi-vendor control equipment at every level of the pyramid. In the future, it will support broadband, carrierband and proprietary networks.

Today's typical industrial plant contains large numbers of relatively low-cost programmable devices and operator interfaces, directly controlling machines and processes at the lowest levels of the Productivity Pyramid. These must communicate with each other, and report upward through the pyramid. Relatively small amounts of data are involved, communications are usually event-driven, and response times must be very fast. Up to now, the only way to accomplish this type of communication has been to employ proprietary communications subnetworks, which are then linked into the overall broadband LAN.

Allen-Bradley now offers products which link various proprietary subnetworks into the MAP broadband LAN, allowing the integration of existing equipment from different manufacturers into the overall system.

How Quality fits in the Productivity Pyramid

Quality management means more to Allen-Bradley than the attainment of consistent quality. That is aiming too low.

Allen-Bradley industrial automation is geared toward:

- Progressively higher quality
- Progressively lower costs
- Making quality a competitive edge

The Productivity Pyramid symbolizes a highly flexible, highly responsive production system where quality is prevention-based rather than inspection-driven. Data collection at the machinery/process and station levels is attuned to gathering the data most relevant to process quality. Data is provided in real-time to the appropriate decision-making levels. Analysis is designed to highlight trends and patterns that give advance notice of a process problem. In addition, it provides data archiving for historical tracking.

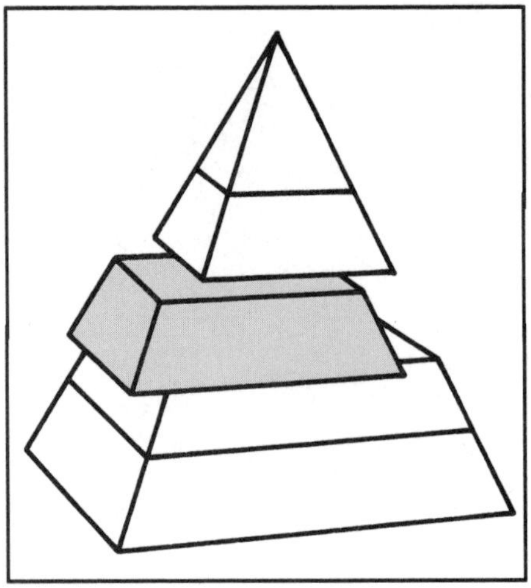

Fig. 21.1.2

The Allen-Bradley quality management offering fits into the pyramid as follows:

Level 5 — Machinery/Process Level

- Sensors to PLCs
- Automatic Test Equipment
- Torque Sensing (instrumented tools)

Level 4 — Station Level

- PLCs
- DataMyte Fixed Station Data Collectors
- DataMyte Handheld Data Calculators
- Fastening System Controllers
- Programmable Vision System

Level 3 — Cell Level

- Series 7890 Productivity System
- A-B/CAMM Industrial Computers
- Fastener Remote Modules
- DataMyte FAN system

Level 2 — Center Level

- Central Data Collection System (Host Computer)

Earlier chapters in this book will acquaint the reader with DataMyte product offerings, with Chapter 15 providing an overall summary. The rest of this chapter covers these Allen-Bradley systems:

- EXPERT Programmable Vision System
- PLC-3
- A-B/CAMM
- 7890 Productivity System
- Automated Quality System for Threaded Fasteners

21.2 EXPERT PROGRAMMABLE VISION SYSTEM

The EXPERT Programmable Vision System allows inspection of 100% of products at production line speeds. This system allows identification, location and sorting of objects by pattern recognition. The marriage of video imagery and computer technology offers the manufacturer a means of reducing product waste, costly inspection errors, and human fatigue.

In cases of product nonconformance, corrective action can be taken to reduce shipped waste. Overall product quality increases are possible, while product warranty losses can be decreased. A constant production rate can be maintained 24 hours a day, 7 days a week, without endangering product integrity. And A-B's communications capability means the system is compatible with existing Allen-Bradley products.

21.3 PLC-3 FAMILY STATISTICAL PROCESS ANALYSIS

The PLC-3 Family Statistical Process Analysis Software Package is designed for use with the PLC-3 Family of Programmable Controllers and the 1775-GA Module. It is a station level SPC system that analyzes data directly from a programmable controller. See Figure 21.3.1.

Fig. 21.3.1 PLC-3 Programmable Controller.

The SPA package calculates statistics on machine performance and product conformity, allowing a fast and easy means for prevention rather than inspection-based quality control.

Statistical data, which is more compact than raw data, is easier to read, comprehend and distribute to plant employees and supervisors. As a result, operators can react more quickly to production fluctuations avoiding costly errors and minimizing inspection time.

How the SPA Package Operates

The PLC-3 can automatically collect data, such as analog gage readings, from the industrial processes it controls or monitors, and then read that data into a binary or decimal file. The file is then accessed by the software package from the GA module. Manual data entry is also an option.

The Allen-Bradley GA module, with its extended math capabilities, allows you to command an entire function library from single or multiple industrial terminals. The SPA package computes averages, medians, control limits, ranges, standard deviations and frequencies based on the data collected. These values are then stored for use with one of four control charts: histogram, $\bar{x}$, range or median. The statistical data can then be displayed on the industrial terminal as a data list or graph. Hardcopy is available in list or graph form from any RS-232 printer.

Applications for SPA Package

Applications for the SPA package include any machining process using the PLC-3 family of programmable controllers. The SPA package provides:

- Statistical summarization of PLC data
- Display graphics of the process
- Both manual data entry and direct input from sensors

The data can be collected automatically by the PLC. The system allows the operator to set a time interval between samples or take samples according to I/O conditions in the program. All operations are menu driven. Lists or graphs of the data are readily available on the Industrial Termainal screen or in hardcopy from a printer. Data can be stored for future reference in the 1770-M11 Universal Mass Storage System.

21.4 A-B/CAMM INDUSTRIAL COMPUTER SYSTEM

Fig. 21.4.1 6120 Industrial Computer.

The Allen-Bradley plant floor information system is called The Information Manager®, and consists of A-B/CAMM software and Allen-Bradley's 6120/6121/6122 Industrial Support Computer Family. The computer system itself can reside on the plant floor near programmable controllers, capturing the data that regularly passes through those controllers before it is lost forever.

The 6120/6121/6122 Industrial Support Computer Family, manufactured for Allen-Bradley by IBM, is three times more reliable then office-grade equipment and is designed for continued use in areas where there may be extended termperatures, vibration, power and voltage fluctuations, and particulate contaminants. See Figure 21.4.1. The hardware family is fully compatible with the software products available for the IBM PC/XT and PC/AT personal computers, as well as IBM's industrially hardened 5531, 7531 and 7532 computers.

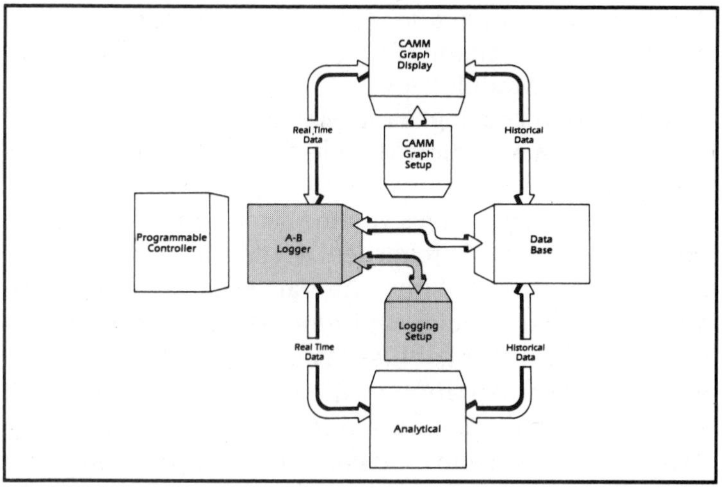

Fig. 21.4.2 Schematic of on-line data collection modules.

The A-B/CAMM brings data into the industrial computer from the programmable controllers via the A-B Data Highway or Data Highway II. Data is stored on the computer's hard disk.

A-B/CAMM Software Modules

Various A-B/CAMM software module combinations provide:

- Communication with programmable controllers, including data collection and storage
- Analysis of stored data in a powerful spreadsheet format
- Graphically monitor logged data in real time or historically, with the ability to forecast events or process trends

The following packages can be configured to meet these information needs:

On-Line Data Collection

- A-B/CAMM System Kit
- A-B Logger Module
- A-B/CAMM Logging Setup Module

This configuration lets you define command sets, logging models and sensor files for the Allen-Bradley Data Highway. See Figure 21.4.2. You can select and invoke logging models to collect data via the Data Highway from A-B programmable controllers and log collected data on a real-time data base. You can also select and invoke command sets to send data via the Data Highway to programmable controllers.

On-Line Data Collection, Analysis and Reporting

- A-B/CAMM System Kit
- A-B Logger Module
- A-B/CAMM Logging Setup Module
- A-B/CAMM Analytical Module for standard or enhanced graphics

This combination gives you the same capabilities as the previous package. Spreadsheet models also help you to analyze data collected from the Data Highway in real-time and to perform trending and forecasting based on previously logged historical files. You can display or print a graphical representation of the spreadsheet data using standard or enhanced graphics hardware. See Figure 21.4.3. You can send calculated data to programmable controllers. You can also share data with other software packages and other computers, using DIF file formats.

On-Line Data Collection and Dynamic Color Graphic Analysis

- A-B/CAMM System Kit
- A-B Logger Module
- A-B/CAMM Logging Setup Module
- A-B/CAMM Graph Display Module (requiring and enhanced graphics color monitor)

This package will let you monitor your process via the Allen-Bradley Data Highway from Allen-Bradley programmable controllers and store collected data in a real-time database. The CAMMGraph Module provides a 640 x 350 pixel resolution color graphic interface for real-time or historical display of process or sensor states. See Figure 21.4.4.

Fig. 21.4.3 Schematic of on-line data collection analysis and reporting.

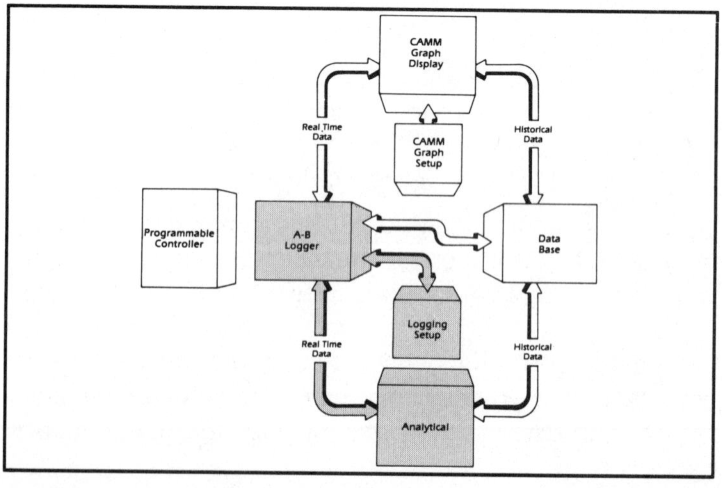

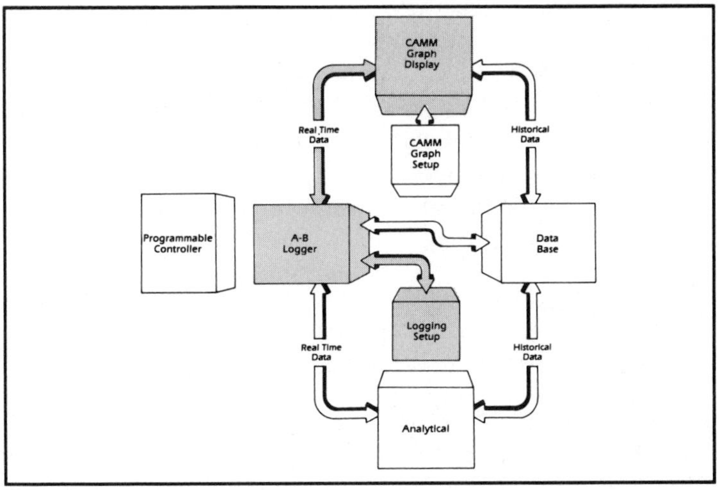

Fig. 21.4.4 Schematic of on-line data collection and dynamic color graphic analysis.

21.5 7890 PRODUCTIVITY SYSTEM

The 7890 Productivity System is a Cell-Level on-line SQC system. It organizes and manages data in a way which shows where improvement efforts must be focused. Plant and test data are collected and processed by the 7890 System on-line and presented to plant personnel in summary form. Operators, technicians, supervisors, engineers and managers can take action in time to effect appropriate changes in process or machine operation in order to improve quality and productivity.

The powerful advantage of the 7890 system is that it can handle thousands of parameters simultaneously. It allows a user to get a much quicker representation of what is happening on the plant floor.

System Architecture

The 7890 system would typically be at the Cell Level of the Productivity Pyramid. It obtains data from devices at the Station Level via the Data Highway. The 7890 system can configure up to four Data Highway networks.

The 7890 system gathers information in raw data form. It then converts the data into a format that is meaningful for SQC functions, and usable for the operator. In the case of multiple production lines, it is possible to have 7890s at the Cell Level clock into a 7890 system at the Center Level of the pyramid.

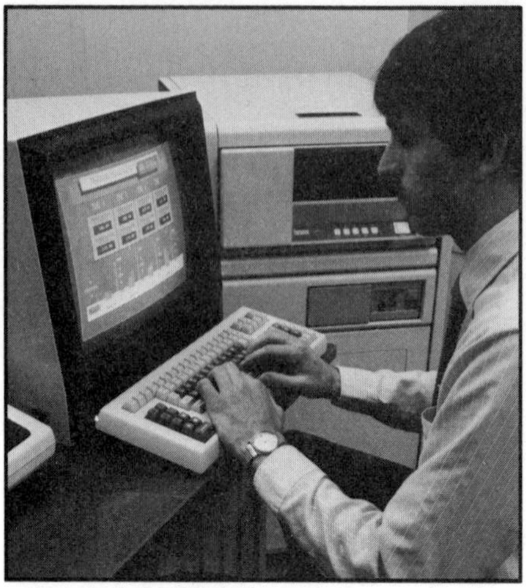
Fig. 21.5.1 Main 7890 processor.

The system consists of the following hardware:

Main 7890 processor — This is a DEC PDP11/73 featuring a hard disk for dynamic data storage and a tape drive for system back-up. See Figure 21.5.1. The processor pulls up data from the data highway and generates pictures of machine, raw material and production data as well as quality performance over time.

Data Highway local area network — The network links data sources such as Allen-Bradley programmable controllers with the processor as well as peripheral operator's terminals, displays, and printers.

Operator color graphic display terminals and printers — The operators's color graphic display terminal generates graphs, such as $\bar{x}$ & R charts, and also provides tables of data. The terminals can graphically depict plant floor operation. The operator has a picture of the machines and process, with colors indicating machine status.

The operator's display terminal also provides quality management information, such as current status and historical information, operating system messages and alarm messages. Downtime can be logged manually at the terminal. The processor merges the manual inputs with data that is automatically recorded. A printer provides hard copies of reports or any of the screens.

Configurer's terminal — System configuration is done at the configurer's terminal. The terminal is a black and white terminal for customizing the 7890 to a particular application. Reconfiguration can be done on-line.

Applications for the 7890 System

The 7890 Productivity System can provide on-line SQC and SPC data to operators and management. It can help analyze the cause of a defect in a product coming off a production line. If an operator knows what parameters would cause a defect, the 7890 system can measure all needed data and apply SQC to establish a correlation to the highest probability of failure.

For the startup of new machinery, the 7890 system can be used to develop accurate models of how the machines will actually function. A user can determine if the new equipment will be fast enough to meet desired production levels. The modeling function in some cases have led to paybacks on the 7890 system of just a few months.

One of the most important characteristics of the 7890 system is its simplicity of use and operation. It's easily configurable by non-computer people who are experienced in the plant floor operations. A series of menus prompt the configurer who simply answers the questions. The only information the configurer must know includes the output, the appropriate report or display format, and the control devices that are involved.

The simplicity of the 7890 system greatly reduces the customer's cost of implementation. On-line, as the process is taking place, the 7890 evaluates data and displays it in usable form for the operator. The system can also track raw materials and parts through the process on the plant floor. It keeps a data history so that as productivity improves, current operation of the plant can be compared to prior periods.

21.6 AUTOMATED QUALITY SYSTEMS FOR THREADED FASTENERS

Allen-Bradley Automated Quality Systems are computer-based fastening systems for the automotive, off-highway and aerospace industries. Their function is to improve the quality of threaded fastener operations.

AQS gathers torque and angle data. See Figure 21.6.1. It can play an active role in achieving desired specifications by controlling the fastening operation or it can take a passive role of monitoring and reporting on the fastening operation. The system provides:

- Accurate monitoring of the fastening cycle
- Accurate and flexible control of fastening tools
- Tracking of fastener rundowns throughout the particular assembly process

AQS monitors the state of the fastener at the end of the tightening cycle. It compares this state to a range of engineering specifications, providing a basis for quality control. The AQS can also decrease clamping load variations via the control of tension. By controlling tension, AQS improves the integrity of a joint and therby optimizes the strength of a fastener.

Fig. 21.6.1 Computer-based fastening system in auto plant.

AQS Fastening Concept

Conventional fastening systems measure only torque. To determine if you have quality joint, you must measure and precisely control not only torque, but clamp load as well. Clamp load is the bolt tension required to appropriately hold parts together. That's the primary job of a fastener — to exert clamping load.

Measuring torque alone does not tell you if a fastener is performing its function well. A typical nut and bolt are designed to work together as a clamp load machine. Their sole job is to apply clamping force to a joint. But threaded fasteners are not very efficient clamping machines. They generate a relatively small proportion of clamping force in relation to the work, or torque, that is put into them.

The application of torque generates clamping force but it must also overcome friction:

- Friction of the fastener itself
- Friction under the bearing surface
- Friction in the mating threads

Friction in the treads consumes about half the work put into the fastener when torque is applied. Friction on the bearing face consumes another forty percent. Only ten percent of the work put into the fastener generates clamping load.

Clamp load will vary as the coefficient of friction varies. A small change in bearing face friction, for example, say just three percent, has the effect of reducing clamp load thiry percent. Changes in clamping force can mean the difference between a joint that performs properly and a joint that has poor durability. On the other hand, reduced friction, from oil contamination of the threads for instance, increases the clamp load on the joint. This could result in deformation of a bearing or overload of a joint component.

Many factors affect friction — fastener finishes, coatings, nicks, burrs, rough machined surfaces, sealants, even color identification. Product designers must take friction variables into account when calculating the clamp load needed to hold an assembly together. For tightening critical joints, other strategies besides torque monitoring must be considered because the fundamental concern is with clamp load, not applied torque.

Torque Graphing

An excellent tool for evaluating predicted clamp load and for modeling fastener mechanics is a graph of torque versus clamp load. See Figure 21.6.2. The torque output of a power tool is plotted along one axis. The tension, measured by strain gages, load cells and other devices is plotted along the other axis.

The typical torque curve has three segments:

The prevailing torque— This is the "free" rundown area, before a threaded fastener starts to actually clamp parts together. Using the prevailing torque feature of the AQS system, limits can be assigned to the free rundown area to identify defects, bends, cross-threading, and stripped threads.

Mid-point pause— The next segment of the torque curve is the area between prevailing torque and a mid-point pause. It is a point at which the system analyzes torque/angle data and checks the performance of the instrumented fastening tool. The tool has an overrun characteristic, which is a brief span of time between a command to shut the tool off and the point at which the tool actually stops. During this brief period AQS can build a history of the tools's performance. The angle encoder measures the tool's overrun characteristics.

Torque value— The third segment of the torque curve represents the area between the mid-point pause and the torque value we want to achieve in tightening the fastener. Based on previous measurements of the tool's overrun, the system shuts off the tool at a calculated distance prior to the desired value. When the tool finally stops, the system makes an accept/reject decision.

AQS constantly compares the midpoint overrun values with the tool's final positions. If there's a significant deviation, the system signals marginal tool performance.

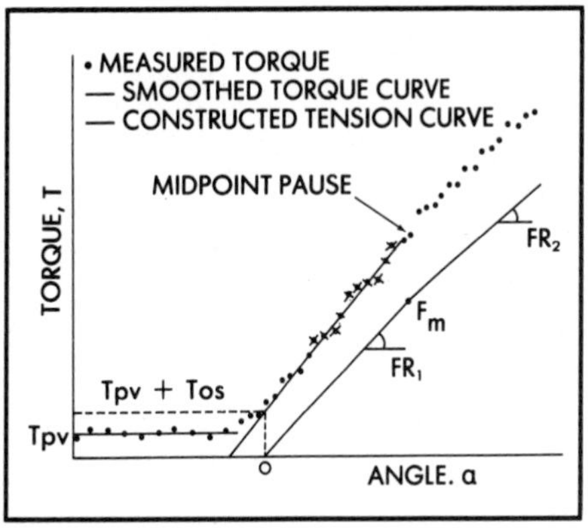

Fig. 21.6.2 Torque Graph.

Torque Synchronization for Mulit-Tool Applications

The AQS system has special features for multiple joint fastening applications, such as automotive wheel hubs. See Figure 21.6.3. Pre-torque pause in conjunction with spindle synchronization evens the clamping load of a multi-fastener joint.

Fig. 21.6.3 Multi-spindle application.

When multiple tools (or spindles) are used for a multiple joing fastening application, all of the tools get an initial command to tighten to a low level of torque — about five to ten percent of the ultimately desired value. As each tool reaches the pre-torque level, it waits to be sure that all the other tools have caught up. What this does is eliminate uneven clamping at the beginning of the run down cycle. When all the tools have reached the pre-torque level, they are simultaneously turned on. They all advance to the midpoint pause, and each tool again waits for the others to arrive at the specified point. Then they are commanded to proceed to the point of shutoff that will achieve the desired torque value.

Origin of Tension

Origin of Tension is a patented concept that allows the Allen-Bradley AQS system to consistently achieve a specified clamp load exclusive of the friction variables in the joint. The Origin of Tension is the point of reference used to calculate clamp load. See Figure 21.6.4. The AQS approach to finding this point is the logarithmic rate method (LRM). The algorithms for tension are derived from logarithmic rate formulas.

Using the LRM approach the AQS fastening system minimizes clamping load variations. By controlling tension, AQS improves the integrity of a joint, maximizes the strength of the fastener and improves the quality of the assembly.

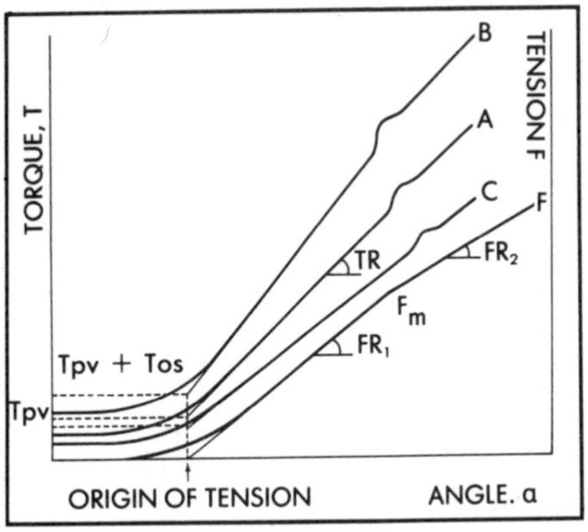

Fig. 21.6.4 Origin of Tension.

AQS System Architecture

An automated Quality System consists of four major components:

Fig. 21.6.5 AQS Architecture.

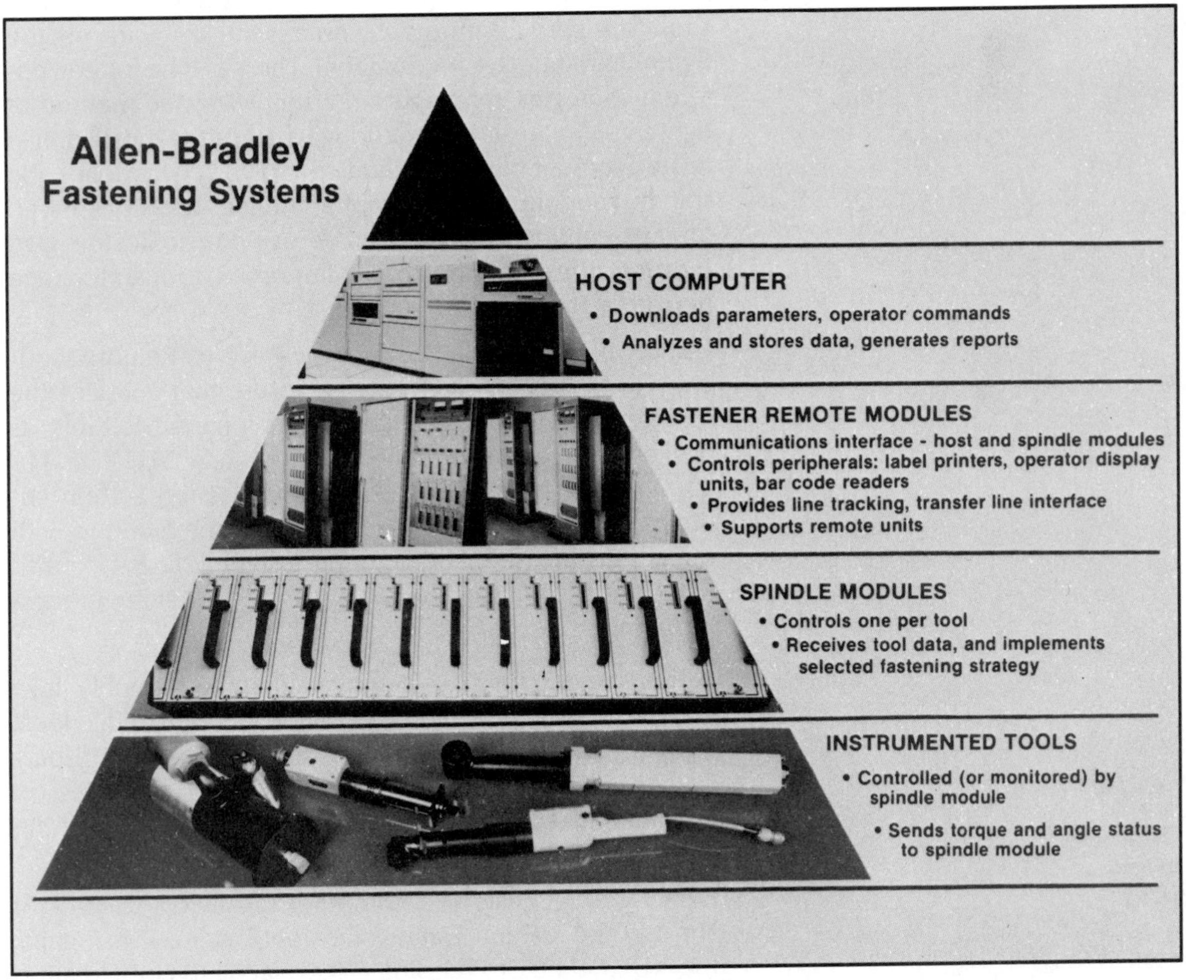

- Instrumented tools or spindles
- Spindle modules to control the tools
- Fastener Remote Module (FRM) for local data collection
- A host computer for central data collection

The four components can be described in terms of the Productivity Pyramid (Figure 21.6.5):

Machinery/Process Level— Instrumented tools or spindles can be both pneumatic or electric. They tighten the fasteners. The instrumented tool sends torque and angle status information to a spindle module at the Station Level of the pyramid. The torque transducer in each tool measures dynamic torque being applied to a threaded fastener. An angle encoder measures the angle and direction of spindle rotation. An on-off device controls torque action.

Station Level— One spindle module is needed for each tool. The spindle modules contain the software for the tightening strategies for each tool. There can be forteen different strategies, ranging from a simple torque method of tightening to tension monitoring which is the most sophisticated form of measuring and controlling clamp load. The spindle module makes accept and reject decisions based on data coming from the tool. Error status indicators give diagnostic information that is important to maintenance personnel.

Cell Level— At the Cell Level is the Fastener Remote Module (FRM). It is an electronic enclosure that contains the spindle modules and DC controllers for electric tools, as well as the Local Data Collection System, a DEC PDP-11/23 minicomputer. The Local Data Collection System coordinates the activities of individual spindle modules with operations of the manufacturing assembly line it coordinates the activities of the tools with the fastening process including:

- Tracking of parts as they move along the assembly line
- Local reporting functions to spindle modules and to local peripherals such as bar code readers, operator display units and label printers.
- Communications between the spindle modules and the Central Data Collection System.

Center Level— The host computer is a DEC PDP 11/73, and has the Central Data Collection System. It maintains the AQS data base, keeping tasks relating to configuration and assignment of spindle modules and tools within a particular FRM enclosure. Two hard disks store fastening strategies and spindle rundown data for each tool as well as calibration data. The host maintains a separate data base, file management and storage system for fastener rundown and assembly line production data. Through video display terminals and printers, operators can access the entire system's data base. The host can also be connected to a mainframe at the Plant Level of the Productivity Pyramid.

For more information about Allen-Bradley Quality Management contact Allen-Bradley, 1201 South Second Street, Milwaukee, Wisconsin 53204.

22. FACTORY AUTOMATION FOR QUALITY

INTRODUCTION

This chapter describes a few types of systems that typically span the departmental boundaries of a company. What these systems share in common is the ability to take data from a DataMyte and use it for analysis and decision making.

The systems from these companies can help engineers design for manufacturing by using analysis of data collected by a DataMyte. They can help a manufacturing manager associate quality data with MRP activities. They can also help planning engineers better plan for factory automation by knowing process capability at any point in time.

22.1 APOLLO SERIES 3000® PERSONAL WORKSTATIONS

Apollo Computer, Inc. supports DataMyte® FAN® II statistical quality control applications on the Series 3000 Personal Workstations. The DataMyte applications run on DOMAIN® Series 3000 workstations using Apollo's IBM®-compatible PC co-processor, the DOMAIN/PCC®, which provides an MS-DOS® operating environment in a window on the display of any workstation. The window can co-exist with other operating system environments, including Berkeley 4.2, AT&T Unix® System V and Apollo's AEGIS®.

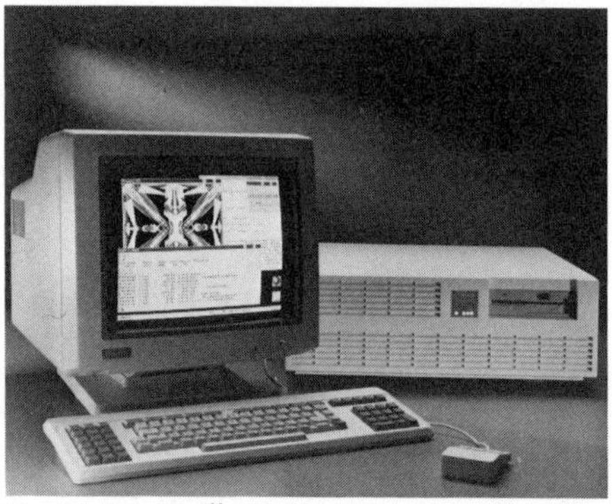

Fig. 22.1.1 Apollo DOMAIN Series 3000 Personal Workstation.

The IBM PC/AT-compatible bus in every Series 3000 workstation also allows IBM PC-compatible add-on boards to be accessed by the DOMAIN/PCC. Included are RS-232 serial communications boards, which enable DataMyte data collectors to be easily connected for fast, accurate data collection and report generation (both text and graphics).

DOMAIN Series 3000 Color Personal Workstation

Apollo's DOMAIN Series 3000 Personal Workstation family offers technical professionals the affordability and convenience of a personal computer, while providing the power of a dedicated, 32-bit workstation and the resource-sharing capabilities of the DOMAIN system. See Figure 22.1.1. These workstations are based on the MC68020 central processor and MC68881 floating point processor.

The system features a 15-inch or 19-inch 60Hz, tilt-and-swivel high resolution monitor, low-profile keyboard (com-

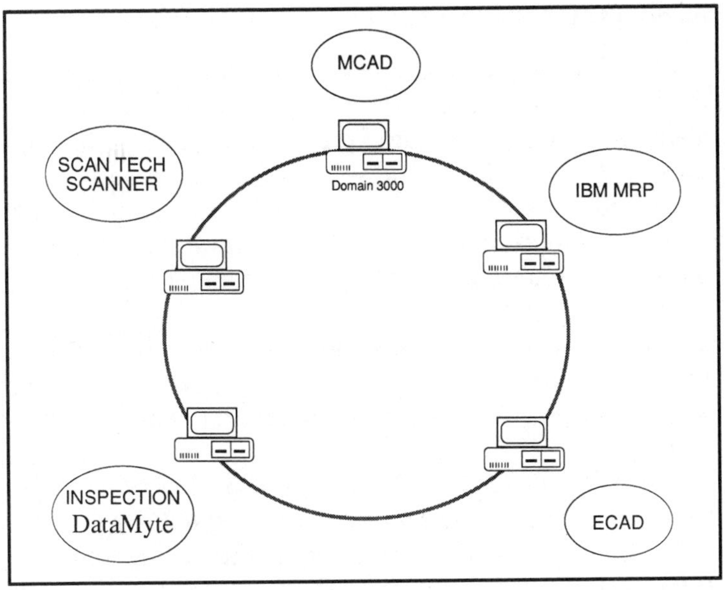

Fig. 22.1.2 Example of a DOMAIN Network.

plete with numeric keypad and ten user-definable function keys), quiet operation, and an IBM PC/AT-compatible bus interface that lets users connect a wide variety of popular, low-cost personal computer peripherals to their workstations.

Apollo's Open Architecture Program provides DOMAIN System support for a wide variety of communications gateways and links. See Figure 22.1.2. DOMAIN Open Architecture helps professionals and work groups share resources in environments that include IBM mainframes and PCs, DEC® systems, ETHERNET® backbone networks, SNA and RJE links, and more.

For more information on Apollo workstations contact Product Marketing, Apollo Computer, Inc., 330 Billerica Road, Chelmsford, MA 01824 (617-256-6600).

22.2 AT&T PC 6300 AND 6300 PLUS INDUSTRIAL WORKSTATIONS

DataMyte FAN II software for quality data management and statistical process control has been tested and used on the AT&T PC 6300 and 6300 Plus Industrial Workstations. These workstations provide host computing and network gateways to the AT&T industrial and laboratory computing environment.

Fig. 22.2.1 AT&T PC 6300.

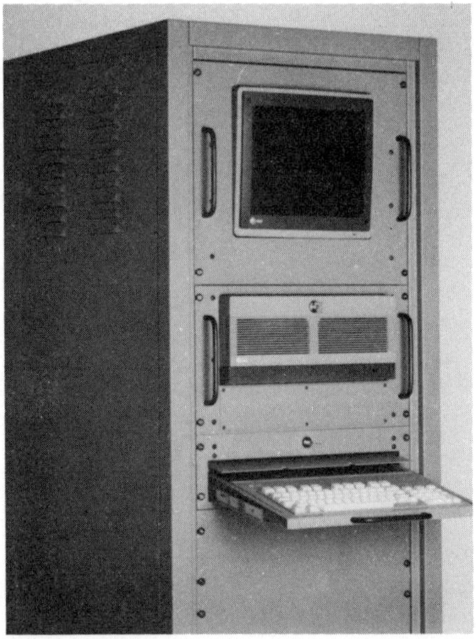

Fig. 22.2.2 AT&T PC 6300 with rack mounting.

Fig. 22.2.3 Equipment used for cosmetics packaging quality control.

AT&T PC 6300 Workstations

The AT&T line of industrial workstations are designed for the MS-DOS user who wants increased speed or is looking ahead to more sophisticated programming needs. See Figures 22.2.1 and 22.2.2. The workstations are based on the 8086 and 80286 CPUs with optional math coprocessors. The workstations feature up to 7 expansion slots, high resolution color graphics, security locking, impact and particulate protection.

The workstation can be a host processor for statistical process control and a network gateway, with interfaces with STARLAN, ISN and other local and wide area networks.

The AT&T PC6300 IWS can run several operating systems. The standard operating system is MS-DOS 2.11. MS-DOS 3.1 is available as well, adding interfacing ability to the AT&T STARLAN network. The system is also compatible with CP/M and XENIX V. XENIX can support two users simultaneously, sharing files and programs and transfering files between MS-DOS and XENIX.

Application at Cosmetics Manufacturer

A major cosmetics manufacturer used the DataMyte FAN system in conjunction with the AT&T PC 6300 IWS to efficiently monitor the fill weight and removal torque of filled product containers. See Figure 22.2.3. The manufac-

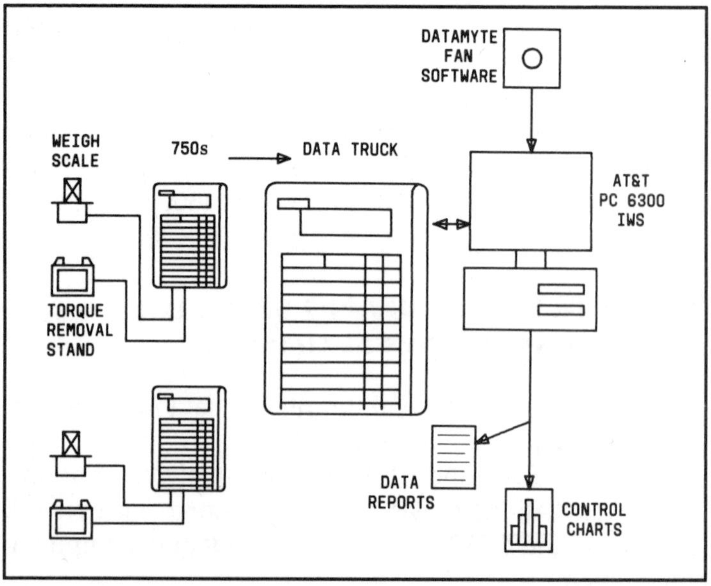

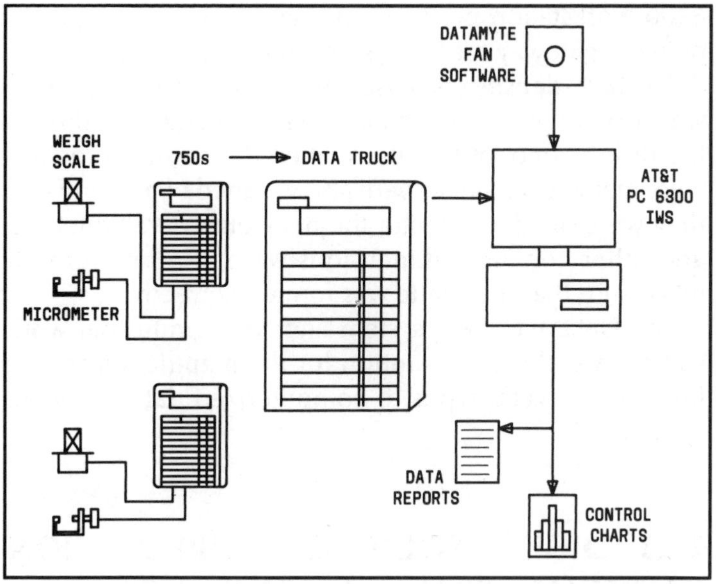

Fig. 22.2.4 Equipment used for plastic container quality control.

turer had to monitor a dozen different fill lines for product containers between 1 and 12 ounces. Both fill weight and removal torque auditing required an operator to sample each product line every 1/2 hour.

The workers had been manually recording the weights and then calculating and plotting control charts. This process took too much time. The solution was to put a DataMyte 762 data collector, electronic weigh scale, and a removal torque test unit on each product line. The DataMyte DataTruck data collector was used to set up the 762 data collectors and to harvest data on a daily basis. The data was then transferred to the AT&T PC 6300 IWS, which was running DataMyte FAN II support software.

The system decreased operator time spend collecting data and recording the control charts, allowing operator review and analysis of process variables, and provided management with an organized data base for evaluating product quality and machine productivity.

Application at Plastic Container Manufacturer

A plastic container manufacturer used the DataMyte FAN system to weigh and take various measurements of their containers for statistical process control. the AT&T PC

6300 workstation provided management reporting and a network gateway for the system. See Figure 22.2.4.

The high-density resin used in manufacturing the bottles was expensive, so the manufacturer wanted to be sure that the proper amount was used when the plastic containers were made. Containers were also weighed before and after they were filled to monitor the net weight. Wall thickness and other container dimensions were also measured to make sure that the bottle was formed correctly.

The DataMyte FAN system and AT&T industrial workstation was the best solution for the manufacturer, who looked at several types of computerized data collection systems.

22.3 DIGITAL EQUIPMENT CORPORATION MICROVAX 2000/VAXSTATION 2000

The DataMyte FAN system can now interface with Digital's multiuser VAX Soution Systems. VAX® Solution Systems are integrated, networked hardware and software systems each addressing a specific application, including manufacturing. A typical manufacturing system would include a MicroVAX II with 456 Mb disk, two VAXmate® desktop computers, one color VAXstation, two MicroVAX 2000s, eight VT 240 terminals and a network server.

Applications software would include RS/1 software from BBN Software Products. RS/1® for the VAXmate desktop computer can take data from DataMyte data collectors and perform statistical analysis. RS/1 software running on a VAX workstation or minicomputer can then receive DataMyte data files sent from the VAXmate along a network.

VAXmate Desktop Computer

The VAXmate is a high-performance desktop computer that enables transparent access to other personal, departmental and corporate computer resources. The system gives users access to both MS-DOS and VMS operating systems. VAXmate is based on the Intel 80286 microprocessor, running at 8 MHz. The base model is equipped with 1 Mbyte of RAM, a 1.2-Mbyte half-height floppy disk drive, a 14-inch high resolution monitor, a three-button mouse, an Lk50 keyboard, 12 feet of ThinWire® Ethernet cable, and a ThinWire Ethernet port. Options include a 2 Mbyte RAM upgrade module, an Intel 80287 math co-processor, and a 20-Mbyte hard disk and expansion chassis.

RS/1 Software System

RS/1 is an easy-to-use, versatile and fully integrated computer software system designed to meet the unique data management needs of engineers and laboratory scientists. RS/1 eliminates the need to write programs to satisfy each routine data analysis, statistics, graphics and modeling need.

Using simple English commands, you direct the system to:

Enter and Store Data — Data is automatically stored and used in the familiar table format or rows and columns, like a laboratory notebook. There is no setup required. There are no limits on the size or number of tables you may have, or the kind of data you can include.

Analyze data — Numerical, text, date, and time data in tables can be edited, sorted, subsetted, transposed, searched, manipulated and extended logically or mathematically.

Display graphics — You can produce and edit a variety of presentation-quality graphical forms: scatter plots, line graphs, histograms, bar-graphs, pie charts, three-dimensinal plots and control charts.

Fit curves — Linear and nonlinear regression analysis can be performed on data in tables and graphs. The fitted curve appears on the graph, accompanied by numerous goodness-of-fit statistic.

Perform statistical analysis — An extensive set of parametric and nonparametric tests may be applied to data in tables. If desired, RS/1 will help you select the right test for your data.

Develop analytical models — RS/1 tables can be extended to define models of complex systems, from chemical absorption to budget spread sheets.

Produce final reports — RS/1 helps you combine text, data, table and graphs into presentation-quality reports.

22.4 HP QUALITY DECISION MANAGEMENT/10000

The Vital Link to Quality in Manufacturing

Hewlett-Packard Company has developed a powerful application software package which helps analyze and monitor manufacturing process and product quality — HP Quality Decision Management/1000.

QDM/1000 Software Package

HP Quality Decision Management/1000 is an applications software package for analyzing manufacturing processes and product quality. The package provides control charts and Pareto charts that help production and quality assurance engineers identify and prioritize statistically significant product defects and manufacturing process problems. Engineering departments can use data collected on-line to generate scattergrams, histograms, and tabular reports. These outputs identify the manufacturing process causes of product quality deviations.

A menu and prompt/response approach allows engineers without programming experience to configure data collection transactions, specify report and graph formats, archive data, and perform system maintenance functions. Extensive "hooks" for user programs provide additional data input, output, and analysis flexibility.

QDM/1000 fits very well with the "Fix the Process" idea. It can help engineers and management identify/pinpoint potential manufacturing process/product *problems* (or areas for improvement) with statistical tools (Pareto analysis, scattergrams, histograms, control charts) as well as flexible "what if" reports that the users can also define to test hypotheses.

These reports can also be used to pinpoint *causes* as well. Perhaps more importantly, these tools can be used to objectively determine what is not the problem (e.g. "No, it's not this machine"), so time and resources aren't wasted correcting something that is not broken.

QDM/1000 can then be used to monitor the process to see if actions taken actually solved the problems or improved the process. If not, try something else.

As requirements, products, problems to be solved, etc. change over time, the QDM/1000 menu driven report def-

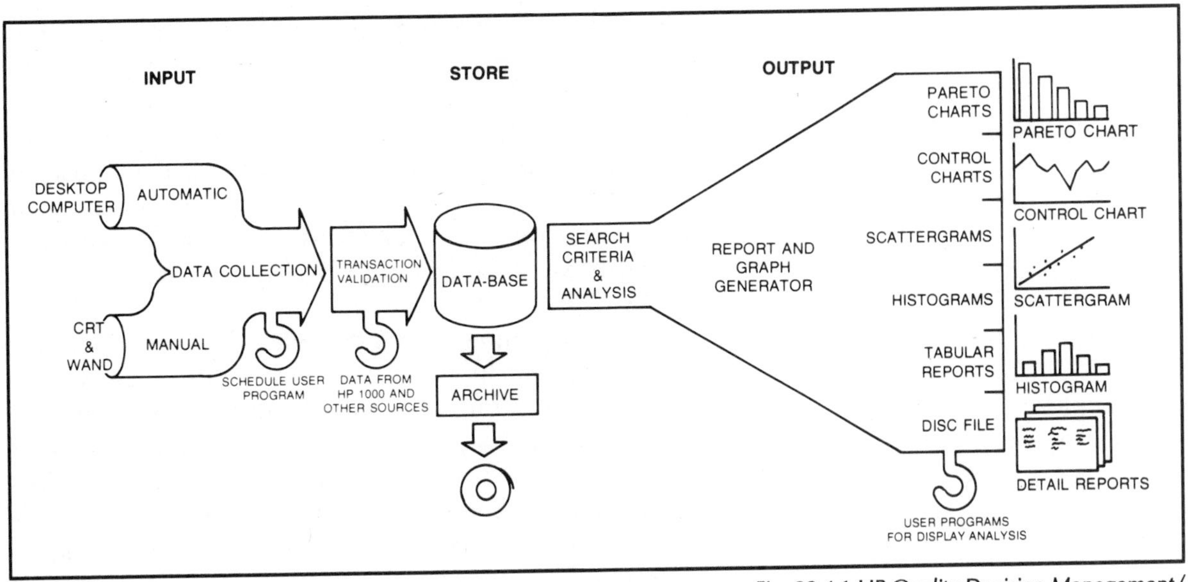

Fig. 22.4.1 HP Quality Decision Management/1000 Functional Diagram.

inition algorithm is flexible enough to handle new reporting needs. Get them the next day instead of next month or next year as you might with home grown systems where MIS resources are nearly impossible to get.

Functional Description

HP Quality Decision Management/1000 provides data collection, validation and storage to a data base, which is the center of the system. Engineers can statistically analyze the data and output the results in tabular or graphical format. A functional diagram is shown in Figure 22.4.1.

The data base is pre-defined and transparently configured by the user during the menu-driven transaction design process. Manual data collection follows a prompt/response sequence on a CRT, while automatic data collection occurs on HP Desktop Computers that accumulate data (for example, from a DataMyte) via user-written BASIC programs. These programs format the data, then forward the entire transaction to HP Quality Decision Management/1000. Transactions are validated and added to the data base. Invalid transactions are posted to an error log. Parameters and attributes are only validated in manual transactions.

User extensions are illustrated by the hooks in Figure 22.4.1. The left hook enables a user to activate an external program from both automatic and manual data collection. In its simplest form, this hook can be used to collect an input automatically. For example, instead of requiring an operator to key in a reading from a digital voltmeter, the value can be collected automatically. Another use in manual and automatic data collection modes is to schedule a program that pre-processes data or diverts it to some specialized storage or validation routine. The transaction validation hook accepts any formatted file.

Users also define search criteria as well as report and graph formats via menus. Once search criteria, analysis requirements, and output formats have been defined, they can be stored as a procedure name. An unsophisticated user can request one of these pre-defined reports. Conversely, a manufacturing engineer or other sophisticated user could interactively define a new report linking various parameters and attributes from different workstations in order to isolate and identify defect causes.

The right hook illustrates the capability of storing the result of a search into a disc file. The user can then access the file through user-written programs that perform specialized data analysis and display functions.

Features:

- Powerful report/graph writer for precise selection and analysis of collected data.
- Menu or prompt/response driven user interface for easy configuration, modification and system use by non-programmers.
- Controlled access via password assignments.
- Pre-defined data base for simplifying system design efforts.
- User-defined data collection prompts for system customization to specific application requirements.
- Extensive user-defined data validation for parametric (numerical) and attribute (descriptive) data.
- Data collection supported from CRTs and HP Desktop Computers.
- Flexible user extensions for data collection from any device that can transfer a formatted file to an HP 1000 computer.
- Data integrity through data base utilities and executive management programs.
- Color graphic CRT output.

Model of Production

The HP Quality Decision Management/1000 data base is designed for work station oriented production environments. The data base implicitly defines a model of production described in the diagram below.

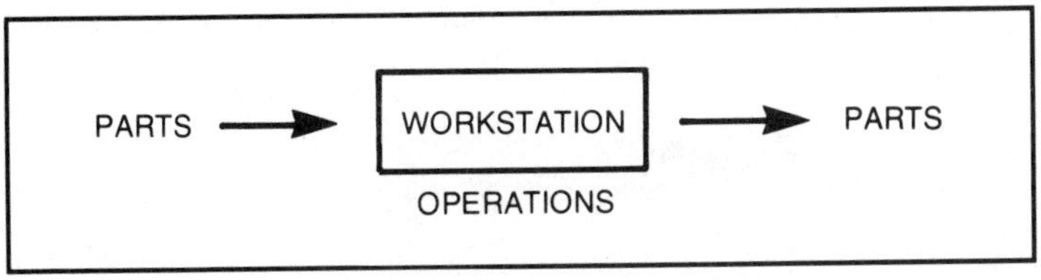

Multiple parts go through the work station and different operations are performed on the parts. For each combination of work station, part number, and operation, a data collection transaction can be identified. Each data collection transaction has three parts:

- Transaction data (e.g., who, what, where)
- Process Common data (common to all of the parts)
- Unit Specific data (specific to an individual part)

The following example illustrates the distinction between the three types of data. Assume a spray painting operation. A work order, A234-22, for five 0142-2009 parts is being painted by Joe Worker at spray station 2. The individual parts have unique serial numbers: 1, 2, 3, 4, and 5. The parts are spray painted different colors, and then placed in a 500-degree F drying oven for 20 minutes. See Table 22.4.1

This example includes just one work station. An actual application would have multiple workstations, such as Receiving/Incoming Inspection, Final Test, Fabrication, Assembly, etc.

User Configurable Prompt			**Operator Response**
Transaction Data (identifies the transaction)			
Workstation		?	: Spray station 2
Part Number		?	: 0142-2009
Operation		?	: Paint
Operator		?	: Joe Worker
Unit ID No.		?	: 1,2,3,4,5
Workorder No.		?	: A234-22
Process Common Data (all parts)			
Drying temperature		?	500 degrees F
Drying time		?	20 minutes
Unit Specific Data (unique to unit ID number)			
Unit 1	Color	?	Blue
Unit 2	Color	?	Red
Unit 3	Color	?	Green
Unit 4	Color	?	Yellow
Unit 5	Color	?	Vermillion

Table 22.4.1

Using HP Quality Decision Management/1000

The next two pages provide a few examples of reports produced by HP Quality Decision Management/1000. Table 22.4.2 indicates some of the key application areas and the product features and benefits of each area. HP Quality Decision Management/1000 executes on an HP 1000 minicomputer with HP's powerful RTE-A with VC+ operating system.

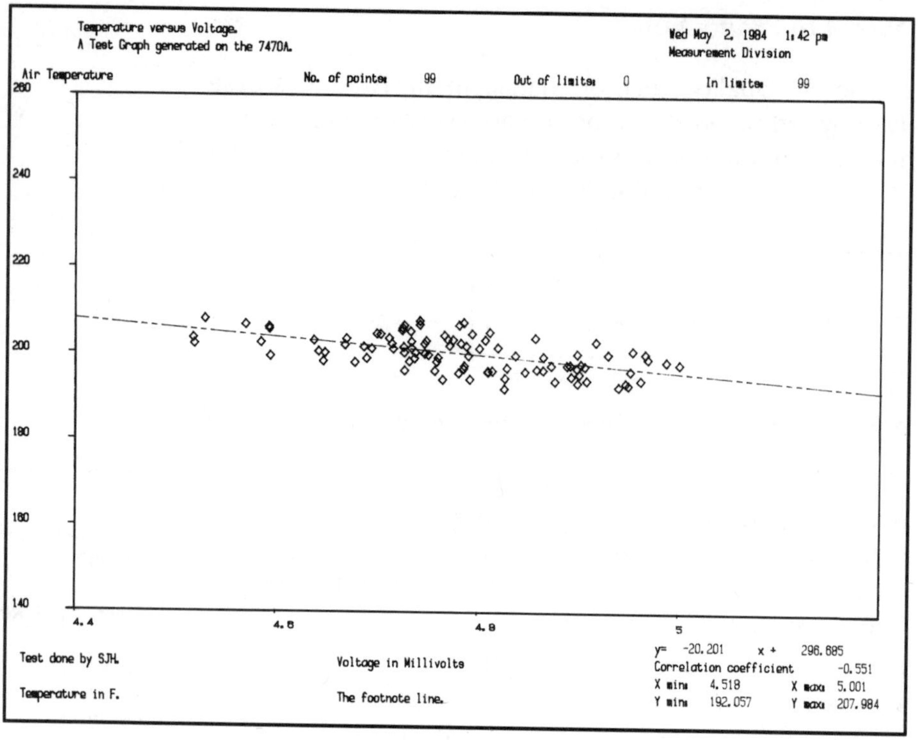

A scattergram of temperature versus voltage, printed by a pen plotter.

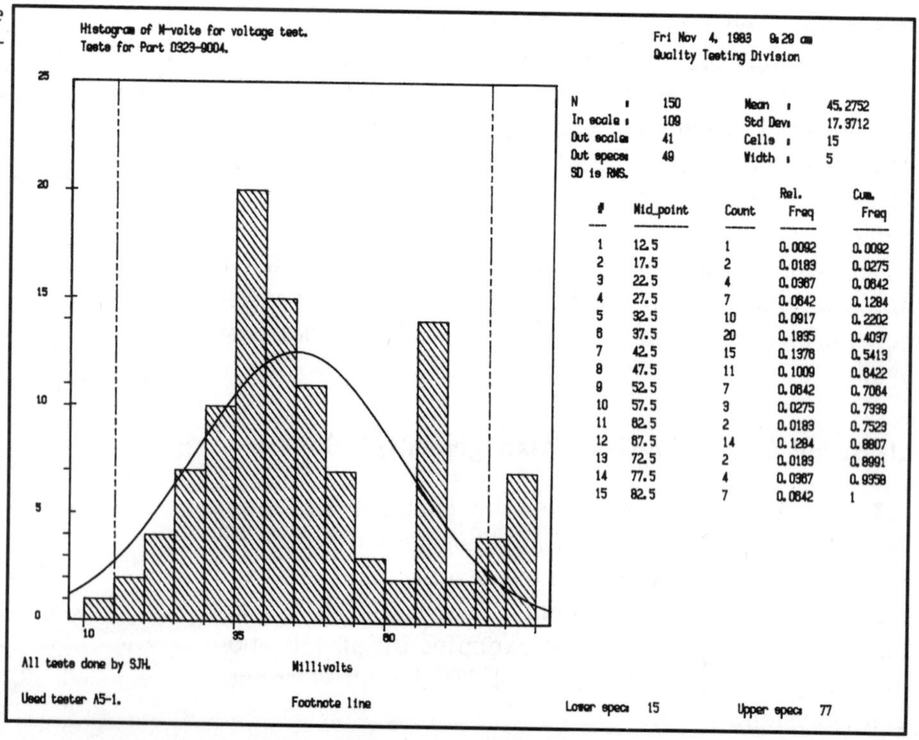

A histogram of a voltage test, done on a pen plotter.

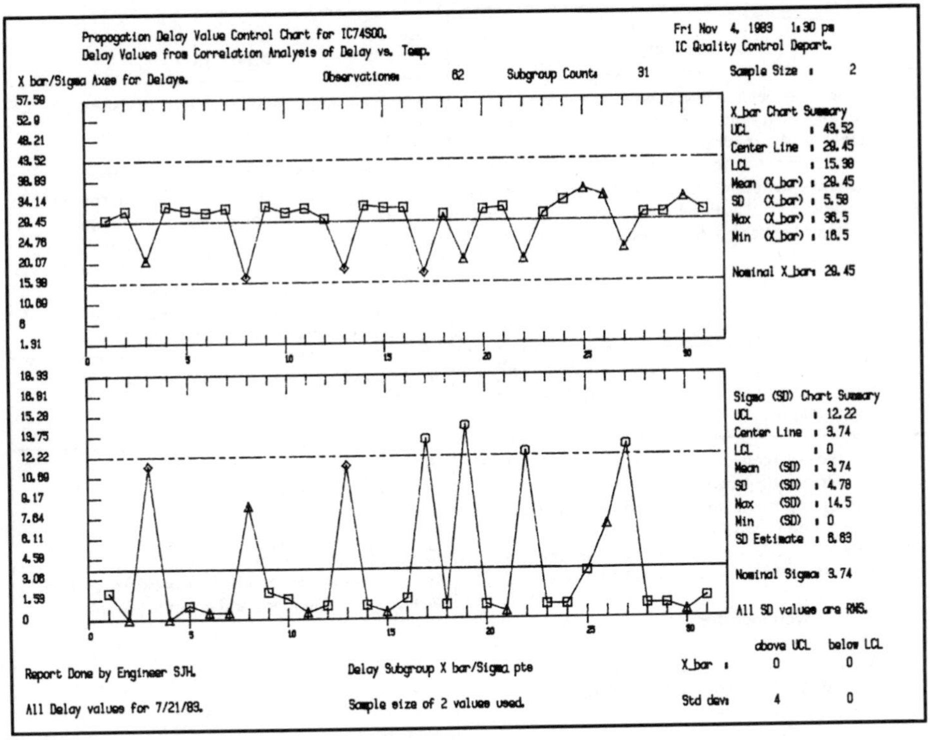

$\bar{x}$ & R chart for propagation delay value, done on a pen plotter.

The is c test Pareto Chart for the GRPKG program.
The test name is TESTB2 xxxxxxxxxxxxxxxxxxxxxxxx

The test made by SJH. xxxx
Thu May 10, 1984 2:31 pm

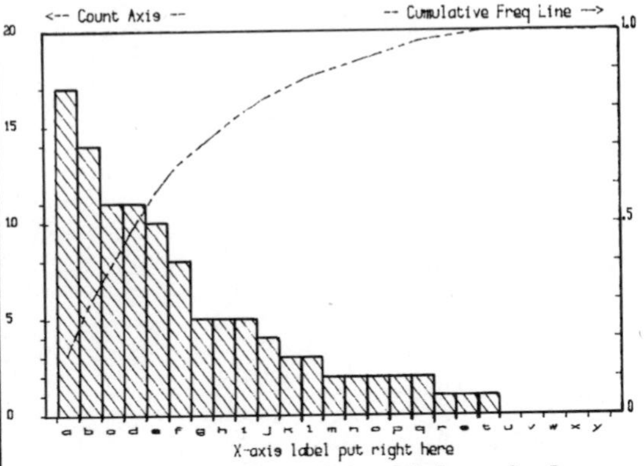

Cell	Rel. Freq.	Cum. Freq.	Cell	Rel. Freq.	Cum. Freq.
a	0.15596	0.15596	n	0.01835	0.91743
b	0.12844	0.2844	o	0.01835	0.93578
c	0.10092	0.38532	p	0.01835	0.95413
d	0.10092	0.48624	q	0.01835	0.97248
e	0.09174	0.57798	r	0.00917	0.98165
f	0.07339	0.65138	s	0.00917	0.99083
g	0.04587	0.69725	t	0.00917	1
h	0.04587	0.74312	u	0	1
i	0.04587	0.78899	v	0	1
j	0.0367	0.82569	w	0	1
k	0.02752	0.85321	x	0	1
l	0.02752	0.88073	y	0	1
m	0.01835	0.89908			

Cell	Count	Description of cell parameter
a	17	Error class 565
b	14	Tucked Pin
c	11	Open circuit
d	11	Static discharge on board
e	10	Not Soldered
f	8	Bridge Break
g	5	Solder Bridge
h	5	Missing Resistor
i	5	Operator test error
j	4	Wrong value
k	3	Confidential
l	3	Capacitor failure
m	2	Cracked board
n	2	Missing component
o	2	Reversed component
p	2	Gold Bridge
q	2	Dropped on floor
r	1	Wrong Component
s	1	Unidentified failure
t	1	Test Machine Error
u	0	
v	0	
w	0	
x	0	
y	0	

Comment line is here. xxxxx
This is a comment line also
This is a footnote line xxx

Total Occurrence Count: 109
Number of Cells : 25

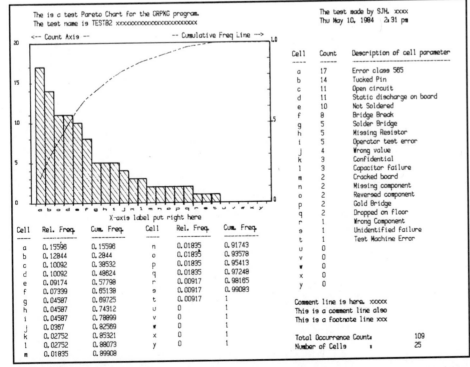

Pareto chart, with a table of counts and descriptions.

APPLICATION AREA	FEATURES	BENEFITS
Incoming Inspection	Displays inspection instructions, generates vendor rating reports, control charts of defect rates, vendor quality.	Prioritize vendors, reduce number of vendors, and increase vendor responsiveness to your quality demands.
Product Test: Electronic, electro-mechanical, final, in-process, component	Manual and automatic on-line data collection, test procedure display. Provides statistical monitoring of defect levels and decision support graphics and reports.	■ Optimize test process, schedule calibrations, determine minimum number of readings necessary, identify tester vs product defects. ■ Reaction to statistically significant defect rates ■ Production defect data available for correlation to manufacturing process data, identification of causes of quality problems.
History Tracking/Audit Trail	On-line data collection of pertinent traceability facts, archived but available for recall to satisfy regulatory requirements.	■ Respond to regulatory requirements.
Statistical process/product monitoring	On-line data collection from incoming inspection, manufacturing process, and test areas. Statistical graphs/reports to monitor manufacturing process quality and product defect rates. Correlation between product defect data and defect cause data allows identification of specific defect causes: ■ poor workmanship ■ faulty material ■ weak manufacturing process execution ■ wrong manufacturing process definition ■ faulty product design	■ High, predictable yields ■ Lower production costs ■ Reduced rework costs ■ Lower scrap levels ■ Reduced labor content ■ Accurate vendor quality feedback-correlation. ■ Reduced cycle times and inventory levels

Table 22.4.2.

APPENDIX

TABLE A-1 CONSTANTS FOR CALCULATING CONTROL LIMITS

The formulas for calculating control limits are shown below. They are based on the normal distribution curve.

Number of Observations in subgroup	Constants for $\bar{x}$ Chart		Divisors for Estimate of Standard Deviation	Range Chart Lower Control Limit	Range Chart Upper Control Limit	Constant for $\bar{x}$ Chart	Divisors for Estimate of Standard Deviation	Sigma Chart Lower Control Limit	Sigma Chart Upper Control Limit
n	A	A_2	d_2	D_3	D_4	A_3	c_4	B_3	B_4
2	2.12	1.880	1.128	—	3.267	2.659	0.7979	—	3.267
3	1.73	1.023	1.693	—	2.574	1.954	0.8862	—	2.568
4	1.50	0.729	2.059	—	2.282	1.628	0.9213	—	2.266
5	1.34	0.577	2.326	—	2.114	1.427	0.9400	—	2.089
6	1.22	0.483	2.534	—	2.004	1.287	0.9515	0.030	1.970
7	1.13	0.419	2.704	0.076	1.924	1.182	0.9594	0.118	1.882
8	1.06	0.373	2.847	0.136	1.864	1.099	0.9650	0.185	1.815
9	1.00	0.337	2.970	0.184	1.816	1.032	0.9693	0.239	1.761
10	0.95	0.308	3.078	0.223	1.777	0.975	0.9727	0.284	1.716
11	0.90	0.285	3.173	0.256	1.744	0.927	0.9754	0.321	1.679
12	0.87	0.266	3.258	0.283	1.717	0.886	0.9776	0.354	1.646
13	0.83	0.249	3.336	0.307	1.693	0.850	0.9794	0.382	1.618
14	0.80	0.235	3.407	0.328	1.672	0.817	0.9810	0.406	1.594
15	0.77	0.223	3.472	0.347	1.653	0.789	0.9823	0.428	1.572
16	0.75	0.212	3.532	0.363	1.637	0.763	0.9835	0.448	1.552
17	0.73	0.203	3.588	0.378	1.622	0.739	0.9845	0.466	1.534
18	0.71	0.194	3.640	0.391	1.608	0.718	0.9854	0.482	1.518
19	0.69	0.187	3.689	0.403	1.597	0.698	0.9862	0.497	1.503
20	0.67	0.180	3.735	0.415	1.585	0.680	0.9869	0.510	1.490
21	0.65	0.173	3.778	0.425	1.575	0.663	0.9876	0.523	1.477
22	0.64	0.167	3.819	0.434	1.566	0.647	0.9882	0.534	1.466
23	0.63	0.162	3.858	0.443	1.557	0.633	0.9887	0.545	1.455
24	0.61	0.157	3.895	0.451	1.548	0.619	0.9892	0.555	1.445
25	0.60	0.153	3.931	0.459	1.541	0.606	0.9896	0.565	1.435

FORMULAS

$\bar{x}$ Control Limits based on $\bar{R} = \bar{\bar{x}} \pm A_2\bar{R}$

$\bar{x}$ Control Limits based on $\bar{s} = \bar{\bar{x}} \pm A_3\bar{s}$

$\bar{x}$ Control Limits based on the sigma of the data $= \bar{x}' \pm A\sigma'$

$\bar{x}$ Control Limits based on the sigma of the x-bars $= \bar{\bar{x}} \pm 3\sigma_{\bar{x}}$

$\bar{x}$ Control Limits based on moving range $= \bar{\bar{x}} \pm 2.66\text{m}\bar{R}$

Range Upper Control Limit $= D_4\bar{R}$

Range Lower Control Limit $= D_3\bar{R}$

Sigma Upper Control Limit $= B_4\bar{\sigma}$

Sigma Lower Control Limit $= B_3\bar{\sigma}$

Estimated Sigma Hat based on $\bar{R} = \hat{\sigma} = \bar{R}/d_2$

Estimated Sigma Hat based on $\bar{s} = \hat{\sigma} = \bar{s}/c_4$

*Adapted from ASTM publicaton STP-15D, **Manual on the Presentation of Data and Control Chart Analysis**, 1976; pp 134-136. Copyright ASTM, 1916 Race Street, Philadelphia, Pennsylvania 19103. Reprinted, with permission.

TABLE A-2 AREAS UNDER THE NORMAL CURVE

$\frac{X_i - \bar{X}'}{\sigma'}$	0.09	0.08	0.07	0.06	0.05	0.04	0.03	0.02	0.01	0.00
−3.5	0.00017	0.00017	0.00018	0.00019	0.00019	0.00020	0.00021	0.00022	0.00022	0.00023
−3.4	0.00024	0.00025	0.00026	0.00027	0.00028	0.00029	0.00030	0.00031	0.00033	0.00034
−3.3	0.00035	0.00036	0.00038	0.00039	0.00040	0.00042	0.00043	0.00045	0.00047	0.00048
−3.2	0.00050	0.00052	0.00054	0.00056	0.00058	0.00060	0.00062	0.00064	0.00066	0.00069
−3.1	0.00071	0.00074	0.00076	0.00079	0.00082	0.00085	0.00087	0.00090	0.00094	0.00097
−3.0	0.00100	0.00104	0.00107	0.00111	0.00114	0.00118	0.00122	0.00126	0.00131	0.00135
−2.9	0.0014	0.0014	0.0015	0.0015	0.0016	0.0016	0.0017	0.0017	0.0018	0.0019
−2.8	0.0019	0.0020	0.0021	0.0021	0.0022	0.0023	0.0023	0.0024	0.0025	0.0026
−2.7	0.0026	0.0027	0.0028	0.0029	0.0030	0.0031	0.0032	0.0033	0.0034	0.0035
−2.6	0.0036	0.0037	0.0038	0.0039	0.0040	0.0041	0.0043	0.0044	0.0045	0.0047
−2.5	0.0048	0.0049	0.0051	0.0052	0.0054	0.0055	0.0057	0.0059	0.0060	0.0062
−2.4	0.0064	0.0066	0.0068	0.0069	0.0071	0.0073	0.0075	0.0078	0.0080	0.0082
−2.3	0.0084	0.0087	0.0089	0.0091	0.0094	0.0096	0.0099	0.0102	0.0104	0.0107
−2.2	0.0110	0.0113	0.0116	0.0119	0.0122	0.0125	0.0129	0.0132	0.0136	0.0139
−2.1	0.0143	0.0146	0.0150	0.0154	0.0158	0.0162	0.0166	0.0170	0.0174	0.0179
−2.0	0.0183	0.0188	0.0192	0.0197	0.0202	0.0207	0.0212	0.0217	0.0222	0.0228
−1.9	0.0233	0.0239	0.0244	0.0250	0.0256	0.0262	0.0268	0.0274	0.0281	0.0287
−1.8	0.0294	0.0301	0.0307	0.0314	0.0322	0.0329	0.0336	0.0344	0.0351	0.0359
−1.7	0.0367	0.0375	0.0384	0.0392	0.0401	0.0409	0.0418	0.0427	0.0436	0.0446
−1.6	0.0455	0.0465	0.0475	0.0485	0.0495	0.0505	0.0516	0.0526	0.0537	0.0548
−1.5	0.0559	0.0571	0.0582	0.0594	0.0606	0.0618	0.0630	0.0643	0.0655	0.0668
−1.4	0.0681	0.0694	0.0708	0.0721	0.0735	0.0749	0.0764	0.0778	0.0793	0.0808
−1.3	0.0823	0.0838	0.0853	0.0869	0.0885	0.0901	0.0918	0.0934	0.0951	0.0968
−1.2	0.0985	0.1003	0.1020	0.1038	0.1057	0.1075	0.1093	0.1112	0.1131	0.1151
−1.1	0.1170	0.1190	0.1210	0.1230	0.1251	0.1271	0.1292	0.1314	0.1335	0.1357
−1.0	0.1379	0.1401	0.1423	0.1446	0.1469	0.1492	0.1515	0.1539	0.1562	0.1587
−0.9	0.1611	0.1635	0.1660	0.1685	0.1711	0.1736	0.1762	0.1788	0.1814	0.1841
−0.8	0.1867	0.1894	0.1922	0.1949	0.1977	0.2005	0.2033	0.2061	0.2090	0.2119
−0.7	0.2148	0.2177	0.2207	0.2236	0.2266	0.2297	0.2327	0.2358	0.2389	0.2420
−0.6	0.2451	0.2483	0.2514	0.2546	0.2578	0.2611	0.2643	0.2676	0.2709	0.2743
−0.5	0.2776	0.2810	0.2843	0.2877	0.2912	0.2946	0.2981	0.3015	0.3050	0.3085
−0.4	0.3121	0.3156	0.3192	0.3228	0.3264	0.3300	0.3336	0.3372	0.3409	0.3446
−0.3	0.3483	0.3520	0.3557	0.3594	0.3632	0.3669	0.3707	0.3745	0.3783	0.3821
−0.2	0.3859	0.3897	0.3936	0.3974	0.4013	0.4052	0.4090	0.4129	0.4168	0.4207
−0.1	0.4247	0.4286	0.4325	0.4364	0.4404	0.4443	0.4483	0.4522	0.4562	0.4602
−0.0	0.4641	0.4681	0.4721	0.4761	0.4801	0.4840	0.4880	0.4920	0.4960	0.5000

Reproduced with permission from Eugene L. Grant and Richard S. Leavenworth, "Statistical Quality Control," 5th ed., 1980, McGraw-Hill Book Company.

HOW TO USE THIS TABLE: Subtract the mean ($\bar{x}$) from the specification (x_i) and divide by sigma (σ'). Negative numbers indicate areas to the left of the mean and positive to the right. Use the value in the table that corresponds to units and tenths (first column), and hundredths (top row) digits of the number. For example, .38 corresponds to 0.6480. Subtract from 1.0 to get the percent area from the specification out to infinity on a normal curve. For .38, it is 35%.

TABLE A-2, CONTINUED

$\frac{X_i-\bar{X}'}{\sigma'}$	0.00	0.01	0.02	0.03	0.04	0.05	0.06	0.07	0.08	0.09
+0.0	0.5000	0.5040	0.5080	0.5120	0.5160	0.5199	0.5239	0.5279	0.5319	0.5359
+0.1	0.5398	0.5438	0.5478	0.5517	0.5557	0.5596	0.5636	0.5675	0.5714	0.5753
+0.2	0.5793	0.5832	0.5871	0.5910	0.5948	0.5987	0.6026	0.6064	0.6103	0.6141
+0.3	0.6179	0.6217	0.6255	0.6293	0.6331	0.6368	0.6406	0.6443	0.6480	0.6517
+0.4	0.6554	0.6591	0.6628	0.6664	0.6700	0.6736	0.6772	0.6808	0.6844	0.6879
+0.5	0.6915	0.6950	0.6985	0.7019	0.7054	0.7088	0.7123	0.7157	0.7190	0.7224
+0.6	0.7257	0.7291	0.7324	0.7357	0.7389	0.7422	0.7454	0.7486	0.7517	0.7549
+0.7	0.7580	0.7611	0.7642	0.7673	0.7704	0.7734	0.7764	0.7794	0.7823	0.7852
+0.8	0.7881	0.7910	0.7939	0.7967	0.7995	0.8023	0.8051	0.8079	0.8106	0.8133
+0.9	0.8159	0.8186	0.8212	0.8238	0.8264	0.8289	0.8315	0.8340	0.8365	0.8389
+1.0	0.8413	0.8438	0.8461	0.8485	0.8508	0.8531	0.8554	0.8577	0.8599	0.8621
+1.1	0.8643	0.8665	0.8686	0.8708	0.8729	0.8749	0.8770	0.8790	0.8810	0.8830
+1.2	0.8849	0.8869	0.8888	0.8907	0.8925	0.8944	0.8962	0.8980	0.8997	0.9015
+1.3	0.9032	0.9049	0.9066	0.9082	0.9099	0.9115	0.9131	0.9147	0.9162	0.9177
+1.4	0.9192	0.9207	0.9222	0.9236	0.9251	0.9265	0.9279	0.9292	0.9306	0.9319
+1.5	0.9332	0.9345	0.9357	0.9370	0.9382	0.9394	0.9406	0.9418	0.9429	0.9441
+1.6	0.9452	0.9463	0.9474	0.9484	0.9495	0.9505	0.9515	0.9525	0.9535	0.9545
+1.7	0.9554	0.9564	0.9573	0.9582	0.9591	0.9599	0.9608	0.9616	0.9625	0.9633
+1.8	0.9641	0.9649	0.9656	0.9664	0.9671	0.9678	0.9686	0.9693	0.9699	0.9706
+1.9	0.9713	0.9719	0.9726	0.9732	0.9738	0.9744	0.9750	0.9756	0.9761	0.9767
+2.0	0.9773	0.9778	0.9783	0.9788	0.9793	0.9798	0.9803	0.9808	0.9812	0.9817
+2.1	0.9821	0.9826	0.9830	0.9834	0.9838	0.9842	0.9846	0.9850	0.9854	0.9857
+2.2	0.9861	0.9864	0.9868	0.9871	0.9875	0.9878	0.9881	0.9884	0.9887	0.9890
+2.3	0.9893	0.9896	0.9898	0.9901	0.9904	0.9906	0.9909	0.9911	0.9913	0.9916
+2.4	0.9918	0.9920	0.9922	0.9925	0.9927	0.9929	0.9931	0.9932	0.9934	0.9936
+2.5	0.9938	0.9940	0.9941	0.9943	0.9945	0.9946	0.9948	0.9949	0.9951	0.9952
+2.6	0.9953	0.9955	0.9956	0.9957	0.9959	0.9960	0.9961	0.9962	0.9963	0.9964
+2.7	0.9965	0.9966	0.9967	0.9968	0.9969	0.9970	0.9971	0.9972	0.9973	0.9974
+2.8	0.9974	0.9975	0.9976	0.9977	0.9977	0.9978	0.9979	0.9979	0.9980	0.9981
+2.9	0.9981	0.9982	0.9983	0.9983	0.9984	0.9984	0.9985	0.9985	0.9986	0.9986
+3.0	0.99865	0.99869	0.99874	0.99878	0.99882	0.99886	0.99889	0.99893	0.99896	0.99900
+3.1	0.99903	0.99906	0.99910	0.99913	0.99915	0.99918	0.99921	0.99924	0.99926	0.99929
+3.2	0.99931	0.99934	0.99936	0.99938	0.99940	0.99942	0.99944	0.99946	0.99948	0.99950
+3.3	0.99952	0.99953	0.99955	0.99957	0.99958	0.99960	0.99961	0.99962	0.99964	0.99965
+3.4	0.99966	0.99967	0.99969	0.99970	0.99971	0.99972	0.99973	0.99974	0.99975	0.99976
+3.5	0.99977	0.99978	0.99978	0.99979	0.99980	0.99981	0.99981	0.99982	0.99983	0.99983

TABLE A-3 METRIC SYSTEM

METRIC SYSTEM		
	LENGTH (METERS)	
unit	abbr.	
myriameter	mym	10,000
kilometer	km	1,000
hectometer	hm	100
decameter	dkm	10
meter	m	1
decimeter	dm	0.1
centimeter	cm	0.01
millimeter	mm	0.001
	AREA (SQUARE METERS)	
square kilometer	sq km *or* km^2	1,000,000
hectare	ha	10,000
are	a	100
centare	ca	1
square centimeter	sq cm *or* cm^2	0.0001
	VOLUME (CUBIC METERS)	
decastere	dks	10
stere	s	1
decistere	ds	0.10
cubic centimeter	cu cm *or* cm^3 *also* cc	0.000001
	CAPACITY (LITERS)	
kiloliter	kl	1,000
hectoliter	hl	100
decaliter	dkl	10
liter	l	1
deciliter	dl	0.10
centiliter	cl	0.01
milliliter	ml	0.001
	MASS AND WEIGHT (GRAMS)	
metric ton	MT *or* t	1,000,000
quintal	q	100,000
kilogram	kg	1,000
hectogram	hg	100
decagram	dkg	10
gram	g *or* gm	1
decigram	dg	0.10
centigram	cg	0.01
milligram	mg	0.001

TABLE A-4 SI SYSTEM

Characteristic	Unit of measure	Symbol	Formula
	Fundamental units		
Length	meter	m	
Mass	kilogram	kg	
Time	second	s	
Electric current	ampere	A	
Temperature	degree Kelvin	K	
Luminous intensity	candela	cd	
	Supplementary units		
Plane angle	radian	rad	
Solid angle	steradian	sr	
	Derived units		
Area	square meter	m^2	
Volume	cubic meter	m^3	
Frequency	hertz	Hz	(s^{-1})
Density	kilogram per cubic meter	kg/m^3	
Velocity	meter per second	m/s	
Angular velocity	radian per second	rad/s	
Acceleration	meter per second squared	m/s^2	
Angular acceleration	radian per second squared	rad/s^2	
Force	newton	N	$(kg\text{-}m/s^2)$
Pressure	newton per sq meter	N/m^2	
Kinematic viscosity	sq meter per second	m^2/s	
Dynamic viscosity	newton-second per sq meter	$N\text{-}s/m^2$	
Work, energy, quantity of heat	joule	J	(N-m)
Power	watt	W	(J/s)
Electric charge	coulomb	C	(A-s)
Voltage, potential difference, electromotive force	volt	V	(W/A)
Electric field strength	volt per meter	V/m	
Electric resistance	ohm		(V/A)
Electric capacitance	farad	F	(A-s/V)
Magnetic flux	weber	Wb	(V-s)
Inductance	henry	H	(V-s/A)
Magnetic flux density	tesla	T	(Wb/m^2)
Magnetic field strength	ampere per meter	A/m	
Magnetomotive force	ampere	A	
Luminous flux	lumen	lm	(cd-sr)
Luminance	candela per sq meter	cd/m^2	
Illumination	lux	lx	(lm/m^2)

TABLE A-5 CONVERSION FACTORS

Unless otherwise specified, the units *oz* and *lb* in the following tables are *units of force.*

LENGTH	m	metre	1 m = 10^{-3} km 10^{2} cm 10^{3} mm 10^{6} μm 10^{9} nm 10^{10} Å	1 m = 39.370 in 3.2808 ft 1.0936 yd
	km	kilometre	1 in = 25.4 mm (exactly)	
	cm	centimetre	1 ft = 12 in = 0.3048 m	
	mm	millimetre	1 yd = 3 ft = 0.9144 m	
	μm	micrometre	1 mi (statute mile) = 1609.344 m = 5280 ft	
	nm	naometre	1 nautical mile = 1852 m	
	Å	angstrom	1 mil = 10^{-3} in = 0.0254 mm	
AREA	m^2	square metre	1 m^2 = 10^4 cm^2 10^6 mm^2	1 m^2 = 1550.0 in^2 10.764 ft^2 1 cm^2 = 0.155 in^2
	km^2	square kilometre	1 in^2 = 645.16 mm^2 = 6.4516 cm^2 6.9444 x 10^{-3} ft^2	
	ha	hectare	1 ft^2 = 144 in^2 = 0.0929 m^2	
	a	are	1 km^2 = 100 ha 10^4 a 10^6 m^2 0.3861 mi^2	1 ha = 10^4 m^2 = 100 a 2.471 acres 1 a = 100 m^2 0.01 ha
	cm^2	square centimetre	1 mi^2 = 640 acres 2.59 km^2	1 acre = 0.40469 ha 4046.9 m^2
	mm^2	square millimetre		
VOLUME	m^3	cubic metre	1 m^3 = 10^3 dm^3 10^3 ℓ 10^6 cm^3 10^6 mℓ 10^9 mm^3	1 m^3 = 6.1024 x 10^4 in^3 35.315 ft^3 1 cm^3 = 6.1024 x 10^{-2} in^3
	dm^3	cubic decimetre	1 in^3 = 16.387 cm^3	
	ℓ	litre (=dm^3)	1 ft^3 = 1728 in^3 = 2.8317 x 10^{-2} m^3	
	mℓ	millilitre (=cm^3)	1 mℓ = 0.0338 fl oz	1 fl oz = 29.5737 mℓ 1.8047 in^3
	cm^3	cubic centimetre	1 ℓ = 33.8 fl oz 1.0567 qt 0.26417 gal	1 qt = 0.94636 ℓ 1 gal = 3.7854 ℓ
	mm^3	cubic millimetre		

<table>
<tr><td>LINEAR VELOCITY</td><td>m/s metre per second
mm/s millimetre per second
km/h kilometre per hour</td><td>1 m/s = 10^3 mm/s
3.6 km/h
1 m/s = 29.370 in/s
3.2808 ft/s
1 in/s = 2.54×10^{-2} m/s = 25.4 mm/s
1 mph = 1.6093 km/h
1 km/h = 0.6214 mph</td></tr>
<tr><td>LINEAR ACCELER-ATION</td><td>m/s^2 metre per square second</td><td>1 m/s^2 = 39.370 in/s^2
3.2808 ft/s^2
1 in/s^2 = 2.54×10^{-2} m/s^2</td></tr>
<tr><td>PLANE ANGLE</td><td>rad radian
r revolution
o angular degree
′ angular minute
″ angular second</td><td>1 rad = 57.296° = $(360/2\pi)$ ° = 0.15915 r
1° = 60′
3600″
1.7453×10^{-2} rad
2.7778×10^{-3} r
1 r = 360°
6.2832 rad = (2π) rad</td></tr>
<tr><td>ANGULAR VELOCITY</td><td>rad/s radian per second
r/s (rps) revolution per second
r/min (rpm) revolution per minute
°/s angular degree per second</td><td>1 rad/s = 0.15915 rps
9.5493 rpm
1 rpm = 10^{-3} krpm
1.6667×10^{-2} rps
6 °/s
0.10472 rad/s
1 krpm = 104.72 rad/s
1 rps = 60 rpm
360 °/s
6.2832 rad/s</td></tr>
<tr><td>ANGULAR ACCELERATION</td><td>rad/s^2 radian per square second
r/s^2 revolution per square second
rpm/s revolution per minute per second
$°/s^2$ angular degree per square second</td><td>1 rad/s^2 = 0.15915 r/s^2
9.5493 rpm/s
1 rpm/s = 10^{-3} krpm/s
1.6667×10^{-2} r/s^2
6 $°/s^2$
0.10472 rad/s^2
1 r/s^2 = 60 rpm/s
360 $°/s^2$
6.2832 rad/s^2</td></tr>
</table>

MASS	kg kilogram g gram t tonne (metric ton)	1 kg = 10^3 g = 10^{-3} t 35.274 oz (mass) 2.2046 lb (mass) 6.8522×10^{-2} slug
		1 oz (mass) = 28.3495 g
		1 lb (mass) = 16 oz (mass) 0.45359 kg
		1 slug = 14.5939 kg
		1 t = 10^3 kg 2204.6 lb (mass) 1.1023 short ton
		1 short ton = 2000 lb (mass) 907.185 kg 0.907185 t
FORCE	N newton kp kilopond kgf (= kp) kilogram-force p pond gf (=p) gram-force	1 N = 0.10197 kp 0.22481 lb 3.5969 oz 7.2330 poundals
		1 kp = 9.80665 N 2.2046 lb 35.274 oz
		1 oz = 0.27801 N 2.83495×10^{-2} kp 28.3495 p
		1 lb = 16 oz 4.4482 N 0.45359 kp
		1 poundal = 0.138255 N
PRESSURE, STRESS	Pa pascal kPa kilopascal MPa megapascal kp/cm^2 kilopond per square centimetre at (=kp/cm^2) technical atmosphere kp/mm^2 kilopond per square millimetre	1 Pa = 1.0197×10^{-5} at 1.45034×10^{-4} lb/in^2
		1 kPa = 1.0197×10^{-2} at 0.145034 lb/in^2
		1 MPa = 10.197 at 145.034 lb/in^2
		1 at = 1 kp/cm^2 98.0665 kPa 14.223 lb/in^2
		1 kp/mm^2 = 100 at 9.80665 MPa 1422.3 lb/in^2
		1 lb/in^2 = 6.895 kPa = 0.07031 at

	Units	Conversions
TORQUE	Nm newton metre kpm kilopond metre	1 Nm = 0.10197 kpm 0.73756 lb-ft 8.85075 lb-in 141.612 oz-in
		1 kpm = 9.80665 Nm 1.3887×10^3 oz-in
		1 oz-in = 7.0615×10^{-3} Nm 7.2008×10^{-4} kpm
		1 lb-ft = 192 oz-in = 12 lb-in 1.3558 Nm 0.13825 kpm
MOMENT OF INERTIA	$kg\,m^2$ kilogram-square metre $kg\,cm^2$ kilogram-square centimetre $kg\,mm^2$ kilogram-square millimetre $g\,cm^2$ gram-square centimetre	$1\ kg\,m^2 = 10^4\ kg\,cm^2 = 10^6\ kg\,mm^2 = 10^7\ g\,cm^2$ 8.85075 $lb\text{-}in\text{-}s^2$ 141.612 $oz\text{-}in\text{-}s^2$
		$1\ kg\,cm^2 = 0.01416\ oz\text{-}in\text{-}s^2$
		$1\ oz\text{-}in\text{-}s^2 = 6.25 \times 10^{-2}\ lb\text{-}in\text{-}s^2$ $7.06155 \times 10^{-3}\ kg\,m^2$ $70.6155\ kg\,cm^2$
ENERGY, WORK, AMOUNT OF HEAT	J joule Ws wattsecond kWh kilowatthour kpm kilopond metre kcal kilocalorie (nutrition calorie) cal calorie	1 J = 1 Ws 2.7778×10^{-7} kWh 0.10197 kpm 2.38846×10^{-4} kcal 9.4781×10^{-4} Btu
		1 kcal = 10^3 cal 4186.8 J 1.1630×10^{-3} kWh 3.9683 Btu
		1 kWh = 3.6×10^6 J 859.845 kcal 3.4121×10^3 Btu
		1 Btu = 1055.06 J 2.9307×10^{-4} kWh 0.251997 kcal

TABLE A-6 TORQUE CONVERSION FACTORS

A \ B	Nm	kpm (kg*-m)	g*-cm	oz-in	lb-in	lb-ft
Nm	1	0.101972	1.01972×10^{4}	141.612	8.85075	0.737562
kpm (kg*-m)	9.80665	1	10^{5}	1.38874×10^{3}	86.7962	7.23301
g*-cm	9.80665×10^{-5}	10^{-5}	1	1.38874×10^{-2}	8.67962×10^{-4}	7.23301×10^{-5}
oz-in	7.06155×10^{-3}	7.20077×10^{-4}	72.0077	1	6.25×10^{-2}	5.20833×10^{-3}
lb-in	0.112985	1.15212×10^{-2}	1.15212×10^{3}	16	1	8.33333×10^{-2}
lb-ft	1.35582	0.138255	1.38255×10^{4}	192	12	1

*units of force

To convert from A to B, multiply by entry in table.

Example: 1 oz-in = 7.06155×10^{-3} Nm

TABLE A-7 RANDOM NUMBERS

07	28	68	61	81	38	11	98	34	74	64	03	48	09	18	10	15	25	98	80
29	24	86	11	41	21	16	12	96	17	56	61	49	32	48	35	43	29	34	12
76	05	58	54	35	55	35	59	07	19	00	92	65	95	34	88	26	32	61	36
95	01	20	28	66	31	15	92	14	33	39	98	55	85	71	35	82	04	51	64
73	89	25	53	83	33	75	79	98	20	09	06	76	92	43	42	55	86	41	67
41	58	46	41	68	72	73	78	34	65	87	08	10	93	46	00	32	48	29	68
53	46	33	57	86	99	47	87	14	55	98	93	72	15	77	23	13	26	37	20
39	46	65	77	16	92	33	65	57	49	18	41	87	68	05	23	73	33	55	49
40	98	58	06	54	13	55	31	86	06	34	94	43	59	08	54	86	44	59	84
06	45	65	80	97	46	95	38	82	01	88	12	28	75	93	39	33	60	00	48
84	72	36	35	94	11	36	23	17	09	95	90	26	46	90	70	81	40	77	38
61	14	68	60	77	44	75	28	56	67	36	58	03	82	16	76	39	12	73	70
07	47	15	19	64	62	17	97	36	08	22	55	58	81	17	77	83	65	75	05
70	43	84	46	41	98	44	54	23	72	39	79	53	16	88	04	66	00	66	43
57	10	02	26	17	12	56	48	43	97	65	06	21	97	65	97	95	77	93	01
95	01	58	34	51	77	89	80	79	72	60	94	43	05	89	83	88	15	09	58
53	00	18	66	58	39	02	95	62	79	35	52	01	06	50	18	98	88	87	81
51	86	20	34	89	54	54	61	15	00	96	89	11	34	05	18	26	77	17	23
38	63	42	41	87	99	37	18	91	08	55	42	27	51	69	48	94	14	70	96
47	77	39	28	14	56	98	96	73	22	31	67	20	90	85	04	01	87	42	17
26	20	46	66	36	28	98	66	97	56	78	29	19	53	46	08	20	30	55	61
58	58	28	68	36	45	83	66	12	05	17	37	74	90	81	86	99	04	17	90
80	83	75	20	32	63	09	41	69	12	43	82	63	40	08	89	71	89	68	44
40	90	05	68	85	00	90	91	49	16	23	00	26	56	52	66	71	22	63	40
77	38	50	26	29	57	56	31	37	52	88	88	37	72	14	52	73	79	23	79
51	62	77	67	70	21	17	88	22	26	66	77	78	55	87	14	39	07	31	67
66	81	52	18	87	47	01	60	71	73	90	72	90	39	37	64	44	26	82	07
67	72	78	24	07	12	61	67	78	85	92	68	95	24	69	57	74	13	28	64
14	29	00	91	50	43	64	63	85	17	54	46	92	58	58	52	97	54	84	09
30	89	99	07	56	26	49	27	83	67	52	35	36	93	63	60	15	71	16	34
26	42	43	27	81	79	67	35	84	28	64	59	79	16	11	54	85	34	01	49
98	05	34	47	71	14	87	98	70	21	53	51	01	46	60	71	19	33	62	43
02	82	10	42	11	62	87	83	16	96	34	46	04	25	33	69	55	37	82	29
99	88	34	85	46	77	12	00	89	17	04	48	85	62	32	77	08	24	88	65
83	59	57	38	84	22	08	75	21	10	58	75	87	70	19	07	94	83	09	37
76	27	52	23	67	14	39	88	57	00	72	71	21	68	81	49	24	94	19	37
03	80	24	56	17	64	66	90	80	09	62	03	65	61	66	39	83	87	41	95
40	86	98	74	63	72	14	00	08	38	25	25	37	93	89	96	74	66	36	06
38	02	78	20	39	15	04	67	68	27	46	22	43	79	26	45	45	17	66	13
19	51	85	12	56	95	63	15	44	74	88	26	02	10	68	09	84	86	26	81

TABLE A-8 ASCII CHARACTER CODES

Decimal	Hexadecimal	ASCII Code	Decimal	Hexadecimal	ASCII Code	Decimal	Hexadecimal	ASCII Code
032	20	(space)	064	40	@	096	60	
033	21	!	065	41	A	097	61	a
034	22	"	066	42	B	098	62	b
035	23	#	067	43	C	099	63	c
036	24	$	068	44	D	100	64	d
037	25	%	069	45	E	101	65	e
038	26	&	070	46	F	102	66	f
039	27	'	071	47	G	103	67	g
040	28	(	072	48	H	104	68	h
041	29	)	073	49	I	105	69	i
042	2A	*	074	4A	J	106	6A	j
043	2B	+	075	4B	K	107	6B	k
044	2C	,	076	4C	L	108	6C	l
045	2D	-	077	4D	M	109	6D	m
046	2E	.	078	4E	N	110	6E	n
047	2F	/	079	4F	O	111	6F	o
048	30	0	080	4G	P	112	70	p
049	31	1	081	50	Q	113	71	q
050	32	2	082	51	R	114	72	r
051	33	3	083	53	S	115	73	s
052	34	4	084	54	T	116	74	t
053	35	5	085	55	U	117	75	u
054	36	6	086	56	V	118	76	v
055	37	7	087	57	W	119	77	w
056	38	8	088	58	X	120	78	x
057	39	9	089	59	Y	121	79	y
058	3A	:	090	5A	Z	122	7A	z
059	3B	;	091	5B	[	123	7B	{
060	3C	<	092	5C	\	124	7C	|
061	3D	=	093	5D	]	125	7D	}
062	3E	>	094	5E	^	126	7E	~
063	3F	?	095	5F	—			

INDEX